Third Edition

Bill Bowerman's High-Performance Training for Track and Field

William J. Bowerman
William H. Freeman

ISBN: 978-1-60679-031-1
Library of Congress Control Number: 2008940537
Cover design: Roger W. Rybkowski
Book layout: Studio J Art & Design; Roger W. Rybkowski
Front cover photo: ©L.E. Baskow/ZUMA Press

Coaches Choice
P.O. Box 1828
Monterey, CA 93942
www.coacheschoice.com

Dedication

For Barbara Bowerman and the Men of Oregon

Acknowledgments

In developing this revision, I was helped by the gracious cooperation of the staff of the University of Oregon Archives, in particular Heather Briston, Leslie Larson, and James Fox, with their assistance at digging out and scanning many of the photographs of Bowerman's athletes. I am most appreciative of the work of Greg Walker of the University of Oregon Athletic Media Services in locating and providing further photographs of athletes. Barbara Bowerman assisted with pictures from her own collection, as well as her always kind and enthusiastic support. Dan Long and Kristi Kieffer at the Nike Archives also contributed to the project, and Geoff Hollister of Nike gave helpful guidance. Kenny Moore, whose masterful biography of Bowerman replaces my small, ancient biographical dissertation, contributed the foreword with his own words of wisdom.

Contents

Foreword

In 1962, when I was an Oregon freshman and dedicating myself to distance running, I didn't have this book. I had the man who wrote it, Oregon coach William J. Bowerman. A lot of times, I'd rather have had the book.

Bill Bowerman was—and is, and ever shall be—a generous, ornery, profane, beatific, unyielding, antic, impenetrably complex Oregon original. As a freshman, I found him deeply disturbing. One of my best friends was his middle son, Jay, who became an Olympic biathlete. That didn't matter. We both found him disturbing.

The principles of high performance training set down in this book (with a clarity traceable to a collaborator named Freeman) had long been assembled and put into practice when I joined Bowerman's team, but he was—and is, and ever shall be—working on refinements. We paid our freshman dues by being guinea pigs in experiments that compared different sorts and intensities of training.

On the fundamentals, Bowerman delivered a 40-second speech. "You stress an organism, for example a freshmen," he told us, "and you let it rest. What happens? It responds by overcompensating. It becomes some increment stronger, faster, or more enduring. That's all training is. You'd think any damn fool could figure out how to do it. The only trick is finding what works best for a specific athlete."

I still share some of Bowerman's amazement that so few damn fools do learn to train to optimum effect. This general ignorance is something I've always been grateful for, given that I've had to race athletes more talented than I am. The equalizer has always been there, the fact that talent can almost be counted on to blunder in training. But if we were to gain an edge from that, Bowerman had to teach us to prepare intelligently.

Stress. Rest. Response. Individuality. They seem dry, clinical terms. But Bowerman hurled them upon us—not with the reasoned good humor of this book, but with all the force of his Old Testament personality.

Stress: The actual workouts were the least of our worries. The man was the thing, the man in all his mystifying incarnations. He spoke in parables, in Hammurabi's Code, in ringing declamations from Delphi. (I think the only one that survives in this book is the big one: "Know thyself"). He made us study. Instead of giving any of us full scholarships, he made us work weekends on the graveyard shift in Eugene's plywood mills. When we were new, he would assign an interval workout and, standing on the infield, call out our time civilly enough but completely ignore us otherwise. If you asked him a question ("Was my form correct?"), he would stonily, silently lift his gaze to the swallows in their flight above Hayward Field.

He made our shoes. He was disdainful of the excessive weight and nonexistent cushioning of the shoes then on the market, so he improved them.

As you sat, a little weary, at your locker after a long run, a bear would suddenly loom up before you—no, a man, covered in black hoarfrost, smelling evilly of burned rubber. It was Bowerman, fresh from grinding down the rough edges of the rubber soles he'd cemented to your training shoes. He either never ground them enough (so you had to finish the job) or ground holes in the uppers. Had we known these were the beginnings of Nike's vast success, would we have been more respectful of his cobbling?

Bowerman seemed to glory in the tyranny permitted a head coach. He played with us, yanking us from races on the starting line because the dual meet score was growing lopsided, kicking people off the team because they ran unauthorized mileage behind his back.

Once he bet me a case of Nutrament® that I couldn't break 2:00 minutes for the 880 on a freezing Saturday morning. I ran with control, hitting the 440 in 60. I could feel myself accelerating in the last lap. Near the finish, I knew I'd done it. I heard him stop to watch. I slowed, and turned, gasping, to hear the time. "2:00.3," he said. "Good try." I leaped upon him, screaming, made insane by outrage. He allowed me to wrestle the watch away from him. It read: "1:56.6."

He loved to sit in the sauna until his heavy ring of brass keys had been heated to 180 degrees, and then brand us with them. And when we yelled that nowhere in Plato or Isaiah was his behavior justified, he answered us with the defining parable. All of this—*all* of it—was in the manner of the two-by-four.

"Farmer couldn't get his mule to work," he'd say. "Couldn't even get him to eat or drink. Mule just stood there. Finally he brought in a mule expert who took a look, went in the barn, and came out with a six-foot two-by-four. *Hit* that mule as hard as he could between the eyes.

" '*That's* supposed to teach him to *drink*?' said the farmer. '*That's* supposed to *teach* him something?'

" 'Well,' said the mule expert, 'first you have to get his attention.' "

Rest: "Are you in this to do mindless labor?" he asked when I announced my lunatic intention of running 200 miles per week over the summer after my first year. "Or do you want to improve? You can't improve if you're sick or injured."

Before June was half over, I was sick and injured. Bowerman, fed up by the spring of my sophomore year, forced me—by threat of bodily harm—to do two or even three easy days between each remotely taxing work out. My schedule seemed little more than a life of 3-A and 3-B. You can look it up. In three weeks, I improved from 9:30 to 8:48 in the two mile.

That was my personal two-by-four. It finally began to penetrate my thick skull that I had to rise above the world's fixation with work. I had to attend to my own slow-recovering physiology. I had to rest.

Response: Work for its own dumb sake is a hard habit to break, but slowly I embraced those deceptively simple basics. I accepted easy days into my life. I stopped counting miles. I grew stronger, gradually extending the one long run permitted me every 10 days from 20 to 25, to 30, even 35 miles. Over time, those runs transformed me into a marathoner capable of running 2:11:36 in 1970 and of finishing fourth in the 1972 Olympic marathon.

Coming to terms with my individual raw material also had a wider liberating effect. Eccentricity—and in Bowerman, I sure had an example of that—no longer seemed all that silly. Quitting Stanford Law School and trying to be a writer no longer seemed an imbecilic thing to do.

Now, looking around at a world largely inhabited by people who have never learned how to compete without letting it take over their life, people who've never learned how to peak when it counts, or take a joke, or stand up to a tyrant, or have faith in their thinking even if it is kind of strange, I begin to appreciate my good fortune in having been born into the Bowerman Kingdom.

Individuality: How much of what the man did to and for me can his book of training principles do for you? It's a good question. The technical instruction Freeman and Bowerman provide in these chapters is first-rate. Yet, as I found, a lot of what seems common sense is hard to apply. It goes against the damn fool compulsive achiever's grain. "Rest?" "Have fun?" "Finish your training feeling exhilarated, not exhausted?" Those are fighting words, and this book has no two-by-four.

I feel a lot more like a farmer than a man who knows mules. All I can say is, "Here is the water. Drink."

Kenny Moore
Two-time Olympic marathoner
Author, *Bill Bowerman and the Men of Oregon*

Preface

In the preface to the first edition of this book, Bill Bowerman reflected on the changes in his life and work over a 40-year period. As the surviving co-author, I look back almost 40 years to the start of the writing of that first edition. A Ph.D. student when I first met Bowerman in 1970, I look back on my life as a teacher and coach, even if not at the level of a Bill Bowerman. My dissertation was a 1972 biographical study of Bowerman,[1] and Kenny Moore has recently produced an outstanding work on Bowerman and his Men of Oregon,[2] following his screenplay for the movie *Without Limits*, which depicted Steve Prefontaine and Bowerman

This revision gives me an opportunity to put Bill Bowerman into the context of his time. He coached at Medford, Oregon, High School, his own alma mater, having great success as a football and track coach. In 1948, he returned to his other alma mater, the University of Oregon, where he had been quarterback of successful football teams and a convert to Bill Hayward's track team as a 440-yard runner.

His 25 years at Oregon made him a legend, or rather, his work there created his legend. Coaches from other nations sometimes discount his impact, largely due to a failure to understand his working context. They sometimes suggest that Bowerman was not a great coach because he did not produce large numbers of world and Olympic champions. My reply is simple: his job, his mission was training undergraduate university students between the ages of 18 and 22. He was not a national coach starting with the best talent in a nation and with 10 years of adulthood to develop them. He had his athletes for four years, and then they were out into the adult world for which he sought to prepare them.

Bill Bowerman throughout his career did two things few international coaches did then or do today: he personally designed and oversaw the training plan for every athlete in every track and field event, producing national- and world-class athletes in almost every event, and his Oregon days were working with men mostly from 18 to 22 years old. He rarely worked with anyone other than undergraduate university students. One example of his coaching of a post-collegiate athlete was Henry Marsh, who ran 8:09 in the steeplechase—over 20 years ago.

Compare the starting ages and talent level of his young athletes, and then look at what he produced in those brief years of their young lives. Most nations have not produced a single coach as accomplished in producing high-level success while working almost exclusively with university undergraduates—and all while coaching every event, rather than specializing in a single event as is more common in the outside world.

In a time when hardly any coach in the world had produced more than one, occasionally two, sub-4:00 milers, Bill Bowerman produced about 20, almost all of them under the age of 22. His athletes cut almost 15 seconds from the

4 x 1 mile relay world record set by the New Zealand national team that included two Olympic champions and was anchored by world-record holder Peter Snell. 16:08.9 in 1962 on cinders, with young men of 20 to 21 years of age. In the same year, his sprint relay set a world record for the 440-yard relay, running 40.0 (39.7m) on cinders with three hurdlers and a sprinter. In 1964, his javelin throwers took the first three places in the NCAA championship. He had four different NCAA one-mile champions between 1954 and 1960.

Bowerman coached world-record holders in the 60-yard (indoors), 100-yard, 100m, 400m, 440-yard relay, two-mile and three-mile (indoors), 4 x 1 mile relay, shot (indoors), and discus (his athletic conference did not compete in the hammer at that time).

He coached U.S. record holders in the 60-yard (indoors), 100-yard, 100m, 400m, 440-yard relay, high hurdles, 1,000-yard, 1,000m, 1500, 1-mile, 3 km, two-mile (indoors and outdoors) and three-mile (indoors and outdoors), 5 km, six-mile, 10 km, 4 x 1 mile relay, shot (indoors), and discus.

He coached athletes who went to the Olympics in the 100m, 200m, 400m, 800m, 1500m, steeplechase, 5 km, marathon, shot, discus, javelin, pole vault, and decathlon.

He coached national or collegiate national champions in the 100, 200, 800, 1500/mile, steeplechase, two-mile, three-mile/5 km, high hurdles, low hurdles, 400 hurdles, high jump, long jump, shot, discus, and javelin.

The event chapters give further information on his best athletes. This is in part, along with the athletes' photos, to honor his and their accomplishments. It also serves to drive home a critical point: those athletes used the workouts in this book. Even though these workouts are as much as 40 years old, they produced sub-4:00 miles, 10.0 100m dashes, a 44.9 400m, 1:45.0 800m, 60-foot shot-putters, and 26-foot long-jumpers.

Bill Bowerman was a master coach, in large part because he saw himself as far more than a coach, or even a teacher. His goal was to lead young, unformed boys to become men, men of accomplishment in a bigger world than the enclave of sport. He used the fire of sport to harden and then polish them, producing his "Men of Oregon."

The core elements of Bill Bowerman's coaching success were his belief in discovering what worked best for each individual, coupled with the curiosity that kept him seeking improvements in training, equipment, and facilities, in every disparate element that affected performance. Nike grew from Bowerman's quest for a lighter shoe, for the purpose of carrying less weight, for the purpose of applying more of the athlete's energy into running faster.

Working with him over the years, I came to admire his wide-ranging curiosity, his never-ceasing quest to improve, well, everything he encountered.

Where most coaches copy, Bill examined, analyzed, and dug deeper, until he could understand not simply *what* worked, but *why* it worked. Knowing *why* could lead to the discovery of a more effective process.

I also appreciated the breadth of his interest. I saw the contributions that Bill and Barbara Bowerman made to the University and State of Oregon, as well as to their home communities, and appreciated how wide was the reach of their interest and help into the realms of education and the arts.

When we were writing the first edition of this book, Bill would say, "Coaches just want to know what works. They don't care why. So let's give them the 'what' and skip the 'why.' They can get that somewhere else."

This book is Bill Bowerman's "what" book. If you want to succeed in track and field, this is what you do. The wise coaches will pick apart the nuts and bolts to see the underlying "why" (as Bill hoped they would), and then apply the training principles more effectively to the talents and needs of their own individuals. The performance marks at the start of each chapter, along with scattered photos of many athletes, are the proof that these training plans work.

Bill Bowerman was a master coach. This book is part of the great legacy that he left to the sport he loved.

As Kenny Moore wrote, "Here is the water. Drink."

Bill Freeman

Preface to the First Edition

It was almost 40 years ago that circumstances led me, a prospective medical student, into an unforeseen teaching career. Two years after the great Los Angeles Olympiad of 1932, the lean times of the Depression encouraged me to take a fling at teaching. Teachers are always needed, I reasoned, and more importantly, teaching would allow me to save tuition money and go on to medical school. But the two years I allotted to this detour were filled with so many exciting experiences that medicine was left to those dedicated to the sick, while I continued to work with the healthy. The pre-med background has nonetheless been of inestimable value to me.

Teaching was and still is fun. Like any other job, it has its tribulations and boredom, but the rewards have been generous: for one, the satisfaction of contributing to the growth of several generations of Americans.

I am proud to be a teacher and to be associated with a group of men and women who, on the whole, love youngsters and do not give a whoop if their critics, the vocal few, cause them to be underpaid, underestimated, and overworked.

I think that our schools are among the best in the world because of such teachers. Their efforts and the support of involved parents and students have made our schools the educational, cultural, and athletic centers of our communities. As both a teacher and a coach, I feel fortunate to be part of this great program.

Coaching Track and Field is an outgrowth of my years of coaching in schools. There are a number of ways to present a text on track and field, and in fact, many excellent books on the subject have been published. I have tried to read them all and continue to run into old ones, as well as those that are "hot off the press." Each has something good to offer, and many are so full of "meat" that rereading often turns up appetizing new morsels.

Nonetheless, I believe that *Coaching Track and Field* has something new and unique to offer. Through the years, it has been my pleasure to attend clinics on track, both as a listener and as an "expert" in presentations to athletes and coaches. My observation has been that most teacher-coaches and athletes would prefer to know *how* to train for, or to train a person for, an event, rather than *why* to train that way. This presentation will therefore be devoted to the "how," with training schedules that have been used by champion athletes as a special feature. Other materials related to training methods are included, plus bibliographies directing the reader to further materials in each area.

It is my hope that this book will have value in its entirety as a step-by-step guide for the teacher-coach in his first years. I would hope, too, that the experienced coach will find its systematic and complete analyses of form and training methods a useful addition to his own methods. Finally, it should be possible for the individual working alone to adapt the workout materials in single sections, such as "Distance training and racing," to a training program tailored to his own goals and informed by the experience of decades of champion athletes.

WJB

Preface to the Second Edition

This book grew from *Coaching Track and Field*, which described the Bill Bowerman's Oregon training system, the most influential in the United States today. It presents

- The theory of training
- How the theory is applied in the training program
- Extensive real-life daily training schedules for each event

Use *High-Performance Training for Track and Field* for a training year, even if you do no more than copy the workouts, and we guarantee that your athletes will perform well. Most training books cover either the "why" (the latest training theories) or the "how" (applying the theory to an actual training program). This text gives *both*, and it blends them into the single most useful text for track and field coaches and athletes.

The earlier book included a training year of workouts for each event. All of the schedules were used by national- or world-class American athletes, some of them U.S.- and world-record holders. The result was the most comprehensive set of real-life training schedules available in any track and field book.

This book adds the theoretical bases that underlie training, summarizing what researchers know about training and competition and discussing the most advanced, scientifically monitored, foreign endurance training system in the world today. It tells, briefly and simply, what you need to know about periodization in training, overload theory, and the effects of nutrition and psychology on today's training.

Our scientific knowledge of training has expanded during the last decade, but today's knowledge has not changed the principles that underlie the Oregon System. Our training patterns reflect the very latest scientific training methods.

The heart of the Oregon system is intact, including the training schedules, with a minimum of six months of daily training sessions per event. Although the schedules have indeed been used by elite athletes, they can be used as they appear by almost any healthy athlete—male or female. As these schedules demonstrate, there is an art to coaching. The schedules were carefully crafted to develop athletes without losing them to injury or burnout.

The schedules emphasize developing the fundamental skills and necessary conditioning of the events, with performance levels scaled to individual abilities. The schedules are most appropriate for junior and young senior athletes (high school and university athletes, ages 14 to 22).

High-Performance Training for Track and Field is a step-by-step guide for teacher-coaches in their first years, who will find it to be a model for success. Experienced coaches will find its systematic analyses of training methods an invaluable addition to their own expertise.

Experienced coaches can use the schedules as an example and a starting point in developing or modifying their own training systems. Less experienced coaches can use them as models. Some coaches have simply copied and posted the schedules for their athletes to follow. Although we do not recommend that method, it will work. An individual athlete can adapt the training schedules to a training program tailored to his own goals.

No other text has ever been so usable for coaches and athletes alike. By studying and using this book properly, even the most inexperienced coach can produce well-prepared athletes.

Whether you are a coach or an athlete, a beginner or an expert, *High-Performance Training for Track and Field* will be more useful to you than any other track text in print.

Bill Bowerman
Bill Freeman

Endnotes

1. William H. Freeman. (1972). *A Biographical Study of William J. Bowerman.* Unpublished Ph.D. dissertation, University of Oregon, Eugene.
2. Kenny Moore. (2006). *Bowerman and the Men of Oregon: The Story of Oregon's Legendary Coach and Nike's Cofounder.* Rodale.

BEGINNING IN TRACK AND FIELD ATHLETICS

Introduction

Bill Bowerman

1

How to Use This Book

Who Can Use This Book

This text is written for a broad audience. It is equally useful to men and women, to coaches and athletes, to beginners and elite athletes. It fills a need for more detailed information on *how* to train, but it includes the *why* that provides the theory base of training. While it gives training schedules used by elite athletes, it is more useful to the inexperienced coach and athlete than any other training text because it gives detailed workout schedules based on solid experience. While the schedules are elite schedules, they can be very easily adapted to athletes at any level. This book gives months of real training for every event; national and Olympic champions have used these workouts.

Approach and Changes From Previous Editions

The first edition of the text emphasized the practical aspects of training and coaching. Its emphasis was on one thing: how. It told how to train, but it limited the explanations of why the training was done that way. This edition continues the strength of giving months of genuine training schedules that have been used by elite athletes.

The changes from the first edition are highly useful additions. Chapters that summarize the science of training and conditioning are included. The scientific overview in each event is more thorough. The text provides the best combination of understanding and usability in training and technique. For resources, a number of highly useful supplementary sources are suggested for each topic.

Organization of the Text

After these introductory chapters, the text has three broad sections. The first part discusses the science and theory of training and conditioning. The second part covers the events of track and field athletics. The third part shows the coaching and administrative techniques used in building and coaching a team and in organizing training and competitions.

Photographic sequences of the performances of champion athletes are not included as in the first edition for two reasons: the cost to the authors is prohibitive, and many video studies are available on DVDs and on many websites. Coaches and athletes should study performance videos because they show how skilled athletes perform the events. Each athlete's performance has unique points. There is no "perfect" method of training or skill performance. If an athlete rigidly copies a training system or technique, the result will be a second-rate athlete. The champion is the person who takes the basic form of an event and molds it to accommodate his personal strengths and limitations.

A new chapter discusses how to become a great coach. It looks at critical knowledge and experience, and it closes with a bibliography of useful source books for track and field coaches from the neophyte to the highly experienced.

The chapters on the science and theory explain what coaches and scientists know and believe about training and conditioning at this time. They emphasize the scientific basis that underlies training in all events and sports.

The chapters on the events begin with an overview of the science that affects training and performance in that event. The training methods for the event are studied next. The most common training techniques for the event are explained, showing how the fundamentals of training are actually applied.

The training schedules are the most valuable portion of the book. The workouts in this book are all taken from real training files; they follow an athlete through daily training for an entire training year, from the fall until June, when the most important meets are contested. The workouts were used by national-class and world-class athletes, Olympic team members, sub-4:00 milers, 1:45 800-meter runners, 60-foot shot-putters, 10.0- to 10.2-second 100-meter runners, 13.3-second high hurdlers, and so on. The training schedules are proven effective.

These competitors have been national-class and world-class athletes. Where actual times, paces, heights, and distances are given, the coach or athlete should experiment with the workouts and adapt them to their own individual capabilities. For younger athletes, the quantity of work should also be lowered. Other than those precautions, the workouts are absolutely usable by any athlete. They solve a great problem for the inexperienced coach or athlete: What should an athlete do to train well?

Following the training schedules, the meaning of the symbols on the training schedule sheets is explained in detail. In addition, the origin of the schedule sheets and a presentation of their use and interpretation, as well as a general discussion of training, appear in Chapter 6. In this edition, we have reprinted the training schedules in their original form from the 1974 edition, when American athletes still raced primarily at distances in yards and miles. The workout sheets will be preceded in each case by a blank schedule form updated to the metric system, as in the 1991 edition.

The explanation of the training fundamentals is followed by a list of useful sources for more information about the event. It is a selection of materials, mostly periodical articles, which have appeared in print since the 1991 edition. The authors do not necessarily agree with the content of every article, but this book tries to stress that there is no single way to reach success.

The section on administrative techniques briefly discusses how to build an all-around track program, including how to test students for track talent. The techniques and problems involved in planning and directing track and field athletics competitions, both small and large, are also discussed in some detail.

Applying the Knowledge

The schedules in this text can be used as they are. Some athletes may need to modify the workouts, but this adaptation will not often be the case. Some coaches have simply copied the workouts and told athletes to follow the schedules, with no explanation. While an athlete can progress even with that method of coaching, we do not approve.

We prefer that coach and athlete first learn what the parts of the schedule mean:

- Learn the scientific principles of training. Those principles provide the foundation for wise training.
- Practice and develop the performance techniques, the skills needed for good form. Those skills make performance more effective, while making the likelihood of injuries much smaller.
- Study how the patterns are organized, how each part fits with the other parts, and why each part is used. Coupled with a knowledge of the scientific background, this understanding will allow you to adapt training more effectively. Good coaches and athletes are always experimenting with new ways of training. Useful experiments require a broad knowledge of these foundations.

Some Basic Sources for Track and Field Athletics

Many valuable publications are devoted to this sport. Several of them are cited frequently in this book. While many periodicals cover specific events or event groups, such as the throwing events, the two most useful coaching journals are *Track Coach* (formerly *Track Technique*), which is the coaching journal for USA

Track and Field, and *New Studies in Athletics*, the technical journal of the International Association of Athletics Federations (IAAF). No American coach will be well informed without those journals. *Track Coach* offers more practical, applied information, while *New Studies in Athletics* offers more technical material from experts around the world.

Many nations around the world also produce invaluable coaching and technical journals, such as *Modern Athlete and Coach* in Australia. Any coach who aspires to success will subscribe to the appropriate journals in his part of the world.

Other periodicals deal with current news and statistics in track and field athletics. *Track and Field News* is an absolutely essential monthly publication to any person interested in what is going on around the world in track and field. The core focus is on athletes and major competitions around the world, but under the imprint of Tafnews, the publisher produces many excellent books on track and field.

To play the game, you must know the rules. Every coach should have the appropriate rulebook for their level of competition, whether it is the international level and Olympic Games (IAAF *Competition Rules*), the national level (USA Track and Field), intercollegiate competition (the NCAA or other college rule books), or the high school rule book from the National Federation of State High School Associations.

Another useful publication, especially in a nation that still uses the Imperial measure more comfortably than the metric system is the *Big Gold Book* (Tafnews, 2005) which gives metric conversion tables, combined event scoring tables, and many other useful aids to the coach, athlete, and fan.

2

How to Develop as a Great Coach

Every coach wants to become as knowledgeable and skilled as possible. However, many young coaches do not fully understand what is involved in becoming a great coach. Many traits can be suggested, but this chapter discusses seven factors that contribute to coaching success: scientific knowledge, pedagogical knowledge, sports knowledge, communication skills, charismatic factors, practical experience, and curiosity.

Scientific Knowledge

As Harmon Brown wrote:

> *The scientific basis of modern athletic coaching and training is often overlooked, or taken for granted. Many believe that coaching is primarily an art, involving understanding of athlete-coach inter-relationships in order to impart information, and the ability to teach skills. However, the educational background for modern qualified coaches world-wide involves a university or sports school curriculum which is soundly based in the sciences: anatomy, physiology, kinesiology, biomechanics, psychology, nutrition, and pedagogy (skills teaching). This knowledge base provides the coach with a solid foundation on which to learn how to select athletes, design appropriate training programs, and teach the skills essential to each event.*[1]

Too many young coaches do not take scientific knowledge seriously. They foolishly believe that coaching is largely an attitude, combined with using the methods that were used in their own training.

The reality is that the coach cannot improve human performance if he does not understand how the body works. If he does not have a working knowledge of anatomy, he will not understand how the parts interrelate and work together. Without a basic understanding of biomechanics, a coach can never be effective in improving movement skills, which are based on the laws of mechanics. Without an understanding of exercise physiology, he cannot plan effective programs of exercise, because he will not understand how the body adapts to training or which training applications are most appropriate and effective.

While it is not necessary for a good coach to have the knowledge of a research scientist, he does need to have at least basic knowledge of the areas mentioned, as well as basic mathematics skills. An understanding of simple trigonometry (as taught in middle school) helps with solving questions in biomechanics. An understanding of elementary statistics enables a coach to evaluate research papers to determine their value and potential application.

Pedagogical Knowledge

Pedagogical knowledge means a basic understanding of how to teach. As Bill Bowerman always stressed, a coach is first and foremost a teacher. A coach teaches an athlete, whether teaching skills, behaviors, or simply the ability to grow in experience and maturity.

This approach to pedagogy takes the coach into several areas, such as requiring an elementary understanding of motor development, so he will know what improvements can be gained simply through maturation, as well as what skills and exercises are or are not appropriate for students to learn at a given age. He also needs to understand motor-skill learning, which deals with skill improvements that are not simply a result of maturation. The coach needs to understand instructional methodology, effective ways of teaching skills. Sports psychology is also important. Some people will consider psychology to be scientific knowledge, while others may classify it under pedagogy.

Sport-Specific Knowledge

A coach needs to grow in his knowledge of the sport. No highly successful coach will claim to know it all or will stop trying to learn more about the sport. This need is met with textbooks, coaching journals, applied scientific journals, coaching clinics, certification programs, and regular discussions with other coaches.

An extremely valuable way to gain knowledge is through national programs of coach certification. In the United States, certification is obtained through the USA Track and Field Coach Education program. Currently, this program offers certification at Levels I, II, and III. Similar programs can be found in most developed nations, as well as an international program through the IAAF.

Level I courses are offered across the United States as an inexpensive, focused, single-weekend course designed to meet the needs of beginner coaches. Schedules are listed on the USATF website. With Level I certification and more experience, a coach can then move to Level II certification, which is a one-week in-depth focus on a single group of events, such as the jumps or throws. This certification prepares the coach to work with athletes from the youth levels through collegiate and national levels. Level III is aimed at coaches who work with national- and international-level athletes. The value of going through the coach education program cannot be overestimated, regardless of the coach's educational background.[2]

Communication Skills

Communication skills are critical for a coach. The coach must be able to speak both informally to an athlete and more formally to a team or a group of coaches or to the media. The coach must also be able to write competently, allowing the sharing of knowledge through coaching magazines, journals, and books.

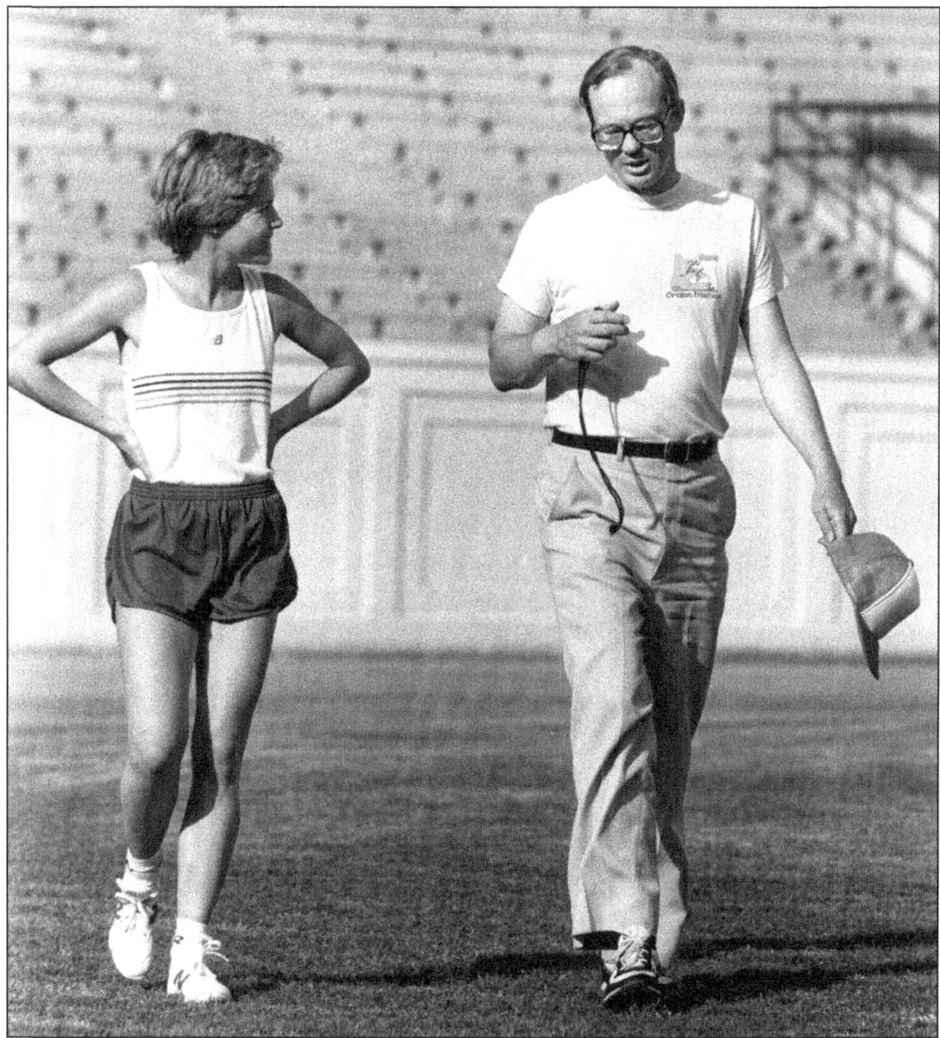

Photo 2-1. Bill Freeman and Joan Nesbit

Charismatic Factors

These factors get into the question of why people, such as athletes, will work for someone, trust them, and cooperate with them in trying to achieve their goals. Very successful coaches are charismatic. People pay attention to what they say and tend to treat them with respect. Charismatic factors can sometimes lead to problems, as some athletes are looking for a guru who seems to have all of the answers—and he often does not. Steve Myrland warned about false gurus, suggesting that athletes and coaches need to analyze the "experts" they meet to determine whether they really know what they claim to know, and whether their focus is genuine expertise or simply self-promotion.[3]

Practical Experience

Practical experience is critical. A sad reality of coaching, especially in the early years, is that coaches learn at the expense of their athletes. Every coach makes mistakes, but it is the athlete who pays the physical price. Theoretical and technical knowledge is very important, but it must be balanced with practical experience. What works in theory may not fit so easily into the real world.[4]

The number of experienced track and field coaches sometimes seems smaller than it should be. One reason for this small number is that coaches in

Photo 2-2. Bill Bowerman and Steve Prefontaine

the public schools are not paid well for their time, so many eventually leave coaching. Rather than raising pay levels, often the schools will simply open a revolving door of inexperienced coaches-in-training, who will themselves soon leave.[5] A shortage of women coaches can also be found at all levels, but especially in the university ranks, which tend to be run by male athletic directors who generally hire male head coaches, even for the women's teams.[6]

Curiosity

Curiosity is a critical component of coaching success. It means that the coach is always seeking new methods, better techniques, and answers to the many questions that appear during the annual training cycle. Some of the research is done through books and technical journals. Some progress comes as ideas from athletes or from other coaches. Some knowledge comes through experimentation, both formal and informal.

Coaches are always seeking new and better ways to analyze performance. The boom in microtechnology since the first edition of this book in 1974 has created opportunities undreamed of by coaches 30 years ago. Software

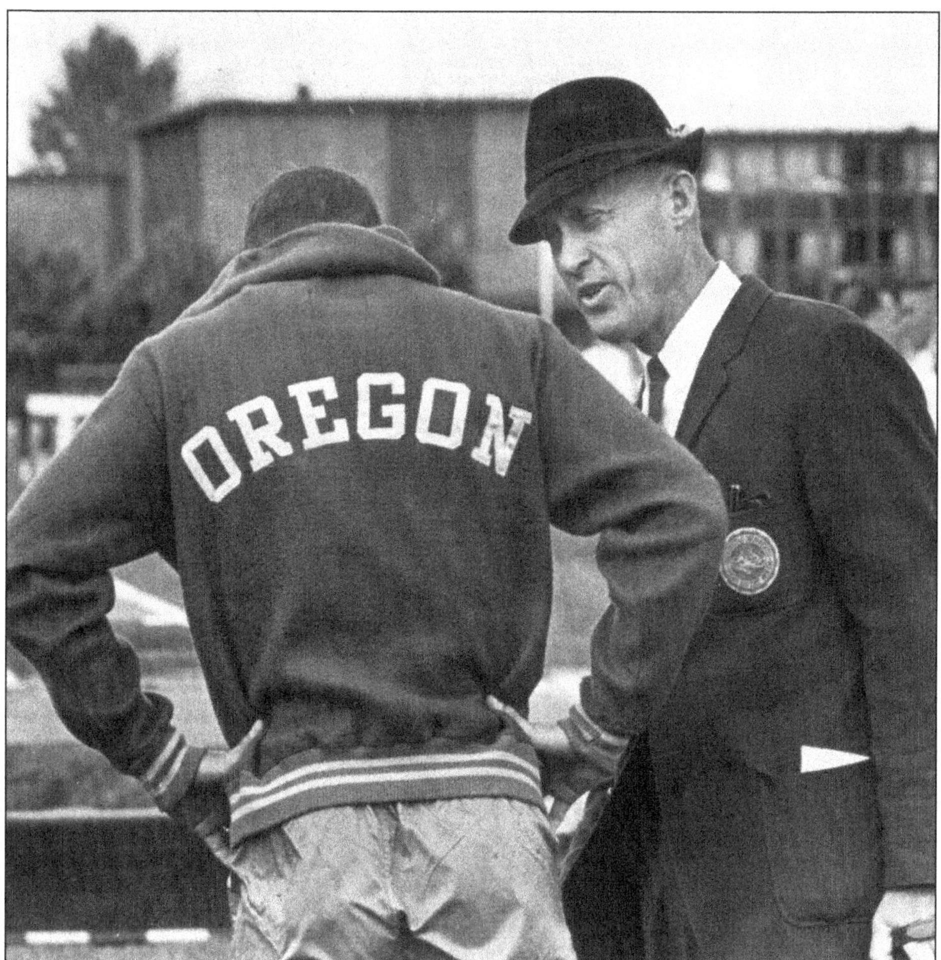

Photo 2-3. Bill Bowerman with one of the Men of Oregon

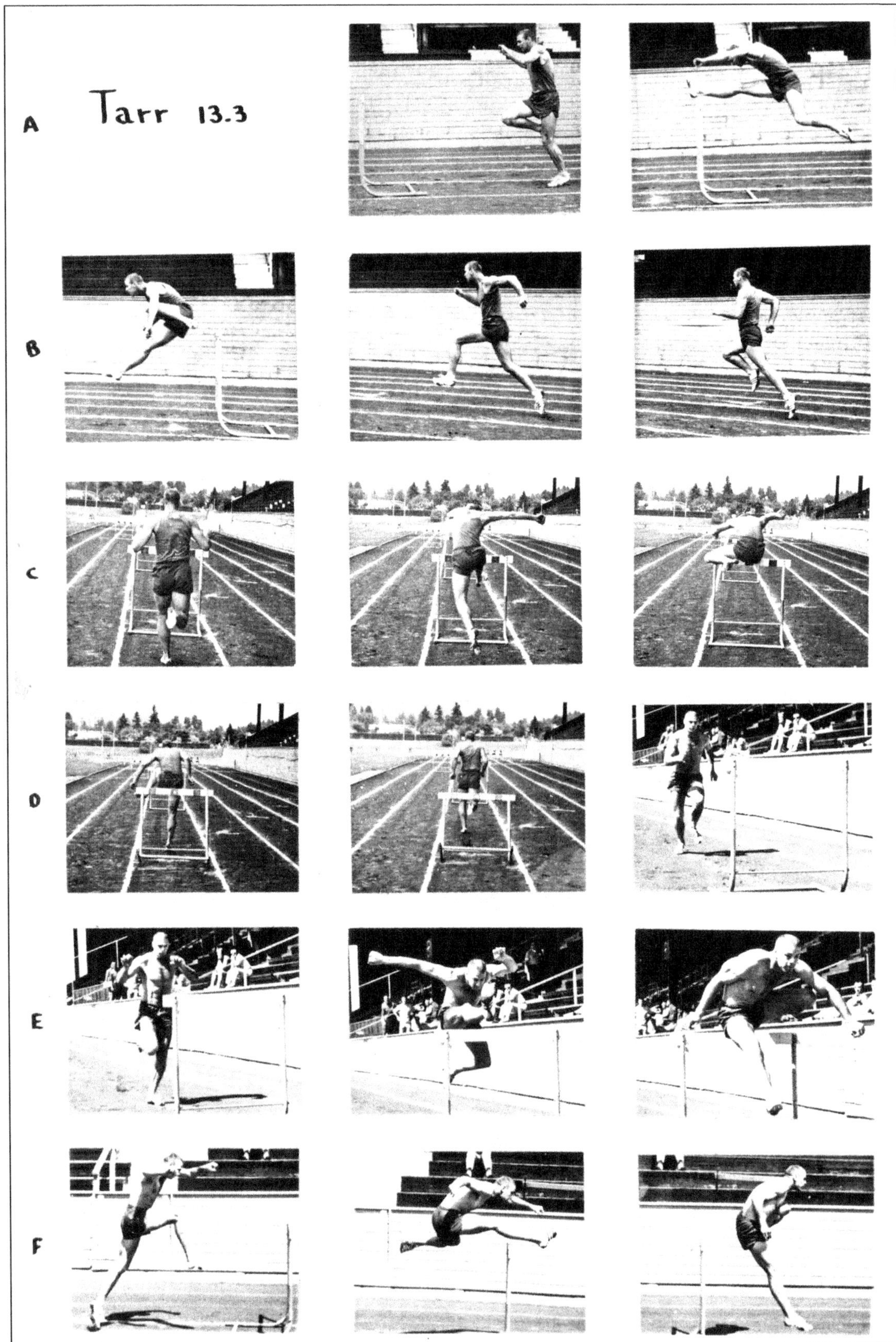

Photo 2-4. Jerry Tarr, 1962 #1 world ranking and two-time NCAA champion in high hurdles, 1962 #2 world ranking and one-time NCAA champion in 440-yard hurdles (*Note*: This technique study was probably taken by Bill Bowerman.)

programs allow the planning of training and the storage and analysis of training records. Expert systems software is allowing new applications to skill analysis and training evaluations. Video analysis has advanced rapidly in recent years, allowing many potential uses to make the coach's job easier and more effective.[7, 8]

Video analysis programs, such as Dartfish®, are now available around the world, greatly improving the coach's ability to analyze skills and design training and teaching programs for other coaches, teachers, and athletes. The Internet supports numerous websites devoted to sport training, to individual sports, and to events or event groups, and they often include video collections of athletic performances. Many national and international groups include useful articles and programs on their websites. Today coaches have a wealth of information easily available.

Resources for the Track Coach

Following the endnotes and reading list is a second listing of books that can serve as major resources for the track coach. This list offers more books than a coach may need, but in the science area, every coach should have at least one book that deals with basic biomechanics and another dealing with core-level exercise physiology. A book dealing with the care and prevention of athletic injuries would also be useful, though none are cited in the list.

Endnotes

1. Harmon Brown. (1993). Does science belong in sport? *Track Technique*, *123*, 3926-397.
2. Dennis J. Grady. (Winter 2007). Confessions of a Level II alumnus. *Track Coach*, *178*, 5673-5676.
3. Steve Myrland. (Fall 2005). Guru-ism and the decline of coaching. *Track Coach*, *173*, 5526-5528, 5537.
4. Wilf Paish. (Spring 2001). Quis custodiat ipsos custodes? [Who educates the Educators: Coach education in the UK]. *Track Coach*, *155*, 4941-4942, 4946.
5. Skip Stolley. (1989). Where have all the coaches gone? *Track Technique*, *106*, 3387, 3397.
6. Michelle Hopper Buchicchio. (1995). Where are the [women] coaches? *Track Coach*, *133*, 4244-4245.
7. Peter McGinnis. (Summer 2000). Video technology for coaches. *Track Coach*, *152*, 4857-4862.
8. Christina Hunneshagen. (2006). "Coaches' Eye"–Technical analysis and fault finding as an Internet application for coaching high jump. *New Studies in Athletics*, *21*(4), 39-47.

Recommended Readings

Digel, Helmut. (2001). Future outlook for the coaching profession. *New Studies in Athletics, 16*(1/2), 9-22.

Freeman, William H. (1994). Coaching, periodization, and the battle of artist versus scientist. *Track Technique, 127* (Spring 1994), 4054-4057; revised in Modern Athlete and Coach, 33 (January 1995), 19-23.

Gould, Daniel, et al. (Fall 2000). Positive and negative factors influencing U.S. Olympic athletes and coaches: Nagano Games assessment. *Track Coach, 153*, 4889-4893.

Huntsman, Stan. (1999). The fourth dimension. *Track and Field Coaches Review, 72*(4), 15-17.

NSA Round Table 26: Technology. (1994). *New Studies in Athletics, 9*(4), 13-24. [José Manuel Ballesteros, Neil Craig, Frank W. Dick, Vern Gambetta, Craig Hillyard, Elio Locatelli, Jarmo Mäkelä, Canadian Panel, & Chinese Group].

Robins, Michael. (1991). Training of NCAA Division II men's track coaches. *Track Technique, 114*, 3637-3638.

Sands, William A. (1996). How can coaches use sport science? *Track Coach, 134*, 4280-4283, 4292.

Schiffer, Jürgen. (2000). Selected and annotated bibliography 53: Coaching and coaches. *New Studies in Athletics, 15*(2), 75-102.

Schiffer, Jürgen. (1998). World list of periodicals relevant to athletics [and supplement]. *New Studies in Athletics, 13*(2), 45-90; 13(4), 79-82.

Straub, William F. (1991). Beyond the X's and O's: Sport leadership. *Track Technique, 117*, 3734-3736.

Ungerleider, Steven, & Jacqueline Golding. (1991). Beyond strength: Psychological profiles of Olympic athletes. *Track Technique, 116*, 3704-3709.

Vernacchia, Ralph A. (1998). Competitive refocusing and the performance of USA international junior elite track and field athletes. *New Studies in Athletics, 13*(1), 25-30.

Resources for the Coach

Coaching Basics

Carr, Gerry A. (1999). *Fundamentals of track and field* (2nd ed.). Champaign, IL: Human Kinetics.

Doherty, Ken. (2007). *Track & field omnibook* (5th ed.). Ed. John N. Kernan. Mountain View, CA: Tafnews.

Freeman, William H. (2001). *Peak when it counts: Periodization for American track and field* (4th ed.). Mountain View, CA: Tafnews.

Gambetta, Vern. (2007). *Athletic development: The art and science of functional sports conditioning*. Champaign, IL: Human Kinetics.

Guthrie, Mark. (2003). *Coaching track and field successfully*. Champaign, IL: Human Kinetics.

Hazen, Jack. (2004). *Training for cross country*. Mountain View, CA: Tafnews.

Martens, Rainer. (1997). *Successful coaching* (2nd ed.). Champaign, IL: Human Kinetics.

Newton, Joe, & Joe Henderson. (1998). *Coaching cross country successfully*. Champaign, IL: Human Kinetics.

Parker, Ron. (2005). *Getting started in track and field* (2nd ed.). Mountain View, CA: Tafnews.

Powell, John T. (1971). *Track and field fundamentals for teacher and coach* (3d ed.). Champaign, IL: Stipes.

Stolley, Skip, & E. Derse. (1991). *AAF/CIF track and field coaching manual*. Los Angeles: Amateur Athletics Federation.

USA Track and Field coaching manual. (2000). Champaign, IL: Human Kinetics.

More Advanced Coaching

Bompa, Tudor O. (1999). *Periodization: Theory and methodology of training* (4th ed.). Champaign, IL: Human Kinetics.

Bompa, Tudor O., Mauro di Pasquale & Lorenzo Cornacchia. (2003). *Serious strength training*. Champaign, IL: Human Kinetics.

Chu, Donald A. (1996). *Explosive power and strength: Complex training for maximum results*. Champaign, IL: Human Kinetics.

Cissick, John. (2003). *Strength training for track & field*. Mountain View, CA: Tafnews.

Clarkson, Michael. (1999). *Competitive Fire*. Champaign, IL: Human Kinetics.

Costill, David L., & Scott Trappe. (2002). *Running: The athlete within*. Traverse City, MI: Cooper.

Dintiman, George, & Bob Ward. (2003). *Sports speed* (3rd ed.). Champaign, IL: Human Kinetics.

Fleck, Steven J., & William J. Kraemer. (1997). *Designing resistance training programs* (2nd ed.). Champaign, IL: Human Kinetics.

Fleck, Steven J., & William J. Kraemer. (1996). *Periodization breakthrough!* New York: Advanced Research Press.

Gambetta, Vern, & Gary Winckler. (2001). *Sport specific speed: The 3 S systems*. Sarasota, FL: Gambetta Sports Training Systems.

Kraemer, William J., & Steven J. Fleck. (1993). *Strength training for young athletes*. Champaign, IL: Human Kinetics.

Kurz, Thomas. (1991). *Science of sports training: How to plan and control training for peak performance*. Island Pond, VT: Stadion.

Matveyev, Lev Pavlovich. (1981). *Fundamentals of sports training*. Trans. Albert P. Zdornykh. Moscow: Progress.

O'Shea, Patrick. (1996). *Quantum strength and power training: Gaining the winning edge: Textbook of applied athletic strength training and conditioning for peak performance, ages 16-80*. Corvallis, OR: Patrick's Books.

Payne, Howard, & Rosemary Payne. (1981). *The science of track and field athletics*. London: Pelham Books.

Peterson, James A., Cedric X. Bryant & Susan L. Peterson. (1995). *Strength training for women*. Champaign, IL: Human Kinetics.

Reaburn, Peter, & David Jenkins. (Eds.). (1996). *Training for speed and endurance*. St. Leonards, Australia: Allen & Unwin.

Siff, Mel, & Yuri V. Verkhoshansky. (1999). *Supertraining* (4th ed.). Denver, CO: Supertraining International.

Science Basics

Costill, David L. (1986). *Inside running: Basics of sports physiology*. Indianapolis: Benchmark.

Dick, Frank W. (2002). *Sports training principles* (4th ed.). London: A & C Black.

Dyson, Geoffrey, B.D. Woods, & Peter R. Travers. (1986). *Dyson's mechanics of athletics* (8th ed.). New York: Holmes & Meier.

Ecker, Tom. (1996). *Basic track and field biomechanics* (2nd ed.). Mountain View, CA: Tafnews.

Foss, Merle E. (1998). *Fox's physiological basis for exercise and sport* (6th ed.). Boston: WCB/McGraw-Hill.

Hay, James G. (1993). *The biomechanics of sports techniques* (4th ed.). Englewood Cliffs, NJ: Prentice-Hall.

McGinnis, Peter M. (2004). *Biomechanics of sport and exercise* (2nd ed.). Champaign, IL: Human Kinetics.

Schiffer, Jürgen. (1996). *An annotated dictionary of athletics and training*. Cologne: Sport und Buch Strauß.

Suinn, Richard M. (1986). *Seven steps to peak performance: The mental training manual for athletes*. Toronto: Hans Huber.

Thompson, Peter. (1991). *Introduction to training theory*. London: IAAF.

Ungerleider, Steven. (1996). *Mental training for peak performance*. Emmaus, PA: Rodale.

Vernacchia, Ralph, & Traci A. Statler (Eds.). (2005). *The psychology of high-performance track and field*. Mountain View, CA: Tafnews.

Wilmore, Jack H., David L. Costill, & W. Harry Kenney. (2008). *Physiology of sport and exercise* (4th ed.). Champaign, IL: Human Kinetics.

Zatsiorsky, Vladimir M. & William J. Kraemer. (2006). *Science and practice of strength training* (2nd ed.). Champaign, IL: Human Kinetics.

Specialized Knowledge

Armstrong, Lawrence E. (2000). *Performing in extreme environments*. Champaign, IL: Human Kinetics.

Astrand, Per-Olof (Ed.). (2003). *Textbook of work physiology: Physiological bases of exercise* (4th ed.). Champaign, IL: Human Kinetics.

Australian Sports Commission. (2000). *Physiological tests for elite athletes*. Champaign, IL: Human Kinetics.

Bar-Or, Oded. (Ed.). (1996). *The child and adolescent athlete*. Oxford: Blackwell Scientific.

Burke, Edmund R. (Ed.). *Precision heart rate training*. (1998). Champaign, IL: Human Kinetics

Hanin, Yuri L. (Ed.). (2000). *Emotions in sport*. Champaign, IL: Human Kinetics.

Hardy, Lew, Graham Jones & Daniel Gould. (1996). *Understanding psychological preparation for sport: Theory and practice of elite performers*. Chichester, England: John Wiley.

Hargreaves, Mark (Ed.). (1995). *Exercise metabolism*. Champaign, IL: Human Kinetics.

Heyward, Vivian H. (2002). *Advanced fitness assessment and exercise prescription* (4th ed.). Champaign, IL: Human Kinetics.

Houston, Michael E. (2006). *Biochemistry primer for exercise science* (2nd ed.). Champaign, IL: Human Kinetics.

Jackson, Susan A., & Mihaly Csikszentmihalyi. (1999). *Flow in sports*. Champaign, IL: Human Kinetics.

Janssen, Peter. (2001). *Lactate threshold training*. Champaign, IL: Human Kinetics.

Johnson, Rebecca, & Bill Tulin. (1995). *Travel fitness: Feel better, perform better on the road*. Champaign, IL: Human Kinetics.

Karinch, Maryann. (2002). *Diets designed for athletes*. Champaign, IL: Human Kinetics.

Kellmann, Michael (Ed.). (2002). *Enhancing recovery: Preventing underperformance in athletes*. Champaign, IL: Human Kinetics.

Komi, Paavo V. (Ed.). (2003). *Strength and power in sport*. Oxford, Eng.: Blackwell Science.

Kraemer, William J., & Keijo Hakkinen (Eds.). (2002). *Strength training for sport*. Oxford: Blackwell Science.

Kreider, Richard B., Andrew C. Fry, & Mary L. O'Toole (Eds.). (1998). *Overtraining in sport*. Champaign, IL: Human Kinetics.

Lohman, Timothy G. (1992). *Advances in body composition assessment*. Champaign, IL: Human Kinetics.

MacDougall, J. Duncan, Howard A. Wenger & Howard J. Green (Eds.). (1991). *Physiological testing of the high-performance athlete*. Champaign, IL: Human Kinetics.

Maud, Peter J., & Carl Foster (Eds.). (1995). *Physiological assessment of human fitness*. Champaign, IL: Human Kinetics.

Mougios, Vassilis. (2006). *Exercise biochemistry*. Champaign, IL: Human Kinetics.

Orlick, Terry. (2000). *In pursuit of excellence: How to win in sport and life through mental training* (3rd ed.). Champaign, IL: Human Kinetics.

Sheikh, Anees A., & Errol R. Korn. (Eds.). (1994). *Imagery in sports and physical performance*. Amityville, NY: Baywood.

Shephard, Roy J., & Per-Olof Astrand (Eds.). (1992). *Endurance in sport* [The Encyclopedia of Sports Medicine]. Oxford, Eng.: Blackwell Scientific.

Sparrow, William A. (Ed.). (2000). *Energetics of human activity*. Champaign, IL: Human Kinetics.

Starkes, Janet L., & K. Anders Ericsson (Eds.). (2003). *Expert performance in sports: Advances in research on sport expertise*. Champaign, IL: Human Kinetics.

Thompson, Ron A., & Roberta Trattner Sherman. (1992). *Helping athletes with eating disorders*. Champaign, IL: Human Kinetics.

Verhoshansky, Yuri I. (1986). *Fundamentals of special strength-training in sport* [1977 ed.]. Trans. Andrew Charniga, Jr. Livonia, MI: Sportivny.

Viru, Atko A. (1995). *Adaptation in sports training*. Boca Raton, FL: CRC.

Weinberg, Robert S., & Daniel Gould. (2007). *Foundations of sport and exercise psychology* (4th ed.). Champaign, IL: Human Kinetics.

Wells, Christine L. (1991). *Women, sport, and performance* (2nd ed.). Champaign, IL: Human

Williams, Melvin H. (1998). *The ergogenics edge: Pushing the limits of sports performance*. Champaign, IL: Human Kinetics.

THE ESSENTIALS OF SCIENTIFIC TRAINING

Part 1

Frank Shorter and Steve Prefontaine, 1971 AAU 3 mile

3

Foundations of Training

Though many athletes compete in sports, only a few reach the highest performance levels. Why is that true? Certainly not everyone has the same potential when beginning. Even so, many athletes who seem only ordinary in their early years later blossom into national- or world-class performers. Why are they able to make it to the top when athletes who were initially more talented are not? The answer lies in their training.

The Three Cornerstones of Training

Training and competition are complex activities; many variables contribute to success. However, three very basic rules should always be followed in training. These cornerstones of any successful system of training are:

- Moderation
- Consistency
- Rest

Moderation

Moderation is the first cornerstone of training. It means not going to extremes in any aspect of training. Inexperienced distance runners should not run 100 miles a week in training because they may develop serious injuries that could end their running careers early. Extended hours of training are not necessary. Athletes at most levels of competition can compete successfully with two hours of daily training if it is well planned and seriously conducted. Only at the most advanced levels of sport (after 6 to 10 years of training) does the need for more extensive training appear.

It is true that athletes in some events have trained more than this specified amount. However, the long-term results of more extreme training programs are inconsistent, with more athletes failing than succeeding in reaching the top.

Some athletes develop serious injuries, and many become burned out, psychologically drained by the heavy training loads.

The human body can take far more stress than we generally give it. However, it needs to adapt to heavier stresses gradually. Moderation means a carefully planned training program that avoids extremes in physical or psychological stress. Training and competing can be a beautiful, exciting part of life, but they are not all there is to life. The principle of moderation permits the athlete to enjoy the other parts of life as much as sports.

Consistency

Consistency is the second cornerstone of training. One way to avoid extremes in training is to train at a reasonable level every day. However, the same training load should not be used each day. When an athlete trains consistently, the body has more time to adapt to the stress of training, easing its way to higher levels of fitness. If a few days of training are missed, the body loses tone and endurance. A day or two of extra-hard training does not make up for that loss. In fact, the athlete may overstress the body, resulting in an injury or an illness. Extra physical strain does more than simply tire the body, so the consistency of training is critical. The athlete who trains daily at a moderate level will outperform the equally talented athlete who trains extremely hard at times and skips training at other times.

Consistency has another reward for the athlete. As training continues, a solid fitness base develops. The longer the time used to develop the base, the less effect an interruption of training has. Although any athlete loses conditioning when training is interrupted, an athlete with a long-term base loses conditioning more slowly and regains it more quickly.

Rest

Rest is the third cornerstone of training, perhaps the most important one for younger athletes. An athlete *must* get enough rest. This training rule may be the least followed by young athletes. A simple rule of training: when in doubt, get more rest. Athletes feeling tired or weak should not try to have hard training sessions. Instead, they should have very light training sessions or simply skip sessions. Athletes must be aware of how much sleep they are getting. Athletes in training need more rest and sleep than non-athletes.

Why do they need more rest? First, the extra work creates extra physical stress, which calls for more recovery time. Second, the body makes its adaptations to stress when the body is at rest rather than during the stress. It is part of the overload aspect of training. If the body does not have enough rest, it cannot recover and adapt fully, so it does not benefit fully from the training.

The body is like a massive computer, with many complex working parts. When it is worked very hard, occasionally the body tires or overloads, becoming less efficient. With a computer, a problem requires "down time," a rest period while the operators repair the problem. The body repairs its own problems (unless they are extreme), but it requires its own down time every day. The amount varies from one person to another, but most athletes need at least 8 to 10 hours of sleep each night.

Generally speaking, the younger the athlete is, the more rest that is needed. An athlete must learn to be tuned in to his body, which tells when it needs more rest and when it has had enough. The body runs on rest, just as it runs on fuel. If it has too little rest, it begins to run poorly.

These three cornerstones are critical to any training plan that a coach or athlete may use. If an athlete trains consistently at a moderate level while getting enough rest, his performances should continue to improve for years. The principles of the training system described in this book are built around these cornerstones.

The Principles of Training

Training is based on a set of principles, fact-based beliefs that are followed in deciding how the athlete's training should be carried out. These basic principles set the tone for the whole program. Developed over a period of years, each principle plays an important part in helping to plan an effective program. No set of principles is sacred, but the following discussion covers the principles adhered to in the Oregon System (Table 3-1).

Principle 1: Each Person Is an Individual

The entire training program is built on this principle. Though all people have common structural and physiological characteristics, each has their own particular talents, strengths, and weaknesses. In planning the program, take advantage of and develop the strengths, even as you strive to strengthen the weak areas. The program should meet the athlete's personal, specific needs. For this reason, never simply copy another person's training. The strengths and needs may not be the same; what is good for one person may not be appropriate for another. Therefore, find what makes that person's program successful, and then decide whether such factors might work well within your own program.

Principle 2: Set Reasonable (but Challenging) Goals

To get anywhere, you must know where you are going. Goals should be a challenge, for life is a process of rising to meet challenges. At the same time, goals need to be reasonably attainable. An athlete's goals should be based on what the athlete can do now (or has done recently). If the athlete's best mile was 5:00, a goal of 4:00 or even 4:30 is not reasonable. A goal such as breaking 4:50 is still a challenge, but it is one that a good training program may deliver. A person moves by steps, not by leaps. The purpose of setting

Foundations of Training

The Three Cornerstones of Training

- Moderation
- Consistency
- Rest

The Principles of Training

Principle 1: Each person is an individual.

Principle 2: Set reasonable (but challenging) goals.

Principle 3: Have a master plan.

Principle 4: Base the plan on event-specific abilities.

Principle 5: Be flexible in the plan.

Principle 6: Develop good mechanics.

Principle 7: Variety is the spice of life.

Principle 8: Follow the hard-easy approach.

Principle 9: It is better to undertrain than to overtrain.

Principle 10: Observe the rules of good nutrition.

Principle 11: Use recreation for the "whole" person.

Principle 12: Get enough rest.

The Overriding Principle: Make it fun.

Table 3-1. Foundations of training

reasonable goals is to help lead the athlete in a gradual progression toward larger goals. Athletes need goals that are challenging, but not discouraging because they are too extreme.

Principle 3: Have a Master Plan

Every athlete needs a master plan. The plan sets goals and shows how the athlete will progress toward them. A master plan looks at the total picture and takes the long view. For a young or beginning athlete, the plan may simply be for a season or a year. For a more experienced athlete, the plan should set broad goals for several years: Where does the athlete want to be next year and the year after that? A master plan is the competitive road map; it shows where the athlete is going and how to get there.

Principle 4: Base the Plan on Event-Specific Abilities

For an athlete to be better in any event, the physical traits that are specific to that event must be developed. One of the components of a good periodized training program is the development of a model of the event. Coaches and scientists try to determine what measurable physiological and psychological traits are found in elite performances in each event. Training is planned to develop those traits. The model is improved each year, and the training plan is modified to conform to the performance model. For example, if the anaerobic component is extremely important to success in a running event, the plan should emphasize training of that type. The athlete should be trained very specifically for the event.

Principle 5: Be Flexible in the Plan

Nature cannot be controlled, nor can a training plan result in a perfect progression mapped across a sheet of graph paper. The master plan must be flexible enough that it can be adapted to changing conditions or needs. Unusual weather may affect training or force a temporary change in the training site. The master plan must be able to meet changing circumstances, just as the athlete must prepare for changing situations in competition. For these reasons, athletes need to learn to be independent, for in major meets they are not allowed to communicate with their coaches.

Principle 6: Develop Good Mechanics

Good performance mechanics should be developed early in an athlete's career. For an athlete, good mechanics means easier, more effective training and competing. The time spent in perfecting the performance mechanics will be repaid again and again in competition. A noticeable characteristic of the world-class athlete is a high level of technical skill.

Principle 7: Variety Is the Spice of Life

A good training plan uses a variety of training methods. The more predictable the training program is, the duller it will be. This trait leads to staleness in the athlete because it lessens the challenge of training. It is one reason the Oregon System developed as an eclectic training system, one that took its methods from several different systems. The more variety a training program has, the more challenging and interesting the training will be for the athlete.

Principle 8: Follow the Hard-Easy Approach

A day of hard training should be followed by a day of easy or recovery training. Though the Oregon System used this approach for decades, it was not until the 1980s that East German research proved its worth. Using daily blood tests on their athletes to determine how they responded to training (when they should train hard and when they needed rest), the Germans also came up with a hard-easy pattern, with light training on every other day, for most athletes. The body needs about 48 hours for full recovery from very hard exercise. To stress this idea, use Arthur Lydiard's watchword for joggers: train; don't strain. Moderation requires recovery periods.

Principle 9: It Is Better to Undertrain Than to Overtrain

Because moderation is needed, every athlete must avoid the temptation to train ever harder. Human nature tells us that if so much work results in so much progress, twice as much work should yield twice the progress. However, human nature neglects mentioning that the athlete may break down under the increased training load.

The use of very heavy training leads to effects of the Law of Diminishing Returns. As the workload continues to rise, the results begin to flatten out, eventually giving worse results for the increased loads. The results of overtraining are staleness, fatigue, and a loss of interest in training or competing.

Principle 10: Observe the Rules of Good Nutrition

Proper energy intake is very important to successful sport. The term "good nutrition" (rather than "diet") is used deliberately because strange or fad diets need to be discouraged. A normal, well-balanced eating plan will meet most athletes' nutritional needs for successful competition. The only real difference is in quantity, rather than in magic foods. At the same time, the idea of dieting should be discouraged, especially with female athletes. Too often, female distance runners are encouraged to maintain very low body weights, which has serious long-term health risks. Most athletes who train intelligently and eat sensibly gradually reach a reasonable competition weight. An athlete who is significantly overweight or underweight may have unaddressed problems that are not physical.

Principle 11: Use Recreation for the "Whole" Person

Every athlete needs to develop a balanced approach to life to learn to enjoy it more fully. Recreation specialists like to use the term *re-creation*, for recreation helps people rebuild after the stresses of life take their toll. Recreation is not simply killing time, nor does it necessarily mean doing "useful" work. Everyone needs time spent in escaping the routine pattern of life, adding variety to life. The key is enjoying the gift of life. An athlete who has no dimensions other than being an athlete and student or worker misses much of the interest of life. An athlete should be a whole person.

Principle 12: Get Enough Rest

Rest is one of the most neglected needs of less successful or younger athletes. For an athlete in doubt, rest will probably be more useful than an extra workout. Although many experienced athletes train twice a day, younger athletes need to approach this practice with caution. Students often keep late hours while studying. The extra sleep in the morning (to ensure adequate rest) may be more useful than an extra training session. Younger athletes need more rest than older athletes. The athlete should never neglect rest because, like oxygen debt, such neglect always catches up with the body.

The Overriding Principle: Make It Fun

People develop an interest in sports because it is fun. The coach should strive to make training and competition fun, regardless of the athlete's level of ability. Even very hard training can be enjoyable if it is not monotonous or an unattainable challenge. By making the sport fun, the coach helps the athlete maintain an appetite for training and competing. Maintain that appetite, and the athlete will continue to train and improve.

4

The Science of Sport Training and Conditioning

Though a great coach is always an artist in arranging a training system, the sport sciences are the underlying foundation of any successful training program. An overview of training science basics is the best starting point for every coach who wants to be a success.

Physiological Laws of Training

All training systems are affected by three physiological laws:[1]

- Law of overload
- Law of specificity
- Law of reversibility

Law of Overload

Any improvement in fitness requires an increased training load. That load is a stimulus to which the athlete's body reacts. If the load is greater than normal, the body becomes fatigued, and its fitness level falls. As the body recovers, though, its fitness level returns to normal. If the training load was optimal, the athlete will be more fit after recovery (overcompensation) than before the load was applied (Figure 4-1).

Overcompensation is the central purpose of training. The coach plans a training load that produces a fitness increase after the athlete recovers. If the training load is too small, the training effect is less. If the load is too great, the athlete may not even rise to the original fitness level. Because each athlete reacts differently to training stimuli, training must be planned in terms of the individual's abilities, needs, and potential.

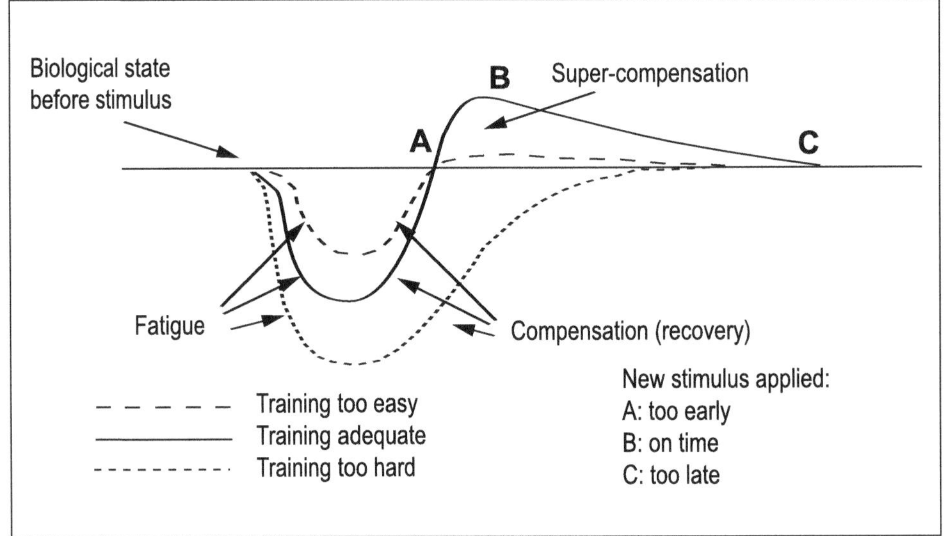

Figure 4-1. Effective and ineffective training loads

The most effective training develops a base of general skills and fitness before developing the more specialized skills of each event. This goal is the major focus of the early part of the training year. The more balanced the body's early development is, the higher the performance levels it can attain later. This fact should be the major focus in training children and junior athletes.

Law of Specificity

The nature of the training load determines the training effect. An athlete needs training methods tailored to the specific demands of the event. The training load becomes specific when it has the proper training ratio (of load to recovery) and structure of loading (of intensity to load).

Intensity is the quality of the training load. Running speed is measured in meters per second (m/sec) or stride rate (s/sec). Strength is measured in pounds, kilograms, or tonnage moved. Jumps and throws are measured by height, distance, or number of efforts. The heart rate is a good guide for endurance running. The intensity of the effort is based on the percentage of the athlete's best effort (Table 4-1 and Figure 4-2).

The *extent* of the training load is the sum of training in terms of time, distance, accumulative weight, or other measures, while the *duration* is that part of the load that is devoted to a single unit or type of training. An athlete may run for 75 minutes (extent) yet elevate the heart rate over 150 beats per minute (BPM) for only 10 minutes (duration) of that time.

Specialization refers to training exercises that develop the capacities and techniques needed for a specific activity or event. Any thrower needs strength in specific areas of the body, while more specific motor skills are needed for

Estimating the Intensity of Effort

Intensity	*Work (% of max)*	*Strength (% of max)*	*Heart Rate* (% of max)*	*Endurance (% $\dot{V}O_{2max}$)*
Maximum	95-100	90-100	190+	100
Sub-maximum	85-95	80-90	180-190	90
High	75-85		165	75
Medium	65-75	70-80	150	60
Light	50-65	50-70		
Low	30-50	30-50	130	50

*Heart rate should be based on a percentage of the athlete's maximum heart rate, which varies considerably among individuals.

Table 4-1. Estimating the intensity of effort

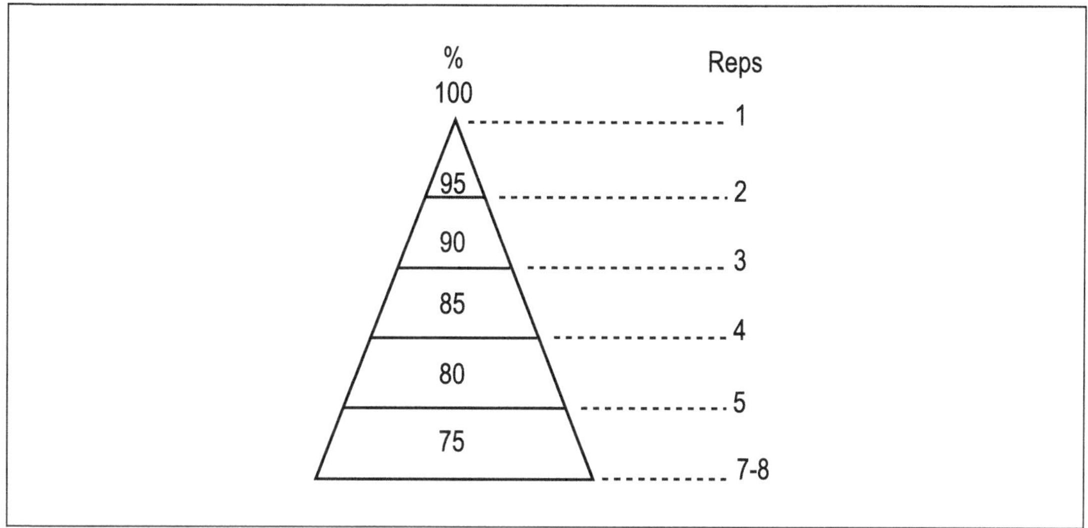

Figure 4-2. Intensity of effort for strength

each different throwing event. A runner needs speed and endurance, but the ratio depends on the length of the race. A runner must develop a technique that is most efficient for the racing distance. All of these traits are developed by using specialized training. Elite training gradually changes the emphasis from general to specific training as the athlete ages.

Modeling is developing a model of the competitive event. The model is then used to develop a training pattern that simulates the competitive requirements of the event. Many years are needed to develop and perfect a model. It begins with the coach's analysis of the competitive event, but afterward the emphasis is upon trial-and-error refinement of the model.

Law of Reversibility

The training effect can reverse itself. If the training does not become more challenging, the fitness level plateaus (flattens out). If the training ends, the fitness level gradually falls. In fact, the training load must continue to increase if the athlete's general and specific fitness are to improve. If the training load remains at the same level, the fitness rises for a time, then begins to fall. The training load must increase regularly (progressive overload) for the performance level to improve (Figure 4-3), though the load may rise and fall (allowing recovery and compensation) across a given period of time. The training ratio (of load to recovery) is critical. The coach must determine how much recovery is needed within a session and between sessions.

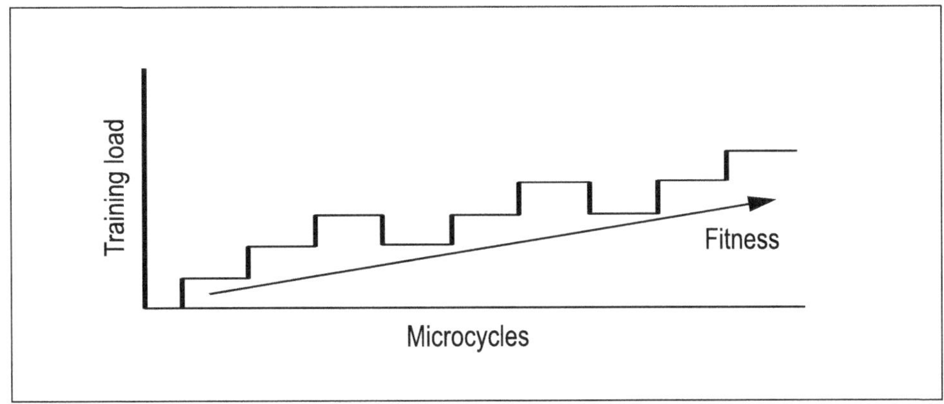

Figure 4-3. Progressive overload

At the same time, the planned training load must be realistic. The demand should not exceed the athlete's capabilities or rise too quickly, or it may be psychologically (and perhaps physically) destructive to the athlete's progress. The object of training is improvement, not discouragement or defeat.

Restoration is recovery from a high training load. Restoration is just as critical to the training effect as the training load itself. If too little restoration is allowed, the athlete will gradually lose fitness.

Active rest is a form of restoration (also used in the transition phase) that includes light physical activity. It may be jogging, or it may be participating in other sports. It allows the athlete to recover physically and psychologically, yet it helps maintain a base of general fitness.

The Components of Sports Fitness

Sports fitness has four basic components:

- Endurance
- Strength
- Flexibility
- Speed

Endurance

Endurance must be developed first, for without it most other types of training cannot be repeated enough to develop the other components of fitness. The amount of this emphasis depends on the event, with the short races and field events requiring considerably less endurance than the longer runs. Too much endurance training can hamper performance in some events.

Endurance can be aerobic or muscular. The most common method of developing aerobic endurance is with steady-state running for a length of time on a regular basis. It should be fast enough to raise the pulse to the 130- to 150-BPM range and should be maintained for at least 20 to 30 minutes. Muscular endurance is developed by many repetitions of low-resistance exercises. Circuit training can be used to combine the two types of endurance. Endurance training should not overwhelm the need for specific speed.

Strength

Strength can be whole-body strength, as in general conditioning, and specific strength, most effective within the range of motion of a given event. Strength is critical to every track and field event. The level of strength has a positive effect on both speed and endurance.

Flexibility

Sometimes called "mobility," flexibility determines the body's range of motion. The stretching exercises of the warm-up are designed to improve the athlete's flexibility. Because strength training results in shortening of the muscles, flexibility work is needed to keep the muscles loose through their full range of motion. The ability to hold stretched positions permits higher levels of performance, so stretching is a critical part of the training program.

Speed

Speed is critical to elite performance in every event. A thrower must be very quick, and even male marathoners at the world-class level can usually run a mile in 4:00 or less. While speed comes from the contractile quality of the muscles, the efficiency of movement comes from specific training, leading to improved speed. Though the basic quality of speed (reaction time) is largely inherited, it can be improved through training.

Types of Running Training

All types of running training are used to some degree in any training program, depending upon the athlete's needs. The basic types of running training are:

- Overdistance training
- Interval training
- Repetition running

- Fartlek
- Sprint training
- Time trials

Overdistance Training

Overdistance training is the essential element in the development of the endurance base. Coaches and athletes are learning that the intensity of training is more important than mileage. The super-heavy training loads of the 1960s and 1970s declined during the 1980s. Today, a typical training load for an elite runner at 10,000 meters and the marathon may be 80 to 90 miles per week, with considerably smaller loads for less experienced athletes. American marathoners who ran under 2:15 to qualify for the 2004 U.S. Olympic Trials reported an average training load of 96.7 miles per week, compared to 89.6 weekly miles for men who ran under 2:22. Women who qualified in under 2:40 averaged 84.4 miles a week, while those who ran under 2:48 averaged 69.2 miles a week.[2]

Today, overdistance runs are becoming shorter and more intense. Runners use *tempo running*, shorter runs at a pace that causes an optimal pulse reading for a length of time, rather than "grinding out the miles" on long, slow runs. The training effect is much greater. More detail is provided in Chapter 7.

Interval Training

Interval training means running short distances (intervals), usually on a track. Interval training has five variables:

- Length of the interval
- Speed or intensity of the variable
- Number of intervals
- Length of the recovery
- Nature of the recovery

Though interval training traditionally involves distances and times for those distances (such as 300m in 45 seconds), the work may be in terms of running set lengths of time at a given pulse rate or intensity level (such as 30 seconds at 170 to 180 BPM). The length of the work interval depends on the type of physiological improvement needed. The energy reserve of the muscles comes from ATP (adenosine triphosphate). It is produced by three pathways:

- ATP-PC (phosphocreatine) system
- Lactic acid (LA) system
- Oxygen (O_2) system

The ATP-PC and LA systems are anaerobic, working with little or no oxygen, while quickly producing ATP for a short time. The O2 system is aerobic (using oxygen) and produces ATP for a longer period of time. The choice of the interval depends upon the length of the race (Table 4-2).

Racing Time and Energy Systems for Training		
Race Length	*Major Energy System*	*Race*
Under 30 seconds	ATP-PC	100/200/high hurdles
30-90 seconds	ATP-PC-LA	200/400/intermediate hurdles
1:30-3:00	LA-O_2	800
More than 3:00	O_2	1500 and longer

Table 4-2. Racing time and energy systems for training

Repetition Running

Repetition running is a more intensive version of interval training. The intervals are run at a faster pace, with a nearly complete recovery between repetitions. Some coaches define intervals and repetitions according to their training emphasis. An interval focuses on the stress created by the pace and short recovery, while a repetition focuses on the pace itself, thus allowing a fuller recovery. In some training systems, repetitions are longer intervals, such as 800 meters or more.

Fartlek

Fartlek (speed play) is a less formal version of interval training that is especially suited to training away from the track. It mixes bursts of faster paced intervals of work with slower running within the context of a longer run on trails or a golf course. The length and the intensity of the faster runs are decided by the runner, depending upon what he needs and feels at the time. For more speed, shorter and faster bursts are used, while longer and less intense intervals are used for more endurance. Ideally, the training takes place on relatively soft surfaces, such as grass or sawdust trails.

Fartlek is a valuable training method because it allows a wide range of intensities, while also helping prevent the stress injuries that result from training on hard surfaces, such as pavement or running tracks. At the same time, it gives a more relaxing psychological setting and a chance to avoid the monotony of the track. It is more difficult for less experienced athletes, because they tend to turn it into a long, easy run with a few short accelerations. It has to be carefully taught to young runners. The use of heart monitors allows structured fartlek, a highly controlled training process, by monitoring and limiting the effort and recovery levels.

Sprint Training

Sprint training involves very short bursts of very fast running used primarily to improve the athlete's speed. It is also used for technique training. The recovery interval is almost complete, much like a short form of repetition running. Only a small number of repetitions are used, because fatigue changes the nature of the training. For distance runners, this technique is used in the final stages of sharpening or peaking.

Time Trials

Time trials are mentioned because they are an easily abused aspect of the training program. Time trials have two functions: assessing progress and simulating competition. They should be conducted under meet conditions, more formal than a training session. They should be held no more often than two to three weeks apart, or they become meaningless. Unless a trial serves a specific training function, it should not be used, because it reduces the number of effective training days. Frequent time trials are a sign of insecurity: the coach wants reassurance that the training system is working.

Strength-Development Programs

The order of strength-training exercises is critical in two respects. First, the larger muscle groups should be exercised before the smaller ones. Otherwise, overloading the large muscles is difficult because the smaller muscle groups tire more quickly. Second, no two exercises should train the same group of muscles consecutively, for the muscles would have too little recovery time.

The principle of specificity is extremely important. Strength development is specific to both the muscle group exercised and the pattern of movement used. You should duplicate the event movement pattern as closely as possible in the strength-training program. This specificity includes the joint angle at which the muscle is exercised and the type of contraction performed. Using the proper joint angle and contraction is especially important in isometric training because the major strength gain in isometrics is only at the angle used in exercising the muscle.

Resistance-Training Procedures

Exercises are measured in repetitions (reps), usually divided into larger groups called sets. One set is a number of reps performed without interruption. Three sets of five reps (3 x 5) means to repeat the exercise five times without stopping, take a recovery rest, perform the exercise five more times, take a rest, then perform the exercise for a final five times, completing the three sets.

Resistance exercises are generally used three times a week, on alternating days to permit the muscles to recover. Strength specialists may train every day, but the muscle groups are divided so that no muscle group is trained on consecutive days. During the early competitive season, strength work drops to two days per week, then to once a week as the season nears its peak. At that stage, the emphasis is on maintenance of strength. Improved technique makes up for any loss of strength. If strength training stops when the season begins, much of the strength gain would be lost before the end of the season.

Intensity is also a factor in strength activities. To lessen fatigue and improve efficiency, active rest is useful between lifts at higher intensities. This involves light or non-lifting movements directed toward other parts of the body after an intense exercise is completed.

Every athlete encounters "sticking points," performance plateaus that the athlete cannot pass. These points can result both from overtraining and from undertraining. Often a change in the workout load helps. Other causes may be poor diet or physical or mental fatigue (often called "staleness").

The starting weights are largely a matter of opinion and personal feeling. The coach or athlete should check the more scientifically oriented strength-training books. Starting weights may be based on a percentage of either the athlete's body weight or his best performance in each exercise. Strength training emphasizes either body development (hypertrophy) or strength, depending upon the weight and number of repetitions of an exercise (Table 4-3).

Weight Training Load and Emphasis

Load	*Percent of Maximum*	*Number of Repetitions*	*Training Emphasis*
Heavy	90%	1-3	Strength
Medium	80%	5-6	Muscular endurance
Light	70%	8-12	Muscular endurance

Table 4-3. Weight training load and emphasis

A General Weight-Training Program

This book will not suggest specific strength-training programs at this point, because it is better for coaches and athletes to develop their own programs. Many books deal primarily with such programs (refer to the Additional Readings section at the end of Chapter 2). In general, as athletes become more experienced, they will learn which exercises are most helpful on their own.

Plyometrics

Plyometrics (jump training) is used to develop leg strength and resilience for explosive power. The most common forms of training are with multiple jumps (on one or both legs) on the ground and with jumps using boxes of varying heights. The training involves work with the muscles' stretch reflex. It will be discussed in more depth later. Plyometrics involves a high injury risk if too many jumps are attempted, so caution is important.

Circuit Training

Circuit training uses a series of resistance exercises and calisthenics that follow a sequence, usually within an indoor area. The athlete moves quickly from one exercise station to the next, performing each exercise within a time limit. The circuit is finished when the performer completes the sequence. This approach is good for physical conditioning in limited areas, when bad weather conditions force athletes indoors, and for group exercises (athletes start at different stations, then move to the next station on a signal).

The *parcourse* is an outdoor version of circuit training, an exercise trail laid around a park or wooded area, with jogging or running between the stations. Oregon's 1984 Olympic 800-meter champion Joaquim Cruz used a similar course for his base conditioning, with a 10-station circuit at 100-meter intervals around a kilometer packed-sawdust loop.[3]

Concerns in Training and Conditioning

Sex Differences in Sport Training

The training for both sexes is largely the same, differing primarily in terms of the loading. Until puberty, boys and girls have essentially the same abilities and capacities. During puberty, the differences are as great within a single sex as between the sexes. From about ages 10 to 16, adolescents show widely varying body sizes, strength, and levels of coordination, depending upon when a child goes through puberty and how quickly it happens. At this time (about the fifth through tenth grades), a teacher or coach needs to be as careful with single-sex classes as with a mixed class. However, both sexes can work at the same relative intensity.

After physical maturity (about age 18), several differences between the sexes affect physical capacity and performance. The typical male has about 12 to 15 percent body fat, compared to 26 percent for females. Women have more difficulty in reaching higher levels of performance because the additional body fat is "drag weight"; that is, it limits performance.

Body-fat levels may be very low in elite distance runners (2 to 6 percent in men and 10 to 15 percent in women). Menstrual irregularities may occur when a woman drops below 15 percent body fat, though research suggests training intensity or stress is a factor in this effect.[4] Among the potentially harmful effects of very low fat levels in women athletes are anorexia and the development of osteoporosis, a dangerous thinning of bone density, which may not be recoverable in later years.

Women are more likely than men to suffer from anemia (iron deficiency). Heavy training increases this deficiency, so women in training may need iron supplements, though supplements should not be taken without medical consultation.[5] Women's performances at different times in the menstrual cycle may vary, but the effect is highly individualized. Olympic medals have been won at all stages of the cycle.

Another major difference is the higher proportion of muscle tissue in men (about 60 percent) compared to women (about 40 percent). Because male hormones are a major factor in the development of muscular strength, women do not have the same potential for strength development that men have. Also, because of female hormones, it is very difficult for women to develop the "bulky" muscles associated with male athletes.[6] However, though a female athlete can become much stronger through training, even heavy weight training will not develop a "masculine-looking" woman. Women are both shorter and lighter than men, which has many effects in terms of biomechanics and potential power.

Although coaches are aware that some athletes may take steroids to help increase their strength, they should not forget a common hormonal treatment used by many women: birth-control pills. Younger women may be placed on the Pill by a physician to control menstrual disorders. Among the Pill's effects is an increase in weight. Nausea may be a side effect when treatment starts, so the coach should be cautious in any interpretation of physical problems. However, never assume that any athlete's problem is only in their head.

Remember that the differences between the sexes are based on averages. An elite female athlete may be more capable than an average male athlete. Both women and men can benefit from intensive training programs; their capacities to endure such training are essentially the same. Some male coaches suggest that female athletes are less likely than men to complain about heavier training loads.

Men and women who perform at the same level can be trained together, for their abilities are essentially the same. Coed teams have many benefits; the men's and women's teams usually are very supportive of each other, particularly if they are coached and trained together.

Warm-Up: Prelude to Exercise

A careful warm-up raises the body and muscle temperatures, which increase their working effectiveness. A warm-up stretches the muscles, which helps prevent injury. It should not be done to the point of fatigue, however. Because long-distance runners use a more limited range of motion than athletes in other events, they often do minimal warming up.

The athlete should wear a sweatsuit or other covering to promote the warming effect. Rubber suits should *never* be used because they prevent normal evaporation of sweat. The use of rubber suits raises the body temperature and can result in heat exhaustion or heart attacks (even in teenagers) in some situations.

A warm-up begins with a short, light jog, just long enough to raise the muscle temperature. Then, stretching exercises are used, beginning with light, gradual stretching and progressing over 10 to 20 minutes to more thorough exercises. All of the major muscle groups should be stretched. No sudden movements (such as bouncing or jerking) should be used, so the muscles are never strongly forced to stretch. The progress should be gentle and gradual. Brief calisthenics may follow stretching. The athlete should be warm and sweating after the warm-up, but not tired.

The closing part of the warm-up should be event-specific. The runners do a bit of running, with a few short bursts of faster runs. Sprinters take a few easy-to medium-effort starts, while hurdlers begin to work with lower hurdles. Throwers simulate parts of their throwing routine.

Warm-Up Exercises

Stretching improves performance because loose muscles perform more easily and are less prone to injury. Relaxation is a part of stretching. No sudden pulling or yanking motions should be used. Be careful of pairing athletes for stretching; no fast moves or forcing of stretching should be done. Lasting injuries may result from sudden stretching. The final stretched position should be held for 20 to 30 seconds, keeping in mind that it is a *relaxed* extension of the muscles, not a forced one. Table 4-4 illustrates 10 suggested stretching exercises for class instruction and team training.[7]

Warm-Up Stretching Routine
• Achilles tendon and gastrocnemius • Back • Hamstring • Groin • Spine and waistline • Quadriceps • Shoulder and chest • Ankle • Abdominal • Hip

Table 4-4. Warm-up stretching routine

Some calisthenics are also useful as warm-up and conditioning exercises. They should not be used too much because younger athletes quickly become bored with them. The following are suggested exercises for specific body areas:[8]

- Shoulders and groin: jumping jacks
- Ankles, toes and gastrocnemius: toe raises and running in place
- Quadriceps: half-squats (no weights)
- Shoulders, arms, and chest: push-ups
- Abdominals: bent-knee sit-ups and bent-knee leg-raises

Straight-leg sit-ups and leg-raises should not be used because they create back strain rather than help develop the abdominals.

Special Environments

Much of the American training year involves dealing with weather that interferes with training. The most common concerns are heat and cold.

Heat

Much of the general or base training occurs during the hot summer months and is unsupervised. Only a few places in the United States do not have some problems of extremes in heat and humidity. In many heat conditions, the athlete's sweat does not evaporate quickly enough, which limits the ability to cool the body and may result in heat stress.

Heat alone, common in the Southwest, can be dangerous; combined with high humidity, as in the Midwest, East, and South, it can be deadly. If the humidity is high, heat stress can appear in athletes before the temperature reaches 70 degrees F (22 degrees C). Even with low humidity, temperatures above 80 degrees F (27 degrees C) can create the risk of stress. Symptoms of heat stress include headaches, dizziness, sudden tiring or weakness, a pounding sensation in the head, tingling or goose-bump sensations across the body, or the cessation of sweating.

The five levels of heat effects are cramps, syncope, two types of exhaustion (from water depletion and from salt depletion), and stroke. Muscle cramps result from excessive loss of salt through sweating. Taking salt tablets may increase the problem unless enough fluid is taken at the same time. In most cases, an athlete can eat enough salt with meals to avoid this problem.[9]

Heat exhaustion causes collapse or fainting as the body tries to end the work that is causing stress. It results from severe loss of fluids or electrolytes that the body uses to assist in cooling itself.

Heat stroke is most noticeable when sweating stops. Failure to cool the body quickly may result in brain damage, coma, or even death. Although it does not commonly happen, runners die every year from heat stress, usually because they fail to exercise proper caution.

Sweating is the body's way of coping with heat and humidity. The humidity is important because the higher the level of water in the air, the less sweat that evaporates from the athlete. The evaporation, not the act of sweating, does the actual cooling. The athlete must stay aware of the following concerns:

- Am I sweating?
- Is my sweat evaporating?
- Am I getting enough fluids?

In warm or humid training conditions, fluid intake is extremely important. The best, most easily, and most quickly absorbed fluid is water. Waiting until the training session is completed to drink fluids is extremely dangerous and does not help an athlete adapt to heat.

Adapting to heat is done best under natural conditions. To be able to race in heat, an athlete must train in heat. An athlete can train harder and longer, and run faster, in cooler conditions. However, if an important race will be run in hot or humid conditions, the athlete needs to train under those conditions. Adapting to heat takes about 10 to 14 days. The most useful training is to take longer, easier runs, being careful to drink enough fluids. However, as much as 50 percent of the body's adaptation to heat may come from the heat generated by interval training, regardless of the climate.

Cold

Cold weather creates its own training problems. Athletes must dress carefully for protection. Modern fabrics and layering allow less bulky training dress than in the past.

The most vulnerable parts of the body are the extremities. Thermal socks or layers of socks are needed for the feet, just as gloves are used for the hands. The material should absorb sweat so the body can cool itself properly within the warm bundles of protective gear (an athlete can suffer from heat exhaustion even in very cold weather). A cap that can cover the ears, or added earmuffs, helps to protect the head. In extreme climates, an athlete may wear a ski mask to protect the face from frostbite.

A sunny, cold day or a windy day can create special problems. A well-dressed runner may overheat if the sun is out and the air is calm. The same effect is possible with a strong tailwind. On windy, cold days, an out-and-back run is best. The athlete is dressed to begin facing the wind, removing clothing while returning with the wind. If the process were reversed, the athlete would overheat early, then chill and tire rapidly when running into the wind.

Athletes should be aware of the effects of the wind-chill factor: A strong wind in cool conditions may create far harsher cold than expected. Cold is as deadly as heat, and strong winds heighten the effect. Insisting on an outdoor run regardless of the weather conditions is not a virtue. It may be far wiser to skip a session or train indoors than to risk injury or worse. The smart coach and athlete always consider the possible effects of weather conditions on training and racing.

Sports Psychology and Motivation

Sport psychology is critical to the preparation of elite athletes. Psychology is used for more than just motivation. As Thomas Tutko noted, "On the whole, the psyching-up idea is more part of the problem than a solution."[10] because often it simply increases the athlete's anxieties, reducing performance effectiveness. Performers simply try *too* hard.

Richard M. Suinn's training book for athletes recommends a seven-step program of mental training to prepare athletes for competition:11

- Relaxation training
- Stress management
- Positive thought control
- Self-regulation
- Mental rehearsal (visual motor behavior rehearsal)
- Concentration
- Energy control

The focus is upon learning to control the athlete's emotions and channel them, dealing constructively with stress and maintaining a positive focus on training. The old concept of psyching up acted more as sensory overkill, putting some athletes almost out of control. Elite performance requires very calm, deliberate control of energy and skills, while a heated, emotional approach provides an unstable platform for performance. Thus, much of the focus of sport psychology is on relaxation, or stress and tension control.

The other aspect is the accent on the positive. The old coaching approach was to criticize and pressure athletes, forcing them to improve. It was similar to the old Theory X in business, the idea that people were inherently lazy and unwilling to perform unless threatened and forced to do well. The emphasis on the positive skips past Theory Y (people do want to perform well) to Theory Z, a cooperative approach between athlete and coach to training and performance.[12] The coach tries to reinforce the positive aspects of training, encouraging and supporting the athletes as they proceed. Confident athletes perform far better than insecure ones.

The coach should evaluate athletes' performances objectively but should conclude with and emphasize the positive. Encourage the athletes and show them how they are progressing. An athlete who faces constant criticism will eventually quit and will leave with a poor self-image. Every performance has some positive aspects. The coach who encourages his athletes and maintains a positive attitude will generally be the most successful coach in the long run.

The Goal: Consistency in Training

Ultimately, the most successful training program is the one that is most consistent. Athletes must train for weeks, months, and years at a consistent, moderate level. This stability creates a solid foundation for future success. The athletes are not forced up and down the emotional scale by extreme psyching or negative criticism. They are not put through destructively hard training sessions as "character builders." Instead, they are brought along with a carefully designed, positively oriented program that gives them emotional support, encouragement, and pride at every step along the way. This approach is what good training is all about; it is the heart of sport for life.

Endnotes

1. William H. Freeman. (2001). *Peak when it counts: Periodization for the American coach* (4th ed.). Mountain View, CA: Tafnews, 23-31.
2. Karp, Jason R. (2007). Training characteristics of U.S. Olympic Marathon Trials qualifiers. *Track Coach*, 178, 5693-5698.
3. Bill Dellinger & Bill Freeman. (1984). *The competitive runner's training book*. New York: Collier, 49-55.
4. Edward L. Fox, Richard W. Bowers, & Merle L. Foss. (1989). *The physiological basis of physical education and athletics*. Dubuque, IA: Wm. C. Brown, 401-402.
5. *Ibid.*, 405.
6. *Ibid.*, 393-394.
7. *Ibid.*, 190-193.
8. *Ibid.*, 299.
9. *Ibid.*, 492-493, 499.
10. Thomas Tutko & Umberto Tosi. (1976). *Sports psyching*. Los Angeles: J.P. Tarcher, 11.
11. Richard M. Suinn. (1986). *Seven steps to peak performance: The mental training manual for athletes*. Toronto: Hans Huber.
12. William G. Ouchi. (1981). *Theory Z: How American business can meet the Japanese challenge*. Reading, MA: Addison-Wesley, 48-49, 58-59.

Recommended Readings

Abernethy, P., G. Wilson, & P. Logan. (1995). Strength and power assessment: Issues, controversies and challenges. *Sports Medicine*, *19*(6), 401-417.

Adirim, Terry A., & Tina L. Cheng. (2003). Overview of injuries in the young athlete. *Sports Medicine*, *33*(1), 75-81.

Arbeit, Ekkart. (1998). Practical training emphases in the first and second decades of development. *New Studies in Athletics*, *13*(1), 13-20.

Arbeit, Ekkart. (1998). Principles of the multi-year training process. *New Studies in Athletics*, *13*(4), 21-28.

Bergeron, Joil. (Summer 2006). Selection & design of event-specific exercises. *Track Coach*, *176*, 5609-5614.

Bishop, David. (2003). Warm up I: Potential mechanisms and the effects of passive warm up on exercise performance. *Sports Medicine*, *33*(6), 439-454.

Bishop, David. (2003). Warm up II: Performance changes following active warm up and how to structure the warm up. *Sports Medicine*, *33*(7), 483-498.

Brown, C. Harmon. (1999). Over-training: A brief review. *New Studies in Athletics*, *14*(1), 67-70.

Brown, C. Harmon. (Fall 1996). Strength training for women: Some hormonal considerations. *Track Coach*, *137*, 4367-4368, 4370.

Cissik, John M. (Winter 2007). Program design: Linking it all together. *Track Coach*, *178*, 5688-5692.

Cissick, John. (Spring 2001). You need a needs analysis. *Track Coach*, *155*, 4952-4954.

De Jonge, Xanue A. K. Janse. (2003). Effects of the menstrual cycle on exercise performance. *Sports Medicine*, *33*(11), 833-851.

Ebbets, Russ, ed. (Summer 2001).Core strength roundtable. *Track Coach*, *156*, 4969-4974. Participants: Troy Engle, Larry Judge, Joe Miller, Dave Nielsen & Irving "Boo" Schexnayder.

Gambetta, Vern. (2007). *Athletic development: The art and science of functional sports conditioning*. Champaign, IL: Human Kinetics.

Godik, Mark A. (1998). A comparative analysis of the preparation process of men and women athletes. *New Studies in Athletics*, *13*(2), 19-25.

Grund, Martin, & Wolfgang Ritzdorf. (2006). From talent to elite athlete: A study of the performance development of the finalists at the 1999 IAAF World Youth Athletics Championships. *New Studies in Athletics*, *21*(2), 43-55.

Henschen, Keith, & Craig Poole. (Summer 1998). How to repeat a gold medal performance. *Track Coach*, *144*, 4595-4596, 4612

Hohmann, A., & I. Seidel. (2003). Scientific aspects of talent development. *International Journal of Physical Education*, *40*(1), 9-20.

Hooper, Sue L., & Laurel Traeger Mackinnon. (1995). Monitoring overtraining in athletes: Recommendations. *Sports Medicine*, *20*(5), 321-327.

Karp, Jason R. (2000). Training the energy systems. *Track & Field Coaches Review*, *73*(2), 18-20.

Kenttä, Göran, & Peter Hasmén. (1998). Overtraining and recovery: A conceptual model. , *26*(1), 1-16.

Kernan, John. (Summer 1999). The 24 consensus principles of athletic training and conditioning. *Track Coach*, *148*, 4720-4722.

Keul, Joseph, Daniel König, Martin Huoneker, Martin Halle, Bernd Wohlfahrt, & Aloys Berg. (1996). Adaptation to training and performance in elite athletes. *Research Quarterly for Exercise and Sport 67*(3, suppl.), 29-36.

Kibler, W. Ben, Joel Press, & Aaron Sciascia. (2006). The role of core stability in athletic function. *Sports Medicine*, *36*(3), 189-198.

Koutedakis, Yiannis. (1993). The female athlete: Physiological aspects of fitness. *Track Technique*, *122*, 3889-3892.

Kraemer, William J. (1997). A series of studies—The physiological basis for strength training in American football: Fact over philosophy. *Journal of Strength and Conditioning Research, 11*(3), 131-142.

Kraemer, William J., & Nicholas A. Ratamess. (2004). Fundamentals of resistance training: Progression and exercise prescription. *Medicine & Science in Sports & Exercise*, *36*(4), 674-688.

Kratina, Karin. (Summer 2001). 10 things coaches can do to help prevent eating disorders in their athletes. *Track Coach*, *156*, 4979.

Kuipers, Harm, & HA Keizer. (1988). Overtraining in elite athletes. *Sports Medicine*, *6*, 79-92.

Laursen, Paul B., & David G. Jenkins. (2002). The scientific basis for high-intensity interval training: Optimising training programmes and maximising performance in highly trained endurance athletes. *Sports Medicine*, *32*(1), 53-73.

Leddy, Matthew H., Michael J. Lambert & Benjamin M. Ogles. (1994). Psychological consequences of athletic injury among high-level competitors. *Research Quarterly for Exercise and Sport 65*, 347-354.

Luo, Jin, Brian McNamara & Kieran Moran. (2005). The use of vibration training to enhance muscle strength and power. *Sports Medicine*, *35*(1), 23-41.

Mackinnon, Laurel T., & Sue L. Hooper. (2000). Overtraining and overreaching: Causes, effects, and prevention. In *Exercise and Sport Science*, eds. William E. Garrett & Donald T. Kirkendall (pp. 487-498). Philadelphia: Lippincott Williams & Wilkins.

Martin, David. (1995). Appearances are deceiving: The female athlete triad. *Track Technique*, *130*, 4144-4147.

Martin, David E. (1995). Overview: Physiology—Its role in explaining athletic performance. *New Studies in Athletics*, *10*(1), 9-12.

Mujika, Iñigo, & Sabino Padilla. (2003). Scientific bases for precompetition tapering strategies. *Medicine & Science in Sports & Exercise*, *35*(7), 1182-1187.

Mujika, Iñigo, Sabino Padilla, David Pyne & Thierry Busso. (2004). Physiological changes associated with the pre-event taper in athletes. *Sports Medicine*, *34*(13), 891-927.

Plyometrics roundtable [James C. Radcliffe, Vern Gambetta, Larry Judge, Dave Kerin, John Cissik & Chris Polakowski]. (Fall 2006). *Track Coach*, *177*, 5646-5659, 5669.

Portugalov, Sergej. (1998). Characteristics of the specialised nutrition of top women athletes. *New Studies in Athletics*, *13*(2), 27-29.

Quod, Marc J., David T. Martin & Paul B. Laursen. (2006). Cooling athletes before competition in the heat: Comparison of techniques and practical considerations. *Sports Medicine*, *36*(8), 671-682.

Raglin, John S. (2001). Psychological factors in sport performance: The mental health model revisited. *Sports Medicine*, *31*(12), 875-890.

Rowland, Thomas W. (2000). Exercise science and the child athlete. In *Exercise and Sport Science*, eds. William E. Garrett & Donald T. Kirkendall (pp. 339-350). Philadelphia: Lippincott Williams & Wilkins.

Rundell, Kenneth W., & David M. Jenkinson. (2002). Exercise-induced bronchospasm in the elite athlete. *Sports Medicine*, *32*(9), 583-600.

Smith, David J. (2003). A framework for understanding the training process leading to elite performance. *Sports Medicine*, *33*(15), 1103-1126.

Suslov, Felix. (2001). Annual training programmes and the sport specific fitness levels of world class athletes. *New Studies in Athletics*, *16*(1/2), 63-70.

Taha, Tim, & Scott G. Thomas. (2003). Systems modelling of the relationship between training and performance. *Sports Medicine*, *33*(14), 1061-1089.

Tancred, Bill, & Geoff Tancred. (1995). An examination of the benefits of warm up: A review. *New Studies in Athletics*, *10*(4), 35-41.

Tarnopolsky, Mark A. (2000). Gender differences in metabolism, nutrition and supplements. *Journal of Science and Medicine in Sport*, *3*(3), 287-298.

Training theory roundtable [Russ Ebbets, Rob Graham, Matt Lydum, Tyler Wingard & Phil Lundin]. (Winter 2007). *Track Coach*, *178*, 5677-5687, 5701.

Tranckle, Peter, & Christopher J. Cushion. (2005). Rethinking giftedness and talent in sport. *Quest*, *58*, 265-282.

Tschiene, Peter. (1995). A necessary direction in training: The integration of biological adaptation in the training program. *Coaching and Sport Science Journal*, *1*(3), 2-14.

Urhausen, Axel, & Wilfried Kindermann. (2002). Diagnosis of overtraining: What tools do we have? *Sports Medicine*, *32*(2), 95-102.

Venderley, Angela M., & Wayne W. Campbell. (2006). Vegeterian diets: Nutritional considerations for athletes. *Sports Medicine*, *36*(4), 293-305.

Verkhoshansky, Yuri. (1998). Main features of a modern scientific sports training theory. *New Studies in Athletics*, *13*(3), 9-20.

Vernacchia, Ralph A. (Spring 2007). Psychological restoration: Assessing underrecovery and underperforming in track and field athletes. *Track Coach*, *179*, 5705-5712.

Wann, Daniel L., & Brian Church. (Summer 1998). A method for enhancing the psychological skills of track and field athletes. *Track Coach*, *144*, 4597-4605.

Weerapong, Poruratshanee, Patria A. Hume & Gregory S. Kolt. (2005). The mechanisms of massage and effects on performance, muscle recovery and injury prevention. *Sports Medicine*, *35*(3), 235-256.

Wells, Christine L., & Muriel Gilman. (1991). An ecological approach to training. *The Academy Papers*, *24*, 15-29.

Yonamine, Mauricio, Paula Rodrigues Garcia & Regina Lúcia De Moraes Moreau. (2004). Non-intentional doping in sports. *Sports Medicine*, *34*(11), 697-704.

Zelichenok, Vadim. (2005). The long term competition activity of the world's top athletes. *New Studies in Athletics*, *20*(2), 19-24.

Zelichnok, Vadim. (2006). From junior star to elite performer [abstract]. *New Studies in Athletics*, *21*(1), 66.

5

Designing the Training Program

A major concern for coaches is the process of designing a training program. How do you plan the training year? What factors determine the training emphases? How are training sessions designed? This discussion is adapted from *Peak When It Counts*, a detailed explanation of periodization and how to apply it to the American training year.[1]

Periodization Defined

The term *periodization* simply means dividing the training process into *periods* of time with different training emphases, goals, and lengths. Each period prepares the athlete for the next, a more advanced training period, until the athlete peaks at the most important competition of the year.

Periodization is an attempt to make training an objective process. It points the training effort toward the major goal. Training is a very complex process, involving both internal and external variables. It is affected by the quantity and quality of training, by rest, and by the competitive experiences of the athlete.

Training graphs show the training emphases at different times during the training year. Periodization tries to quantify training in a meaningful way so you can summarize it in tables and charts. This approach allows you to see more clearly how the athlete is expected to progress.

An athlete uses periodized training so he can:

- Peak at the ideal moment.
- Achieve the optimal training effect from each phase of training.
- Make training a more objective process.

Also, because the training plan produces objective records of training and progress, it can be compared to future training. The coach can objectively measure how much more training is being done in the new year, what types of training are different, and the amount of improvement in the performance characteristics along the way. It gives more objective standards to measure how improvement in the control tests translates into event success.

The Language of Periodization

The training periods in periodization are called *cycles*. A training year contains seven categories of cycles (from the largest unit of time down to the smallest):

- Macrocycle
- Mesocycle
- Period
- Phase
- Microcycle
- Training session
- Training unit

A training year with a single macrocycle (primary goal or training emphasis) leads to a single peak competition (*single periodization*, Figure 5-1). Although the single training emphasis often is appropriate, many training years include two major competitions or peaks (*double periodization*), such as the indoor and outdoor seasons in American track and field.

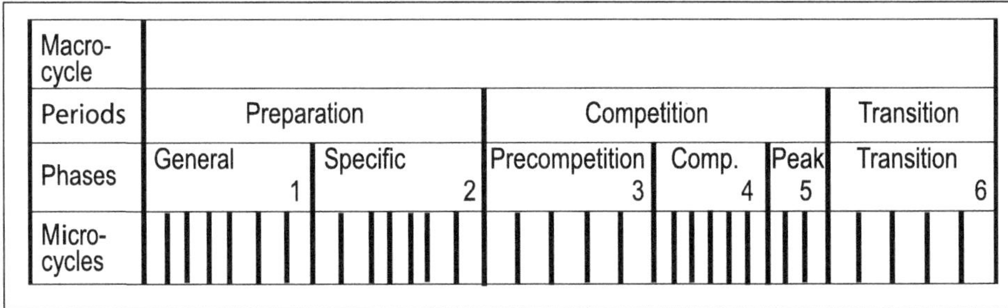

Figure 5-1. Single periodization

Although some distance runners may try for three peaks (cross country, indoor track, and outdoor track), it is very difficult to achieve against elite competition. Proper preparation for elite competitive efforts requires too much time for an athlete to achieve a true peak three times a year. Most athletes who have been able to perform at that level maintain such a high training load that they cannot really predict a peak. A peak is more a matter of chance.

Triple periodization is more appropriate for explosive technical events (jumps, throws, sprints, and hurdles). Indeed, European athletes commonly divide their long summer season into two mesocycles of competition separated by a mesocycle of transition, regeneration, or modified base training that lasts for two to four weeks.

The Periodization Training Cycle

A *macrocycle* is a complete training cycle, from the start of training to a peak at a major competition, then through the concluding transitional or recovery period. A calendar year consists of one to three macrocycles.

A *mesocycle* is a subdivision of a macrocycle. It means a middle (in length) cycle between the long cycle (macrocycle) and the short cycle (microcycle). The term is not used consistently in the literature. It can include periods and phases but is often used as a subdivision of a phase.

A typical macrocycle includes three *periods*:

- Preparation
- Competition
- Transition or recovery

Each period is a different training emphasis and load within a macrocycle. A period lasts for one to six months.

The *preparation* period prepares the athlete for competition. In traditional terms, it includes the preseason training. The second period of the cycle is the *competition* period, including the athlete's competitive season. The meets are chosen to prepare the athlete for the single meet selected as the goal of the season, where the athlete expects to peak.

The third period of the cycle is the *transition* period (sometimes called recuperation or regeneration), a bridge between competition and the start of the next preparation period. It allows the athlete to recover from the physical and psychological stress of competition. This period does not include any event-training activities; it is a time of active rest, designed as much for the psychological as for the physical recovery.

Each training period consists of one or more phases. For example, the preparation period includes two phases. The first phase emphasizes general conditioning, while the second phase emphasizes the special conditioning needed for the event. A phase usually lasts between two weeks and four months.

Each phase consists of a number of microcycles (usually from two to six). A typical microcycle lasts for one week, though it can be as long as three weeks or as short as three days.

A training session (also called a lesson) is a single workout with a single training focus, such as the afternoon workout at the track. An athlete might have from zero (on a rest day) to three training sessions in a single day.

Each session includes a number of *training units*. A training unit is a single component of the training session. Usually, a training session includes between one and five training units.

Types of Periodized Training

Periodized training falls into three categories: general, special, and competition-specific. *General training* (basic conditioning) is "training for the general functioning capacity of the athlete. It is the foundation of endurance, strength and mobility through training units... The objective here is to ensure that the athlete will be fit to accept and benefit from special training."[2]

Special training develops the conditioning, traits, and technique that are specific to success in the athlete's event. The terms *special training* and *specific training* can be confusing. Special training uses partial movements involving the technical skills being learned. Specific training involves the whole action.

Competition-specific training is "training where technique and conditioning are completely rehearsed by applying the fitness acquired through special training to the event itself."[3] It is done either within competition or with special simulations that are similar to competition.

Planning Periodized Training Programs

Periodized training is planned from the top down, beginning with a period of several years and moving downward to the components of a single training session. Experienced athletes should plan their training from the multiple-year perspective. Younger or less-experienced athletes should plan their training for only one year at a time because they have less predictable improvement curves. A young athlete may suddenly mature physically, with a sharp rise in performance over a very short time. Also, the early learning and performance curve is steep for athletes in a new event. Major improvements are rare for more experienced, older athletes, so their training needs can be planned farther ahead.

Long-Term Planning

A long-term training plan must consider the following four factors:

- Number of years of organized training needed to achieve a high performance level
- Average age when high performance is achieved
- Amount or degree of the athlete's natural ability
- Age that the athlete began specialized training

Long-term training plans change the proportions of general training and specialized training. An effective long-term plan meets the following objective criteria:

- It relates the performance objectives to factors specific to the sport.
- It increases the training and competition load in successive training years, assuming that the athlete improves. At the highest stages of development, the number of major competitions should level off; it may even decrease.

- It forecasts the annual increase of volume and intensity of training according to the event's dominant component and the athlete's needs.
- It changes the emphasized training exercises yearly.
- It specifies the control tests and standards to be met.
- It specifically covers all of the needs of the event.
- It shows the progression of the number of training lessons and hours per year.

Long-term training requires much careful thought. It requires good training records for the athlete, with the control tests spread carefully across the training year. Well-planned training is measurable, so you can make tables, charts, or graphs of the training progress. The coach should be able to show how much of the training load (time and percentage) was devoted to developing each performance component.

A record sheet can list the objectives for each year in a four-year (Olympiad) plan. The coach and the athlete work together to develop the long-term plan, though the coach's role is larger with younger athletes (because of their lack of practical experience).

The basic steps in developing the long-term plan include the following:

- Set performance goals (the athlete's time, distance, or height) for each year.
- Set the objectives of each type of preparation (physical, technical, tactical, and psychological) for each year.
- Select the control tests that will be used to evaluate the athlete's progress, along with the standards that will show whether the athlete is making satisfactory progress.
- Graph the athlete's training factors (training volume, training intensity, and progress toward peaking) across the bottom of the plan. This graph gives a condensed version of each year's training plan.

An example of a hypothetical four-year plan for an 800-meter runner (Figure 5-2) shows how a four-year plan is constructed. It lists the objectives planned for each year, with the performance goals, the tests and standards, and a rough graph of the training progress and periods of training over the four-year period.

Annual Planning

Planning the competitions. You can design a rough pattern for the year by fixing the date(s) when the athlete must peak, then developing a training curve similar to that in Figure 5-3. The entire year's program is simply a process of preparing for that peak. It is a cycle of training, competition, and regeneration (recovery). Meets are classified into two groups, the main competitions and the preparatory meets.

Club:
Athlete:
Event: 800m

	Objectives			
	Year 1	Year 2	Year 3	Year 4
Performance	2:14	2:06	2:01	1:58 - 1:59
Physical preparation	• Develop general physical preparation • Develop aerobic endurance	• Improve general physical preparation • Develop muscular endurance • Improve aerobic endurance • Develop anaerobic endurance	• Improve specific physical preparation • Improve muscle endurance • Perfect aerobic endurance • Improve anaerobic endurance	• Perfect specific physical preparation • Perfect aerobic endurance • Perfect anaerobic endurance
Technical preparation	• Correct arm carriage • Correct position of head	• Efficient stride length • Minimum vertical bouncing	• Relaxed running • Efficient technical movement	→ →
Tactical preparation	• Steady pace throughout the race	• Fast, alert in the first 400m • Steady pace in the body of the race	• Secure good position before the finish • Perfect the start	• Cope with various strategies • Perfect the finish
Psychological preparation	• Develop mental awareness • Attempt to modify the above	→ • Develop self-concept	• Identify anxieties and stressors and how to handle them • Relaxation techniques	→ →
Tests and standards	100m = 12.4 400m = 57.0 1500m = 4:22 $\dot{V}O_{2max}$ = 3.08L	12.0 55.5 4:16 3.7L	11.7 53.0 4:09 4.1L	11.5 51.5 4:04 4.5L

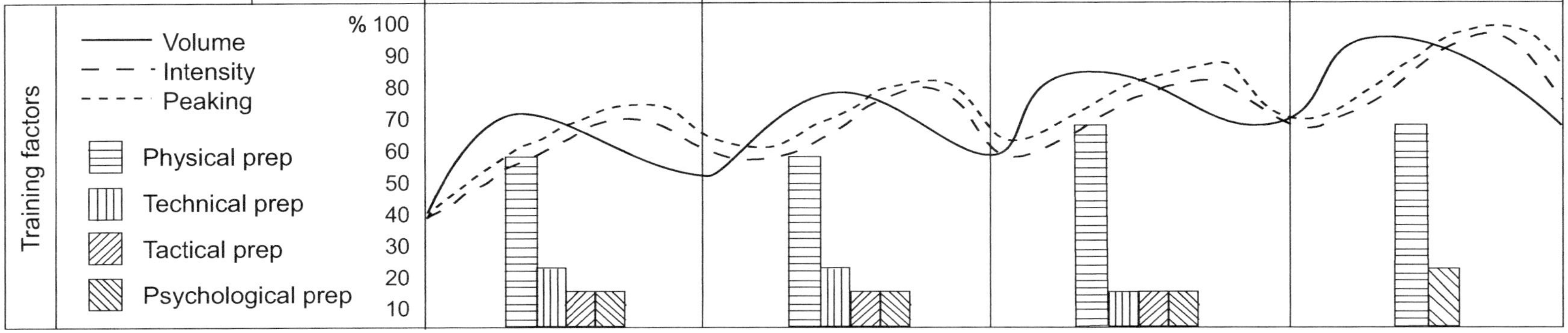

Figure 5-2. Hypothetical four-year training plan for 800 meters

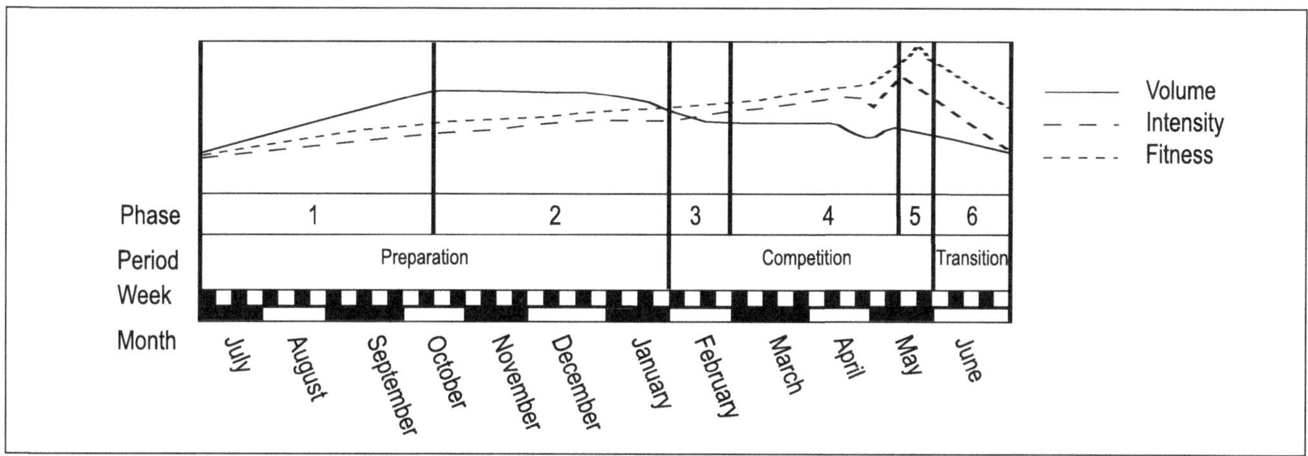

Figure 5-3. Hypothetical training curve for one year

Concern about win-loss records may be a factor in the process, so no meet that is important this way should be scheduled for the last two or three weeks before the season's main competition; the effort affects the season's final preparation. Preparatory meets are tests to assess the athlete's progress. The coach should include meets that create the same meet conditions (time schedules, level of competition) and meets at the same facility (track) or course (cross country, road racing). At those meets, the primary goal is to adjust to the environment for the sake of future success rather than to win at that time.

The number of competitions is critical because the athlete should peak at the proper time rather than compete too often and lose fitness. Table 5-1 suggests the number of meets per year by event.

Suggested Number of Meets Per Year

Event	Beginning Athletes		Elite Athletes	
	Winter	*Summer*	*Winter*	*Summer*
Sprints, Hurdles, Jumps, and Throws				
Primary event	3-4	12-16	3-5	16-20
Secondary event	2-3	4-6	1-3	3-5
Middle Distances				
800-1500	—	4-8	2-3	10-16
Shorter distances	2-3	8-10	2-4	8-10
Marathon	—	1	—	2-3
50 km Walk	—	6-8	—	8-10
Combined Events				
Decathlon	—	1-2	—	2-3
Heptathlon	—	2	—	2-4
Individual events	2-4	10-12	3-5	12-16

Table 5-1. Suggested number of meets per year

Consider the following factors in planning the athlete's meet schedule:

- The most important meet of the year is the *only* one that determines the athlete's ranking. All other meets are steps to prepare the athlete for that one competition.
- If the meets are planned properly, the athlete will peak at the most important meet of the year.
- Having too many meets interferes with the balance of competition and training. It lessens the athlete's physical and psychological potential.
- The athlete should compete *only* when capable of meeting a meet's objectives for each training factor (physical, technical, tactical, and psychological).
- Each meet should be a more difficult competition for the athlete than the previous meet.
- A meet with too little competition provides no motivation.
- Superior opponents should not be avoided.

Planning the training year. The training year is divided into one or more macrocycles, with one macrocycle for each peak. Each macrocycle has three periods: preparation, competition, and transition. If an athlete peaks for both indoor and outdoor track, several weeks of low-key transitional activities should follow the major indoor competition. The athlete's fitness level will drop during this period, but that drop enables the athlete to undertake more effective training later, resulting in improved performances during the outdoor competitions. If the transition period were not included, the athlete would "hit the wall" at some point, ending further progress and effectively ending the season.

Records for the annual plan. The annual planning process begins by planning the year's competition schedule. The schedule gives a starting point to the training structure. It is combined with the four-year plan's objectives for that year, which is then modified based on the evaluation of the previous year. Then, the annual training plan is developed, giving the year's plans, control tests, and progression. Next, detailed exercises and tests are placed into the training plan. As the year progresses, the coach keeps a record of the athlete's performances on the control tests and in the meets.

Planning the macrocycles. The macrocycle is planned to result in a peak performance at a major meet. Explosive events (such as sprints, jumps, and throws) may allow up to three major peaks (therefore, three macrocycles in a year), but for other events only one or two peaks are possible. The greater the influence of endurance (the aerobic component) on the performance, the fewer peaks that are possible in a year. For the highest possible performance level, a marathoner should plan only one major peak in a year.

The schedule of macrocycles is largely a function of the meet schedule that you develop. After you choose the athlete's most important meets of the year, you will know when the athlete's macrocycles will occur. Each major meet (one to three in a year) requires a macrocycle. The macrocycle ends after the transition period that follows the major meet (one to four weeks after the major meet). At that point, the next macrocycle begins.

Planning the training periods. Each of the three training periods should have specific training objectives consistent with the annual plan. The objectives should be listed in the order of their importance to performance so you can assess the relative training time that is applied to their development. The athlete's success or progress in meeting the goals or objectives should be evaluated and recorded at the end of each period.

The preparation period develops the basic conditioning and technique that is needed for competition. The length of this period depends on the athlete's fitness level. A more fit, more highly skilled athlete needs much less preparation time than a young, inexperienced, or unfit one.

The competition period tests the athlete in steps along the way toward the season's major meet. This progress is evaluated after each meet, refinements are made in the next microcycle's training, and the athlete trains to improve again. The goal of the entire macrocycle is the major meet at the end of the competition period.

The transition period provides recovery from the competition season and prepares the athlete to start the next macrocycle. If the year includes more than one macrocycle and peak, the midyear transition periods may be as brief as a week or so. The transition period at the end of the training year should last for at least one month.

Planning the phases. A macrocycle is usually divided into six subdivisions called *phases* (Table 5-2). A phase lasts for three to six weeks. Table 5-3 shows the primary objectives of each phase.

Phases of the Macrocycle

Period	*Phase*	*Phase Type*	*Length*
Preparation	1	General preparation	3-6 weeks
	2	Specific preparation	3-6 weeks
Competition	3	Pre-competition	3-6 weeks
	4	General competition	3-6 weeks
	5	Special competition	2 weeks
Transition	6	Transition or recovery	1-4 weeks

Table 5-2. Phases of the macrocycle

Objectives of the Phases			
Period	*Phase*		*Objectives*
Preparation	1	General preparation	• Diagnosis of problems from competition • Development of endurance, strength, mobility • Fine-tuning of technical model • Preparation for Phase 2
	2	Specific preparation	• Development of event-specific fitness • Development of the advanced technical model • Preparation for Phase 3
Competitive	3	Pre-competitive	• Progressive intensity of meets • Improvement of meet performances • Technical evaluation in meet setting • Expansion of meet experiences (if appropriate) • Qualifying for advanced meets (if appropriate)
	4	General competition	• Refining of the advanced technical model • Preparation for the peak performance
	5	Special competition	• Achievement of peak performance at major meet
Transition	6	Transition	• Active recovery from season • Preparation for Phase 1

Table 5-3. Objectives of the phases

For training programs that stress a repeated cycle based on the biological model, a phase is divided into three parts, each lasting for one to four microcycles:

- Preparation: general conditioning for the phase goal
- Adaptation: specific conditioning for the phase goal
- Application: control testing, simulations, or competition

This pattern repeats from the level of the individual training session up to that of the macrocycle. It can be applied to multi-year training plans, with a year devoted to each part.

Phase 1 (*general preparation*) improves the athlete's base fitness and technique levels. This "training to train" prepares the athlete for the training in Phase 2.

Phase 2 (*specific preparation*) prepares the athlete for the third phase, but it also develops event-specific fitness and models the advanced technique in the athlete.

Phase 3 (*pre-competition*) covers the early part of the competitive season. It uses a series of meets that increase in intensity or in the opponents' skill, challenging the athlete to improve his performance.

The whole point of training is to achieve excellence in the major meet. The athlete's technical performance in these early meets is a critical indicator of progress. The use of inexpensive video recording and analysis tools helps immensely in this area because coaches can more easily evaluate the recorded performances later.

Phase 4 (*general competition*) has two tasks: refining the advanced technical model and preparing for the peak performance. For elite athletes, this time may include few meets, lasting for four to six weeks. It is used as a breather from competition, a time to concentrate on the final adjustments in the technique and fitness levels. The training reaches its peak intensity (quality) at this time, but the loading (quantity) will be falling sharply.

Phase 5 (*special competition*) is the peak of the season, with the most important meet of the year. The training load is very light, allowing the athlete to be rested and fresh, so the highest level of performance is possible. It may include one or more final tune-up meets before the major meet. This phase usually lasts for only one or two weeks.

Phase 6 (*transition*) is also called the recovery or regeneration (rebuilding) phase. It involves active recovery from the season, with other physical activities in low-key, relaxing situations. The activity level is high enough that the athlete will be physically ready to begin general training with Phase 1 after Phase 6 is ended. At the same time, the activity level is low enough for the athlete to be physically and psychologically rested and recovered, thus enthusiastic to return to Phase 1.

Planning the Microcycles

Characteristics of microcycles. Each phase is divided into a series of microcycles. A typical microcycle is one week long, though it may vary in length from 3 to 21 days. Microcycles have four features:

- The structure (the volume relative to the intensity) of the load demand changes during the cycle.
- The load degree differs from one training session to the next, alternating between lower and higher loads according to the athlete's load tolerance and ability to recover.
- The training sessions have differing main tasks, which use either special or general training exercises.
- The training load rises for as long as is necessary to meet the objectives of the training phase.[4]

Each training session is followed by a recovery period long enough to remove the fatigue that prevents the athlete from meeting the required standard of performance in the next training session. Sessions with general exercises are useful as active recovery, which makes the recovery process shorter than passive rest does. Depending on the activity, an athlete may not need a full recovery before the next training session. Training without a full recovery is possible if the coach plans sessions with varying tasks, methods, and loads, so the stress on a given bodily system is not consistently high. The coach may plan some training sessions that focus on a single task, rather than trying to mix conflicting systems (such as speed and endurance) during the same session.

The cycle should be planned so that sessions with special demands on speed, speed-strength, and high-level technique are performed before sessions that emphasize endurance. Generally, more than 24 hours of recovery is needed after very hard training. Meets should occur during the overcompensation phase that follows such recovery (usually two or three days after the optimum-load training session). However, no pattern of training microcycles has proven to be infallible.

The optimum succession (best order of training activities) for a microcycle is to:

- Learn and perfect technique with medium intensity.
- Perfect technique at submaximal and maximal intensity.
- Develop speed of short duration (up to personal limit).
- Develop anaerobic endurance.
- Improve strength with a load of 90 to 100 percent of personal maximum.
- Develop muscular endurance with medium and low loads.
- Develop muscular endurance with high and maximal intensity.
- Develop cardiorespiratory endurance with maximal intensity.
- Develop cardiorespiratory endurance with moderate intensity.[5]

This succession of training is very similar to Korobov's recommended progression for the single training session, which is to develop (in this progression):

- Technique and/or tactical training
- Speed and/or coordination
- Strength
- General endurance

You should use the following factors to plan the content of a microcycle:

- Set the objectives, particularly the dominant training factors.
- Decide the type of microcycle:
  - ✓ Development microcycle (improves fitness)
  - ✓ Tuning microcycle (maintains fitness)
  - ✓ Unloading microcycle (peaking cycle)

- Set the absolute level of work:
  - ✓ Number of training sessions
  - ✓ Volume of training
  - ✓ Intensity of training
  - ✓ Complexity of training
- Set the relative level of effort (how many peak sessions, which alternate with less intensive training sessions).
- Decide on the character of training (training methods and means for each training session).
- Set control testing or meet days.
- Begin with low- to medium-intensity sessions, progressing to more intensive sessions later.
- Before an important meet, use a microcycle with only one training peak, occurring three to five days before the meet.

Microcycle patterns. A one-week microcycle usually has two peak sessions. Training lessons should be repeated two to three times per microcycle for each different objective. Learning technical skills requires much repetition. The frequency of repetition varies, depending on the type of training, as follows:

- Daily training
  - ✓ General endurance
  - ✓ Flexibility
  - ✓ Strength in small-muscle groups
- Every other day
  - ✓ Strength for large-muscle groups
- Three sessions per week
  - ✓ Specific endurance (submaximal intensity)
- Two sessions per week
  - ✓ Specific endurance (maximal intensity)
  - ✓ Maintenance of strength
  - ✓ Maintenance of flexibility
  - ✓ Maintenance of speed
- Two to three sessions per week
  - ✓ Bounding drills and speed exercises under strenuous conditions (sand or snow)

During the competitive period, the microcycles should include some modeling of the conditions of the most important meet of the year. If the athlete must compete for two days in a row, this practice should be simulated every second or third week. In some cases, an athlete qualifies in the morning, and then competes in the finals in the afternoon.

Planning the Peak

Peaking is as much a psychological state as a physical one, "with an intense emotional arousal... An important attribute of peaking seems to be the athlete's capacity to tolerate various degrees of frustration which occur before, during and after competition."[6]

Although peaking is a very complex process, the primary factors that facilitate it are the athlete's high working potential, quick rate of recovery, near-perfect neuromuscular coordination (technical skill), overcompensation, unloading, recovery, psychological factors (motivation, arousal, and psychological relaxation), and nervous cell working capacity (increased only for the last 7 to 10 days before the main meet).

The peaking process involves a final use of overcompensation in the training schedule. Overcompensation usually occurs from 24 to 36 hours after an optimal training session. During the racing season, the training plan may alternate maximal- and low-intensity stimuli, resulting in a wavelike pattern of fitness. This approach helps prevent exhaustion from overtraining while competing.

The correct unloading (tapering) procedure is critical to performance in the major meet. The training load during the last five microcycles (Figure 5-4) before

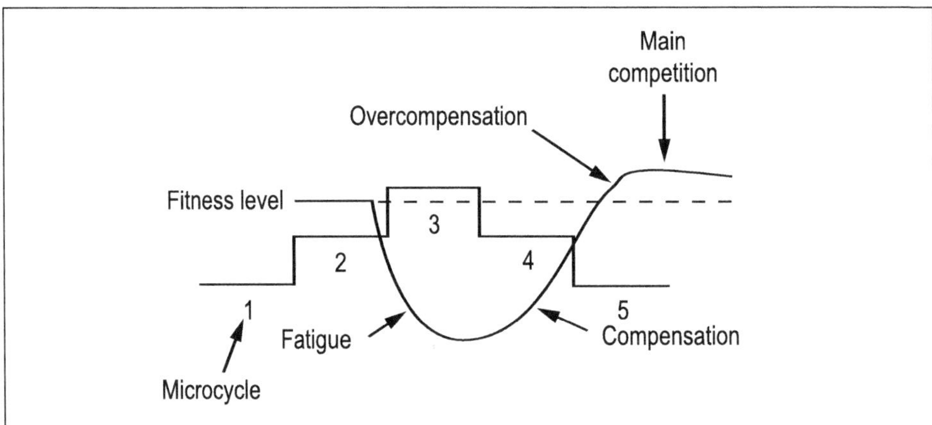

Figure 5-4. Loading for peaking

the main meet shows the increase of the training load from low to medium to high (causing fatigue), with a drop back to medium and then low loads that results first in compensation, then in overcompensation for the main meet.

Recovery and regeneration are extremely important during the competitive season. Massage and sauna are useful, and proper diet is also a critical factor in the energy level.

The psychological aspects of training are also critical at this time. Although the athlete may be motivated to perform at a high level, reasonable goals and expectations should be set. Otherwise, unnecessary frustration will become a post-meet factor. The athlete should not be overmotivated or too aroused; his psychological state will already be "on edge." At this time, the coach is more useful in the role of encouraging relaxation than in "pumping up" the athlete.

The length of time that a peak can be maintained depends upon the length and quality of the underlying preparation period, as well as other factors that are very individualized. The Zone 1 level (performance within 2 percent of one's best) may last as long as two to three-and-a-half months, with three to five minor peaks during that time, if the preparation period was long enough and the training process during the competition period is handled properly. The peaking process itself is about 7 to 10 days in length, after which the performance level falls off.

Maintaining that performance level requires a short phase of regeneration after each peak for a major meet, followed by more training. If those conditions were not met, the peak period would be shortened considerably. The number of competitions is also a factor; too many competitions cause a performance plateau, instead of improving performances.

To avoid the onset of fatigue during the competitive season, the training plan should follow this constant pattern:

- Competition
- Regeneration
- Training
- Unloading
- Next competition

An athlete usually needs four to six microcycles to rise from the pre-competition phase to the Zone 1 performance level. Extending the Zone 1 performances beyond the eighth microcycle of competition (two months) requires careful planning and monitoring of the athlete's training.

In deciding how many meets an athlete can compete in during a season, note that the events fall into four groups according to their recovery needs: the throws, the short sprints and jumps, the long sprints and middle distances, and the long distances and combined events. The stress of competition rises from the first group to the fourth. Table 5-4 shows the recommended number of meets and recovery time for each group.

Planning the Training Sessions

The training session has three or four primary parts. A three-part session includes the following:

- Preparation (usually the warm-up)
- Body (content)
- Conclusion (usually the cool-down)

Event Group	Event	Time to Overcompensation	Meets per Year
Recommended Competitions by Event Groups			
Throws			
	Throws	2-3 days	16-20
Short sprints and jumps			
	Short sprints	3-5 days	16-20
	Jumps	3-5 days	16-20
Long sprints and middle distances			
	Long sprints	6-7 days	16-20
	Middle distances	6-7 days	10-15
Long distances and combined events			
	Long distances	2 weeks or more	6-10
	Marathon	More than 2 weeks	3-5
	50 km walk	More than 2 weeks	3-5
	Combined events	2 weeks or more	3-5

Table 5-4. Recommended competitions by event groups

A four-part session adds an introduction before the preparation. The three-part session is used by more advanced athletes. It is the dominant form during the competition period. The four-part version is best for beginners and group sessions because it allows the goals of the lesson to be explained.

Previously, Korobov's four-step progression for the body of the training session was outlined, from learning or perfecting technique and/or tactics, to developing speed and/or coordination, then strength work, and finally training for general and specific endurance. Technique and tactics are practiced first because they require a rested body. If other types of training were performed first, fatigue would interfere with the learning rate.

When perfecting technique that is fatiguing or heavy in its workload (such as in the throwing events or weight lifting), the speed and coordination exercises should be performed before the technique development exercises. When developing maximum speed, the speed training should be performed first, immediately after the warm-up.

In learning or perfecting technique, the sequence of learning should be to:

- Consolidate the skills learned in the last session.
- Perfect the skills that are most important to the event.
- Apply the skills under simulated competitive conditions.

The complete training session should not last more than two hours. Younger athletes may improve more rapidly with shorter training sessions. This time includes the warm-up and cool-down, leaving 90 minutes or less for the body of the training session. With less skilled athletes, the concluding part of the training session may include supplementary conditioning exercises, especially if the entire session is not too demanding and the athletes are not exhausted.

The conclusion, or cool-down, is often neglected by coaches. It is critical in enhancing the body's recovery. Light running, jogging, and walking, along with light stretching, aids the body's recovery from training sessions. Every athlete should learn a relaxing cool-down procedure and follow it after every training session. It is even more critical following intensive competition. Even 10 minutes of cool-down activities are very helpful to the athlete's recovery.

A lesson plan for a group of athletes has four parts, beginning with an introduction. It includes notes of points that the coach wants to stress, including points relating to individual athletes. Not only does such a plan help the coach focus the training session, but it provides a good record for reviewing the training process later in the year or during later years.

Each athlete should keep a training diary as a record of his individual training. The coach and the athlete can decide what information should be included in the diary. Various versions of training diaries have included the morning's resting pulse, details of diet and sleep, fatigue indexes, and other items in addition to the workout session details themselves.

Remember that thorough planning combined with good records of what was actually done are essential if you are to make the training process optimally effective.

Changing Approaches to Periodization

Periodization is *not* a rigid approach to training.

The traditional periodization described in this chapter works well in the school and developmental setting, as it is based on the concept of increasingly challenging competition, leading to a seasonal or yearly peak performance. This pattern is used by most school and university athletes as well as developmental athletes. "Periodization aims at producing the best possible performance at a specific point in time, the major competition or peak. Professional sport, for the most part, does not. It aims to entertain with acceptably high levels of performance over a period of time."[7]

Professional athletes follow a different form of periodization in which the early phases are brief, the training and competition levels are high for a long period of time, and the concept of a peak is not of critical importance. In this case, the training aims at the maximum number of high-level performances, which increases the athlete's income. Their more advanced training patterns use more frequent variations in the volume and intensity of training while keeping the overall training level relatively high until unloading for the peak meet. Neither methodology genuinely challenges the other.

Remember that even though the Russians experimented with this type of training for many years, they warned their own coaches against applying the research in too rigid a manner.[8] It is preferable to accept a slightly slower rate of improvement in performance than to try to force the athlete to progress too quickly. A physical breakdown from overtraining can cost the athlete a season, and it may even result in one or more years of lost progress. For younger athletes (into their early 20s), mononucleosis sometimes occurs during times of overstress (too much training combined with too many other activities or needs). It most often appears in the first two years of college as young athletes make the transition to harder training, along with their new academic demands, increased personal responsibilities, and wider social opportunities.

Endnotes

1. William H. Freeman. (2001). *Peak when it counts: Periodization for the American coach* (4th ed.). Mountain View, CA: Tafnews, 17-68.
2. Frank W. Dick. (1978). *Training theory*. London: British Amateur Athletic Board, 41.
3. *Ibid.*
4. Dietrich Harre (Ed.). (1982). *Principles of sports training: Introduction to the theory and methods of training* (2nd ed.). Berlin: Sportverlag, 80-87.
5. N.G. Ozolin. (1971). Athlete's training system for competition. In Harre, ibid., 210.
6. Tudor O. Bompa. (1987). Peaking for the extended athletics calendar. *New Studies in Athletics, 2*(4), 29-43.
7. William H. Freeman. (Fall 1999). A reply to Verhoshansky on periodization. *Track Coach*, , 4767-4768.
8. Yevgeniy Kashkalov. (1971). Varying work loads in middle distance training. *Track Technique*, , 1375-1377.

Recommended Readings

Anderson, Owen. (1997). Things your mom forgot to tell you about the periodization of your training. *Running Research, 13*(6), 1-9.

Arbeit, Ekkart. (1998). Practical training emphases in the first and second decades of development. *New Studies in Athletics, 13*(1), 13-20.

Arbeit, Ekkart. (1998). Principles of the multi-year training process. *New Studies in Athletics, 13*(4), 21-28.

Avery, Guy. (1997). Training by phases. *Peak Running Performance, 6*(1), 1-7.

Balyi, Istvan. (1998, September). Long term planning of athlete development: The training to train phase. *Faster Higher Stronger, The UK's Quarterly Coaching Magazine, No. 1*, pp. 8-11.

Balyi, Istvan. (1998, December). Long-term planning of athlete development. Part 2: The training to compete phase. *Faster Higher Stronger, no. 2*, 8-11.

Balyi, Istvan, & Anne Hamilton. (1999). Long-term planning of athlete development. Part 3: The training to win phase. *Faster Higher Stronger, no. 3*, 7-9.

Balyi, Istvan, & Anne Hamilton. (1999). Long-term planning of athlete development. Part 4: Multiple periodization, modelling and normative data. *Faster Higher Stronger, no. 4*, 7-9.

Banister, E. W., & T. W. Calvert. (1980). Planning for future performance: Implications for long term training. *Canadian Journal of Applied Sport Science*, *5*(3), 170-176.

Bartonietz, Klaus, & Bill Larsen. (1997). General and event-specific considerations in peaking for the main competition. *New Studies in Athletics*, *12*(2-3), 75-86.

Brown, Lee E., & Richard Knee. (1999). Monitoring periodization with a spreadsheet. *Strength and Conditioning Journal*, *21*(6), 45-49.

Cissik, John. (Winter 2005). Is periodization dead or just very sick? *Track Coach*, *170*, 5422-5426.

Conroy, Michael. (1999). The use of periodization in the high school setting. *Strength and Conditioning Journal*, *21*(1), 52-54.

Ebbets, Russ. (Summer 2003). Track Coach talks with Tudor Bompa. *Track Coach*, *164*, 5243-5247.

Fairall, Dennis. (1994). Matveyev periodization of training adapted to high school programs. *Track and Field Quarterly Review, 94*(2), 16.

Fleck, Steven J. (1999). Periodized strength training: A critical review. *Journal of Strength and Conditioning Research*, *13*(1), 82-89.

Freeman, William H. (1994). Factors in planning periodized training in a flexible world. Presented at the 10th Commonwealth and International Scientific Congress, University of Victoria, BC, Canada.

Friel, Joe. (1995). Twin peaks. *Track Coach*, *131*, 4182-4183.

Fry, R. W., A.R. Morton & D. Keast. (1992). Periodisation and the prevention of overtraining. *Canadian Journal of Sports Science*, *17*, 241-248.

Fry, Rod W., Alan R. Morton & David Keast. (1992). Periodisation of training stress–A review. *Canadian Journal of Sport Science*, *17*(3), 234-240.

Gambetta, Vern. (2002). Rethinking periodization. *Training & Conditioning*, *12*(2), 16-21.

Karp, Jason R. (Winter 2001). Periodization training. *Track Coach*, *154*, 4905-4908.

Killing, Wofgang. (Spring 2001). Views on the transition period [abstract]. *Track Coach*, *155*, 4962.

Lange, Günter. (2004). The "Puzzle" – a teaching aid for training session and microcycle planning. *New Studies in Athletics*, *19*(31), 57-68.

Laursen, Paul B., & David G. Jenkins. (2002). The scientific basis for high-intensity interval training: Optimising training programmes and maximising performance in highly trained endurance athletes. *Sports Medicine*, *32*(1), 53-73.

Lidor, Ronnie. (1995). Another view of the concept of consistency in track and field. *New Studies in Athletics*, *10*(3), 7-11.

Lyden, Robert. (1990). Cycles of acquisition and training periodization. *Track and Field Quarterly Review*, *90*(2), 21-42.

Matveyev, L. P. (Spring 2005). Projection of training in the preparation period [abstract]. *Track Coach*, *171*, 5477.

Morton, R. H. (1990). Modeling human performance in running. *Journal of Applied Physiology*, *69*, 1171-1177.

Morton, R. Hugh. (1991). The quantitative periodization of athletic training: A model study. *Sports Medicine, Training, and Rehabilitation*, *3*(1), 19-28.

Mujika, Iñigo. (1998). The influence of training characteristics and tapering on the adaptation in highly trained individuals: A review. *International Journal of Sports Medicine*, *19,* 439-446.

Mujika, Iñigo, Sabino Padilla, David Pyne & Thierry Busso. (2004). Physiological changes associated with the pre-event taper in athletes. *Sports Medicine*, *34*(13), 891-927.

Neumann, Georg. (Fall 1997). Short-term competition preparation. *Track Coach*, *141,* 4513.

Palmer, Andy. (1995, September). The fall of periodization and the rise of mediocrity. *Running Times*, pp. 37-38, 40, 42-43.

Platonov, Vladimir N. (1999). The concept of "periodisation of training" and the development of a training theory. [abridged translation]. *Leistungssport*, *29*(1).

Platonov, Vladimir N. (1996). Formation of athletes' preparation within [the] year. *Athletic Asia*, *21*(1), 37-74.

Platonov, Vladimir. (Winter 2005). The high performance maintenance phase in the long-term training system [abstract]. *Track Coach*, *170*, 5444-5445.

Rowbotton, David G. (2000). Periodization of training. In *Exercise and Sport Science*, William E. Garrett & Donald T. Kirkendall, Eds. (pp. 499-512). Philadelphia: Lippincott Williams & Wilkins.

Schiffer, Jürgen. (2001). Selected and annotated bibliography 55: Performance diagnosis. Part I: Lactate and heart rate measurement. *New Studies in Athletics*, *16*(1/2), 105-150.

Schiffer, Jürgen. (2001). Selected and annotated bibliography 56: Performance diagnosis. Part II: General medical and biomechanical methods and assessment systems based on training science. *New Studies in Athletics*, *16*(3), 63-85.

Smith, David J. (2003). A framework for understanding the training process leading to elite performance. *Sports Medicine*, *33*(15), 1103-1126.

Suslov, Felix. (2001). Annual training programmes and the sport specific fitness levels of world class athletes. *New Studies in Athletics*, *16*(1/2), 63-70.

Taha, Tim, & Scott G. Thomas. (2003). Systems modelling of the relationship between training and performance. *Sports Medicine*, *33*(14), 1061-1089.

Tschiene, Peter. (1999). Discussion of "periodisation" comments. [abridged translation]. *Leistungssport*, *29*(1).

Ückert, Sandra, & Winfried Joch. (2007). The effects of warm-up and pre-cooling on endurance performance in high ambient temperatures. *New Studies in Athletics*, *22*(1), 33-39.

Verchoshanskiy, Juri. (1999). The skills of programming the training process. *New Studies in Athletics*, *14*(4), 45-54.

Verhoshansky, Yuri. (Summer 1999). The end of periodization in high performance sport [abstract]. *Track Coach*, *148*, 4737; Freeman, William H. (Fall 1999). A reply to Verhoshansky on periodization. *Track Coach*, *149*, 4767-4768.

Zelichenok, Vadim. (2005). The long term competition activity of the world's top athletes. *New Studies in Athletics*, *20*(2), 19-24.

Zelichnok, Vadim. (2006). From junior star to elite performer [abstract]. *New Studies in Athletics*, *21*(1), 66.

6

The Oregon Training Schedule Sheets

The Oregon workout sheets were first developed while Bill Bowerman was teaching coaching clinics in Pakistan for the U.S. State Department in the 1950s. He needed to communicate with coaches and athletes who spoke several different languages. To save time and improve the coaches' understanding, he had an interpreter translate a single list of fundamentals for each event into the coaches' native languages. Those charts were copied, together with weekly training schedules.

Then Bowerman could refer to each exercise by its number. For example, if he wanted the runners to run 8 x 400m in 70 to 73 seconds, he wrote "8 x 5E1." The number 5 was "Intervals," E was "440 yards" (at that time, all U.S. races and tracks were measured in yards and miles), and 1 was "70 to 73 seconds"(see Sheet 6-1). He knew what he was assigning because his copy was in English, and the runner knew what the coach wanted because each coach's copy, with the same numbering system, was printed in Urdu, Hindustani, or his other native tongue. Thus, the coach could communicate with the athletes in another language "by the numbers." The system worked so well that he used it with his own athletes when he returned to Oregon.

The format of the charts was revised slightly every year, so slight variations are found from year to year. Sheet 6-2 shows the February 1960 workouts of Jim Grelle, who made the U.S. Olympic Team at 1500m that year. As an example, look at his workout on the 10th of that month. He warmed up, then ran 4 x 440 yards in 64 seconds. The current versions of the schedule sheets, which represent workouts of real athletes who trained under Bowerman at Oregon, are in the chapters for each of the specific events.

Runner's Schedule NAME DATE

1. A. Jog 1 to 3 miles
   B. Weights & jog
2. Fartlek A. Varied (1) 30 min. (2)
   B. Steady (1) 2-4 mi. (2) 4-6 mi. (3) 7-10 mi.
   (4)
3. Weights
4. High knee and power run
5. Intervals
   A. 110 (1) 18-16-14 (2) 17-15-13
   B. 165 (1) 25 (2)
   C. 220 (1) 35 (2)
   D. 330 (1) 52 (2) 48 (3) 45 (4)
   E. 440 (1) 70-73 (2)
   F. 660 (1) 1:45 (2)
   G. 880 (1) 70 (2)
   H. 3/4 (1) 70 (2)
   I. Mile (1) 72 (2) 68-70 (3) 64-67 (4)
   J.
   K.
   L.
6. Sets A. 660-440-330-220-110
   (1) 1:45-68-49-32-15 (2)
   B. 440-660-440-220 (1) 63 (2)
   C. 550-165-165 (1) 55 pace (2)
   D.
7. Squad meeting
8. Special A. Sauna B. Swim C.
9. Drills A. Sprint-float-sprint (165)
   B. 1-step acceleration (165)
   C. 40-30 drill (1) 4 laps (2)
   D. 70-90 drill (1) 1-1 (2) 2-1
   (3) 3-1 (4)
   E. Cut-downs (1) 110 (2) 165 (3) 220
   (4) 330 (5) 440 (6) 880 (7)
   F. Simulate race drills (1) 1st 220-last 220
   (2) 2½–1½ (3) 10 miles–3/4 drill (4)
   G. 2-4 miles at (1) 80 (2) 75 (3)
10. A. Test B. Trial C. Compete
    (1) 3/4 date pace (2) Over (3) Under
11. Hill interval A. 110 B. 220 C.
12. With coach (A) Bill B. (B) Bill D. (C)
14. A. Wind sprint B. Hurdle drill
    C. Spring and bound D.
15. Finish work
16. Acrobatics or apparatus
17. 3/4 effort
18.
19.
20. Secondary event
21. A. Pictures B. Film

M
T
W
T
F
S
S
M
T
W
T
F
S
S
M
T
W
T
F
S
S
M
T
W
T
F
S
S

Sheet 6-1. Sample of an original training schedule

DATE								
			2x	2x	2x			
Feb.	1	1	9D	6C	5D	12	11	F
	2	1	3					
			10x					
	3	1	7F	11				
	4	1	3					
	5	1	3					
	6-7	2	Saturday and Sunday					
			1x	2x				
	8	1	10	4D	11			1/2
	9	1	3					
			4x	4x	4x			
	10	1	7F	6C	5D	3		
	11	1	3					
	12	1	3					
			1x			1x		
	13	1	3/4	64s		660 29s		
	14	1	16	2				
	15	1	2					1/4
	16	1	3					
			10x					
	17	1	7F	3				
	18	1	3					
			1x					
	19	1	9D					
	20-21	2	Saturday and Sunday					1/4
			4x	4x				
	22	1	6C	5C	12	9		
	23		3					
			1x	1x	4x			
	24	1	9	14	5C	9		
	25		3					
	26		3					
			1x			1x		
	27	1	3/4	64s		660 29s		
	28							

1. Warm-up weight work or arm and shoulder work on rope, rings, or apparatus.

2. Fartlek

3. Light fartlek

4. Repeats. 110, A.20; B.18; C.16; D.14; E.12; F.11

5. Repeats. 220, A.38; B.35; C.33; D.31; E29; F.28; G.27; H.26

6. Repeats. 330, A.54 B.51; C.48; D.45; E.42; F.39; G.38; H.37

7. Repeats. 440, A.75; B.72; C.70; D.68; E.66; F.64; G.62; H.60; I.58

8. Selected longer distance repeats.

9. Sets. 660 - 440 - 220

	660	440	220
A.	1:50	70	34
B.	1:45	68	32
C.	1:42	66	30
D.	1:39	64	29
E.	1:36	62	28
F.	1:33	60	27
G.	1:30	58	26

10. Bunches. 2 or 3 660s; 3 to 6 440s; 6 to 10 220s; Use same time as (9) A, B, Etc.

11. Run ot after each competition or workout.

12. Wind sprints.

14. Reduced interval 440s. Run 440, rest, 440, run 440, rest, 220; 440, rest 110, run 440. Use letters as (7).

15. Alternate sprint 55, shag 55.

16. Up and down hill.

NAME Grelle

Sheet 6-2. Early Oregon training schedule sheet

These workout records can be viewed as historical records (of sorts), and they can be saved. The coach can compare the progress of an athlete against his previous progress or that of any earlier athletes in that event, giving a more accurate picture of the athlete's progress. This method is the quickest way to communicate with large numbers of athletes. It is not simply "putting up a workout sheet," because the workouts should be written to the specific talents and needs of the athlete, rather than simply using a "one size fits all" plan.

Periodization and the Oregon System

The Oregon System is an early form of periodized training. Its laws and principles are consistent with those of periodized training. From the start, the athletes' goal was to peak for the outdoor track conference meet and the NCAA championships. All other goals were secondary to that goal. Cross country served primarily as base training and technique work for distance runners rather than as a major competitive season. Indoor track was a short season (one to two meets), used primarily to maintain training interest during the chilly, wet winter in the Willamette Valley.

The training patterns used by the distance runners (Chapters 8 and 9) show the same wave-like hard-easy pattern used by elite athletes in an intricate periodized system of training. Regular testing measured each athlete's progress toward the peak goals. Meet conditions were simulated on a regular basis. Training and progression were recorded and charted in written records. Though the basic patterns were the same for each athlete, the workouts themselves were highly individualized. The end result was almost 100 All-American athletes (at a time when only the top three won the honor) and dozens of Olympians across a wide range of events.

How to Interpret the Training Schedules

Later chapters discuss how to train for each individual track and field event. The daily training schedules in each chapter are not written in the form of today's periodized training patterns. Few examples of such genuine (rather than theoretical) training schedules are available. Instead of designing sets of theoretical periodized workout schedules, the workouts in this book are genuine training schedules of Oregon athletes, each of whom was a national- or world-class athlete at the time that the schedules were used. Those athletes include Olympic champions and world-record holders in the 400m and discus, and national champions (sometimes national record-holders) in most other events.

Though the workouts are the originals, the schedule sheets have been revised slightly and redesigned to make the numbering system more consistent from one event to another. Also, the running distances were converted to the metric system. In the event chapters, the schedule pages are designed to reproduce the schedule sheet for one month. The fundamentals of the event are on the left-hand half of the page, while the workouts are on the right.

Coaches who use the training schedule sheets can write workouts for every athlete. A full month of training can be assigned, and saved, on one sheet. Because of the numbering system for the training fundamentals, the coach can easily review the program to see whether any given training element is included or left out. An individual athlete's training needs can be easily met by modifying the sheet. The current training schedule sheets are shown in the event chapters.

The numbering system allows the training to be recorded in a form of shorthand. Repetitions of an activity are numbered above the code for that activity. Thus, "6C" refers to running a 200m interval. A notation of "4x" above the "6C" means four repeats of 200m. If the assignment is "6C(2)," then the pace of the 200m would be given in the "(2)" space on the schedule sheet.

Many of the numbered activities are essentially the same for every event (see Table 6-1). This repetition makes the job of writing the workouts easier, and it shows a foundational core of training that is common to every athlete. The activities that are specific to an event are discussed in the appropriate event chapters. Following is an explanation of the meaning of the numbers common to all schedules.

1. Warm-Up Routine

The first activity on every schedule sheet is the warm-up. It includes jogging for every athlete. For the sprinters and jumpers, it includes easy work on the relay pass, described in the Chapter 10. Except for distance runners (who cover from one to three miles), the athletes jog about two laps on or near the track. Jogging on grass or some other softer surface is easier on the legs than running on the track.

All athletes follow the jogging with their stretching routine. Then sprinters do the high-knee, fast-leg drill, while hurdlers go through the X drill (hurdle warm-up). Sprinters and hurdlers finish with a few easy starts.

A few other activities may be used instead of or following the warm-up. Field-event athletes might be assigned to run to Hendricks Park, a tree-covered park on a nearby ridge (completing a three-mile running loop), or to the hilly golf course one mile away. These workouts may be conditioning runs themselves, or the athletes may run a hill-training session at the golf course. They may run steps at the track stadium. Usually, such other activities complete the training session, except for a cool-down. Because these schedules represent actual workouts, this volume has kept Hendricks Park (within sight of the University of Oregon track) as an entry. Coaches may assign a comparable park or forest run for their athletes.

2. Fartlek

Fartlek has been an important part of distance training since the late 1940s, when it first came to the United States. Done properly, it has the advantages of interval training but without the boredom of laps on the track or the stress risks of working on harder surfaces.

Common Activities on Training Schedules

1. Warm-up routine
   A. Jog 1-2 laps with relay pass
   B. Slow high knee; fast leg
2. Fartlek
   A. Varied pace: stride, sprint, recover; stride, meet a challenge, recover; finish feeling exhilarated, not exhausted.
      (a) 10 min. (b) 30 min. (c)
   B. Steady pace: slow, 10-30 min.
      (1) Hendricks Park (2) Golf course (3)
3. Strength and flexibility
   A. Weights and jogging
   B. Jogging and stretching
7. Team meeting
8. Special activities
   A. Sauna
   B. Swim
   C.
10. Competition or test
    A. Meet
    B. Test effort
    C. Simulation
    D. Control test
12. With coach
    A. (Name) B. Leader
14. Miscellaneous training
    A. Wind sprints (1) on the straight (2) on the curve
    B. Hurdle (X) drill
    C. Spring and bound
    D. Alternate run and jog, at least 800m
    E. Hills with (1) coach (2) leader
15. Plyometrics
    A. Jumps (1) 1-leg (2) Both legs (3)
    B. Bounding (1) 1-leg (2) Both legs (3)
    C.
20. Work on second event
21. Visual aids
    A. Videotape (1) Record performance (2) Study
    B. DVD (1) Record performance (2) Study
    C. Pictures (1) Record performance (2) Study
30. Experimental work

Table 6-1. Common activities on training schedules

With fartlek, all of the elements of a race are mixed with periods of rest or partial recovery. The length of the training session depends upon the runner's time and energy, though few quality fartlek sessions last more than 45 minutes. Fartlek sessions are usually done on soft surfaces, such as grass or sawdust.

The runner begins by jogging slowly for two or three miles as a warm-up, preparing the cardiovascular and respiratory systems for hard work. The runner then accelerates to race pace or to a planned effort level, running for 400 to 800m or until the fatigue is felt. When fatigue appears, the athlete sprints for 50 to 150m until it begins to "hurt." This acceleration is followed by a very slow jog or a walk to recover. Next may be a series of short sprints of perhaps 50m, alternating sprinting and walking or jogging equal distances until the effort becomes difficult, then recovering with another jog or walk.

Next, the runner imagines a racing setting. He strides at racing pace up to the shoulder of an imagined opponent, passes with a quick burst, then settles into racing pace for 200 to 400m, followed by a recovery jog or walk. Next comes another imaginary race, with the opponent approaching from the rear. The athlete accelerates enough to hold off a challenge or a series of challenges, then finishes with another jogging or walking recovery. Anything that can happen or be imagined in a race can be practiced in a fartlek session. Fartlek is a personal—*not* a group—tool.

At one time, Bill Bowerman and Bill Dellinger referred to Holmer and Lydiard fartlek. This terminology is changed on the schedule sheets to avoid confusion. Holmer fartlek, named for Swedish coach Gosta Holmer (who made fartlek famous), is the traditional varied-pace running, or true fartlek. Lydiard fartlek, named for New Zealand coach Arthur Lydiard, is not really fartlek; it is steady-paced running. In the early stages of training, such steady runs may last from only 20 to 30 minutes, enough for general conditioning and a change of scene. Distance runners eventually run from 45 minutes to one hour or more. The value of Lydiard's contribution is its emphasis on the aerobic component of conditioning.

3. Strength and Flexibility

Few elite athletes fail to include strength training in their training program. This listing is used for "easy day" training, so two variations can be used. The first variation is for weights and jogging, or a strength-training session, followed by easy jogging (preferably on a soft surface). The second variation does not include weights, calling simply for a light session of jogging and stretching.

Traditionally, a set weight-training program is not assigned. Strength training is specific to both the athlete and the event. Although some general suggestions are offered in the event chapters, it is highly recommended that the coach and the athlete study the writings of strength-training specialists. The athlete's input is critical in developing a good strength-training program. The psychological or mental aspect is as important as the physical aspect in strength training.

7. Team Meeting

Team meetings should be a regular feature of the training sessions. These meetings should not be daily events, nor should they interrupt training. They should be held either before the warm-up or after the training session and cool-down are completed. They should, above all, be *brief* because the athletes' time is far more limited than the coach's. An *effective* team meeting should not last longer than 10 to 15 minutes.

These meetings are to give *vital* information, such as future meets or changes in schedules or arrangements, or to ensure that team members are working toward the same goals. Short meetings can help draw the team together, but they are *not* pep rallies. An athlete who must be "psyched" to train well has a limited future as a performer.

8. Special Activities

These activities are primarily alternate training or recovery activities. The two listed activities are sauna and swimming. The sauna can be a useful relaxation experience during a long, dreary winter's training. It also has some benefits in preparing athletes for dealing with heat in summer racing.

Swimming is an excellent easy-day activity because it exercises the muscles without putting any body-support strain on the joints or feet. It provides all-around conditioning. It is also popular as an alternate training activity for some injured athletes (in such forms as running in place in deep water, including fartlek-type workouts).

10. Competition or Test

Several variations of the meet or time trial are listed. This version of the time trial is more properly called a *"test effort"* because it is never a full-effort attempt. Arthur Lydiard spoke of three-quarter-effort trials, where the athlete runs an even-paced effort at a planned pace that is slower than an all-out effort. The aim of these trials is for the athlete to perform each trial better than the previous trial, but always within limits, *knowing that he can perform even better when the time comes.*

The simulation is an imitation of the racing situation, with some changes made so that it will not be a full effort. Bill Dellinger uses a series of simulations for distance runners,[1] having them run the full racing distance at a mixture of the goal pace and slower paces. The athlete becomes accustomed to running the full racing distance, to running an increasingly faster overall pace, and to varying and monitoring the running pace carefully. These simulations are especially useful with younger athletes or with athletes changing to a new event.

Control tests are standard tests that indicate some aspect of the athlete's fitness in relation to their actual performance in the event. They are most useful in the field events.

Photo 6-1. Dyrol Burleson, two-time Olympian (fifth and sixth places), and Vic Reeve

12. With Coach (Name)

At times, an athlete may be assigned to work with a specific or different coach for a training session or part of a training session. The coach's name is written in the blank space.

14. Miscellaneous Training

Several different basic training activities are listed here. Wind sprints, usually about 100m each, are sometimes run on the straight and other times run on the curve (the latter for sprinters in the 200 and 400 or for intermediate hurdlers). The hurdler's drill, which we call the X drill, may be run by steeplechasers as technique work or by jumpers to help regulate their stride patterns.

Springing and bounding activities were once a smaller part of the training, but now are widely used for jumpers as plyometrics (next section). The alternate run and jog, done for at least 800m, is used primarily as a cooling-down activity. Hill training is used most in the fall and winter base-training phases, sometimes directed by a coach and sometimes led by one of the athletes.

15. Plyometrics

Plyometrics are jumping and bounding activities performed on one or both legs, sometimes across the open ground and sometimes on the track. It can include jumping from, onto, or over boxes or platforms of different heights. It improves the strength and resilience of the leg muscles. The result of a good plyometric program is stronger legs with more spring. It must be planned carefully, beginning with a very light load of activities, because the stress on the legs is high. It is strongly recommended that any program be developed carefully, using expert information.[2]

20. Work on Second Event

Many school-age athletes compete in a second event. This number assigns a specific time to train for that event. An athlete should not try to train for too many events, but younger athletes may not be sure of their best event. An athlete's potentially best event may still be hidden at the start of the collegiate experience.

21. Visual Aids

Visual aids are extremely useful to athletes in the technical events. Athletes can learn and imprint proper techniques by studying photos, films, videotapes, and DVDs of the world's best athletes. The advances in technology have made this task far simpler for today's coaches and athletes. Blank tapes, CDs, and DVDs are inexpensive, and machines and software programs allow easy repeated viewing and the use of biomechanical analysis programs such as Dartfish.

All athletes should be taped regularly so their technique can be studied. Ideally, each athlete should be on a tape, CD or DVD devoted to his performance, so progress from one training session or competition to the next can be studied. At the same time, the field-event athletes should study the performances of champion athletes on a regular basis.

30. Experimental Work

Every coach sometimes wants to experiment with a new idea in training or technique. In addition, athletes at the university level may be involved in a research study by faculty or graduate students, particularly outside the competitive season.

Other Activities

You will notice in the event chapters that each event has some numbered activities that no other event has. At the same time, some numbers may be listed without including an activity. This allows for activities that are new or are not used regularly. The coach or the athlete may have his own special drills or workout segments, which can be assigned one of those open numbers. The "Experimental work" listing is "30," so open numbers are available to the coach and the athlete.

Date	Result	3/4	Date	Goal

Date	3/4	7/8	Goal	Date

Figure 6-1. Two types of abbreviated progress records

Figure 6-1 shows two types of boxes in which the coaches can record an athlete's progress during the season. These boxes are useful additions to the training schedules for the field events.

Above all, the schedule sheets are not meant to be static. Just as an athlete's training and a good coach's training system are modified after each year's new experiences and learning, so will the schedule sheets be modified slightly each year. They should change to reflect the needs of your own program. They should be as dynamic as the training process itself.

Adapting the Training Schedules to Your Program

Although the training schedules are highly usable as they are, it is preferable that each coach adapt them to his own program and athletes. Such adaptation requires you to study the workouts and compare their objectives and progression to your own needs. Keep in mind that these training schedules were used by male college-age athletes. However, Bill Bowerman emphasized moderation in training, so the overall training loads are not high. As a result, the athlete has less need to lessen the workload. Consider the following differences in adapting the schedules to your own program.

Age Differences

Older athletes can tolerate higher workloads and more training sessions, while younger athletes cannot effectively train as often or as long. The coach must watch the recovery carefully because less experienced athletes may overtrain, not being as observant of their bodies' reactions to training stresses.

The coach can set a time limit on training sessions for young athletes, such as one hour for the middle school athlete and one-and-a-half hours for the high school athlete (a heavy training day might add half an hour to those figures). In addition, easy days should be clearly specified so young athletes are aware that such days are as important to the training process as the hard days.

Interval training and distance-running loads are the only area in which the training schedules' load might be too high for younger athletes. We usually limit intervals to three times the racing distance, with a maximum load of three miles or 5,000m of intervals (not including recovery jogs). Those figures are reasonable for well-trained high school athletes. For middle school or inexperienced athletes, an interval limit of twice the racing distance, with two miles or 3,000m as an absolute limit is suggested. For middle school athletes, the long runs can be up to six miles, but three to four miles should be sufficient for most such runs.

Sex Differences

Changing the training loads for females, compared to male workloads, is not recommended. Athletes' best marks are the truest gauges of their tolerance for given training loads. Two athletes with a best mark of 5:00 for the mile are essentially the same in their physical capabilities, regardless of their sex. Certainly, no reason exists for giving one of them a lesser (or greater) training load. Instead, base any reductions on age, skill levels, and training tolerances as described in this chapter.

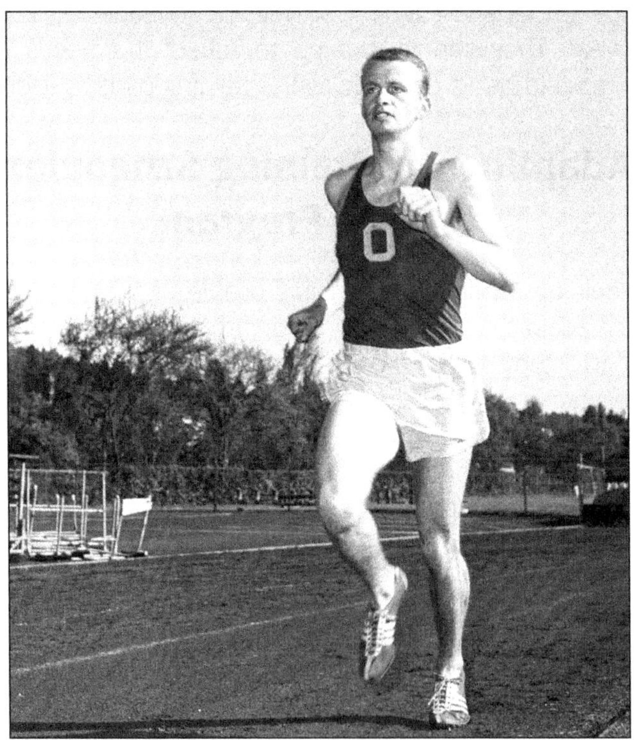

Figure 6-2. Jim Grelle, NCAA champion and Olympic athlete

Skill or Fitness Differences

The primary modification needed for the training schedules is a change in the suggested times for interval training sessions. All of the paces given in the training sheets are based on male college athletes in a national-level program. However, the interval times are also based on a standard progression of paces, based on each athlete's goal pace and date pace.

The *goal pace* (GP) is the pace that the athlete hopes to run for the peak race at the end of the season. For example, if the athlete's goal is to run 800m in 1:48, the GP is 27 seconds for 200m (54 secs. for 400m), the pace that will result in a time of 1:48. For races longer than 800m, the GP is usually the 400m pace. If an athlete hopes to run 5:20 for 1,600m, the GP is 80 (the pace time for 400m).

The *date pace* (DP) is the pace that the athlete can run the race in *at this date*. If the 800 runner can run 1:54 now, the DP is 28.5 for 200m. If the 1,600 runner runs 5:40, the DP is 85 seconds for 400m.

When using an interval workout from the schedules, compare the suggested interval times to the time of year and the schedule's GP (during the last month of the year). Translate that figure to the athlete's own GP and DP. The typical progression is to try to improve by 1 second per 400m per month of training. Thus, two months before peaking, an athlete may be running DP intervals about 2 seconds per 400m slower than the GP. This progression allows the athlete to gradually adapt to the faster racing paces. GP and DP are discussed in more detail in Chapter 6.

Endnotes

1. Bill Dellinger & Bill Freeman. (1984). *The competitive runner's training book.* New York: Collier-Macmillan.
2. James C. Radcliffe & Robert C. Farentinos. (1985). *Plyometrics: Explosive power training* (2nd ed.). Champaign, IL: Human Kinetics.

Recommended Readings

Bowerman, William J., & Freeman, William H. (1974). *Coaching track and field.* Boston: Houghton Mifflin.

Bowerman, William J., & Freeman, William H. (1991). *High performance training for track and field* (2nd ed.). Champaign, IL: Human Kinetics.

Walsh, Chris. (1983). *The Bowerman System.* Mountain View, CA: Tafnews.

Part 2

THE OREGON SCHOOL OF RUNNING

Dyrol Burleson in the first sub-4:00 at Hayward Field

7

The Fundamentals of Distance Training

The Oregon System of Distance Training

Scientific Principles Overview

The training principles and science described in the early chapters of this book apply to all middle distance races. At the elite level, an 800-meter race requires about 60 percent anaerobic endurance (to 40 percent aerobic), while the 1500 meters requires about a 50-50 mixture of aerobic and anaerobic.[1] However, as Jess Jarver notes, "While there appears to be general agreement that aerobic and anaerobic endurance capacities play the most important role in the training of middle distance runners, exactly how this can be best achieved still remains rather vague. This applies, in particular, to the best distribution of work to develop these capacities, as well as the limits of their trainability."[2]

Two points are of particular interest. First, over the last two decades, international training theory has moved away from extreme high-mileage training, becoming closer to the Oregon System. Indeed, no principle of the Oregon System is inconsistent with the most advanced training in the world today.

Second, general agreement can be found that heavy training loads (even of aerobic training) should not be used with young athletes. Low-mileage aerobic training is the best focus for pre-college athletes, with some speed training, but limited training for anaerobic endurance. Early age-group training programs and serious competitions are not recommended. Instead, a middle school student should develop a moderate aerobic base and a basic level of general skills, with a moderate number of meets. High school students can become more specialized, using slightly more intensive training and more meets.

Jarver points out that "the majority of world-class middle distance runners have used very little planned training during their years of growth." Indeed,

Russian researchers recommend that serious training for anaerobic endurance not begin before the age of 18.

The Philosophy of Bowerman's Oregon System

The basic philosophy of the Oregon system is to seek the greatest improvement possible in the athlete while working for his benefit. This approach means that the good of the athlete is the first consideration, rather than the maximum use the school can get from his abilities. To help the athlete reach his potential, his training schedule is planned to improve his performances gradually over a period of time, aiming for peak performances at the time of the conference and national meets.

Until the late 1960s, fall and winter were not emphasized as competitive seasons, but used as part of this training cycle of gradual improvement. Cross country is used to give the runners a solid training background. Though some cross-country meets are entered, these few meets are more for the purpose of stimulating the runners and giving them something to look forward to than for actual competition. The indoor track season is also passed over, for the most part. One "home" meet is held in Portland each year, the Oregon Invitational, but except for that meet, few of the Oregon athletes have any official winter competition. Instead, they run against the clock in 3/4-effort trials every two or three weeks from early winter until just before the competitive season begins.

When spring arrives, Oregon competes almost every week against some of the best teams in the world, the Pacific 10 conference teams. A runner might not compete every week even during this season. A distance man will rarely compete in two events in a single meet. The reasons are simple: the athlete needs to be "hungry," anxious to compete, and a runner reaches his potential more surely (and is more likely to remain there for some time) if he does not go out every week feeling the need to "make up points" for his team. The coach may like to win as much as anyone, but the good of the runner must come first. An athlete who has to compete in two events regularly will usually be holding back in the first event and tired during the second. As a result, he will not be likely to reach his full potential in either event.

Foundation of the Oregon System

The Oregon training system had its genesis in the coaching theories of William H. Hayward, Oregon track coach from 1904 to 1947. "Colonel Bill"—a volunteer assistant coach and trainer for the U.S. Olympic Team at several Olympics and coach of several world record holders—stressed a program of gradual conditioning and a reasonable limit on the number of competitive races. The Oregon system of training has its roots in his four-and-a-half decades of service to the University and to American track and field.

Upon returning to the University as track coach in 1948, Bill Bowerman found a small track team and a "stable" of one distance runner, junior Pete

Mundle. At this time, Bill knew mostly the American theories of distance training, so he had Pete conduct some library research to learn what training methods seemed to offer the best possibilities for success. After some study, Mundle wrote a term paper recommending that they try interval training and fartlek, a method that was not too widely known or understood in the United States at that time.

Pete then became the "guinea pig," and those experiments laid the groundwork from which the Oregon system of distance training grew. This research led to the discovery of the great value of fartlek to the training program and to further development of the "hard-easy" principle of training. Fortunately, some fine young distance runners chose to come to Oregon, and they in turn brought more good runners. For many years, this method was the primary means of recruiting runners.

Photo 7-1. Peter Mundle, Bowerman's first distance runner

The basic system is a combination of interval training and fartlek. It began with the written materials given to Pete Mundle in the late 1940s, was combined with what was learned from coaches around the world since then, and was synthesized through years of coaching practice into the present system. We have found no better system for the athletes for whom it was developed: college students between the ages of 17 and 24. Here the work level is lower than that cited for many world-class athletes. Keep in mind, however, that those athletes are often five or more years older than college students and 10 years older than high school athletes.

The first major outside influence on the system was Gosta Holmer of Sweden, who used fartlek with his athletes. He also contributed a 10-day training pattern that was adapted into our first pattern of training. His writings and assistance were a great contribution to the system. Franz Stampfl provided the framework of interval training with a gradually quickening pace through the year, shown in his 1955 book. It was an attempt to put interval training into a system in which the level of training progressed scientifically. It was probably more widely circulated among English-speaking coaches than the work of interval training's major developer, Woldemar Gerschler of Germany. Bowerman also observed John Landy's training before the 1954 British Empire Games.

Mihaly Igloi's use of interval training, varying paces, and sets made considerable contributions also. Bowerman's first contact with his training methods was through a letter from the Dale Ranson, coach at the University of North Carolina. After Igloi's defection from Hungary following the 1956 Olympics, he and several of his runners spent some time in Chapel Hill, where they were observed by Coach Ranson. Later Oregon's Pete Mundle trained after graduation under Igloi in southern California, providing more information and insight into the methods of that fine, knowledgeable, but misunderstood coach.

Finally, but by no means least, much was learned from personal contacts with Arthur Lydiard of New Zealand. His insights into training opened up new areas of experimentation. His year-round training patterns were very interesting, as were a number of his practices, which were adapted and are now used in one form or another. Bowerman also received useful ideas from many fine American coaches.

Basic Principles of Distance Training

The basic principles are simple. The first was expressed well by Lydiard: "Train, don't strain." The athlete should enjoy training. He should complete his workout feeling exhilarated, not exhausted, as Holmer suggested with fartlek training. Training must be fun, or else why do we train?

It is better for a runner to undertrain than to overtrain. Overtraining results in staleness, a loss of interest in practice and in competition. Staleness also results from competing too often, which interferes with the best performances and progress of athletes. An ideal situation for distance runners is competition every 10 to 14 days, occasionally every three weeks. It is difficult to understand how a team or a coach can accomplish much in the school season with two meets a week. When do they learn or teach?

To those coaches who prefer two or three meets a week and point to the summer European programs where American athletes have performed outstandingly, we emphasize that those distance runners are usually mature, experienced athletes, 25 years old or older. Furthermore, during that time all they do is compete, eat, and rest. The school athlete is not only competing; he is also getting an education, which should be the first concern. Education requires considerable study time and energy.

The Hard-Easy Training Approach

No athlete should compete before being properly conditioned. Competing too soon causes the athlete to risk injury because the body is not properly prepared for the stresses of competition. For that same reason, neither the coach nor the athlete should use meets as a means of conditioning.

The training pattern follows a hard-easy sequence, with each day of hard training being followed by a day of easy or light training, primarily jogging and light fartlek. The reason for this cycle is basic to all training: the body must have rest. Rest is always necessary for the body to recover and replenish itself. Furthermore, taking light days allows more work in the training sessions on the hard days, giving greater progress in the long run. This cycle is basic, but it is not inflexible. Some runners are strong enough to take two hard days for every easy day; others can take only one hard day and then need two easy days.

Years ago, an experiment was conducted with the Oregon runners to see how long they could hold up under conditions of heavy training, with no recovery days. Most of the runners lasted no more than a week, including several who, after returning to the hard-easy cycle, later ran under 4:00 for the mile. Only one runner lasted two weeks: Bill Dellinger, then a 25-year-old graduate student and veteran of two Olympics. At the end of three weeks, even he could no longer take the unrelieved hard days.

We prefer to keep the runners short of their peak, not over the hill. Once an athlete has been properly conditioned and has a good background of training, it takes little extra work to bring him to a peak. However, an athlete cannot remain at a peak for very long. For that reason, we prefer to hold the athletes short of their peak and sharpen them at the end of the season for the most important meets. Many athletes are world-beaters in the early season but cannot make the finals in the national meets. We want to avoid such a situation.[3]

Athletes work toward objectives and goals in their training. If they don't know where they are going, how will they get there? How will they know how close they are? The athletes and the coach set personal goals for the end of the

Photo 7-2. Bill Dellinger, three-time Olympian, 5,000m bronze medal, NCAA champion at mile and 5,000m, prominent collegiate and Olympic distance coach

year, then they gradually progress toward those goals through training sessions and test efforts run at the 3/4-effort level.

The athlete must also train to the competition. No athlete can train without taking account of the competitors. It involves training to reach the same level, or a better one, as the competitors and also includes training in tactics and their uses. One of the purposes of training is to improve the runners' strengths, so that their assets become greater assets, and to overcome their weaknesses, so that those handicaps are removed or minimized.

The athlete should continue with light exercise after hard training or competition. This process is sometimes called "cooling down." The reason is quite simple: during strenuous exercise, the body builds up lactic acid—a by-product of muscular activity—in the muscles. If the lactic acid is not removed from the muscles, it can result in cramping and possibly muscular injury. Easy jogging after heavy exercise keeps the blood circulating rapidly, gradually drawing the excess lactic acid from the muscles. For this reason, also, an easy trot on the morning after heavy exercise is beneficial to the body.

The morning run is now considered an essential of distance training. The practice is excellent, if the runner can handle it. It helps the athlete wake up in the morning and get the metabolic processes started for the day. It also encourages going to bed earlier. If the runner does not get the rest, however, it becomes a destructive process. A runner with heavy studies or involved in a romance should not try the morning run, nor should the coach force the attempt. The athlete is going through the biology of youth. It must be accommodated because it cannot be changed.

Compared to other world-class athletes, Oregon athletes do not train very hard. At one time, 100 or more miles a week was considered by many people to be necessary for success in distance running. We do not believe this, nor has experience proven it. Though Arthur Lydiard has been pointed to as the source for this magic mark, his training schedules call for that amount of training for only about 10 weeks of the year, while at other times they call for only 40 to 60 miles per week of training.

The top Oregon collegiate athletes run from 60 to 80 miles a week, averaging about 70 miles. None of them covers 100 miles a week except in rare circumstances, yet by 1973 over two dozen sub-4:00 milers were produced at Oregon by Bowerman. While mileage helps, it is by no means the only variable involved in training; certainly it is not the most important one. One Oregon runner ran a 4:01 mile on 20 miles a week.

Every athlete's training methods should be taken with a grain of salt, experimented with, and then adapted to the specific needs and abilities of the individual who wishes to use them. The coach must keep in mind that the student-athlete is supposed to be studying and that other things are important in life besides running.

The athletes should learn to maintain their appetite for running, not make it the most important thing in their lives. If athletes pass up other things in life, they will be isolating themselves, which is not good.

The age at which training should begin is simple to pick: the age at which the youngster wants to train. A four-year-old who likes to run is old enough to train (but not be trained). An 18-year-old who must be driven out to the track and flogged around it either is too young to train or has lost their appetite for it. The key is enjoyment: athletes should enjoy what they are doing; they should not have to be forced into training.

Principles and Physiology of Distance Running

The principles of training are discussed in detail in Chapter 3. The major emphases are moderation, consistency, and rest. The scientific foundations that underlie the system are described in Chapter 4. However, a few points need to be discussed in greater detail.

Of the physiological phenomena that are a measure of a person's ability to run a race of over 100 yards, one of the best indicators is oxygen debt and its related reactions. When a miler runs, he is burning internal fuels and using oxygen for the burning, just as a camper burns wood that consumes oxygen. If the lungs can supply enough oxygen to the fuel to carry the runner for a mile at a comfortable pace, there is no distress. If there is insufficient oxygen supplied to maintain the pace, or if the pace is too fast for the amount of oxygen supplied, the runner goes into oxygen debt.

Other related biochemical factors produce the same sort of inability to maintain pace. Producing carbon dioxide and related wastes in greater quantities than can be eliminated by the cardiorespiratory system interferes with oxygen exchange and contributes to oxygen debt, just as too much smoke in the chimney prevents good combustion in the stove.

Some coaches speak of fatigue tolerance or tolerance to oxygen debt. Is it a superior level of fitness that permits an athlete not only to turn in a world-record performance, but to do it repeatedly? We suspect that it is a combination of fitness, tolerance, the coach, and, of course, the runner's superior physical equipment.

Other Distance-Training Principles

We believe in weight training for runners. By "weight training," we do not mean developing Olympic weightlifters or spending hours weekly. We use a short list of exercises that concentrate on the upper body, the back, and the arms, all of which tend to be neglected by most runners. Strengthening those areas, particularly the back and the abdomen, assists in improving the posture, which in turn permits the body to take in more oxygen, permitting the athlete to run faster and farther. This approach is in line with today's strong emphasis on core strength.

Swimming is also beneficial to runners. It is good for relaxing and loosening tight muscles. It is very helpful for a runner with knee or ankle problems because the muscles can be exercised without irritating the joints. In fact, Scott Taylor, a varsity swimmer at Oregon, came out for the mile during his fifth year of school. At the end of the year, he ran a 4:05.2 mile, followed by a 1500-meter race at a faster pace. He later became an Olympic performer in the modern pentathlon.

The final principle might be better described as a practice. During their early season training, all the distance runners at Oregon practice the techniques of the steeplechase occasionally. Since few of them have ever encountered this event before coming to the university, it is a way of finding runners who show natural ability or interest in this event. Those athletes will continue to work on steeplechase activities. This work consists primarily of practicing clearance of the barriers, pace work over the barriers, and work on the water-jump—beginning with stepping onto and then over sections of logs. A number of good steeplechasers began on Oregon's Douglas firs.

Components of Running Ability

Three components are essential to successful racing over the middle distances. The first two are of equal importance, and the third is nice to have, but not absolutely necessary:

- Endurance
- Pace judgment
- Speed

A possible fourth essential was added by Emil Zatopek and Vladimir Kuts in the 1950s: varied-pace or aggressive tactics.

Photo 7-3. Jim Bailey, first sub-4:00 in the United States, 1956; NCAA champion, Australian Olympian.

Endurance is needed to withstand the continued stress of a distance race. Runners must develop the strength to endure before becoming able to compete well. Endurance is not solely physical or physiological; it is also a state of mind and a function of willpower. Champions have not only greater physical endurance, but also greater mental endurance. They can drive themselves closer to their true capacities before their minds tell them to stop. Tolerance to stress requires much mental training along with the physical training.

Pace judgment is extremely important. Most inexperienced runners begin their race at a very fast pace, slow down too much during the race, then try to sprint at the finish. That tactic is not only painful but also physiologically foolish. Physiologically, the easiest way to run a given time is at an even pace. The ability to run even pace, or any pace, requires training in pace judgment, not just endurance training. The world's best distance runners are all excellent judges of pace. It results from years of training and racing experience, and it is essential to success.

The third component of success is speed. Although it is not the most important factor, it is still very helpful. Obviously if all other factors and abilities are the same, the runner with the best speed will win. However, all other factors and abilities are rarely equal, and many tactical variations have been used to equalize the inequities among runners. Speed can be improved in runners in most instances. Where it can be improved, it should be improved.

The tentative fourth essential is varied-pace or aggressive tactics. This method involves shifting from one pace to another during the race, throwing in a short sprint here or a quick extended surge there, and attempting to hold a reasonably fast pace for the rest of the race. It is a difficult type of race to run. It is physiologically much more difficult than an evenly paced race. Also, the runner has the disadvantage of having to lead the race, while hoping to "kill off" his opponents without exhausting his own physiological resources. However, it is as psychologically exhausting on the opponents as it is physically exhausting, for they never know when a fast burst may be used or how long it will last; thus, they are unsure how to cope with it.

Introducing the Runners to Training

Finding Candidates

The best way to find your first candidates is by testing everyone in the physical education classes. Have every student run 800 meters, and record their times. An untrained young man who can run under 2:30, or a young woman who can run under 3:00 has enough natural speed and endurance to be considered a good prospect. Experience in high school and college over a period of years has proven this test to be a reliable indicator of inherent talent. (See Chapter 23 for more information.)

Most of the great middle-distance champions have been of average or slightly over average height, slightly built, and with well-defined (but not bulky) muscles. They generally have had slower-than-average pulse rates. Longer-distance runners tend to be smaller. However, notable exceptions to each of these characteristics have occurred.

Champions must be serious, with abundant energy and tenacity. They must be willing to endure grueling workout schedules, regardless of weather conditions, year after year. They must be eager to push themselves to the limit of their capacities, as well as eager to defeat their opponents. The two greatest characteristics of the champion have always been dedication and hard work.

Equipment

The runner's equipment is almost as meager as the swimmer's, with one exception: the shoes. Every experienced runner should have three pairs of shoes, if possible. One is for wearing to and from the track and during roadwork, the second is for regular practice, and the last is for competition.

For practice sessions, a sturdy but comfortable shoe is essential. A four-spike model is a frequent choice. It must be comfortable and light because every ounce counts. If a pair of shoes weighs 4 ounces more than another pair of shoes, that extra 4 ounces amounts to the runner literally lifting 220 extra pounds in the course of a mile race (4 ounces x 880 strides). That energy can be more profitably spent running faster than in dragging an anchor.

For training clothes, lightweight materials that protect from the weather yet still "breathe" should be used. The running trunks and jersey should also be very light. Names or emblems can be silk-screened rather than sewn on, avoiding useless, weighty junk. The only necessary stripe across the chest is the one at the finish line.

Practice gear can be inexpensive. Cotton long johns can be substituted for spandex tights or sweatpants, not only for economy but also because they do not get clammy when wet and can be worn in competition during cold weather. Stocking caps are good protection against the cold, but a sweatshirt with a hood attached is probably more practical because the hood cannot be forgotten or lost. All of the training clothing should be kept clean, washed as often as possible.

Mechanics and Posture

We try to improve our runners' mechanics because they gain much from it. A champion can do the job with less effort than a non-champion. The reason is that his body has been trained to do that task more efficiently. We want to improve the mechanical efficiency of our runners so they can do the same amount of work with less effort. Thus, they will be able to devote the saved energy to running a faster race. The effort expended will be the same, but the time will be faster because the body works more efficiently, yielding greater output without requiring greater effort.

Good posture comes from good muscle tone. If the muscles of the stomach, the lower back, and the hips are well developed, they assist in maintaining an upright posture. Weight lifting and other exercises can help in this regard.

The best postural position for the middle distance runner is an upright one. A line from the ear straight down to the ground should show that the back is perpendicular to the ground during running. The widely accepted belief that the body needs to lean forward to run well is not true. Research by Dr. Donald Slocum[4] shows that such a belief is incorrect. Champion runners have an upright posture while striding at racing speed. This factor is true even for sprinters, once they have finished accelerating.

Photos 7-4 and 7-5 are side views of runners in an 800m run and a 200m dash. Times on this 800m lap varied from 51 to 53 seconds, so they are running at race pace. Notice that they are all running erectly, with little or no body lean, though there are some personal eccentricities of form. The upright posture is simply more efficient because when any body part is out of alignment, some muscles must strain to keep the body balanced, diverting part of the body's energies from the task of running a fast race. Notice that once acceleration ends, the sprinters are also upright.

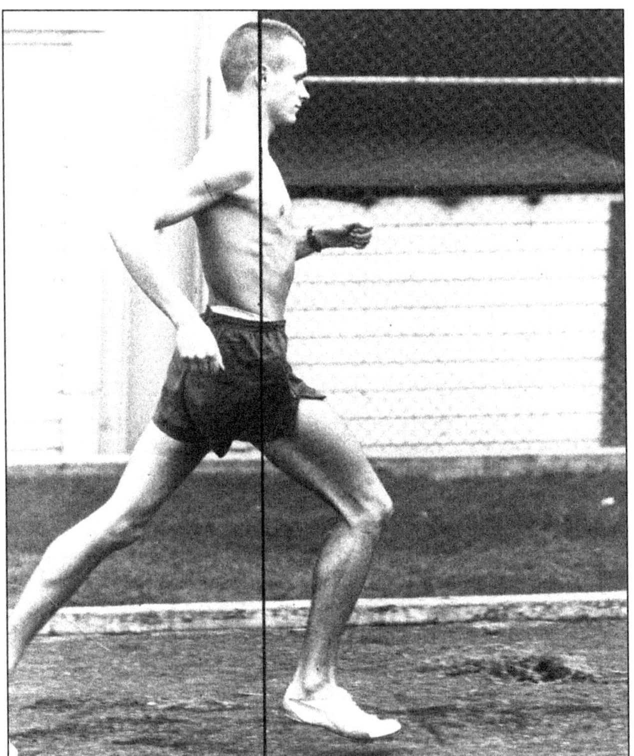

Photo 7-4. Running posture in 1500m, Dyrol Burleson

In our work with runners, we try to point out the mechanical advantages of this upright form. We have the runners practice their form during fartlek and interval training, so it becomes part of their natural technique. We try to remember that this "perfect" form has individual variations. Very few runners can be termed "picture" runners, for most people have some physical characteristics that require minor technical compensations.

Our research found that the pelvic position is the key to control of the runner's posture. The pelvis should be "tucked under," or brought forward in relation to the rest of the body. This positioning assists in straightening the spine, which helps maintain an upright posture. The chest is directly in line above the hips, keeping the back in a straight line perpendicular to the ground. The head is up, the chest is raised, and the arms are swung slightly across the chest. This basic running form permits easier use of the leg muscles and aids in taking air into the lungs. If the horizon seems to be moving up and down, the runner may be overstriding.

The arm carry and swing also affect the posture. We teach an angle of 60 to 90 degrees at the elbow as optimal, though an athlete with very muscular arms might need to use a more open angle. This angle contributes to running efficiency in three ways. First, it improves the circulation. The little bit of downward flow from hand to elbow makes the heart's job that much easier. Centrifugal force also needs to be considered. Like the water in the bucket swung at arm's length, centrifugal force will act to keep the blood from returning from the hands, if the arms are carried very low.

Photo 7-5. Posture in the 200m.

Optimal arm angle also gives a mechanical advantage. The lower the arms are carried, the longer the stride tends to be. The longer the stride, the greater the energy output required to maintain the pace and stride length. Because the arms and legs work in opposing pairs, we try to develop a short, quick, economical stride by keeping the arms moving in a shorter working radius.

Third, the arm swing contributes to the athlete's balance or imbalance. Exaggerated swinging of the arms must be compensated for by shifting the weight on the opposite side of the center of gravity or by expending more energy. A fresh runner can swing an arm way out of line and get away with it. However, coming down the home stretch, fatigued and tense, the runner may wander all over the track, or if too fatigued may even fall.

We recommend that runners use their arms in this manner: With an elbow bend of 60 to 90 degrees, swing the hand in an arc from about the top of the hipbone to the breastbone in the center of the body, with the arms naturally alternating this movement. Swing the hand and arm from the shoulder; the elbow does not open and close. At times, the runner may want to rest or save the arms for the final drive by carrying them for a while. This motion is one where the hands remain about three to six inches apart and swing in a rhythmical tempo back and forth across the chest.

A quick, light stride is the most economical. It is most easily maintained when running upright rather than leaning forward. The leg swing should be as effortless as possible. The knee lift is moderately high, but no conscious effort is made to reach with the knee. The leg and foot are dropped directly under the body for the stride, and the leg is not fully extended in front of the body. A slightly short stride is the most efficient.

It is better to understride than to overstride. The runner should watch an object on the horizon to see whether it appears to be moving up and down. If the object is bounding, then the runner is bouncing, lifting the body on every stride. He is probably overstriding, a very common fault, or at least running inefficiently.

The three ways to plant the foot while running are: heel to ball, flat-footed, and ball to heel. The ball-to-heel plant is basically running on the toes, as sprinters do, and is out of place in distance running. It is less efficient for a runner because it requires more energy and puts additional strain on the calf muscles. Most great runners use either the heel-to-ball or the flat-footed stride. Runners should experiment to see which is most comfortable for them. The flat style involves landing flat-footed and rocking forward; the heel-to-ball style lands in the area of the heel of the foot and rolls forward, pushing off with the toes.

Three of the items discussed (stride length, body mechanics, and body posture) are worth repeating. Stride length is important because it, combined with stride cadence and economy of energy, determines in part how soon the race will be finished. The "long, beautiful stride" is often a disadvantage because it acts as a brake when the foot lands ahead of the center of gravity. Also, it requires more energy because it lifts and drops the body with every stride. Overstriding is the most common fault of high school distance runners. A short, economical, quick stride is better and more efficient.

Body mechanics are important because improper mechanics create a much greater energy drain. The body should be moved as efficiently as possible so the energy saved by good mechanics can be diverted to faster running. Posture is also critical to efficiency. If the mechanical and postural advantages are ignored, two advantages of the upright running posture remain:

- The body can take more air into the lungs because the upright trunk allows the lungs more space in the body cavity.
- The knees can be lifted higher, allowing the runner to swing the legs more freely and easily while running.

Pace Judgment

Pace judgment is a critical ability of the champion runner. The most efficient way to run a race is with even pacing. Pace judgment is not inherent–it is learned. Once it is acquired, the athlete can plan the race more easily and can better utilize his strengths. The significant thing is that pace judgment is one of the weapons with which an athlete is armed. The athlete knows what his pace is and deviates from it only as a weapon.

Poor races result from an inability to judge pace. By running too fast in the early stages of races, athletes build up an oxygen debt that they cannot repay without slowing down greatly. Practice perfects rhythm at any pace. A person can be strong of wind and heart and in good condition, but not have practiced pace work long enough to establish his rhythm.

To start teaching pace to our runners, we put a small stake in the middle of each straight and each turn of the track, dividing the track into four 100m segments. The runners are shown a pace card with the 400-, 200-, and 100-meter splits for 1600m times of 4:32, 5:00, 6:00, 7:00, and 8:00, which is illustrated in Table 7-1.

Pace Card

1600m	4:32	5:00	6:00	7:00	8:00
400m	68	75	90	105	2:00
200m	34	37.5	45	52.5	60
100m	17	19	22.5	26.25	30

Table 7-1. Pace card sample

Practice consists of watching a large pace clock and jogging into a paced 100m when the second hand reaches any of the quarter-circle points: 0, 15, 30, or 45 seconds. Men try to reach the 100m mark in 20 to 25 seconds (25 to 30 seconds for women), then walk or jog a 100m, and repeat the paced run until they have run ten 100s. It is interesting how many men run at a pace faster than a four-minute mile on the first 100m, but reassuring to see how soon pain teaches the first lesson of 20 to 25 seconds per 100. When the runners can do this, we drop down to the five-minute 1600 pace for men (or six-minute pace for women) and increase the distances to a 200, a 300, or even a 400m.

It is doubtful that any runner can be dead sure of the pace. Our runners have a margin of error of 2 seconds per 400m in the 1500, mile and 5,000 meters, and of 1 second per 400m in the 800 meters. Table 7-2 is an example of a pace chart for men.

Theoretical Race Paces

1600 Meters and One Mile

100	*200*	*400*	*800*	*1200*	*1600*
18-19-20	36-37-38	73-75-77	2:26-2:30-2:34	3:39-3:45-3:51	4:52-5:00-5:08
	34-35-35	68-70-72	2:16-2:20-2:24	3:24-3:30-3:35	4:32-4:40-4:48
	33-34-35	65-68-70	2:11-2:15-2:19	3:15-3:22-3:25	4:22-4:30-4:38
	32-33-34	63-65-67	2:06-2:10-2:14	3:09-3:15-3:21	4:12-4:20-4:28
	30-31-32	60-62-54	2:00-2:04-2:00	3:00-3:06-3:12	4:02-4:10-4:18
14-15-16	29-30-31	58-60-62	1:56-2:00-2:04	2:54-3:00-3:06	3:52-4:00-4:05
Margin of Error					
+1	+1	+2	+4	+6	+8

800 Meters

100	*200*	*400*	*600*	*800*
15-17-18	33-34-35	66-68-70	1:40-1:42-1:44	2:11-2:15-2:19
15-16-17	31-32-33	63-65-67	1:35-1:37-1:39	2:06-2:10-2:14
14-15-16	30-31-32	50-62-64	1:31-1:33-1:35	2:01-2:05-2:09
14-15-16	29-30-31	58-60-62	1:28-1:30-1:32	1:56-2:00-2:04
13-14-15	28-29-30	56-58-50	1:25-1:27-1:29	1:52-1:56-2:00
13-14-15	27-28-29	54-56-58	1:22-1:24-1:26	1:45-1:52-1:55
Margin of Error				
-1 +1	-1 +1	-2 +2	-2 +2	-4 +4

Table 7-2. Theoretical race paces

In practicing pace, we not only expect errors in judgment, but we permit runners to be off a bit, as long as they remain within allowable limits. We expect the margin to appear in any of the segments of the race, but we do not want a big deviation, for example, in the third or fourth quarter of the race. If a male runner is trying for 1:56 in the 800m and he hits 28 and 29 for a 57 at the 400m, that is acceptable. If he then rests with a 32, he is running like a beginner and either is not capable of running a 1:56 or has not yet found the courage to pour it on and make his own race.

It is frustrating to see a well-conditioned good judge of pace hold back and save something for the last 100 meters against a competitor who is known to have a better kick. If the other athlete is going to win, make him earn it. Through pace judgment, the weapons for the slower, stronger athlete are either to build a lead that a sprinter cannot overcome, or force the opponent into a pace that will remove his kick.

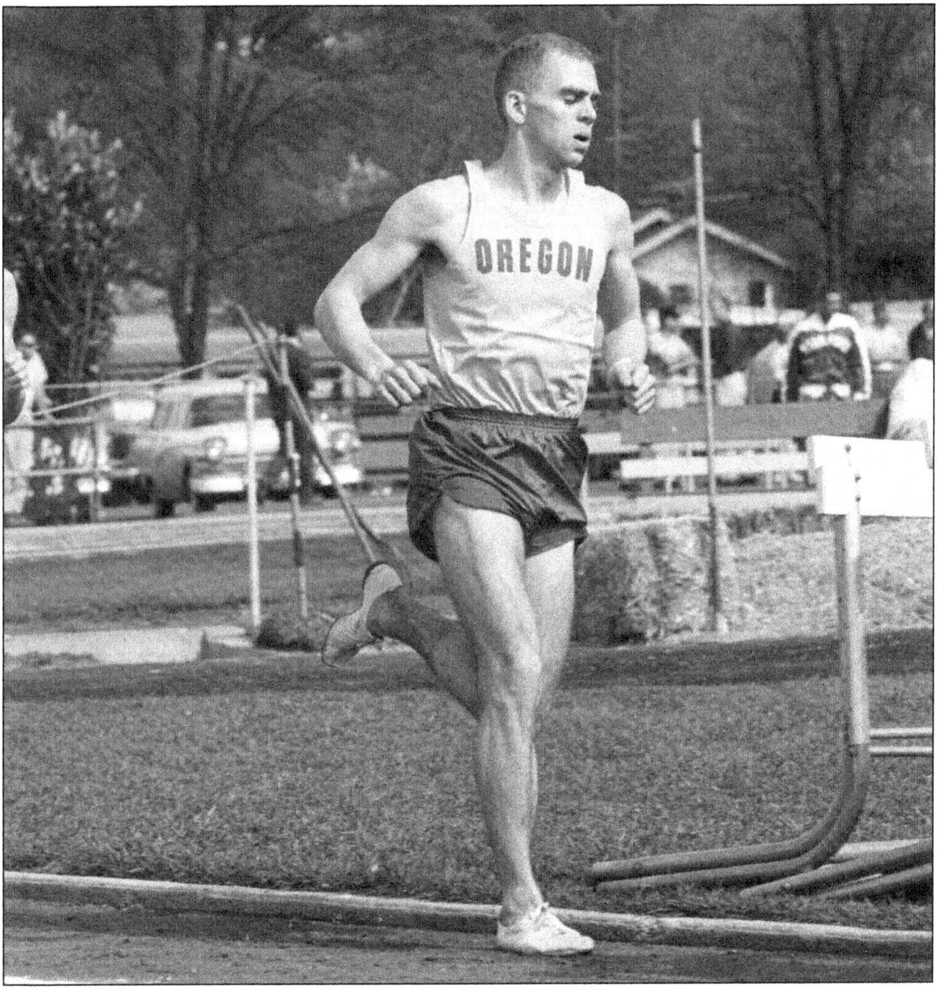

Photo 7-6. Keith Forman, 3:58.3 mile

Timing Intervals

Eugene, Oregon, is a distance man's paradise, with the most knowledgeable and enthusiastic track fans in the world. We probably have more stopwatches per capita than any city in the world. With all these watches available, how do we time intervals? We use a large clock. With a squad of 60 or more men in 17 events, it is impossible to spend an hour with each man or be with every event every day. It is also expensive to turn a watch over to a runner or a group of runners, so we use our clock.

Our clock is homemade. We took a piece of sheet tin three feet square, cut a round hole which was two inches in diameter in the middle, and painted the face black. A ruler compass was used to lay out the major sixty points of a circle with a three-foot diameter. Each fifth or five-second mark was painted yellow, and the other four points were painted smaller and white. We now had a three-foot clock face.

Our original clock was "begged" from a drugstore. We made a second hand, which was three feet long and painted one half black and the other half yellow. We then mounted it on the "axle" of the clock and carefully counterbalanced it so that the small motor could make it go steadily. Our clock can be used anywhere that we have an electrical outlet, and when mounted above the ground, it is visible clearly from all points around the track.

Vandals have occasionally disabled our clock, since it is left outdoors. It would be easy to say, "If they're going to act that way, we will not leave our equipment out." Because of a few troublemakers, 60 or more people who want to participate may be denied a facility. For this reason, we try to keep our clock and some of our other equipment out and available for anyone's use. As Ray Hendrickson has said, "The real test of a facility is that it is being used."

Workout Sheets

The chart form of workout sheets that we use (Sheet 6-1) developed from necessity. These charts were mimeographed, together with a weekly training calendar. The coach then had to refer to each exercise only by its number. For example, if he wanted the runners to run 8 x 440 yards in 70 to 73 seconds, he wrote 8 x 5E1. A fartlek assignment was 2 (this was pre-Lydiard). Thus, the coach can communicate with his athletes "by the numbers."

The charts are updated every year, so slight variations can be found from year to year. As an example of how we record the workouts, Sheet 6-2 shows a copy of the February 1960 workouts of Jim Grelle, who made the U.S. Olympic Team that year, running 4:00.1 in the mile. In 1966, he ran a 3:55.4 mile and an 8:25.2 2-mile as a 30-year-old veteran. As an example, note his workout on the tenth of that month. He warmed up, then ran 4 x 440 yards in 64 seconds.

The workout record saves much of this space. The records are retained, with some of them going back to the late 1940s. The coach is then able to compare the progress of one miler against his previous progress or that of any of his predecessors, giving a more concrete comparison of the runner's current progress. We believe that it is the quickest way to communicate with our runners.

The General Training Patterns

The Annual Cycle

At Oregon, a master plan is developed for each three-month period. The early training during October, November, and December consists of conditioning, cross country and testing. The pre-track and long distance training in January, February, and March stresses fundamentals and increasing strength. During the competitive season (April, May, and June), all efforts are directed toward keeping the athletes in top physical and psychological condition.

The volume of work is rather modest at the start of a training period. It builds up as the year progresses, reaches a peak just before the competitive season, and then is somewhat reduced as the weekly competition demands maximum energy and attention. During all the seasons, the schedules generally follow a pattern of a hard day (one to two hours of work) followed by an easy day (about 30 minutes of work).

During the early season, group assignments are made to the runners. During the competitive season, each person has a separate workout sheet on which his workouts are written for one week at a time. An example of the rough progression of training throughout the year for a male miler who can already run in the 4:00 range is shown in Table 7-3. The pace given is for a 440-yard interval, the volume is the workout mileage in terms of the number of times the racing distance ("2" for a miler would be two miles), and the rest interval is proportionate to the interval being run. If the athlete is running 440s and the interval is 1/2, the rest interval is 220 yards of walking or jogging.

This general workout pattern can be adapted to the individual runner in both pace and volume. The goal pace (60 seconds per lap) is scheduled for May, so time adjustments can easily be made. For a woman with a goal of 5:00 for 1600m, the May pace for 400m is 75, which is 15 seconds more than the 60 pace in the table. Thus, all of the 400m paces are increased by 15 seconds, starting with 90 seconds in October, dropping to 85 seconds in November, and so forth.

Above all, the runners must have variety. The pleasurable variety offered by fartlek, the discipline of interval training, some special speed work, and regular exercises all increase the runner's strength. The runner needs a bit of almost everything, including a balanced training diet, both for overall improvement and for the prevention of the boredom that is sometimes called "staleness."

Oregon Training Schedule Outline (For a 4:00 miler)				
Month	*Week*	*400 Pace*	*Volume*	*Rest Interval*
October	1	75	2	Full
	2	75	2-3	1/2
	3	75	2	1/4
	4	75	2-3	1/4
November	1	70	2	Full
	2	70	2-3	1/2
	3	70	2	1/4
	4	70	2-3	1/4
December	1	68	2	Full
	2	68	2-3	1/2
	3	68	2	1/4
	4	68	2-3	1/4
January	1	66	2	Full
	2	66	2-3	1/2
	3	66	2	1/4
	4	66	2-3	1/4
February	1	64	2	Full
	2	64	2-3	1/2
	3	64	2	1/4
	4	64	2-3	1/4
March	1	62	2	Full
	2	62	2-3	1/2
	3	62	2	1/4
	4	62	2-3	1/4
April	1	61	2	Full
	2	61	2-3	1/2
	3	61	2	1/4
	4	61	2-3	1/4
May	1	60	2	Full
	2	60	2-3	1/2
	3	60	2	1/4
	4	60	2-3	1/4
June	1	59	2	Full
	2	59	2-3	1/2
	3	59	2	1/4
	4	59	2-3	1/4
July	1	58	2	Full
	2	58	2-3	1/2
	3	58	2	1/4
	4	58	2-3	1/4
August	1	57	2	Full
	2	57	2-3	1/2
	3	57	2	1/4
	4	57	2-3	1/4

Table 7-3. Oregon training schedule outline (for a 4:00 miler)

Date pace and goal pace need to be defined at this point. Date pace (DP) is the actual pace at which the runners are clocked in a test effort or time trial that they try to run 3/4 effort. This figure is usually expressed as their pace for 400m. If the runner can already run 4:24 for 1600m, the DP is 66. After the next test effort, the DP is adjusted to reflect the runner's improvement. We try to get the runner to improve by 1 second per 400m during each training period (two to three weeks).

Goal pace (GP) is the 400m pace that the runner wants to run at the peak of the season. If the athlete wants to run a 4:08 for 1600, the GP is 62. If the goal is 5:24 for the 1600, the GP is 81.

The 10-day, 14-day, and 21-day schedules are named for the times that their training cycle requires at a set pace. Each pattern concludes with a test effort. The test effort, often marked simply as "test," is a time trial run at 3/4 effort. It is not an all-out effort.

The Running Patterns

The athletes' schedules should be tailored to fit their needs, ambitions, and goals. These schedules are a mixture of training methods that we have tried and found helpful. The first pattern was a seven-day pattern. It was developed years ago simply as a way to plan ahead where to put the training emphasis for a given period. At that time, most runners did not begin regular training until the first of January or February, and they did not train or compete with any regularity after mid-June. The pattern, based on the hard-easy sequence, is shown in Table 7-4.

Seven-Day Training Pattern

Day		*Training Level*
Monday	(1)	Heavy
Tuesday	(2)	Light
Wednesday	(3)	Heavy
Thursday	(4)	Light
Friday	(5)	Heavy
Saturday	(6)	Light
Sunday	(7)	Heavy

Table 7-4. Seven-day training pattern

You will notice that this schedule throws two hard days, Sunday and Monday, together. In applying the principle of hard-easy, or heavy-light, training, it is important to recall that every person is different. Some runners benefit from the two heavy days, but others need to make Sunday a light or rest day also.

The idea of the 10-day pattern came from Sweden. It fits the progress of conditioning, testing, and preparation better than the one that most of us are forced into by the Gregorian and school calendars of seven days to a week, which usually puts us into a 14-day training period. A 10-day schedule is shown in Table 7-5.

Ten-Day Training Pattern

Day		*Training Level*
Monday	(1)	Heavy
Tuesday	(2)	Light
Wednesday	(3)	Heavy
Thursday	(4)	Light
Friday	(5)	Heavy
Saturday	(6)	Light
Sunday	(7)	Heavy
Monday	(8)	Light
Tuesday	(9)	Light
Wednesday	(10)	Test effort

Table 7-5. Ten-day training pattern

This schedule points out another principle: Usually, the athlete should have at least two days of light training before a hard test effort or a competition. Our school calendar being what it is, we must use the 14-day training pattern. This two-week pattern also brings up our strong belief that runners compete best if their major efforts are at least two weeks apart.

Major meets may have trials and final races over a period of two, three, or even four days. We plan and train for such situations with the individual runner. The basic two-week pattern calls for alternating days of heavy and light training, beginning with a hard day on the first Sunday and including two light days, the second Thursday and Friday, before the competition or test effort on the second Saturday. The specific 14-day pattern that we follow is shown in Table 7-6.

Some of the preceding words will be clearer if we elaborate a bit. *Overdistance* work is understandable. *Goal* refers to intervals run at the goal pace. The athlete runs intervals totaling the racing distance at that pace. For example, a 1600 runner with a goal pace of 60 seconds per 400 would run 4 x 400m in 60 seconds. Each as the "goal" part of the workout; perhaps run a set of 600-, 400-, 300-, 200-, and 100-meter intervals all at that pace; or run any other combination totaling 1600 meters.

Date refers to intervals run at the date pace. If a runner is at 5:20 in the date pace, he might next run 1600 to 3200 meters of intervals on a pace of 80 seconds per 400 meters. The workout would conclude with some fartlek.

Fourteen-Day Training Pattern		
Day		*Training Level*
Sunday	(1)	Steady fartlek: 6 to 15 miles (10-25 km.)
Monday	(2)	Varied fartlek (light)
Tuesday	(3)	Goal pace, date pace, light fartlek
Wednesday	(4)	Steady fartlek (light)
Thursday	(5)	Rhythm or quick, fartlek, cutdowns
Friday	(6)	Light fartlek
Saturday	(7)	Overdistance, underdistance, date pace, fartlek
Sunday	(8)	Steady fartlek: 6 to 15 miles (10-25 km.)
Monday	(9)	Varied fartlek (light)
Tuesday	(10)	Goal pace, steady fartlek, light running
Wednesday	(11)	Steady fartlek (light)
Thursday	(12)	Quick fartlek (light); cutdowns, or simulated race
Friday	(13)	Light fartlek
Saturday	(14)	Test effort (date pace), steady fartlek, cutdowns

Table 7-6. Fourteen-day training pattern

Sprints consist of a small number of fast, short intervals. They are followed by a moderate to heavy amount of fartlek. The workout is concluded with increasingly fast, short intervals, or *cutdowns*. These cutdowns are usually 100s run at a pace that gradually quickens, such as 4x100m, one each in 16, 15, 14, and 13 seconds.

The *overdistance* or *underdistance* in the schedule for the first Saturday refers to a test effort at either a longer or shorter distance than the usual racing distance. For example, 1600m runners might run 800m, or they might run 3000 or 5000m. The workout for the second Thursday consists of a small number of short, quick sprints, followed by a moderate, but not heavy, fartlek workout. The final day is a test effort conducted at the date pace.

The 21-day pattern combines two 10-day patterns, with a day of rest tossed in at a convenient spot. Most of our training before the meets begin is just this type of pattern. The schedule progresses as shown in Table 7-7.

Rhythm is simply the opposite of lack of rhythm; it is not a pace. *Tempo* is similar to rhythm, but we use it as an action—an exercise in which the hands are held about six inches apart and swung quickly back and forth across the chest as a break in the monotony of running, a breather or a wake-up exercise.

Speed is the same thing as the short sprints that are done as speed work. We might do 4 x 50m fast sprints, or one or two 150s with the middle 50m extremely fast. Fewer intervals of this type should be used because the risk of injury is high.

Twenty-One-Day Training Pattern

Day		*Training Level*
Sunday	(1)	Steady fartlek: 6 to 15 miles (10-25 km.)
Monday	(2)	Varied fartlek (light)
Tuesday	(3)	Goal pace, date pace, light fartlek, cutdowns
Wednesday	(4)	Steady fartlek (light)
Thursday	(5)	Rhythm, light fartlek, cutdowns
Friday	(6)	Light fartlek
Saturday	(7)	Overdistance trial, steady fartlek, cutdowns
Sunday	(8)	Steady fartlek: 6 to 15 miles (10-25 km.)
Monday	(9)	Varied fartlek (light)
Tuesday	(10)	Heavy intervals, light fartlek, cutdowns
Wednesday	(11)	Steady fartlek (light)
Thursday	(12)	Quick intervals; light fartlek; cutdowns
Friday	(13)	Light fartlek
Saturday	(14)	Underdistance, date pace, light fartlek, cutdowns
Sunday	(15)	Steady fartlek: 6 to 15 miles (10-25 km.)
Monday	(16)	Varied fartlek (light)
Tuesday	(17)	Goal pace, steady fartlek, cutdowns
Wednesday	(18)	Steady fartlek
Thursday	(19)	Quick intervals; light fartlek; cutdowns; or simulated race
Friday	(20)	Light fartlek
Saturday	(21)	Date pace trial, steady fartlek, cutdowns

Table 7-7. Twenty-one-day training pattern

Trials and What They Mean

We use test efforts or time trials to assess the runners' progress at different points throughout the year. However, our trials are not all-out efforts. Our trials are similar to the system of trials used by Arthur Lydiard, 3/4-effort trials in which the runner tries to achieve a predetermined time (the date pace) by running an evenly paced race.

For example, if a female athlete ran 4:56 for 1600m in her trial three weeks ago, her present goal (date pace) would probably be 4:52 (73 pace). Actually, to avoid trying to push her along too fast, we average several times to get her new goal. We add twice her previous trial time to her new tentative goal (4:52) and divide by three, yielding a more accurate goal for her new pace (4:54).

She runs her trial as closely as possible to an even pace (73.5, 2:27, 3:50.5), following the suggested limits of variance in Table 7-2. Her run is a controlled effort in which she knows she could have run faster and in which she kicks or runs under her date pace only in the last quarter or less of her racing distance. The race thus shows how far she has progressed toward her goal, while giving her practice in the most efficient way of running her race: even pace.

Photo 7-7. Arne Kvalheim (3:38.5m and 3:58.5 mile) and Dave Wilborn (3:39.9 and 3:56.2 mile)

Setting Goals

Each individual should have a goal, and for a good runner, the goal should be high. If a young man was a 4:28 high school miler, we sit down with him and ask, "How fast do you want to run next year?" Too many freshmen say, "Four minutes." That is a good goal, but we want to know what to aim for during the immediately coming year. After all, 4:28 is only four times 67 seconds.

Assume that 4:16 is a reasonable goal for this 18- or 19-year-old freshman. Also assume that if he is capable of better than 4:16, he will be helped as far as his ability will carry him; and if he falters somewhere in his progress toward 4:16, his schedule will be adjusted to the slower time of 4:20 or 4:24 or possibly 4:28, which may be as fast as he will ever run.

Each runner should have a goal. It should be a challenging goal, but it should be realistic. We want our runners to make steady progress year after year, rather than progress rapidly one year, only to stagnate or regress during the next several years. Now that you have the rudiments of our distance training system, the next several chapters will get down to the specific training for the individual middle distance and distance races.

Training Methods

The basic training methods were discussed in Chapters 3 through 6. The Oregon version of interval training includes ideas from Franz Stampfl, Billy Hayes, Woldemar Gerschler, and Mihaly Igloi, to name a few. We try to fit the workout to the individual. Some athletes can handle more work than others. Some show more improvement on intervals, and others on fartlek. The two are combined with a little speed work until we learn what kind of fertilizer makes our flowers grow best.

Interval Training

For interval training, one to two-and-a-half times the racing distance, preceded by a warm-up and followed by some fartlek or speed work, is a heavy workout. Experience shows that one quarter of the racing distance is the ideal distance for practicing intervals for shorter races. Distances shorter and longer than the quarter distance are used, and the intensity is increased by reducing the rest or recovery intervals.

A male runner working toward a 4:40 1600m would run 4-12 x 400m in 70 seconds each, while a female trying to run 5:40 would run 4-12 x 400m in 85 seconds each. For variety, they might run some 200s at a slightly faster pace or some 600s at a slightly slower pace. The total distance covered during a workout would be one to three times the racing distance, or one to three miles (1600 to 5,000m) total (we prefer not to go over three miles of intervals). Their full rest would be an equal interval. If they want the workout to be a bit more intense, they shorten the rest interval to 200m or even 100m after running each fast 400.

Experience suggests that you gain nothing by training ahead of pace (such as a 4:40 1600 runner training at a 65- or 60-second pace for 400m). The runner will reach higher goals by getting in a greater volume of work than by trying to carry too fast a pace and not completing the workout. How many freshmen males have said, "But I can run faster than 75s (or 70s). I can run 10x400m in 64 seconds."

The answer should be a question: "But can you run a mile in 4:16?" The courage of the young athlete who wants to try is admirable, but after he tries and finds himself wanting, we question his judgment if he will not turn himself over to his coach.

There are five variables involved in interval training:

- Duration of the effort (the length or time run)
- Intensity of the effort (speed of the run)
- Number of repetitions
- Duration of the recovery (length of the rest intervals)
- Nature of the recovery interval (jogging, walking, or complete rest)

Repetition Running

Repetition running is a useful variant of interval training. While interval training technically includes only short runs (not over 600m) with only partial recovery between each run, repetition running involves longer intervals run at a slower pace, usually with long or complete rest between each run, allowing complete or near-complete recovery. Repetition running is done less often than interval training, but it is still very useful to the overall training pattern.

Photo 7-8. Roscoe Divine (3:56.3 mile)

Fartlek

Gosta Holmer of Sweden is generally recognized as the man who introduced his *fartlek*, or "speed play," training to running. We are indebted to him for the ideas of "Holmer-type" fartlek. How does an athlete train with Holmer fartlek? All the elements of a race are interspersed with periods of rest or partial recuperation. The length of the training session depends upon the amount of time available and the energy of the runner.

Assume that a period of 30 minutes, 45 minutes, an hour, or even longer will be used. Begin by having the runner jog slowly at a pace of seven to eight minutes per mile for two or three miles. This 15 or 20 minutes is for warming up, to bring the cardiovascular and respiratory systems into a condition of readiness for hard work. Then, have the runner pick up to what feels like race pace and carry it for 400m, 600m, 800m, or however far until a sense of fatigue is felt. Then, without letting him rest, have him sprint for 50 to 150m until it begins to "hurt." This work is followed by a very slow jog or a walk to recover. Next comes a series of short sprints of perhaps 50m, alternating sprinting and walking that distance until it is quite an effort, then recovering with another jog or walk.

Now have him imagine that it is a race. The athlete will stride at racing pace up to the shoulder of an imaginary opponent, pass with a quick burst, then settle into racing pace for 200 to 400m, followed by a recuperative jog or walk. Have another imaginary race, this time with his opponent on his shoulder. The athlete should accelerate enough to hold off a challenge or series of challenges, and then finish with another walking or jogging rest. Anything that can happen or be imagined in a race can be practiced in Holmer's fartlek. Fartlek is a personal, not a group, "tool."

Where should a runner practice fartlek? Soft surfaces are best. Holmer suggests the woods and fields. Runners might use the local golf courses. However, you should get written permission to use the courses from the president and board of each course every year. The ground rules for the runners are simple:

- Always stay on the outside of a fairway and "run with the grain" or direction of play.
- Do not cut across a fairway.
- Go behind the tees and around the greens.
- If a player is addressing a ball, stop until it is hit.

The second type of fartlek is "Lydiard fartlek." Lydiard also uses variations of the speed play. However, to differentiate between what we want our runners to do, we call the steady running "Lydiard fartlek," even though it is not really fartlek. We agree with Lydiard that no runner is ready to start training until he can run steadily without stopping for 45 minutes to one hour. How does a runner reach that stage? He should wear a watch and start at an 8- to

10-minute-per-mile pace (60 to 75 seconds per 200m), head down the street for 10 minutes, and then return, all at that same pace. Add time gradually until he can go out for 30 minutes and then return, a total of one hour. Then, he is ready to go on a schedule.

We continue to use Lydiard's slow, steady running fartlek and Holmer's speed play throughout the year, following the principles which each of them suggested. Holmer said, "You should finish the workout feeling exhilarated, not exhausted." Lydiard said, "You should train, not strain." Both men produced champions and world-record holders.

Steady-paced running is also very valuable. Runners are not ready to start training until they can run steadily without stopping for 45 to 60 minutes. How does a runner reach that stage? The runner wears a watch and starts at 8 to 10 minutes per mile (60 to 75 seconds per 200m), heads down the street for 10 minutes, then returns, all at that same pace. The runner adds time gradually until he can go out for 30 minutes and return, a total of one hour. Then, the runner is ready to begin a distance-training schedule.

Overdistance and Road Training

Overdistance training is essential to a balanced program of training for the distance races. This training consists simply of long runs, usually at a steady pace. As for what constitutes a "long" run, it depends to some extent on the athlete's normal racing distance. To most 800m runners, a 6- or 8-mile (10 to 12 km.) run is a long distance, but for a 5- or 10-km racer, it is not long at all. Generally speaking, a long run would be any distance over 10 kilometers. The longest distance any of our runners uses with any regularity is 14 to 16 miles (23 to 26 km), though some older marathon runners occasionally run as far as 30 miles (50 km) in a long training session.

We have a series of loops or training courses laid out around the town and surrounding countryside. These loops are almost entirely on roads, as a matter of simple necessity: The Willamette Valley is a bit damp for six or eight months a year. Our shortest loop is a three-mile (5 km) loop through Hendricks Park on a low ridge near campus, and our longest loop (16 miles/26 km) wanders around nearby Spencer's Butte, a small mountain south of town. A much longer course runs up the McKenzie River, but it is used only on rare occasions. Local training loops should include both easy and difficult terrain, depending upon what the training program needs.

Arthur Lydiard suggested a period of training that he termed "marathon training." Thus, his recommendation of a minimum of 100 miles a week is considered something of a sacred rite for any runner who wishes to be successful. In the first place, that training period was no more than 15 percent of his suggested annual cycle. In the second place, we don't consider that much mileage to be entirely necessary. The purpose of the heavy mileage was to lay an endurance basis for the later speed work and races. We are not entirely convinced that runs of more than 10 miles (16 km) at a time are necessary to successful running. We definitely do not believe that over 70 or 80 miles (110 to 130 km) a week are needed for success on the international level.

One cardinal principle should never be forgotten: Variety is the spice of life. Every runner needs variety, if for no other reason than to prevent mental staleness. The system must always recognize that individuals are different. Schedules are only guides. Just as a balanced diet makes for a healthier, happier person, so does a varied and balanced training schedule make for a more efficient, eager runner. A continuous, non-varied schedule usually makes an automatic, unimaginative runner.

Endnotes

1. Peter Janssen. (2001). *Lactate threshold training*. Champaign, IL: Human Kinetics, 16.
2. Jess Jarver. (1985). What is new in middle distance running? In Jess Jarver (Ed.), *Middle distances: Contemporary theory, technique and training* (2nd ed.). Los Altos, CA: Tafnews, 6-8.
3. William H. Freeman. (2001). *Peak when it counts: Periodization for the American coach* (4th ed.). Mountain View, CA: Tafnews.
4. Donald B. Slocum & William J. Bowerman. (1981). The biomechanics of running. In *Proceedings of the Second National Conference on the Medical Aspects of Sports*. Chicago: American Medical Association, 55-58.

Core Works

Ackland, Jon. (2003). *The complete guide to endurance training* (2nd ed.). London: A & C Black.

Benson, Tony, & Irv Ray. (2001). *Run with the best* (2nd ed.). Mountain View, CA: Tafnews.

Daniels, Jack. (2004). *Daniels' running formula* (2nd ed.). Champaign, IL: Human Kinetics.

Dellinger, Bill, & Bill Freeman. (1984). *The competitive runner's training book*. New York: Collier.

Doherty, Ken. (2007). *Track & field omnibook* (5th ed.). Ed. John N. Kernan. Mountain View, CA: Tafnews.

Gibbons, Tim. (2000). Common characteristics of successful endurance programs. Part I: Factors of success. *Track and Field Coaches Review, 73*(2), 15-17; Part II: Application to U.S. distance running, 73(3), 24-27.

Greene, Laurence S., & Russell R. Pate. (2004). *Training for young distance runners* (2nd ed.). Champaign, IL: Human Kinetics.

Jarver, Jess. (Ed.). (2002). *Middle and long distances: Contemporary theory, technique and training*. Mountain View, CA: Tafnews.

Lyden, Robert M. (2003). *Distance running*. Ann Arbor, MI: The Running Book.

Lydiard, Arthur, & Garth Gilmour. (1999). *Distance training for young athletes*. Aachen, Germany: Meyer & Meyer Sport.

Martin, David E., & Peter Coe. (1997). *Better training for distance runners* (2nd ed.). Champaign, IL: Human Kinetics.

Noakes, Tim. (2003). *Lore of running* (4th ed.). Champaign, IL: Human Kinetics.

Squires, Bill, & Bruce Lehane. (2006). *Speed with endurance*. Boston: Authors.

Vigil, Joe I. (1994). *Road to the top*. Place: Morning Star Communications.

Recommended Readings

Alonso, Juan Manuel. (2004). Methods to increase the delivery of oxygen. *New Studies in Athletics*, *19*(1), 33-43.

Anderson, Owen. (2000). Get your training in order: How sequencing determines your overall fitness. *Peak Performance, no. 127*, 1-5.

Anderson, Owen. (1999). Millennium review: As we reach year 2YK, here's a critical survey of the latest thinking about the ins and outs of training. *Peak Performance, no. 126*, 1-4.

Anderson, Tim. (1996). Biomechanics and running economy. *Sports Medicine*, *22*(2), 76-89.

Aragon, Angelo. (Summer 2002). Distance runners–Go with the flow! *Track Coach*, *160*, 5114-5118.

Arrese, Alejandro Legaz, Diego Munguía Izquierdo & Diego Moliner Urdiales. (2005). A review of the maximal oxygen uptake values necessary for different running performance levels. *New Studies in Athletics*, *20*(3), 7-20.

Bailey, Stephen P., & Russell R. Pate. (1991). Feasibility of improving running economy. *Sports Medicine*, *12*(4), 228-236.

Baquet, Georges, Emmanuel Van Praagh & Serge Berthoin. (2003). Endurance training and aerobic fitness in young people. *Sports Medicine*, *33*(15), 1127-1143.

Beck, Kevin. (1999, December). A tempo run by any other name. *Running Times*, pp. 6-7.

Berg, Kris. (2003). Endurance training and performance in runners: Research limitations and unanswered questions. *Sports Medicine*, *33*(1), 59-73.

Billat, Véronique L., Pascal Sirvent, Guillaume Py, Jean-Pierre Koralsztein & Jacques Mercier. (2003). The concept of maximal lactate steady state: A bridge between biochemistry, physiology and sport science. *Sports Medicine*, *33*(6), 407-426.

Billat, L. Véronique. (2001). Interval training for performance: A scientific and empirical practice. Special recommendations for middle- and long-distance running. Part I: Aerobic interval training. *Sports Medicine*, *31*(1), 13-31; Part II: Anaerobic interval training. *31*(2), 75-90.

Billat, L. Véronique. (1996). Use of blood lactate measurements for prediction of exercise performance and for control of training. *Sports Medicine*, *22*(3), 157-175.

Bompa, Tudor O. (1989). Physiological intensity values employed to plan endurance training. *Track Technique*, *108*, 3435-3442.

Bosquet, Lauren, Luc Léger & Patrick Legros. (2002). Methods to determine aerobic endurance. *Sports Medicine*, *32*(11), 675-700.

Brandon, L. Jerome. (1995). Physiological factors associated with middle distance running performance. *Sports Medicine*, *19*(4), 268-277.

Brill, Patricia A., & Caroline A. Macera. (1995). The influence of running patterns on running injuries. *Sports Medicine*, *20*(6), 365-368.

Burrows, Melonie, & Steve Bird. (2000). The physiology of the highly trained female endurance runner. *Sports Medicine*, *30*(4), 281-300.

Cairns, Simeon P. (2006). Lactic acid and exercise performance: Culprit or friend? *Sports Medicine*, *36*(4), 279-291.

Casa, Douglas J. (Spring 2004). Proper hydration for distance running– Identifying individual fluid needs. *Track Coach*, *167*, 5321-5328.

Cheuvront, Samuel N., Robert Carter III, Keith C. DeRuisseau & Robert J. Moffatt. (2005). Running performance differences between men and women: An update. *Sports Medicine*, *35*(12), 1017-1024.

Christensen, Scott. (1996). Distance running training theory. *Track Coach*, *136*, 4340-4347.

Christensen, Scott. (Spring 2001). A psychological application for distance runners. *Track Coach*, *155*, 4955-4959.

Christensen, Scott. (Summer 2000). Strength training for endurance runners. *Track Coach*, *152*, 4841-4845.

De Oliveira, Luiz. (1988). Middle distance training. *Track Technique*, *104*, 3319-3321, 3333.

Dionisi, Enrico. (1991). The secrets behind Morocco's running achievements [abstract]. *New Studies in Athletics*, *6*(4), 80-82.

Driscoll, Dennis G. (Summer 2004). Barefoot running: A natural step for the endurance athlete. *Track Coach*, *168*, 5373-5377.

Duffield, Bob, & Brian Dawson. (2003). Energy system contribution in track training. *New Studies in Athletics*, *18*(4), 47-56.

Ebbets, Russ. (Winter 2004). 11 keys to a successful distance running program. *Track Coach*, *166*, 5296-5298, 5304.

Fallowfield, Joanne L. (Ed.). (1999). *Improving sports performance in middle and long distance running: A scientific approach to race preparation*. New York: John Wiley.

Foster, Carl. (1998). Monitoring training in athletes with reference to overtraining syndrome. *Medicine & Science in Sports & Exercise*, *30*(7), 1164-1168.

Foster, Carl, Erin Daines, Lisa Hector, Ann C. Snyder & Ralph Welsh. (1996, June). Athletic performance in relation to training load. *Wisconsin Medical Journal*, 370-374.

Foster, Carl, Jessica A. Florhaug, Jodi Franklin, Lori Gottschall, Lauri A. Hrovatin, Suzanne Parker, Pamela Doleshal & Christopher Dodge. (2001). A new approach to monitoring exercise training. *Journal of Strength and Conditioning Research*, *15*, 109-115.

Foster, Carl, Lisa L. Hector, Ralph Welsh, Mathew Schrager, Megan A. Green & Ann C. Snyder. (1995). Effects of specific versus cross-training on running performance. *European Journal of Applied Physiology and Occupational Physiology*, *70*, 367-372.

Foster, Carl, Matthew Schrager, Ann C. Snyder, & Nancy N. Thompson. (1994). Pacing strategy and athletic performance. *Sports Medicine*, *17*(2), 77-85.

Fowler, Robert. (1998). A critical analysis of performance trends in distance running. *Modern Athlete and Coach*, *36*(4), 3-7.

Frederickson, Michael. (1996). Common injuries in runners: Diagnosis, rehabilitation and prevention. *Sports Medicine*, *21*(1), 49-72.

Fredericson, Michael, & Tammara Moore. (2005). Core stabilisation training for middle- and long-distance runners. *New Studies in Athletics*, *20*(1), 25-37.

Freeman, William H. (1985). Concerns in training women distance runners. *Track and Field Quarterly Review*, *85*(3), 29-36.

Freeman, William H. (1975). Distance training methods, past and present. *Track and Field Quarterly Review, 75*(4), 4-11.

Freeman, William H. (2001). Periodized training for [distance] runners. In *Peak When It Counts: Periodization for American track and field* (4th ed., pp. 86-105). Mountain View, CA: Tafnews.

Garcia-Manso, Juan M., Juan M. Martin-González, Enrique Arriaza & Lucia Quintero. (2006). Middle- and long-distances races viewed from the perspective of complexity: Macroscopic analysis based on behaviour as a power law. *New Studies in Athletics, 21*(1), 17-25.

Galloway, Jeff. (2000, June). How low [mileage] can you go? *Runner's World*, 44.

Garcin, M., A. Fleury, N. Ansart, L. Mille-Hamard & V. Billat. (2006). Training content and potential impact on performance: A comparison of young male and female endurance-trained runners. *Research Quarterly for Exercise and Sport*, 77(3), 351-361.

Gerweck, Jim. (2004, July/August). Hot to trot: Principles and practices for running in the heat. *Running Times*, p. 49.

Gilman, Muriel B. (1996). The use of heart rate to monitor the intensity of endurance training. *Sports Medicine, 21*(2), 73-79.

Gonschinska, Idrill. (1996). The speed and strength training of middle-distance runners from a functional point of view [abstract]. *New Studies in Athletics, 11*(4), 98-102.

Green, Howard J. (2000). Altitude acclimatization, training and performance. *Journal of Science and Medicine in Sport, 3*(3), 299-312.

Grogan, Thomas J., Bradley R. A. Wilson & Jeffrey D. Camm. (1991). The relationship between age and optimal performance of elite athletes in endurance events. *Research Quarterly for Exercise and Sport 62*, 333-339.

Hanon, Christine, J.M. Levêque, L. Vivier & C. Thomas. (2007). Oxygen uptake in the 1500 metres. *New Studies in Athletics, 22*(1), 15-22.

Hawley, John A., & Will G. Hopkins. (1995). Aerobic glycolytic and aerobic lipolytic power systems: A new paradigm with implications for endurance and ultraendurance events. *Sports Medicine, 19*(4), 240-250.

Hirsch, Lothar, & Werner Klein. (Summer 2003). Evaluation of an altitude training camp [abstract]. *Track Coach, 164*, 5252.

Hogg, John M., & Marisa A. Hayden. (1997). Pain perceptions among competitive runners. *New Studies in Athletics, 12*(2-3), 95-99.

Horwill, Frank J. (Fall 1998). Beyond our reach forever? *Track Coach, 145*, 4617-4618, 4639.

Houmard, J. A., B.K. Scott, C.L. Justice & J.C. Chenier. (1994). The effects of taper on performance in distance runners. *Medicine & Science in Sports & Exercise, 26*, 624-631.

Hreljac, Alan. (2004). Impact and overuse injuries in runner. *Medicine & Science in Sports & Exercise, 36*(5), 845-849

Hsieh, Margaret. (2004). Recommendations for treatment of hyponatraemia at endurance events. *Sports Medicine, 34*(4), 231-238.

Johnson, Nathan A., Stephen R. Stannard & Martin W. Thompson. (2004). Muscle triglyceride and glycogen in endurance exercise: Implications for performance. *Sports Medicine, 34*(3), 151-164.

Jones, Andrew M., & Helen Carter. (2000). The effects of endurance training on parameters of aerobic endurance. *Sports Medicine, 29*(6), 373-386.

Jung, Alan P. (2003). The impact of resistance training on distance running. *Sports Medicine, 33*(7), 539-552.

Karp, Jason R. (Summer 2006). Carbohydrates and the distance runner: A scientific perspective. *Track Coach, 176*, 5622-5627.

Karp, Jason R. (Winter 2002). Heart rate training for improved running performance. *Track Coach, 158*, 5035-5039.

Karp, Jason R. (Spring 2006). "I can't catch my breath": Lungs and distance running performance. *Track Coach, 175*, 5577-5579.

Karp, Jason R., & Lisa C. Kelley. (Summer 2002). Running at altitude. *Track Coach, 160*, 5097-5100.

Kubukeli, Zuko N., Timothy D. Noakes & Steven C. Dennis. (2002). Training techniques to improve endurance exercise performance. *Sports Medicine, 32*(8), 489-509.

Kuipers, Harm. (1996). How much is too much? Performance aspects of overtraining. *Research Quarterly for Exercise and Sport 67*(3, suppl.), 65-69.

Ladd, Lowell. (Fall 2002). Cross training for distance runners. *Track Coach, 161*, 5151-5152.

Landa, Luis Miguel. (Fall 1996). The Spanish distance running training system [abstract]. *Track Coach, 137*, 4383.

Lange, Günter. (1999). Principles of female distance training in Asia–A report from experience. *New Studies in Athletics, 14*(1), 57-65.

La Torre, Antonio, Franco Impellizzeri, Antonio Dotti & Enrico Arcelli. (2005). Do Caucasian athletes need to resign themselves to African domination in middle- and long-distance running? *New Studies in Athletics, 20*(4), 39-49.

Lehmann, M., Carl Foster & J. Keul. (1993). Overtraining in endurance athletes: A brief review. *Medicine & Science in Sports & Exercise, 25*, 854-862.

Lowes, David. (Spring 2005). Is some of your endurance training a waste of time? [abstract]. *Track Coach, 171*, 5477.

Lyden, Robert M. (1993). The importance of strength training for middle distance and distance runners. *Track and Field Quarterly Review, 93*(2), 35-59.

Lyden, Robert M. (1994). The sharpening period. *Track and Field Quarterly Review, 94*(2), 39-60.

Martin, David. (1994). The challenge of using altitude to improve performance. *New Studies in Athletics, 9*(2), 51-57.

Martin, D. T., & M. B. Andersen. (2000). Heart rate-perceived exertion relationship during training and taper. Journal of *Sports Medicine and Physical Fitness, 40*, 201-208.

Maulbecker, Klaus, & Jobst Kuger. (1990). Are long distance runners permanently overtrained? [abstract]. *Track Technique, 113*, 3619.

Midgley, Adrian W., Lars R. McNaughton & Michael. Wilkinson. (2006). Is there an optimal training intensity for enhancing the maximal oxygen uptake of distance runners?: Empirical research findings, current opinions, physiological rationale and practical recommendations. *Sports Medicine, 36*(2), 117-132.

Mikesell, K. A., & G. A. Dudley. (1984). Influence of intense endurance training on aerobic power of competitive distance runners. *Medicine & Science in Sports & Exercise, 16*, 371-375.

Mikkelsson, Lasse. (1996). How to train to become a top distance runner. *New Studies in Athletics, 11*(4), 37-44. Reprinted in Jarver, *Middle and Long Distances*, 11-15.

Molvar, John, & Mick Grant. (Fall 2006). Improving the high school competition structure for middle and long distance runners. *Track Coach, 177*, 5660-5662.

Montrucchio, Noel. (Spring 2000). A goal-setting strategy for endurance athletes. *Track Coach, 151*, 4809-4813. Reprinted in Jarver, *Middle and Long Distances*, 34-39.

Neuhof, Joachim. (1990). Structure and yearly training build-up in middle and long distance running. *New Studies in Athletics, 5*(2), 69-81.

Nurmekivi, Ants. (1997). A combination of different training means in the preparation of elite middle distance runners. In Jess Jarver (Ed.), *Middle Distances* (4th ed., pp. 65-69). Los Altos, CA: Tafnews.

Nurmekivi, Ants. (Spring 2002). Physiological and pedagogical factors in the planning of endurance training. *Track Coach, 159*, 5078-5081.

O'Connell, Colm. (1996). Environmental conditions, training systems and performance development of Kenyan runners. *New Studies in Athletics, 11*(4), 25-36.

Palmer, Andy. (1995, September). The fall of periodization and the rise of mediocrity. *Running Times*, pp. 37-38, 40, 42-43.

Pikó, Károly. (1999). Endurance performers and iron deficiency. *New Studies in Athletics, 14*(2), 43-46.

Popov, Ilia. (1994). Viewpoint: The pros and cons of altitude training. *New Studies in Athletics, 9*(2), 15-22.

Prendergast, Kevin. (1997). Energy systems and duration of effort. In Jess Jarver (Ed.), *Middle Distances* (4th ed., pp. 31-35). Los Altos, CA: Tafnews.

Reed, Jack. (Fall 2000). A visit with Jack Reed [high school coach]. *Track Coach, 153*, 4873-4877, 4888.

Reiss, Manfred. (1999). Guidance and advice in the use and methodology of altitude training for endurance sports. *New Studies in Athletics, 14*(3), 13-27.

Reiss, Manfred, Olaf Ernest & Dieter Gohlitz. (1993). Analysis of the 1989-1992 Olympic cycle with conclusions for coaching distance running and walking events. *New Studies in Athletics, 8*(4), 7-18.

Reiss, Manfred, & Peter Tschiene. (1997). Performance level and developmental reserves in endurance events. In Jess Jarver (Ed.), *Middle Distances* (4th ed., pp. 36-41). Los Altos, CA: Tafnews.

Saunders, Philo U., David B. Pyne, Richard D. Telford & John A. Hawley. (2004). Factors affecting running economy in trained distance runners. *Sports Medicine, 34*(7), 465-485.

Schiffer, Jürgen. (1996). Selected and annotated bibliography 40-41: Distance running. *New Studies in Athletics, 11*(4), 85-97; 12(1), 109-124.

Schiffer, Jürgen. (2003). Selected and annotated bibliography 62: Altitude training. *New Studies in Athletics, 18*(2), 59-107.

Sherman, Cheyne, & Steve Selig. (1997). Physiological testing—An important factor in the training of junior middle distance runners. In Jess Jarver (Ed.), *Middle Distances* (4th ed., pp. 50-52). Los Altos, CA: Tafnews.

Shiquin, P., & W. Wenshen. (1995). An analysis of Ma Junren's training methods. *Modern Athlete and Coach, 33*(3), 40-41.

Simmons, Scott. (Spring 2003). A case study in support of research of staggered altitude stimuli in distance runners. *Track Coach, 163*, 5205-5208.

Snell, Peter, & Robert Vaughan. (1990). Longitudinal physiological testing of elite female middle and long distance runners. *Track Technique, 111*, 3532-3534.

Snell, Peter, & Robert Vaughan. (1991). Physiological testing of high performance distance runners [abstract]. *Track Technique, 118*, 3777.

Suslov, Felix P. (1994). Basic principles of high altitude training. *New Studies in Athletics, 9*(2), 45-49.

Swan, Gerry. (1992). Developing young distance runners. *Track Technique, 121*, 3868-3872.

Tegen, Peter. (1994). Middle distance and distance training. *Track and Field Quarterly Review, 94*(2), 21-22.

Thibault, Guy. (2003). A graphical model for interval training. *New Studies in Athletics, 18*(3), 49-55.

Thibault, Guy, & François Pèronnet. (2006). It is not lactic acid's fault. *New Studies in Athletics, 21*(1), 9-15.

Tomlin, Dona L., & Howard A. Wenger. (2001). The relationship between aerobic fitness and recovery from high intensity intermittent exercise. *Sports Medicine, 31*(1), 1-11.

Tschiene, Peter. (1995). A necessary direction in training: The integration of biological adaptation in the training program. *Coaching and Sport Science Journal, 1*(3), 2-14.

Van Niekerk, Owen. (2002). Developing of young endurance athletes. *Modern Athlete and Coach, 40*(3), 27-30.

Vigil, Joe. (1996). Training parameters and philosophies in international competition. *American Swimming Coaches Association World Clinic Series, 27*, 315-332.

Walker, James. (1993). Nutritional status of men and women collegiate distance runners. *Track Technique, 124*, 3952-3956; Brown, C. Harmon. (1994). Letter to the editor. *Track Technique, 128*, 4100-4101.

Walsh, Christopher M. (1990). Bowerman Oregon distance tradition meets Bompa training theory: Periodized Bowerman mile and 5 km training. *Track and Field Quarterly Review, 90*(2), 12-20.

Walsh, Chris. (1983). *The Bowerman System*. Mountain View, CA: Tafnews.

Wilber, Randall L. (2001). Current trends in altitude training. *Sports Medicine, 31*(4), 249-265.

Williams, Keith. (1996). Biomechanical relationships in middle distance running. *Track Coach*, 134, 4269-4275.

Zarkadas, P. C., J. B. Carter & E. W. Banister. (1995). Modeling the effect of taper on performance, maximal oxygen uptake, and the aerobic threshold in endurance triathletes. *Adv Exp Med Biol, 393*, 179-186.

Zavorsky, Gerald S. (2000). Evidence and possible mechanism of altered maximum heart rate with endurance training and tapering. *Sports Medicine, 29*(1), 13-26

Zelentsova. Tatyana. (Fall 1998). Soviet middle distance training. *Track Coach, 145*, 4637-4638.

8

The Distance Runner's Sprint and the Golden Mile

Bowerman's Best

800m	1:45.0	Wade Bell	1967
1500m	3:38.1	Steve Prefontaine	1973
	3:38.5	Arne Kvalheim	1968
One mile	3:54.6	Steve Prefontaine	1973
	3:56.2	Dave Wilborn	1967
4 x 1 mile	16:08.9	Archie San Romani, Vic Reeve, Keith Forman, Dyrol Burleson	1962; World and U.S. Record

Record Setters

Dyrol Burleson	Three-time NCAA 1500 and mile champion; two-time U.S. champion; two-time Olympic 1500m finalist; five U.S. records at 1500m, one mile, and two mile
Jim Bailey	First sub-4:00 mile in the United States, 1956; NCAA mile champion, 1955; 2nd NCAA 1500, 1956; Australian Olympic Team
Bill Dellinger	NCAA mile champion, 1954; 2nd NCAA mile, 1955; U.S. record, 1500m (3:41.5).
Jim Grelle	NCAA mile champion; three-time All-American (worst finish was 2nd); 1960 Olympic 1500m finalist

Training for the 800-meter run, the 1500 meter, and the mile follow essentially the same pattern. The first object of the training is to get good, solid cardiovascular work that will permit the athlete to run up to six miles in a session. The longer training runs take away the athlete's basic speed, but it can return to its maximum level with three to six weeks of quality, or "sharpening," work. However, no athlete can build up the cardiovascular system in 6 weeks.

The training program should combine the speed-developing training activities and the conditioning training from the fall of the year to the end of the racing season. Although this approach is contrary to some training theories, experience has proved it to be as successful as any other system. Now, it is supported by more recent training theory. It has a further advantage, largely psychological, but still important: The athletes get more pleasure out of their training if the quality and the quantity training are combined, rather than used separately at different times in the year.

The training cycle for 800 and 1500 runners should begin in the fall and continue throughout the year for the best results. After school begins, the athletes will participate in the cross country training described in Chapter 9. The fall training concentrates on cardiovascular development. At the end of the cross country season, in late November, the athletes begin training patterns aimed at their track racing distance.

As in other events, the "hard-easy" principle is followed in planning the athletes' training programs. This area can be dangerous, if the coach attempts to overwork the athlete. The runner must not be sent beyond his personal tolerance level in training. The basic cycle used is one day of hard or heavy training, followed by a day of light or easy training. However, this pattern is not universal. Some athletes need two light days after each heavy day of training. An example of this was Kenny Moore, who developed into an Olympic marathoner after graduating from college. Many athletes are not really physically mature until they have reached their early 20s, so the coach should be careful of the workload assigned to young athletes.

Other athletes are extremely strong and can go two hard days for every easy day. Examples in this case are Dyrol Burleson, who was a three-time NCAA mile champion and ran on two Olympic Teams, and Steve Prefontaine, who set an American record in the five kilometers as a college sophomore and was a three-time NCAA cross country champion and four-time NCAA three-mile/5000m champion. These athletes might even be able to progress on a program of three hard days for each easy day, but the coach must be very cautious in following up such possibilities. Each individual has his own tolerance level for work. If he is pushed beyond that level, his performance will go into a nosedive. Once he is pushed too far, it is very difficult to reverse the process and get the athlete's performances moving in the right direction.

The training patterns for the longer distances are the same as for the shorter distances, but the mileage covered is greater. In other words, where a miler or half-miler might run 6 to 10 miles (10 to 16 km) for his long run of the week on Sunday, the 5000m racer may go as many as 15 miles (25 km) or more. Interval work is essentially proportionate to the racing distance, varying from one-and-a-half to three times the racing distance. Where an 800 runner will cover no more than 2000 to 2400m in a long interval session, the 5000 racer may cover from 3 to 6 miles (5 to 10 km) of intervals. Even so, most athletes at Oregon would rarely cover more than 70 or so miles in the heavier load training weeks of the winter.

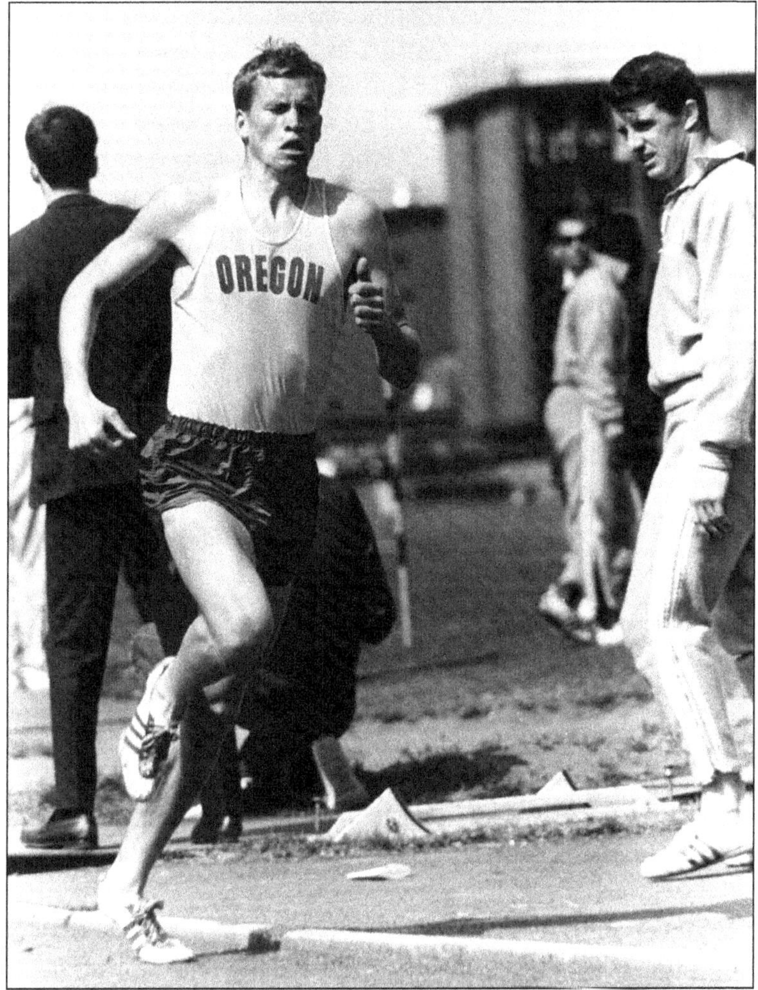

Photo 8-1. Wade Bell, 1967 NCAA champion, world ranking #1 in 1:45.0; 3:59.8 mile

Actually, from the 5000m run to the marathon the training is very similar. A 5000m runner can train for a marathon by working over some longer distance intervals (but not run any more miles of intervals), but about the only real change in his training would be the addition of a long run of 20 to 30 miles (30 to 45 km) once a month for his Sunday run. Five and ten km runners have discovered that super-high mileage is not as necessary to successful marathoning as theorists would suggest. Also, running the marathon does not mean that the athlete cannot compete in the track races successfully. Experience has proven that it can be done with success.

The tactics of the longer distance runs are essentially the same, regardless of the racing distance: find out what the opponent can do, then determine how he can be beaten.

The schedules can be adapted by the athlete for training for almost any racing distance between the 1500-meter run and the marathon, for the principles and patterns are the same. Only the paces and quantities differ.

Some athletes prefer interval training, while others prefer the long runs. Some do not thrive on the "who can get in the most miles" philosophy. Men have run a 4:00 mile on less than 30 miles a week in training. Those "quick types" usually perform best on 50 to 80 miles per week in training. Other athletes may be the slower "warriors," who love the long-distance training and destroy an opponent with work, trying to set a devastating pace to get out of the range of the sprinter. Coaches must know their runners, just as the athletes must know themselves. In training, many roads lead from A to B, and the shortest is not always the quickest or the best, any more than is the longest.

In using the following training schedules, which have been used by successful athletes, remember that they should be viewed as a starting point, an example of how the theories of training have been applied, rather than seen as *the* way to train. The training schedule sheets were interpreted in Chapter 7. The only different activities are the drills.

The *sprint-float-sprint* goes for 150m, the runner sprinting for the first 50m, then relaxing and "floating" for the middle 50m before sprinting again. The runner is learning to take a breather without slowing down during a race.

The *150, middle one-step acceleration* is a paced 150m run, with an attempt to sharply increase the pace within a single step. It helps develop the ability to "change gears" quickly to react to a racing situation, whether it is a chance to move quickly or a response to another runner's move.

The *40-30 drill* and the *70-90 drill* are used to practice varied-pace racing. The 40-30 drill divides the run into 200m segments. The athlete runs continuously for a set number of laps, alternating between 40-second and 30-second 200s. The 70-90 drill alternates 400s of 70 and 90 seconds. The 1-1 option calls for an even mix of the paces, while 2-1 and 3-1 mean to run either two or three of the fast 400s for each slow 400m. This type of mixed-pace training session can also be used to simulate racing at the goal pace, mixing goal pace running with slower paces.

Cutdowns are a series of intervals run at increasing speeds. For instance, 4 x 100m cutdowns might mean running the first 100 in 18 seconds, the next one in 17 seconds, the third one in 16 seconds, and the last one in 15 seconds. A set of 6 x 300m cutdowns might be run in pairs, with the first two 300s in 54 seconds, the next two in 51 seconds, and the last two in 48 seconds. It helps to accustom the runner to finishing strongly. It is also a refreshing way to finish a training session.

Simulated race drills are used to practice race situations. The *first 200, last 200 drill* practices running the first 200m of the race, followed by the finishing 200m. Racers in the 800 should practice starting in different lanes for the run around the first turn.

The *2 1/2, 1 1/2 drill* breaks the mile or 1500/1600m race into two parts. The athlete runs the first two-and-a-half laps (1000m) of the race at pace, strides 400m, then runs the last one-and-a-half laps (600m) at pace. This drill simulates the race, and it is long enough to require specific endurance for the event.

The *10-mile, 3/4 drill* (16 km, 1200m) is a 10-mile run on the roads. At some point during the run, the coach appears and has the athlete run a timed 3/4-mile (1200m) at close to mile pace. This drill teaches the runner to combat a long, hard surge by an opponent or else to be able to drop an opponent by forcing the pace for a very long surge. Runners such as Steve Prefontaine sometimes ran the 1200m in 3:05 or faster. Note that after the 1200m, the athlete slows down only to the earlier running pace, *not* to a slow jog. That aspect is what makes the drill very difficult. It is primarily a drill for the race of 5000 meters or longer distances.

An athlete may run two to four miles (three to six km) at a moderate (but not taxing) pace, such as 80 seconds per 400m for a male college runner. This drill is good to simulate trial heats for longer distance runners. For example, a 3000m runner who must run a qualifying race on Friday, followed by a final on Saturday, can use this as a Friday workout before Saturday meets. It is run at a pace fast enough to require more than just a light effort, but not a moderate effort. A variation is to run the drill on the day after a meet instead of the day before.

Racing Tactics

An athlete who wants to run the best possible time for a race is usually better off running as closely as possible to even pace for the entire distance. However, many racing situations call for tactics that consider not what will yield the fastest time, but what will give the greatest chance of victory against a particular opponent. A knowledge of tactics is vital.

To use tactics well, the runner must know two things. The first was inscribed at the entrance to the temple of the Delphic Oracle: "Know thyself." What are the athlete's personal strengths and weaknesses as a racer? Can he carry a solid pace for the entire racing distance? How far can he carry a final sprint? These aspects are learned in the test efforts, then put to practice in racing situations. The athletes must learn their capabilities and weaknesses well, both to know how they can use them to their advantage and to know how their opponents might use those weaknesses against them.

The second thing that athletes must know is their opponents. What are their strong and weak points? Those factors point the way to how they can be beaten. The comparison between the athlete and the opponent indicates which of the following tactical considerations might be of the greatest value.

If the athlete is clearly better than the opponent, then practice some facet of the race during the competition. This work on strengthening one particular

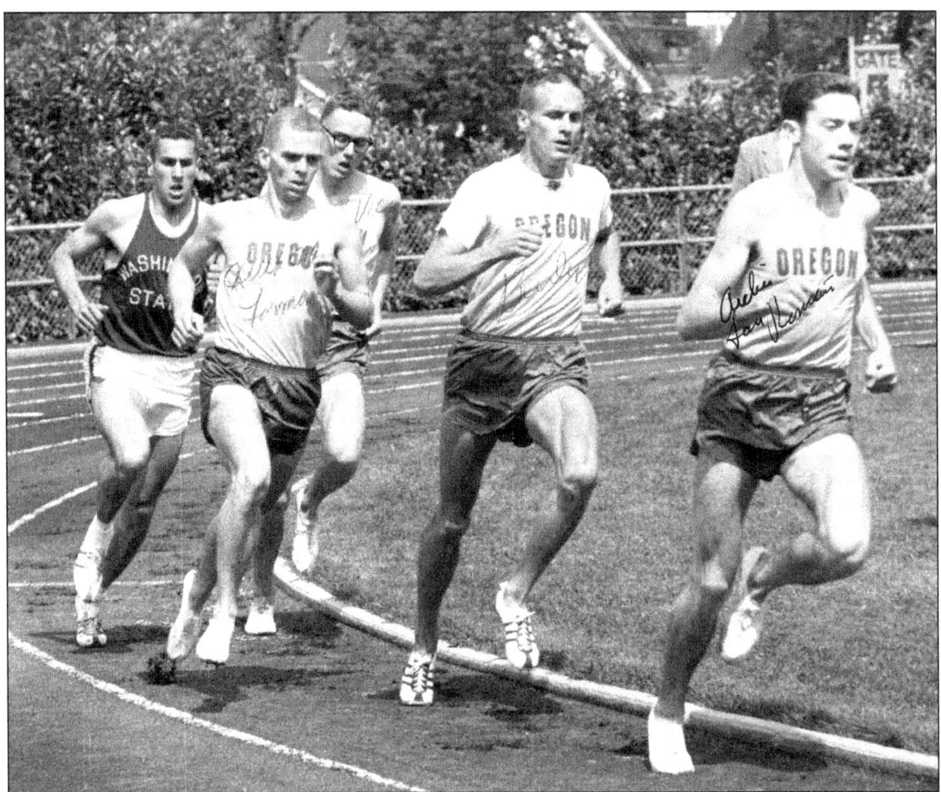

Photo 8-2. Members of the 4 x mile relay world-record team

phase of the race helps in an obvious way, but it also serves another purpose: it conceals the athlete's strengths. Athletes should no more show all of their racing weapons against a weak opponent than they should use a sledgehammer on an ant. Instead, concentrate on some section of the race, such as the first, middle, or last part.

This concealment of the athlete's weapons leads to another aspect of tactics: an athlete should not always run the same kind of race. He should have a plan for *every* race, and it should be a different one in some respect. If the athlete runs only one kind of a race, a good tactician will notice it, analyze it, and beat that runner. Being obvious is never a tactical virtue, unless it is a deliberate effort to mislead an opponent.

An athlete whose strong point is the last part of the race should work to make it his best weapon. The athlete should work to improve what he is endowed with, rather than accepting it as it is and working only on other areas of ability. This approach does not mean to work only on the strengths; the runner must also train to overcome the weaknesses. A person with only one weapon in his bag may meet someone else with the same weapon, only to find that the other racer's weapon is bigger. Again, an athlete should beware of tipping his hand. The athlete might in fact use his greatest weapon only once in a year, at the time of the most important race.

One tactic is varied-pace running. It is also a tactic of which the runner should beware. Some athletes can use it, but other runners are destroyed by it.

It is a very big weapon for the person who can use it. However, the athlete who knows that he cannot use it should beware of a contest with someone who can use it. He must let the other runner go, then reel them in like a fish, making sure not to let them get too far ahead. A runner should not at any time go when the opponent surges. Rather, as soon as the runner is close enough to the finish to hold it to the end, he should go into the sprint finish. An athlete who runs their opponent's race will have a very bad experience, because it is a devastating way to run a race.

Whenever an athlete is tempted to try to beat an opponent while letting the opponent use his favorite club in the contest, the athlete should remember one thing: wisdom and judgment are a great deal more important than determination. More pleasure is to be found in being a wise victor than a determined loser.

The runner must be cautious in the first part of the race, for it is very important. It is easily the most dangerous part of the race. Most athletes tend to start too fast, which puts them quickly into oxygen debt and makes the late stages of the race very difficult. Few athletes are strong enough to lead all the way. Pace judgment is extremely important in this case, for by running too fast in the first 1/8 to 1/4 of the racing distance the runner stands the greatest chance of looking like a fool. The runner with good pace judgment should be onto the correct pace by the end of the first 1/4 of the racing distance. A runner without good pace judgment need not worry, because he has little chance in top competition anyway. When tempted to overwhelm the opponents with a fast start, the runner must remember one vital fact: all of the rewards are at the finish line.

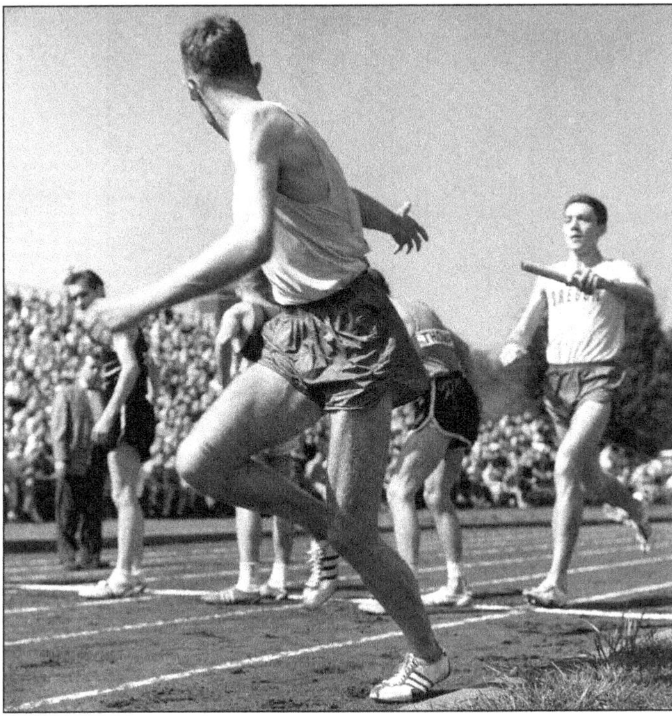

Photo 8-3. Archie San Romani (3:57.6 mile) hands off to Vic Reeve in the 4 x mile relay

Every runner, no matter how good, *must* know what is going on at the front of the race. If an athlete trots along in the rear of the pack, someone may break away and not be noticed until it is too late. A runner probably has some advantage in running in the rear for the first half of the racing distance, but he must progress to one of the first three places by the halfway point in the race to keep an eye on what is going on at the front. To stay in the first three places, an athlete must be careful not to get "boxed in," or blocked, as other runners move up in position. Each time a competitor moves up to go by, the athlete should "take one," moving out a lane or so and going with the new competitor to ensure a place at the front of the race. Moving out from the curb also helps prevent being boxed in and unable to move if an opponent tries to break away from the leaders.

In the last 300 meters of the race, a good competitor should attempt to get in front, *if* he can sprint that far. Once in front, the runner becomes the other runners' problem. The runner should use up to 90 percent of his effort to get in front. The runner should not use 100 percent because a bit of reserve is needed to prevent being passed in the last 50m of the race. A runner should not try to win from fifth place on the last straight of the track, a very foolish tactic. An athlete who prefers to race with that tactic should enter the 100-meter dash instead.

Sheet 8-1 is an updated training schedule form, followed by the original sheets for the 800m (Sheets 8-2 through 8-10) and 1500m/one mile (Sheets 8-11 through 8-19) training.

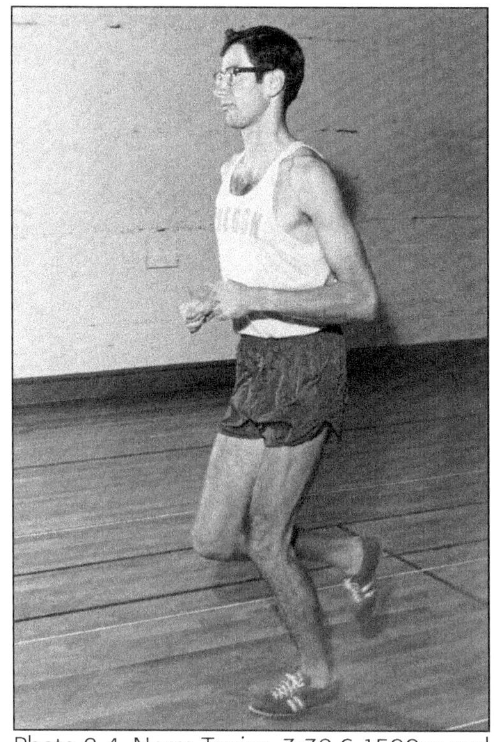

Photo 8-4. Norm Trerise, 3:39.6 1500m and Canadian Olympian

RUNNERS SCHEDULE NAME ______________________ DATE ______________

1. Warmup: Jog 1-3 mi., stretching
2. Fartlek A. Varied (1) 30 min. (2)
   B. Steady (1) 2-4 mi. (2) 4-6 mi.
   (3) 6-10 mi. (4)
3. Weights and jogging
4. High knee and power run
5. Intervals
   A. 100 (1) 18-16-14 (2) 17-15-13
   B. 150 (1) 25 (2)
   C. 200 (1) 35 (2)
   D. 300 (1) 52 (2) 48 (3) 45 (4)
   E. 400 (1) 70-73 (2)
   F. 600 (1) 1:45 (2)
   G. 800 (1) 70 pace (2)
   H. 1200 (1) 70 pace (2)
   J. 1600 (1) 72 pace (2) 68-70 (3) 64-67 (4)
   K.
   L.
6. Sets A. 600-400-300-200-100
   (1) 1:45-68-49-32-15 (2)
   B. 400-600-400-200 (1) 63 (2)
   C. 500-150-150 (1) 55 pace (2)
   D.
7. TEAM MEETING
8. Special A. Sauna B. Swim C.
9. Drills A. 150 sprint-float-sprint
   B. 150 middle 1-step acceleration
   C. 40-30 drill (1) 4 laps (2) 6 laps (3)
   D. 70-90 drill (1) 1-1 (2) 2-1 (3) 3-1 (4)
   E. Cut-downs (1) 100 (2) 150 (3) 200
   (4) 300 (5) 400 (6) 800 (7)
   F. Simulated race drills (1) 1st 200, last 200
   (2) 2-1/2, 1-1/2 (3) 15 km, 1200 drill
   (4)
   G. 2-4 mi. at (1) 80 (2)
10. A. Meet B. Trial C. Simulation D. Control test
   (1) 3/4 date pace (2) Over (3) Under
11. Hill intervals A. 100 B. 200 C.
12. With Coach A. B.
14. A. Wind sprints (1) Straight (2) Curve
   B. Hurdle (X) drill C. Spring and bound
   D.
15. Plyometrics A. Jumps B. Bounding C.
   (1) 1-leg (2) Both legs (3)
16. Finish work
17. Acrobatics or apparatus
18. 3/4 effort
19.
20. Work on second event
21. A. Videotape B. Film C. Pictures
   (1) Record performance (2) Study
30. Experimental

Date	Distance	3/4 pace	Date Pace	Goal Pace

M
T
W
T
F
S
S
M
T
W
T
F
S
S
M
T
W
T
F
S
S
M
T
W
T
F
S
S

Sheet 8-1. Metric distance runners training schedule sheet

800-Meter Training Schedules

880-Yard Run NAME DATE September/October

1. A. Jog 1 to 3 miles
   B. Weights & jog
2. Fartlek A. Varied (1) 30 min. (2) 45 min.
   B. Steady (1) 2-4 mi. (2) 4-6 mi. (3) 7-10 mi.
   (4)
3. Weights and jog
4. High knee and power run
5. Intervals
   A. 110 (1) 18-16-14 (2) 17-15-13
   B. 165 (1) 25 (2)
   C. 220 (1) 35 (2) 28
   D. 330 (1) 52 (2) 48 (3) 45 (4)
   E. 440 (1) 70-73 (2)
   F. 660 (1) 1:45 (2)
   G. 880 (1) 70 (2)
   H. 3/4 (1) 70 (2)
   I. Mile (1) 72 (2) 68-70 (3) 64-67 (4)
   J.
   K.
   L.
6. Sets A. 660-440-330-220-110
   (1) 1:45-68-49-32-15 (2)
   B. 440-660-440-220 (1) 63 (2)
   C. 550-165-165 (1) 55 pace (2)
   D. 440-330-220
7. Squad meeting
8. Special A. Sauna B. Swim C.
9. Drills A. Sprint-float-sprint (165)
   B. 1-step acceleration (165)
   C. 40-30 drill (1) 4 laps (2)
   D. 70-90 drill (1) 1-1 (2) 2-1
   (3) 3-1 (4)
   E. Cut-downs (1) 110 (2) 165 (3) 220
   (4) 330 (5) 440 (6) 880 (7)
   F. Simulate race drills (1) 1st 220-last 220
   (2) 2½-1½ (3) 10 miles-3/4 drill (4)
   G. 2-4 miles at (1) 80 (2) 75 (3)
10. A. Test B. Trial C. Compete
    (1) 3/4 date pace (2) Over (3) Under
11. Hill interval A. 110 B. 220 C.
12. With coach (A) Bill B. (B) Bill D. (C)
14. A. Wind sprint B. Hurdle drill
    C. Spring and bound D.
15. Finish work
16. Acrobatics or apparatus
17. 3/4 effort
18. Steeplechase A. Hurdle drill B. Water jump C.
19. Park A. Around B. Hill
20. Secondary event
21. A. Pictures B. Film
22. Golf course A. Around B. Short C. Long

Day	Workout
M	7 (organization-lockers-equipment)
T	3-2B
W	2x 2x 1A-5D-5C-2A(1)
T	3-2B
F	1A
S	10 a.m.:3 mile or 6 mile fall road run
S	
M	3
T	2x 2x 2x 3x 2x 4x 1A-18A-5G-5A-5F-5E-6D
W	Light and 3
T	19A (45 min.)-5A
F	Light
S	2A(2) (park)
S	
M	4x 10x 1A-5D-19A-5A(16-18)
T	3
W	8x 3x 1A-5C(2)-6A(1)-22A
T	16 (rope climbing)-3-2 (20 min.)
F	3x 4x 5A(1)-30 min. out-30 min. back-5A
S	6A(1) (grass)-easy jog
S	

Day	A.M.	Workout
M	A.M. Jog	6-10x 5C or D (110 rest-20 secs.)
T		16-3 (20 min. jog)
W	Jog	6x 3x 5D(2-3) (220 rest)-6A(1)-1A
T		16 (rope and parallel bars)
F	Jog	3x/5A(1)-30 out-30 back (7-10 min./mile)
S		1A
S		

Sheet 8-2. 800-meter training schedule sheet

880-Yard Run NAME DATE October/November

1. A. Jog 1 to 3 miles
   B. Weights & jog
2. Fartlek A. Varied (1) 30 min. (2) 60 min.
   B. Steady (1) 2-4 mi. (2) 4-6 mi. (3) 7-10 mi.
   (4)
3. Weights and jog
4. High knee and power run
5. Intervals
   A. 110 (1) 18-16-14 (2) 17-15-13
   B. 165 (1) 25 (2)
   C. 220 (1) 35 (2)
   D. 330 (1) 52 (2) 48 (3) 45 (4)
   E. 440 (1) 70-73 (2)
   F. 660 (1) 1:45 (2) 1:39
   G. 880 (1) 70 (2) 68
   H. 3/4 (1) 70 (2)
   I. Mile (1) 72 (2) 68-70 (3) 64-67 (4)
   J.
   K.
   L.
6. Sets A. 660-440-330-220-110
   (1) 1:45-68-49-32-15 (2) 1:42-66-46-30-14
   B. 440-660-440-220 (1) 63 (2) 28-30/220y.
   C. 550-165-165 (1) 55 pace (2) Date pace (880)
   D. 220-440-220 (1) 29 pace
7. Squad meeting
8. Special A. Sauna B. Swim C.
9. Drills A. Sprint-float-sprint (165)
   B. 1-step acceleration (165)
   C. 40-30 drill (1) 4 laps (2)
   D. 70-90 drill (1) 1-1 (2) 2-1
   (3) 3-1 (4)
   E. Cut-downs (1) 110 (2) 165 (3) 220
   (4) 330 (5) 440 (6) 880 (7)
   F. Simulate race drills (1) 1st 220-last 220
   (2) 2½-1½ (3) 10 miles-3/4 drill (4)
   G. 2-4 miles at (1) 80 (2) 75 (3)
10. A. Test B. Trial C. Compete
    (1) 3/4 date pace (2) Over (3) Under
11. Hill interval A. 110 B. 220 C.
12. With coach (A) Bill B. (B) Bill D. (C)
14. A. Wind sprint B. Hurdle drill
    C. Spring and bound D.
15. Finish work
16. Acrobatics or apparatus
17. 3/4 effort
18.
19.
20. Secondary event
21. A. Pictures B. Film

Day	Workout
M	4x 5H(1)-2-5A(1)
T 1A	3-8A
W	1A
T 1A	3x 6A(2)-2A(2)
F	1A-3
S	440-440-440-220-220 10A(68- 68- 68- 34-9/10)-2A(1)
S	
M 1A	2x 2x 1A-5G(2)-5F(2)-2A(2)
T	1A-3-8A
W 3-6x 5A(1)	440-440-440-220-220 Mile(80- 80- 80- 29-9/10-2A(1)
T	Jog and stretch
F 1A	9A(660 to 1320)- 2A-9A(330 to 660)
S	6A(2)-6D(1)-2A
S	
M 1A	4x 1A-5G(2)-1A
T	3-8A
W 3-6x 5A(1)	3x 1A-6D-6A(1)-2A(2)
T	9A(880 to 1320)-2A
F	1A-3
S	
S	220 6x 10A(880)(30-30-28-9/10)-2A-5A(1)
M	1A-2A-5A(1)
T 1A	4x 2x 6C(2)-5E-6A(1)-1A
W	3-8A
T 5A(1)	4x 1A-6B(2)-2A-5A(1)
F	3-8A
S	2-3x 1A-6A (60 sec. pace)-6A(1)-1A
S	

Sheet 8-3. 800-meter training schedule sheet

880-Yard Run NAME DATE November/December

1. A. Jog 1 to 3 miles
   B. Weights & jog
2. Fartlek A. Varied (1) 30 min. (2) 60 min.
   B. Steady (1) 2-4 mi. (2) 4-6 mi. (3) 7-10 mi.
   (4) 10 miles
3. Weights
4. High knee and power run
5. Intervals
   A. 110 (1) 18-16-14 (2) 17-15-13
   B. 165 (1) 25 (2) 7/8 effort
   C. 220 (1) 35 (2)
   D. 330 (1) 52 (2) 48 (3) 45 (4) 42
   E. 440 (1) 70-73 (2) 59 (3) 58
   F. 660 (1) 1:45 (2) 1:27
   G. 880 (1) 70 (2)
   H. 3/4 (1) 70 (2)
   I. Mile (1) 72 (2) 68-70 (3) 64-67 (4)
   J. 770 (1) 58 at 440
   K.
   L.
6. Sets A. 660-440-330-220-110
   (1) 1:45-68-49-32-15 (2)
   B. 440-660-440-220 (1) 63 (2)
   C. 550-165-165 (1) 55 pace (2)
   D.
7. Squad meeting
8. Special A. Sauna B. Swim C.
9. Drills A. Sprint-float-sprint (165)
   B. 1-step acceleration (165)
   C. 40-30 drill (1) 4 laps (2)
   D. 70-90 drill (1) 1-1 (2) 2-1
   (3) 3-1 (4)
   E. Cut-downs (1) 110 (2) 165 (3) 220
   (4) 330 (5) 440 (6) 880 (7)
   F. Simulate race drills (1) 1st 220-last 220
   (2) 2½-1½ (3) 10 miles-3/4 drill (4)
   G. 2-4 miles at (1) 80 (2) 75 (3)
10. A. Test B. Trial C. Compete
    (1) 3/4 date pace (2) Over (3) Under
11. Hill interval A. 110 B. 220 C.
12. With coach (A) Bill B. (B) Bill D. (C)
14. A. Wind sprint B. Hurdle drill
    C. Spring and bound D.
15. Finish work
16. Acrobatics or apparatus
17. 3/4 effort
18.
19.
20. Secondary event
21. A. Pictures B. Film

M 1A	1A-(2x)5F(2)-5E(2)-(8x)5D(1-2)-1A-(4x)5A
T	3-8A
W 5A	2A(2)(grass)
T	Light jog
F	10A(880 date pace)-2A(45min)-5A(1)
S	2B(3)(7-9 min. pace per mile)
S	

M 1A	1A-5J(1)-5E(3)-(2x)5D(3-4)-(3x)6A(1)-1A-5A(1)
T	3-8A
W	9A(660)-2A(45min)-(2x)5B(2)
T 1A	1A-3-8A
F	10A(Mile)(68-68-68-9/10 effort) 440-440-440-440
S	2B(4)(8-10min pace)
S	

M
T
W
T
F
S
S

M
T
W
T
F
S
S

Sheet 8-4. 800-meter training schedule sheet

880-Yard Run NAME DATE *January*

1. A. Jog 1 to 3 miles
   B. Weights & jog
2. Fartlek A. Varied (1) 30 min. (2) *60 min.*
   B. Steady (1) 2-4 mi. (2) 4-6 mi. (3) 7-10 mi.
   (4)
3. Weights *and jog*
4. High knee and power run
5. Intervals
   A. 110 (1) 18-16-14 (2) 17-15-13 *(3) 15*
   B. 165 (1) 25 (2) *22½ (3) 19½*
   C. 220 (1) 35 (2) *30*
   D. 330 (1) 52 (2) 48 (3) 45 (4)
   E. 440 (1) 70-73 (2) *59-62*
   F. 660 (1) 1:45 (2)
   G. 880 (1) 70 (2)
   H. 3/4 (1) 70 (2)
   I. Mile (1) 72 (2) 68-70 (3) 64-67 (4)
   J.
   K.
   L.
6. Sets A. 660-440-330-220-110
   (1) 1:45-68-49-32-15 (2)
   B. 440-660-440-220 (1) 63 (2)
   C. 550-165-165 (1) 55 pace (2)
   D.
7. Squad meeting
8. Special A. Sauna B. Swim C.
9. Drills A. Sprint-float-sprint (165)
   B. 1-step acceleration (165)
   C. 40-30 drill (1) 4 laps (2)
   D. 70-90 drill (1) 1-1 (2) 2-1
   (3) 3-1 (4)
   E. Cut-downs (1) 110 (2) 165 (3) 220
   (4) 330 (5) 440 (6) 880 (7)
   F. Simulate race drills (1) 1st 220-last 220
   (2) 2½-1½ (3) 10 miles-3/4 drill (4)
   G. 2-4 miles at (1) 80 (2) 75 (3)
10. A. Test B. Trial C. Compete
    (1) 3/4 date pace (2) Over (3) Under
11. Hill interval A. 110 B. 220 C.
12. With coach (A) Bill B. (B) Bill D. (C)
14. A. Wind sprint B. Hurdle drill
    C. Spring and bound D.
15. Finish work
16. Acrobatics or apparatus
17. 3/4 effort
18.
19.
20. Secondary event
21. A. Pictures B. Film

Day	Workout
M	*Recheck organization-1A or 3*
T	*2B-3-8A*
W	*5I or 5G (¾ effort)-2A-8A*
T	*3-8A*
F	*1A-8A*
S	*Reestablish date pace 5I or 5G (½ effort)-2A2-8A*
S	
M	*1A-4x 5C-3x 5D-2x 6A(1)-2A(1)-2x 5A(1)*
T	*Jog and stretch-8A*
W	*3-6B-2B-2x 5C(1)*
T	*1A-3-8A*
F	*1A-8x 5C(2)-4x 9A-2A-5C(1)*
S	*10A(1)*
S	
M *1A*	*1A-11x 5B(2)-2A(1)-2x 5C(1)*
T *Jog*	*2x 6A(1)-1A-6x 5B(3)-2x 5C(1)*
W	*1B-8A*
T *1A*	*5B(3)-2A or B-5x 5A(3)*
F *Jog*	*1B-8A*
S	*Mile (80-80-60-9/10 effort)-2A*
S	
M *Jog*	*4x 5E(2)-3x 5B(3)-2A-8A*
T *Jog*	*9A (660)-2A(1)-8A*
W *2x 5A(1)*	*1B*
T	*1A-6x 5B-2A-4x 5A(3)*
F *Jog*	*Check indoor gear-1A*
S	*Indoor 1,000 or 2B(1)*
S	

Sheet 8-5. 800-meter training schedule sheet

880-Yard Run NAME DATE February

1. A. Jog 1 to 3 miles
   B. Weights & jog
2. Fartlek A. Varied (1) 30 min. (2) 60 min.
   B. Steady (1) 2-4 mi. (2) 4-6 mi. (3) 7-10 mi.
   (4)
3. Weights and jog
4. High knee and power run
5. Intervals
   A. 110 (1) 18-16-14 (2) 17-15-13
   B. 165 (1) 25 (2)
   C. 220 (1) 35 (2) 28 (3) 25-26
   D. 330 (1) 52 (2) 48 (3) 45 (4)
   E. 440 (1) 70-73 (2) 60
   F. 660 (1) 1:45 (2)
   G. 880 (1) 70 (2)
   H. 3/4 (1) 70 (2)
   I. Mile (1) 72 (2) 68-70 (3) 64-67 (4)
   J.
   K.
   L.
6. Sets A. 660-440-330-220-110
   (1) 1:45-68-49-32-15 (2)
   B. 440-660-440-220 (1) 63 (2)
   C. 550-165-165 (1) 55 pace (2)
   D. 220-440-220
7. Squad meeting
8. Special A. Sauna B. Swim C.
9. Drills A. Sprint-float-sprint (165)
   B. 1-step acceleration (165)
   C. 40-30 drill (1) 4 laps (2)
   D. 70-90 drill (1) 1-1 (2) 2-1
   (3) 3-1 (4)
   E. Cut-downs (1) 110 (2) 165 (3) 220
   (4) 330 (5) 440 (6) 880 (7)
   F. Simulate race drills (1) 1st 220-last 220
   (2) 2½-1½ (3) 10 miles-3/4 drill (4)
   G. 2-4 miles at (1) 80 (2) 75 (3)
10. A. Test B. Trial C. Compete
    (1) 3/4 date pace (2) Over (3) Under
11. Hill interval A. 110 B. 220 C.
12. With coach (A) Bill B. (B) Bill D. (C)
14. A. Wind sprint B. Hurdle drill
    C. Spring and bound D.
15. Finish work
16. Acrobatics or apparatus
17. 3/4 effort
18.
19.
20. Secondary event
21. A. Pictures B. Film

Day	Workout
M Jog	4x 2x 1A-5E(2)-5C(2)-6A(1)
T 2x 5A(1)	1A-4-3-8A
W Jog	2A
T	2x 4x 2x 2x 10A(Mile)-5B-5D-5B-2A-5A(1)
F 5x 5A(1)	2A(1)-3-8A
S	2x 10A(500 or 1,000)-2A-5A(1)
S	2B(3)
M Jog	3x 4x 1B-5C(1)-2A(1)-55y.
T 2x 5A(1)	2x 4x 1A-6D-6A(1)-2A(2)-5A (grass)
W Jog	1B-8A
T 2x 5A(1)	1A-6C-9A (880)-2A(1)
F	2x Light jog-5B(7/8 effort)
S	10A(1,000 or 500)-2A
S	2B(3)
M Jog	2x 1A-5B(9/10 effort)-2A
T 2x 5A(1)	2x 2x 1A-5C(3)-6C-6B-6A(1)-5A(1)
W Jog	3x 3x 1A-5A(1)-2B(2)-5A(1)-8A
T Jog	3x 2A-5A(1)
F 2x 5A(1)	2x 2x 1A-9A-9A(220)
S	2A(2)
S	Country jog
M Jog	3-6x 2A(2)-5A(1)
T 2x 5A(1)	2x 3x 1A-6C-2B(2)-5A(1)
W Jog	3x 1A-5B(9/10 effort)-2A(1)-5A(1)
T 2x 5A(1)	1A-3-8A
F	1A
S	10A (600y.)
S	Run-choice

Sheet 8-6. 800-meter training schedule sheet

880-Yard Run NAME DATE *March*

1. A. Jog 1 to 3 miles
   B. Weights & jog
2. Fartlek A. Varied (1) 30 min. (2) *60 min.*
   B. Steady (1) 2-4 mi. (2) 4-6 mi. (3) 7-10 mi.
   (4) *45 min.*
3. Weights *and jog*
4. High knee and power run
5. Intervals
   A. 110 (1) 18-16-14 (2) 17-15-13 *(3) 12.5 (4) 12.0*
   B. 165 (1) 25 (2) *19*
   C. 220 (1) 35 (2) *25-27 (3) 27*
   D. 330 (1) 52 (2) 48 (3) 45 (4)
   E. 440 (1) 70-73 (2) *65-70 (3) 63*
   F. 660 (1) 1:45 (2)
   G. 880 (1) 70 (2)
   H. 3/4 (1) 70 (2)
   I. Mile (1) 72 (2) 68-70 (3) 64-67 (4)
   J.
   K.
   L.
6. Sets A. 660-440-330-220-110
   (1) 1:45-68-49-32-15 (2) *1:42-66-46-30-14*
   B. 440-660-440-220 (1) 63 (2)
   C. 550-165-165 (1) 55 pace (2)
   D. *220-440-220*
7. Squad meeting
8. Special A. Sauna B. Swim C.
9. Drills A. Sprint-float-sprint (165)
   B. 1-step acceleration (165)
   C. 40-30 drill (1) 4 laps (2)
   D. 70-90 drill (1) 1-1 (2) 2-1
   (3) 3-1 (4)
   E. Cut-downs (1) 110 (2) 165 (3) 220
   (4) 330 (5) 440 (6) 880 (7)
   F. Simulate race drills (1) 1st 220-last 220
   (2) 2½-1½ (3) 10 miles-3/4 drill (4)
   G. 2-4 miles at (1) 80 (2) 75 (3)
10. A. Test B. Trial C. Compete
    (1) 3/4 date pace (2) Over (3) Under
11. Hill interval A. 110 B. 220 C.
12. With coach (A) Bill B. (B) Bill D. (C)
14. A. Wind sprint B. Hurdle drill
    C. Spring and bound D.
15. Finish work
16. Acrobatics or apparatus
17. 3/4 effort
18.
19.
20. Secondary event
21. A. Pictures B. Film

Day		
M	*1A*	*3X 9E(3)(33-30-27)-2A(1)-3X 5A(1)*
T	*2A(2)*	*1A-4X 5A(3)-4X 5C(2)-6A(1)-2A(2)*
W	*1A*	*2A(1)-3-2X 5A(1)*
T	*2A(1)*	*1A-5B(9/10)-2B(4)-2X 9E(4)(48-45-42)*
F		*1A-3-4X 9E(3)(36-33-30-27)*
S	*1A*	*1A-6C-2A(2)-2-3X 5C(1)*
S		*Runner's choice*
M	*2X 5A(1)*	*3*
T	*1A*	*10A(330 at pace, 220 jog, 330 at pace)-2X 6A(2)-3-5X 5A(1)*
W	*2X 5A(1)*	*1A-3-8A*
T	*1A*	*6X 5B(2)-2A(2)-2-3X 9F(4)(51-48-45)*
F	*3X 5A(1)*	*5B-2A-4X 5A(3)*
S	*2A*	*10A (880 at date pace)-2A(2)*
S		*Runner's choice*
M	*1A*	*1A-5E(2)-4X 5C(3)-2A(2)-2X 9E(4)(48-45-42)*
T	*2B*	*4X 5A(4)-2A-3X 5A(1)*
W	*1A*	*1A-5E(2)-2X 5B(9/10 effort)-2A*
T	*2A*	*2A or 2B-5A(1)*
F	*1A*	*2X 5A-3-2X 5A*
S		*10C or 10A*
S		*Travel to spring trip*
M	*2A*	*1A-2A or 2B-2X 5A(1)*
T	*2B(1)*	*1A-4X 5E(3)-6D-2A(1)-4X 5A*
W	*2A*	*2A or 2B-2X 5A(1)*
T	*2X 5A(1)*	*4X 5C(3)-2A*
F	*2X 5A(1)*	*Jog*
S		*10C*
S		*Home and re-register (spring term)*

Sheet 8-7. 800-meter training schedule sheet

880-Yard Run NAME DATE April

1. A. Jog 1 to 3 miles
   B. Weights & jog
2. Fartlek A. Varied (1) 30 min. (2) 45 min.
   B. Steady (1) 2-4 mi. (2) 4-6 mi. (3) 7-10 mi.
   (4)
3. Weights and jog
4. High knee and power run
5. Intervals
   A. 110 (1) 18-16-14 (2) 17-15-13 (3) 11.5-12
   B. 165 (1) 25 (2)
   C. 220 (1) 35 (2)
   D. 330 (1) 52 (2) 48 (3) 45 (4)
   E. 440 (1) 70-73 (2)
   F. 660 (1) 1:45 (2)
   G. 880 (1) 70 (2)
   H. 3/4 (1) 70 (2)
   I. Mile (1) 72 (2) 68-70 (3) 64-67 (4)
   J.
   K.
   L.
6. Sets A. 660-440-330-220-110
   (1) 1:45-68-49-32-15 (2) 1:42-66-46-30-14
   B. 440-660-440-220 (1) 63 (2)
   C. 550-165-165 (1) 55 pace (2)
   D. 220-440-220 (1) 26 pace for 220
7. Squad meeting
8. Special A. Sauna B. Swim C.
9. Drills A. Sprint-float-sprint (165)
   B. 1-step acceleration (165)
   C. 40-30 drill (1) 4 laps (2)
   D. 70-90 drill (1) 1-1 (2) 2-1
   (3) 3-1 (4)
   E. Cut-downs (1) 110 (2) 165 (3) 220
   (4) 330 (5) 440 (6) 880 (7)
   F. Simulate race drills (1) 1st 220-last 220
   (2) 2½-1½ (3) 10 miles-3/4 drill (4)
   G. 2-4 miles at (1) 80 (2) 75 (3)
10. A. Test B. Trial C. Compete
    (1) 3/4 date pace (2) Over (3) Under
11. Hill interval A. 110 B. 220 C.
12. With coach (A) Bill B. (B) Bill D. (C)
14. A. Wind sprint B. Hurdle drill
    C. Spring and bound D.
15. Finish work
16. Acrobatics or apparatus
17. 3/4 effort
18.
19.
20. Secondary event
21. A. Pictures B. Film
22. Golf course A. Around B. Short C. Long

Day	Workout
M 1A	3x 4x 3x 1A-9A-6D(1)-2A(2)-5A(1)
T	3-2A
W 3x 5A(1)	3x 3x 1A-6D-9E(4)(50-47-44)-2A-5A(1)
T	Light
F 1A	10A:880(220 in 35; go last 550:13-26-52-65)-2A
S	10C or 660 at date pace-2B
S	Runner's choice
M 2x 5A(1)	4x 2x 1A-5C-6D-6A(2)-2A(1)
T	3-1A-8A
W 1A	3x 6C-22A or 22B-5A(1)
T	2x 5B(9/10 effort)-2B
F	Gear ready-light jog
S	10C-880 and Relay
S	Runner's choice
M	4x 2x 1A-5C-5C-2A(1)-9E(4)(48-45-42)
T 1A	4x 3x 5A(3)-2A(1)-5A(1)
W	2x 1A-6B-5B(9/10 effort)-2B
T 2x 5A(1)	9A-2B
F	4-6x 5A(quick)-relay work
S	10C (mile and relay)
S	Runner's choice
M 1A	2-3x 2A-5A(1)(grass)
T	6x 2x 1A-6D-5D(2-3)-6A(1)-2A(2)-5A(1)
W 2x 5A(1)	1B-2A-8A
T	1A-5F(14-26-54-68-1:22- 6x/5C-2A-2x/5A(1)
F 1A	Jog
S	10C (Easy, perhaps relay only)
S	Runner's choice

Sheet 8-8. 800-meter training schedule sheet

880-Yard Run NAME DATE May

1. A. Jog 1 to 3 miles
   B. Weights & jog
2. Fartlek A. Varied (1) 30 min. (2) 45 min.
   B. Steady (1) 2-4 mi. (2) 4-6 mi. (3) 7-10 mi.
   (4)
3. Weights and jog
4. High knee and power run
5. Intervals
   A. 110 (1) 18-16-14 (2) 17-15-13
   B. 165 (1) 25 (2)
   C. 220 (1) 35 (2) 27
   D. 330 (1) 52 (2) 48 (3) 45 (4) 39-42
   E. 440 (1) 70-73 (2)
   F. 660 (1) 1:45 (2)
   G. 880 (1) 70 (2)
   H. 3/4 (1) 70 (2)
   I. Mile (1) 72 (2) 68-70 (3) 64-67 (4)
   J. 770 (1) Race pace
   K.
   L.
6. Sets A. 660-440-330-220-110
   (1) 1:45-68-49-32-15 (2) 1:42-66-46-30-14
   B. 440-660-440-220 (1) 63 (2)
   C. 550-165-165 (1) 55 pace (2) 52 pace
   D. 220-440-220
7. Squad meeting
8. Special A. Sauna B. Swim C.
9. Drills A. Sprint-float-sprint (165)
   B. 1-step acceleration (165)
   C. 40-30 drill (1) 4 laps (2)
   D. 70-90 drill (1) 1-1 (2) 2-1
   (3) 3-1 (4)
   E. Cut-downs (1) 110 (2) 165 (3) 220
   (4) 330 (5) 440 (6) 880 (7)
   F. Simulate race drills (1) 1st 220-last 220
   (2) 2½-1½ (3) 10 miles-3/4 drill (4)
   G. 2-4 miles at (1) 80 (2) 75 (3)
10. A. Test B. Trial C. Compete
    (1) 3/4 date pace (2) Over (3) Under
11. Hill interval A. 110 B. 220 C.
12. With coach (A) Bill B. (B) Bill D. (C)
14. A. Wind sprint B. Hurdle drill
    C. Spring and bound D.
15. Finish work
16. Acrobatics or apparatus
17. 3/4 effort
18.
19.
20. Secondary event
21. A. Pictures B. Film
22. Golf course

Day		
M	2x 5A(1)	4x 1A-5C(2)-2A(2)
T	1A	2x 1A-5B(9/10 effort)-8A-8B
W	2x 5A(1)	1A-5J(1)-6A(1)
T	1A	4x 2x 5C-5B(9/10 effort)-2A(1)
F		Gear ready-1A
S	2x 5A(1)	10C (880 and Relay)
S		Runner's choice
M	2A	3-1A-8A-8B
T	2x 5A(1)	3x 2x 5D(4)-6A(1)-22-5A(1)
W	2A	4x 2-3x 5C(2)-2B-5A(1)
T	2x 5A(1)	2x 5B(7/8 effort)-2A
F		Gear ready-baton work
S	2A	10C (440 or mile and relay)
S		Runner's choice
M	1A	1A
T	2x 5A(1)	1A-6D-6B-6A(2)-2A
W	1A	Light-8A-8B
T	2x 5A(1)	Gear ready-5C-5B-5A-2A
F		2-4x 2A(1)-5B(quick)
S	1A	10C(880) Northern Division
S		Runner's choice
M		2-4x 6C(2)-2A(1)-5B
T	1A	5C(2)-5D(4)-5C(2) -5B(9/10 effort)-2B
W		1-2x Jog-5B-2A(1)
T		2x Jog-5A(quick)
F	1A	10C-Trials-Pac 8 Meet
S	1A	10C-Finals
S		2A or 2B

Sheet 8-9. 800-meter training schedule sheet

880-Yard Run NAME DATE *Late May or June*

1. A. Jog 1 to 3 miles
   B. Weights & jog
2. Fartlek A. Varied (1) 30 min. (2) *60 min.*
   B. Steady (1) 2-4 mi. (2) 4-6 mi. (3) 7-10 mi.
   (4)
3. Weights
4. High knee and power run
5. Intervals
   A. 110 (1) 18-16-14 (2) 17-15-13
   B. 165 (1) 25 (2) *19½*
   C. 220 (1) 35 (2) *26–28 (3) 26*
   D. 330 (1) 52 (2) 48 (3) 45 (4)
   E. 440 (1) 70-73 (2) *59 (3) 53*
   F. 660 (1) 1:45 (2)
   G. 880 (1) 70 (2)
   H. 3/4 (1) 70 (2)
   I. Mile (1) 72 (2) 68-70 (3) 64-67 (4)
   J. *2½ laps (1) 60-65*
   K.
   L.
6. Sets A. 660-440-330-220-110
   (1) 1:45-68-49-32-15 (2) *1:42-66-46-30-14*
   B. 440-660-440-220 (1) 63 (2)
   C. 550-165-165 (1) 55 pace (2)
   D.
7. Squad meeting
8. Special A. Sauna B. Swim C.
9. Drills A. Sprint-float-sprint (165)
   B. 1-step acceleration (165)
   C. 40-30 drill (1) 4 laps (2)
   D. 70-90 drill (1) 1-1 (2) 2-1
   (3) 3-1 (4)
   E. Cut-downs (1) 110 (2) 165 (3) 220
   (4) 330 (5) 440 (6) 880 (7)
   F. Simulate race drills (1) 1st 220-last 220
   (2) 2½-1½ (3) 10 miles-3/4 drill (4)
   G. 2-4 miles at (1) 80 (2) 75 (3)
10. A. Test B. Trial C. Compete
    (1) 3/4 date pace (2) Over (3) Under
11. Hill interval A. 110 B. 220 C.
12. With coach (A) Bill B. (B) Bill D. (C)
14. A. Wind sprint B. Hurdle drill
    C. Spring and bound D.
15. Finish work
16. Acrobatics or apparatus
17. 3/4 effort
18.
19.
20. Secondary event
21. A. Pictures B. Film

M	*5B–1A*	*Jog*
T	*1A*	*Twilight meet*
W	*5A*	*2A*
T		*4X 5C(2) – 2X 6A(2) – 2A*
F	*4X 5A*	*2A – 8B*
S	*2A*	*5E(2) or 5C(2) – 2A(2) – 6X 5B(2)*
S		*Jog*
M	*Jog*	*5C (9/10 effort) – 2A – 6X 5A (1)*
T	*Jog*	*5J(1) – 2B – 4X 5C*
W	*Jog*	*4 – 1A – 8A and B*
T	*Jog*	*6C – 2X 5B – 2A – 3X 5A (1)*
F		*5C(3) – 5E(3) – 5C (9/10 effort) – 1A – 2X 5A*
S		*6X 5B(2) – 2B – 2X 5A (7/8 effort)*
S		*Jog*
M		*6X 5B(2) – 2A – 4X 5A (7/8 effort)*
T		*Light*
W		*Light*
T		*Trials*
F		*Semi-finals*
S		*Finals*
S		*Jog*
M		
T		
W		
T		
F		
S		
S		

Sheet 8-10. 800-meter training schedule sheet

1500-Meter and One-Mile Training Schedules

One-Mile Run NAME DATE September/October

1. A. Jog 1 to 3 miles
   B. Weights & jog
2. Fartlek A. Varied (1) 30 min. (2) 45 min.
   B. Steady (1) 2-4 mi. (2) 4-6 mi. (3) 7-10 mi.
   (4)
3. Weights
4. High knee and power run
5. Intervals
   A. 110 (1) 18-16-14 (2) 17-15-13
   B. 165 (1) 25 (2)
   C. 220 (1) 35 (2) 32-35
   D. 330 (1) 52 (2) 48 (3) 45 (4)
   E. 440 (1) 70-73 (2)
   F. 660 (1) 1:45 (2)
   G. 880 (1) 70 (2)
   H. 3/4 (1) 70 (2)
   I. Mile (1) 72 (2) 68-70 (3) 64-67 (4)
   J.
   K.
   L.
6. Sets A. 660-440-330-220-110
   (1) 1:45-68-49-32-15 (2)
   B. 440-660-440-220 (1) 63 (2)
   C. 550-165-165 (1) 55 pace (2)
   D. 220-440-220 (1) 29-58-29
7. Squad meeting
8. Special A. Sauna B. Swim C.
9. Drills A. Sprint-float-sprint (165)
   B. 1-step acceleration (165)
   C. 40-30 drill (1) 4 laps (2)
   D. 70-90 drill (1) 1-1 (2) 2-1
   (3) 3-1 (4)
   E. Cut-downs (1) 110 (2) 165 (3) 220
   (4) 330 (5) 440 (6) 880 (7)
   F. Simulate race drills (1) 1st 220-last 220
   (2) 2½-1½ (3) 10 miles-3/4 drill (4)
   G. 2-4 miles at (1) 80 (2) 75 (3)
10. A. Test B. Trial C. Compete
    (1) 3/4 date pace (2) Over (3) Under
11. Hill interval A. 110 B. 220 C.
12. With coach (A) Bill B. (B) Bill D. (C)
14. A. Wind sprint B. Hurdle drill
    C. Spring and bound D.
15. Finish work
16. Acrobatics or apparatus
17. 3/4 effort A. Mile
18. Steeplechase A. Hurdle drill B. Water jump
19. Park A. Around B. Short Hill
20. Secondary event
21. A. Pictures B. Film

Day	A.M.	P.M.
M	Jog in the	Organization-lockers-equipment-1A
T	mornings if	3-2B
W	time permits	1B-5D 2x-5C 2x-2A(1)
T	1A	3-2B
F	1A	1A-6D(1) 2x-9A(880-mile)-2B
S		2A(1)
S		2B(3)
M	1A	3
T	1A	1A-18A 2x-5G 2x-5A 2x-5F 3x-5E,D,C 4x-7
W	1A	1A
T	1A	18-17A
F	1A	2(light)
S		2A(2)
S		2(light)
M	1A	1A-5C 4x-19A-5A 10x (16-18)
T	1A	1B
W	1A	1A-5D 4x(1-2)-6A 3-4x(1)-5A 3x(1)
T	1A	1B
F	1A	1A-5C 4x(2)-2A(2)-5A 3x(1)
S		2(light)
S		2A(2)-19A
M	1A	2(light)
T	1A	10A-6A 2-3x
W	1A	2B(1)-3
T	1A	2A(2)
F	1A	2(light)
S		10A or cross country
S		2(light)

Sheet 8-11. 1500-meter training schedule sheet

One-Mile Run NAME DATE *October/November*

1. A. Jog 1 to 3 miles
   B. Weights & jog
2. Fartlek A. Varied (1) 30 min. (2) *45 min.*
   B. Steady (1) 2-4 mi. (2) 4-6 mi. (3) 7-10 mi. (4)
3. Weights
4. High knee and power run
5. Intervals
   A. 110 (1) 18-16-14 (2) 17-15-13
   B. 165 (1) 25 (2)
   C. 220 (1) 35 (2)
   D. 330 (1) 52 (2) 48 (3) 45 (4)
   E. 440 (1) 70-73 (2) *65-70*
   F. 660 (1) 1:45 (2)
   G. 880 (1) 70 (2)
   H. 3/4 (1) 70 (2)
   I. Mile (1) 72 (2) 68-70 (3) 64-67 (4)
   J.
   K.
   L.
6. Sets A. 660-440-330-220-110
   (1) 1:45-68-49-32-15 (2) *1:42-66-46-30-14*
   B. 440-660-440-220 (1) 63 (2)
   C. 550-165-165 (1) 55 pace (2)
   D.
7. Squad meeting
8. Special A. Sauna B. Swim C.
9. Drills A. Sprint-float-sprint (165)
   B. 1-step acceleration (165)
   C. 40-30 drill (1) 4 laps (2)
   D. 70-90 drill (1) 1-1 (2) 2-1 (3) 3-1 (4)
   E. Cut-downs (1) 110 (2) 165 (3) 220 (4) 330 (5) 440 (6) 880 (7)
   F. Simulate race drills (1) 1st 220-last 220 (2) 2½-1½ (3) 10 miles–3/4 drill (4)
   G. 2-4 miles at (1) 80 (2) 75 (3)
10. A. Test B. Trial C. Compete
    (1) 3/4 date pace (2) Over (3) Under
11. Hill interval A. 110 B. 220 C.
12. With coach (A) Bill B. (B) Bill D. (C)
14. A. Wind sprint B. Hurdle drill
    C. Spring and bound D.
15. Finish work
16. Acrobatics or apparatus
17. 3/4 effort *A. Mile*
18. *Steeplechase A. Hurdle drill B. Water jump*
19. *Park run A. Around B. Short hill*
20. Secondary event
21. A. Pictures B. Film
22. *Golf course run A. Around*

	A.M.	P.M.
M	1A	2-19A-2B(3)(7-8 min. pace)
T	1A	2B(1)-3
W	1A	2-18A-2X 5D(2-3)-4X 19A-1-2X 19B-2A(2)
T	1A	2A(1)
F	1A	9A (1320-mile)-4
S		3
S		6A-2A(2)
M	1A	3
T	1A	10A(17A)-2A-19A
W	1A	3
T	1A	10A(17A)-22
F	1A	2 (light)
S		5-9X 22A
S		2A (light)
M	1A	2A (light)
T	1A	1A-4-2X 6A (1 or 2)-2A(2)
W	1A	3
T	1A	1A
F	1A	Light
S		10C-Cross country regional meet
S		2 (light)
M	1A	3-2A
T	1A	4X 5E(2)-2X 6A(1)-2B(2)
W	1A	3
T	1A	6-10X 22A
F	1A	2 (light)
S		4X 5E(2)-2X 5H(1)-5-6X 5A-2A
S		2 (light)

Sheet 8-12. 1500-meter training schedule sheet

One-Mile Run NAME DATE November/December

1. A. Jog 1 to 3 miles
   B. Weights & jog
2. Fartlek A. Varied (1) 30 min. (2)
   B. Steady (1) 2-4 mi. (2) 4-6 mi. (3) 7-10 mi.
   (4)
3. Weights
4. High knee and power run
5. Intervals
   A. 110 (1) 18-16-14 (2) 17-15-13
   B. 165 (1) 25 (2)
   C. 220 (1) 35 (2)
   D. 330 (1) 52 (2) 48 (3) 45 (4)
   E. 440 (1) 70-73 (2) 60
   F. 660 (1) 1:45 (2)
   G. 880 (1) 70 (2)
   H. 3/4 (1) 70 (2)
   I. Mile (1) 72 (2) 68-70 (3) 64-67 (4)
   J.
   K.
   L.
6. Sets A. 660-440-330-220-110
   (1) 1:45-68-49-32-15 (2)
   B. 440-660-440-220 (1) 63 (2)
   C. 550-165-165 (1) 55 pace (2)
   D.
7. Squad meeting
8. Special A. Sauna B. Swim C.
9. Drills A. Sprint-float-sprint (165)
   B. 1-step acceleration (165)
   C. 40-30 drill (1) 4 laps (2)
   D. 70-90 drill (1) 1-1 (2) 2-1
   (3) 3-1 (4)
   E. Cut-downs (1) 110 (2) 165 (3) 220
   (4) 330 (5) 440 (6) 880 (7)
   F. Simulate race drills (1) 1st 220-last 220
   (2) 2½-1½ (3) 10 miles-3/4 drill (4)
   G. 2-4 miles at (1) 80 (2) 75 (3)
10. A. Test B. Trial C. Compete
    (1) 3/4 date pace (2) Over (3) Under
11. Hill interval A. 110 B. 220 C.
12. With coach (A) Bill B. (B) Bill D. (C)
14. A. Wind sprint B. Hurdle drill
    C. Spring and bound D.
15. Finish work
16. Acrobatics or apparatus
17. 3/4 effort
18. Steeplechase A. Hurdle drill
19. Park run A. Around
20. Secondary event
21. A. Pictures B. Film
22. Golf course A. Around

Day	A.M.	P.M.
M	1A	2A(1)-3
T	1A	4x 4x 3-5x 5E(2)-18A-6A
W	1A	1B
T	1A	9A(1-1½ miles)-2B
F	1A	1B
S		4x 6A-19A
S		Pleasant jog
M	1A	10C-area cross country race
T	1A	Home-1A
W	1A	4x 6-10x 18A-5G(1)
T	1A	1B
F	1A	2A or 2B
S		Light
S		10A(1½ miles)-19A
M		Vacation:
T		Fartlek runs
W		+rest
T		+recreation
F		
S		
S		
M		
T		
W		
T		
F		
S		
S		

Sheet 8-13. 1500-meter training schedule sheet

One-Mile Run NAME DATE January

1. A. Jog 1 to 3 miles
   B. Weights & jog
2. Fartlek A. Varied (1) 30 min. (2) 45 min.
   B. Steady (1) 2-4 mi. (2) 4-6 mi. (3) 7-10 mi.
   (4) 45 min. out, 45 min. back
3. Weights
4. High knee and power run
5. Intervals
   A. 110 (1) 18-16-14 (2) 17-15-13
   B. 165 (1) 25 (2)
   C. 220 (1) 35 (2)
   D. 330 (1) 52 (2) 48 (3) 45 (4)
   E. 440 (1) 70-73 (2) 60
   F. 660 (1) 1:45 (2)
   G. 880 (1) 70 (2) 61
   H. 3/4 (1) 70 (2)
   I. Mile (1) 72 (2) 68-70 (3) 64-67 (4)
   J.
   K.
   L.
6. Sets A. 660-440-330-220-110
   (1) 1:45-68-49-32-15 (2)
   B. 440-660-440-220 (1) 63 (2)
   C. 550-165-165 (1) 55 pace (2)
   D.
7. Squad meeting
8. Special A. Sauna B. Swim C.
9. Drills A. Sprint-float-sprint (165)
   B. 1-step acceleration (165)
   C. 40-30 drill (1) 4 laps (2)
   D. 70-90 drill (1) 1-1 (2) 2-1
   (3) 3-1 (4)
   E. Cut-downs (1) 110 (2) 165 (3) 220
   (4) 330 (5) 440 (6) 880 (7)
   F. Simulate race drills (1) 1st 220-last 220
   (2) 2½-1½ (3) 10 miles-3/4 drill (4)
   G. 2-4 miles at (1) 80 (2) 75 (3)
10. A. Test B. Trial C. Compete
   (1) 3/4 date pace (2) Over (3) Under
11. Hill interval A. 110 B. 220 C.
12. With coach (A) Bill B. (B) Bill D. (C)
14. A. Wind sprint B. Hurdle drill
   C. Spring and bound D.
15. Finish work
16. Acrobatics or apparatus
17. 3/4 effort A. Mile
18. Steeplechase A. Hurdle drill
19. Park run A. Around B. Short hill
20. Secondary event
21. A. Pictures B. Film

Day	A.M.	P.M.
M		Class or squad organization
T		Register and 1B
W		2-3x 4x 4x 2x 1A-18A-5D(2-3)-5G-6A-1A
T		2B(1)
F		1B-2B
S		2B(4)
S		Recreation
M		1B-2B
T	1A	11x4x 4x 2x 7-5B-9A-19B-5A(1)
W		1B-2B
T		10x 3x 2x 1A-9A-6A(1)-5D-2B
F		1A-3
S		Easy 220's
S		2
M	1A	1B-1A
T	1A	10x 8x 5D(3)-5F-2B
W	1A	1B
T	1A	1A
F		Gear ready-1A
S		10C-Indoor mile or 10A
S		Pleasant jog
M	1A	1B
T	1A	10x 4x 1A-5B-5C-14A
W	1A	1B
T	1A	7
F	1A	Gear ready-1A
S		10C-2 mile indoor
S		Recreation

Sheet 8-14. 1500-meter training schedule sheet

One-Mile Run NAME DATE February

1. A. Jog 1 to 3 miles
   B. Weights & jog
2. Fartlek A. Varied (1) 30 min. (2)
   B. Steady (1) 2-4 mi. (2) 4-6 mi. (3) 7-10 mi.
   (4) 12-15 min.
3. Weights
4. High knee and power run
5. Intervals
   A. 110 (1) 18-16-14 (2) 17-15-13
   B. 165 (1) 25 (2)
   C. 220 (1) 35 (2) 28 (3) 29
   D. 330 (1) 52 (2) 48 (3) 45 (4) 42
   E. 440 (1) 70-73 (2) 65-70 (3) 62
   F. 660 (1) 1:45 (2) 1:30
   G. 880 (1) 70 (2)
   H. 3/4 (1) 70 (2)
   I. Mile (1) 72 (2) 68-70 (3) 64-67 (4)
   J.
   K.
   L.
6. Sets A. 660-440-330-220-110
   (1) 1:45-68-49-32-15 (2) 1:42-66-46-30-14
   B. 440-660-440-220 (1) 63 (2)
   C. 550-165-165 (1) 55 pace (2)
   D. 220-440-220
7. Squad meeting
8. Special A. Sauna B. Swim C.
9. Drills A. Sprint-float-sprint (165)
   B. 1-step acceleration (165)
   C. 40-30 drill (1) 4 laps (2)
   D. 70-90 drill (1) 1-1 (2) 2-1
   (3) 3-1 (4)
   E. Cut-downs (1) 110 (2) 165 (3) 220
   (4) 330 (5) 440 (6) 880 (7)
   F. Simulate race drills (1) 1st 220-last 220
   (2) 2½-1½ (3) 10 miles-3/4 drill (4)
   G. 2-4 miles at (1) 80 (2) 75 (3)
10. A. Test B. Trial C. Compete
    (1) 3/4 date pace (2) Over (3) Under
11. Hill interval A. 110 B. 220 C.
12. With coach (A) Bill B. (B) Bill D. (C)
14. A. Wind sprint B. Hurdle drill
    C. Spring and bound D.
15. Finish work
16. Acrobatics or apparatus
17. 3/4 effort A. Mile
18. Steeplechase A. Hurdle drill B. Water jump
19. Park run A. Around B. Short hill C. Long hill
20. Secondary event
21. A. Pictures B. Film
22. Golf course A. Around

Day	A.M.	P.M.
M	1A	4x 2x 19A-5A(1)
T	1A	4x 6x 4x 5E(2)-5D(3)-5A(9/10 effort)-5C(2)-2B(1)
W	1A	1B
T	1A	2-4x 2x 2-3x 19A-19B-5A(1)
F		2
S		10C
S		2B(3)
M	1A	1A
T	1A	4-6x 3x 22A-5A(1)
W	1A	1B-1A
T	1A	3x 2x 4x 2x 2x 5F(2)-5A(9/10 effort)-5E(3)-5A(9/10 effort)-6A(2)
F		1A
S		2
S		1A
M	1A	3x 5A(1)-2B(1)
T	1A	4x 4x 2A(1)-6B-5D(2-3)-5C(3)-9A(880)
W	1A	3x 5A(1)-2B(1)
T	1A	1A-6D-22A-5C(1)
F		Light
S		10A(17A)-19A-19C-19B
S		2
M	1A	4x 4x 4x 2x 4x 3x 2B-18A-18B-5E-5A-5D(4)-5A(1)
T	1A	6x 2A-19A
W	1A	2A
T	1A	2B(4)
F		4x 4x 12x 18A-18B-5D(3)(9/10 effort every 3d)-2B
S		2A(1)-3
S		2

Sheet 8-15. 1500-meter training schedule sheet

One-Mile Run NAME DATE March

1. A. Jog 1 to 3 miles
   B. Weights & jog
2. Fartlek A. Varied (1) 30 min. (2)
   B. Steady (1) 2-4 mi. (2) 4-6 mi. (3) 7-10 mi.
   (4)
3. Weights
4. High knee and power run
5. Intervals
   A. 110 (1) 18-16-14 (2) 17-15-13
   B. 165 (1) 25 (2)
   C. 220 (1) 35 (2)
   D. 330 (1) 52 (2) 48 (3) 45 (4) 42
   E. 440 (1) 70-73 (2) 66 (3) 60
   F. 660 (1) 1:45 (2)
   G. 880 (1) 70 (2) 63
   H. 3/4 (1) 70 (2)
   I. Mile (1) 72 (2) 68-70 (3) 64-67 (4)
   J.
   K.
   L.
6. Sets A. 660-440-330-220-110
   (1) 1:45-68-49-32-15 (2) 1:42-66-46-30-14
   B. 440-660-440-220 (1) 63 (2)
   C. 550-165-165 (1) 55 pace (2)
   D.
7. Squad meeting
8. Special A. Sauna B. Swim C.
9. Drills A. Sprint-float-sprint (165)
   B. 1-step acceleration (165)
   C. 40-30 drill (1) 4 laps (2)
   D. 70-90 drill (1) 1-1 (2) 2-1
   (3) 3-1 (4)
   E. Cut-downs (1) 110 (2) 165 (3) 220
   (4) 330 (5) 440 (6) 880 (7)
   F. Simulate race drills (1) 1st 220-last 220
   (2) 2½-1½ (3) 10 miles-3/4 drill (4)
   G. 2-4 miles at (1) 80 (2) 75 (3)
10. A. Test B. Trial C. Compete
    (1) 3/4 date pace (2) Over (3) Under
11. Hill interval A. 110 B. 220 C.
12. With coach (A) Bill B. (B) Bill D. (C)
14. A. Wind sprint B. Hurdle drill
    C. Spring and bound D.
15. Finish work
16. Acrobatics or apparatus
17. 3/4 effort A. Mile
18. Steeplechase A. Hurdle drill B. Water jump
19. Park run A. Around B. Short hill
20. Secondary event
21. A. Pictures B. Film

Day	A.M.	P.M.
M	1A	1A-4-2B(1)
T	1A	2-6x 4-6x 2x 1B-19B-19A-5A(1)
W	1A	1A-1B
T	1A	4x 4x 18A-18B-9A(1320)-2B(1)
F		Light
S		10B(17A)-2
S		2
M	1A	1B-4
T	1A	2
W	1A	1B-4
T	1A	2-4x 6B-18AB-6A(2)-2A
F		1B-4-2B
S		Light
S		2
M		Exam week-2A(1)
T		2x 2x 3-4x 2x 4-6x 6x 5G(3)-5A-5F(1)-5A-5E(2)-5D-2A
W		1B-2B(1)
T		2B
F		Gear ready-14A
S	Travel	10C-Dual meet
S		Travel-Spring trip
M	1A-14A	4x 3x 5E(3)-2A(1)-6A(1)-2A(1)
T	1B-14B	3x 2x 5D(4)-5A(9/10 effort)-2
W	1A	Light
T	1A-14A	2 (Hills)
F		1B
S		10C-Triangular meet
S		Travel home-registration

Sheet 8-16. 1500-meter training schedule sheet

One-Mile Run NAME DATE April

1. A. Jog 1 to 3 miles
   B. Weights & jog
2. Fartlek A. Varied (1) 30 min. (2)
   B. Steady (1) 2-4 mi. (2) 4-6 mi. (3) 7-10 mi.
   (4)
3. Weights
4. High knee and power run
5. Intervals
   A. 110 (1) 18-16-14 (2) 17-15-13
   B. 165 (1) 25 (2)
   C. 220 (1) 35 (2)
   D. 330 (1) 52 (2) 48 (3) 45 (4)
   E. 440 (1) 70-73 (2)
   F. 660 (1) 1:45 (2)
   G. 880 (1) 70 (2)
   H. 3/4 (1) 70 (2)
   I. Mile (1) 72 (2) 68-70 (3) 64-67 (4)
   J. 1100y (1) 60
   K.
   L.
6. Sets A. 660-440-330-220-110
   (1) 1:45-68-49-32-15 (2) 1:42-66-46-30-14
   B. 440-660-440-220 (1) 63 (2)
   C. 550-165-165 (1) 55 pace (2)
   D.
7. Squad meeting
8. Special A. Sauna B. Swim C.
9. Drills A. Sprint-float-sprint (165)
   B. 1-step acceleration (165)
   C. 40-30 drill (1) 4 laps (2)
   D. 70-90 drill (1) 1-1 (2) 2-1
   (3) 3-1 (4)
   E. Cut-downs (1) 110 (2) 165 (3) 220
   (4) 330 (5) 440 (6) 880 (7)
   F. Simulate race drills (1) 1st 220-last 220
   (2) 2½-1½ (3) 10 miles-3/4 drill (4)
   G. 2-4 miles at (1) 80 (2) 75 (3)
10. A. Test B. Trial C. Compete
    (1) 3/4 date pace (2) Over (3) Under
11. Hill interval A. 110 B. 220 C.
12. With coach (A) Bill B. (B) Bill D. (C)
14. A. Wind sprint B. Hurdle drill
    C. Spring and bound D.
15. Finish work
16. Acrobatics or apparatus
17. 3/4 effort
18.
19. Park run
20. Secondary event
21. A. Pictures B. Film
22. Golf course run

	A.M. P.M.
M 2A	1A-1B
T 2B	4-6x 1A-6A-9G(1)-2A
W 2A	1A-1B
T 2B	1A-19
F	Gear ready-1A
S	Relay Meet-10C(2 mile)
S	2
M 2A	4x 4x 4-5x 7-1A-5F(2)-5F(3)-6A(2)-2B(1)
T 2B	1B-9F(2)(60's)-22
W 2A	Light
T 2B	14A
F	Gear ready-1A
S	10C-dual meet-mile
S	2
M 2B	1A-2(easy)-1B
T 2A	2-3x 5A(1)-5J(1)-5F(2)-2B
W 2B	1A-1B
T 2A	2 (easy)
F	Gear ready
S	10C-Dual Meet
S	2(easy)
M 2A	7-2B(grass)
T 2B	4x 3x 1A-5E(3)-6A(1:39-64-45-29-13½)-2A(1)
W 2A	2-1B
T 2B	2 (easy)
F	Travel-1A
S	Dual meet-10C (2 miles)
S	Home-loosen up

Sheet 8-17. 1500-meter training schedule sheet

One-Mile Run NAME DATE May

1. A. Jog 1 to 3 miles
   B. Weights & jog
2. Fartlek A. Varied (1) 30 min. (2)
   B. Steady (1) 2-4 mi. (2) 4-6 mi. (3) 7-10 mi.
   (4)
3. Weights
4. High knee and power run
5. Intervals
   A. 110 (1) 18-16-14 (2) 17-15-13
   B. 165 (1) 25 (2)
   C. 220 (1) 35 (2)
   D. 330 (1) 52 (2) 48 (3) 45 (4)
   E. 440 (1) 70-73 (2) 60
   F. 660 (1) 1:45 (2)
   G. 880 (1) 70 (2) 61
   H. 3/4 (1) 70 (2)
   I. Mile (1) 72 (2) 68-70 (3) 64-67 (4)
   J.
   K.
   L.
6. Sets A. 660-440-330-220-110
   (1) 1:45-68-49-32-15 (2) 1:42-66-46-30-14
   B. 440-660-440-220 (1) 63 (2) 59
   C. 550-165-165 (1) 55 pace (2)
   D. 880-660-220 E. 330-660-330
7. Squad meeting
8. Special A. Sauna B. Swim C.
9. Drills A. Sprint-float-sprint (165)
   B. 1-step acceleration (165)
   C. 40-30 drill (1) 4 laps (2)
   D. 70-90 drill (1) 1-1 (2) 2-1
   (3) 3-1 (4)
   E. Cut-downs (1) 110 (2) 165 (3) 220
   (4) 330 (5) 440 (6) 880 (7)
   F. Simulate race drills (1) 1st 220-last 220
   (2) 2½-1½ (3) 10 miles-3/4 drill (4)
   G. 2-4 miles at (1) 80 (2) 75 (3)
10. A. Test B. Trial C. Compete
    (1) 3/4 date pace (2) Over (3) Under
11. Hill interval A. 110 B. 220 C.
12. With coach (A) Bill B. (B) Bill D. (C)
14. A. Wind sprint B. Hurdle drill
    C. Spring and bound D.
15. Finish work
16. Acrobatics or apparatus
17. 3/4 effort
18. Steeplechase A. Hurdle drill B. Water jump
19.
20. Secondary event
21. A. Pictures B. Film

Day	Workout
M A.M. 1A	P.M. 4x 4x 7-18A-5E(2)-2A
T 2A	2x 1A-6B-6D(2:14-1:37½-63-30)-2A(1)
W 2x 1A-5A(1)	Light
T 2A	14A-2 (easy)
F	Gear ready-1A
S	10C-Dual meet-mile
S	2
M 7	3x 2x 1A-5D(3)-5A(9/10 effort)-2A(1)
T 1A	2x 2A(1)-5E(2)-5G(2)-5E(2)-6A(2)-2B
W 2A	Light
T 1A	2B (easy)
F 2A	Gear ready
S	10C-Traditional dual meet
S	2
M 2A	4x 4x 2x 1A-5E(2)-5E(2)-9B-2A(1)
T 1A	2x 1A-6E-6A
W 2A	1A-1B-2A(1)
T 1A	2
F	Travel
S	10C-Relay (4 x 1 mile)
S	Home-2
M 1A	2x 7-18AB-2A(2)
T 2A	2-4x 18A(330's)-6B(2)-2A(1)
W	1A
T	2B (easy)-14A
F	Gear ready
S	10C-Division championship
S	2

Sheet 8-18. 1500-meter training schedule sheet

One-Mile Run NAME DATE June

1. A. Jog 1 to 3 miles
   B. Weights & jog
2. Fartlek A. Varied (1) 30 min. (2)
   B. Steady (1) 2-4 mi. (2) 4-6 mi. (3) 7-10 mi.
   (4)
3. Weights
4. High knee and power run
5. Intervals
   A. 110 (1) 18-16-14 (2) 17-15-13
   B. 165 (1) 25 (2)
   C. 220 (1) 35 (2) 27
   D. 330 (1) 52 (2) 48 (3) 45 (4) 42
   E. 440 (1) 70-73 (2) 60 (3) 58
   F. 660 (1) 1:45 (2) 1:30 (3) 1:27
   G. 880 (1) 70 (2) 59 (3) 60
   H. 3/4 (1) 70 (2)
   I. Mile (1) 72 (2) 68-70 (3) 64-67 (4)
   J.
   K.
   L.
6. Sets A. 660-440-330-220-110
   (1) 1:45-68-49-32-15 (2)
   B. 440-660-440-220 (1) 63 (2)
   C. 550-165-165 (1) 55 pace (2)
   D.
7. Squad meeting
8. Special A. Sauna B. Swim C.
9. Drills A. Sprint-float-sprint (165)
   B. 1-step acceleration (165)
   C. 40-30 drill (1) 4 laps (2)
   D. 70-90 drill (1) 1-1 (2) 2-1
   (3) 3-1 (4)
   E. Cut-downs (1) 110 (2) 165 (3) 220
   (4) 330 (5) 440 (6) 880 (7)
   F. Simulate race drills (1) 1st 220-last 220
   (2) 2½-1½ (3) 10 miles-3/4 drill (4)
   G. 2-4 miles at (1) 80 (2) 75 (3)
10. A. Test B. Trial C. Compete
    (1) 3/4 date pace (2) Over (3) Under
11. Hill interval A. 110 B. 220 C.
12. With coach (A) Bill B. (B) Bill D. (C)
14. A. Wind sprint B. Hurdle drill
    C. Spring and bound D.
15. Finish work
16. Acrobatics or apparatus
17. 3/4 effort A. Mile
18.
19. Park run A. Around B. Short hill
20. Secondary event
21. A. Pictures B. Film
22. Golf course A. Around B. Short C. Long

Day	A.M.	P.M.
M	1A	1A - 3
T	2A	5G(2)-5F(2)-5E(2)-5C(2)-2A(1)
W	1A	1A
T	2A	22 (easy)
F		Travel
S		10C - Mile
S	Home	2x 19A - 2x 19B - 3x 5A(1)
M	2A	2A
T	1A	1A
W		10C-Twilight Meet (2 mile)
T		3
F		17A - 2A
S		2x 6C - 2B
S		2
M	2x 5A(1)	5G(3)-5F(3)-5E(3)-5D(4)-5C(2)-2A(1)
T	1A	2B-14A
W	2x 5A(1)	1A
T		Trials - NCAA Meet
F		Semifinals
S		Finals (Mile)
S		
M		
T		
W		
T		
F		
S		
S		

Sheet 8-19. 1500-meter training schedule sheet

Recommended Readings

Avery, Guy. (1996). A simple but proven way to train for a faster mile. *Track and Field Coaches Review, 96*(2), 10-16.

Bennett, Steve. (Winter 1999). Training for the 800. *Track Coach, 146*, 4649-4656. Reprinted in Jarver, *Middle and Long Distances*, 111-123.

Bessel, Jennifer. (Winter 2006). The 800 and 1500 meters: Racing fast and controlled. *Track Coach, 174*, 5545-5549.

Bondarenko, Vladimir. (1991) The structure of the last cycle of the training year: 1988 Olympic Champion Olga Bondarenko. *Track and Field Quarterly Review, 91*(2), 51-53.

Boyle, Tommy. (1992). Preparation for the women's 3000 meters at the elite level. *Track Technique, 120*, 3818-3821.

Chalmers, Angela, Wynn Gmitroski & David Johns. (1994). Defining success through performance goals: An account of the scientific preparation of a middle distance runner. In *Access to living: Proceedings of the 10th Commonwealth & International Scientific Congress*, eds. Frederick I. Bell & Geraldine H. Van Gyn (pp. 424-429). Victoria, BC, Canada: The University of Victoria.

Coe, Peter. (1983). Training a world class 800/1500m athlete. *Track and Field Quarterly Review, 83*(3), 19-26.

De Oliveira, Luiz, & John Cobley. (1988). Middle distance training with Luiz de Oliveira. *Track Technique, 104*, 3319-3321, 3333.

Ebbets, Russ. (Spring 2001). An interview with Ruth Wysocki. *Track Coach, 155*, 4947-4951, 4954.

Ebbets, Russ. (Fall 2001). Track Coach talks with Peter Coe. *Track Coach, 157*, 5001-5007, 5029.

Freeman, William H. (2001). Periodized training for [distance] runners. In *Peak When It Counts: Periodization for American track and field* (4th ed.). Mountain View, CA: Tafnews, 86-105.

Gamboa, Jorge Diaz, Ray Elrick, Amarilis Hernández Mora, David E. Martin, Manuel Pascua Piqueras, Matt Paterson, Paul Schmidt & Carlo Vittori. (1996). NSA Round Table 32: Speed in the 800 metres. *New Studies in Athletics, 11*(4), 7-22.

Gmitroski, Wynn. (1998). Definition of success via performance goals: A report about the scientific preparation of middle distance runners. *New Studies in Athletics, 13*(1), 87-89.

Gonschinska, Idrill. (1996). The speed and strength training of middle-distance runners from a functional point of view, *New Studies in Athletics, 11*(4), 98-102.

Hanon, C., C. Thomas, J. M. Le Chevalier, B. Gajer & H. Vandewalle. (2002). How does $\dot{V}O_2$ evolve during the 800m? *New Studies in Athletics, 17*(3/4), 61-68.

Lindstrom, Sieg. (2004, May). At home with the world's greatest miler. *Track & Field News, 57*(5), 16-17. [Hicham El Guerrouj, Morocco]

Litovchenko, M. (1991). High level women's training program: 800, 1500, 3000 meters. *Track and Field Quarterly Review, 91*(2), 54-56.

McDonnell, John. (2004), Arkansas middle distance and long distance training. Presentation at NCAA Track Coaches Clinic, Somewhere in Arkansas, March 2004.

Mikkelsson, Lasse. (1996). How to train to become a top distance runner. *New Studies in Athletics, 11*(4), 37-44. Reprinted in Jarver, *Middle and Long Distances*, 11-15.

Moore, Philip. (Fall 2001). Middle distance athlete development. *Track Coach, 157*, 5021-5024. Originally in Jarver, *Middle and Long Distances*, 18-22.

Moss, Dick. (Summer 2003). Stay off the curb in middle distance events [abstract]. *Track Coach, 164,* 5253.

Murray, Yvonne. (1992). Practical preparation for the 1988 Olympics [3 km]. *Track Technique, 120*, 3821, 3843.

Nurmekivi, Ants. (Winter 2004). Specificity of middle distance training [abstract]. *Track Coach, 166*, 5316-5317. Full version in Jarver, *Middle and Long Distances*, 91-93.

Poehlein, Mike. (2000). 800 meters to mile. In *USA Track and Field coaching manual.* Champaign, IL: Human Kinetics, 93-107.

Pöhlitz, Luther. (Winter 2004). How to develop 800m talents [abstract]. *Track Coach, 166*, 5315.

Prendergast, Kevin. (2002). Optimum speed distribution in 800m and training implications. In Jarver, *Middle and Long Distances*, 131-136.

Remingo, Lindy. (1994). Coaching the elite 800 meter runner. *Track and Field Quarterly Review, 94*(2), 23-28.

Schmidt, Paul. (1993). Tactics in middle distance running. *Track Technique, 122*, 3901-3902, 3907.

Spencer, Matt R., Paul B. Gastin & Warren R. Payne. (1996). Energy system contribution during 400 to 1500 metres running. *New Studies in Athletics, 11*(4), 59-65. Reprinted in Jarver, *Middle and Long Distances*, 76-83.

Storkina, Svetlana. (Winter 2002). How Olympic Champion Svetlana Masterkova trained [abstract]. *Track Coach, 158*, 5060.

Tanser, Toby. (Winter 2001). A profile of Olympic [1500m] champion Noah Ngeny. *Track Coach, 154*, 4928-4929.

Wilson, Harry. (1983). Preparation of 1500m runners. *Track and Field Quarterly Review, 83*(3), 14-17.

9

The Longer Distances and Cross Country

Bowerman's Best

Cross Country		Steve Prefontaine, three-time NCAA Champion
Steeplechase	8:29.6	Steve Savage, 1971; three-time All-American; 1972 U.S. Olympic Team
5 km	13:22.4	Steve Prefontaine, 1973
10 km	27:43.6	Steve Prefontaine, 1974
Marathon	2:11:35.8	Kenny Moore, 1970

Record Setters

Bill Dellinger — Olympic bronze medal, 1964; three-time Olympian; NCAA mile champion, 1954; 2nd NCAA mile, 1955; NCAA 5 km champion, 1956; four U.S. records at 1500m and 5,000m; two world indoor records at two miles and three miles.

Steve Prefontaine — Four-time NCAA champion, 3 mile and 5 km, 1970-1973; three-time NCAA cross country champion, 1970, 1971, 1973; U.S. three-mile Champion, 1971 and 1973; 4th place, 5 km, 1972 Olympic Games

Set 13 U.S. records between 2 km and 10 km

2 km	5:01.4	U.S. record, 1975
3 km	7:42.6	U.S. record, 1974
2 Mile	8:19.4	U.S. record, 1972
5 km	13:22.2	U.S. record, 1974
10 km	27:43.6	U.S. record, 1974

Kenny Moore — Three-Mile All-American; two-time Olympian; 4th in 1972 Olympic Marathon; U.S. record in marathon, 2:11:35.8.

As an athlete moves on to the longer races, the aerobic component of training becomes more important. However, speed is a factor even in the longest races. Today's world-class marathoner is also a world-class 10,000-meter runner. For men, that means well under 28:00 for the track race, while for women it means sub-32:00 speed. For an athlete to maintain that speed for an extended distance requires good leg speed. The top male marathoners can run under 4:00 for a mile or under 3:42 for 1500 meters. Though that high-speed component in the short races is not yet vital for women, it will be within a decade as a larger talent pool enters the arena.

This discussion of speed points out a critical fact: the long distances and the steeplechase are not refuges for the athlete with no talent. The races do allow more progress based on extended hard work, so they are excellent frameworks for the traditional work ethic. However, at the world-class level, no events are "weak." Through 2006, the world records at 10,000 meters require paces of just over 63 seconds per 400m lap for a man and under 71 seconds per lap for a woman, both maintained for 25 laps. The marathons require paces of 71 and 77 seconds per 400m lap for over 105 laps (though not run on the track) for a man and a woman, respectively.

More attention is now paid to developing the anaerobic threshold. The idea of very high mileage at a relatively easy pace is discredited as an effective training method for the distances.[1] As David Martin of the USOC's Elite Athlete Project says, "This 7:00 a mile stuff for a 100 miles a week isn't necessarily going to hack it."[2] Instead, higher intensity training at lower mileages is more effective.

The most effective training appears to depend upon paces based on the athlete's aerobic and anaerobic thresholds, the levels at which the athlete accumulates certain levels of lactic acid:

- Aerobic threshold: 2 mmol per liter of lactate
- Anaerobic threshold: 4 mmol per liter of lactate

These thresholds are "breaking points" on the rising curve of lactic acid produced by the body as exercise becomes more strenuous. The *aerobic threshold* is the point at which the athlete is beginning to "work," having to use more oxygen to maintain the training effort. The *anaerobic threshold* is the point at which the athlete can no longer take in enough oxygen to fuel the exercise, thus beginning to go into oxygen debt (recovery oxygen) and drawing on the body's reserves to maintain the effort.[3] This discussion is based on Finnish research and practice, but some exercise physiologists question the validity of the thresholds.[4]

The most effective training speeds are in the transitional range between those two levels. Although an athlete's potential $\dot{V}O_{2max}$ has genetic limits, the ability to race at a given level (percentage) of that figure is not so limited. In other words, the $\dot{V}O_{2max}$ is not the only factor limiting an athlete's potential. As an example, Steve Prefontaine had a $\dot{V}O_{2max}$ of above 80, compared to about 70 for Frank Shorter, yet both had roughly the same best marks at 5,000 meters (both world class). Shorter had more efficient running technique and was able to run at a higher percentage of his maximum than was Prefontaine.

Thus, two important aspects can be identified for long distance training: proper running technique and training at more effective levels of effort. The proper technique is discussed in Chapter 7. The more intensive training sessions that theory recommends make the hard-easy principle even more important.

The benefit of—and reason for—the hard-easy principle is that the body needs time to recover from a workload. The recovery time that is needed depends on the intensity of the workload. A light run may require only a few hours of recovery. A 10-mile run at close to the anaerobic threshold may require from one to three days of recovery, depending on the athlete's training background.

With that understood, how to determine the most effective training levels? Although the $\dot{V}O_{2max}$ and the aerobic and anaerobic thresholds are best determined by treadmill tests in a lab setting, rough measures can be made from the best racing times at longer distances.

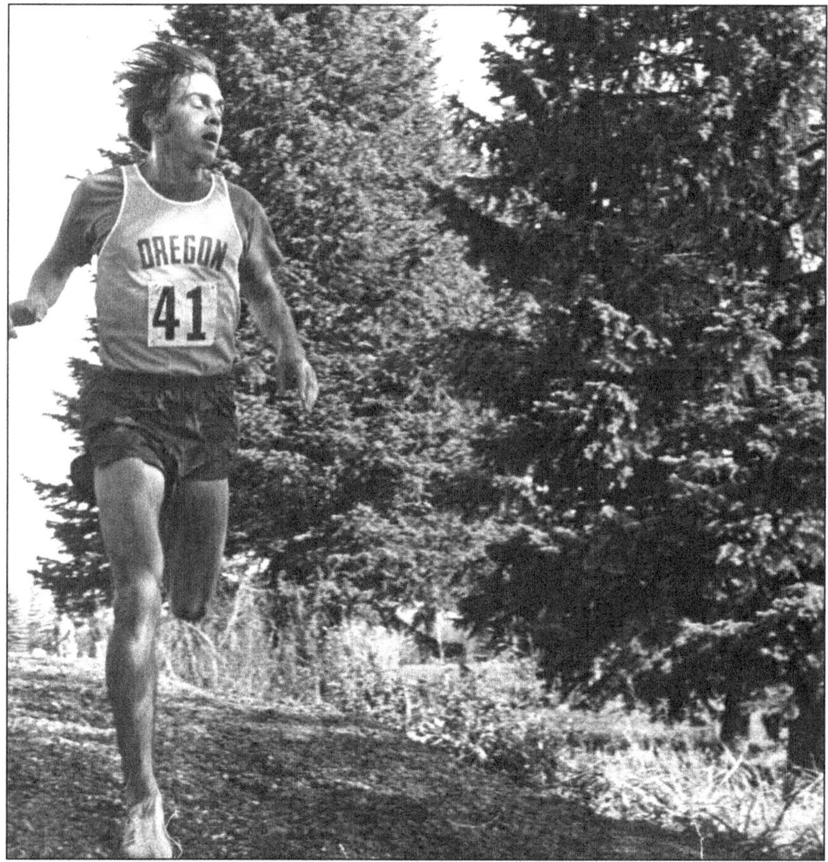

Photo 9-1. Steve Prefontaine, three-time NCAA cross country champion

Finnish researchers have suggested that when more scientific testing is not possible, the thresholds can be estimated from the beats per minute (BPM) of the maximum heart rate (HRmax, which can also be estimated).[5] The training zones are:

- $\dot{V}O_{2max}$ training:
  - ✓ Within 5 BPM of the HRmax
- Anaerobic training:
  - ✓ 20 to 30 BPM below HRmax for long-distance runners
  - ✓ 15 to 25 BPM below HRmax for middle-distance runners
- Aerobic training:
  - ✓ 40 to 60 BPM below HRmax for long-distance runners
  - ✓ 35 to 50 BPM below HRmax for middle-distance runners

Table 9-1 gives an example based on a maximum heart rate of 200 BPM. The maximum rate varies by age, sex, and fitness.

Estimating the Heart Rate for Training Levels

	Heart Rate	
Training Zone	*Middle Distance*	*Long Distance*
Maximum	200	200
$\dot{V}O_{2max}$ training	195-200	195-200
Anaerobic training	175-185	170-180
Aerobic training	150-165	140-160

Table 9-1. Estimating the heart rate for training levels

After the limits are set for each type of training, the athlete can easily find the most effective training speeds for steady runs. By running at varied paces on the track and taking the pulse, the runner can find what speed gives a pulse of 150, 160, and so forth. Those speeds will be the training speeds. The theory suggests the following types of training during the base conditioning period:

- $\dot{V}O_{2max}$ training: one session per week
  - ✓ Usually three to five minutes total of fast intervals
  - ✓ Long recoveries (10 to 20 minutes)
  - ✓ Recovery runs at lower aerobic training speed. *Note*: The heart rate should be maintained at this lower level after a race because it speeds the removal of lactic acid from the muscles.
- Anaerobic training: one session per week
  - ✓ Usually 12 to 15 minutes of intervals
  - ✓ Shorter recoveries (four to five minutes)
  - ✓ Recovery runs at lower aerobic training speed

- Aerobic training: five sessions per week
  - ✓ Steady-state running
  - ✓ Three days at the upper limit (such as 160 BPM)
  - ✓ Two days at the lower limit (such as 140 BPM)

Note that these training ideas are still experimental. Many gaps still exist in the knowledge base. Understanding training is like putting together a huge puzzle: the edges are formed, with isolated clusters of knowledge in the open middle. Coaching is still far from a hard science. However, all of the training principles in Chapter 3 hold firm in the face of newer scientific knowledge.

Research under the USOC's Elite Athlete Project in the early 1980s found that the best indicators of fitness changes from training by elite male runners were:

- Percentage of body fat
- Anaerobic threshold
- Blood hemoglobin
- Serum ferritin and haptoglobin6

As a note on the tests for iron, such as the serum ferritin level, male distance runners were anemic nearly as often as women runners were. The iron level is critical to distance runners because of its role in oxygen transport. Though women runners must be especially careful that a proper iron level is maintained, male runners are also vulnerable to depletion. Tests such as the serum ferritin level show a drop in the iron level much sooner than the blood hemoglobin measure, which may give little useful indication until the problem is beyond quick remedy. Runners should be aware that a program of taking iron supplements should include regular blood tests, if possible, because different types of supplements are absorbed at different rates. In some cases, no more than 10 percent of the iron supplement may be absorbed by the body.

Cross Country

Cross country means many things to many people. For this discussion, the primary purpose of the cross country season is to build a cardiovascular base for the spring track season. We consider the big meets in May and June to be the most important of the year.

The cross country season begins after the opening of school, though the first organized practice may be held as soon as early August, depending on the school system's schedule. We begin the program with a "run," not a race. The distance is equal to the racing distance at the end of the season, which (for university competition) is 5 to 6 kilometers for women and 8 to 10 kilometers for men. The male athletes run their distance at a pace of 6 to 7 minutes per mile, aiming for a time of 37 to 43 minutes for 10 km. The women run their distance at a pace of 7 to 8 minutes per mile, aiming for a time of 23 to 26 minutes for 5 km. This pace is submaximal, but it should be a comfortable, successful run for the athlete.

Before the start of the run, each athlete declares a pace. The times are given at the one- and two-mile points to give the runners an idea of how close they are to their paces. If athletes reach a mark in a time much faster than their declared paces, they must stop until their pace times come up on the watch. After the two-mile point, the next time for men is given at four miles, and then times are recorded at five miles. The athletes are allowed to run the last mile as fast as they wish. When the last mile split is calculated, the athlete's pace for interval training is determined. If the last mile was 4:40, the training pace for intervals will be 70 seconds per 400, as in the case of a runner like Prefontaine. If the last mile was 6:00, the pace will be 90 seconds. The pace is changed as the runner improves during the racing season. The training pace usually will be set at an average of the last three times in the cross country runs.

The Oregon cross country pattern is a 14-day cycle based upon years of training patterns. Like any other dynamic training program, it undergoes periodic changes and improvements. The terms used in the training schedule have already been described. The heavy use of fartlek and steady-pace runs is evident. The present system was described by Bill Dellinger, Bowerman's successor at Oregon, coach of four NCAA cross country championship teams and co-coach of Steve Prefontaine (primary coach after Bowerman's retirement), as following the pattern in Table 9-2.

Fourteen-Day Training Pattern

Day		*Training Level*
Sunday	(1)	Steady-pace run
Monday	(2)	Fartlek
Tuesday	(3)	Cutdown intervals; date pace intervals; light fartlek; cutdowns
Wednesday	(4)	Steady-pace run
Thursday	(5)	Hill intervals; light fartlek
Friday	(6)	Light fartlek
Saturday	(7)	Overdistance; simulated race; fartlek
Sunday	(8)	Steady-pace run
Monday	(9)	Fartlek over hills
Tuesday	(10)	Date pace intervals; steady-pace run; cutdowns
Wednesday	(11)	Steady-pace run
Thursday	(12)	Quick; light fartlek; cutdowns
Friday	(13)	Light fartlek
Saturday	(14)	Competition or test effort

Table 9-2. Fourteen-day training schedule

The athletes need to learn to run on hills as well as on the flat. Their posture should still be relatively upright, as on the track, though the slopes cause some leaning. Runners should try not to let the slopes cause them to lean too much, though. When they run uphill or downhill, they should keep their legs a bit bent at the knee to allow for more play in a joint in case of unexpected changes in the ground. When going uphill, they should try not to lean too far forward, which could result in back strain and "stabbing" at the ground with the feet. When running downhill, they should try to avoid leaning back because hitting a wet spot might cause a rough landing on the wrong part of the anatomy. Cross country is the season for developing a base that will help the runner throughout the year.

During the cross country season, the training uses more fartlek and steady-pace running than interval training because the primary object is cardiovascular development. Interval training generally is used only one day a week, usually Tuesdays, and it is run at the date pace, as explained in Chapter 8. The athletes should have a minimum of three weeks of training before they compete in any meets. No more than one meet should be scheduled per week. If the athletes were to race twice a week, they would have a difficult time making any real progress. With such a heavy racing schedule, they would be better off with a bookkeeper than a coach.

The training schedules are included at the end of this chapter. The training dates can be changed to reflect the local season.

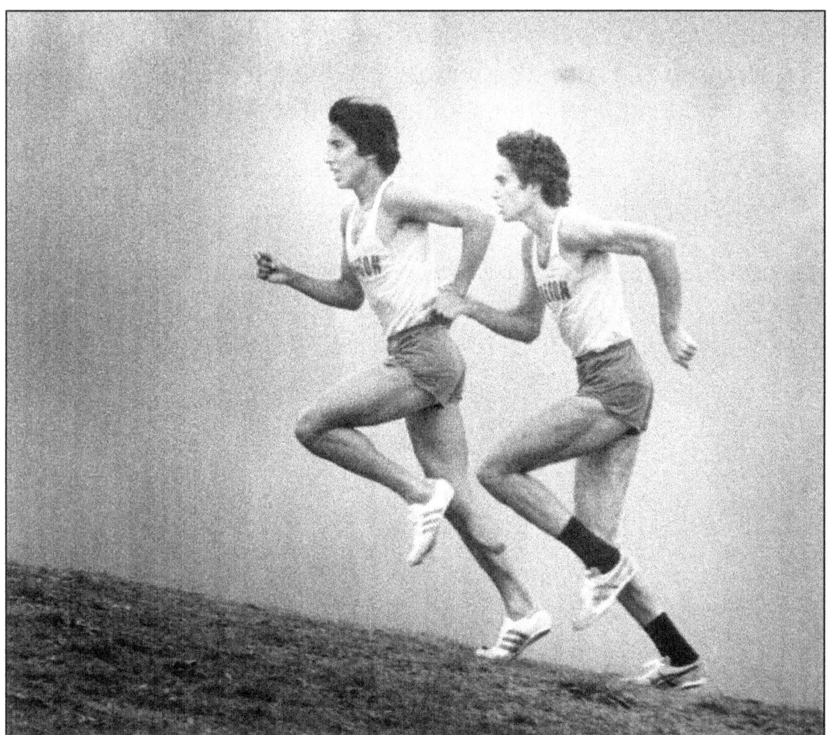

Photo 9-2. Alberto Salazar (U.S. records at 5 km, 10 km; marathon world record) and Rudy Chapa (U.S. record at 3,000m; NCAA champion 5,000m)

Racing Tactics in Cross Country

Cross country is a sport that allows runners to use a variety of tactical maneuvers. Because the terrain varies, the course turns, rises, and falls, and the weather and the opponents affect the racing conditions, successful runners must consider many factors before the race. Some examples of cross country tactics follow.[7]

Check the entire course before the race. Ideally, the athletes should see the course before the day of the race so they do not get exhausted by the warm-up. They should learn what dangers and benefits the course has.

Go for position at the start. In dual meets, this tactic is rarely so important, but in major races, no course is wide enough to allow freedom of movement to slow starters. Some courses turn into narrow trails very soon. Athletes must run fast enough in the first 400m to get into position without risking later oxygen debt. Some long training runs should begin with a fast 400m from a group start, so this skill can be learned.

Surge to get out of heavy traffic. Sometimes, runners must use a faster pace to get ahead of the crowd. They should be careful that the pace does not overextend them, however.

Run against the opponents, not the watch. Because of course conditions, even-pace running may not be possible, as it is in road or track races.

Be ready to take advantage of an opponent's moment of weakness. Some runners slow down at a curve or after reaching the top of a hill. Runners should look for such sudden opportunities to make an effective move.

Photo 9-3. Bill McChesney, 13:14.80 and Olympic athlete for Bill Dellinger

Make a move just after turning a corner or crossing the top of a hill. Making sudden gains in position while out of sight can be unnerving to an opponent.

Float up the hills, then surge on the downhill. This tactic takes less energy, and most people slow down as they top the hill.

Be careful not to slow down too much after a surge. The surging runner may fall too far off the pace and be caught by an opponent.

Think of strength rather than speed at the end of the race. An opponent's superior 400m or mile speed means nothing. No runner is starting fresh at this point. The finishing kick comes down to who has more strength and determination, not who has greater speed.

The Steeplechase

The steeplechase is the real test of an athlete. The training for the steeplechase is basically the same as that for a 3,000 or 5,000m runner. The only real difference involves the hurdling activities. Ideally, the athlete will run a steeplechase about once a month, or hopefully no more often than every two weeks until he gets into a situation where he has to race twice as part of a single meet. Otherwise, running the steeplechase too often can cause the steeplechaser to be "flattened out" from giving too much in his practice and early competitive seasons.

The difference between training for the flat races and for the steeplechase is the hurdle training. Place hurdles and small logs (up to three feet in diameter, lying on their sides) around the track and off-track athletics areas of the campus for the runners to use for informal practice. One principle of training is that

Photo 9-4. Technique over the water jump

every male distance runner does some steeplechase training, whether or not he ever runs a steeplechase in competition. This practice helps the coach discover potential steeplechasers, some of whom might not be inclined to volunteer for such a tough event. The runners practice jumping over the obstacles or stepping on and then over them while running on their own.

Some pace work is done over a distance of 200m on the track over the hurdles. This pace work is done with two arrangements of hurdles. In one case, only two hurdles are used, one set at the end of the first straight and the other at the end of the turn as the second straight begins. In the other case, about five hurdles are run, set 15 to 20 meters apart and included in a 200m run. In both cases, the athlete runs about four intervals while working on his hurdling. He tries to hurdle as a hurdler would. During the early part of the year, the hurdles are set at 30 inches in height; as the training year progresses, the hurdles are raised to the three-foot height of the steeplechase barriers.

The steeplechasers practice over the water jump and barriers once a week. Except during regular competitions, the water jump does not have any water in the pit. The athletes run in a loop, going over the barrier or water jump perhaps four times. Except for this practice situation, they practice with the regular hurdles. The reason for this is simple: You can hit the regular hurdles and they move. The water-jump barrier does not move at all. The other barriers are over 12 feet long and weigh well over 200 pounds (90 kg). They do not move too freely, either. Finally, if an athlete prefers to step on the barriers rather than hurdle over them, he must work on this regularly. The athlete may place a barrier at the edge of the long-jump pit and practice running down the runway and stepping onto and going over the barrier and into the sand.

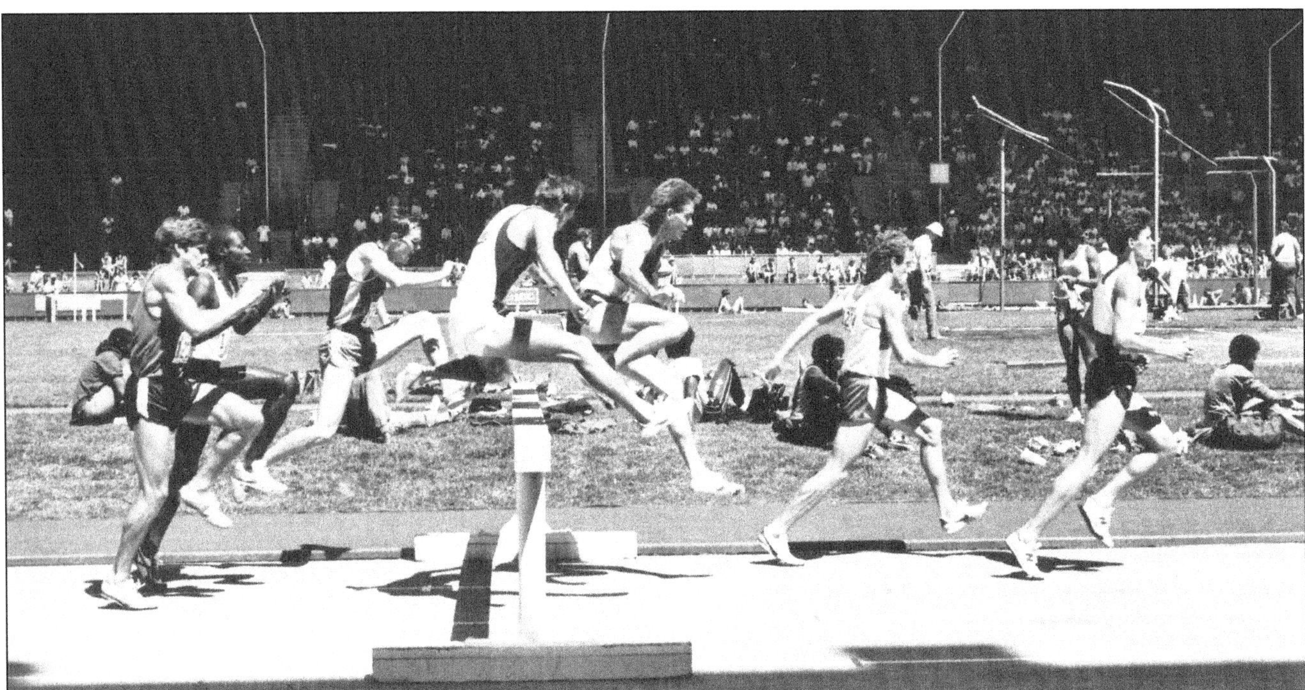

Photo 9-5. Technique over the hurdles

The steeplechaser should not compete too much in his event for it causes a lot of wear and tear. Also, he should not hurdle too much, for it can be hard on the legs.

American steeplechasing would be helped greatly if the race were added to the high school competitive schedule. Unfortunately, few athletes are exposed to steeplechasing before college. A short, 2,000m (five-lap) race is an excellent high school event. When the race is longer than a mile, it begins to highlight the experts. This event can provide pre-college experience to many runners, and it would be one more event for competitors, allowing more participants. The real objective of the entire sport is the joy of competition. The steeplechase training schedules can be found at the end of this chapter.

Steeplechase Racing Tactics

Most distance-running tactics hold true for the steeplechase. However, the hurdles add another dimension to the race: Some runners fall, especially at the first barrier. Athletes should run wide approaching the first hurdle so they have a clear look at where the barrier is. Some runners have run into the barrier, not realizing where it was until the runner ahead of them jumped suddenly. One way to stay safe is to step on the first barrier rather than hurdle it.

At every barrier, it is safer to move out to the side and have a clear view than to follow closely behind a runner, for two reasons. First, the athlete needs to judge exactly where the barrier is so he can time the clearance properly. Second, if the runner ahead falls while clearing the barrier, the trailing runners may fall over him or be injured while trying to avoid stepping on him.

Photo 9-6. Steve Savage, 1972 Olympian, 8:29.6 steepler and 3:59.2 miler, off the hurdle

The steeplechasers should try to get a straight line for the last three or four steps to the water-jump barrier. After the first lap, their feet will be wet and may slip on the barrier if they hit it at an angle. The runner should stride onto the barrier with the heel down so that their foot rolls across the top, and the toe of the shoe (and some spikes) pushes off from the far side of the barrier, propelling him across the water. The runner should not try to clear the water completely because it wastes energy. Some athletes hurdle over the barrier rather than step on it. This procedure can be marginally faster, but it may be more stressful on the legs, and the runner may land in deeper water.

The best way to run the race is to begin cautiously, avoiding getting caught in the crowd or following the early leader's pace, which is often too fast. The runner moves into position after four laps, moving into the front three positions, just as suggested for the middle distances. He finishes strongly over the last one or two laps, but he must be especially careful of the barriers on the last lap. Some runners get carried away with the head-to-head competition and hit a barrier. The steeplechase is an event for the more courageous and determined athletes.

The Long Middle Distances: Two Miles to Ten Kilometers

The training principles and patterns for the longer distance races are the same as those given for the shorter, middle-distance runs. The fall training is usually the cross country training described previously. At the end of the cross country season, in late November, the distance runners switch to training schedules that more specifically apply to their racing distances on the track.

Photo 9-7. Some of Bill Dellinger's best

As in other events, follow the hard-easy principle in planning the athletes' training programs. This area can be dangerous if the coach attempts to overwork the athlete. Runners must not be sent beyond their personal tolerance levels in training. The basic cycle used is one day of hard or heavy training followed by one day of light or easy training. However, this pattern is not universal, as described in Chapter 7. Most male athletes rarely need to cover more than 70 or 80 miles (50 or 60 miles for females) in the longer training weeks of the winter.

Coaches and athletes should not assume that speed is less important for distance runners. A finishing sprint is always a potent weapon, and all highly competitive distance runners are swift at shorter distances. Though he had become an Olympic 5,000m runner, in 1958 Bill Dellinger ran an American record of 3:41.5 for 1500m, equivalent to a 3:59 mile. As a world-class marathoner in the early 1970s, Kenny Moore ran a 4:01 mile.

The tactics of the longer distance runs are essentially the same regardless of the racing distance: find out what the opposition can do, then determine how he or she can be beaten.

The training schedules are given fully at the end of this chapter. They can be adapted by the athlete for almost any racing distance between 1500m and the marathon because the principles and patterns are the same. Only the paces and the quantities differ.

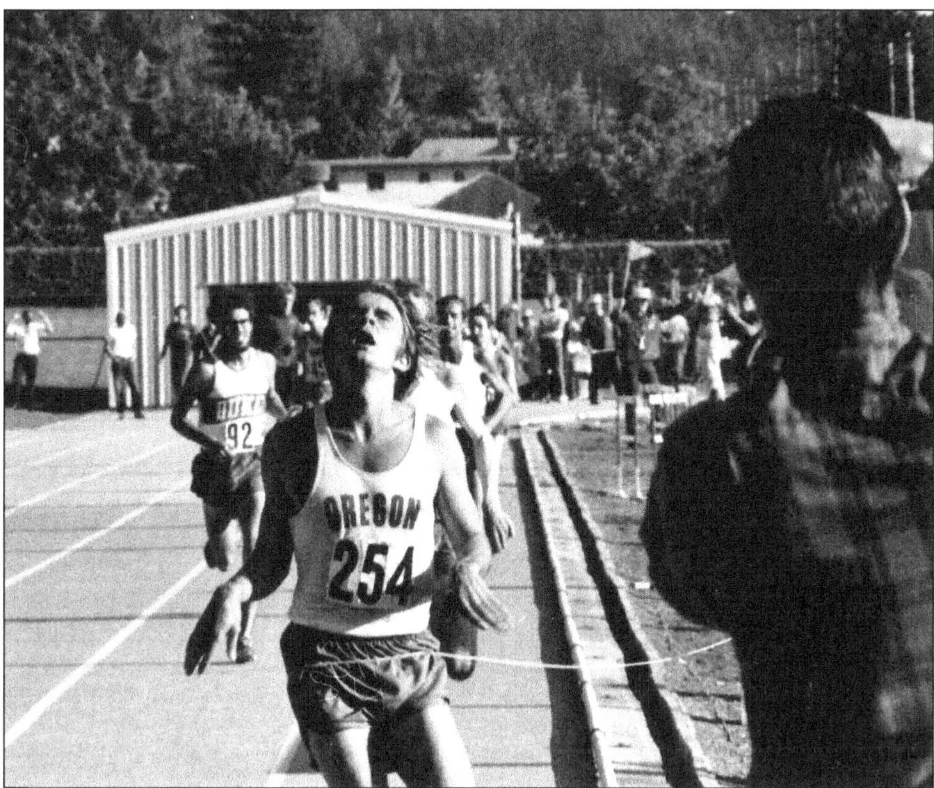

Photo 9-8. Steve Prefontaine winning the 1971 AAU three mile

Training for the Marathon

The marathon is an event for the mature athlete, starting no sooner than their mid-20s. Success at the highest levels requires great talent, just as in the other events. The most influential factors on marathon performance are shown in Table 9-3.[8]

Performance Factors in the Marathon
Physiological Factors
• Slow twitch muscle fiber dominance (genetic)
• Relatively large $\dot{V}O_{2max}$, depending on:
✓Genetic heritage
✓Body weight
✓Heart volume
✓Blood chemistry
• High utilization of the $\dot{V}O_{2max}$
• High level of running economy (limits oxygen consumption)
• Optimal glycogen storage system
• Optimal fluid supply (prevents overheating and dehydration):
✓Quality and quantity are factors
✓Aided by reduced body weight (reduces energy needs)
Training Factors
• Training structures based on:
✓Sufficiently high total volume
✓Principles of periodization and regeneration
• Tempo endurance runs that develop the aerobic capacity (near the anaerobic threshold)
• Sufficiently high volume of single endurance loads (runs of 30 km. or longer):
✓Consolidates aerobic capacity
✓Allows adjustments to overheating and dehydration
✓Assists in development of willpower
• Anaerobic loads adjusted to energy needs of marathon:
✓Short-interval training 1to 2 times per week

Table 9-3. Performance factors in the marathon

Photo 9-9. Pete Mundle in the 1971 AAU Marathon

Photo 9-10. Kenny Moore, 4th in 1972 Olympics, 200m from finish in 1971 AAU Marathon

Cross Country Training Schedules

Cross Country NAME DATE *October*

1. A. Jog 1 to 3 miles
   B. Weights & jog
2. Fartlek A. Varied (1) 30 min. (2) *Light*
   B. Steady (1) 2-4 mi. (2) 4-6 mi. (3) 7-10 mi.
   (4) *3-5 mi.* *(5) Easy run* *(6) 8-15 mi.*
3. Weights
4. High knee and power run
5. Intervals
   A. 110 (1) 18-16-14 (2) 17-15-13
   B. 165 (1) 25 (2) *24-26*
   C. 220 (1) 35 (2)
   D. 330 (1) 52 (2) 48 (3) 45 (4)
   E. 440 (1) 70-73 (2) *72-75* *(3) 62*
   F. 660 (1) 1:45 (2)
   G. 880 (1) 70 (2)
   H. 3/4 (1) 70 (2) *69* *(3) 68* *(4) 66*
   I. Mile (1) 72 (2) 68-70 (3) 64-67 (4)
   J.
   K.
   L.
6. Sets A. 660-440-330-220-110
   (1) 1:45-68-49-32-15 (2)
   B. 440-660-440-220 (1) 63 (2)
   C. 550-165-165 (1) 55 pace (2)
   D.
7. Squad meeting
8. Special A. Sauna B. Swim C.
9. Drills A. Sprint-float-sprint (165)
   B. 1-step acceleration (165)
   C. 40-30 drill (1) 4 laps (2)
   D. 70-90 drill (1) 1-1 (2) 2-1
   (3) 3-1 (4)
   E. Cut-downs (1) 110 (2) 165 (3) 220
   (4) 330 (5) 440 (6) 880 (7) *Mile*
   F. Simulate race drills (1) 1st 220-last 220
   (2) 2½-1½ (3) 10 miles-3/4 drill (4)
   G. 2-4 miles at (1) 80 (2) 75 (3)
10. A. Test B. Trial C. Compete
    (1) 3/4 date pace (2) Over (3) Under
11. Hill interval A. 110 B. 220 C.
12. With coach (A) Bill B. (B) Bill D. (C)
14. A. Wind sprint B. Hurdle drill
    C. Spring and bound D.
15. Finish work
16. Acrobatics or apparatus
17. 3/4 effort
18.
19.
20. Secondary event
21. A. Pictures B. Film

Day	A.M.	P.M.
M	2B(4)	2A(1) - 6x 5A (grass)
T	2B(4)	12-16-20x 5E(2) - 2B(1) - 6x 9E(1)
W	2B(4)-8x 5A	2B(3)
T	2B(4)	16-24x 5B(2) - 1A - 7
F	1A	1A
S		5E(3)-2B(3)-6x 9E(4)
S		2B(5)
M	2B(4)	2B(2)-6x 5A (grass)
T	2B(4)	4x 5H(2 or 3)-3x 9E(7)[72-70-68 or 80-75-70]
W	1A	1A
T	2B(4)	12x 5D (grass)
F	1A	1A
S		12x 5I.(3)-9E(5)[72-70-68]
S		2B(6)
M	2B(5)	2B(5)
T	2B(4)	12x 5D(1)-2B(1)-6x 9E(1)
W	2B(4)	2B(3)
T	2B(4)	16x 9E(2) -2B(5)(grass)
F	1A(grass)	1A(grass)
S		10B (6 miles)
S		2B(6)
M	2B(4)	2B(2)-4x 9E(1)
T	2B(4)	3x 5H(1-3-4)-3x 9E(6)-3x 9E(5)-3x 9E(3)-1A-9E(4)
W	2B(4)-9x 9E(1)	2B(3)
T	2B(4)	12x 5D(grass)
F	1A	1A
S		9F(3)-3x 5A
S		1A

Sheet 9-1. Cross country training schedule sheet

Cross Country NAME DATE *November*

1. A. Jog 1 to 3 miles
   B. Weights & jog
2. Fartlek A. Varied (1) 30 min. (2) *Light*
   B. Steady (1) 2-4 mi. (2) 4-6 mi. (3) 7-10 mi.
   (4) *3-5 mi. (5) Easy run (6) 8-15 mi.*
3. Weights
4. High knee and power run
5. Intervals
   A. 110 (1) 18-16-14 (2) 17-15-13
   B. 165 (1) 25 (2) *21-22*
   C. 220 (1) 35 (2) *27 (3) 30*
   D. 330 (1) 52 (2) 48 (3) 45 (4)
   E. 440 (1) 70-73 (2) *66-68*
   F. 660 (1) 1:45 (2) *1:42*
   G. 880 (1) 70 (2) *68*
   H. 3/4 (1) 70 (2)
   I. Mile (1) 72 (2) 68-70 (3) 64-67 (4)
   J.
   K.
   L.
6. Sets A. 660-440-330-220-110
   (1) 1:45-68-49-32-15 (2)
   B. 440-660-440-220 (1) 63 (2)
   C. 550-165-165 (1) 55 pace (2)
   D.
7. Squad meeting
8. Special A. Sauna B. Swim C.
9. Drills A. Sprint-float-sprint (165)
   B. 1-step acceleration (165)
   C. 40-30 drill (1) 4 laps (2) *6 laps*
   D. 70-90 drill (1) 1-1 (2) 2-1
   (3) 3-1 (4)
   E. Cut-downs (1) 110 (2) 165 (3) 220
   (4) 330 (5) 440 (6) 880 (7)
   F. Simulate race drills (1) 1st 220-last 220
   (2) 2½-1½ (3) 10 miles-3/4 drill (4)
   G. 2-4 miles at (1) 80 (2) 75 (3)
10. A. Test B. Trial C. Compete
    (1) 3/4 date pace (2) Over (3) Under
11. Hill interval A. 110 B. 220 C.
12. With coach (A) Bill B. (B) Bill D. (C)
14. A. Wind sprint B. Hurdle drill
    C. Spring and bound D.
15. Finish work
16. Acrobatics or apparatus
17. 3/4 effort
18.
19.
20. Secondary event
21. A. Pictures B. Film

	A.M.	*P.M.*
M	*1A*	*2B(2)*
T	*2B(4)*	*5H(1)-2x 5G(2)-6x 5D(2)-2A(2)-3x 9E(1)*
W	*2B(4)*	*2A(1)*
T	*1A*	*4x 9E(2)-2A(2)-4x 9E(1)-7*
F	*1A*	*1A*
S		*10C-Northern Division Meet*
S		*2B(6)*
M	*2B(4)*	*2B(4)*
T	*2B(4)*	*9F(3)-9x 9E(4)*
W	*2B(4)*	*2B(2)-9x 9E(1)*
T	*12x 9E(4)*	*2x 5C(2)-2B(2)-6x 5C(1)*
F	*1A*	*1A*
S	*3x 5I(2)-12x 5D*	*2B(2)*
S		*2B(6)*
M	*1A*	*4x 9E(1)*
T	*2B(4)*	*4x 5F(2)-4x 5E(2)-4x 5D(2)-4x 5C(3)-1A*
W	*2B(4)*	*2B(3)*
T	*1A*	*2x 5B(2)-9G(1)-4x 9E(1)*
F		*Travel-light over course*
S		*10C-Pac 8 Meet*
S		*2B(5)*
M		*2B(5) (6 miles)-4x 9E(1)*
T	*2B(2)*	*2-3x 9C(2)-2B(5)-6x 9E(4)*
W	*2B(4)*	*2B(5) (45 min)*
T	*2B(2)*	*8-12x 5D(1-2)-2B(2)-6x 9E(4)*
F		*2B(5)*
S		*Travel*
S	*Jog course*	*Monday=N.C.A.A. Meet*

Sheet 9-2. Cross country training schedule sheet

Steeplechase Training Schedules

STEEPLECHASE NAME ______________________ DATE ______________

1. Warmup: Jog 1-3 mi., stretching
2. Fartlek A. Varied (1) 30 min. (2)
   B. Steady (1) 2-4 mi. (2) 4-6 mi.
   (3) 6-10 mi. (4)
3. Weights and jogging
4. High knee and power run
5. Intervals X. Over hurdles
   A. 100 (1) 18-16-14 (2) 17-15-13
   B. 150 (1) 25 (2)
   C. 200 (1) 35 (2)
   D. 300 (1) 52 (2) 48 (3) 45 (4)
   E. 400 (1) 70-73 (2)
   F. 600 (1) 75 (2) 72 (3) 68 (4)
   G. 800 (1) 72-75 (2) 68-70 (3)
   H. 1200 (1) 72-75 (2) 69-71 (3)
   J. 1600 (1) 72-75 (2) 69-72 (3)
   K.
6. Sets A. 600-400-300-200-100
   (1) 1:45-68-49-32-15 (2)
   B. 400-600-400-200 (1) 64 (2)
   C.
7. TEAM MEETING
8. Special A. Sauna B. Swim C.
9. Drills X. Hurdle X-drill (1) LH (2) IH
   A. 150 sprint-float-sprint
   B. 150 middle 1-step acceleration
   C. 40-30 drill (1) 4 laps (2) 6 laps (3)
   D. 70-90 drill (1) 1-1 (2) 2-1
   (3) 3-1 (4)
   E. Cut-downs (1) 100 (2) 150 (3) 200
   (4) 300 (5) 400 (6) 800 (7)
   F. Simulated race drills (1) 1st 800, last 800
   (2) 10 mile, 1200 drill
   (3)
   G. Last 150 (water jump and hurdle)
   H. Intermediate hurdles (1) 150 (2) 200
   J. 5 km - 4 hurdles
   (1) 90 (2) 85 (3) 80 (4)
   K.
10. A. Meet B. Trial C. Simulation D. Control test
    (1) 3/4 date pace (2) Over (3) Under
11. Hill intervals A. 100 B. 200 C.
12. With Coach A. B.
14. A. Wind sprints (1) Straight (2) Curve
    B. Hurdle (X) drill C. Spring and bound
    D.
15. Plyometrics A. Jumps B. Bounding C.
    (1) 1-leg (2) Both legs (3)
16. Finish work
17. Acrobatics or apparatus
18. 3/4 effort
19.
20. Work on second event
21. A. Videotape B. Film C. Pictures
    (1) Record performance (2) Study
30. Experimental

Date	Distance	3/4 pace	Date Pace	Goal Pace

M
T
W
T
F
S
S
M
T
W
T
F
S
S
M
T
W
T
F
S
S
M
T
W
T
F
S
S

Sheet 9-3. Metric steeplechase training schedule sheet

Steeplechase NAME DATE *December*

1. A. Light jogging B.
2. Fartlek A. Varied (1) 30 min. (2) *40 min.*
   B. Steady (1) 2-4 mi. (2) 4-6 mi. (3) 7-10 mi.
   (4) *8-15 mi.*
3. Weight program
4. High knee and power run
5. Intervals
   A. 110 (1) 18-16-14 (2) 17-15-13
   B. 165 (1) 25 (2)
   C. 220 (1) 35 (2) *27-29*
   D. 330 (1) 52 (2) 48 (3) 45 (4)
   E. 440 (1) 70-73 (2)
   F. 660 (1) 75 (2) 72 (3) 68 (4)
   G. 880 (1) 72-75 (2) 68-70 (3)
   I. 3/4 (1) 72-75 (2) 69-71 (3)
   J. Mile (1) 72-75 (2) 69-72 (3)
   K.
   L.
5. H. Same interval as above with hurdles
6. Sets A. 660-440-330-220-110
   (1) 1:45-68-49-32-15 (2)
   B. 440-660-440-220 (1) 64 (2)
   C.
7. Squad meeting
8. Special A. Sauna B. Swim C.
9. Drills A. Hurdle; X drill (1) 30 in. (2) 36 in.
   B. 165 sprint-float-sprint
   C. 165 middle 1-step accelerate
   D. Last 165 (WJ & hurdle)
   E. Intermediate hurdles (1) 165 (2) 220
   F. 3 mi.-4 hurdles (1) 90 (2) 85 (3) 80 (4)
   G. 40-30 drill (1) 4 laps (2) 6 (3)
   H. 70-90 drill (1) 1-1 (2) 2-1 (3) 3-1 (4)
   I. Cut-downs (1) 110 (2) 165 (3) 220 (4) 330
   (5) 440 (6) 880 (7)
   J. Simulate race drill (1) 1st 880-last 880
   (2) 10 mi.-3/4 drill (3) *2 mi. at 80 pace*
   K.
10. A. Test B. Trial C. Compete
    (1) 3/4 date pace (2) Over (3) Under
11. Hill interval A. 110 B. 220 C.
12. With coach (A) Bill B. (B) Bill D. (C)
14. A. Wind sprint B. Hurdle drill
    C. Spring and bound D.
15. Finish work
16. Acrobatics or apparatus
17. 3/4 effort
18.
19.
20. Secondary event
21. A. Pictures B. Film

Day	
M	*9A-2A(2)-(4X) 9I(1)*
T	*(2) 5F-(6) 5D-2B(2)-(4) 9I(4)*
W	*2B(3)*
T	*(4X) 5BH-9J(3)-5A(1)*
F	*/A*
S	*10B(1)(3 mi.)-2B(2)-(6X) 9I(4)*
S	*2B(4)*
M	*2A(2)*
T	*(12-24) 5D*
W	*2B(3)*
T	*2A(2)*
F	*/A*
S	*2B(3)*
S	*2B(3)*
M	*2A(2)*
T	*(3X) 5I-(3X) 5G-(3) 5E-(6) 5D*
W	*2B(3)-5A(1)*
T	*(4) 5C(2)-2B(2)-5A(1)*
F	*2B(2)*
S	*9G(2)-2B(1)-(6) 5D*
S	*2B(3)*
M	
T	
W	
T	
F	
S	
S	

Sheet 9-4. Steeplechase training schedule sheet

Steeplechase NAME DATE January

1. A. Light jogging B. 45 min.
2. Fartlek A. Varied (1) 30 min. (2)
   B. Steady (1) 2-4 mi. (2) 4-6 mi. (3) 7-10 mi.
   (4) 12-15 mi.
3. Weight program
4. High knee and power run
5. Intervals
   A. 110 (1) 18-16-14 (2) 17-15-13
   B. 165 (1) 25 (2)
   C. 220 (1) 35 (2)
   D. 330 (1) 52 (2) 48 (3) 45 (4)
   E. 440 (1) 70-73 (2)
   F. 660 (1) 75 (2) 72 (3) 68 (4)
   G. 880 (1) 72-75 (2) 68-70 (3)
   I. 3/4 (1) 72-75 (2) 69-71 (3)
   J. Mile (1) 72-75 (2) 69-72 (3)
   K.
   L.
5. H. Same interval as above with hurdles
6. Sets A. 660-440-330-220-110
   (1) 1:45-68-49-32-15 (2)
   B. 440-660-440-220 (1) 64 (2)
   C.
7. Squad meeting
8. Special A. Sauna B. Swim C.
9. Drills A. Hurdle; X drill (1) 30 in. (2) 36 in. (3) Water barrier drill
   B. 165 sprint-float-sprint
   C. 165 middle 1-step accelerate
   D. Last 165 (WJ & hurdle)
   E. Intermediate hurdles (1) 165 (2) 220
   F. 3 mi.-4 hurdles (1) 90 (2) 85 (3) 80 (4)
   G. 40-30 drill (1) 4 laps (2) 6 (3)
   H. 70-90 drill (1) 1-1 (2) 2-1 (3) 3-1 (4)
   I. Cut-downs (1) 110 (2) 165 (3) 220 (4) 330
   (5) 440 (6) 880 (7)
   J. Simulate race drill (1) 1st 880-last 880
   (2) 10 mi.-3/4 drill (3)
   K.
10. A. Test B. Trial C. Compete
    (1) 3/4 date pace (2) Over (3) Under
11. Hill interval A. 110 B. 220 C.
12. With coach (A) Bill B. (B) Bill D. (C)
14. A. Wind sprint B. Hurdle drill
    C. Spring and bound D.
15. Finish work
16. Acrobatics or apparatus
17. 3/4 effort
18.
19.
20. Secondary event
21. A. Pictures B. Film

Day	Workout
M	2A(2)-9A(1)
T	1A-9F(3)-5A(2)
W	7-9A(3)-2B(2)-5A(1)
T	5J-5G-9I(4)-1A (2x, 3x)
F	1A
S	5D(123) (15x)
S	2B(3)
M	2A(2)-9A(1)
T	1A-5HG-5E-1A-9I(4) (4x, 4x)
W	9A(3)-2B(2)-5A(1)
T	5HC-1A-5A(2) (4x)
F	1A
S	5B(1)-2A(1)-5A(1) (16x)
S	2B(3)
M	2A(2)-9H(2)
T	1A-5D-1A-5A(1) (8x)
W	9A(3)-2B(2)-5A(1)
T	9F-5A(1)
F	1A
S	Oregon indoor meet
S	2B(3)
M	
T	
W	
T	
F	
S	
S	

Sheet 9-5. Steeplechase training schedule sheet

Steeplechase NAME DATE February

1. A. Light jogging B.
2. Fartlek A. Varied (1) 30 min. (2) 45 min.
   B. Steady (1) 2-4 mi. (2) 4-6 mi. (3) 7-10 mi.
   (4) 12-15 mi.
3. Weight program
4. High knee and power run
5. Intervals
   A. 110 (1) 18-16-14 (2) 17-15-13
   B. 165 (1) 25 (2)
   C. 220 (1) 35 (2)
   D. 330 (1) 52 (2) 48 (3) 45 (4)
   E. 440 (1) 70-73 (2)
   F. 660 (1) 75 (2) 72 (3) 68 (4)
   G. 880 (1) 72-75 (2) 68-70 (3)
   I. 3/4 (1) 72-75 (2) 69-71 (3)
   J. Mile (1) 72-75 (2) 69-72 (3)
   K.
   L.
5. H. Same interval as above with hurdles
6. Sets A. 660-440-330-220-110
   (1) 1:45-68-49-32-15 (2)
   B. 440-660-440-220 (1) 64 (2)
   C.
7. Squad meeting
8. Special A. Sauna B. Swim C.
9. Drills A. Hurdle; X drill (1) 30 in. (2) 36 in. (3) Water barrier
   B. 165 sprint-float-sprint
   C. 165 middle 1-step accelerate
   D. Last 165 (WJ & hurdle)
   E. Intermediate hurdles (1) 165 (2) 220
   F. 3 mi.–4 hurdles (1) 90 (2) 85 (3) 80 (4)
   G. 40-30 drill (1) 4 laps (2) 6 (3)
   H. 70-90 drill (1) 1-1 (2) 2-1 (3) 3-1 (4)
   I. Cut-downs (1) 110 (2) 165 (3) 220 (4) 330
   (5) 440 (6) 880 (7)
   J. Simulate race drill (1) 1st 880-last 880
   (2) 10 mi.-3/4 drill (3)
   K.
10. A. Test B. Trial C. Compete
    (1) 3/4 date pace (2) Over (3) Under
11. Hill interval A. 110 B. 220 C.
12. With coach (A) Bill B. (B) Bill D. (C)
14. A. Wind sprint B. Hurdle drill
    C. Spring and bound D.
15. Finish work
16. Acrobatics or apparatus
17. 3/4 effort
18. Regular steeplechase course A. Mile B. 880 C. 440
19.
20. Secondary event
21. A. Pictures B. Film

Day	Workout
M	9A – 2A(2)
T	6x 5D – 2B(1) – 6x 9I(1)
W	4x 9A(3) – 2B(3)
T	4x 5HG – 4x 5E – 2B(1) – 6x 9I(4)
F	1A
S	12x 5C – 10A(2) – 6x 9I(1) (6 mile run)
S	2B(4)
M	3x 9E(2) – 2A(2)
T	4x 5D – 4x 5C – 2B(1) – 5A(1)
W	4x 9A(3) – 2B(3)
T	2x 5I – 2x 5HG – 2x 5E – 2B(1) – 4x 9I(1)
F	1A
S	8x 5C – 2B(2) – 6x 9I(4)
S	2B(4)
M	2x 9E(2) – 2A(2)
T	12x 5D – 1A – 4x 9I(1)
W	4x 9A(3) – 2B(2)
T	2x 5C – 9F(3) – 4x 9I(1)
F	1A –
S	18A(72-75) – 18B(70-72) – 18C(64-66) – 2B(1) – 5A
S	2B(4)
M	9A – 2A(2) – 4x 9I(1)
T	6x 5D – 2B(3) – 6x 5D
W	2B(2)
T	6x 9E(1) – 2B(1) – 6x 9I(1)
F	1A – 9A
S	2x 5I – 3x 5G – 4x 9I(5) – 1A – 4x 9I(3)
S	2B(4)

Sheet 9-6. Steeplechase training schedule sheet

Steeplechase NAME DATE March

1. A. Light jogging B. 45 min.
2. Fartlek A. Varied (1) 30 min. (2)
   B. Steady (1) 2-4 mi. (2) 4-6 mi. (3) 7-10 mi.
   (4) 12-15 mi.
3. Weight program
4. High knee and power run
5. Intervals
   A. 110 (1) 18-16-14 (2) 17-15-13
   B. 165 (1) 25 (2)
   C. 220 (1) 35 (2)
   D. 330 (1) 52 (2) 48 (3) 45 (4)
   E. 440 (1) 70-73 (2)
   F. 660 (1) 75 (2) 72 (3) 68 (4)
   G. 880 (1) 72-75 (2) 68-70 (3)
   I. 3/4 (1) 72-75 (2) 69-71 (3)
   J. Mile (1) 72-75 (2) 69-72 (3)
   K.
   L.
5. H. Same interval as above with hurdles
6. Sets A. 660-440-330-220-110
   (1) 1:45-68-49-32-15 (2)
   B. 440-660-440-220 (1) 64 (2)
   C. 300-220-110
7. Squad meeting
8. Special A. Sauna B. Swim C.
9. Drills A. Hurdle; X drill (1) 30 in. (2) 36 in. (3) Water barrier
   B. 165 sprint-float-sprint
   C. 165 middle 1-step accelerate
   D. Last 165 (WJ & hurdle)
   E. Intermediate hurdles (1) 165 (2) 220
   F. 3 mi.-4 hurdles (1) 90 (2) 85 (3) 80 (4)
   G. 40-30 drill (1) 4 laps (2) 6 (3)
   H. 70-90 drill (1) 1-1 (2) 2-1 (3) 3-1 (4)
   I. Cut-downs (1) 110 (2) 165 (3) 220 (4) 330
   (5) 440 (6) 880 (7)
   J. Simulate race drill (1) 1st 880-last 880
   (2) 10 mi.-3/4 drill (3)
   K.
10. A. Test B. Trial C. Compete
    (1) 3/4 date pace (2) Over (3) Under
11. Hill interval A. 110 B. 220 C.
12. With coach (A) Bill B. (B) Bill D. (C)
14. A. Wind sprint B. Hurdle drill
    C. Spring and bound D.
15. Finish work
16. Acrobatics or apparatus
17. 3/4 effort
18. Regular steeplechase course D. 3/4 mi.
19.
20. Secondary event
21. A. Pictures B. Film

Day	Workout
M	2A(2)
T	4x 4x 4x 5E-5HD-2B(1)-9I(3)
W	2B(2)
T	6C-2B(1)-6C
F	1A
S	4x 10B(Mile)-1A-9I(4)
S	2B(3)
M	2A(2)
T	6x 6x 5D-2B(1)-9I(3)
W	2B(2)
T	2x 4x 4x 18D(72)-5G-5E-1A-9I(1)
F	1A
S	6x 5G-2B(2)-9I(4)
S	2B(3)
M	9A-2A(2)
T	4x 4x 6x 5D-5HD-1A-9I(3)
W	2A(4)
T	4x 4x 5C-2B(1)-9I(1)
F	1A
S	10C-Fresno
S	2B(4)
M	3x 3x 2x 2x 2x 5HD-5D-2B(1)-5D-5C-9D
T	2B(2)
W	2A(1)
T	5F-5D-5A-1A-5A(2)
F	1A
S	10C
S	2B(4)

Sheet 9-7. Steeplechase training schedule sheet

Steeplechase NAME DATE April

1. A. Light jogging B.
2. Fartlek A. Varied (1) 30 min. (2) 45 min.
   B. Steady (1) 2-4 mi. (2) 4-6 mi. (3) 7-10 mi.
   (4) 12-15 mi.
3. Weight program
4. High knee and power run
5. Intervals
   A. 110 (1) 18-16-14 (2) 17-15-13
   B. 165 (1) 25 (2)
   C. 220 (1) 35 (2)
   D. 330 (1) 52 (2) 48 (3) 45 (4)
   E. 440 (1) 70-73 (2)
   F. 660 (1) 75 (2) 72 (3) 68 (4)
   G. 880 (1) 72-75 (2) 68-70 (3)
   I. 3/4 (1) 72-75 (2) 69-71 (3)
   J. Mile (1) 72-75 (2) 69-72 (3)
   K.
   L.
5. H. Same interval as above with hurdles
6. Sets A. 660-440-330-220-110
   (1) 1:45-68-49-32-15 (2)
   B. 440-660-440-220 (1) 64 (2) 62
   C. 660-330-110 D. 330-220-110
7. Squad meeting
8. Special A. Sauna B. Swim C.
9. Drills A. Hurdle; X drill (1) 30 in. (2) 36 in. (3) Water barrier
   B. 165 sprint-float-sprint
   C. 165 middle 1-step accelerate
   D. Last 165 (WJ & hurdle) (1) 220
   E. Intermediate hurdles (1) 165 (2) 220 (3) 440
   F. 3 mi.-4 hurdles (1) 90 (2) 85 (3) 80 (4)
   G. 40-30 drill (1) 4 laps (2) 6 (3)
   H. 70-90 drill (1) 1-1 (2) 2-1 (3) 3-1 (4)
   I. Cut-downs (1) 110 (2) 165 (3) 220 (4) 330
   (5) 440 (6) 880 (7)
   J. Simulate race drill (1) 1st 880-last 880
   (2) 10 mi.-3/4 drill (3) 4 mi. at 80 pace
   K.
10. A. Test B. Trial C. Compete
    (1) 3/4 date pace (2) Over (3) Under
11. Hill interval A. 110 B. 220 C.
12. With coach (A) Bill B. (B) Bill D. (C)
14. A. Wind sprint B. Hurdle drill
    C. Spring and bound D.
15. Finish work
16. Acrobatics or apparatus
17. 3/4 effort
18. Regular steeplechase course A. 3/4 mi.
19.
20. Secondary event
21. A. Pictures B. Film

Day	Workout
M	2A(2)
T	6B(2)
W	2B(2)
T	2x 2x 2x 2x 5I-5HG-5E-9D(1)
F	1A
S	6x 9E(3)-2B(3)-9I(3)
S	2B(3)
M	2A(2)
T	2x 3x 3x 18A-5G-9I(5)-1A-9E(2)
W	7-2B(2)
T	6C-1A-6D
F	1A
S	10C
S	2B(4)
M	9A-2A(2)
T	3x 3x 3x 5HD-9I(6)-2B(1)-5HD
W	4x 2B(2)-9I(1)
T	9J(3)-9D(1)-9D-5A
F	2B(1)-5A(2)
S	1A
S	10C-Twilight meet
M	2B(3)
T	2x 4x 2x 2x 5HG-9I(5)-2B(1)-9D(1)-9C
W	2B(2)
T	2x 2x 2x 2x 5D-5C-5A-2B(1)-5A
F	1A
S	10C-Washington
S	2B(3)

Sheet 9-8. Steeplechase training schedule sheet

Steeplechase NAME DATE *May*

1. A. Light jogging B. *1-3 miles*
2. Fartlek A. Varied (1) 30 min. (2) *45 min.*
   B. Steady (1) 2-4 mi. (2) 4-6 mi. (3) 7-10 mi.
   (4) *12-15 mi.* *(5) 8-12 mi easy*
3. Weight program
4. High knee and power run
5. Intervals
   A. 110 (1) 18-16-14 (2) 17-15-13
   B. 165 (1) 25 (2)
   C. 220 (1) 35 (2) *32*
   D. 330 (1) 52 (2) 48 (3) 45 (4) *46*
   E. 440 (1) 70-73 (2) *62 (3) hurdles in 68*
   F. 660 (1) 75 (2) 72 (3) 68 (4)
   G. 880 (1) 72-75 (2) 68-70 (3) *64 (4) hurdles in 70*
   I. 3/4 (1) 72-75 (2) 69-71 (3)
   J. Mile (1) 72-75 (2) 69-72 (3)
   K.
   L.
5. H. Same interval as above with hurdles
6. Sets A. 660-440-330-220-110
   (1) 1:45-68-49-32-15 (2)
   B. 440-660-440-220 (1) 64 (2)
   C.
7. Squad meeting
8. Special A. Sauna B. Swim C.
9. Drills A. Hurdle; X drill (1) 30 in. (2) 36 in. *(3) Water barrier*
   B. 165 sprint-float-sprint
   C. 165 middle 1-step accelerate
   D. Last 165 (WJ & hurdle) *(1) 220*
   E. Intermediate hurdles (1) 165 (2) 220
   F. 3 mi.-4 hurdles (1) 90 (2) 85 (3) 80 (4)
   G. 40-30 drill (1) 4 laps (2) 6 (3)
   H. 70-90 drill (1) 1-1 (2) 2-1 (3) 3-1 (4)
   I. Cut-downs (1) 110 (2) 165 (3) 220 (4) 330
   (5) 440 (6) 880 (7)
   J. Simulate race drill (1) 1st 880-last 880
   (2) 10 mi.-3/4 drill (3)
   K. *Pace over 4 hurdles per 440*
10. A. Test B. Trial C. Compete
    (1) 3/4 date pace (2) Over (3) Under
11. Hill interval A. 110 B. 220 C.
12. With coach (A) Bill B. (B) Bill D. (C)
14. A. Wind sprint B. Hurdle drill
    C. Spring and bound D.
15. Finish work
16. Acrobatics or apparatus
17. 3/4 effort
18. *Regular steeplechase course*
19.
20. Secondary event
21. A. Pictures B. Film

M	*2A(2)*
T	*3X 9I(6) – 3X 9I(5) – 3X 9I(3) – 2B(1) – 3X 9I(3)*
W	*2B(2)*
T	*2X 9E(2) – 2B(1) – 2X 9D(1)*
F	*1A*
S	*Mile trial*
S	*2B(3)*

M	*2A(2)*
T	*5G(3) – 9K(880 in 2:20) 5G(3) – 5D(4) – 9K(330 in 57) – 5D(4) – 2A*
W	*2B(2)*
T	*6X 5C(2) – 2B(1) 2X 5C (water barrier + 1 hurdle)*
F	*Light*
S	*10C – Northern Division meet*
S	*2B(5)*

	A.M.	*P.M.*
M	*2B(1)*	*2A(2)*
T	*Light*	*9K(880 in 2:20) – 3X 9I(5)(66-64-62) – 1A – 3X 9I(4)(49-47-45)*
W	*Light*	*2X 9(3) – 1A*
T	*Travel*	*Light grass*
F		*10C – Pac 8 Meet*
S		*Light grass – 8X 5A*
S		*2B(5)*

M	*2B(1)*	*2A(2)*
T	*2B(1)*	*6X 5E(2) – 2A(1) – 6X 9I(4)*
W	*2B(1)*	*2B(2)*
T	*Light*	*4X 5G(3-4) – 4X 5E(2-3) – 4X 9I(3)(33-31-29-27)*
F	*Light*	*Light*
S		*3X 9I(4)(hurdles in 52-50-48) – 2B(3) – 3X 9I(4)(48-45-42)*
S		

Sheet 9-9. Steeplechase training schedule sheet

Steeplechase NAME DATE June

1. A. Light jogging B.
2. Fartlek A. Varied (1) 30 min. (2)
   B. Steady (1) 2-4 mi. (2) 4-6 mi. (3) 7-10 mi.
   (4)
3. Weight program
4. High knee and power run
5. Intervals
   A. 110 (1) 18-16-14 (2) 17-15-13
   B. 165 (1) 25 (2)
   C. 220 (1) 35 (2) 27
   D. 330 (1) 52 (2) 48 (3) 45 (4) 51 over hurdles
   E. 440 (1) 70-73 (2)
   F. 660 (1) 75 (2) 72 (3) 68 (4)
   G. 880 (1) 72-75 (2) 68-70 (3)
   I. 3/4 (1) 72-75 (2) 69-71 (3)
   J. Mile (1) 72-75 (2) 69-72 (3)
   K.
   L.
5. H. Same interval as above with hurdles
6. Sets A. 660-440-330-220-110
   (1) 1:45-68-49-32-15 (2)
   B. 440-660-440-220 (1) 64 (2)
   C.
7. Squad meeting
8. Special A. Sauna B. Swim C.
9. Drills A. Hurdle; X drill (1) 30 in. (2) 36 in.
   B. 165 sprint-float-sprint
   C. 165 middle 1-step accelerate
   D. Last 165 (WJ & hurdle)
   E. Intermediate hurdles (1) 165 (2) 220
   F. 3 mi.-4 hurdles (1) 90 (2) 85 (3) 80 (4)
   G. 40-30 drill (1) 4 laps (2) 6 (3)
   H. 70-90 drill (1) 1-1 (2) 2-1 (3) 3-1 (4)
   I. Cut-downs (1) 110 (2) 165 (3) 220 (4) 330
   (5) 440 (6) 880 (7)
   J. Simulate race drill (1) 1st 880-last 880
   (2) 10 mi.-3/4 drill (3) 6 laps – 80 sec. pace
   K.
10. A. Test B. Trial C. Compete
    (1) 3/4 date pace (2) Over (3) Under
11. Hill interval A. 110 B. 220 C.
12. With coach (A) Bill B. (B) Bill D. (C)
14. A. Wind sprint B. Hurdle drill
    C. Spring and bound D.
15. Finish work
16. Acrobatics or apparatus
17. 3/4 effort
18.
19.
20. Secondary event
21. A. Pictures B. Film

M Light	Light grass – 5A(2)
T Light	5D(4) – 2x 5C(2) – 9J(3)
W Light	1A
T	10C – Trials – NCAA meet
F	1A
S	10C – Finals – NCAA meet
S	
M	
T	
W	
T	
F	
S	
S	
M	
T	
W	
T	
F	
S	
S	
M	
T	
W	
T	
F	
S	
S	

Sheet 9-10. Steeplechase training schedule sheet

Distance Training Schedules

Middle Distances NAME DATE *November*

1. A. Jog 1 to 3 miles
   B. Weights & jog
2. Fartlek A. Varied (1) 30 min. (2) *45 min.*
   B. Steady (1) 2-4 mi. (2) 4-6 mi. (3) 7-10 mi.
   (4) *8-12 mi.*
3. Weights
4. High knee and power run
5. Intervals
   A. 110 (1) 18-16-14 (2) 17-*16-15-14*
   B. 165 (1) 25 (2)
   C. 220 (1) 35 (2) *28 (3) 27*
   D. 330 (1) 52 (2) 48 (3) 45 (4) *42*
   E. 440 (1) 70-73 (2)
   F. 660 (1) 1:45 (2) *1:39*
   G. 880 (1) 70 (2)
   H. 3/4 (1) 70 (2)
   I. Mile (1) 72 (2) 68-70 (3) 64-67 (4)
   J.
   K.
   L.
6. Sets A. 660-440-330-220-110
   (1) 1:45-68-49-32-15 (2)
   B. 440-660-440-220 (1) 63 (2)
   C. 550-165-165 (1) 55 pace (2)
   D.
7. Squad meeting
8. Special A. Sauna B. Swim C.
9. Drills A. Sprint-float-sprint (165)
   B. 1-step acceleration (165)
   C. 40-30 drill (1) 4 laps (2)
   D. 70-90 drill (1) 1-1 (2) 2-1
   (3) 3-1 (4)
   E. Cut-downs (1) 110 (2) 165 (3) 220
   (4) 330 (5) 440 (6) 880 (7) *3/4 effort (8) Mile*
   F. Simulate race drills (1) 1st 220-last 220
   (2) 2½-1½ (3) 10 miles-3/4 drill (4)
   G. 2-4 miles at (1) 80 (2) 75 (3)
10. A. Test B. Trial C. Compete
    (1) 3/4 date pace (2) Over (3) Under
11. Hill interval A. 110 B. 220 C.
12. With coach (A) Bill B. (B) Bill D. (C)
14. A. Wind sprint B. Hurdle drill
    C. Spring and bound D.
15. Finish work
16. Acrobatics or apparatus
17. 3/4 effort *A. 3 miles on date pace*
18.
19.
20. Secondary event
21. A. Pictures B. Film

	A.M.	*P.M.*
M	*1A*	*2B(2)-5A(2)*
T	*2B(2)*	*8-12x 5D(on hill)-2B(1)*
W	*2B(1)*	*2A(2)*
T	*1A*	*3x 9E(7)(67-66-64)-3x 9E(8)(75-70-68 or 69)-6x 9E(4)-7*
F	*1A*	*1A (grass)*
S		*6x 5D(on hill)-2B(2)-6x 5D (track)*
S		*Easy run*
M		*Light-5A(2)*
T	*2B(1)*	*2x 5F(1)-2x 5F(2)-2x 5F(1)-2x 5D(1-2)-2x 5D(3-4)-2x 5D(2)-2B(1)*
W	*2B(2)*	*2B(3)*
T	*Easy*	*2x 5C(2)-9G(1) (sawdust)-5A(2)*
F	*Light*	*Light*
S		*10B(17A)-2B(2)-6x 9E(4)*
S		*Easy run*
M		*2A(1)-5A(2)*
T	*2B(1)*	*9C(1)-880 rest-9C(1)-880 rest-9C(1)-1A-6x 9E(4)*
W	*2B(1)*	*2B(3)*
T	*2B(2)*	*2x 5C(3)-2B(2)-5A(2)*
F	*Light*	*Light*
S		*16-24x 5D(1-2) (sawdust)*
S		*Easy-long*
M		*2A(1)-5A(2)*
T		*2B(3)*
W		*2A(2)*
T		*Light run-Thanksgiving*
F		*2B(4)*
S		*12-24x 5D(50-52)*
S		*Easy running*

Sheet 9-11. Distance training schedule sheet

Middle Distances NAME DATE December

1. A. Jog 1 to 3 miles
   B. Weights & jog
2. Fartlek A. Varied (1) 30 min. (2) 45 min.
   B. Steady (1) 2-4 mi. (2) 4-6 mi. (3) 7-10 mi.
   (4) 12-15 mi. (5) 8-12 mi.
3. Weights
4. High knee and power run
5. Intervals
   A. 110 (1) 18-16-14 (2) 16-15-14
   B. 165 (1) 25 (2)
   C. 220 (1) 35 (2) 27-28
   D. 330 (1) 52 (2) 48 (3) 45 (4)
   E. 440 (1) 70-73 (2)
   F. 660 (1) 1:45 (2)
   G. 880 (1) 70 (2)
   H. 3/4 (1) 70 (2)
   I. Mile (1) 72 (2) 68-70 (3) 64-67 (4)
   J. 4 miles (1) 6:30-7:00
   K.
   L.
6. Sets A. 660-440-330-220-110
   (1) 1:45-68-49-32-15 (2)
   B. 440-660-440-220 (1) 63 (2)
   C. 550-165-165 (1) 55 pace (2)
   D.
7. Squad meeting
8. Special A. Sauna B. Swim C.
9. Drills A. Sprint-float-sprint (165)
   B. 1-step acceleration (165)
   C. 40-30 drill (1) 4 laps (2) 6-12 laps
   D. 70-90 drill (1) 1-1 (2) 2-1
   (3) 3-1 (4)
   E. Cut-downs (1) 110 (2) 165 (3) 220
   (4) 330 (5) 440 (6) 880 (7)
   F. Simulate race drills (1) 1st 220-last 220
   (2) 2½-1½ (3) 10 miles-3/4 drill (4)
   G. 2-4 miles at (1) 80 (2) 75 (3)
10. A. Test B. Trial C. Compete
    (1) 3/4 date pace (2) Over (3) Under
11. Hill interval A. 110 B. 220 C.
12. With coach (A) Bill B. (B) Bill D. (C)
14. A. Wind sprint B. Hurdle drill
    C. Spring and bound D.
15. Finish work
16. Acrobatics or apparatus
17. 3/4 effort A. 3 miles at 70 $\pm$ 1 sec.
18.
19.
20. Secondary event
21. A. Pictures B. Film

	A.M.	P.M.
M	2B(2)	2A(2)
T	2B(2)	3x 9D-5J(1)-9E(4)(52-49-46)
W	2B(2)	2B(3)(6:30-7:00 pace)
T	2B(2)	6x 6x 6x 2A(2)(include 5G-5E-5B)
F	2B(2)	2B(2)
S		3x 4x 9F(3)(5H)-9E(4)-2B(2)
S		2B(4)
M	2B(2)	2A(2)
T	2B(1)	6x 6x 5D(2)-2B(3)-9E(4)
W	2B(2)	2B(3)(easy)
T	2B(1)	2x 5C(2)-2A(1)-5A(2)
F	Light	Light grass
S		6x 10B(17A)-2B(2)-9E(4)
S		2B(4)
M	2B(1)	2A(2)
T	2B(2)	12-24x 5D(1-2)
W	2B(1)	2B(3)
T	2B(2)	4x 4x 4x 4x 2A(2)(include 5G-5E-5C-5A)
F	2B(1)	Light run
S		2B(5)
S		2B(5)(Light)
M	2B(1)	2A(2)
T	2B(2)	3x 3x 3x 6x 5H-5G-5E-5C
W	2B(1)	2B(5)-5A(2)
T	2B(2)	4x 5C(1)-2A(1)-5A(2)
F	2B(2)	Light run (30-40 min.)
S		2B(5)
S		6x 9C(2)-2B(1)-9E(4)

Sheet 9-12. Distance training schedule sheet

Middle Distances NAME DATE January

1. A. Jog 1 to 3 miles
   B. Weights & jog
2. Fartlek A. Varied (1) 30 min. (2) 45 min.
   B. Steady (1) 2-4 mi. (2) 4-6 mi. (3) 7-10 mi.
   (4) 12-15 mi.
3. Weights
4. High knee and power run
5. Intervals
   A. 110 (1) 18-16-14 (2) 17-16-15-14
   B. 165 (1) 25 (2) 24
   C. 220 (1) 35 (2) 29
   D. 330 (1) 52 (2) 48 (3) 45 (4) 54 (5) 50
   E. 440 (1) 70-73 (2) 68
   F. 660 (1) 1:45 (2)
   G. 880 (1) 70 (2)
   H. 3/4 (1) 70 (2)
   I. Mile (1) 72 (2) 68-70 (3) 64-67 (4)
   J.
   K.
   L.
6. Sets A. 660-440-330-220-110
   (1) 1:45-68-49-32-15 (2)
   B. 440-660-440-220 (1) 63 (2)
   C. 550-165-165 (1) 55 pace (2)
   D.
7. Squad meeting
8. Special A. Sauna B. Swim C.
9. Drills A. Sprint-float-sprint (165)
   B. 1-step acceleration (165)
   C. 40-30 drill (1) 4 laps (2)
   D. 70-90 drill (1) 1-1 (2) 2-1
   (3) 3-1 (4)
   E. Cut-downs (1) 110 (2) 165 (3) 220
   (4) 330 (5) 440 (6) 880 (7) Mile (8) 1320
   F. Simulate race drills (1) 1st 220-last 220
   (2) 2½-1½ (3) 10 miles-3/4 drill (4)
   G. 2-4 miles at (1) 80 (2) 75 (3)
10. A. Test B. Trial C. Compete
    (1) 3/4 date pace (2) Over (3) Under
11. Hill interval A. 110 B. 220 C.
12. With coach (A) Bill B. (B) Bill D. (C)
14. A. Wind sprint B. Hurdle drill
    C. Spring and bound D.
15. Finish work
16. Acrobatics or apparatus
17. 3/4 effort
18.
19.
20. Secondary event
21. A. Pictures B. Film

	A.M.	P.M.
M		2A(2)
T	2B(2)	15x 5E(2)-2B(2)-6x 9E(4)
W	2B(2)-5A(2)	2B(2)
T	2B(2)	4x 5D(3)-2A(1)-7
F	2B(2)	2B(1)
S		9D(4)-2 (light)
S		2B(4)
M	2B(2)	2A(2)
T	2B(2)	1A-8F(1)-5A(1)
W	2B(1)	7-2B(2)
T	2B(2)	5I(3)-9G(1)-1x 9E(7) (80-75-70-65)
F	1A	1A
S		12x 5D(1-2)-2B(2)-5A(2)
S		2B(4)
M		2A(2)
T	2B(2)	8x 5D(1-2)-2B(2)-5A(2)
W	2B(2)	2A(2)
T	2B(2)	4x 9E(8)(72-70-68-66)-3x 9E(7)(75-72-68)-1A
F	1A	1A
S		22x 5B(2)-9G(1)-5A(2)
S		2B(4)
M		2A(2)
T	2B(2)	6x 5D(4)-6x 5D(5-1)-6x 5D(2-5)-1A-5A(2)
W	2B(1)	2 (easy - 1 hour)
T	2B(1)	2x 5C(2)-9G(1)-6x 9E(4)(2x 52-50-2x 48-46)
F	1A	1A
S		10C - Portland Indoor
S		

Sheet 9-13. Distance training schedule sheet

Middle Distances NAME DATE February

1. A. Jog 1 to 3 miles
   B. Weights & jog
2. Fartlek A. Varied (1) 30 min. (2) 45 min.
   B. Steady (1) 2-4 mi. (2) 4-6 mi. (3) 7-10 mi.
   (4) 12-15 mi. easy
3. Weights
4. High knee and power run
5. Intervals
   A. 110 (1) 18-16-14 (2) 17-16-15-14
   B. 165 (1) 25 (2)
   C. 220 (1) 35 (2) 30 (3) 32-34 (4) 27-28
   D. 330 (1) 52 (2) 48 (3) 45 (4)
   E. 440 (1) 70-73 (2) 68 (3) 62
   F. 660 (1) 1:45 (2)
   G. 880 (1) 70 (2) 62-64
   H. 3/4 (1) 70 (2)
   I. Mile (1) 72 (2) 68-70 (3) 64-67 (4) 63
   J. 6 miles (1) 6 min./mile
   K.
   L.
6. Sets A. 660-440-330-220-110
   (1) 1:45-68-49-32-15 (2)
   B. 440-660-440-220 (1) 63 (2)
   C. 550-165-165 (1) 55 pace (2)
   D.
7. Squad meeting
8. Special A. Sauna B. Swim C.
9. Drills A. Sprint-float-sprint (165)
   B. 1-step acceleration (165)
   C. 40-30 drill (1) 4 laps (2)
   D. 70-90 drill (1) 1-1 (2) 2-1
   (3) 3-1 (4)
   E. Cut-downs (1) 110 (2) 165 (3) 220
   (4) 330 (5) 440 (6) 880 (7)
   F. Simulate race drills (1) 1st 220-last 220
   (2) 2½-1½ (3) 10 miles-3/4 drill (4)
   G. 2-4 miles at (1) 80 (2) 75 (3)
10. A. Test B. Trial C. Compete
    (1) 3/4 date pace (2) Over (3) Under
11. Hill interval A. 110 B. 220 C.
12. With coach (A) Bill B. (B) Bill D. (C)
14. A. Wind sprint B. Hurdle drill
    C. Spring and bound D.
15. Finish work
16. Acrobatics or apparatus
17. 3/4 effort
18.
19.
20. Secondary event
21. A. Pictures B. Film

Day	Workout
M	2A(1-2) (light)
T 2B(2)	6x 6x 5D(4)-2B(2)-9E(1)
W 2B(2)	2B(3)
T 2B(1)	4x 8x 5G(2)-1A(light)-9E(4)(50-48-46-44)
F 1A	1A
S	8x 6x 5C(2)-2B(2)-9E(1)
S	2B(4)
M	2A(2)
T 2B(2)	6x 5E(2)-5J(1)-5A(2)
W 1A	2B(2)
T 2B(2)	3-4x 5H(1)-2B(1)
F 2B(1)	2B(1)
S	12-20x 5C(3)-1A
S	2B(4)
M 2B(1)	2A(2)
T 2B(2)	4x 8x 5E(3)-5E(2)-2B(1)
W 2B(2)	2B(3)
T 2B(2)	2x 6x 5C(4)-2B(2)-9E(1)
F 2B(2)	1A
S	6x 5I(4)-9G(1)-9E(4) 2B(4)
S	2B(4)
M	2A(2)
T 2B(2)	6x 6x 5D(4)-2B(2)-9E(1)
W 2B(2)	2B(3)
T 2B(2)	3-4x 5H(1)-2B(1)
F 2B(2)	2B(1)
S	16x 5D-1A
S	2B(4)

Sheet 9-14. Distance training schedule sheet

Middle Distances NAME DATE March

1. A. Jog 1 to 3 miles
   B. Weights & jog
2. Fartlek A. Varied (1) 30 min. (2) 45 min.
   B. Steady (1) 2-4 mi. (2) 4-6 mi. (3) 7-10 mi.
   (4) 12-15 mi. easy (5) 8-12 mi.
3. Weights
4. High knee and power run
5. Intervals
   A. 110 (1) 18-16-14 (2) 17-16-15-14
   B. 165 (1) 25 (2)
   C. 220 (1) 35 (2) 32-34 (3) 27
   D. 330 (1) 52 (2) 48 (3) 45 (4) 46-47
   E. 440 (1) 70-73 (2) 68
   F. 660 (1) 1:45 (2)
   G. 880 (1) 70 (2)
   H. 3/4 (1) 70 (2)
   I. Mile (1) 72 (2) 68-70 (3) 64-67 (4)
   J.
   K.
   L.
6. Sets A. 660-440-330-220-110
   (1) 1:45-68-49-32-15 (2)
   B. 440-660-440-220 (1) 63
   C. 550-165-165 (1) 55 pace (2)
   D.
7. Squad meeting
8. Special A. Sauna B. Swim C.
9. Drills A. Sprint-float-sprint (165)
   B. 1-step acceleration (165)
   C. 40-30 drill (1) 4 laps (2)
   D. 70-90 drill (1) 1-1 (2) 2-1
   (3) 3-1 (4) 2-2
   E. Cut-downs (1) 110 (2) 165 (3) 220
   (4) 330 (5) 440 (6) 880 (7)
   F. Simulate race drills (1) 1st 220-last 220
   (2) 2½-1½ (3) 10 miles-3/4 drill (4)
   G. 2-4 miles at (1) 80 (2) 75 (3)
10. A. Test B. Trial C. Compete
    (1) 3/4 date pace (2) Over (3) Under
11. Hill interval A. 110 B. 220 C.
12. With coach (A) Bill B. (B) Bill D. (C)
14. A. Wind sprint B. Hurdle drill
    C. Spring and bound D.
15. Finish work
16. Acrobatics or apparatus
17. 3/4 effort
18.
19.
20. Secondary event
21. A. Pictures B. Film

Day	A.M.	P.M.
M	/A	2A(2)
T	2B(2)	6x 5E(2)-9G(1)-5A(2)
W	2B(2)	2B(2)
T	2B(2)	3-4x 5H(1)-2B(1)
F	/A	2B(1)
S		12-20x 5C(2)
S		2B(4)
M	2B(1)	2A(2)
T	2B(2)	6x 5D(4)-2B(2)-6x 9E(4)
W	2B(2)	2B(3)
T	2B(2)	9D(4)
F	/A	/A
S		10A(880)-2B(3)-6x 9E(4)
S		2B(4)
M	2B(1)	2A(1-2)-5A(2)
T	2B(1)	6x 9E(4)-2B(1)-6x 9E(3)(32-30-28)
W	2B(1)	2B(2)-5A(2)
T	/A	2x 5C(3)-9G(1)(2 mi.)-5A(2)
F	/A	/A
S		10C-Fresno meet
S		2B(5)
M	2B(1)	2A(2)-5A(2)
T	2B(1)	6x 5D(4)-2B(1)-6x 9E(4)
W	2B(1)	2B(2)
T	2B(1)	2x 5C(3)-9G(1)-5A(2)
F	/A	/A
S		10C
S		2B(4)

Sheet 9-15. Distance training schedule sheet

Middle Distances NAME DATE April

1. A. Jog 1 to 3 miles
   B. Weights & jog
2. Fartlek A. Varied (1) 30 min. (2) 45 min.
   B. Steady (1) 2-4 mi. (2) 4-6 mi. (3) 7-10 mi.
   (4) 8-12 mi. easy (5) 8-15 mi. easy
3. Weights
4. High knee and power run
5. Intervals
   A. 110 (1) 18-16-14 (2) 17-16-15-14
   B. 165 (1) 25 (2)
   C. 220 (1) 35 (2)
   D. 330 (1) 52 (2) 48 (3) 45 (4) 47
   E. 440 (1) 70-73 (2) 66
   F. 660 (1) 1:45 (2)
   G. 880 (1) 70 (2) 90
   H. 3/4 (1) 70 (2) 67-68
   I. Mile (1) 72 (2) 68-70 (3) 64-67 (4)
   J.
   K.
   L.
6. Sets A. 660-440-330-220-110
   (1) 1:45-68-49-32-15 (2)
   B. 440-660-440-220 (1) 63 (2) 62
   C. 550-165-165 (1) 55 pace (2)
   D. 330-220-110 (1) 48-31-14
7. Squad meeting
8. Special A. Sauna B. Swim C.
9. Drills A. Sprint-float-sprint (165)
   B. 1-step acceleration (165)
   C. 40-30 drill (1) 4 laps (2)
   D. 70-90 drill (1) 1-1 (2) 2-1
   (3) 3-1 (4)
   E. Cut-downs (1) 110 (2) 165 (3) 220
   (4) 330 (5) 440 (6) 880 (7) 1320
   F. Simulate race drills (1) 1st 220-last 220
   (2) 2½-1½ (3) 10 miles-3/4 drill (4)
   G. 2-4 miles at (1) 80 (2) 75 (3)
10. A. Test B. Trial C. Compete
    (1) 3/4 date pace (2) Over (3) Under
11. Hill interval A. 110 B. 220 C.
12. With coach (A) Bill B. (B) Bill D. (C)
14. A. Wind sprint B. Hurdle drill
    C. Spring and bound D.
15. Finish work
16. Acrobatics or apparatus
17. 3/4 effort
18.
19.
20. Secondary event
21. A. Pictures B. Film

	A.M.	P.M.
M		2B(2)
T	2B(2)	4x/5E(2)-Rest/5G(2)-4x/5E(2)-2B(1)-4x/9E(4) (51-49-47-45)
W	2B(2)	2B(2)
T	2B(1)	5F(1)-5D(4)-5A(14)-1A-5A(2)
F	1A	1A
S		10C (2 mile)
S		2B(4)
M	2B(2)	2A(2)
T	2B(2)	6x 6B(2)-2B(2)-9E(4)
W	2B(2)	2B(2)
T	2B(2)	4x 9G(1)-9E(4) (52-50-48-46)
F	2B(2)	2B(1)
S		3x 5H(2)-2x 5I(1, 2)-1A-4x 9E(4)
S		2B(5)
M	2B(1)	2A(1)
T	2B(1)	8x 7-5D(2)-1A-6x 9E(3) (34-32-30)
W	1A	7-2B(2)
T	1A	2x 6D(1)-1A-5A(2)
F	1A	1A
S		10C (2 or 3 mile)
S		2B(4)
M	2B(2)	2A(2)
T	2B(2)	4x 5D(4)-3x 9E(7) (70-68-66)
W	2B(1)	2B(2)-2x 9A
T	2B(1)	Light grass-2x 5A(14)
F	1A	9G(1)
S	1A	1A
S		10C-Twilight meet

Sheet 9-16. Distance training schedule sheet

Middle Distances NAME DATE *May*

1. A. Jog 1 to 3 miles
   B. Weights & jog
2. Fartlek A. Varied (1) 30 min. (2) *45 min.*
   B. Steady (1) 2-4 mi. (2) 4-6 mi. (3) 7-10 mi.
   (4) *8-12 mi. easy*
3. Weights
4. High knee and power run
5. Intervals
   A. 110 (1) 18-16-14 (2) 17-*16-15-14*
   B. 165 (1) 25 (2) *8-6-8*
   C. 220 (1) 35 (2) *33* *(3) 31*
   D. 330 (1) 52 (2) 48 (3) 45 (4) *46*
   E. 440 (1) 70-73 (2) *62*
   F. 660 (1) 1:45 (2)
   G. 880 (1) 70 (2) *64*
   H. 3/4 (1) 70 (2) *66*
   I. Mile (1) 72 (2) 68-70 (3) 64-67 (4)
   J.
   K.
   L.
6. Sets A. 660-440-330-220-110
   (1) 1:45-68-49-32-15 (2)
   B. 440-660-440-220 (1) 63 (2)
   C. 550-165-165 (1) 55 pace (2)
   D.
7. Squad meeting
8. Special A. Sauna B. Swim C.
9. Drills A. Sprint-float-sprint (165)
   B. 1-step acceleration (165)
   C. 40-30 drill (1) 4 laps (2)
   D. 70-90 drill (1) 1-1 (2) 2-1
   (3) 3-1 (4)
   E. Cut-downs (1) 110 (2) 165 (3) 220
   (4) 330 (5) 440 (6) 880 (7)
   F. Simulate race drills (1) 1st 220-last 220
   (2) 2½-1½ (3) 10 miles-3/4 drill (4)
   G. 2-4 miles at (1) 80 (2) 75 (3)
10. A. Test B. Trial C. Compete
    (1) 3/4 date pace (2) Over (3) Under
11. Hill interval A. 110 B. 220 C.
12. With coach (A) Bill B. (B) Bill D. (C)
14. A. Wind sprint B. Hurdle drill
    C. Spring and bound D.
15. Finish work
16. Acrobatics or apparatus
17. 3/4 effort
18.
19.
20. Secondary event
21. A. Pictures B. Film

Day	*A.M.*	*P.M.*
M		*2A(2)*
T	*2B(1)*	*8x 5D(2)-2B(2)-5F(1)-5D(4)-5A(13)*
W	*2B(2)*	*2B(2)*
T	*2B(1)*	*2x 5B(2)-9G(1)(2 miles)-5A(2)*
F	*1A*	*1A*
S		*10C - Dual meet*
S		*2B(4)*
M		*2 (light)*
T	*2B(1)*	*9x 9E(4)(50-48-46)-2B(2)-3x 9E(4)(48-46-44)*
W	*2B(1)*	*2B(2)*
T	*1A*	*4x 9E(4)(52-50-48-46)-1A-5A(2)*
F	*1A*	*1A*
S		*10C - 3 mile*
S		*2B(4)*
M	*2B(1)*	*2A(2)*
T	*2B(1)*	*5H(2)-5G(2)-5E(2)-1A-6x 9E(4)(50-48-46)*
W	*2B(1)*	*2B(2)*
T	*2B(1)*	*6x 5C(2)-2B(1)-5A(2)*
F	*1A*	*1A*
S		*10C - Northern Division meet*
S		*2B(4)*
M	*2B(1)*	*2A(2)(easy)*
T	*2B(1)*	*6x 5D(2)-2B(1)-3x 9E(4)(48-46-43)*
W	*2B(2)*	*2B(2)*
T	*2B(1)*	*4x 5C(3)-Light grass-3x 9E(3)(31-29-27)*
F		*Light grass*
S		*10C - Pac 8 meet*
S		*2B(4)*

Sheet 9-17. Distance training schedule sheet

Middle Distances NAME DATE *June*

1. A. Jog 1 to 3 miles
   B. Weights & jog
2. Fartlek A. Varied (1) 30 min. (2) *45 min.*
   B. Steady (1) 2-4 mi. (2) 4-6 mi. (3) 7-10 mi.
   (4) *8-12 mi.*
3. Weights
4. High knee and power run
5. Intervals
   A. 110 (1) 18-16-14 (2) 17-15-13 *(3) 15-14-13*
   B. 165 (1) 25 (2)
   C. 220 (1) 35 (2) *27-28*
   D. 330 (1) 52 (2) 48 (3) 45 (4)
   E. 440 (1) 70-73 (2) *60-64*
   F. 660 (1) 1:45 (2)
   G. 880 (1) 70 (2)
   H. 3/4 (1) 70 (2) *62-68*
   I. Mile (1) 72 (2) 68-70 (3) 64-67 (4)
   J. *7 miles (1) 6 min. pace*
   K.
   L.
6. Sets A. 660-440-330-220-110
   (1) 1:45-68-49-32-15 (2)
   B. 440-660-440-220 (1) 63 (2)
   C. 550-165-165 (1) 55 pace (2)
   D.
7. Squad meeting
8. Special A. Sauna B. Swim C.
9. Drills A. Sprint-float-sprint (165)
   B. 1-step acceleration (165)
   C. 40-30 drill (1) 4 laps (2)
   D. 70-90 drill (1) 1-1 (2) 2-1
   (3) 3-1 (4)
   E. Cut-downs (1) 110 (2) 165 (3) 220
   (4) 330 (5) 440 (6) 880 (7)
   F. Simulate race drills (1) 1st 220-last 220
   (2) 2½-1½ (3) 10 miles-3/4 drill (4)
   G. 2-4 miles at (1) 80 (2) 75 (3)
10. A. Test B. Trial C. Compete
    (1) 3/4 date pace (2) Over (3) Under
11. Hill interval A. 110 B. 220 C.
12. With coach (A) Bill B. (B) Bill D. (C)
14. A. Wind sprint B. Hurdle drill
    C. Spring and bound D.
15. Finish work
16. Acrobatics or apparatus
17. 3/4 effort
18.
19.
20. Secondary event
21. A. Pictures B. Film

Day		
M	*A.M. 2B(1)*	*P.M. 2A(2)*
T	*2B(2)*	*6x 5E(2) - 2A(1) - 6x 9E(4)*
W	*2B(2)*	*2B(2)*
T	*2B(2)*	*4x 5H(2) - 12x 5D(1-2) - 1A*
F	*2B(2)*	*Light run*
S		*3x 9E(4)(48-45-43) - 5J(1) - 3x 9E(4)(48-45-43)*
S		*2B(4)*
M	*2B(1)*	*Light grass – 5A(3)*
T	*2B(1)*	*1-2x 5C(2) - 9G(1) - 5A(2)*
W		*Light grass*
T		*10C-5km. Trials or light grass (NCAA)*
F		*Light grass or 10C-Finals-10km (NCAA)*
S		*10C-Finals-5km (NCAA)*
S		
M		
T		
W		
T		
F		
S		
S		
M		
T		
W		
T		
F		
S		
S		

Sheet 9-18. Distance training schedule sheet

Endnotes

1. Manuel Bueno. (1985). Current conceptions of endurance training. In Jess Jarver (Ed.), *Middle distances: Contemporary theory, technique and training* (2nd ed.). Los Altos, CA: Tafnews, 10-15.
2. David Hinz. (1986). U.S. Elite Athlete Project. *The Harrier*, 12(10), 6.
3. Brian J. Sharkey. (1984). *Physiology of fitness* (2nd ed.). Champaign, IL: Human Kinetics, 10-11.
4. George A. Brooks & Thomas D. Fahey. (1985). *Exercise physiology: Human bioenergetics and its applications*. New York: Macmillan, 208-213.
5. John Underwood. (1985). Personal communication.
6. David E. Martin. (1985). Distance running: The Elite Athlete Athlete Project. *Track Technique*, *93*, 2969.
7. Tricks of the trail. (1987). *Track and Field Quarterly Review*, *87*(2), 25-27.
8. Jürgen Schiffer. (1988). Performance factors in the marathon. *Track Technique, 105*, 3360.

Recommended Readings

Cross Country

Canova, Renato. (1998). Can cross-country running be considered an athletics event in its own right? *New Studies in Athletics, 13*(4), 13-20.

Coffman, Wayne. (1994). Cross country: Theory and training schedule. *Track and Field Quarterly Review, 94*(2), 11-12.

Hazen, Jack. (2004). *Training for cross country*. Mountain View, CA: Tafnews.

Kissane, John A. (2001, November). Razor's edge [Arkansas XC]. *Running Times*, 24, 26-27.

Koskei, Mike, & Walter Abmayr. (1988). Cross country training in Kenya. *New Studies in Athletics, 3*(4), 53-59.

Mikkelsson, Lasse. (1996). Strengthen the strengths: Annemari Sandell's training. *New Studies in Athletics, 11*(4), 45-50.

Newton, Joe, & Joe Henderson. (1998). *Coaching cross country successfully*. Champaign, IL: Human Kinetics.

Parker, Derek. (Spring 2000). How to succeed on the cross country circuit [abstract]. *Track Coach, 151*, 4836.

Schaffer, Ray. (1991). Periodization of cross country training for high school women. *Track Technique, 117*, 3725-3727.

Schiffer, Jürgen. (1998, 1999). Selected and annotated bibliography 46-48: Cross country running–Parts I-III. *New Studies in Athletics, 13*(3), 61-88; 13(4), 55-78; 14(1), 81-104.

Stevenson, Carol. (1987). Cross country training for women. *Track and Field Quarterly Review, 87*(2), 19-21.

Stevenson, Carol. (1988). Mileage illusions and limitations in women's distance running. *Track and Field Quarterly Review, 88*(2), 30-31.

Tulloh, Bruce. (1998). The role of cross-country in the development of a runner. *New Studies in Athletics, 13*(4), 9-12.

Steeplechase

Belishko, A., & V. Sirenko. (2002). A structure for steeplechase training. In Jarver, *Middle and Long Distances*, 160-164.

Bowerman, Bill. (1985). Steeplechase training. *Track and Field Quarterly Review, 85*(3), 15-17.

Dimova, Alla. (2002). The 2000m steeplechase for women. In Jarver, *Middle and Long Distances*, 156-159.

Freeman, William H. (1985). Pacing chart for the steeplechase. *Track Technique, 92*, 2930-2931.

Hislop, Chick. (1985). Steeplechase technique. *Track and Field Quarterly Review, 85*(3), 18-22.

Schiffer, Jürgen. (1999). Selected and annotated bibliography 50: Steeplechase. *New Studies in Athletics, 14*(3), 75-89.

Scholich, Manfred. (1993). Technique-orientated conditioning of steeplechasers [abstract]. *Track Technique, 122*, 3904.

The Longer Distances: 5km to the Marathon

Andersen, John. (1983). Breaking the thirteen minute barrier. *Track and Field Quarterly Review, 83*(3), 27-34.

Anderson, Owen. (Spring 2000). Ronaldo da Costa's unique marathon training [abstract]. *Track Coach, 151*, 4834-4835.

Arcelli, Enrico. (1996). Marathon and 50km walk race: Physiology, diet and training. *New Studies in Athletics, 11*(4), 51-58.

Billat, Véronique. (2005). Current perspectives on performance improvement in the marathon: From universalisation to training optimisation. *New Studies in Athletics, 20*(3), 21-39.

Bompa, Tudor O. (1989). Physiological intensity values employed to plan endurance training. *Track Technique, 108*, 3435-3442.

Costill, David L. (1986). *Inside running: Basics of sports physiology*. Indianapolis: Benchmark.

Cheuvront, S. N. (Summer 2002). Thermoregulation and marathon running [abstract]. *Track Coach, 160*, 5122.

Clarke, Brian. (2006). *5k and 10k training*. Champaign, IL: Human Kinetics.

Ebbets, Russ. (Spring 2006). Interview with Joe Vigil: The gospel according to Joe. *Track Coach, 175*, 5580-5589.

Ebbets, Russ. (Winter 2002). Wings of an eagle [interview with Billy Mills]. *Track Coach, 158*, 5041-5046.

Ferreira, Raimundo Luiz, & Ramiro Rolim. (2006). The evolution of marathon training: A comparative analysis of elite runners' training programmes. *New Studies in Athletics, 21*(1), 29-37.

Garcia-Manso, Juan M., Juan M. Martin-González, Enrique Arriaza & Lucia Quintero. (2006). Middle- and long-distances races viewed from the perspective of complexity: Macroscopic analysis based on behaviour as a power law. *New Studies in Athletics, 21*(1), 17-25.

Gigliotti, Lucia. (1991). Marathon training–Gelindo Bordin's programme [abstract]. *New Studies in Athletics, 6*(4), 72-74.

Gilimov, A., & V. Kulakov. (1992). Anaerobic threshold to guide marathon training [abstract]. *Track Technique, 120*, 3838.

Harter, Lance, & Harry Groves. (2000). 3000 to 10,000 meters. In *USA Track and Field coaching manual*. Champaign, IL: Human Kinetics, 109-122.

Hartmann, Robert. (2003). Why are the Kenyan runners so good? *New Studies in Athletics, 18*(2), 7-11.

Karp, Jason R. (Winter 2007). Training characteristics of U.S. Olympic Marathon Trials qualifiers. *Track Coach, 178*, 5693-5698.

Kepka, Tadeusz. (1991). Training for long-distance track events—Arturo Barrios [abstract]. *New Studies in Athletics, 6*(4), 73-79.

Keska, Stefan. (1991). Training principles of Arturo Barrios' coach [abstract]. *Track Technique, 115*, 3684.

Lange, Günter. (1993). Trends in long distance training. *New Studies in Athletics, 8*(4), 23-25.

La Torre, Antonio, Franco Impellizzeri, Antonio Dotti & Enrico Arcelli. (2005). Do Caucasian athletes need to resign themselves to African domination in middle- and long-distance running? *New Studies in Athletics, 20*(4), 39-49.

Lear, Chris. (2004, July/August). Return of the king: Bob Kennedy's comeback. *Running Times*, 32, 34, 36.

Lenzi, Giampaolo. (1987). The marathon race: Modern training methodology. *New Studies in Athletics, 2*(2), 41-50.

Lowes, David. (Fall 2006). Advanced sessions for the brave. *Track Coach, 177*, 5666-5669.

Martin, David E. (2003). Challenges for ensuring quality performance in the 2004 Athens Olympic marathon. *New Studies in Athletics, 18*(3), 57-66.

Mayes, Randall E. (2005). *The cybernetics of Kenyan running: Hurry, hurry has no blessing*. Durham: Carolina Academic Press.

Morris, Al. (2006). Nutrition before, during, and after a marathon [abstract]. *New Studies in Athletics, 21*(1), 63.

Pfitzinger, Pete, & Scott Douglas. (2001). *Advanced marathoning*. Champaign, IL: Human Kinetics.

Pfitzinger, Pete, & Scott Douglas. (1999). *Road racing for serious runners*. Champaign, IL: Human Kinetics.

Raevuori, Antero, & Rolf Haikkola. (1978). *Lasse Viren: Olympic Champion*. Trans. Matti Hannus. Portland, OR: Continental.

Rehrer, Nancy J. (2001). Fluid and electrolyte balance in ultra-endurance sport. *Sports Medicine, 31*(10), 167-194.

Salazar, Alberto, & Richard A. Lovett. (2003). *Alberto Salazar's guide to road racing*. Camden, ME: Ragged Mountain Press/McGraw Hill.

Schiffer, Jürgen. (2002). Selected and annotated bibliography 59-60: Medical aspects of marathon running. *New Studies in Athletics, 17*(2), 57-88; 17(3/4), 85-155.

Sparks, Ken, & Bjorklund, Garry. (1984). *Long distance runner's guide to training and racing: Build your endurance, strength, and efficiency*. Englewood Cliffs, NJ: Prentice-Hall.

Stevenson, Carol. (1988). Mileage illusions and limitations in women's distance running. *Track and Field Quarterly Review, 88*(2), 30-31.

Tanser, Toby. (2001). *Train hard, win easy: The Kenyan way.* (2nd ed.). Mountain View, CA: Tafnews.

Usami, Akio. (1988). The development of Japanese marathon runners. *New Studies in Athletics, 4*(4), 61-69.

Vigil, Joe. (1987). Distance training. *Track Technique, 100*, 3189-3192.

Vigil, Joe. (2006). Endurance training for distance events [abstract]. *New Studies in Athletics, 21*(1), 61-62.

SPRINTS, HURDLES, AND RELAYS

Part 3

Otis Davis edges Karl Kauffman in 44.9 world record at the 1960 Rome Olympics

10

The Short Sprints and Relays

Bowerman's Best

60-yard	6.0i	Roscoe Cook, world indoor record, 1959, 1960, and 1961
100-yard	9.2	Harry Jerome, world record, 1962
100m	10.0ht	Harry Jerome, world record, 1960
200m	20.79	Harry Jerome, 1964
440-yard	40.0	World record, 1962 equivalent to 39.7m

Record Setters

Harry Jerome	Olympic 100m Bronze Medal; four world records: 100m, 100-yard (two times), 440-yard relay; two-time NCAA Champion; five-time All American; Canadian Olympic Team
Roscoe Cook	Four world records: 100-yard, indoor 60-yard (three times)
440-yard relay	Jerry Tarr, Mike Gaechter, Mel Renfro, Harry Jerome

The first thing that a prospective sprinter must learn is that training is not a "sometime" thing. Sprint training requires the same training consistency that any other event requires. Several general principles of training should be kept in mind:

- The training should be full time in the sense that it continues throughout the year, as opposed to training for only four to six months of the year.
- The athlete's fitness should be raised to a high level and maintained at that level throughout the year.
- The hard-easy principle is the best approach for long-term progress.
- Outside influences upon the athlete must be considered.

The coach must help the athletes to understand their priorities while they are competing for a school team. The first priority is, and must always be, to graduate. The athletes' academic work always takes precedence. Hopefully, the next priority is preparation for athletic competition. Much of the athletes' eventual achievement depends upon how good they want to be and how much they are willing to work to succeed. The coach should exert a good influence on the athletes in helping them to determine their priorities.

Sprinters are not picked by size or body build, but by raw speed. Sprinters come in all sizes, including very short, and all shapes, occasionally including round. Although sprinters may be "born" to the event, they do not fit an easily defined mold.

The Start

A good start is essential to successful sprinting. The three types of starts are each named for the position of the sprinter's feet relative to each other.

- *Bunch start*: feet close together, bringing the athlete close to the starting line
- *Medium start*: feet a bit farther apart, with the athlete not as close to the line
- *Elongated start*: feet farther apart, with the sprinter not very close to the starting line

Though the bunch setting gives the fastest start from the blocks for about 30m, it is not the fastest for the whole race. Usually the medium setting results in the fastest time for the entire race. However, the block settings are very much a personal matter with sprinters. Individual anthropometric and strength measures are the deciding factor.

For figuring out each athlete's settings, experimentation in practice is necessary. The blocks might first be set two foot-lengths from the line to the first block and three to four foot-lengths from the line to the rear block. The position of the hands should be marked to become as standard as the block settings. They need to be wide enough for the legs to come through without hindrance, but not so wide that the sprinter's first move would be to fall on his chin.

The athlete should take starts at many different settings. Some timed starts should be run for 30 or 40m from each of the settings to learn which actually is fastest for the sprinter. The times should not be announced until the tests are completed; otherwise, the athlete may subconsciously "prove" a setting is better in relation to the others than it really is, simply because of a belief that the setting is faster.

The commands of the starter are "on your marks" and "set," and then the gun is fired. At the command of "on your marks," the sprinter gets into the down position on the blocks, setting into the starting position. The hips should be about four inches higher than the shoulders, and the angle at the knee should be about 100 degrees. The athlete should not try to anticipate the gun (doing so leads to false starts), but should have practiced reacting to any sharp sound.

When the gun is fired, the athlete should concentrate on getting the back leg forward and down. This method was the practice of Harry Jerome, who ran 9.2 (for 100 yards) and 10.0 for 100m for world records at Oregon. Though he did not concentrate on driving off the rear block with his back leg, he did drive with the leg in actual practice. The chest is driven upward and forward. If the left foot is forward in the blocks, then the left hand is thrust forward as the right leg is brought out of the rear block. While the athlete is leaving the blocks, the hips are kept relatively level. They should not rise or fall while starting. Each athlete has personal idiosyncrasies, so he must work to master that individual style.

Photo 10-1. Harry Jerome of Canada, 100m world-record holder (10.0), Olympic medalist, three-time Olympian

Relaxation is extremely important in sprinting. All great sprinters have it, and it can be taught. The shoulders and the hands need to be relaxed, for they can cause the runner to tense the upper body. If the shoulders and hands are tense, the arms will move more slowly, consequently slowing down the leg speed. Many runners have been taught to judge their relaxation by whether or not their jaw is relaxed: It will seem to be flopping or bouncing along when relaxed.

One good exercise for learning to relax while sprinting is running 150s (sprint-float-sprint). The first 50m are worked hard, the next 50m are floated (relaxed running), and the last 50m are worked hard. The runner should try to run the floated 50 within 1/10th of a second as fast as the worked 50s. The object is to develop the ability to relax and float briefly in a race, with little or no real slowing down of the running speed.

Finally, the sprinter should finish strongly, learning to reach out for the tape with a properly timed lean or lunge. Some runners use a quick "dip" toward the tape, others lunge toward it, while still others lunge and at the same time turn the shoulder for additional reach toward the tape. The timing is crucial, and it requires considerable practice. Racers should sprint through the tape, continuing to drive forward for at least 10m. The reason for this is that many runners are subconsciously slowing down as they approach the tape, when they should be moving strongly through it.

Sprinting Mechanics

According to studies sponsored by the United States Olympic Committee, the following are the significant variables in a successful full-speed sprint performance:

- Greater forward speed of the body
- Greater stride rate
- Lesser support time
- Minimal upper-leg extension at takeoff
- Greater upper-leg rotational speed during the support phase
- Greater lower-leg rotational speed at touchdown
- Short foot-to-body distance at touchdown
- Greater backward foot speed relative to the body at touchdown1

The stride support time is a major part of successful sprinting. The higher stride rate of the elite sprinter results from spending significantly less time on the ground. The average sprinter places the foot too far ahead of the body at touchdown, overemphasizing the upper- and lower-leg extension at takeoff. This placement results from improper preparation for ground contact and poor upper-leg strength, increasing support time and decreasing the stride rate. The primary function of the arms is to counterbalance the actions of the legs.

A weakness in stride length or rate can be analyzed from freeze-frame video taken from the side at these three points in the stride:

- Takeoff—overextension of the upper and lower leg?
- Maximum upper-leg recovery
  - ✓ Lower-leg position at the knee—held to a minimum?
  - ✓ Upper-leg positionhigh knee lift?
- Touchdown too far ahead of the body?

One weakness of this evaluation is that the upper- and lower-leg rotational speeds cannot be measured, but those speeds are directly related to the leg positions just given. If the sprinter overextends the leg at takeoff, upper-leg speed during support is poor. If the knee lift during recovery is poor, upper-leg recovery speed is poor. If the foot lands too far ahead of the body, lower-leg speed at touchdown is poor, resulting in a braking action. Table 10-1 summarizes which problems in stride rate and length are strength-related and which are mechanical.

Strength and Mechanical Relationships of Sprinting Errors

Weakness	*Mechanics Problem*	*Strength Problem*
Poor stride length	• Poor upper-leg recovery • Poor lower-leg recovery	
Poor stride rate	• Poor lower-leg speed at touchdown • Excessive foot distance at touchdown	• Poor upper-leg speed at touchdown and during support time • Overextension of upper leg at takeoff and at full extension • Overextension of lower leg at takeoff

Table 10-1. Strength and mechanical relationships of sprinting errors

Drills for Sprint Mechanics

Drills for improving sprinting mechanics may concentrate on improving leg strength or on technique (Table 10-2). Strength drills include both bounding drills (plyometrics) and traditional strength training. Sprinting technique drills such as the following concentrate on improving the overall mechanics, the stride rate, the recovery mechanics, and preparing the leg for touchdown.[2]

Leg cycling drill. Lean against a wall or hurdle with both hands, swinging one leg through with the sprinting motion. Concentrate on not overextending the leg behind the body, instead allowing the heel to touch the buttocks during recovery, followed by a high knee lift, then "pawing" the ground to complete the cycle. Ten cycles with each leg constitute one set.

Quick stride drill. While jogging, increase the stride rate, and take as many steps as possible in 10m. Jog for 10m, then repeat the drill. Emphasize the fastest possible turnover, moving the legs in front of the body, not behind it.

Sprint Mechanics Training Drills

Strength Improvement Drills

Bounding Drills: improve dynamic leg strength

Static Strength Exercises: focus on hamstrings or gluteals

- Hamstring strength exercises
  - ✓ Hamstring curls
  - ✓ Hamstring/gluteal machine
- Gluteal strength exercises
  - ✓ Squats
  - ✓ Step-ups
  - ✓ Hamstring/gluteal machine
  - ✓ Inverted leg presses

Sprinting Drills

Concentrate on:

- Overall mechanics
  - ✓ Leg cycling drill
- Stride rate
  - ✓ Quick stride drill
  - ✓ Quick support drill
  - ✓ Stick drill
- Recovery mechanics
  - ✓ Hip-kickers drill
- Preparing the leg for touchdown
  - ✓ Pawing drill
  - ✓ Pull-through drill

Table 10-2. Sprint mechanics training drills

Quick support drill. From the high-knee position, emphasize dropping the foot to the ground, then lifting it as quickly as possible. The foot pushes from the ground and lifts into the high knee position. Ten touchdowns with the leg is one set.

Stick drill. Using 20 ground markers (tape or sticks) placed 14 inches (35 cm) apart (increasing gradually to 20 inches (50 cm) or more), step between the sticks as quickly as possible, emphasizing high knee lift and quick contact with the ground. A set is one time across the markers.

Hip-kickers drill. While jogging, swing the heel backward until it bounces off the hip. Keep the upper leg relatively straight, concentrating the effort on moving the heel to the hip as quickly as possible. Ten kicks with each leg is one set.

Pawing drill. While jogging, reach forward with the foot, pulling the ground toward you in a pawing action, keeping all of the effort ahead of your body. Do not drive forward or upward off the ground. One set is 10 pawing actions with each leg.

Pull-through drill. Extend the leg in front of the body like a hurdler, then bring it down in a powerful motion through its contact with the ground. Ten pull-throughs with each leg is one set.

Posture in Sprinting

One of the earliest American studies of posture for sprinters was done by Dr. Donald B. Slocum, an orthopedic physician and surgeon, and Bill Bowerman.[3] It examined the posture of 100m and 400m champions in full sprint, using both still and motion pictures. Without exception, their posture was almost 90 degrees in relation to the surface being covered.

The question is how to correct the posture for an average athlete so that he can perform more effectively. Muscle tone is more important than the command to "stand straight." The most important muscles are the abdominals, the pectorals, and the latissimi dorsi (the stomach, chest, and upper back). The weakest set of muscles in many athletes is the abdominal muscles. Core strength is critical. To correct that weakness and also to prescribe exercises for general body activity, a set of 10 self-testing and self-exercising weight activities is used.

Strength affects the posture, and posture affects the sprinting mechanics. If the sprinter's head leans forward, something must balance that 5 kilograms of weight. It is usually the hips, which move into an awkward position. Several simple exercises are helpful, following the idea that better muscle tone results in better posture. Two simple exercises for the athletes are the following:

- Standing with your heels about four inches from a door, a post, or another flat surface, bend the knees slightly. Rotate the hips forward and under while tightening the abdominal muscles. Walk in that position for about four to eight seconds, and then relax the abdominal muscles. Return to the door, and repeat the exercise four or five times.
- Lie on your back, and then raise your knees, keeping your heels on the floor. Contract the abdominal muscles, and rotate the hips upward until your back is flat. Lift one foot, and gradually straighten that leg during a slow five-count. Bring the leg back in a five-count, and relax. Perform the exercise with the other foot and leg.

Lateral bodily movement should also be eliminated through practice. Swaying the head from side to side, swinging the arms too far across the chest, or making similar motions results in a compensating action by the legs. The coach and the athlete—through work, observation, pictures, and video—can make the training interesting as well as productive.

When a sprinter is in full stride and clear of the blocks, the upper body is relatively erect, rather than leaning forward. Photographic studies of Olympic runners have proven the validity of this statement. In the erect position, the athlete can more easily raise the knees and reach out with the feet. This positioning enables a longer stride. The arms swing roughly from hip level to shoulder level. If they are swung higher than this, the runner's strides have a tendency to be shorter. Usually the faster the arms move, the faster the legs move. The sprinter should keep on the toes and run with a high-knee action, as practiced in the high-knee drill. If the sprinter tends to toe out (pointing the toes at an angle toward the side of the track, which is a weaker driving position than when the toes point straight ahead in the running direction), it helps to practice running along a straight line. The head should be kept up at all times, rather than down facing the ground or back facing the sky.

Training Theory

If a prospect is not already quick, the chance of reaching the elite level is slim. The United States is not known for its innovative methods in training sprinters, yet it dominates the world in sprinters. By the end of 2006, 106 male sprinters worldwide had run 100m in 10.06 or faster. Of them, 50 were from the United States.

In essence, the primary needs are talent and opportunity. Jess Jarver summarized sprint training theory by noting that no general agreement exists on the most effective training methods.[4] He noted Nikolay Ozolin's warning of the "speed barrier" effect in training, created by running many repetitions at the same speed (even if that speed is very fast). Such one-speed training teaches the body to run at that single speed, but not to become any faster. Instead, a variety of paces, intensities, and efforts is more effective (and consistent with the training schedules that follow).

Frank Dick suggests the following fitness characteristics for the sprinter (giving a basis for training emphases):

- General conditioning
  - ✓ Aerobic endurance
  - ✓ Strength endurance
  - ✓ Mobility (flexibility)
  - ✓ Maximum strength
- Special conditioning
  - ✓ Speed endurance
  - ✓ Speed
  - ✓ Elastic strength
  - ✓ Special strength: relative to event
  - ✓ Special endurance: 200m and 400m
- Competition specific conditioning
  - ✓ Sprint technique
  - ✓ Starting technique
  - ✓ Time trials
  - ✓ Baton speed technique[5]

Hans Torim notes that five physical performance capacities give results in the sprints.[6] These capacities and their importance to different types of sprints are shown in Table 10-3.

Physical Performance Capacities for the Sprints

	Importance (Ranked 1 to 5)		
Capacity	*100m*	*200m*	*400m*
Reaction speed	3	4	4-5
Acceleration	2	3	3
Maximal speed	1	1-2	2
Speed endurance	4	1-2	1
General endurance	5	5	4-5

Table 10-3. Physical performance capacities for the sprints

A thorough two-peak periodized year used to train sprinters at the University of Tennessee concentrates on six major training factors:

- *Speed training*: focuses on absolute speed
- *Speed endurance training*: uses three types of workouts
  - ✓ Low anaerobic stress training
  - ✓ Medium to high anaerobic stress training
  - ✓ High anaerobic stress training
- *Weight training*: develops both total conditioning and specific-event strength
- *Plyometrics*: increases ability to apply force to the ground very quickly
- *Technique work*: used more for warm-up, developing the holistic movement sense, and muscular strengthening
- *Relaxation*: includes relaxation both at rest (for calming and visualization) and at speed[7]

The sprinters are given control tests at distances up to 300m, along with related tests and a body-fat test by the hydrostatic (underwater) method. The training year falls into six phases and is an excellent example of applying periodized training to the American college competitive year.

The TAC/USA Level II Coaching Education Curriculum Development Committee on Sprints and Hurdles described the training components of sprinting within two major subgroups, technical components and energy system components.[8] The technical components are:

- *Speed skill*: developing effective sprinting mechanics
- *Speed acceleration*: developing effective starting and acceleration techniques

The energy system components are:

- Speed (absolute speed)
- Speed endurance
  - ✓ Short speed endurance (alactic and glycolytic)
  - ✓ Long speed endurance
  - ✓ Lactate tolerance
- Tempo endurance
  - ✓ Extensive (aerobic capacity and aerobic power)
  - ✓ Intensive (anaerobic capacity)
  - ✓ Strength endurance

Gary Winckler of the University of Illinois developed a table (Table 10-4) showing the intervals, intensities, and recoveries needed for developing the different systems needed for elite sprinting.[9]

The direct competition (peaking) phase is three successive microcycles (accumulation, intensification, and transformation) lasting for a total of four

Energy Systems Training for Sprinters						
	Physiological Objectives			**Training Run Pattern**		
Work Type	*Biomotor Component Trained*	*Energy System Trained*	*Length (m)*	*Intensity (% of best performance)*	*Rest Intervals* Between Reps*	*Sets*
Extensive tempo	Aerobic capacity Aerobic power	Aerobic Aerobic	>200 >100	<70 70-79	<45 s 30-90 s	<2 2-3
Intensive tempo	Anaerobic capacity	Mixed aerobic and anaerobic	>80	80-89	30 s-5	3-10
Speed	Speed, anaerobic power	Anaerobic alactic	20-80	90-95 95-100	3-5	6-8
Speed endurance	Alactic short speed endurance, anaerobic power	Anaerobic alatic	50-80	90-95 95-100	1-2 2-3	5-7 7-10
	Glycolytic short speed endurance, anaerobic capacity, anaerobic power	Anaerobic glycolytic	<80	90-95 95-100	1 1	3-4 4
	Speed endurance, anaerobic power	Anaerobic glycolytic	80-150	90-95 95-100	5-6 6-10	– –
Special endurance I	Long speed endurance, anaerobic power	Anaerobic glycolytic	150-300	90-95 95-100	10-12 12-15	– –
Special endurance II	Lactic acid tolerance	Lactic acid tolerance	300-600	90-95 95-100	15-20 Full recovery	– –

Developed by Gary Winckler, 1986.
*Rest intervals in minutes, unless number is followed by s (seconds). Times given are between reps or sets.

Table 10-4. Energy systems training for sprinters

weeks.[10] The accumulation microcycle is primarily recovery from previous competition. Although the volume of training rises, the intensity is generally low. The intensification microcycle (14 days) requires very-high-intensity training. The athlete will need one week of transformation training to recover from the intensification process and rise to a higher performance level. This microcycle, ending with a day of rest followed by the major competition, uses a low training load and short, intensive training sessions mixed with easier sessions to peak the sprinter.

Applying the Theory

Training begins in the fall with group workouts, changing to individual schedules after the start of the new year. The fall program consists of conditioning and technique workouts two or three days a week. An additional program consists of hill running one day a week, beginning with six 40m runs up a moderately steep hill. The sprinters concentrate on their arm drive and knee lift. They do not go full effort. The hill run is lengthened by 10m per week until the athletes are running 90m up the hill six times. They can then go to six times 40 to 60m at 7/8 effort. The full workout consists of a one-mile jog to the golf course, the hill training session, a one-mile jog back to the track, and then four medium-effort sprints of 50 or 100m.

A test effort is scheduled every two weeks. The testing is partly to give the runner experience at the race, though the trials are rarely run at a very fast pace. Usually, several races are run at 1/2 to 3/4 effort. Underdistance or overdistance runs, such as 60, 100, 200, 300, and 400m, may also be included for 100- and 200-meter runners. The 400 athletes occasionally run 300 or 500m, and a 350-meter run is a good test for a potential 400 racer. The hardest effort ever done in practice is 3/4 to 9/10 effort; the sprinter never runs at full effort in practice. The risk of injury (such as muscle pulls) in training is not worth taking.

A helpful practice for the coach is a Sunday training session. The biggest reason for this practice is to speed the recovery of the Saturday night "party people." If not for this practice, they will do nothing on Sunday, then take Monday and Tuesday to recover, thus effectively missing most of the practice week, particularly if the competitive season is in full swing.

The sprinters should have a routine for beginning their practice sessions. Our routine begins by jogging one or two laps with several other sprinters while practicing the relay pass. The sprinter might work with two, three, or even five people. The sprinters form a straight line, jog forward, and the runner in the rear starts by passing the baton forward. The next runner in the line drops the left hand back, receives the baton, brings it forward, and switches it to the right hand, then passes it ahead to the next runner in line. The runner who has passed the baton moves out and trots to the head of the line to wait for the baton to reach him again.

The runner receives the baton with the left hand; thus, when the runner behind has the baton, the receiver swings the arms back in the regular cadence five times (the left arm is back on counts one, three, and five). On the fifth count, the left hand stays extended downward and to the rear, awaiting the baton.

After the jogging and relay drill, the athlete works on the combined high-knee, fast-leg drill. This two-part drill ideally is done on a grass or sawdust surface. The high-knee part of the drill is done slowly and is used to exercise the small groin muscles. The runner jogs either in place or slowly across the grass, moving on the toes and lifting the knee until the thigh is parallel to the ground, then dropping the foot back to the grass. The knees are not lifted beyond this thigh-parallel-to-the-ground position because that is as high as the knees ever go in normal sprinting. Any more stretching simply risks injury. The fast-leg part of the drill is done next, and at a fast stride rate. The arms are moved very quickly, as in a sprint race, and the feet are sprinting in place, but they are just barely lifted off the ground. The faster the arms move in sprinting, the faster the legs move. A similar drill is used in football.

The warm-up routine is concluded by having the sprinters go through two to four easy starts. These drills are done very easily and are primarily designed to give the sprinters more starts without imposing any additional strain. For training sessions, the track is marked at 50m intervals. The 100s are run from the middle of the turn to the middle of the straight. When told to run 13 to 15 seconds, the athlete should run progressively from the slower to the faster time. Running 4 x 100m in 13 to 15 seconds is done in 15, 14, 13.5, and 13 seconds.

Photo 10-2. Roscoe Cook, multiple world-record holder in the short sprints

The long runs for the sprinters are usually two to three miles. To gain real benefits from an overdistance run, an athlete must raise the pulse rate to at least 150 beats per minute and hold it at that level for at least 20 minutes. After a long run, the sprinter should run several 50s. These runs are not fast or hard. Because of the variability of fall and winter weather, the whole training pattern may be changed to take advantage of a good day. If the weather conditions permit nothing else, the runners can jog in hallways.

Weight training is also beneficial to the sprinter. Most runners who have been very successful have done some sort of weight training. We do not have a specific workout; instead, we recommend that the athletes develop their own programs. An example is the training done by Oregon's Harry Jerome (an Olympic medalist and former world-record holder at 10.0 seconds for 100m), whose weight workouts are shown in Table 10-5.

Sample Weight Training Program for Sprinters

Exercise	*Repetitions*	*Sets*	*Times Per Week*
Military press	6	2	3
Half or quarter squats	6	2	2
Bench press	6	2	3
Sit-ups	15	2	3
Pullovers (bent or straight)	6	2	3
Dead lift (bent leg)	6	2	2

Table 10-5. Sample weight training program for sprinters

Another common exercise for sprinters is a step-up lunge onto a 24-inch-tall bench while carrying weights on their shoulders.

The athlete's equipment is perhaps as important as the training. A shoe is needed that is sturdy, comfortable, and light. A sweatshirt with a hood is the only practical kind for practice sessions. Tights or leggings in a school color are warmer than regular sweatpants. Cotton long-johns, dyed in the school colors, are equally usable. They are not bulky and can be worn either over or under the running shorts. They will last about a year. Competition gear should be light and comfortable. Some runners do not wear socks or wear them only in cold weather or practice sessions. How and when to wear socks is largely a matter of personal preference.

The athlete should not train with a cold or other sickness or infection. An athlete with a cold can return to hard training, fully recovered, in about six days if the cold is cared for. If the cold is not cared for, and the athlete continues to train, the cold may linger for weeks. If the ailment is physical, such as an injury of some sort, the athlete should be cared for in the training room, then get out on the track.

The athlete should try to avoid certain outside influences, although not all outside activities are bad ones. The best influence, from the team's standpoint, is to have a strong team esprit de corps. Some athletes meet "hangers-on" who want to be seen with them, consequently taking the athletes to places or situations that are detrimental to them. Parties are always great to have, but they should not be too big, nor should they be planned without anything to celebrate.

Above all, the athlete must have dedication and perseverance. Athletes must act like champions every day if they expect to be champions someday. The activities on the days of meets need to be considered, also. For a dual meet held on a Saturday, the sprinters train hard on Monday and Wednesday, going light on Tuesday, Thursday, and Friday.

If a meet begins at 1:30 p.m., the squad meets to eat together between 8:30 and 9:00 a.m. It does not really matter what the meal is, however, because it is too early to affect the meet. An athlete might have a small steak, a cup of tea, some Jell-o®, and a cup of bouillon. Just a cup of tea and some toast might be the best meal, but many athletes are too psyched to limit themselves to such a light meal. The primary function of this meal is to get the athletes up and functioning.

The athletes dress about one-and-a-half hours before they run. They go out for the warm-up one hour before the race; the warm-up concludes about 15 minutes before the race begins. They might do striding on the grass or sawdust, running perhaps a 100, a 150 or a 200 at an easy pace. When time for the race comes, they jog a bit, set the blocks, and go.

For a conference meet, the procedure depends upon the schedule of the meet. An athlete may run on two consecutive afternoons. In the case of morning trials, the team may get up at 6 a.m. if the race is at 10:00 a.m. For a national meet, where a sprinter might have to run three days in a row, he will try to have meals no later than four hours before the race. If ample time is given between races, provide liquids or toast, but nothing that is slow to digest. During the week before the conference or NCAA meets, almost no training should be done beyond taking a few starts and some passing of the baton.

Multiple-Event Considerations

Sprinters in the short races tend to compete in a large number of events. The image of the immortal Jesse Owens with four golds in the 1936 Olympics (the 100, the 200, the long jump, and the 4 x 100 relay) is reflected in Carl Lewis's 1984 four-gold performance. A top 400 sprinter may compete in both relays.

Unfortunately, such feats have a price. Unless an athlete is far superior to his opponents, such multiple-event performances come at the risk of defeat or injury due to fatigue. Regardless of the time an effort requires, whether it is a long jump or a marathon, top performance requires that the athlete be fresh. Fatigued muscles cannot perform as well, and they are very susceptible to injury if forced to surpass their limits. Many observers failed to realize the wisdom of Carl Lewis's much-criticized skipping of his last attempts in the long jump at the 1984 Olympics. His reasoning was absolutely correct: he was tired and risking serious injury, with events yet to run.

Competing in even two events means that at least one event will not be an all-out effort. The fatal flaw to doubling is the subconscious tendency to hold back a bit during the first race (because another race follows), but still be too tired for an all-out effort in the second race. You may emphasize a team effort in some meets, having athletes in multiple events, but it should not be a regular occurrence. An athlete who regularly competes in multiple events (unless a combined-events athlete) is not being prepared to reach the top. Some meets should be full-effort competitions. Note that Carl Lewis rarely set an individual world record, though he was in a number of races where world records were set. This observation is not meant to criticize him; it is to point out the difficulty of peak efforts when doubling.

Training for the 4 x 100 Relay

The relays are very tactical races, even though they are run at top speed. The placement of personnel in a 4 x 100 relay is based on several considerations. They might be placed by their best sprinting times. The best starter might be the first runner. The poorest receiver in the group might be the first runner. A runner with more endurance than the others might take the first leg, which tends to be the longest, just as the runner with the least endurance might be made anchorman, having the shortest run. Some runners perform better around a turn than others. Many situations involving personal strengths and weaknesses of the sprinters must be considered. The fastest runner might be put in the third leg to upset the opponents with what appears to be a sudden breakthrough. Some teams run better from in front than from behind, which might be a reason to start the fastest runner first. The sprinters should be timed around a turn to find which ones are fastest. They should be timed twice at this, once starting from a down position and once from a stand. Some athletes are faster from a running start than they are from a crouch.

With a sprint relay, the underhand (blind) handoff is used. Fewer teams now switch the baton from one hand to the other while running, as opposed to keeping it in the same hand throughout the run. The advantage of switching the baton from the receiving hand (left) to the passing hand (right) is stability. A relay team must practice together often. The athletes have other races to run, though, and occasionally one of the regulars will not be able to run on the relay. When a different person goes into a spot, if that person is not as practiced at the technique or has not practiced in that position in the sequence of passes, a pass may be missed.

For younger teams, the inside pass is preferred. The athlete receives the baton with the left hand and switches it to the right hand while running. The pass is from the right hand into the next runner's left hand. The receiver is in the outside of the lane, which allows him to move on a relatively straight line into the turn. Also, the runner who must look back will tend to run along the curve, rather than veer into the outer lane. Successful relay racing is the result of repeated practice and precision. One Oregon team that used this technique set a world record for the 440-yard relay of 40.0 (39.7m) on a cinder track, though three of the men were hurdlers.

The warm-up routine, which includes relay practice, has already been described. For further practice on the relay, the regular team members work on the passes using two check marks: one called "lean," and the other called "go." Practice begins with the first check 5m before the fly zone, and the other check 5m before that, or 10m out. The passer and the receiver run through the handoff at half speed on this round. When the runner with the baton hits the first mark, 10m from the fly zone, the receiver leans forward, preparatory to running. When hitting the second mark, 5m away, the receiver begins his own sprint. The same five-count arm swing is used as described previously, and on the fifth count, the left hand stays back, ready to receive the baton. The sprinter does not look back at any time after starting his own run. Gradually, the practice speed is increased, and the check marks are moved out until they are determined correctly for a full-speed run.

Each pair of relay runners practices two or three passes at each of the exchange zones. The alternate team member practices as both the first and the last person in the relay. By taking this approach, little chance for damage to the interior of the relay team is possible, so mistakes by the alternate cannot hurt the relay team too much. The coach should remember that a team of not-too-good sprinters can form a very respectable relay team if they are trained well enough to be very precise and consistent in their relay techniques. U.S. relay teams have lost a number of major races to teams whose fastest member is slower than the slowest American runner.

100- and 200-Meter Training Schedules

The training schedule sheets are given at the end of this chapter. The following training fundamentals are listed on the sheets. The elements common to all events are described in Chapter 6, along with how to adapt the workouts to the athletes' level of performance.

4. High Knee, Fast Leg

The high-knee (slow), fast-leg drill is described with the typical warm-up activities. It is extremely useful for working on the stride rate and reaction speed of the legs.

5. Starts, 3 at 1/2 Speed, 3 at 7/8

Starts are never done at full effort because the risk of injury is very high. Instead, several starts are taken at half speed, then several are taken at 3/4 to 7/8 speed. Sometimes, the athletes practice the starts on their own, while at other times gun starts are taken to simulate meet conditions. Ideally, gun starts should be given by the starter for your local meets.

6. Intervals

Interval training is basic, with two exceptions. The 100m interval may be run as single intervals, or it may be run as cutdowns, as in 6A(1). A notation of "2 x 6A(1)" means two sets of three times 100m, with the speed increasing through each set. The first 100 is run in 18 seconds, the next in 16 seconds, then the last in 14 seconds. The second set is run in the same manner.

The other exception is the 6Z, which calls for the middle 20 to 50m of the interval to be run faster than the assigned pace. This drill helps the athlete learn to vary the pace or put an acceleration or a surge into the race.

9. Relay Work

The relay routine was described previously.

11. Sets

Sets are groups of intervals run in descending order. Run each interval in a set a slightly faster pace than the longer interval before it. Thus, as the intervals become shorter, the pace speeds up. The rest interval ranges from an equal distance to twice the length of the fast interval.

16. Finish Work

This drill simulates trying to accelerate and finish the race strongly. The interval is the full racing distance, running at a moderate pace for 50 to 75 percent of the distance, then accelerating to 9/10 effort through the finish.

17. Back to Back

The back-to-back drill consists of running the interval twice in quick succession. The athlete runs a 50m dash, walks back to the starting line, and immediately runs a second 50.

18. 3/4 Effort

19. Run at 8/10 Effort, Float at 7/10 (Three Steps), Then Go

This drill develops the ability to take a very brief breather during the race, so the athlete can then surge or accelerate toward the finish. It may be practiced over the full racing distance, or the sprinter may work on segments of the race.

22. Turn Work (40 at 9/10 , 30 at 1/2, 40 at 9/10)

This drill develops the skills of racing through the turn, but it allows a bit of relaxed floating during the interval. The elite sprinter can be very relaxed at very high speeds, but that ability must be developed carefully.

100-200 SCHEDULE NAME ______________________ DATE ______________

1. Warmup routine: A. Jog 1-2 laps with relay pass
B. Slow high knee; fast leg
2. Fartlek A. Varied pace: stride, sprint,
recover-- stride, meet a challenge, recover.
Finish feeling exhilarated, not exhausted.
(a) 10 min. (b) 30 min. (c)
B. Steady pace: slow, 10-30 min.
(1) Hendricks Park (2) Golf course
(3)
3. A. Weights and jogging
B. Jogging and stretching
4. High knee and fast leg
5. Starts, 3 at 1/2 speed, 3 at 7/8ths
A. 30m B. 50m C. On grass D.
(1) On your own (2) Gun
6. Intervals Z. Fast 20-50 meters in middle
A. 100 (1) 18-16-14 (2)
B. 150 (1) 22 (2)
C. 200 (1) 30 (2)
D. 100-200-100 (1)
E. 300 F.
7. TEAM MEETING
8. Special A. Sauna B. Swim C.
9. Relay work A. Routine
B. 50 meters C. Trial
10. A. Meet B. Trial C. Simulation D. Control test
11. Sets A. 500-300-100 (1) 80-48-14 (2)
B. 300-200-100 (1)
C. 300-150-75 (1)
D. 150-100-50 (1)
12. With Coach A. B.
14. A. Wind sprints (1) Straight (2) Curve
B. Hurdle (X) drill C. Spring and bound
D. Alternate run and jog, at least 800
E. Hills with A. B.
15. Plyometrics A. Jumps B. Bounding C.
(1) 1-leg (2) Both legs (3)
16. Finish work: 50-70 at 3/4ths,
last 30-50 at 9/10ths
A. 100 B. 200
17. Back-to-back A. 50 B.
18. 3/4 effort A. 100 B. 300 C. 500
19. Run at 8/10ths: float at 70 (3 steps), then go
A. 100 B. 200 C. Parts
20. Work on second event
21. A. Videotape B. Film C. Pictures
(1) Record performance (2) Study
22. Turn work (40 at 9/10ths,
30 at 1/2, 40 at 9/10ths)
30. Experimental work

Date	Distance	3/4 pace	Date Pace	Goal Pace

M
T
W
T
F
S
S
M
T
W
T
F
S
S
M
T
W
T
F
S
S
M
T
W
T
F
S
S

Sheet 10-1. Metric 100- and 200-meter training schedule sheet

Short Sprint NAME DATE September/October

1. A. Jog 1 or 2 laps with relay pass B. High knee (slow) and fast leg
2. Fartlek: A. Holmer (varied-pace)—stride, sprint, recover—stride, meet a challenge or challenge, recover. Finish feeling exhilarated, not exhausted.
   B. Lydiard (steady pace)—slow, 10-30 min. (1) Hendricks (2) Golf course (3)
3. A. Weights and jogging—get chart B. Jogging and stretching
4. High knee and fast leg
5. Starts A. 3 at 1/2 speed, 3 at 7/8—30 yds.
   (1) On your own (2) Gun
   B. 50 yds. C. Grass D.
6. Intervals Y. Fast 20-55 in middle A. 110
   (1) 18-16-14 (2)
   B. 165 (1) 22 (2)
   C. 220 (1) 30 (2)
   D. 110-220-110 (1)
   E.
7. Squad meeting
8. Special A. Sauna B. Swim C.
9. Relay work A. Routine B. 55 C. Trial
10. A. Trial B. Compete
11. Bunches A. 330 B. 165 C. 80
12. Hill with: A. Coach B. Leader
14. A. Wind sprints B. Hurdle drill C. Spring and bound
    D. Alternate run and jog, at least 880
15. Finish work—50-70 at 3/4—last 30-50 at 9/10
    A. 100 B. 220
16. Back to back A. 55 B.
17. 3/4 effort A. 100 B. 300 C. 500
18.
19.
20.
21. A. Pictures B. Film
22. A. 100 yds. at 8/10—float at 70 (3 steps), then go
    B. 220 C. Parts
23. A. 550-330-110 (80-48-14) B. 300-200-100 (1)
    C. 165-110-55
24. Turn work (40 at 9/10) (30 at 1/2) (40 at 9/10)

Date	Dist.	3/4	Date P.	Goal P.

Day	Work
M	7-Organization-equipment-lockers
T	Meet on use of weights
W	7 Discussion of facilities-14A
T	3A
F	1A-1B-2A(1)
S	Registration completed
S	recreation
M	1B-23A-6A(1) 2x-880 jog
T	
W	12B-6A(1) 2x
T	
F	10A-200 meters at 7/8 effort to 9/10 effort
S	
S	
M	1A-23A-6A(1) 2x-jog 880
T	3A
W	12B
T	3A
F	1A-11ABC 2x-6B(1)
S	
S	
M	1A-1B-23A-6B 3x-6A-2B(1)
T	3A
W	12B
T	
F	10A-100 and 300
S	
S	

Sheet 10-2. Training schedule for 100- and 200-meter sprinters

Short Sprint NAME DATE October/November

1. A. Jog 1 or 2 laps with relay pass B. High knee (slow) and fast leg
2. Fartlek: A. Holmer (varied-pace)—stride, sprint, recover—stride, meet a challenge or challenge, recover. Finish feeling exhilarated, not exhausted.
   B. Lydiard (steady pace)—slow, 10-30 min. (1) Hendricks (2) Golf course (3)
3. A. Weights and jogging—get chart B. Jogging and stretching
4. High knee and fast leg
5. Starts A. 3 at 1/2 speed, 3 at 7/8—30 yds.
   (1) On your own (2) Gun
   B. 50 yds. C. Grass D.
6. Intervals Y. Fast 20-55 in middle A. 110
   (1) 18-16-14 (2)
   B. 165 (1) 22 (2)
   C. 220 (1) 30 (2)
   D. 110-220-110 (1)
   E.
7. Squad meeting
8. Special A. Sauna B. Swim C.
9. Relay work A. Routine B. 55 C. Trial
10. A. Trial B. Compete
11. Bunches A. 330 B. 165 C. 80
12. Hill with: A. Coach B. Leader
14. A. Wind sprints B. Hurdle drill C. Spring and bound
    D. Alternate run and jog, at least 880
15. Finish work—50-70 at 3/4—last 30-50 at 9/10
    A. 100 B. 220
16. Back to back A. 55 B.
17. 3/4 effort A. 100 B. 300 C. 500
18.
19.
20.
21. A. Pictures B. Film
22. A. 100 yds. at 8/10—float at 70 (3 steps), then go
    B. 220 C. Parts
23. A. 550-330-110 (80-48-14) B. 300-200-100 (1)
    C. 165-110-55
24. Turn work (40 at 9/10) (30 at 1/2) (40 at 9/10)

Date	Dist.	3/4	Date P.	Goal P.

Day	Workout
M	1B – 5A – 21A – 23A – 2X 6C – 2B(1)
T	3A – 21B
W	12B – 2X 6A(1)
T	3A
F	2X 300y – 4X 100y – 2A(1)
S	1A – 1B
S	

Day	Workout
M	1A – 5A – 23A – 4X 6A – 2A(1)
T	3A – 21B
W	12B – 6A(1)
T	
F	10X 100y
S	10A – 300 yards
S	

Day	Workout
M	1A – 5A – 1X 500y – 2X 300y – 3X 200y – 4X 100y – 2A(1)
T	3B – 21B
W	12
T	3A
F	10X 100y (sets of 4-4-2) – 2A(1)
S	
S	

Day	Workout
M	1A – 5A – 23A – 3X 6B – 10A(1)
T	3A
W	12 – 3X 6B
T	
F	10A – 100y and relay
S	10A – Relay and 300y
S	recreation

Sheet 10-3. Training schedule for 100- and 200-meter sprinters

Short Sprint NAME DATE November/December

1. A. Jog 1 or 2 laps with relay pass B. High knee (slow) and fast leg
2. Fartlek: A. Holmer (varied-pace)—stride, sprint, recover—stride, meet a challenge or challenge, recover. Finish feeling exhilarated, not exhausted.
   B. Lydiard (steady pace)—slow, 10-30 min. (1) Hendricks (2) Golf course (3)
3. A. Weights and jogging—get chart B. Jogging and stretching
4. High knee and fast leg
5. Starts A. 3 at 1/2 speed, 3 at 7/8—30 yds.
   (1) On your own (2) Gun
   B. 50 yds. C. Grass D.
6. Intervals Y. Fast 20-55 in middle A. 110
   (1) 18-16-14 (2)
   B. 165 (1) 22 (2)
   C. 220 (1) 30 (2)
   D. 110-220-110 (1)
   E.
7. Squad meeting
8. Special A. Sauna B. Swim C.
9. Relay work A. Routine B. 55 C. Trial
10. A. Trial B. Compete
11. Bunches A. 330 B. 165 C. 80
12. Hill with: A. Coach B. Leader
14. A. Wind sprints B. Hurdle drill C. Spring and bound
    D. Alternate run and jog, at least 880
15. Finish work—50-70 at 3/4—last 30-50 at 9/10
    A. 100 B. 220
16. Back to back A. 55 B.
17. 3/4 effort A. 100 B. 300 C. 500
18.
19.
20.
21. A. Pictures B. Film
22. A. 100 yds. at 8/10—float at 70 (3 steps), then go
    B. 220 C. Parts
23. A. 550-330-110 (80-48-14) B. 300-200-100 (1)
    C. 165-110-55
24. Turn work (40 at 9/10) (30 at 1/2) (40 at 9/10)

Date	Dist.	3/4	Date P.	Goal P.

Day	Workout
M	1A-1B-6D-23B (2-3X)
T	5A-3A
W	12
T	
F	10A-100 (2X)-300 (1X)-14A
S	
S	2A
M	1A-1B-5A-23B-23C (2-3X)
T	7-3A-21B
W	1-5A-9A-6D-23A
T	
F	10A-Relay (1X)-100 (1X)
S	10A-100 (1X)-300 (1X)
S	
M	
T	
W	
T	
F	
S	
S	
M	
T	
W	
T	
F	
S	
S	

Sheet 10-4. Training schedule for 100- and 200-meter sprinters

Short Sprint NAME DATE January

1. A. Jog 1 or 2 laps with relay pass B. High knee (slow) and fast leg
2. Fartlek: A. Holmer (varied-pace)—stride, sprint, recover—stride, meet a challenge or challenge, recover. Finish feeling exhilarated, not exhausted.
   B. Lydiard (steady pace)—slow, 10-30 min. (1) Hendricks (2) Golf course (3)
3. A. Weights and jogging—get chart B. Jogging and stretching
4. High knee and fast leg
5. Starts A. 3 at 1/2 speed, 3 at 7/8—30 yds.
   (1) On your own (2) Gun
   B. 50 yds. C. Grass D.
6. Intervals Y. Fast 20-55 in middle A. 110
   (1) 18-16-14 (2)
   B. 165 (1) 22 (2)
   C. 220 (1) 30 (2)
   D. 110-220-110 (1)
   E.
7. Squad meeting
8. Special A. Sauna B. Swim C.
9. Relay work A. Routine B. 55 C. Trial
10. A. Trial B. Compete
11. Bunches A. 330 B. 165 C. 80
12. Hill with: A. Coach B. Leader
14. A. Wind sprints B. Hurdle drill C. Spring and bound
    D. Alternate run and jog, at least 880
15. Finish work—50-70 at 3/4—last 30-50 at 9/10
    A. 100 B. 220
16. Back to back A. 55 B.
17. 3/4 effort A. 100 B. 300 C. 500
18.
19.
20.
21. A. Pictures B. Film
22. A. 100 yds. at 8/10—float at 70 (3 steps), then go
    B. 220 C. Parts
23. A. 550-330-110 (80-48-14) B. 300-200-100 (1)
    C. 165-110-55
24. Turn work (40 at 9/10) (30 at 1/2) (40 at 9/10)

Date	Dist.	3/4	Date P.	Goal P.

M	New Year activities
T	Travel-settle in
W	Register-check equipment-organization
T	3A-14A or jog the halls
F	
S	Relay work or stairs
S	recreation
M	2x 1A-1B-5A-23C-14A
T	7-3A-14A
W	12, if no rain. If rain, 1B-5A-9A
T	3A
F	1A-1B-9A
S	
S	
M	2x 1A-23B-23C-2A(1)
T	3A-21B
W	2x 1A-12-6A(1)
T	1A-3A
F	2x 1A-5A-23B-2B(1)
S	1x 1x 10A-100-300-2B(1)
S	
M	1A-5A-10A (40 or 60 at 9/10)-1B-14A
T	1A-5A (easy)
W	1A-5A-10A (40 to 60 at 9/10)-2A(1)
T	7 at 4:30 pm
F	Gear ready-jog
S	10A here or 10B-Portland
S	recreation

Sheet 10-5. Training schedule for 100- and 200-meter sprinters

Short Sprint NAME DATE February

1. A. Jog 1 or 2 laps with relay pass B. High knee (slow) and fast leg
2. Fartlek: A. Holmer (varied-pace)—stride, sprint, recover—stride, meet a challenge or challenge, recover. Finish feeling exhilarated, not exhausted.
   B. Lydiard (steady pace)—slow, 10-30 min. (1) Hendricks (2) Golf course (3)
3. A. Weights and jogging—get chart B. Jogging and stretching
4. High knee and fast leg
5. Starts A. 3 at 1/2 speed, 3 at 7/8—30 yds.
   (1) On your own (2) Gun
   B. 50 yds. C. Grass D.
6. Intervals Y. Fast 20-55 in middle A. 110
   (1) 18-16-14 (2)
   B. 165 (1) 22 (2)
   C. 220 (1) 30 (2)
   D. 110-220-110 (1)
   E.
7. Squad meeting
8. Special A. Sauna B. Swim C.
9. Relay work A. Routine B. 55 C. Trial
10. A. Trial B. Compete
11. Bunches A. 330 B. 165 C. 80
12. Hill with: A. Coach B. Leader
14. A. Wind sprints B. Hurdle drill C. Spring and bound
    D. Alternate run and jog, at least 880
15. Finish work—50-70 at 3/4—last 30-50 at 9/10
    A. 100 B. 220
16. Back to back A. 55 B.
17. 3/4 effort A. 100 B. 300 C. 500
18.
19.
20.
21. A. Pictures B. Film
22. A. 100 yds. at 8/10—float at 70 (3 steps), then go
    B. 220 C. Parts
23. A. 550-330-110 (80-48-14) B. 300-200-100 (1)
    C. 165-110-55
24. Turn work (40 at 9/10) (30 at 1/2) (40 at 9/10)

Date	Dist.	3/4	Date P.	Goal P.

Day	Workout
M	2x 4x 1A-1B-14A-5A-6C(2)-6A(2)-14A
T	12
W	1x 2x 6x 1A-1B-300-200-100-14A
T	12 or 1A
F	1x 2x 4x 1A-5A-300-200-100-14A
S	22A or 12
S	grass run or recreation
M	4x 4x 1A-5A-6A(3)-9A-6C(2)-2A(1)
T	3A-14A-7 (5 pm)
W	1A-2B(1)
T	4x 4x 1A-5A-6C(2)-6A(4)-14A
F	3A
S	2A(1)
S	
M	1x 2x 4x 1A-14A-5A-300-200-100-2B(1)
T	3A
W	1A-1B-2B(1)
T	3B
F	1A-9A-9B
S	1x 1x 10A-75y-300y-9A
S	recreation
M	2x 4x 1x 1A-5A-9A-200-100-300
T	3A-2B(1)
W	12
T	9A
F	1A-5A-14A-easy 500y.
S	
S	2B(1)

Sheet 10-6. Training schedule for 100- and 200-meter sprinters

Short Sprint NAME DATE *March*

1. A. Jog 1 or 2 laps with relay pass B. High knee (slow) and fast leg
2. Fartlek: A. Holmer (varied-pace)—stride, sprint, recover—stride, meet a challenge or challenge, recover. Finish feeling exhilarated, not exhausted.
   B. Lydiard (steady pace)—slow, 10-30 min. (1) Hendricks (2) Golf course (3)
3. A. Weights and jogging—get chart B. Jogging and stretching
4. High knee and fast leg
5. Starts A. 3 at 1/2 speed, 3 at 7/8—30 yds.
   (1) On your own (2) Gun
   B. 50 yds. C. Grass D.
6. Intervals Y. Fast 20-55 in middle A. 110
   (1) 18-16-14 (2)
   B. 165 (1) 22 (2)
   C. 220 (1) 30 (2)
   D. 110-220-110 (1)
   E.
7. Squad meeting
8. Special A. Sauna B. Swim C.
9. Relay work A. Routine B. 55 C. Trial
10. A. Trial B. Compete
11. Bunches A. 330 B. 165 C. 80
12. Hill with: A. Coach B. Leader
14. A. Wind sprints B. Hurdle drill C. Spring and bound
    D. Alternate run and jog, at least 880
15. Finish work—50-70 at 3/4—last 30-50 at 9/10
    A. 100 B. 220
16. Back to back A. 55 B.
17. 3/4 effort A. 100 B. 300 C. 500
18.
19.
20.
21. A. Pictures B. Film
22. A. 100 yds. at 8/10—float at 70 (3 steps), then go
    B. 220 C. Parts
23. A. 550-330-110 (80-48-14) B. 300-200-100 (1)
    C. 165-110-55
24. Turn work (40 at 9/10) (30 at 1/2) (40 at 9/10)

Date	Dist.	3/4	Date P.	Goal P.

M	*3A-4-5A-23B-6D-500 (1x)-2B(1)*
T	*9A-7 (5pm)*
W	*1B-12-6A (4x)*
T	*1A-9A-2A(1)-8C*
F	*Grass run*
S	*10A-Relay-300y (1x)*
S	*recreation*
M	*1B-5A-23B-6D-2A(1)*
T	*9A-2-7 (5pm)*
W	*1A-4-2B(1)-6A(1) (2x)*
T	*21-9A*
F	*1A-5A-6C-6A (4x)-9A-2 (grass)*
S	*Exams start-9A-grass*
S	
M	*Exams-easy workout-2B*
T	*Relay in pairs-14A*
W	*1A-5A (if no exams)-2B(1)*
T	
F	*Gear ready*
S	*Travel-10B-100 and/or 220*
S	*Jog and settle in-spring trip*

	A.M.	P.M.
M	*Jog*	*1A-5A-11ABC (2x)-grass*
T	*14A*	*9A-23A-2B*
W	*Jog*	*1A-5A-6A (4x)-500 (1x)-2*
T	*14A*	*9A-2*
F		*Light and swim*
S	*10B-Meet and bus home*	
S		

Sheet 10-7. Training schedule for 100- and 200-meter sprinters

Short Sprint NAME DATE *April*

1. A. Jog 1 or 2 laps with relay pass B. High knee (slow) and fast leg
2. Fartlek: A. Holmer (varied-pace)—stride, sprint, recover—stride, meet a challenge or challenge, recover. Finish feeling exhilarated, not exhausted.
   B. Lydiard (steady pace)—slow, 10-30 min. (1) Hendricks (2) Golf course (3)
3. A. Weights and jogging—get chart B. Jogging and stretching
4. High knee and fast leg
5. Starts A. 3 at 1/2 speed, 3 at 7/8—30 yds.
   (1) On your own (2) Gun
   B. 50 yds. C. Grass D.
6. Intervals Y. Fast 20-55 in middle A. 110
   (1) 18-16-14 (2)
   B. 165 (1) 22 (2)
   C. 220 (1) 30 (2)
   D. 110-220-110 (1)
   E.
7. Squad meeting
8. Special A. Sauna B. Swim C.
9. Relay work A. Routine B. 55 C. Trial
10. A. Trial B. Compete
11. Bunches A. 330 B. 165 C. 80
12. Hill with: A. Coach B. Leader
14. A. Wind sprints B. Hurdle drill C. Spring and bound
    D. Alternate run and jog, at least 880
15. Finish work—50-70 at 3/4—last 30-50 at 9/10
    A. 100 B. 220
16. Back to back A. 55 B.
17. 3/4 effort A. 100 B. 300 C. 500
18.
19.
20.
21. A. Pictures B. Film
22. A. 100 yds. at 8/10—float at 70 (3 steps), then go
    B. 220 C. Parts
23. A. 550-330-110 (80-48-14) B. 300-200-100 (1)
    C. 165-110-55
24. Turn work (40 at 9/10) (30 at 1/2) (40 at 9/10)

Date	Dist.	3/4	Date P.	Goal P.

M	*New term – Register 1A – 1B – 5A – 9A – 6B (4x) – 6A (4x) – 300 (1x)*
T	*9A*
W	*1A – 1B – 12*
T	*9A*
F	*9A – gear ready*
S	*10B – relay carnival*
S	*2B – 6A (4x)*
M	*1A – 6D – 6B (4x) – 500 (1x) – 7 (5pm)*
T	*5A (easy) – light grass*
W	*1A – 2B (1)*
T	*1 – 5A – 9A – 6D*
F	*gear ready – 7 (5pm)*
S	*10B – Home meet*
S	*Easy grass*
M	*1A – 1B – 14A – 300 (1x) (easy)*
T	*1 – 5A – 100 (7/8 effort) – 200 (7/8 effort) 2 – (grass)*
W	*1 – 14A – 14 or 2B*
T	*Light*
F	*Light*
S	*10B – Conference / Dual meet*
S	*Easy grass*
M	*1A – 1B – 14A – 300 (1x) (easy)*
T	*1 – 5B – 100 (2x) (7/8 effort) – 14B – grass*
W	*1 – 4 – 14A*
T	*Light*
F	*Travel*
S	*10B – Competition*
S	*Home – loosen up*

Sheet 10-8. Training schedule for 100- and 200-meter sprinters

Short Sprint NAME DATE May

1. A. Jog 1 or 2 laps with relay pass B. High knee (slow) and fast leg
2. Fartlek: A. Holmer (varied-pace)—stride, sprint, recover—stride, meet a challenge or challenge, recover. Finish feeling exhilarated, not exhausted.
   B. Lydiard (steady pace)—slow, 10-30 min. (1) Hendricks (2) Golf course (3)
3. A. Weights and jogging—get chart B. Jogging and stretching
4. High knee and fast leg
5. Starts A. 3 at 1/2 speed, 3 at 7/8—30 yds.
   (1) On your own (2) Gun
   B. 50 yds. C. Grass D.
6. Intervals Y. Fast 20-55 in middle A. 110
   (1) 18-16-14 (2)
   B. 165 (1) 22 (2)
   C. 220 (1) 30 (2)
   D. 110-220-110 (1)
   E.
7. Squad meeting
8. Special A. Sauna B. Swim C.
9. Relay work A. Routine B. 55 C. Trial
10. A. Trial B. Compete
11. Bunches A. 330 B. 165 C. 80
12. Hill with: A. Coach B. Leader
14. A. Wind sprints B. Hurdle drill C. Spring and bound
    D. Alternate run and jog, at least 880
15. Finish work—50-70 at 3/4—last 30-50 at 9/10
    A. 100 B. 220
16. Back to back A. 55 B.
17. 3/4 effort A. 100 B. 300 C. 500
18.
19.
20.
21. A. Pictures B. Film
22. A. 100 yds. at 8/10—float at 70 (3 steps), then go
    B. 220 C. Parts
23. A. 550-330-110 (80-48-14) B. 300-200-100 (1)
    C. 165-110-55
24. Turn work (40 at 9/10) (30 at 1/2) (40 at 9/10)

Date	Dist.	3/4	Date P.	Goal P.

Day	Workout
M	1A-1B-2B(1)-4x 6A-7(4:15 pm)
T	9B
W	1A-1B-5A-grass run
T	7 (3:15 pm)-9A-5A
F	Light
S	10B-Home meet
S	14A (easy)
M	7 (3:15 pm)-9B-4-14A
T	1A-5A-1x 300-1x 165-4x 110-1x 500 (easy)
W	9A-9B-14A
T	7 (3:30 pm)-5A
F	Gear ready
S	10B-Dual meet
S	2B(1) (easy)
M	7 (3:30)-4-9A-1x 300 (easy)
T	1-5A-4x 6D-6A-grass run
W	9A-light grass
T	7 (3:30)-1-5A-4x 6D (grass)
F	Gear ready
S	10B-Invitational or relay meet
S	Home and jog
M	1A-9A-9B-easy 300-14A
T	1A-1B-light
W	1-5A-6D-14A
T	7 (3:30 pm)-Light, gear ready
F	Preliminaries, Pac 8 Meet
S	Finals, Pac 8 Meet
S	Loosen up

Sheet 10-9. Training schedule for 100- and 200-meter sprinters

Short Sprint NAME DATE June

1. A. Jog 1 or 2 laps with relay pass B. High knee (slow) and fast leg
2. Fartlek: A. Holmer (varied-pace)—stride, sprint, recover—stride, meet a challenge or challenge, recover. Finish feeling exhilarated, not exhausted.
   B. Lydiard (steady pace)—slow, 10-30 min. (1) Hendricks (2) Golf course (3)
3. A. Weights and jogging—get chart B. Jogging and stretching
4. High knee and fast leg
5. Starts A. 3 at 1/2 speed, 3 at 7/8—30 yds.
   (1) On your own (2) Gun
   B. 50 yds. C. Grass D.
6. Intervals Y. Fast 20-55 in middle A. 110
   (1) 18-16-14 (2)
   B. 165 (1) 22 (2)
   C. 220 (1) 30 (2)
   D. 110-220-110 (1)
   E.
7. Squad meeting
8. Special A. Sauna B. Swim C.
9. Relay work A. Routine B. 55 C. Trial
10. A. Trial B. Compete
11. Bunches A. 330 B. 165 C. 80
12. Hill with: A. Coach B. Leader
14. A. Wind sprints B. Hurdle drill C. Spring and bound
    D. Alternate run and jog, at least 880
15. Finish work—50-70 at 3/4—last 30-50 at 9/10
    A. 100 B. 220
16. Back to back A. 55 B.
17. 3/4 effort A. 100 B. 300 C. 500
18.
19.
20.
21. A. Pictures B. Film
22. A. 100 yds. at 8/10—float at 70 (3 steps), then go
    B. 220 C. Parts
23. A. 550-330-110 (80-48-14) B. 300-200-100 (1)
    C. 165-110-55
24. Turn work (40 at 9/10) (30 at 1/2) (40 at 9/10)

Date	Dist.	3/4	Date P.	Goal P.

M 1A - 1B - 2X 15A - 1X 300
T 1 - 9A - 14A
W 1 - 5A - 24 - 4 - grass run
T 1 - 9A - jog
F 1 - 5A - 14A
S 10B - Relay
S Squad picnic
M 1A - 1B - grass run
T 1A - 14A
W 1 - 5A - grass 14A - 1X 100 (7/8 effort) - 1X 220 (7/8 effort) - Jog
T 1 - grass run - 100 (7/8 effort) - 220 (7/8 effort) - grass run
F 1A - (light) 14A
S 7 - 1A - 14A (light)
S 1 - 5A - 1X 100 (7/8 effort) - 2X 200 (7/8 effort) - 4 - 14A
M 1 - easy grass
T 1 - 5 (easy) - 14A (easy)
W Light
T 10B Championship, or light run
F 10B Championship
S 10B Championship
S
M
T
W
T
F
S
S

Sheet 10-10. Training schedule for 100- and 200-meter sprinters

Endnotes

1. Ralph V. Mann, Ben F. Johnson, John W. Kotmel, John A. Herman, et al. (1982-1984). *The Elite Athlete Project* (Technical Reports 1-11). Colorado Springs, CO: United States Olympic Training Center.
2. Ben F. Johnson, John W. Kotmel, & John A. Herman. (1987). *Applying mechanics research to sprint coaching*. Unpublished manuscript.
3. Donald B. Slocum & William J. Bowerman. (1961). The biomechanics of running. In *Proceedings of the Second National Conference on the Medical Aspects of Sports*. Chicago: American Medical Association, 53-58.
4. Jess Jarver. (1983). What is happening in sprinting? In Jess Jarver (Ed.), *Sprints and relays: Contemporary theory, technique and training* (2nd ed.). Los Altos, CA: Tafnews, 11-13.
5. Frank Dick. (1978). *Training theory*. London: British Amateur Athletic Board, 64-65.
6. Hans Torim. (1988). Maximal speed in the sprints. *Track Technique, 104*, 3331.
7. Bernie Dare & Beverly Kearney. (1988). Speed training. *Track Technique, 103*, 3289-3295.
8. Vern Gambetta, Gary Winckler, Joe Rogers, John Orognen, Loren Seagrave, & Sonny Jolly. (1989). Sprints and relays. In *The Athletic Congress's track and field coaching manual* (2nd ed.). Champaign, IL: Leisure Press, 55-71.
9. Gary Winckler & Vern Gambetta. (1987). Classifications of energy systems in sprint training. *Track Technique, 100*, 3193-3195.
10. Adam Zajac. (1987). Direct competition preparation for elite sprinters. *Track Technique, 98*, 3114-3115.

Core Readings

Freeman, William H. (2001). Periodized training for sprinters and hurdlers. In *Peak When It Counts: Periodization for American track and field* (4th ed.). Mountain View, CA: Tafnews, 106-119.

Frye, Curtis. 100 and 200 meters. (2000). In *USA Track and Field coaching manual*. Champaign, IL: Human Kinetics, 35-50.

Jarver, Jess, ed. (2000). *Sprints and relays: Contemporary theory, technique and training* (5th ed.). Mountain View, CA: Tafnews.

Johnson, Rob, & Karen Dennis. Relays. (2000). In *USA Track and Field coaching manua*l. Champaign, IL: Human Kinetics, 123-137.

Level II Coaching Education Curriculum Development Committee on Sprints and Hurdles, The. (1989). Sprints and relays. In *The Athletics Congress's Track and Field Coaching Manual* (2nd ed.). Champaign, IL: Human Kinetics, 55-71.

USA Track & Field Coaching Education Program. (2001). *Level II Course: Sprints hurdles relays*. USA Track & Field. Invaluable; revised regularly.

Vittori, Carlo. (1995). Monitoring the training of a sprinter. *New Studies in Athletics, 10*(3), 39-44. Reprinted in Jarver (5th ed., 2000), 45-50.

Recommended Readings

Sprinting

Ayres, Thomas R., & Marc S. Gottlieb. (2006). Occurrence of right vs. left side injury location in elite sprinters who train on an oval 400m track. *New Studies in Athletics, 21*(4), 51-56.

Baughman, Mark, Mike Takaha & Tom Tellez. (1984). Sprint training: Including strength training. *Track and Field Quarterly Review, 84*(2), 9-12.

Bidder, Tudor, Emperatriz Gonzalez Henao, Victor Lopez, Carlo Vittori, & Gary Winckler. (1995). NSA Round Table 27: Sprinting. *New Studies in Athletics, 10*(1), 13-22.

Blount, Jeff, Jeff L. Hoskisson, & Remi Korchemny. (1990). Summary of results from TAC Junior Elite Sprint Camp. *Track Technique, 113*, 3593-3602.

Bompa, Tudor. (1991). A model of an annual training programme for a sprinter. *New Studies in Athletics, 6*(1), 47-51.

Bompa, Tudor O. (1987). Peaking for the extended athletics calendar. *New Studies in Athletics, 2*(4), 29-43.

Bowerman, William J., & Brown, Gwilim S. (1971, August 2). The secrets of speed. *Sports Illustrated, 35*, 22-29.

Coh, Milan, & Katia Tomazin. (2006). Kinematic analysis of the sprint start and acceleration from the blocks. *New Studies in Athletics, 21*(3), 23-33.

Collier, Curtis. (Spring 2002). Foundational concepts of sprinting: Spatial and movement perspectives. *Track Coach, 159*, 5071-5077.

Connolly, Pat. (1985). Five cycle sprint training for Evelyn Ashford. *Track and Field Quarterly Review, 85*, 15-20.

Delecluse, Christophe. (1997). Influence of strength training on sprint running performance: Current findings and implications for training. *Sports Medicine, 24*(3), 147-156.

Delecluse, Christophe, Herman Van Coppenolle, Marina Goris & Rudi Diels. (1992). A model for the scientific preparation of high level sprinters. *New Studies in Athletics, 7*(4), 57-64. Reprinted in Jarver (5th ed., 2000), 124-129.

Delecluse, Christophe, Rudi Diels, Maria Goris & Herman van Coppenolle. (1996). The F.A.S.T. project–A scientific follow-up of sprinting abilities. *New Studies in Athletics, 11*(2-3), 141-143.

Donati, Alessandro. (1995). The development of stride length and stride frequency in sprinting. *New Studies in Athletics, 10*(1), 51-66.

Ebbets, Russ. (Fall 2002). An interview with Charlie Francis. *Track Coach, 161*, 5144-5148. Coach of Ben Johnson.

Faccioni, Adrian. (1995). The role of the mid-torso in maximizing sprint performance. *Track Coach, 133*, 4233-4237, 4245, 4261.

Ferro, Amelia, Alicia Rivera, Itzar Pagola, Miguel Ferreruela, Álvaro Martin & Valentin Rocandio. (2001). Biomechanical Research Project at the 7th World Champiuonships in Athletics Seville 1999. *New Studies in Athletics, 16*(1/2), 25-60. Analysis of the 100m finals, 28-43. Analysis of the 200m finals, 44-51.

Gajer, B., C. Thépaut-Mathieu & D. Lehénaff. (1999). Evolution of stride rate and length during a 100m race. *New Studies in Athletics, 14*(3), 43-50.

Gambetta, Vern. (1991). Essential considerations for the development of a teaching model for the 100 metres sprint. *New Studies in Athletics, 6*(2), 27-32.

Gardiner, Phil. (Summer 2005). Specific strength exercises for sprinters. *Track Coach, 172*, 5486-5490.

Harland, M.J., & J.R. Steele. (1997). Biomechanics of the sprint start. *Sports Medicine, 23*(1), 11-20.

Helmick, Karen. (Spring 2003). Biomechanical analysis of sprint start positioning. *Track Coach, 163*, 5209-5214.

Headly, David. (Fall 2003). Radar technology as a tool for the sprint coach. *Track Coach, 165*, 5257-5264.

Ito, Akira, Masaki Ishikawa, Juha Isolehto & Paavo V. Komi. (2006). Changes in the step width, step length, and step frequency of the world's top sprinters during the 100 metres. *New Studies in Athletics, 21*(3), 35-39.

Kearney, Beverly. (1993). Sprints & sprint hurdles. *Track and Field Quarterly Review, 93*(1), 29-36.

Kirksey, Brett, & Michael H. Stone. (1998). Periodizing college sprint program: Theory and practice. *Strength and Conditioning, 20*(3), 42-47. Reprinted in Jarver (5th ed., 2000), 73-78.

Korchemny, Reni. (1994). Speed development training menu. Ed. John Millar. *Track Technique, 129*, 4105-4110.

Lacour, René. (1996). Physiological analysis of qualities required in sprinting. *New Studies in Athletics, 11*(2-3), 59-70.

Letzelter, Stefan. (Winter 2002). Supramaximal sprints [abstract]. *Track Coach, 158*, 5057.

Lidor, Ronnie, & Dapeng Chen. (2003). A 3-step learning and performance strategy for the 100 metres sprint start. *New Studies in Athletics, 18*(1), 29-34.

Lidor, Ronnie, & Yoav Meckel. (2004). Physiological, skill development and motor learning considerations for the 100 metres. *New Studies in Athletics, 19*(1), 7-11.

Linthorne, Nick. (1994). Wind assistance in the 100m sprint. *Track Technique, 127*, 4049-4051.

Locatelli, Elio. (1996). The importance of anaerobic glycolysis and stiffness in the sprints (60, 100 and 200 metres). *New Studies in Athletics, 11*(2-3), 121-125.

Locateli, Elio, & Laurent Arsac. (1995). The mechanics and energetics of the 100m sprint. *New Studies in Athletics, 10*(1), 81-87. Reprinted in Jarver (5th ed., 2000), 23-28.

Mach, Gerard. (1985). Individual Olympic sprint events. *Track and Field Quarterly Review, 85*(2), 11-14.

McClements, James D., Lyle K. Sanderson & Robert E. Gander. (1996). Kinetic and kinematic factors related to sprint starting as measured by the Saskatchewan Sprint Start Team. *New Studies in Athletics, 11*(2-3), 133-135; Using immediate kinetic and kinematic feedback measured by the Saskatchewan Sprint Start System to improve sprinting performance. 137-139.

Mureika, Jonas R. (2000). The legality of wind and altitude assisted performances in the sprints. *New Studies in Athletics, 15*(3/4), 63-58.

Parjsuk, Vladimir. (1996). The European School in sprint training: The experiences in Russia. *New Studies in Athletics, 11*(2-3), 71-76.

Parry, Tom, Phillip Henson & John Cooper. (Fall 2003). Lateral foot placement analysis of the sprint start [abstract]. *Track Coach, 165*, 5284-5285.

Ritzdorf, Wolfgang. 100m & 200m. In Harald Müller & Helmar Hommel, eds., Biomechanical Research Project at the VIth World Championships in Athletics, Athens 1997: Preliminary Report. *New Studies in Athletics, 12*(2-3), 45-48; 48-49.

Ross, Angus, Michael Leveritt & Stephen Riek. (2001). Neural influences on sprint running: Training adaptations and acute responses. *Sports Medicine, 31*(6), 409-425.

Ryan, Gary J., & Andrew J. Harrison. (2003). Technical adaptations of competitive sprinters induced by bend running. *New Studies in Athletics, 18*(4), 57-67.

Salo, Aki, & Ian Bezodis. (2004). Which starting style is faster in sprint running–Standing or crouch start? *Sports Biomechanics, 3*(1), 43-54.

Schiffer, Jürgen. (1995). Selected and annotated bibliography 34: Sprints and relays. *New Studies in Athletics, 10*(1), 99-120.

Schiffer, Jürgen. (1996). Selected and annotated bibliography 39: Sprints, relays and speed training. *New Studies in Athletics, 11*(2-3), 169-181.

Schiffer, Jürgen. (2006-2007). Selected and annotated bibliography 76-77: Sprints. *New Studies in Athletics, 21*(4), 79-109; 22(1), 73-107.

Seagrave, Loren. (1996). Introduction to sprinting. *New Studies in Athletics, 11*(2-3), 93-113.

Shi, Duamu, & Tanhua Tong. (Spring 2003). The effects of stride length and frequency on the speeds of elite sprinters [abstract]. *Track Coach, 163*, 5218.

Stefanovic, Dorde, & Irina Juhas. (1996). Fartlek for sprinters. *New Studies in Athletics, 11*(2-3), 147-148.

Stefanyshyn, Darren, & Ciro Fusco. (2004). Increased shoe bending stiffness increases sprint performance. *Sports Biomechanics, 3*(1), 55-66.

Stefanyshyn, Darren, & Ciro Fusco. (Spring 2002). The shoe in sprinting. *Track Coach, 159*, 5082-5084, 5093.

Tellez, Tom, & Doolittle, Dorothy. (1984). Sprinting: From start to finish. *Track Technique, 88*, 2802-2805.

Van Coppenolle, H., C. Delecluse, M. Goris, R. Diels, L. Seagrave & H. Kraayenhof. (1990). An evaluation of the starting action of world class female sprinters. *Track Technique, 112*, 3581-3582.

Vittori, Carlo. (1996). The European School in sprint training: The experiences in Italy. *New Studies in Athletics, 11*(2-3), 85-92.

Winckler, Gary. (1986). An application of Doherty's power indexing to sprint/hurdle training. *Track Technique, 94,* 2986-2987.

Winckler, Gary. (1991). An examination of speed endurance. *New Studies in Athletics, 6*(1), 27-33.

Winckler, Gary, & Vern Gambetta. (1987). Classifications of energy systems sprint training. *Track Technique, 100*, 3193-3195.

Winter, Lloyd C. "Bud". (1964). *The jet sprint relay pass.* San Jose, CA: Winter Enterprises.

Wood, Graeme A. (1986). Optimal performance criteria and limiting factors in sprint running. *New Studies in Athletics, 1*(2), 55-63.

Young, Michael. (Spring 2007). Maximal velocity sprint mechanics. *Track Coach, 179*, 5723-5729.

Relay Racing

Grady, Dennis. (Winter 2006). Better baton passing for the sprint relays: How to decrease our exchange failure rate. *Track Coach, 174*, 5555-5558.

Hart, Clyde. (1983). Baylor sprint relay exchange. *Track and Field Quarterly Review, 83*(2), 26-27.

Lurie, M. (1982). Technical bases used for preparation of the French national 4 x 100m relay team. *Track and Field Quarterly Review, 82*(2), 49-52.

Maisetti,Georges. (1996). Efficient baton exchange in the sprint relay. *New Studies in Athletics, 11*(2-3), 77-82. Reprinted in Jarver (5th ed., 2000), 138-142.

Rogers, Joe. (1983). Calculating the "go" mark for sprint relay exchanges. *Track Technique, 86*, 2740.

Sanderson, Lyle. (1997). Some thoughts on sprint relay racing from a Canadian perspective. *New Studies in Athletics, 12*(4), 49-52. Reprinted in Jarver (5th ed., 2000), 157-160.

Schiffer, Jürgen. (2006). Selected and annotated bibliography 75: Relay racing. *New Studies in Athletics, 21*(3), 73-92.

Sugiura, Yusaku, Hideo Numazawa & Michiyoshi Ae. (1995). Time analysis of elite sprinters in the 4 x 100 metres relay. *New Studies in Athletics, 10*(3), 45-49. Reprinted in Jarver (5th ed., 2000), 147-151.

Tansley, John. (1991). The alternating, underhand, upsweep, straight-tube, twist pass. *Track Technique, 114*, 3630-3631.

Wiemeyer, Josef, & Walter Oberste. (1993). Linematic analysis of three 4 x 100 baton passing techniques. *Track Technique, 125*, 3995-3998, 4000.

Wolfe, Vern. (1981). 400m relay. *Track and Field Quarterly Review, 81*(2), 35.

11

The Long Sprint: 400 Meters

Bowerman's Best

400m	44.9	Otis Davis	Rome, 1960	
	45.07	Otis Davis	Rome, 1960	back-up auto-timing system
4 x 440 yards	3:06.3		1971, 1972	

Record Setters

Otis Davis	400m world and U.S. record, two Olympic gold medals (400m and 4 x 400 relay); two-time U.S. champion

The theoretical and applied sprint training methods were discussed in Chapter 10. This chapter discusses applied training for the 400m and the 4 x 400 relay.

Training for the 400-Meter Dash

At one time, the one-lap race was considered a distance race similar to the 800m, but that day is long gone. Today, the athlete who runs a world-class 400m is a sprinter with top speed to which has been added much endurance.

As with other events, no perfect training prescription has been found. Clyde Hart of Baylor stressed a greater load of slower intervals to increase the endurance of racers already fast at shorter distances. The results include Michael Johnson and Jeremy Wariner, both sub-44 second racers. Curtis Mills of Texas A&M reached a world-best level on relatively hard work every day, and his coach's basic pattern (Table 11-1) was intervals up to 600m. Jim Bush's world-record holders at UCLA had a pattern (Table 11-2) that carried through the competitive season and was varied only to meet the competitive situation. Stan Wright had a pattern (Table 11-3) that was flexible enough to accommodate the backgrounds of seven world-class athletes at Texas Southern. However, their temperaments were such that his day was divided into from four to seven sections to accommodate the "secret" parts of their formulas.

Training Schedules for Curtis Mills

Early Fall (September to December)

Monday:	2 x 200, 660, 2 x 200, 400, 2 x 200 or 2 x 100, 2 x 200, 600, 2 x 200, 2 x 100
Tuesday:	2 x 100, 2 x 300, 500, 300, 2 x 100 or 2 x 200, 600, 2 x 200, 300, 2 x 100
Wednesday:	2 x 200, 600, 400, 200
Thursday:	Seven-man continuous 800 relay
Friday:	300, 200, 100, 200, 300

January and February

Monday:	2 x 100, 2 x 200, 600 or 400, 2 x 200, 2 x 100
Tuesday:	2 x 200, 500, 2 x 200 or 2 x 600
Wednesday:	5 x 300 or 7 x 200 or 10 x 150
Thursday:	5 x 200 or 6 x 150
Friday:	10 x 150 (six medium, four fast)
Saturday:	3 x 150, 3 x 100

March and April

Monday:	2 x 500 (400 in 50 seconds), 2 x 150 fast
Tuesday:	4 x 300 (31.5-second average)
Wednesday:	4 x 200 (22.0 average)
Thursday:	5 x 150 or 6 x 100, flying start
Friday:	Rest
Saturday:	Track meet

Table 11-1. Training schedules for Curtis Mills

Jim Bush Training Schedules for UCLA 400 Men

Monday:	1 to 2 slow 500s, 2 to 3 medium 300s, 3 to 5 comfortable 150s
Tuesday:	Run a 200, slow on the turn and quickening on the straight, with emphasis on either "arms" or "legs," given audibly
Wednesday:	Hill work, if one is available (the 400 men were urged to use the hill as often as possible)
Thursday:	150s, using "arms" and "legs"
Friday:	300s, 200s, and 100s, and follow with the hill

Table 11-2. Jim Bush training schedules for UCLA 400 men

Photo 11-1. Otis Davis, 1960 Olympic champion and world-record holder

Stan Wright Training Schedules	
Monday:	1 x 500 or 600, 3 x 300 6 x 100
Tuesday:	1 x 300 3 x 200, 6 x 100
Wednesday:	1 x 400, 3 x 200, 6 x 100
Thursday:	3 x 200 6 x 100
Friday:	6 x 100

Table 11-3. Stan Wright training schedules

From the three sets of training patterns shown in Tables 11-1 through 11-3, all of which produced world-class runners, three things can be learned:

- A flexible plan is there, but it must be followed.
- Success is in direct proportion to the talent present.
- If the training pattern is not enjoyable, no lasting success is possible.

The program presented in this chapter's training schedules is flexible, is geared to the needs of the individual, and has produced one Olympic champion and world-record holder, as well as numerous other national

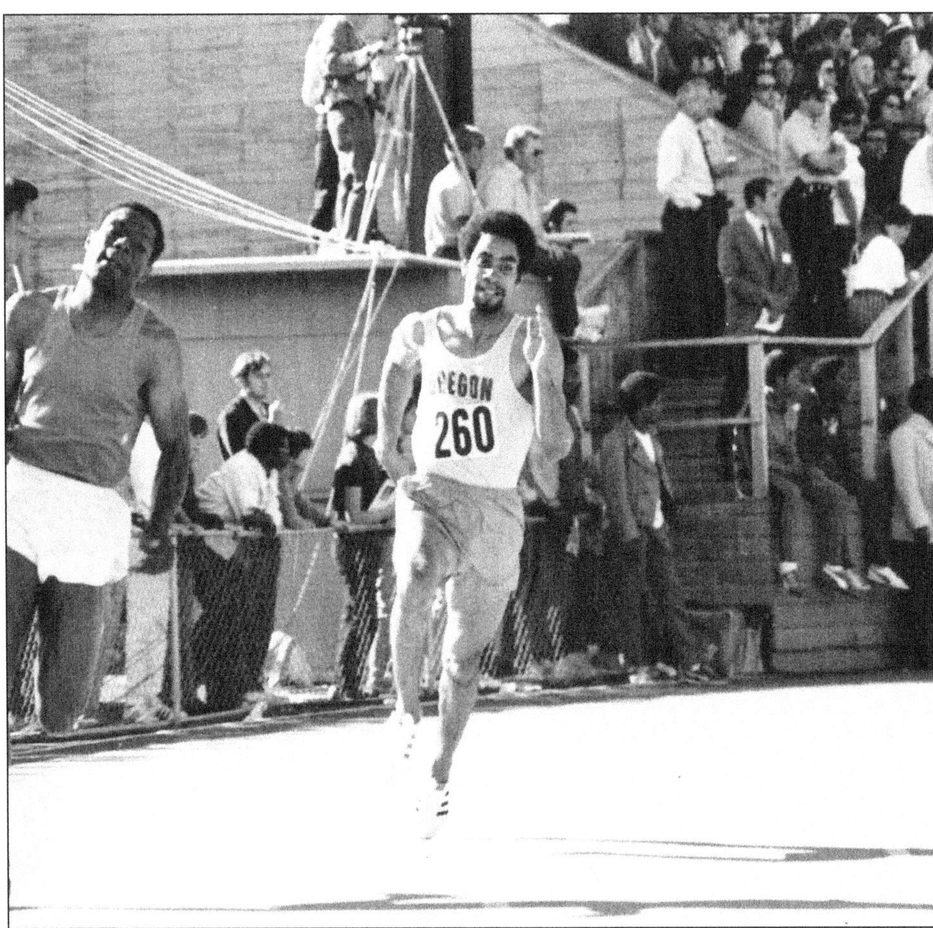

Photo 11-2. Welden Vance (46.7y), 400m start

contenders and international relay runners. In many respects, the training is similar to that of the short sprints, so Chapter 10 should also be studied.

A top 400 runner has the speed of an elite 200 runner but must add the strength to continue the pace, combined with the ability to relax while running at nearly top speed. When Butch Reynolds ran 43.29 to break Lee Evans's 20-year-old record, his splits were 21.4 and 21.9 seconds for the first and second 200m, respectively. A 1971 photograph of world-class sprinter John Smith, coach of the 1988 Olympic champion, at top speed shows that relaxation (Photo 11-3). This photograph was taken at 300m in a world-record race (44.5 seconds for 440 yards, 44.2 seconds for 400m).

The sprinter trains with a combination of short, fast intervals and longer intervals run at a gradually accelerating race pace. The total training distance for an interval workout is from two-and-a-half to three times the racing distance, or about 1200 meters.

Strength is developed through fartlek running at a comfortable pace, and hill work and overdistance runs (such as 500 to 600m) at paces a bit slower than the usual race pace. Too much long work temporarily cuts down on quickness, but it can be regained quickly.

Photo 11-3. John Smith (lane 2) at 300m in 440-yard world record (44.5, 44.2m)

Quarter-milers tend not to like longer runs. An 800m run helps endurance, but a runner lacking in confidence and courage will look out the window when the 800 is mentioned. Having the desire to run this distance is most important.

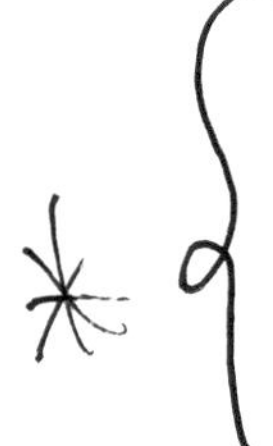

The runner must develop a floating sprint stride. In running 100s, the runner sprints the first 50m then floats the next 50m, trying to relax as much as possible with a minimum of slowing of the pace. The athlete must relax and loosen up the hips. The runner does not take longer strides; the stride length should be the same or shorter. Instead of trying to change the stride length, he should simply relax while running. When relaxed running is learned well, the sprinter may find that the speed actually increases during floating.

Tactics in the 400 relate more to the runner's pace than to the opponent's. Races are run entirely in lanes, so relative positions are difficult to determine before entering the final straight, 100m or so from the finish. The athlete should

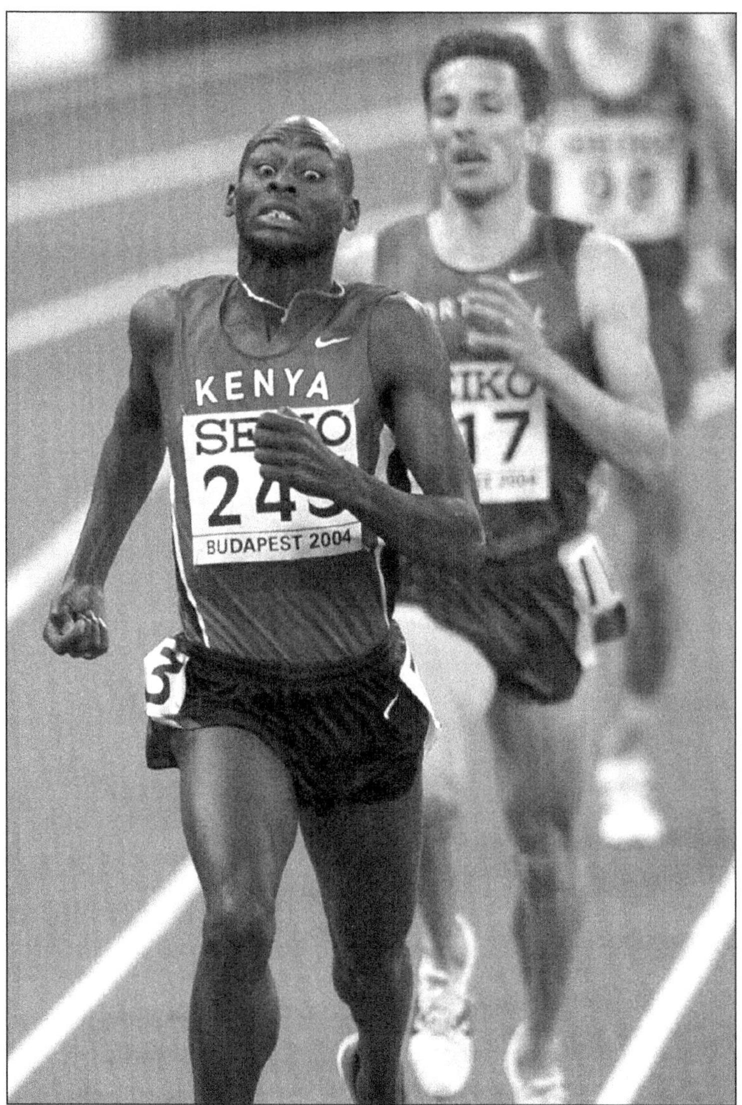

Photo 11-4. Tactics in the 400 relate more to the runner's pace than to the opponent's.

sprint as far as he can comfortably go from the start, anywhere from 50 to 150m. Carry a sprinter's stride until the cadence slows, then accelerate to a sprint for 20 to 30m and go into the float. At the highest levels today, most 400m runners try to reach the 200m mark about one second slower than their 200m best mark.

Again, the float is relaxation, *not* a period of slowing down the pace. The pace should be maintained as much as possible, as long as relaxation can be achieved. The athlete should accelerate when that acceleration can be maintained through the finish line. An athlete in the lead should float until challenged, rather than driving hard until tying up short of the finish line.

Training for the 4 x 400 Relay

Whether athletes run the 100, 200, or 400m, and run in the 4 x 100m or 4 x 400m relay, they must be concerned with the methods and training of all the sprinting races.

The 4 x 400 relay is worth 5 points in a dual meet, so it is important. If possible, the team should try to win the meet before the relay so no athlete will be overworked by having to run the relay. The object of the race is not to please the spectators—a point often lost on network television when it covers contests.

Photo 11-5. Vince Buford in 4 x 400 relay

If the meet depends upon the 4 x 400 relay, put a runner who gives a good position in the first leg. The weakest person runs second, the second-best runner goes third, and the top runner is the anchor. As a variation, if a weak runner is in the third position on the opposing team, the coach might put the best runner up against that athlete to build a lead to carry through the last runner.

The training for the 4 x 400 relay should be a regular, meaningful routine. On the schedule, it appears as number 9 as well as part of the warming-up activities. For the warm-up, two or three athletes jog around the track or across the training area. The receiver watches the incoming runner, takes two to five steps, presents the left hand (inside hand on the track), continues running while receiving the baton, immediately transfers it to the right (outside) hand, and (if three athletes are in the warm-up drill) prepares to pass it to the third runner when that runner's hand is presented. When the front runner has the baton, he peels off and drops to the rear of the line, preparing to repeat the procedure. This pattern is continued during the one or two laps of warm-up activities.

Photo 11-6. The victorious USA women's team in the 4 x 400 relay edges the Russian team in the 2008 Beijing Olympics.

As in the short-relay blind pass, the inside pass is used because dropping the inside arm tends to pull the receiver to the inside. That place in the running lane is where you want the runners as they go into and around the turn. The receiver is to look back over the left shoulder. The left arm is "pumped" in coordination with the stride two, three, or possibly as many as five times as the incoming athlete approaches. When the passer appears to be in position (the receiver watches the approach), the receiver swings the left arm out from the elbow and to the rear, keeping the palm up and the thumb slightly elevated.

The passer swings the arms during the approach, and as the receiver presents an upturned hand, the passer places the baton on it with a forward, downward swing. Practice for the relay is best done in the actual exchange zone. The zone for the 4 x 400 relay is 20 meters long and does not have the extra 10-meter acceleration zone allowed in the 4 x 100 relay.

One drill is to have the first runner approach at jog pace while the second runner waits in the zone. Put a mark about five meters before the zone; as the number 1 runner crosses the mark, the number 2 runner leaves the rear of the passing zone, swinging both arms as in sprinting. However, his eyes never leave the incoming teammate. The receiver presents the left hand on the second or third count, depending upon the speed of the approach, receives the baton, and continues accelerating into the bend at the 400m pace, then tapers off. The next part of the drill is for the number 2 runner to pass to number 3, then number 3 to number 4, and then number 4 to number 1.

A second drill, used after the mechanics of passing are learned, is to have number 1 pass to number 2, and at the same time have number 3 pass to number 4 in a lane just inside or outside the lane used by 1 and 2. After each pass, the two-runner groups change lanes and partners, such as 2 passing to 3, and 4 to 1.

In dual meets, the usual practice is to put the best runner at the anchor position, second-best runner on the third leg, third-best runner as the leadoff, and the weakest runner in the second slot. The only logical reason for such placement is the prestige connected with the anchor position. In a very competitive dual-meet situation, a coach sometimes calls for the best runner to run first to build up a lead that may cause the opposing team to make an error and tie up or choke in either the first or the second leg of the relay. If the outcome of the meet has already been decided, you still have good reasons for running the relay:

- It is a regularly scheduled event, an obligation to the spectator as well as to the opponent.
- It is an opportunity for the team members to practice for coming meets and to learn whether they are capable of racing well after one of the flat races. If a runner cannot come back well from an earlier race, it is better not enter a major relay.
- It helps the runners in maintaining a regular approach to top condition.

400-Meter Training Schedules

400 SCHEDULE NAME ____________________ DATE ______________

1. Warmup routine: Jog 1-2 laps with relay pass
2. Fartlek A. Varied pace: stride, sprint,
   recover-- stride, meet a challenge, recover.
   Finish feeling exhilarated, not exhausted.
   B. Steady pace: slow, 10-30 min.
   (1) Hendricks Park (2) Golf course
   (3)
   (a) 10 min. (b) 30 min. (c)
3. A. Weights and jogging
   B. Jogging and stretching
4. High knee and fast leg
5. Starts
   A. 2 at 1/2 speed, 2 at 7/8ths on curve, 50m
   (1) On your own (2) Gun
   B. Curve 100 meters C. On grass
   D.
6. Intervals Z. Fast 20-50 meters in middle
   A. 100-200-100 (1) 14-30-14 (2)
   B. 150 (1) 22-20-18 (2)
   C. 200 (1) 30 (2)
   D. 300 (1)
   E. 100 (1) 13 (2)
   F.
7. TEAM MEETING
8. Special A. Sauna B. Swim C.
9. Relay work A. Routine
   B. 50 meters C. Trial
10. A. Meet B. Trial C. Simulation D. Control test
    CA. Simulate 400 (1) 100-100-100 (2) 150-150-150
    CB. Simulate 200 (1) 100-100 (2) 150-150
11. Bunches
    A. 500 (1) 70-75 (2)
    B. 300 (1) 42-45 (2)
    C. 150 (1) 20-22 (2)
12. With Coach A. B.
14. A. Wind sprints (1) Straight (2) Curve
    B. Hurdle (X) drill C. Spring and bound
    D. Alternate run and jog, at least 800
    E. Hills with A. B.
15. Plyometrics A. Jumps B. Bounding C.
    (1) 1-leg (2) Both legs (3)
16. Finish work:
    A. First 100, jog 300, last 100
    B.
17. Back-to-back A. B.
18. 3/4 effort A. 200 B. 300 C.
19.
20. Work on second event
21. A. Videotape B. Film C. Pictures
    (1) Record performance (2) Study
30. Experimental work

Date	Distance	3/4 pace	Date Pace	Goal Pace

M
T
W
T
F
S
S
M
T
W
T
F
S
S
M
T
W
T
F
S
S
M
T
W
T
F
S
S

Sheet 11-1. Metric 400m training schedule sheet

440-Yard Run NAME DATE *September/October*

1. A. Warm-up routine: Jog 1 or 2 laps with relay pass.
2. Fartlek A. Holmer (varied-pace)—stride, sprint, recover—stride, meet a challenge or challenge, recover. Finish feeling exhilarated, not exhausted.
   B. Lydiard—slow, steady, 10-30 min. (1) Hendricks (2) Golf course (a) 10 min. (b) 30 min. (c)
3. A. Weights and jogging—get chart B. Jogging and stretching
4. High knee and fast leg
5. Starts A. 2 at 1/2, 2 at 7/8 on curve, 50 yds.
   B. Curve 110 (1) On your own (2) Gun C. Grass
   D.
6. Intervals Y. Fast 20-55 in middle
   A. 110-220-110 (1) 14-30-14 (2)
   B. 165 (1) 22-20-18 (2)
   C. 220 (1) 30 (2)
   D. 330 (1)
   E. 110 (1) 13 (2)
7. Squad meeting
8. Special A. Sauna B. Swim C. *Hill*
9. Relay work A. Routine B. 55 C.
10. A. Trial B. Compete
11. Bunches A. 550 (1) 70-75 (2)
    B. 330 (1) 42-45 (2)
    C. 165 (1) 20-22 (2)
12. With A. Coach B. *Leader*
14. Wind sprints A. Straight B. Curve
15. Finish work A. 1st 110, jog 330, last 110
    B.
16. Back to back A. B.
17. 3/4 effort A. 220 B. 300 C.
18. *Alternate run and jog at least 880*
19.
20.
21. A. Pictures B. Film
22. Simulated 440 A. 110-110-110 B. 165-165-165
23. Simulated 220 A. 110-110 B. 165-165

Date	Dist.	3/4	Date P.	Goal P.

M	*Organization - lockers - equipment*
T	*Leaders meet on use of weights*
W	*7 - Discuss nonschool facilities - 14A*
T	*3A*
F	*1A - 4*
S	*Registration complete*
S	*recreation*
M	*1-4-11A-14A*
T	*3A (light)*
W	*8C - 4x 100y (easy on grass)*
T	
F	*10A - 200 meters of 7/8 effort to 9/10 - 18*
S	
S	
M	*1-11A-11B-6E-6A(1)-18*
T	
W	*12A - 8C*
T	*3A*
F	*1A-11A-11B-6E-4*
S	
S	
M	*1-4-11ABC (1-2x) - 6C (3x) - 2B(1)*
T	*3A*
W	*8C (12B)*
T	*10A - 100y and 300y*
F	
S	
S	

Sheet 11-2. Training schedule for 400-meter sprinters

440-Yard Run NAME DATE October/November

1. A. Warm-up routine: Jog 1 or 2 laps with relay pass.
2. Fartlek A. Holmer (varied-pace)—stride, sprint, recover—stride, meet a challenge or challenge, recover. Finish feeling exhilarated, not exhausted.
   B. Lydiard—slow, steady, 10-30 min. (1) Hendricks (2) Golf course (a) 10 min. (b) 30 min. (c)
3. A. Weights and jogging—get chart B. Jogging and stretching
4. High knee and fast leg
5. Starts A. 2 at 1/2, 2 at 7/8 on curve, 50 yds.
   B. Curve 110 (1) On your own (2) Gun C. Grass
   D.
6. Intervals Y. Fast 20-55 in middle
   A. 110-220-110 (1) 14-30-14 (2)
   B. 165 (1) 22-20-18 (2)
   C. 220 (1) 30 (2)
   D. 330 (1)
   E. 110 (1) 13 (2)
7. Squad meeting
8. Special A. Sauna B. Swim C. Hill
9. Relay work A. Routine B. 55 C.
10. A. Trial B. Compete
11. Bunches A. 550 (1) 70-75 (2)
    B. 330 (1) 42-45 (2)
    C. 165 (1) 20-22 (2)
12. With A. Coach B.
14. Wind sprints A. Straight B. Curve
15. Finish work A. 1st 110, jog 330, last 110
    B.
16. Back to back A. B.
17. 3/4 effort A. 220 B. 300 C.
18.
19.
20.
21. A. Pictures B. Film
22. Simulated 440 A. 110-110-110 B. 165-165-165
23. Simulated 220 A. 110-110 B. 165-165

Date	Dist.	3/4	Date P.	Goal P.

M	1-4-5A (easy) - 11 ABC
T	3A
W	4-5 (easy) - 8C
T	21A - 3A
F	1-6A - 14A
S	1-4-5A - 10A (500y) - 2B(1)
S	recreation
M	1-11ABC - 2A (1 or 2)
T	3-14A
W	1-6E(2) 4x - 8C - 6E 4x
T	3A
F	10A - Relay - 300y or 100y
S	Choice
S	
M	1-4-5A - 11ABC
T	3A
W	4-6A - 8C - 6E 4x
T	3A
F	Light
S	10A - Relay 1x - 385y 1x - 2B (1)
S	recreation
M	1-4-5A - 11ABC 1-2x - 2B(1)
T	4-8B
W	1-6A - 2B(1)
T	3A
F	1-9A - 2B(1)
S	Choice
S	recreation

Sheet 11-3. Training schedule for 400-meter sprinters

440-Yard Run NAME DATE November/December

1. A. Warm-up routine: Jog 1 or 2 laps with relay pass.
2. Fartlek A. Holmer (varied-pace)—stride, sprint, recover—stride, meet a challenge or challenge, recover. Finish feeling exhilarated, not exhausted.
   B. Lydiard—slow, steady, 10-30 min. (1) Hendricks
   (2) Golf course (a) 10 min. (b) 30 min. (c)
3. A. Weights and jogging—get chart B. Jogging and stretching
4. High knee and fast leg
5. Starts A. 2 at 1/2, 2 at 7/8 on curve, 50 yds.
   B. Curve 110 (1) On your own (2) Gun C. Grass
   D.
6. Intervals Y. Fast 20-55 in middle
   A. 110-220-110 (1) 14-30-14 (2)
   B. 165 (1) 22-20-18 (2) 9/10 effort
   C. 220 (1) 30 (2) 28
   D. 330 (1)
   E. 110 (1) 13 (2)
7. Squad meeting
8. Special A. Sauna B. Swim C. Hill
9. Relay work A. Routine B. 55 C.
10. A. Trial B. Compete
11. Bunches A. 550 (1) 70-75 (2)
    B. 330 (1) 42-45 (2)
    C. 165 (1) 20-22 (2)
12. With A. Coach B.
14. Wind sprints A. Straight B. Curve
15. Finish work A. 1st 110, jog 330, last 110
    B.
16. Back to back A. B.
17. 3/4 effort A. 220 B. 300 C.
18.
19.
20.
21. A. Pictures B. Film
22. Simulated 440 A. 110-110-110 B. 165-165-165
23. Simulated 220 A. 110-110 B. 165-165

Date	Dist.	3/4	Date P.	Goal P.

Day	Workout
M	1-11ABC-2B(1)
T	3A
W	4x 4x 1-6C(2)-6E(1)-8C
T	3A
F	3x 4x 4-6B(2)-2B(1)-6E
S	
S	recreation
M	1-3x 1-4-11ABC-2B(1)
T	3A
W	4x 1-5A-8C-6E(1)
T	3A
F	10A (Relay-880 or 440)
S	
S	
M	
T	
W	
T	
F	
S	
S	
M	
T	
W	
T	
F	
S	
S	

Sheet 11-4. Training schedule for 400-meter sprinters

440-Yard Run NAME DATE January

1. A. Warm-up routine: Jog 1 or 2 laps with relay pass.
2. Fartlek A. Holmer (varied-pace)—stride, sprint, recover—stride, meet a challenge or challenge, recover. Finish feeling exhilarated, not exhausted.
   B. Lydiard—slow, steady, 10-30 min. (1) Hendricks (2) Golf course (a) 10 min. (b) 30 min. (c)
3. A. Weights and jogging—get chart B. Jogging and stretching
4. High knee and fast leg
5. Starts A. 2 at 1/2, 2 at 7/8 on curve, 50 yds.
   B. Curve 110 (1) On your own (2) Gun C. Grass
   D.
6. Intervals Y. Fast 20-55 in middle
   A. 110-220-110 (1) 14-30-14 (2)
   B. 165 (1) 22-20-18 (2)
   C. 220 (1) 30 (2)
   D. 330 (1)
   E. 110 (1) 13 (2)
7. Squad meeting
8. Special A. Sauna B. Swim C. Hill
9. Relay work A. Routine B. 55 C.
10. A. Trial B. Compete
11. Bunches A. 550 (1) 70-75 (2)
    B. 330 (1) 42-45 (2)
    C. 165 (1) 20-22 (2)
12. With A. Coach B.
14. Wind sprints A. Straight B. Curve
15. Finish work A. 1st 110, jog 330, last 110
    B.
16. Back to back A. B.
17. 3/4 effort A. 220 B. 300 C.
18. 330-220-110
19. 110s-1st, 2d, 3d, 4th
20.
21. A. Pictures B. Film
22. Simulated 440 A. 110-110-110 B. 165-165-165
23. Simulated 220 A. 110-110 B. 165-165

Date	Dist.	3/4	Date P.	Goal P.

Day	Workout
M	Register-orientation-equiment
T	2-4x 1-4-2B-6B
W	8C or 8A
T	3A
F	3x Easy 10A-Relay-300y or 100y-18
S	
S	
M	2x 4x 1-4-6B-19-2
T	3A
W	2-3x 2-3x 1-14-6B - 6A-jog
T	Light
F	7
S	10B-Indoor meet
S	
M	2-3x 3-5x 1-11A-11B-11C-2B(1)
T	3A
W	6x 1-6E-14 or 8C
T	3A
F	10-Relay-385y-jog
S	
S	
M	1-14A-2
T	3A
W	4x 14A-8C-6E
T	1-14A
F	1-4-6A-18
S	2B(1)
S	

Sheet 11-5. Training schedule for 400-meter sprinters

440-Yard Run NAME DATE February

1. A. Warm-up routine: Jog 1 or 2 laps with relay pass.
2. Fartlek A. Holmer (varied-pace)—stride, sprint, recover—stride, meet a challenge or challenge, recover. Finish feeling exhilarated, not exhausted.
   B. Lydiard—slow, steady, 10-30 min. (1) Hendricks
   (2) Golf course (a) 10 min. (b) 30 min. (c)
3. A. Weights and jogging—get chart B. Jogging and stretching
4. High knee and fast leg
5. Starts A. 2 at 1/2, 2 at 7/8 on curve, 50 yds.
   B. Curve 110 (1) On your own (2) Gun C. Grass
   D.
6. Intervals Y. Fast 20-55 in middle
   A. 110-220-110 (1) 14-30-14 (2)
   B. 165 (1) 22-20-18 (2)
   C. 220 (1) 30 (2)
   D. 330 (1)
   E. 110 (1) 13 (2)
7. Squad meeting
8. Special A. Sauna B. Swim C.
9. Relay work A. Routine B. 55 C. Hill
10. A. Trial B. Compete
11. Bunches A. 550 (1) 70-75 (2)
    B. 330 (1) 42-45 (2)
    C. 165 (1) 20-22 (2)
12. With A. Coach B.
14. Wind sprints A. Straight B. Curve
15. Finish work A. 1st 110, jog 330, last 110
    B.
16. Back to back A. B.
17. 3/4 effort A. 220 B. 300 C.
18. 300-200-100
19.
20. Alternate sprint and float
21. A. Pictures B. Film
22. Simulated 440 A. 110-110-110 B. 165-165-165
23. Simulated 220 A. 110-110 B. 165-165

Date	Dist.	3/4	Date P.	Goal P.

Day	Workout
M	2-3x 3-5x 1x 1-2B(1)(a)-6D-11C - 6E - 11A
T	4x 6E-3A
W	4x 1x 4x 1-6E-11A-20-55y
T	3A
F	2
S	10B or 10A (Relay-385y)
S	recreation
M	1-5A-11A-6B(1)-2B(1)
T	3A
W	4x 8C-6E
T	3A
F	2x 4-9A-500y
S	Light
S	Light
M	2x 4x 1-4-18-6A-6E-2B(b)
T	9A-3A-8A
W	8C
T	9A-3A
F	Light
S	10A-Relay-330y or 385 y
S	easy run
M	4x 1x 1-4-18-6A-6E-500y (1/2 effort)
T	3A
W	1x 2x 1-4-6C-100y-2B(1)
T	9 (easy)
F	9 (easy)
S	10A or 10B (indoor)
S	

Sheet 11-6. Training schedule for 400-meter sprinters

440-Yard Run NAME DATE *March*

1. A. Warm-up routine: Jog 1 or 2 laps with relay pass.
2. Fartlek A. Holmer (varied-pace)—stride, sprint, recover—stride, meet a challenge or challenge, recover. Finish feeling exhilarated, not exhausted.
   B. Lydiard—slow, steady, 10-30 min. (1) Hendricks (2) Golf course (a) 10 min. (b) 30 min. (c)
3. A. Weights and jogging—get chart B. Jogging and stretching
4. High knee and fast leg
5. Starts A. 2 at 1/2, 2 at 7/8 on curve, 50 yds.
   B. Curve 110 (1) On your own (2) Gun C. Grass
   D. *165 yds.* *E. 265 yds.*
6. Intervals Y. Fast 20-55 in middle
   A. 110-220-110 (1) 14-30-14 (2)
   B. 165 (1) 22-20-18 (2)
   C. 220 (1) 30 (2)
   D. 330 (1)
   E. 110 (1) 13 (2)
7. Squad meeting
8. Special A. Sauna B. Swim C. *Hill*
9. Relay work A. Routine B. 55 C.
10. A. Trial B. Compete
11. Bunches A. 550 (1) 70-75 (2)
    B. 330 (1) 42-45 (2)
    C. 165 (1) 20-22 (2)
12. With A. Coach B.
14. Wind sprints A. Straight B. Curve
15. Finish work A. 1st 110, jog 330, last 110
    B. *Jog 220, 440 moves in last 220*
16. Back to back A. B.
17. 3/4 effort A. 220 B. 300 C.
18. *330 – 220 – 110*
19. *165s - 1st, 2nd, last – race moves*
20.
21. A. Pictures B. Film
22. Simulated 440 A. 110-110-110 B. 165-165-165
23. Simulated 220 A. 110-110 B. 165-165

Date	Dist.	3/4	Date P.	Goal P.

M	*1-4-5B-600y(1x)-6E(4x)-440(65-70)(1x)-2B (1 or 2)*
T	*9A – 3A*
W	*4-5B(2)-18-8C-5C(4x)*
T	*9A-21A*
F	*1-10A (Relay-385y)*
S	*2*
S	*2*
M	*4-19-11ABC-2A(1)-6E(4x)*
T	*9A-3A*
W	*1-5D(2)-8C*
T	*3A*
F	*3B*
S	*10A-Relay-15B-2B(1)*
S	*2 (easy)*
M	*Exam week-5E-5D-6B(1)-2B*
T	*9A*
W	*1-5B(2x)-6C(2x)(2)-8C*
T	*9A-3A*
F	*Gear ready*
S	*10B – Meet – 1 event*
S	*Travel for spring vacation*
M	*10A (165-220-165) – 18 – 2B*
T	*9A (easy)-2B-6E(4x)*
W	*18-2B*
T	*6E(4x)-9A (easy)*
F	*Gear ready – jog*
S	*10B – Relay and 1 event*
S	*Home – reregister and settle in*

Sheet 11-7. Training schedule for 400-meter sprinters

440-Yard Run NAME DATE *April*

1. A. Warm-up routine: Jog 1 or 2 laps with relay pass.
2. Fartlek A. Holmer (varied-pace)—stride, sprint, recover—stride, meet a challenge or challenge, recover. Finish feeling exhilarated, not exhausted.
   B. Lydiard—slow, steady, 10-30 min. (1) Hendricks (2) Golf course (a) 10 min. (b) 30 min. (c)
3. A. Weights and jogging—get chart B. Jogging and stretching
4. High knee and fast leg
5. Starts A. 2 at 1/2, 2 at 7/8 on curve, 50 yds.
   B. Curve 110 (1) On your own (2) Gun C. Grass
   D.
6. Intervals Y. Fast 20-55 in middle
   A. 110-220-110 (1) 14-30-14 (2)
   B. 165 (1) 22-20-18 (2)
   C. 220 (1) 30 (2)
   D. 330 (1)
   E. 110 (1) 13 (2)
7. Squad meeting
8. Special A. Sauna B. Swim C. *Hill*
9. Relay work A. Routine B. 55 C.
10. A. Trial B. Compete
11. Bunches A. 550 (1) 70-75 (2)
    B. 330 (1) 42-45 (2)
    C. 165 (1) 20-22 (2)
12. With A. Coach B.
14. Wind sprints A. Straight B. Curve
15. Finish work A. 1st 110, jog 330, last 110
    B.
16. Back to back A. B.
17. 3/4 effort A. 220 B. 300 C.
18. *110s – 1st, 2nd, 3rd, last –*
19. *330 – 220 – 110*
20.
21. A. Pictures B. Film
22. Simulated 440 A. 110-110-110 B. 165-165-165
23. Simulated 220 A. 110-110 B. 165-165

Date	Dist.	3/4	Date P.	Goal P.

Day		
M	*7-4-6C (2x)-18-6E (4x)-11A-2B*	
T	*4-9A*	
W	*1-4-10A (165-275)-6E (4x)-8C*	
T	*9A*	
F	*Gear ready*	
S	*10B*	
S	*Loosen up*	
M	*A.M. 1*	*P.M. 1-19-grass run*
T	*4*	*1-10A (275-165)-6A (2x)-11A*
W	*1*	*8C-8B*
T	*4*	*9A-6C (2x)-grass run*
F	*9A-grass*	
S	*10B*	
S	*grass run*	
M	*1*	*6A-10A(165-275)-6E (4x)-500y (1x)*
T	*Jog*	*1-9A-grass-3A*
W	*4*	*1-10A(165-330)-5C (4x)-1*
T	*Jog*	*1A*
F	*Gear ready*	
S	*10B*	
S	*loosen up*	
M	*3A*	*1-5-9A-grass*
T	*4*	*1-6A-6B(1)-500y (1x)-2(grass)*
W	*3A*	*4-9A-grass-8C*
T	*4*	*9A*
F	*Gear ready*	
S	*10B*	
S	*8B*	

Sheet 11-8. Training schedule for 400-meter sprinters

440-Yard Run NAME DATE *May*

1. A. Warm-up routine: Jog 1 or 2 laps with relay pass.
2. Fartlek A. Holmer (varied-pace)—stride, sprint, recover—stride, meet a challenge or challenge, recover. Finish feeling exhilarated, not exhausted.
   B. Lydiard—slow, steady, 10-30 min. (1) Hendricks (2) Golf course (a) 10 min. (b) 30 min. (c)
3. A. Weights and jogging—get chart B. Jogging and stretching
4. High knee and fast leg
5. Starts A. 2 at 1/2, 2 at 7/8 on curve, 50 yds.
   B. Curve 110 (1) On your own (2) Gun C. Grass
   D.
6. Intervals Y. Fast 20-55 in middle
   A. 110-220-110 (1) 14-30-14 (2)
   B. 165 (1) 22-20-18 (2)
   C. 220 (1) 30 (2) *22.5*
   D. 330 (1)
   E. 110 (1) 13 (2) *7/8 effort*
7. Squad meeting
8. Special A. Sauna B. Swim C. *Hill*
9. Relay work A. Routine B. 55 C.
10. A. Trial B. Compete
11. Bunches A. 550 (1) 70-75 (2)
    B. 330 (1) 42-45 (2)
    C. 165 (1) 20-22 (2)
12. With A. Coach B.
14. Wind sprints A. Straight B. Curve
15. Finish work A. 1st 110, jog 330, last 110
    B. *1st 165, jog, last 165*
16. Back to back A. B.
17. 3/4 effort A. 220 B. 300 C.
18.
19.
20.
21. A. Pictures B. Film
22. Simulated 440 A. 110-110-110 B. 165-165-165
23. Simulated 220 A. 110-110 B. 165-165

Date	Dist.	3/4	Date P.	Goal P.

Day	A.M.	P.M.
M	*Jog*	*1x 100y – 2x 6C – 4x Short hill – 4x Medium hill – 2B*
T	*9A*	*9A*
W	*Jog*	*5A – 1x 300 – 1x 200 – 5x 100 – 1x 500*
T	*9A*	*9A*
F	*1-10A (400y at 3/4 to 7/8 effort)*	
S	*10B*	
S	*Loosen up*	
M	*Jog*	*6B(1) – 2B(1)*
T	*9A*	*1-10A (385-165) – 1x 500 – Jog*
W	*Jog*	*5B – 15B – 8C*
T	*9A*	*9A*
F	*Gear ready for trials*	
S	*10B – Northern Division meet*	
S	*Loosen up*	
M	*7 – Jog*	
T	*2x 6C(2) – 6E(2) – 1x 250 (3/4 effort)*	
W	*9A – 5 (easy) – 4x 6E – 1x 500*	
T	*Travel and loosen up*	
F	*10B – Conference – trials*	
S	*10B – Conference – finals*	
S	*Loosen up at home*	
M		
T		
W		
T		
F		
S		
S		

Sheet 11-9. Training schedule for 400-meter sprinters

440-Yard Run NAME DATE *June*

1. A. Warm-up routine: Jog 1 or 2 laps with relay pass.
2. Fartlek A. Holmer (varied-pace)—stride, sprint, recover—stride, meet a challenge or challenge, recover. Finish feeling exhilarated, not exhausted.
   B. Lydiard—slow, steady, 10-30 min. (1) Hendricks (2) Golf course (a) 10 min. (b) 30 min. (c)
3. A. Weights and jogging—get chart B. Jogging and stretching
4. High knee and fast leg
5. Starts A. 2 at 1/2, 2 at 7/8 on curve, 50 yds.
   B. Curve 110 (1) On your own (2) Gun C. Grass
   D.
6. Intervals Y. Fast 20-55 in middle
   A. 110-220-110 (1) 14-30-14 (2)
   B. 165 (1) 22-20-18 (2)
   C. 220 (1) 30 (2)
   D. 330 (1)
   E. 110 (1) 13 (2)
7. Squad meeting
8. Special A. Sauna B. Swim C. *Hill*
9. Relay work A. Routine B. 55 C.
10. A. Trial B. Compete
11. Bunches A. 550 (1) 70-75 (2)
    B. 330 (1) 42-45 (2)
    C. 165 (1) 20-22 (2)
12. With A. Coach B.
14. Wind sprints A. Straight B. Curve
15. Finish work A. 1st 110, jog 330, last 110
    B.
16. Back to back A. B.
17. 3/4 effort A. 220 B. 300 C.
18. *165s – 1st, 2nd, last – race moves*
19. *110s – 1st, 2nd, 3rd, 4th*
20. *220 – 1st, last – race moves*
21. A. Pictures B. Film
22. Simulated 440 A. 110-110-110 B. 165-165-165
23. Simulated 220 A. 110-110 B. 165-165

Date	Dist.	3/4	Date P.	Goal P.

M	*1-2A(1) – 18-19 – 500y (1X) – 2 (grass)*
T	*9A – 14A (grass)*
W	*1-2A(1) – 20 – Relay 110s*
T	*10B – 440 of 50y dashes*
F	*9B*
S	*10A – 330y – Relay*
S	*Grass Jog -- 9A*
M	*100 (7/8 effort) – 220 (2X) – 9 (passing)*
T	*2-3X 90 (grass) – 9*
W	*Travel – check facility*
T	*10B – Trials*
F	*10B – Semifinal – mile relay trial*
S	*10B – Final – mile relay final*
S	
M	
T	
W	
T	
F	
S	
S	
M	
T	
W	
T	
F	
S	
S	

Sheet 11-10. Training schedule for 400-meter sprinters

Core Readings

Evans, Lee. (1985). Planning training and racing for quality 400 meters. *Track and Field Quarterly Review, 85*(2), 22-24.

Freeman, William H. (2001). Periodized training for sprinters and hurdlers. In *Peak When It Counts: Periodization for American track and field* (4th ed.). Mountain View, CA: Tafnews, 106-119.

Hart, Clyde. 400 meters. (2000). In *USA Track and Field coaching manual.* Champaign, IL: Human Kinetics, 51-61.

Jarver, Jess, ed. (2000). *Sprints and relays: Contemporary theory, technique and training* (5th ed.). Mountain View, CA: Tafnews.

Smith, John. (1990). U.C.L.A. 100-400 sprint training. *Track and Field Quarterly Review, 90*(1), 10-15.

USA Track & Field Coaching Education Program. (2001). *Level II Course: Sprints hurdles relays*. USA Track & Field. Invaluable; revised regularly.

Recommended Readings

Bidder, Tudor, Emperatriz Gonzalez Henao, Victor Lopez, Carlo Vittori, & Gary Winckler. (1995). NSA Round Table 27: Sprinting. *New Studies in Athletics, 10*(1), 13-22.

Black, William. (1988). Training for the 400m. *Track Technique, 102*, 3243-3245.

Blount, Jeff, Jeff L. Hoskisson, & Remi Korchemny. (1990). Summary of results from TAC Junior Elite Sprint Camp. *Track Technique, 113*, 3593-3602.

Coh, Milan. (Summer 2001). Cathy Freeman's sprinting technique. *Track Coach, 156*, 4988-4992.

Ferro, Amelia, Alicia Rivera, Itzar Pagola, Miguel Ferreruela, Álvaro Martin & Valentin Rocandio. (2001). Analysis of the 400m finals. Biomechanical Research Project at the 7th World Championships in Athletics Seville 1999. *New Studies in Athletics, 16*(1/2), 52-60.

Holloway, Mike. (2006). Endurance training for the 400m [abstract]. *New Studies in Athletics, 21*(1), 62.

Jolly, Sonny, & Vernon Crowder. (1991). The effects of hydraulic ladder climbing on 400-meter dash times. *Track Technique, 116*, 3716-3717.

Lisovsky, Josef. (Fall 2003). Energy sources in 400m training [abstract]. *Track Coach, 165*, 5285.

Nummela, Ari, & Heikki Rusko. (Spring 2001). Acclimatization to altitude and normoxic training improve 400m performance at sea level [abstract]. *Track Coach, 155*, 4962.

Otte, Brett, & Dave Hunt. (Fall 1998). Speed Endurance vs. Special Endurance 1 vs. Special Endurance 2. *Track Coach, 145*, 4627-4629. Reprinted in Jarver (5th ed., 2000), 105-107.

Ritzdorf, Wolfgang. 400m. In Harald Müller & Helmar Hommel, eds., Biomechanical Research Project at the VIth World Championships in Athletics, Athens 1997: Preliminary Report. *New Studies in Athletics, 12*(2-3), 49-51.

Salo, Aki, & Ian Bezodis. (2004). Which starting style is faster in sprint running–Standing or crouch start? *Sports Biomechanics, 3*(1), 43-54.

Smith, Mike. (1995). 400m pace control. [abstract]. *Track Coach, 131*, 4192-4193.

Spencer, Matt R., Paul B. Gastin & Warren R. Payne. (1996). Energy system contribution during 400 to 1500 metres running. *New Studies in Athletics, 11*(4), 59-65.

12

The High Hurdles

Bowerman's Best

120-yard hurdle	13.3	Jerry Tarr	1962
110m hurdle	13.7	Ivory Harris	1972

Record Setters

Jerry Tarr	Member 440-yard relay world-record team; three-time NCAA champion: 120-yard high hurdles (twice) and 440-yard intermediate hurdles; U.S. record, 120-yard high hurdles; two-time U.S. champion: 120-yard high hurdles and 220-yard low hurdles
Ivory Harris	Two-time All-American

Hurdlers are usually agile people with quick reactions. They should be strong and fiercely competitive, and usually they are not easily agitated or distracted. Do *not* expect hurdlers to fall into a single physical group. Though most hurdlers are tall and tend toward ranginess, there have been world-class male hurdlers as short as 5′ 8″ and successful high school hurdlers even shorter.

Because the women's races use lower hurdles, only a woman who is unusually short or has very short legs may be at a disadvantage. Gail Devers (5′ 2 3/4″) ran the race in 12.33 in 2000. Leg speed can overcome a height disadvantage.

Always remember one thing where hurdlers are concerned: They are sprinters first and hurdlers second. A slow person on the flat will be slow over the hurdles. Though your hurdlers may not be as fast as your best sprinters, they will not likely be far behind. In 1962, the University of Oregon set a world record for the 440-yard relay (40.0, 39.7m, on a cinder track) with a team of three hurdlers and one sprinter. Because hurdlers must be able to sprint to be successfully, you should study Chapters 10 and 11 on sprint training as a part of hurdle preparation.

In the beginning, God did not create hurdlers. They either develop themselves, or they are developed by the teacher/coach. If the coach has to develop hurdlers, an organized training plan is needed. This chapter will look at teaching athletes to hurdle, and then discuss training methods and procedures for the high hurdles and intermediate hurdles.

Teaching the Hurdles

Teaching prospects to hurdle can be discouraging to them, because it is human nature to avoid anything that might hurt. The prospect of hitting a hurdle and perhaps falling on the track may cause runners to shy away from trying to hurdle.

The athletes cannot fear the hurdles. You can do two things to minimize their fears: perform most hurdle practices on the grass, at least in the learning and early practice stages, and use soft-top hurdles. Those simple precautions will do much to limit the fears of athletes.

The hurdler must know the difference between the lead leg and the trail leg. The leg that goes over the hurdle first is the lead leg, while the leg that follows the body over the hurdle is the trail leg.

It makes no difference which leg the high hurdler uses as the lead leg. Athletes find that they naturally prefer one leg to the other. For a race that goes around a turn on the track, leading with the left leg has advantages. However, not all of the best runners of such races lead with the left leg.

The arm opposite the lead leg is called the "lead arm" because it leads over the hurdle in conjunction with the lead leg. If a person leads with the right leg, the left arm will be the lead arm, and the right arm will be the trail arm.

The hurdler should be observed regularly from three different vantage points. The common one is from the side. Many problems can be detected from this angle, but the coach should also watch from in front of and behind the hurdler. Balance and mechanical problems that are too subtle to detect from the side can be seen from the front or the rear.

The hurdler should at all times remember that the primary objective is to get to the finish line as quickly as possible. Hurdles is a sprint race with obstacles in the way. The hurdling form should not be developed in a way that gains beauty only to lose speed.

Photo 12-1. Jerry Tarr (first, NCAA) and Mel Renfro (second NCAA)

Learning to Hurdle With the X Drill

The athletes should first try walking over the hurdles. Pull three hurdles over backward and place them five yards apart. Boxes or other objects about 12 to 15 inches in height can be used as well. Have the hurdlers walk over the obstacles, concentrating on lifting the lead knee. After several repetitions of this exercise, they should walk through while concentrating on the trail leg and turning the trailing toe outward and upward, until they have the feel of the basic hurdling action. Then, they will be ready to learn the X drill, used to teach hurdling and review the basic techniques regularly.

The term "X" has no meaning other than as a name for the routine. Begin the drill with three hurdles set at the low height (30 inches). If lower hurdles are available, they may be preferable for female candidates. The high hurdle settings are shown in Table 12-1. For the teaching drill, begin with closer hurdle settings. For men, use 14 yards to the first hurdle and 8 yards between the hurdles, then move to 14 and 9 yards, then finally to 15 and 10 yards. For women, use 12 yards to the first hurdle and 7 yards between the hurdles, then move to 13 and 8 yards, and then move finally to the full distances.

The first step in the X drill is walking to the side of the hurdles. The athletes walk past the hurdles, keeping them on their lead-leg side. As they approach each hurdle, they lift the lead knee and step over the hurdle with that leg only,

High Hurdle Settings					
		Height	*To First Hurdle*	*Between Hurdles*	*Last Hurdle to Finish*
Men	110m	1.067m 3′ 6″	13.72m 45′ 0″	9.14m 30′ 0″	14.02m 46′ 0″
Women	100m	0.840m 2′ 9″	13m 42′ 8″	8.50m 27′ 10 3/4″	10.50m 34′ 5 1/2″

Table 12-1. High hurdle settings

keeping the trail leg out to the side of the hurdle. This exercise is repeated, and then the athletes move to the other side of the hurdles to practice with the trail leg. Again, they walk past the hurdles, taking care to place the lead foot past the hurdle, then bring the trail leg over the hurdle with the toe turned out so the foot crosses the hurdle parallel to its top. This exercise is also repeated.

The hurdlers next progress to trotting past the hurdles, using the same exercises as previously described, but taking only five steps between each hurdle. After they acquire the habit of leading with the knee, you no longer need to use the lead-leg exercises as part of the X drill. First, they trot through two repetitions to the side, exercising the trail leg, and then they complete this stage of the drill by five-stepping over the top of the hurdles, using all aspects of correct form. This stage is also repeated twice.

The final stage in the drill is a switch to using three steps between the hurdles. First, two repetitions are run to the side using the trail leg, then two are run straight across the tops of the hurdles. While the previous exercises must be rather slow, the three-stepping exercises must be rather fast.

Training With the X Drill

Emphasize several points of form when using the X drill:

- The lead leg is directed by lifting the knee. If the knee is lifted in the approach to each hurdle, the foot almost automatically reaches out to clear the hurdle, and it is less likely to be directed off to the side. The leg can also be raised more quickly than if the hurdler led with the foot because a short pendulum (the thigh) can move more swiftly than a longer one (the whole leg). The knee of the lead leg should not lock while crossing the hurdle because a locked knee slows the step to the ground.
- The hurdler should pull the trail knee through and into sprinting position. The trail foot does not have to be thrust forward to reach into the next step if the knee is brought through properly and the hurdler keeps on the toes and tries for a quick-stepping rhythm.

- The toe of the trail foot must be rotated upward (everted) until the foot clears the hurdle in a position parallel to the top, rather than hitting the hurdle.
- The shoulders must be kept level. To keep them level, the trail hand (on the side of the lead foot) reaches about as far forward as the lead knee (but straight ahead, not across the knee), while the lead arm extends fully straight ahead and downward across the hurdle (this combination is called "a hand and a half"). If either hand comes across the body, the hurdler tends to land off balance, moving toward the side of the track.
- The hurdler should work to stay up on the toes, trying not to run flat-footed or land on the heels before or after clearing the hurdle.
- The dive, the lean over the hurdle by the upper body, should be held until the toe is almost on the ground. The trailing foot can then be pulled straight forward, clearing the hurdle with less effort.

The X drill is the conclusion of the warm-up exercises on each day when the hurdlers practice their hurdling, which is usually two or three times a week. When working on technique with the X drill, they practice only one fundamental at a time, such as running through the drill while concentrating on keeping on the toes or getting the rhythm of the dive. Working on everything at once can be too confusing to the athlete (and the coach).

Photo 12-2. 1971 AAU championships high hurdles race

High Hurdle Training Theory

The fitness characteristics for the hurdle races include the following:

- General conditioning
  - ✓ Aerobic endurance
  - ✓ Strength endurance
  - ✓ Mobility
  - ✓ Maximum strength
- Special conditioning
  - ✓ Speed endurance
  - ✓ Special mobility (flexibility)
  - ✓ Speed
  - ✓ Elastic strength
  - ✓ Special strength: relative
  - ✓ Special endurance: 200m and 400m
- Competition-specific conditioning
  - ✓ Hurdles technique
  - ✓ Sprint technique
  - ✓ Start technique
  - ✓ Stride patterns
  - ✓ Time trials[1]

The key to hurdling is speed, with technique following closely. The athlete's height is a factor but not in the expected way. Just as being short creates difficulties for the hurdler, being tall also creates problems.[2] For men, 6′ 0″ to 6′ 2″ seems to be the ideal height, give or take an inch. For taller athletes, the tendency is to shuffle (rather than sprint) between the hurdles. Otherwise, the hurdler will overrun the barriers. For women, the ideal height seems to be 5′ 7″ to 5′ 9″. However, elite performers appear across a wide range of heights.

The first training emphasis should be speed, with much mobility work to improve flexibility at the hip.[3] Bounding, hill running, and strength work are used to develop leg power. Wilbur Ross notes that optical fatigue is a factor that limits performances. He also recommends using music in developing the hurdler's all-important running rhythm.[4]

As in sprinting, no widely accepted general theory of hurdle training has appeared. A contrast can be seen between the United States, with its seemingly bottomless pool of raw talent, and the rest of the world. American sprinters have superior speed but poorly developed technique. European sprinters, who are gaining ground on the Americans, have superior technique but lack the raw speed.[5] Speed is still the bottom line, but the Europeans are closing the gap.

Coaches can evaluate the weak points in an athlete's endurance by recording touchdown times off the hurdles. For example, the start is critical in the high hurdles. How does the athlete's time from start to landing after the first hurdle compare to his flat start for that distance? An athlete's total time can be predicted from the touchdown time after one hurdle, assuming no endurance weaknesses. Recording times is relatively easy with a stopwatch that will store at least 11 times. The coach can easily record the touchdown time after all 10 hurdles while watching the full race. Touchdown times are an extremely valuable coaching tool. Tables 12-2 and 12-3 give samples of projected touchdown times for the high hurdles.

Men's 110-Meter Hurdle Touchdown Times

Target Time	*H1*	*H2*	*H3*	*H4*	*H5*	*H6*	*H7*	*H8*	*H9*	*H10*	*Finish Time*
12.8	2.4	3.4	4.3	5.2	6.2	7.2	8.2	9.2	10.3	11.2	12.8
13.0	2.4	3.4	4.4	5.4	6.4	7.4	8.4	9.4	10.5	11.6	13.0
13.2	2.5	3.5	4.4	5.4	6.4	7.4	8.5	9.6	10.7	11.8	13.2
13.6	2.5	3.6	4.6	5.6	6.6	7.7	8.8	9.9	11.0	12.2	13.6
14.0	2.5	3.6	4.6	5.7	6.8	7.9	9.0	10.1	11.2	12.4	14.0
14.4	2.6	3.6	4.7	5.8	6.9	8.1	9.3	10.5	11.7	12.9	14.4
14.6	2.6	3.7	4.7	5.8	7.0	8.2	9.4	10.6	11.8	13.0	14.6
15.0	2.6	3.7	4.9	6.0	7.2	8.3	9.5	10.7	12.0	13.2	15.0
15.5	2.7	3.8	5.0	6.2	7.4	8.6	9.8	11.0	12.3	13.6	15.5
16.0	2.8	3.9	5.1	6.4	7.6	8.8	10.1	11.3	12.6	14.0	16.0

Table 12-2. Men's 110-meter hurdle touchdown times

Women's 100-Meter Hurdle Touchdown Times

Target Time	*H1*	*H2*	*H3*	*H4*	*H5*	*H6*	*H7*	*H8*	*H9*	*H10*	*Finish Time*
11.8	2.2	3.2	4.1	5.0	5.9	6.9	7.9	8.9	9.9	10.9	11.8
12.0	2.3	3.3	4.2	5.1	6.0	7.0	8.0	9.0	10.0	11.1	12.0
12.3	2.3	3.3	4.2	5.1	6.1	7.1	8.1	9.1	10.2	11.3	12.2
12.8	2.4	3.4	4.4	5.4	6.4	7.4	8.4	9.5	10.6	11.7	12.8
13.2	2.4	3.4	4.4	5.5	6.6	7.7	8.8	9.9	11.0	12.1	13.2
13.8	2.5	3.5	4.6	5.7	6.8	7.9	9.1	10.2	11.4	12.6	13.8
14.0	2.5	3.5	4.6	5.7	6.9	8.1	9.3	10.4	11.6	12.8	14.0
14.3	2.5	3.6	4.7	5.9	7.1	8.3	9.5	10.7	11.9	13.1	14.3
14.8	2.6	3.8	4.9	6.0	7.2	8.4	9.6	10.9	12.2	13.5	14.8
15.0	2.6	3.8	4.9	6.1	7.3	8.5	9.7	11.0	12.3	13.6	15.0

Table 12-3. Women's 100-meter hurdle touchdown times

Application: Training for the High Hurdles

The warm-up routine of the hurdler should ensure that the circulation is moving well, the body temperature is adjusted, and the runner feels warm but not tired. Extreme stretching should be avoided. If extreme or violent stretching exercises are performed in practice, the extra adrenalin flowing on the day of competition makes the hurdler more liable to pull or strain a muscle before the competition ever starts. No muscles need to be stretched any more in warming up than they will be stretched in performing the competitive activities.

From the dressing room, the hurdler jogs to the track, then covers about 800m while alternating jogging and stretching easily. He finishes with another 400m of jogging and is then ready for the day's activities. Note that the X drill is a graduated warm-up routine as well as a training routine.

Practice shows that if an athlete works hard on one day, a recovery period will probably be needed the next day. This need is generally true for all athletic events. By alternating hard and easy days of training, the athlete can prepare well for the competitive events and at the same time use the easy days to benefit from activities such as easy jogging, weight training, and swimming. Often, the hurdlers may work with the sprinters on activities such as relay work on the easier days.

For a hard day, the hurdler begins with warm-up jogging and stretching, then goes through the X drill, working perhaps on the trail leg. He progresses from five-stepping to the sides and over the top to three-stepping to the sides and over the top. The X drill begins with the hurdles set at lower heights, the hurdle gradually being raised as the athlete warms up (such as 30 inches, then 36, 39, and 42 inches for men). Such a range of heights is not as necessary for women athletes because their hurdles are lower relative to their height. The hurdler might then run several intervals, followed by easy fartlek, with the workout concluded by four progressively faster 100s.

As the athlete becomes more fit, the coach will realize that competitive situations may arise where the hurdler may race on two or even three consecutive days. If so, preparation for such a situation should begin about a month ahead of time. On one day, the athlete might warm up with the usual routine, do the X drill, then simulate a racing situation, such as running through a full set of hurdles, running five hurdles back to back, or perhaps running the first three hurdles and the last three hurdles, while striding through where hurdles 3 through 7 have been removed. This routine is followed by a cool-down at the end of practice. It is neither a hard nor an easy day, but the runner is being conditioned mentally and physically for the big races that are coming.

The next day, rather than taking it easy, the hurdler again warms up, perhaps takes three or four starts, works on the hurdles as on the previous day (going through a full flight either in part, in segments, or in the first and last parts), then cools down again.

The third day (when preparing for three consecutive racing days) begins with a warm-up, and then simulates the racing situation again. Following this activity is the hardest workout of the week. When athletes get into shape by planned work, they do not want to rest so much when preparing for the meets ahead that they become less fit. The continuation of this procedure might be to run a series of 100s or 150s, or perhaps do enough relay work to run 800m, and then finish with a jog through the hills or a series of moderate wind sprints.

As a final note on training, a good practice is to have regular test efforts every two weeks until the competitive season begins. These tests usually are not over the full distance. For the high hurdles, they are usually at 60m (four or five hurdles), 70m (five or six hurdles), or 80m (seven hurdles: 75 percent of the racing distance). These tests might be all-out trials, but more often they are aimed at running at a set pace or at a rate of gradual improvement from one trial to the next. Also, they are usually run over hurdles set below the regular competitive height during the winter (36 or 39 inches for men, 30 inches for women).

High Hurdle Training Schedules

Many of the fundamentals on the high hurdle schedule sheet are common to the sheets for other events (Chapter 6). This section will look at the activities that are different.

5. Starts

Starts are done as in the sprints, moving from relaxed effort to harder effort, but never making an all-out effort. Starts may be over 30 or 50m, either on the flat or over the high or intermediate hurdles. 5E and 5F develop the endurance. The back-to-back hurdles are starts from the blocks over the first five hurdles, a walk back to the starting line, and a repeat start over five hurdles. The first three, last three drill runs over the full high hurdle race, without the middle four hurdles. The athlete drives through the first three hurdles, slows to stride through the middle of the race with no barriers, and then accelerates to finish strongly over the last three hurdles and through the finish line.

6. Intervals

Intervals may include some variations in their emphasis. They may be run with a fast 20 to 50m in the middle. They may be run over the intermediate hurdles for strength and endurance work. Shorter intervals may be run on the straight or around the curve. Any situation that the athlete might encounter in a race should be practiced repeatedly in training.

10. Competition

Meets, time trials, and simulations can involve a variety of distances and conditions. For high hurdlers, the most common testing distance is the indoor race of 60m, though a trial may range from 40m to the full outdoor distance.

11. Bunches

Bunches, unlike intervals, are usually run in pairs. An 11A (500m) means to run 500m two times. An 11BC means to run 300m twice, then run 100m twice. The 11D is a set rather than a bunch, running 300m, 200m, and then 100m.

16. Finish Work

These exercises strengthen the finishing endurance and skills. The first three, last three drill is the same as 5F under "Starts." The 16B is run over the full 10 hurdles, but simply with floating or running easily over the first five barriers, then finishing strongly over the last five. The 16C is run like the 16B, but with the first five hurdles removed from the lane.

17. X Drill

This activity calls for parts of the X drill to be run at different heights, such as rising from the intermediate hurdle height to the high hurdle height. The different focal points of the body are numbered. For example, 17B(7a) means to run across the top of the hurdles, using the 30-inch low hurdle setting and working on staying up on the toes. The athlete might work on one or two aspects of technique during a workout. He cannot effectively focus on every aspect in sequence because fatigue will interfere with proper performance. However, every part of the technique can be practiced at least once in a week. During the late season, only the weaker points are practiced.

The training schedules for nine months follow. The school notes are based on the university quarter system. When these schedules were written, the NCAA meet was held in mid-June.

HIGH HURDLE SCHEDULE NAME ______________________ DATE ______________

1. Warmup routine: Jog 1-2 laps with relay pass;
   Hurdle X drill at lower height
   B. Slow high knee; fast leg drill
   C. 2 starts to first hurdle
2. Fartlek A. Varied pace: stride, sprint,
   recover-- stride, meet a challenge, recover.
   Finish feeling exhilarated, not exhausted.
   B. Steady pace: slow, 10-30 min.
   (1) Hendricks Park (2) Golf course
3. A. Weights and jogging
   B. Jogging and stretching
4. High knee and fast leg
5. Starts: 2 at 1/2 speed, 2 at 7/8ths speed
   A. 30m B. 50m C. HH D. IH
   E. Back-to-back highs, 5 hurdles
   F. First 3, jog, last 3
   (1) On your own (2) Gun
6. Intervals Z. Fast 20 to 50 meters in middle
   X. Over intermediate hurdles
   A. 100 (1) 18-16-14-12 (2) 17-15-13
   (a) Curve (b) Straight
   B. 150 (1) 22 (2) 20 (3)
   C. 150-100-50 (1) 22-16-6 (2)
   D. 200 (1) 30 (2) 28 (3)
   E. 300 (1) 3/4 effort (2)
   F. 500 (1) 3/4 effort (2)
7. TEAM MEETING
8. Special A. Sauna B. Swim C.
9. Relay work A. Routine
   B. 50 meters C. Trial
10. A. Meet B. Trial C. Simulation D. Control test
    (1) 40 (2) 60 (3) 80 (4) Full distance
11. Bunches A. 500 (1) 75-80 (2)
    B. 300 (1) 45-48 (2)
    C. 100 (1) 12 (2)
    D. 300-200-100 (1)
12. With Coach A. B.
14. A. Wind sprints (1) Straight (2) Curve
    B. Hurdle (X) drill C. Spring and bound
    D. Alternate run and jog, at least 800
    E. Hills with A. B.
15. Plyometrics A. Jumps B. Bounding C.
    (1) 1-leg (2) Both legs (3)
16. Finish work: A. First 3, jog, last 3
    B. Full 10: float for 5, then go last 5
    C. Last 5 hurdles
17. X Drill:
    (a) 30" (b) 33" (c) 36" (d) 39" (e) 42"
    A. 5 step to side B. 5 step to top
    C. 3 step to side D. 3 step to top
    (1) Lean (2) Lead leg (3) Trail leg
    (4) Lead arm (5) Off arm (6) Quickness
    (7) On toes G. On grass
20. Work on second event
21. A. Videotape B. Film C. Pictures
    (1) Record performance (2) Study
30. Experimental work

Date	Distance	3/4 pace	Date Pace	Goal Pace

M
T
W
T
F
S
S
M
T
W
T
F
S
S
M
T
W
T
F
S
S
M
T
W
T
F
S
S

Sheet 12-1. Metric high hurdle training schedule sheet

High Hurdle NAME DATE September/October

1. A. Warm-up: jog 1 or 2 laps with relay pass. Hurdle X drill at 36 and/or 39 in. B. High knee and fast leg drill
   C. 2 starts to 1 hurdle
2. Fartlek: A. Holmer (varied-pace)—stride, sprint, recover—stride, meet a challenge or challenge, recover. Finish feeling exhilarated, not exhausted.
   B. Lydiard—slow, steady (1) Park run
   (2) Golf course (a) 10 min. (b) 20 min. (c)
3. A. Weights and jogging B. Jogging and stretching
4. High knee and fast leg
5. Starts A. 2 at 1/2 speed, 2 at 7/8 speed, 30 yds.
   B. Same as A, 50 yds. (1) On your own (2) Gun
   C. Highs D. IH E. Back to back highs, 5 hurdles
   F. First 3, jog, last 3
6. Intervals Y. Fast 20-55 in middle
   Z. Over intermediates A. 110 (1) 18-15-14-12
   (2) 17-15-13 (a) Curve (b) Straight (c)
   B. 165 (1) 22 (2) 20 (3)
   C. 165-110-55 (1) 22-13-6 (2)
   D. 220 (1) 30 (2) 28 (3)
   E. 330 (1) (2)
   F. 550 G.
7. Squad meeting
8. Special A. Sauna B. Swim C. Hill
9. Relay work A. Routine B. 55 C. Trial
10. Test effort A. Trial B. Compete (1) 40
   (2) 60 (3) 90 (4) Full
11. Bunches A. 550 (1) 75-80 (2)
   B. 330 (1) 45-48 (2)
   C. 110 (1) 12 (2)
   D. 300-200-100 (1)
12. With A. Coach B.
14. A. Wind sprints (1) Curve (2) Straight
   B. Hurdle X drill C. Spring and bound
   D. Alternate run and jog at least 880
   E.
15. Finish work A. First 3, jog, last 3
   B. Full 10—float at 5, then go last 5
   C. Last 5 hurdles
16. X drill—for fundamentals (a) 36 (b) 39
   (c) 42 A. 5 step to side B. 5 step to top
   C. 3 step to side D. 3 step to top (1) Lean (buck)
   (2) Trail leg (3) Lead leg (4) Off arm
   (5) Lead arm (6) Quickness (7) On toes
17. 3/4 speed A. 330 B. 500 C.
18. 5 hurdles A. First 5 B. Last 5
19. Simulated hurdling on the grass
20.
21. A. Pictures B. Film
22. Simulated race A. 220 B. 440 C.
   (1) Over hurdles

Day	Workout
M	Organization-lockers-equipment
T	Meet on use of weights
W	Discuss off-school courses-14A
T	3A
F	1A-1B-2A(1)-
S	
S	recreation
M	1B-19-2A-6A(1)-14D (4x)
T	3A
W	8C
T	3A
F	10A-200 meters at 7/8 to 9/10 effort
S	
S	
M	1A-19-6A(1)-Jog 880 (2x)
T	3A
W	12-Jog
T	3A
F	1A-11ABC-1B(1) (2x)
S	
S	
M	1A-1B-16ABCD(a)(b)
T	3A
W	8C
T	3A
F	
S	
S	

Sheet 12-2. High hurdle training schedule

High Hurdle NAME DATE October/November

1. A. Warm-up: jog 1 or 2 laps with relay pass. Hurdle X drill at 36 and/or 39 in. B. High knee and fast leg drill C. 2 starts to 1 hurdle
2. Fartlek: A. Holmer (varied-pace)—stride, sprint, recover—stride, meet a challenge or challenge, recover. Finish feeling exhilarated, not exhausted. B. Lydiard—slow, steady (1) Park run (2) Golf course (a) 10 min. (b) 20 min. (c)
3. A. Weights and jogging B. Jogging and stretching
4. High knee and fast leg
5. Starts A. 2 at 1/2 speed, 2 at 7/8 speed, 30 yds. B. Same as A, 50 yds. (1) On your own (2) Gun C. Highs D. IH E. Back to back highs, 5 hurdles F. First 3, jog, last 3
6. Intervals Y. Fast 20-55 in middle Z. Over intermediates A. 110 (1) 18-15-14-12 (2) 17-15-13 (a) Curve (b) Straight (c) Hill B. 165 (1) 22 (2) 20 (3) C. 165-110-55 (1) 22-13-6 (2) D. 220 (1) 30 (2) 28 (3) E. 330 (1) (2) F. 550 G.
7. Squad meeting
8. Special A. Sauna B. Swim C.
9. Relay work A. Routine B. 55 C. Trial
10. Test effort A. Trial B. Compete (1) 40 (2) 60 (3) 90 (4) Full
11. Bunches A. 550 (1) 75-80 (2) B. 330 (1) 45-48 (2) C. 110 (1) 12 (2) D. 300-200-100 (1)
12. With A. Coach B.
14. A. Wind sprints (1) Curve (2) Straight B. Hurdle X drill C. Spring and bound D. Alternate run and jog at least 880 E.
15. Finish work A. First 3, jog, last 3 B. Full 10—float at 5, then go last 5 C. Last 5 hurdles
16. X drill—for fundamentals (a) 36 (b) 39 (c) 42 A. 5 step to side B. 5 step to top C. 3 step to side D. 3 step to top (1) Lean (buck) (2) Trail leg (3) Lead leg (4) Off arm (5) Lead arm (6) Quickness (7) On toes
17. 3/4 speed A. 330 B. 500 C.
18. 5 hurdles A. First 5 B. Last 5
19. Simulated hurdling on the grass
20.
21. A. Pictures B. Film
22. Simulated race A. 220 B. 440 C. (1) Over hurdles

Day	Workout
M	1B-5A-21A-11A-6A(1) 2-4x -2B(1)
T	3A
W	12 or 8-6A(1)
T	3A
F	2x 300y-4x 100y-2A(1)
S	3B
S	
M	1A-5A-19-6A 4x -2A(1)
T	3A-21B
W	12 or 8-6A(1)
T	
F	10A (100y or 5 hurdles)
S	10A (300y)
S	
M	1A-5A-1x 100y-2x 300y-3x 200y-4x 100y
T	3B-21B
W	12 or 8
T	3A
F	10A (100y or Hurdles)-2A(1)
S	
S	
M	1A-5A-19-6B 3x -10A(1)
T	3A
W	8 or 12-6B 3x
T	
F	10A (100y and Relay)
S	10A (Relay and 300y flat)
S	

Sheet 12-3. High hurdle training schedule

High Hurdle NAME DATE November/December

1. A. Warm-up: jog 1 or 2 laps with relay pass. Hurdle X drill at 36 and/or 39 in. B. High knee and fast leg drill C. 2 starts to 1 hurdle
2. Fartlek: A. Holmer (varied-pace)—stride, sprint, recover—stride, meet a challenge or challenge, recover. Finish feeling exhilarated, not exhausted. B. Lydiard—slow, steady (1) Park run (2) Golf course (a) 10 min. (b) 20 min. (c)
3. A. Weights and jogging B. Jogging and stretching
4. High knee and fast leg
5. Starts A. 2 at 1/2 speed, 2 at 7/8 speed, 30 yds. B. Same as A, 50 yds. (1) On your own (2) Gun C. Highs D. IH E. Back to back highs, 5 hurdles F. First 3, jog, last 3
6. Intervals Y. Fast 20-55 in middle Z. Over intermediates A. 110 (1) 18-15-14-12 (2) 17-15-13 (a) Curve (b) Straight (c) B. 165 (1) 22 (2) 20 (3) C. 165-110-55 (1) 22-13-6 (2) D. 220 (1) 30 (2) 28 (3) E. 330 (1) (2) F. 550 G.
7. Squad meeting
8. Special A. Sauna B. Swim C. Hill
9. Relay work A. Routine B. 55 C. Trial
10. Test effort A. Trial B. Compete (1) 40 (2) 60 (3) 90 (4) Full
11. Bunches A. 550 (1) 75-80 (2) B. 330 (1) 45-48 (2) C. 110 (1) 12 (2) D. 300-200-100 (1)
12. With A. Coach B.
14. A. Wind sprints (1) Curve (2) Straight B. Hurdle X drill C. Spring and bound D. Alternate run and jog at least 880 E.
15. Finish work A. First 3, jog, last 3 B. Full 10—float at 5, then go last 5 C. Last 5 hurdles
16. X drill—for fundamentals (a) 36 (b) 39 (c) 42 A. 5 step to side B. 5 step to top C. 3 step to side D. 3 step to top (1) Lean (buck) (2) Trail leg (3) Lead leg (4) Off arm (5) Lead arm (6) Quickness (7) On toes
17. 3/4 speed A. 330 B. 500 C.
18. 5 hurdles A. First 5 B. Last 5
19. Simulated hurdling on the grass
20.
21. A. Pictures B. Film
22. Simulated race A. 220 B. 440 C. (1) Over hurdles

M	1A - 16ABCD - 6ZB (2X) - 11A (2X)
T	3A
W	8 or 12
T	
F	10A (100 (2X) - 300 (1X)) - 14A
S	
S	2A
M	1A - 1B - 5C - 11A - 6ZB (2X)
T	7 - 3A - 21B
W	1 - 5A - 9A - 6D - 11A
T	
F	10A (Relay) - 10A(3) - 2B(1)
S	10A (100-300)
S	
M	
T	
W	
T	
F	
S	
S	
M	
T	
W	
T	
F	
S	
S	

Sheet 12-4. High hurdle training schedule

High Hurdle NAME DATE January

1. A. Warm-up: jog 1 or 2 laps with relay pass. Hurdle X drill at 36 and/or 39 in. B. High knee and fast leg drill C. 2 starts to 1 hurdle
2. Fartlek: A. Holmer (varied-pace)—stride, sprint, recover—stride, meet a challenge or challenge, recover. Finish feeling exhilarated, not exhausted. B. Lydiard—slow, steady (1) Park run (2) Golf course (a) 10 min. (b) 20 min. (c)
3. A. Weights and jogging B. Jogging and stretching
4. High knee and fast leg
5. Starts A. 2 at 1/2 speed, 2 at 7/8 speed, 30 yds. B. Same as A, 50 yds. (1) On your own (2) Gun C. Highs D. IH E. Back to back highs, 5 hurdles F. First 3, jog, last 3
6. Intervals Y. Fast 20-55 in middle Z. Over intermediates A. 110 (1) 18-15-14-12 (2) 17-15-13 (a) Curve (b) Straight (c) B. 165 (1) 22 (2) 20 (3) C. 165-110-55 (1) 22-13-6 (2) D. 220 (1) 30 (2) 28 (3) E. 330 (1) (2) F. 550 G.
7. Squad meeting
8. Special A. Sauna B. Swim C. Hill
9. Relay work A. Routine B. 55 C. Trial
10. Test effort A. Trial B. Compete (1) 40 (2) 60 (3) 90 (4) Full
11. Bunches A. 550 (1) 75-80 (2) B. 330 (1) 45-48 (2) C. 110 (1) 12 (2) D. 300-200-100 (1)
12. With A. Coach B.
14. A. Wind sprints (1) Curve (2) Straight B. Hurdle X drill C. Spring and bound D. Alternate run and jog at least 880 E.
15. Finish work A. First 3, jog, last 3 B. Full 10—float at 5, then go last 5 C. Last 5 hurdles
16. X drill—for fundamentals (a) 36 (b) 39 (c) 42 A. 5 step to side B. 5 step to top C. 3 step to side D. 3 step to top (1) Lean (buck) (2) Trail leg (3) Lead leg (4) Off arm (5) Lead arm (6) Quickness (7) On toes
17. 3/4 speed A. 330 B. 500 C.
18. 5 hurdles A. First 5 B. Last 5
19. Simulated hurdling on the grass
20.
21. A. Pictures B. Film
22. Simulated race A. 220 B. 440 C. (1) Over hurdles

M	Register-lockers-2B
T	4B
W	1A-4A-16ABCD-6A 4x (13-15)-8C or 12
T	9A-3A-4B-6C
F	1-5A-16ABCD-6B 3x-2B(1)
S	11 or 2
S	
M	1A-4A-16-6A 2x 2(a)-6A 2x 2(b)-6A 4x (13)
T	3A-4B-7
W	1A-5A-4 2x hurdles-8 or 12
T	3A (grass)
F	1A-4A-5B 2x (2)-Jog-6A 2x 2(a)-6A 2x 2(b)-2A(1)
S	
S	
M	1-5A-6A(1)-6B-2B(1)
T	1-3 (grass)
W	1-5B(2)-16(2,3)(b,c)
T	1-3-Jog
F	10A (Relay-hurdles)
S	
S	
M	1-5A(2)-16(2,3)-11A
T	3A
W	1-5A(2)-10A(2)-6B
T	3A
F	Gear ready-jog
S	10B-indoors, or 3B
S	

Sheet 12-5. High hurdle training schedule

High Hurdle NAME DATE February

1. A. Warm-up: jog 1 or 2 laps with relay pass. Hurdle X drill at 36 and/or 39 in. B. High knee and fast leg drill C. 2 starts to 1 hurdle
2. Fartlek: A. Holmer (varied-pace)—stride, sprint, recover—stride, meet a challenge or challenge, recover. Finish feeling exhilarated, not exhausted.
   B. Lydiard—slow, steady (1) Park run
   (2) Golf course (a) 10 min. (b) 20 min. (c)
3. A. Weights and jogging B. Jogging and stretching
4. High knee and fast leg
5. Starts A. 2 at 1/2 speed, 2 at 7/8 speed, 30 yds.
   B. Same as A, 50 yds. (1) On your own (2) Gun
   C. Highs D. IH E. Back to back highs, 5 hurdles
   F. First 3, jog, last 3
6. Intervals Y. Fast 20-55 in middle
   Z. Over intermediates A. 110 (1) 18-15-14-12
   (2) 17-15-13 (a) Curve (b) Straight (c)
   B. 165 (1) 22 (2) 20 (3)
   C. 165-110-55 (1) 22-13-6 (2)
   D. 220 (1) 30 (2) 28 (3)
   E. 330 (1) (2)
   F. 550 G.
7. Squad meeting
8. Special A. Sauna B. Swim C. Hill
9. Relay work A. Routine B. 55 C. Trial
10. Test effort A. Trial B. Compete (1) 40
    (2) 60 (3) 90 (4) Full
11. Bunches A. 550 (1) 75-80 (2)
    B. 330 (1) 45-48 (2)
    C. 110 (1) 12 (2)
    D. 300-200-100 (1)
12. With A. Coach B.
14. A. Wind sprints (1) Curve (2) Straight
    B. Hurdle X drill C. Spring and bound
    D. Alternate run and jog at least 880
    E.
15. Finish work A. First 3, jog, last 3
    B. Full 10--float at 5, then go last 5
    C. Last 5 hurdles
16. X drill—for fundamentals (a) 36 (b) 39
    (c) 42 A. 5 step to side B. 5 step to top
    C. 3 step to side D. 3 step to top (1) Lean (buck)
    (2) Trail leg (3) Lead leg (4) Off arm
    (5) Lead arm (6) Quickness (7) On toes
17. 3/4 speed A. 330 B. 500 C.
18. 5 hurdles A. First 5 B. Last 5
19. Simulated hurdling on the grass
20.
21. A. Pictures B. Film
22. Simulated race A. 220 B. 440 C.
    (1) Over hurdles

Day	Workout
M	2x 4x 1A-4AB-5A(2)-16(bc)-6B-6A-Jog
T	3-8A or 8B
W	1A-4A-11A(1)-12 to 8C
T	3A-4B
F	2x 4x 1A-5A(2)-16(bc)-5A-6D(2)-6A(14)-2B(1)
S	8C-3
S	recreation
M	2x 1-4A-16(bc)(5)-11A-11B-2B(1)
T	3A-8A or 8B
W	4x 1-6A(2)-8C
T	3A-8A or 8B
F	1-Jog-
S	10A(4)-36" and 39"-Relay-Jog
S	Jog
M	3x 2x 1A-16(1)(bc)-6B(3)-6D(2-1)-2B(1)
T	2x 4x 1A-6D(2-1)-6A(13)-11ABC
W	8C
T	2x 1A-4A-5B-6A(13)-2B(1)
F	10A (Relay-75y Highs)-11ABC
S	3-2B(1)
S	recreation
M	2x 1-4A-16(4)(bc)-11A-11B-2B(1)
T	3A-8A or 8B
W	4x 6AZ-8C
T	3A-8A or 8B
F	2A(1)
S	10A(3)-10A(300y IH)
S	Recreation

Sheet 12-6. High hurdle training schedule

High Hurdle NAME DATE March

1. A. Warm-up: jog 1 or 2 laps with relay pass. Hurdle X drill at 36 and/or 39 in. B. High knee and fast leg drill C. 2 starts to 1 hurdle
2. Fartlek: A. Holmer (varied-pace)—stride, sprint, recover—stride, meet a challenge or challenge, recover. Finish feeling exhilarated, not exhausted. B. Lydiard—slow, steady (1) Park run (2) Golf course (a) 10 min. (b) 20 min. (c)
3. A. Weights and jogging B. Jogging and stretching
4. High knee and fast leg
5. Starts A. 2 at 1/2 speed, 2 at 7/8 speed, 30 yds. B. Same as A, 50 yds. (1) On your own (2) Gun C. Highs D. IH E. Back to back highs, 5 hurdles F. First 3, jog, last 3
6. Intervals Y. Fast 20-55 in middle Z. Over intermediates A. 110 (1) 18-15-14-12 (2) 17-15-13 (a) Curve (b) Straight (c) B. 165 (1) 22 (2) 20 (3) C. 165-110-55 (1) 22-13-6 (2) D. 220 (1) 30 (2) 28 (3) E. 330 (1) (2) F. 550 G.
7. Squad meeting
8. Special A. Sauna B. Swim C. Hill
9. Relay work A. Routine B. 55 C. Trial
10. Test effort A. Trial B. Compete (1) 40 (2) 60 (3) 90 (4) Full
11. Bunches A. 550 (1) 75-80 (2) B. 330 (1) 45-48 (2) C. 110 (1) 12 (2) D. 300-200-100 (1)
12. With A. Coach B.
14. A. Wind sprints (1) Curve (2) Straight B. Hurdle X drill C. Spring and bound D. Alternate run and jog at least 880 E.
15. Finish work A. First 3, jog, last 3 B. Full 10—float at 5, then go last 5 C. Last 5 hurdles
16. X drill—for fundamentals (a) 36 (b) 39 (c) 42 A. 5 step to side B. 5 step to top C. 3 step to side D. 3 step to top (1) Lean (buck) (2) Trail leg (3) Lead leg (4) Off arm (5) Lead arm (6) Quickness (7) On toes
17. 3/4 speed A. 330 B. 500 C.
18. 5 hurdles A. First 5 B. Last 5
19. Simulated hurdling on the grass
20.
21. A. Pictures B. Film
22. Simulated race A. 220 B. 440 C. (1) Over hurdles

Day	Workout
M	1A - 4A - 6A (4x) (12-13) - 11A(2) - 2B(a)
T	9A - 3A
W	1A - 16AB - 6A (4x) (12-13) - 8C
T	9A - 2B(a)
F	10A (Relay) - 300yds. (1x) - 2B(a)
S	10A (4) - 300yds. - 2B(b)
S	Study - jog
M	Exam week - jog, study, rest
T	
W	1-4-5A - 16ABCD - 6A2 (1-2x) - JOG
T	
F	1-4-5A - 1st. 3 (2x) - 6A(1)2 (2x) - 6A(2)2 - 200yds. (1x) (grass)
S	Meet - 1 race
S	Jog - settle in spring trip

Day	A.M.	P.M.
M	Jog	Hill jog
T	Jog	4A - 5A(2) (2x) - 6B - 6A (4x) (12-13)
W	JOG	9A
T	Jog	1A - 1st. 3 (2x) - 5B - 200yds. (1x) (grass)
F		Light - gear ready
S		Meet
S		Home

Day	Workout
M	Register - 1A - 9A - 6C - 6B - 6A (4x)
T	9A
W	1A - 5A - 5A(1) - 5B - 6A(1) - 300yds (1x) or 500yds.
T	Light - 9A
F	Gear ready
S	Relay meet
S	jog

Sheet 12-7. High hurdle training schedule

High Hurdle NAME DATE April

1. A. Warm-up: jog 1 or 2 laps with relay pass. Hurdle X drill at 36 and/or 39 in. B. High knee and fast leg drill C. 2 starts to 1 hurdle
2. Fartlek: A. Holmer (varied-pace)—stride, sprint, recover—stride, meet a challenge or challenge, recover. Finish feeling exhilarated, not exhausted. B. Lydiard—slow, steady (1) Park run (2) Golf course (a) 10 min. (b) 20 min. (c)
3. A. Weights and jogging B. Jogging and stretching
4. High knee and fast leg
5. Starts A. 2 at 1/2 speed, 2 at 7/8 speed, 30 yds. B. Same as A, 50 yds. (1) On your own (2) Gun C. Highs D. IH E. Back to back highs, 5 hurdles F. First 3, jog, last 3
6. Intervals Y. Fast 20-55 in middle Z. Over intermediates A. 110 (1) 18-15-14-12 (2) 17-15-13 (a) Curve (b) Straight (c) B. 165 (1) 22 (2) 20 (3) C. 165-110-55 (1) 22-13-6 (2) D. 220 (1) 30 (2) 28 (3) E. 330 (1) (2) F. 550 G.
7. Squad meeting
8. Special A. Sauna B. Swim C. Hill
9. Relay work A. Routine B. 55 C. Trial
10. Test effort A. Trial B. Compete (1) 40 (2) 60 (3) 90 (4) Full
11. Bunches A. 550 (1) 75-80 (2) B. 330 (1) 45-48 (2) C. 110 (1) 12 (2) D. 300-200-100 (1)
12. With A. Coach B.
14. A. Wind sprints (1) Curve (2) Straight B. Hurdle X drill C. Spring and bound D. Alternate run and jog at least 880 E.
15. Finish work A. First 3, jog, last 3 B. Full 10—float at 5, then go last 5 C. Last 5 hurdles
16. X drill—for fundamentals (a) 36 (b) 39 (c) 42 A. 5 step to side B. 5 step to top C. 3 step to side D. 3 step to top (1) Lean (buck) (2) Trail leg (3) Lead leg (4) Off arm (5) Lead arm (6) Quickness (7) On toes
17. 3/4 speed A. 330 B. 500 C.
18. 5 hurdles A. First 5 B. Last 5
19. Simulated hurdling on the grass
20.
21. A. Pictures B. Film
22. Simulated race A. 220 B. 440 C. (1) Over hurdles

Day	Workout
M	1A-4-5A-16-6A-7
T	9-3A
W	4x 9A-1A-1B-8C-110
T	16ABCD(c)
F	5A-9A
S	Meet-Relay-120 Highs
S	Home-loosen up
M	1x 9A-16-250y
T	4x 1A-5A(2)-6A-11B-7
W	1x 9A-500 (easy grass)
T	1A-5A(1)-5B-5C-6B
F	Travel-loosen up
S	Dual meet
S	Home-loosen up
M	4x 1x 9A-1A-6B-6A-300y-Jog
T	9A-Jog
W	9A-1A-3A-15B-15C-2B(1)
T	9A
F	Light
S	Meet-home
S	Jog
M	2x 1-5A-16-5B-6B-Light jog
T	9A-3A
W	1-5A-5B-12-8
T	Relay and jog
F	5 (2 starts)-9A-Gear ready
S	Dual meet
S	Loosen up

Sheet 12-8. High hurdle training schedule

High Hurdle NAME DATE *May*

1. A. Warm-up: jog 1 or 2 laps with relay pass. Hurdle X drill at 36 and/or 39 in. B. High knee and fast leg drill C. 2 starts to 1 hurdle
2. Fartlek: A. Holmer (varied-pace)—stride, sprint, recover—stride, meet a challenge or challenge, recover. Finish feeling exhilarated, not exhausted. B. Lydiard—slow, steady (1) Park run (2) Golf course (a) 10 min. (b) 20 min. (c)
3. A. Weights and jogging B. Jogging and stretching
4. High knee and fast leg
5. Starts A. 2 at 1/2 speed, 2 at 7/8 speed, 30 yds. B. Same as A, 50 yds. (1) On your own (2) Gun C. Highs D. IH E. Back to back highs, 5 hurdles F. First 3, jog, last 3
6. Intervals Y. Fast 20-55 in middle Z. Over intermediates A. 110 (1) 18-15-14-12 (2) 17-15-13 (a) Curve (b) Straight (c) B. 165 (1) 22 (2) 20 (3) C. 165-110-55 (1) 22-13-6 (2) D. 220 (1) 30 (2) 28 (3) E. 330 (1) (2) F. 550 G.
7. Squad meeting
8. Special A. Sauna B. Swim C. *Hill*
9. Relay work A. Routine B. 55 C. Trial
10. Test effort A. Trial B. Compete (1) 40 (2) 60 (3) 90 (4) Full
11. Bunches A. 550 (1) 75-80 (2) B. 330 (1) 45-48 (2) C. 110 (1) 12 (2) D. 300-200-100 (1)
12. With A. Coach B.
14. A. Wind sprints (1) Curve (2) Straight B. Hurdle X drill C. Spring and bound D. Alternate run and jog at least 880 E.
15. Finish work A. First 3, jog, last 3 B. Full 10—float at 5, then go last 5 C. Last 5 hurdles
16. X drill—for fundamentals (a) 36 (b) 39 (c) 42 A. 5 step to side B. 5 step to top C. 3 step to side D. 3 step to top (1) Lean (buck) (2) Trail leg (3) Lead leg (4) Off arm (5) Lead arm (6) Quickness (7) On toes
17. 3/4 speed A. 330 B. 500 C.
18. 5 hurdles A. First 5 B. Last 5
19. Simulated hurdling on the grass
20.
21. A. Pictures B. Film
22. Simulated race A. 220 B. 440 C. (1) Over hurdles

M	*1A-5A-16-5B (2x)-6AZ*
T	*9A-14A*
W	*7-5ABC-Jog*
T	*Gear ready*
F	*Light*
S	*Dual meet*
S	*Light*
M	*A.M. 9A* | *P.M. 1-16-5B-5C (grass)-200yds. (1x)*
T	*3A*
W	*1-5ABC-6BZ-jog*
T	*Light*
F	*Travel*
S	*Invitational meet*
S	*Home-loosen up*
M	*9A-19-14A*
T	*1A-5A-16-5B-5C-6B*
W	*1-9A-6A*
T	*1-5A-16-14A*
F	*Gear ready*
S	*Northern Division meet*
S	
M	
T	
W	
T	
F	
S	
S	

Sheet 12-9. High hurdle training schedule

High Hurdle NAME DATE June

1. A. Warm-up: jog 1 or 2 laps with relay pass. Hurdle X drill at 36 and/or 39 in. B. High knee and fast leg drill C. 2 starts to 1 hurdle
2. Fartlek: A. Holmer (varied-pace)—stride, sprint, recover—stride, meet a challenge or challenge, recover. Finish feeling exhilarated, not exhausted.
   B. Lydiard—slow, steady (1) Park run
   (2) Golf course (a) 10 min. (b) 20 min. (c)
3. A. Weights and jogging B. Jogging and stretching
4. High knee and fast leg
5. Starts A. 2 at 1/2 speed, 2 at 7/8 speed, 30 yds.
   B. Same as A, 50 yds. (1) On your own (2) Gun
   C. Highs D. IH E. Back to back highs, 5 hurdles
   F. First 3, jog, last 3
6. Intervals Y. Fast 20-55 in middle
   Z. Over intermediates A. 110 (1) 18-15-14-12
   (2) 17-15-13 (a) Curve (b) Straight (c)
   B. 165 (1) 22 (2) 20 (3)
   C. 165-110-55 (1) 22-13-6 (2)
   D. 220 (1) 30 (2) 28 (3)
   E. 330 (1) (2)
   F. 550 G.
7. Squad meeting
8. Special A. Sauna B. Swim C. Hill
9. Relay work A. Routine B. 55 C. Trial
10. Test effort A. Trial B. Compete (1) 40
    (2) 60 (3) 90 (4) Full
11. Bunches A. 550 (1) 75-80 (2)
    B. 330 (1) 45-48 (2)
    C. 110 (1) 12 (2)
    D. 300-200-100 (1)
12. With A. Coach B.
14. A. Wind sprints (1) Curve (2) Straight
    B. Hurdle X drill C. Spring and bound
    D. Alternate run and jog at least 880
    E.
15. Finish work A. First 3, jog, last 3
    B. Full 10—float at 5, then go last 5
    C. Last 5 hurdles
16. X drill—for fundamentals (a) 36 (b) 39
    (c) 42 A. 5 step to side B. 5 step to top
    C. 3 step to side D. 3 step to top (1) Lean (buck)
    (2) Trail leg (3) Lead leg (4) Off arm
    (5) Lead arm (6) Quickness (7) On toes
17. 3/4 speed A. 330 B. 500 C.
18. 5 hurdles A. First 5 B. Last 5
19. Simulated hurdling on the grass
20.
21. A. Pictures B. Film
22. Simulated race A. 220 B. 440 C.
    (1) Over hurdles

M	1A-4-14A
T	5 (easy)-9A (easy)
W	9A
T	Easy jog
F	Prelims.
S	Conference finals
S	Picnic
M	Exams-light-study
T	light-study
W	1A-5A-5B-14A
T	1A-5A-5C-14A
F	1A-5ABC-14A
S	Light
S	9A
M	Light
T	9A
W	Light
T	Championship
F	Championship
S	Championship
S	
M	
T	
W	
T	
F	
S	
S	

Sheet 12-10. High hurdle training schedule

Endnotes

1. Frank W. Dick. (1978). *Training theory*. London: British Amateur Athletic Board, 64-65.
2. NSA Round Table: The sprint hurdles. (1988). *New Studies in Athletics, 3*(2), 14-17.
3. Jess Jarver. (1981). Hurdling in a nutshell. In Jess Jarver (Ed.), *The hurdles: Contemporary theory, technique and training* (2nd ed.). Los Altos, CA: Tafnews, 9-13.
4. Wilbur L. Ross. (1978). *The hurdler's bible* (3rd ed.). San Juan, PR: Santana, 44-50.
5. Frank Lehmann. (1987). Development of hurdle technique. *Track Technique, 99*, 3172-3173.

Core Readings

Freeman, William H. (2001). Periodized training for sprinters and hurdlers. In *Peak When It Counts: Periodization for American track and field* (4th ed.). Mountain View, CA: Tafnews, 106-119.

Jarver, Jess, ed. (2004). *The Hurdles: Contemporary Theory, Technique and Training* (4th ed.). Mountain View, CA: Tafnews.

Lindeman, Ralph, & John Millar. 100- and 110-meter hurdles. (2000). In *USA Track and Field coaching manual*. Champaign, IL: Human Kinetics, 63-74.

McFarlane, Brent. (2000). *The Science of Hurdling* (4th ed.). Ottawa: Athletics Canada.

Poquette, Jean. (1981). Nehemiah's high school training. In Jess Jarver (Ed.), *The hurdles: Contemporary theory, technique and training* (2nd ed.), 67-72.

USA Track & Field Coaching Education Program. (2001). *Level II Course: Sprints hurdles relays*. USA Track & Field. Invaluable; revised regularly.

Winckler, Gary. (1989). Hurdling. In Vern Gambetta (Ed.), *The Athletic Congress's track and field coaching manual* (2nd ed.). Champaign, IL: Leisure Press, 73-87.

Recommended Readings

Alford, Jim. (1995). NSA Interview 8: Malcolm Arnold on Colin Jackson's development. *New Studies in Athletics, 10*(3), 13-15.

Arnold, Malcolm. (1988). Time analysis of the sprint hurdle events at the II World Championships in Athletics: Interpretation from the point of view of training practice. *New Studies in Athletics, 3*(2), 72-74.

Coh, Milan. (Winter 2003). Colin Jackson's hurdle clearance technique. *Track Coach, 162*, 5161-5167.

Coh, Milan. (Summer 2003). A kinematic and dynamic analysis of hurdle clearance technique [abstract]. *Track Coach, 164*, 5251.

Coh, Milan, & Ale‰ Dolenec. (1996). Three-dimensional kinematic analysis of the hurdles technique used by Brigita Bukovec. *New Studies in Athletics, 11*(1), 63-69.

Dapena, Jesús, & Craig McDonald. (1991). Hurdle clearance technique. Track Technique, 116, 3710-3712.

Hommel, Helmar. (1995). NSA photosequences 33 & 34: Colin Jackson. *New Studies in Athletics, 10*(3), 57-64. Commentary by Malcolm Arnold, 57, 64-65.

Hommel, Helmar. (1996). NSA photosequence 35: 100m hurdles: Gail Devers. *New Studies in Athletics, 11*(1), 71-74. Commentary by Lorna Boothe, 71, 75.

Hommel, Helmar. 110mH & 100mH. In Harald Müller & Helmar Hommel, eds., Biomechanical Research Project at the VIth World Championships in Athletics, Athens 1997: Preliminary Report. *New Studies in Athletics, 12*(2-3), 51-56.

Hucklekemkes, Johannes. (1991). Model technique for the women's 100-meter hurdles. *Track Technique, 118*, 3759-3766; 119, 3802-3808.

Jarver, Jess, ed. (1997). *The Hurdles: Contemporary Theory, Technique and Training* (3rd ed.). Mountain View, CA: Tafnews.

Kearney, Beverly. (1993). Sprints & sprint hurdles. *Track and Field Quarterly Review, 93*(1), 29-36.

Mann, Ralph. (1996). Rules-related limiting factors in hurdling. *Track Coach, 136*, 4335-4337.

McDonald, Craig. (Spring 2003). The angular momentum of hurdle clearance. *Track Coach, 163*, 5199-5204.

McDonald, Craig. (Fall 2002). Hurdling is not sprinting. *Track Coach, 161*, 5137-5143.

McFarlane, Brent. (1994). Hurdles...A basic and advanced technical model. T*rack Technique, 128*, 4073-4079.

McFarlane, Brent. (Winter 2000). A talk with Cuban coach Santiago Antunez. *Track Coach, 150,* 4796-4798.

Otte, Bret, & Van Zanic. (Summer 2006). Blocked vs. random practice, with drills for hurdlers. *Track Coach, 176*, 5628-5632.

Parker, Ron. (Summer 2005). Teaching beginners to hurdle. *Track Coach, 172*, 5504-5508.

Polosin, Andrei. (Spring 2004). The secret to a fast finish in the 110m hurdles [abstract]. *Track Coach, 167*, 5343.

Schiffer, Jürgen. (2006). Selected and annotated bibliography 73-74: Hurdles. *New Studies in Athletics, 21*(1), 71-104; 21(2), 97-122.

Sparrey, Kathleen Raske. (Fall 1997). Identifying and developing elite hurdlers in the United States. *Track Coach, 141*, 4505-4510.

Stein, Norbert. (2000). Reflections on a change in the height of the hurdles in the women's sprint hurdles event. *New Studies in Athletics, 15*(2), 15-19.

Veney, Tony. (Spring 1998). Development of the sprint hurdles. *Track Coach, 143*, 4573-4574.

13

The Intermediate Hurdles

Bowerman's Best

400m hurdle	49.6	Gary Knoke	1968	
440-yard hurdle	50.3	Jerry Tarr	1962	equiv. 50.0-yard

Record Setters

Jerry Tarr	NCAA champion
Gary Knoke	Two-time Australian Olympic Team, 110m and 400m hurdles

The 180-yard low hurdles used to be the old American race for high schools, but fortunately the 300m hurdle race has replaced it. The women's race is at the low hurdle height, so the primary requirement of the race is someone who can run a good flat 400 or 800m and lift her feet, as long as she is not too short-legged. The race requires only moderate hurdling skills at the younger age levels, for with moderate training, a good sprinter can beat a good hurdler 9 times out of 10.

Training Theory: 400 Meter Hurdles

Training theory for the 400m hurdles is consistent with training for the 400m flat race and the high hurdles; that is, no agreement exists on training methods. The 400m hurdles has always been a strong American event because of the mass of raw talent in sprinting and hurdling. One area of agreement is on the importance of developing a sense of rhythm for approaching the hurdles. Overemphasis on the step pattern can cause difficulties for the athlete if race conditions cause the athlete to break stride. The hurdle distances and rough step pattern are shown in Tables 13-1 and 13-2. The number of steps depends on the athlete's speed and body structure.

		Height	To First Hurdle	Between Hurdles	Last Hurdle to Finish
Men	400m	0.914m 3′ 0″	45m 147′ 8″	35m 114′ 10″	40m 131′ 3″
Women	400m	0.762m 2′ 6″	45m 147′ 8″	35m 114′ 10″	40m 131′ 3″

Intermediate Hurdle Settings

Table 13-1. Intermediate hurdle settings

Intermediate Hurdle Step Pattern

Strides to First Hurdle	*Strides Between Hurdles*
21	13
21-22	14
22	15
22-23	16
23-24	17

Table 13-2. Intermediate hurdle step pattern

Coaches and researchers in the Russian system made the following recommendations for improving women's performances in the intermediate hurdles:

- Use double periodization for advanced athletes (allows better distribution of conditioning).
- Use more long runs over the intermediate hurdles (set at the standard distances, these develop specific endurance and rhythm between the hurdles).
- Use more bounding against the clock for 30m to 100m (develops specific power).
- Run more intermediate hurdle races (competition is an excellent preparation method). *Note*: This adjustment may be unnecessary for an athlete on a school team with long competitive seasons.[1]

Application: Training for the Intermediates

The intermediate hurdler should think of himself as having the speed of a sprinter, the skill of a high hurdler, and the endurance of an 800m runner. The athlete who has the courage to believe this self-image has the potential to become a great intermediate hurdler. The intermediate hurdle race, although related to the highs, is an entirely different event. In tough competition, it is a most unusual person who can do both events with the utmost skill. The danger is that the athlete may put so much into the preliminary races that he will be totally exhausted after three days of competition in each event—particularly after meeting other outstanding athletes who are competing in only one event.

It is very difficult to accomplish the double in national competition. Some high hurdlers are unable to cover the entire distance of the intermediates, possibly because physiologically they cannot accommodate the lactate buildup, or perhaps because they are mentally lazy and do not want to prepare themselves to run this tough event. When Jerry Tarr won both events for Oregon in the 1962 NCAA meet, he would not have run both events except that the competition in the highs was limited, with few rounds to race. Most important, only eight intermediate hurdlers declared, allowing him to go through the high hurdle qualifying rounds without having to run an all-out race before the finals in either race.

What does the intermediate hurdler do? He runs off the starting block, attempting to reach the first hurdle in six seconds. This time is accomplished, of course, after the hurdler develops the stride to the point that the first hurdle is reached quickly but comfortably. From the first to the second hurdle takes about four seconds for most world-class males. It is not realistic for a beginning hurdler to try to run fast splits over the early hurdles, as a world-class performer might try to do. Instead, the touchdown tables (Tables 13-3 and 13-4) give a rough idea of projected times at different points in the race, based on the time that the hurdler is trying to run.

Men's 400-Meter Hurdle Touchdown Times

H1	*H2*	*H3*	*H4*	*H5*	*200m*	*H6*	*H7*	*H8*	*H9*	*H10*	*Finish Time*
5.8	9.5	13.2	17.0	20.8	22.5	24.7	28.7	32.9	37.3	41.8	47.0
5.7	9.7	13.5	17.4	21.3	23.0	25.3	29.5	33.8	38.2	42.7	48.0
6.0	9.9	13.8	17.7	21.7	23.5	25.8	30.1	34.5	39.1	43.6	49.0
6.0	10.0	14.0	18.1	22.2	24.0	26.4	30.8	35.3	39.9	44.5	50.0
6.1	10.2	14.3	18.5	22.7	24.5	27.0	31.4	35.9	40.6	45.9	51.0
6.1	10.4	14.7	19.0	23.3	25.0	27.7	32.2	36.8	41.6	46.5	52.0
6.3	10.7	15.1	19.5	23.9	25.5	28.4	32.9	37.6	42.5	47.5	53.0
6.4	10.9	15.4	19.9	24.4	26.0	29.0	33.7	38.5	43.4	48.4	54.0

Table 13-3. Men's 400-meter hurdle touchdown times

Women's 400-Meter Hurdle Touchdown Times

H1	*H2*	*H3*	*H4*	*H5*	*200m*	*H6*	*H7*	*H8*	*H9*	*H10*	*Finish Time*
6.1	10.3	14.5	18.8	23.1	25.0	27.5	32.0	36.7	41.4	46.3	52.0
6.3	10.7	15.1	19.6	24.1	26.5	28.7	33.4	38.2	43.2	48.2	54.0
6.5	11.1	15.7	20.3	25.0	27.0	29.8	34.7	39.7	44.9	50.1	56.0
6.7	11.5	16.3	21.1	25.9	28.0	30.8	35.9	41.1	46.2	51.8	58.0
6.9	11.9	16.9	21.9	26.9	29.5	32.0	37.2	42.5	47.9	53.4	60.0
7.1	12.3	17.5	22.6	27.8	30.0	33.1	38.4	43.9	49.5	55.2	62.0
7.3	12.6	17.9	23.3	28.7	31.0	34.2	39.8	45.4	51.1	57.0	64.0

Table 13-4. Women's 400-meter hurdle touchdown times

As an example, if the athlete is a beginning male hurdler, he should start from a standing start, or down in the traditional sprint start, and run the first hurdle comfortably but quickly in about seven seconds. Next, he should trot back and cover the same distance again, but this time going over the first three hurdles. He takes a recovery, jogging completely around the track; then when he reaches the head of the last straight, he runs the last three hurdles down the straight, trying a pace of between four and five seconds between each hurdle. He takes another full-lap recovery jog, then runs the three hurdles on the bend, again trying to get between four and five seconds between each hurdle. The athlete completes another lap recovery jog, then runs the last two hurdles, or about 80m, and tries to finish up as he would in the 400m hurdle race.

A variation of this exercise is to have the athlete run the first 100, recover with 400m, run the middle 200m of the race, jog another lap, then finish with 100m over the hurdles. Another exercise is to have the athlete run 100m over the hurdles, jog back to the start, run 200m over the hurdles, jog back to the start, then run 300m over the hurdles.

Too much hurdling can produce sore knees and ankles from hitting the hurdles, so the intermediate hurdler should run through the X drill over the low and high hurdles, then run through intervals of low or intermediate hurdles totaling one or two times the racing distance, and then think like an 800m runner. Have the runner use step-down sets, running one or two sets of 600-400-200. This pattern consists of 600m at a pace of 30 to 35 seconds per 200 (1:30 to 1:45 total) for men (35 to 40 seconds for women, 1:45 to 2:00), then a recovery of 600m (or however much is needed). This step is followed by 400m at a slightly faster pace, perhaps at a pace two seconds faster per 200. After a 400 jog, the set is concluded with a 200 at about two seconds faster than the 400 pace, then a 200m recovery jog. The runner might then run a second set, or else take a run for a few miles through the local countryside or other softer surfaces. Two courses through rolling hills are used at Oregon. Hill running is exhilarating, and it is also an excellent resistance exercise, just as is weight training.

The hurdlers also follow a regular schedule of weight training. It is identical to the one used by the sprinters and longer distance runners. Ten exercises are used that work the entire body. Runners can develop their own routines beyond those basic exercises as they become familiar with the training. That routine choice is the prerogative of the individual athlete. The basic routine can be done in 10 minutes, so the athlete can benefit without feeling that excessive time is required.

The most important thing for the hurdler is to establish a routine that looks after the various parts of the race, giving enough attention both to the mechanical fundamentals of the event and to the pleasures of the preparation, so the athlete goes into the competition with the belief that he is fully prepared to turn in the very best effort.

The primary differences in the hurdling form of the intermediate hurdles from that of the high hurdles are few. They result in large part from the lower hurdle height, requiring less lift and effort to clear the hurdle and, therefore, less technical excellence. Because the intermediate race is longer, the pace is slower and the hurdler may be a bit more upright in clearance posture. The additional race length adds a considerable fatigue factor, which further modifies the hurdler's form late in the race.

Intermediate Hurdle Training Schedules

The fundamentals on the intermediate hurdle schedule sheet are essentially the same as those on the high hurdle sheet (explained in Chapter 12). More emphasis is placed on specific endurance by dividing the race into segments of 100, 150, and 200m or more. The start, middle, and finish of the race are practiced. The athlete should practice working in different lanes because the race can be far different in Lane 1 than in Lane 8. Different lanes have varying physical and tactical considerations. The athlete should practice leading with both legs so an interruption in the pace will not result in stutter-stepping to hit the hurdle with the preferred leg. The schedules give nine months of training.

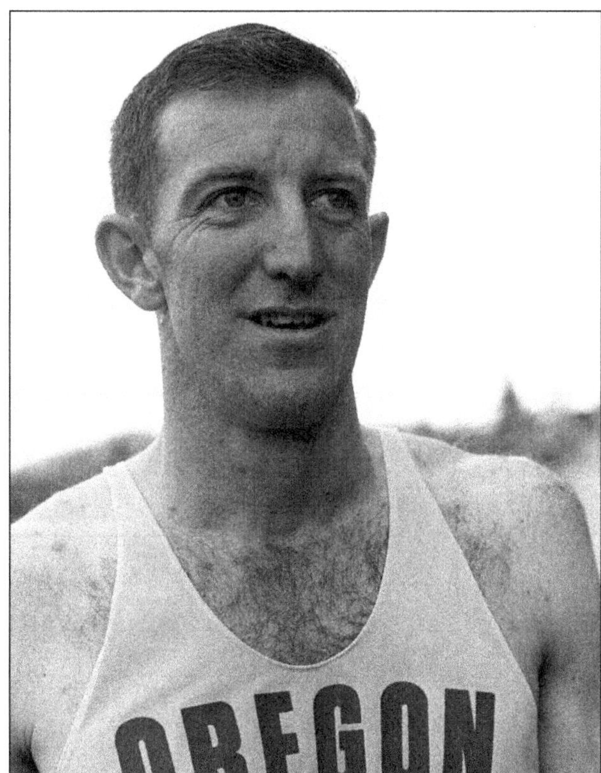

Photo 13-1. Gary Knoke, Australian Olympian

Endnote

1. V. Brezier, et al. (1985). 400m hurdles training for women. *Track Technique, 93*, 2976-2977.

400 HURDLE SCHEDULE NAME ______________________ DATE _______________

1. Warmup routine: Jog 1-2 laps with relay pass.
   Hurdle X drill at lower hurdle height.
   B. Slow high knee; fast leg drill
2. Fartlek A. Varied pace: stride, sprint,
   recover-- stride, meet a challenge, recover.
   Finish feeling exhilarated, not exhausted.
   (a) 10 min. (b) 30 min. (c)
   B. Steady pace: slow, 10-30 min.
   (1) Hendricks Park (2) Golf course (3)
3. A. Weights and jogging
   B. Jogging and stretching
4. High knee and fast leg B. Arms emphasis
5. Starts 2 at 1/2 speed, 2 at 7/8ths speed
   A. Over 2 hurdles (1) LH (2) IH
   B. Back to back (1) 3 hurdles (2)
   C. First 3, slow jog, fast last 3
6. Intervals X. Over hurdles Y. On flat
   Z. Fast 20-50m in middle
   A. 100 (1) 18-16-14 (2)
   B. 150-100-50 (1)
   C. 200 (1) 30 (2) 3/4 effort
   D. 300 E. 150 F. 400 G. 500
7. TEAM MEETING
8. Special A. Sauna B. Swim C.
9. Relay work A. Routine
   B. 50 meters C. 100 meters
10. A. Meet B. Trial C. Simulation D. Control test
   (1) 400 (2) 300 (3) First 3, last 3
   CA. Simulate 200 race CB. Simulate 400 race
   CC. Parts of race F. On the flat
11. Sets A. 500-300-100 (1) 70-75, 42-45, 12-13
   B. 300-200-100 (1) 39-42, 25-27, 12-13
12. With Coach A. B.
14. A. Wind sprints (1) Straight (2) Curve
   B. Hurdle X drill C. Spring and bound
   D. Alternate run and jog, at least 800
   E. Hills with A. B.
15. Plyometrics A. Jumps B. Bounding C.
   (1) 1-leg (2) Both legs (3)
16. Finish work: A. Jog first 300, go last 100
   B. Jog first 200, go last 200 (1) Lanes 2-5-8
17. X Drill:
   (a) 30" (b) 33" (c) 36" (d) 39" (e) 42"
   A. 5 steps to side B. 5 steps over top
   C. 3 steps to side D. 3 steps over top
   (1) On toes (2) Shoulders level
   (3) Lead arm (4) Off arm (5) Hand and a half
17. Parts of race X. Hurdles Y. Flat
   A. 100s: 1st, 2nd, 3rd B. 150s: 1st, mid, last
   C.
18.
20. Work on second event
21. A. Videotape B. Film C. Pictures
   (1) Record performance (2) Study
30. Experimental

Date	Distance	3/4 pace	Date Pace	Goal Pace

M
T
W
T
F
S
S
M
T
W
T
F
S
S
M
T
W
T
F
S
S
M
T
W
T
F
S
S

Sheet 13-1. Metric 400m hurdle training schedule sheet

Intermediate Hurdle NAME DATE September/October

1. Warm-up: jog 1 or 2 laps with relay pass, easy stretch, X drill
   B. High knee (slow) and fast leg
2. Fartlek A. Holmer (varied-pace)
   B. Lydiard—slow, steady (1) Park run (2) Golf course
   (a) 10 min. (2) 30 min. (3)
3. A. Weights and jogging B. Jogging and stretching
4. High knee and fast leg B. Arms emphasis
5. Starts A. 2 at 1/2 effort, 2 at 7/8
   B. Over 2 hurdles (1) 30 in. (2) 36 in.
   C. Back to back (1) 3 hurdles (2)
   D. First 3, slow jog, go last 3
6. Y. Over hurdles Z. Flat A. 110 (1) 18-16-14
   (2) B. 165-110-55
   C. 220 (1) 30 (2)
   D. 330 E. 165 F. 440 G.
7. Squad meeting
8. Special A. Sauna B. Swim C. Hill
9. Relay A. Routine B. 55 C. 110
10. A. Trial B. Compete (1) Full distance
    (2) 3/4 distance (3) First 3, last 3
11. A. 550-330-110 (1) 70-75, 42-45, 12-13
    B. 330-220-110 (1) 39-42, 25-27, 12-13
12. With A. Coach B.
14. A. Wind sprints B. Hurdle X drill
    C. Spring and bound
    D. Alternate run and jog at least 880
15. Finish work A. Jog 1st 330, go last 110
    B. Jog 1st 220, go last 220 C. Go last 330
    D. Finish work lane 2-5-8
16. Parts of race Y. Hurdles Z. Flat
    A. 110s—1st, 2d, 3d B. 165s—1st, 2d, last
    C.
17. 3/4 effort A. 220 B. 330 C. 550 D.
18. X drill A. 36 in. B. 39 in. C. 42 in.
    (1) 5 step to side (2) 5 step the top
    (3) 3 step to side (4) 3 step the top
19. A. Lead arm B. Off arm C. Hand and a half
20. A. On toes B. Shoulders level
21. A. Pictures B. Film
22. Simulated race A. 220 B. 440 C.
    D. Parts of race Y. Over hurdles

Date	Dist.	3/4	Date P.	Goal P.

Day	Workout
M	Organization-equipment-lockers
T	7-use of weights-information
W	7-running courses, procedures-14A
T	1C
F	1A-1B
S	1A-1B
S	recreation
M	1A-11A-14A
T	3A (light)
W	4x 8C-6A (easy on grass)
T	
F	10A (220 at 7/8-9/10ths)-14D
S	
S	
M	4x 1A-11A-11B-6A(1)-14D
T	
W	12-8C
T	3
F	1A-11AB-1B
S	
S	
M	1-2x 3x 1A-1B-11AB-6B-2B(1)
T	3A
W	8C
T	
F	10A (100y and 300y)
S	
S	

Sheet 13-2. Intermediate hurdle training schedule

Intermediate Hurdle NAME DATE October/ November

1. Warm-up: jog 1 or 2 laps with relay pass, easy stretch, X drill
   B. High knee (slow) and fast leg
2. Fartlek A. Holmer (varied-pace)
   B. Lydiard—slow, steady (1) Park run (2) Golf course
   (a) 10 min. (2) 30 min. (3)
3. A. Weights and jogging B. Jogging and stretching
4. High knee and fast leg B. Arms emphasis
5. Starts A. 2 at 1/2 effort, 2 at 7/8
   B. Over 2 hurdles (1) 30 in. (2) 36 in.
   C. Back to back (1) 3 hurdles (2)
   D. First 3, slow jog, go last 3
6. Y. Over hurdles Z. Flat A. 110 (1) 18-16-14
   (2) B. 165-110-55
   C. 220 (1) 30 (2)
   D. 330 E. 165 F. 440 G.
7. Squad meeting
8. Special A. Sauna B. Swim C. Hill
9. Relay A. Routine B. 55 C. 110
10. A. Trial B. Compete (1) Full distance
    (2) 3/4 distance (3) First 3, last 3
11. A. 550-330-110 (1) 70-75, 42-45, 12-13
    B. 330-220-110 (1) 39-42, 25-27, 12-13
12. With A. Coach B.
14. A. Wind sprints B. Hurdle X drill
    C. Spring and bound
    D. Alternate run and jog at least 880
15. Finish work A. Jog 1st 330, go last 110
    B. Jog 1st 220, go last 220 C. Go last 330
    D. Finish work lane 2-5-8
16. Parts of race Y. Hurdles Z. Flat
    A. 110s—1st, 2d, 3d B. 165s—1st, 2d, last
    C.
17. 3/4 effort A. 220 B. 330 C. 550 D.
18. X drill A. 36 in. B. 39 in. C. 42 in.
    (1) 5 step to side (2) 5 step the top
    (3) 3 step to side (4) 3 step the top
19. A. Lead arm B. Off arm C. Hand and a half
20. A. On toes B. Shoulders level
21. A. Pictures B. Film
22. Simulated race A. 220 B. 440 C.
    D. Parts of race Y. Over hurdles

Date	Dist.	3/4	Date P.	Goal P.

Day	Workout
M	4x 1A-4B-5B (easy)-11AB-14D
T	3A
W	1B-5B (easy)-18A-8C
T	21A-3A
F	3x 1A-18A(1)(3)-6D-14A
S	1A-1B-5A-10A (500y)-2B(1)
S	recreation
M	1A-1B-11AB-2A (park)
T	3-14A
W	4x 4x 1A-6A-8C-6A
T	3
F	10A (Relay-300y or 500y)
S	Your choice
S	
M	1A-4B-5B-11A-2A
T	3
W	4x 1B-4A-8C-6A
T	1B
F	2x 1A-6B-Jog
S	10 (Relay-385y)-2B(1)
S	
M	1-2x 1A-1B-5A-11A-2B
T	1B-8B
W	8C
T	3A
F	1A-9A-2B(1)
S	With or observe runners
S	recreation

Sheet 13-3. Intermediate hurdle training schedule

Intermediate Hurdle NAME DATE November/December

1. Warm-up: jog 1 or 2 laps with relay pass, easy stretch, X drill
   B. High knee (slow) and fast leg
2. Fartlek A. Holmer (varied-pace)
   B. Lydiard—slow, steady (1) Park run (2) Golf course
   (a) 10 min. (2) 30 min. (3)
3. A. Weights and jogging B. Jogging and stretching
4. High knee and fast leg B. Arms emphasis
5. Starts A. 2 at 1/2 effort, 2 at 7/8
   B. Over 2 hurdles (1) 30 in. (2) 36 in.
   C. Back to back (1) 3 hurdles (2)
   D. First 3, slow jog, go last 3
6. Y. Over hurdles Z. Flat A. 110 (1) 18-16-14
   (2) 13 B. 165-110-55
   C. 220 (1) 30 (2) 28
   D. 330 E. 165 F. 440 G.
7. Squad meeting
8. Special A. Sauna B. Swim C. Hill
9. Relay A. Routine B. 55 C. 110
10. A. Trial B. Compete (1) Full distance
    (2) 3/4 distance (3) First 3, last 3
11. A. 550-330-110 (1) 70-75, 42-45, 12-13
    B. 330-220-110 (1) 39-42, 25-27, 12-13
12. With A. Coach B.
14. A. Wind sprints B. Hurdle X drill
    C. Spring and bound
    D. Alternate run and jog at least 880
15. Finish work A. Jog 1st 330, go last 110
    B. Jog 1st 220, go last 220 C. Go last 330
    D. Finish work lane 2-5-8
16. Parts of race Y. Hurdles Z. Flat
    A. 110s—1st, 2d, 3d B. 165s—1st, 2d, last
    C.
17. 3/4 effort A. 220 B. 330 C. 550 D.
18. X drill A. 36 in. B. 39 in. C. 42 in.
    (1) 5 step to side (2) 5 step the top
    (3) 3 step to side (4) 3 step the top
19. A. Lead arm B. Off arm C. Hand and a half
20. A. On toes B. Shoulders level
21. A. Pictures B. Film
22. Simulated race A. 220 B. 440 C.
    D. Parts of race Y. Over hurdles

Date	Dist.	3/4	Date P.	Goal P.

M	1A - 18AB(1,3) - 11A - 11B - 2B
T	3A
W	1A - 4x 6C(2) - 4x 6A(2) - 8C
T	3A
F	1B - 3x 6E (9/10 effort) - 2B - 4x 6A (7/8 effort)
S	
S	recreation

M	1A - 1B - 18AB(1,2,3,4) - 11AB - 2B(1)
T	3A
W	1A - 5B - 8C - 4x 6A(2)
T	3A
F	10A (Relay-880 or 440)
S	
S	

M	
T	
W	
T	
F	
S	
S	

M	
T	
W	
T	
F	
S	
S	

Sheet 13-4. Intermediate hurdle training schedule

Intermediate Hurdle NAME DATE January

1. Warm-up: jog 1 or 2 laps with relay pass, easy stretch, X drill
   B. High knee (slow) and fast leg
2. Fartlek A. Holmer (varied-pace)
   B. Lydiard–slow, steady (1) Park run (2) Golf course
   (a) 10 min. (2) 30 min. (3)
3. A. Weights and jogging B. Jogging and stretching
4. High knee and fast leg B. Arms emphasis
5. Starts A. 2 at 1/2 effort, 2 at 7/8
   B. Over 2 hurdles (1) 30 in. (2) 36 in.
   C. Back to back (1) 3 hurdles (2)
   D. First 3, slow jog, go last 3
6. Y. Over hurdles Z. Flat A. 110 (1) 18-16-14
   (2) 13 B. 165-110-55
   C. 220 (1) 30 (2)
   D. 330 E. 165 F. 440 G.
7. Squad meeting
8. Special A. Sauna B. Swim C. Hill
9. Relay A. Routine B. 55 C. 110
10. A. Trial B. Compete (1) Full distance
    (2) 3/4 distance (3) First 3, last 3
11. A. 550-330-110 (1) 70-75, 42-45, 12-13
    B. 330-220-110 (1) 39-42, 25-27, 12-13
12. With A. Coach B.
14. A. Wind sprints B. Hurdle X drill
    C. Spring and bound
    D. Alternate run and jog at least 880
15. Finish work A. Jog 1st 330, go last 110
    B. Jog 1st 220, go last 220 C. Go last 330
    D. Finish work lane 2-5-8
16. Parts of race Y. Hurdles Z. Flat
    A. 110s–1st, 2d, 3d B. 165s–1st, 2d, last
    C.
17. 3/4 effort A. 220 B. 330 C. 550 D.
18. X drill A. 36 in. B. 39 in. C. 42 in.
    (1) 5 step to side (2) 5 step the top
    (3) 3 step to side (4) 3 step the top
19. A. Lead arm B. Off arm C. Hand and a half
20. A. On toes B. Shoulders level
21. A. Pictures B. Film
22. Simulated race A. 220 B. 440 C.
    D. Parts of race Y. Over hurdles

Date	Dist.	3/4	Date P.	Goal P.

Day	Workout
M	Class or squad organization-4A-3
T	Complete registration-7(procedures)-2B
W	1A-4A-1B-5C(1)-8D
T	7-3A-4B-6ZB
F	1-5A-4A-11A-2A
S	Workout
S	
M	2x 4x 1A-4A-4B-5B-16A-6C2(1)-2B
T	1-4A-3A
W	1A-5A-4A-16B-11A-Jog
T	3A-8C
F	1-4A-5A-16B-11B-Jog
S	
S	
M	1-5A-16A-16B-11B-2A
T	3A
W	4x 2x 1-5A-6A(2)-6YB-Jog
T	3A-grass run or 8C
F	2x 2x 2x 1-4A-5B-6YA-6YB-2B
S	10 hurdles
S	
M	1-5A-16A-16B-11B-Jog
T	7-3A
W	1-5A-16B-11B-8A
T	3A
F	Gear ready
S	10A or B-Indoor meet
S	

Sheet 13-5. Intermediate hurdle training schedule

Intermediate Hurdle NAME DATE *February*

1. Warm-up: jog 1 or 2 laps with relay pass, easy stretch, X drill
   B. High knee (slow) and fast leg
2. Fartlek A. Holmer (varied-pace)
   B. Lydiard—slow, steady (1) Park run (2) Golf course
   (a) 10 min. (2) 30 min. (3)
3. A. Weights and jogging B. Jogging and stretching
4. High knee and fast leg B. Arms emphasis
5. Starts A. 2 at 1/2 effort, 2 at 7/8
   B. Over 2 hurdles (1) 30 in. (2) 36 in.
   C. Back to back (1) 3 hurdles (2)
   D. First 3, slow jog, go last 3
6. Y. Over hurdles Z. Flat A. 110 (1) 18-16-14
   (2) *13* (3) *12* B. 165-110-55
   C. 220 (1) 30 (2) *26-28*
   D. 330 E. 165 F. 440 G.
7. Squad meeting
8. Special A. Sauna B. Swim C. *Hill*
9. Relay A. Routine B. 55 C. 110
10. A. Trial B. Compete (1) Full distance
    (2) 3/4 distance (3) First 3, last 3
11. A. 550-330-110 (1) 70-75, 42-45, 12-13
    B. 330-220-110 (1) 39-42, 25-27, 12-13
12. With A. Coach B.
14. A. Wind sprints B. Hurdle X drill
    C. Spring and bound
    D. Alternate run and jog at least 880
15. Finish work A. Jog 1st 330, go last 110
    B. Jog 1st 220, go last 220 C. Go last 330
    D. Finish work lane 2-5-8
16. Parts of race Y. Hurdles Z. Flat
    A. 110s—1st, 2d, 3d B. 165s—1st, 2d, last
    C.
17. 3/4 effort A. 220 B. 330 C. 550 D.
18. X drill A. 36 in. B. 39 in. C. 42 in.
    (1) 5 step to side (2) 5 step the top
    (3) 3 step to side (4) 3 step the top
19. A. Lead arm B. Off arm C. Hand and a half
20. A. On toes B. Shoulders level
21. A. Pictures B. Film
22. Simulated race A. 220 B. 440 C.
    D. Parts of race Y. Over hurdles

Date	Dist.	3/4	Date P.	Goal P.

Day	Workout
M	*1A-18-4A-5A-6A(2) 4X*
T	*1A-4A-6E(18-19) 3X -6A(3) 4X -4A*
W	*7-A-18AB-4A-6A 4X -8C*
T	*1A-3*
F	*Jog and gear ready*
S	*10*
S	*Easy jog*

Day	A.M.	P.M.
M	*1B*	*3A-6YC 4X*
T		*1A-16YB-300yds. 2X -2A-300yds(34) 2X*
W	*1B*	*1A-6A 4X -8C-4-6A*
T		*1A-18-16C-2B-6A 2-4X*
F		*Jog*
S		*Jog*
S		*10A(660yds.)*
M	*1B-6A 3X*	*2B-6A 4X*
T		*1A-18-11B 2X -2B-14A*
W	*1B*	*1A-6F 3-4X (54-56)-2A*
T		*1A-6C 6-8X (2)*
F	*1B*	
S		*1B-(660-440-220) 1X -2A*
S		
M	*1B*	*18AB-16A-(600-300-100) 1X -2A-6A 4X*
T		*1A-4A-16B-6C 2-4X -2A-6A 4X*
W		*3-8C*
T	*1B*	*6C 6-8X (2)-2A-6A 4X*
F		*18AB*
S		*10(440yds. and IH or HH and IH)*
S		*2A*

Sheet 13-6. Intermediate hurdle training schedule

Intermediate Hurdle NAME DATE *March*

1. Warm-up: jog 1 or 2 laps with relay pass, easy stretch, X drill
   B. High knee (slow) and fast leg
2. Fartlek A. Holmer (varied-pace)
   B. Lydiard—slow, steady (1) Park run (2) Golf course
   (a) 10 min. (2) 30 min. (3)
3. A. Weights and jogging B. Jogging and stretching
4. High knee and fast leg B. Arms emphasis
5. Starts A. 2 at 1/2 effort, 2 at 7/8
   B. Over 2 hurdles (1) 30 in. (2) 36 in.
   C. Back to back (1) 3 hurdles (2)
   D. First 3, slow jog, go last 3
6. Y. Over hurdles Z. Flat A. 110 (1) 18-16-14
   (2) B. 165-110-55
   C. 220 (1) 30 (2)
   D. 330 E. 165 F. 440 G. *550* *F. 660*
7. Squad meeting
8. Special A. Sauna B. Swim C. *Hill*
9. Relay A. Routine B. 55 C. 110
10. A. Trial B. Compete (1) Full distance
    (2) 3/4 distance (3) First 3, last 3
11. A. 550-330-110 (1) 70-75, 42-45, 12-13
    B. 330-220-110 (1) 39-42, 25-27, 12-13
12. With A. Coach B.
14. A. Wind sprints B. Hurdle X drill
    C. Spring and bound
    D. Alternate run and jog at least 880
15. Finish work A. Jog 1st 330, go last 110
    B. Jog 1st 220, go last 220 C. Go last 330
    D. Finish work lane 2-5-8
16. Parts of race Y. Hurdles Z. Flat
    A. 110s—1st, 2d, 3d B. 165s—1st, 2d, last
    C. *Last 220 (1) 22*
17. 3/4 effort A. 220 B. 330 C. 550 D.
18. X drill A. 36 in. B. 39 in. C. 42 in.
    (1) 5 step to side (2) 5 step the top
    (3) 3 step to side (4) 3 step the top
19. A. Lead arm B. Off arm C. Hand and a half
20. A. On toes B. Shoulders level
21. A. Pictures B. Film
22. Simulated race A. 220 B. 440 C.
    D. Parts of race Y. Over hurdles

Date	Dist.	3/4	Date P.	Goal P.

Day	A.M.	P.M.
M	*1A*	*18BC – 1x 10HH – 16C(1) – 16A – Jog*
T		*2x 16B*
W	*1B*	*18AB – 1x 10HH – 1x Last 265 at 220 pace – 2A – 4x 6A*
T		*9B*
F	*1B*	*3x 5B(2)*
S		*10A (full 120HH – full 440IH)*
S		
M	*1B*	*18BC – 16B – 11B – 2A*
T	*1A*	*1B – 3*
W	*1B*	*18AB – 5D – 15B – 2A – 4x 6A*
T		*1A – 3*
F	*1B*	*5B – Jog*
S		*10B (IH and mile relay)*
S		*Travel – spring vacation*
M	*1B*	*18AB – 16B – 1x (660 – 440 – 220) – 2A – Jog*
T	*1B*	*18AB – 15C – 15A – 2–4x 6C*
W	*1B*	*18BC – 2A – 4x 6A*
T	*1B*	*18BC · 5 – 16B – 15B – 4x 6A*
F	*1B*	*3A*
S		*10B – Dual meet*
S		*Travel home – re-register*
M	*1B*	*18AB – 5C – Last 265 yds. – 6G – 6F – Jog*
T		*9 – 3A*
W	*1B*	*18AB – 5D(HH) – Last 265 yds. – 2A – 4x 6A*
T	*7*	*Light*
F		*Gear ready*
S		*10B – HH and IH*
S		*Jog*

Sheet 13-7. Intermediate hurdle training schedule

Intermediate Hurdle NAME DATE April

1. Warm-up: jog 1 or 2 laps with relay pass, easy stretch, X drill
   B. High knee (slow) and fast leg
2. Fartlek A. Holmer (varied-pace)
   B. Lydiard—slow, steady (1) Park run (2) Golf course
   (a) 10 min. (2) 30 min. (3)
3. A. Weights and jogging B. Jogging and stretching
4. High knee and fast leg B. Arms emphasis
5. Starts A. 2 at 1/2 effort, 2 at 7/8
   B. Over 2 hurdles (1) 30 in. (2) 36 in.
   C. Back to back (1) 3 hurdles (2)
   D. First 3, slow jog, go last 3
6. Y. Over hurdles Z. Flat A. 110 (1) 18-16-14
   (2) B. 165-110-55
   C. 220 (1) 30 (2)
   D. 330 E. 165 F. 440 G.
7. Squad meeting
8. Special A. Sauna B. Swim C. Hill
9. Relay A. Routine B. 55 C. 110
10. A. Trial B. Compete (1) Full distance
    (2) 3/4 distance (3) First 3, last 3
11. A. 550-330-110 (1) 70-75, 42-45, 12-13
    B. 330-220-110 (1) 39-42, 25-27, 12-13
12. With A. Coach B.
14. A. Wind sprints B. Hurdle X drill
    C. Spring and bound
    D. Alternate run and jog at least 880
15. Finish work A. Jog 1st 330, go last 110
    B. Jog 1st 220, go last 220 C. Go last 330
    D. Finish work lane 2-5-8
16. Parts of race Y. Hurdles Z. Flat
    A. 110s—1st, 2d, 3d B. 165s—1st, 2d, last
    C.
17. 3/4 effort A. 220 B. 330 C. 550 .D.
18. X drill A. 36 in. B. 39 in. C. 42 in.
    (1) 5 step to side (2) 5 step the top
    (3) 3 step to side (4) 3 step the top
19. A. Lead arm B. Off arm C. Hand and a half
20. A. On toes B. Shoulders level
21. A. Pictures B. Film
22. Simulated race A. 220 B. 440 C.
    D. Parts of race Y. Over hurdles

Date	Dist.	3/4	Date P.	Goal P.

Day	Workout
M	1A-4A-5A-16C-11A-Jog
T	9B-2A
W	3x 1A-18BC-16B-6D(39-42)-8C
T	9B-1A
F	Gear ready-14A (grass)
S	10B-Dual meet
S	Loosen up
M	1x 1A-18AB-16C-(660-440-220)-2B
T	3-9A-20 min. jog
W	2x 4x 1A-5A-16C-300yds.-8C-grass 55yds.
T	9A-16A
F	Gear ready-jog
S	10B-Dual meet
S	Loosen up
M	1x 1A-4A-18AB-5C-16B-Jog-500yds.
T	3A
W	1x 4x 1A-5A-5B-18BC-15B-300yds.-6A(grass)
T	3A
F	Gear ready
S	10B-Dual meet
S	1A-10A-2A
M	1A-18A-Jog
T	1A-4A-18AB-16A-15B-16ZA-Jog
W	4x 3-grass hurdle-6ZB
T	1A-5A-18BC-10A (120 yds.-36")- 16YA-16YB-2A
F	Easy
S	10B-Quadrangular meet
S	Jog

Sheet 13-8. Intermediate hurdle training schedule

Intermediate Hurdle NAME DATE May

1. Warm-up: jog 1 or 2 laps with relay pass, easy stretch, X drill
   B. High knee (slow) and fast leg
2. Fartlek A. Holmer (varied-pace)
   B. Lydiard—slow, steady (1) Park run (2) Golf course
   (a) 10 min. (2) 30 min. (3)
3. A. Weights and jogging B. Jogging and stretching
4. High knee and fast leg B. Arms emphasis
5. Starts A. 2 at 1/2 effort, 2 at 7/8
   B. Over 2 hurdles (1) 30 in. (2) 36 in.
   C. Back to back (1) 3 hurdles (2)
   D. First 3, slow jog, go last 3
6. Y. Over hurdles Z. Flat A. 110 (1) 18-16-14
   (2) B. 165-110-55
   C. 220 (1) 30 (2)
   D. 330 E. 165 F. 440 G.
7. Squad meeting
8. Special A. Sauna B. Swim C. Hill
9. Relay A. Routine B. 55 C. 110
10. A. Trial B. Compete (1) Full distance
    (2) 3/4 distance (3) First 3, last 3
11. A. 550-330-110 (1) 70-75, 42-45, 12-13
    B. 330-220-110 (1) 39-42, 25-27, 12-13
12. With A. Coach B.
14. A. Wind sprints B. Hurdle X drill
    C. Spring and bound
    D. Alternate run and jog at least 880
15. Finish work A. Jog 1st 330, go last 110
    B. Jog 1st 220, go last 220 C. Go last 330
    D. Finish work lane 2-5-8
16. Parts of race Y. Hurdles Z. Flat
    A. 110s—1st, 2d, 3d B. 165s—1st, 2d, last
    C.
17. 3/4 effort A. 220 B. 330 C. 550 D.
18. X drill A. 36 in. B. 39 in. C. 42 in.
    (1) 5 step to side (2) 5 step the top
    (3) 3 step to side (4) 3 step the top
19. A. Lead arm B. Off arm C. Hand and a half
20. A. On toes B. Shoulders level
21. A. Pictures B. Film
22. Simulated race A. 220 B. 440 C.
    D. Parts of race Y. Over hurdles

Date	Dist.	3/4	Date P.	Goal P.

M	1A-5A-18AB-5C-16B-Jog-4X 6A
T	Grass hurdle - 4A
W	5A-5D-4A (grass)
T	5A-16A-Jog (grass)
F	Gear ready
S	10B - Dual meet
S	Loosen up
M	1B-4X 6A-4A-grass hurdle
T	1A-18AB-2X 6YE(first)-2X 6YA (last)-2A
W	3
T	1-18- grass hurdle - Jog
F	Gear ready, grass hurdle
S	10B - Northern Division meet
S	1X 500yds - 2B
M	1B-3A-2A
T	1A-18AB-5C-16B-Jog-14A
W	7 - light grass
T	Grass hurdle - 14A (grass)
F	Prelims - Pac 8 meet
S	Finals - Pac 8 meet
S	Loosen up
M	
T	
W	
T	
F	
S	
S	

Sheet 13-9. Intermediate hurdle training schedule

Intermediate Hurdle NAME DATE June

1. Warm-up: jog 1 or 2 laps with relay pass, easy stretch, X drill
   B. High knee (slow) and fast leg
2. Fartlek A. Holmer (varied-pace)
   B. Lydiard—slow, steady (1) Park run (2) Golf course
   (a) 10 min. (2) 30 min. (3)
3. A. Weights and jogging B. Jogging and stretching
4. High knee and fast leg B. Arms emphasis
5. Starts A. 2 at 1/2 effort, 2 at 7/8
   B. Over 2 hurdles (1) 30 in. (2) 36 in.
   C. Back to back (1) 3 hurdles (2)
   D. First 3, slow jog, go last 3
6. Y. Over hurdles Z. Flat A. 110 (1) 18-16-14
   (2) B. 165-110-55
   C. 220 (1) 30 (2)
   D. 330 E. 165 F. 440 G.
7. Squad meeting
8. Special A. Sauna B. Swim C. Hill
9. Relay A. Routine B. 55 C. 110
10. A. Trial B. Compete (1) Full distance
   (2) 3/4 distance (3) First 3, last 3
11. A. 550-330-110 (1) 70-75, 42-45, 12-13
   B. 330-220-110 (1) 39-42, 25-27, 12-13
12. With A. Coach B.
14. A. Wind sprints B. Hurdle X drill
   C. Spring and bound
   D. Alternate run and jog at least 880
15. Finish work A. Jog 1st 330, go last 110
   B. Jog 1st 220, go last 220 C. Go last 330
   D. Finish work lane 2-5-8
16. Parts of race Y. Hurdles Z. Flat
   A. 110s—1st, 2d, 3d B. 165s—1st, 2d, last
   C.
17. 3/4 effort A. 220 B. 330 C. 550 D.
18. X drill A. 36 in. B. 39 in. C. 42 in.
   (1) 5 step to side (2) 5 step the top
   (3) 3 step to side (4) 3 step the top
19. A. Lead arm B. Off arm C. Hand and a half
20. A. On toes B. Shoulders level
21. A. Pictures B. Film
22. Simulated race A. 220 B. 440 C.
   D. Parts of race Y. Over hurdles

Date	Dist.	3/4	Date P.	Goal P.

Day	Workout
M	Light and 9A
T	1x 1A-5A-16C-500yds.-2A
W	2x 1A-5A-16B-300yds.-2A
T	Light-14A
F	Jog
S	1x 1A-5A-16C-500yds.-2A
S	1A-5A-16AY-2A
M	1A-5A-10A (10 highs at 39")-16B-2A
T	Light-gear ready
W	Travel-loosen up
T	Semifinals (N.C.A.A)-14D-14A
F	Trials-14D-14A NCAA
S	Finals NCAA
S	
M	
T	
W	
T	
F	
S	
S	
M	
T	
W	
T	
F	
S	
S	

Sheet 13-10. Intermediate hurdle training schedule

Core Readings

Freeman, William H. (2001). Periodized training for sprinters and hurdlers. In *Peak When It Counts: Periodization for American track and field* (4th ed.). Mountain View, CA: Tafnews, 106-119.

Iskra, Janusz, & Jan Widera. (Summer 2001). The training preparation of the World Junior 400m Hurdles Champion. *Track Coach, 156*, 4980-4984, 4997.

Jarver, Jess, ed. (2004). *The Hurdles: Contemporary Theory, Technique and Training* (4th ed.). Mountain View, CA: Tafnews.

McFarlane, Brent. (2000). *The Science of Hurdling* (4th ed.). Ottawa: Athletics Canada.

USA Track & Field Coaching Education Program. (2001). *Level II Course: Sprints hurdles relays*. USA Track & Field. Invaluable; revised regularly.

Winckler, Gary. 400-meter hurdles. (2000). In *USA Track and Field coaching manual*. Champaign, IL: Human Kinetics, 75-91.

Recommended Readings

Alejo, Bob. (1993). Weight training for the 400m hurdler. *Track Technique*, 123, 3915-3918.

Breizer, Vitaly, & Remi Korchemny. (1993). The preparation of women for the 400 meter hurdles. *Track Technique, 122*, 3895-3897, 3907.

Brown, Garry. (1992). Conditioning for the 400m hurdles. *Track Technique, 121*, 3856-3858.

Ditroilo, Massimiliano, & Maurizio Marini. (Fall 2003). An analysis of race distribution for male 400m hurdlers at the 2000 Sydney Olympics [abstract]. *Track Coach, 165*, 5283.

Iskra, Janus. (1997). Endurance in the 400 metres hurdles. In Jess Jarver, ed., *The Hurdles: Contemporary Theory, Technique and Training* (3rd ed.). Mountain View, CA: Tafnews, 104-109.

Iskra, Janusz. (1995). The most effective technical training in the 100 metres hurdles. *New Studies in Athletics, 10*(3), 51-55.

Iskra, Janusz. (Spring 1999). Pawel Januszewski breaks through at the European Championships. *Track Coach, 147*, 4691-4698.

Iskra, Janusz, Anna Walaszcyk & Ronald Mehlich. (Fall 2006). Principles of 400m hurdle training. *Track Coach, 177*, 5641-5645.

Konig, Eberhard. (1990). Women's 400m hurdles developments [abstract]. *Track Technique, 110*, 3520.

Koszewski, Dietmar. (Summer 2001). Methodical development of young 400m hurdlers [abstract]. *Track Coach, 156*, 4995-4996.

Letzelter, H., M. Letzelter, Y. Honda & W. Steinmann. (1995). Stride rhythm in the junior 400m hurdles. [abstract]. *Track Coach, 133*, 4257-4258.

Lindeman, Ralph. (1995). 400-meter hurdle theory. *Track Coach, 131*, 4169-4171, 4196.

Paish, Wilf. (Summer 2004). A team approach to 400m hurdling. *Track Coach, 168*, 5367-5368.

Robertson, Max. (1990). The merits of speed-orientated as opposed to endurance-orientated training for the 400 metres hurdles. *New Studies in Athletics, 5*(4), 29-32.

Schiffer, Jürgen. (2006). Selected and annotated bibliography 73-74: Hurdles. *New Studies in Athletics, 21*(1), 71-104; 21(2), 97-122.

Stepanova, Marina. (Summer 1997). My experiences in the 400m hurdles. *Track Coach, 140*, 4473-4476.

Vrublevsky, E. (1991). Strength development in the 400m hurdles event [abstract]. *Track Technique, 118*, 3778-3779.

THE JUMPS

Part 4

Bouncy Moore, NCAA champion and two-time U.S. Champion

14

The High Jump

Bowerman's Best

7′ 1/2″	Marty Hill	1971

Record Setters

Emery Barnes	NCAA champion, 1954
Paul Stuber	All-American, 1963

In 1968, an Oregon State high jumper with an eccentric jumping technique stunned the athletic world by winning the Olympic Games and setting an Olympic record. For almost 30 years, the best jumpers had used the straddle style, face down to the crossbar and bodies almost parallel to it during their clearance. Dick Fosbury cleared the bar while lying on his back at a right angle to the bar. Most top jumpers use the Fosbury flop. Another pioneer of the style, also in 1968, was Canadian jumper Debbie Brill with the Brill bend.

Because the flop, or back layout, style dominates high jumping, this theoretical look examines only the flop. The two styles of flop are the *speed flop* and the *power flop*.[1] Thinner jumpers tend to use the speed flop, with its faster approach run, while heavier, slower jumpers rely more on strength development and the power flop (Table 14-1). The speed floppers are concerned with their direction of travel and body lean, with "keeping vertical." Power floppers are more concerned with trying to move faster and apply more force in the jumping action.

Speed Flop Versus Power Flop	
Speed Flop	*Power Flop*
• Run-up at 7.7-8.4 m/second	• Run-up at 7.0-8.0 m/second
• 8-9 stride run-up	• 10-12 stride run-up
• Takeoff in 0.13-0.18 seconds	• Takeoff in 0.17-0.21 seconds
• On toes until last step	• First half of run-up on toes, then flat-footed or on heels
• High knee lift in run-up	• Low trail leg recover, especially on last two strides
• Fast single-arm action in last stride and take off	• Wide, very active double-arm action on takeoff
• Little speed loss in last stride, center of gravity	• More speed loss on last step, center of gravity lower and back or above plant foot
• Farther from bar on takeoff	• Closer to bar on takeoff
• Less arm and leg action while in the air	• More active in air with arms and trail leg
• Trail leg rises close to body soon after takeoff	• Slow trail leg, conscious effort to lift heel and "arch" back
• Less "head-throwing," look at bar for feedback	• Head thrown back; must learn to look at the bar
• Jumpers talk in terms of upper body, components of direction	• Jumpers talk in terms of lower body, components of propulsion
• Usually low body weight, ectomorphic, less power weight trainging	• Usually heavier, more mesomorphic, much power weight training
• Do much speed work (enjoy it).	• Do less speed work (do not enjoy it).

Table 14-1. Speed flop versus power flop

Training Theory

Three basic principles should be the focus of training:

- The ratio of strength to body weight is the foremost training factor, which means concerted work on the takeoff, converting the energy from horizontal to vertical.
- Besides technique, the jumper must develop the speed and power components of training.
- Technical mechanics stay the same at each height. At some height, the jumper's technique breaks down. The jumper must train to locate the breakdowns and correct them.

The technical points that jumpers must perfect include the following:

- Make a fast approach; speed is critical.
- The second half of the run-up must be smooth but done without slowing down (done partly with the arms).
- The shoulders and the neck muscles must stay relaxed.
- Plant the foot at a shallow angle (20 to 30 degrees), with the hips at about 45 degrees, and the shoulders at about 90 degrees to the bar.
- Have a strong plant leg, kept straight on the plant.

- Use aggressive knee-drive action.
- The heel is tucked, arching the back over the bar.
- When the head is back, watch the bar for feedback.

Soviet studies suggest that the most effective power training is at 70 to 90 percent of the athlete's best mark, while speed increases result from weights of 30 to 50 percent of an athlete's maximum.[2] They used a four-week weight-training cycle, followed by three weeks of the other training. Plyometric training is commonly used as a part of the training program, though no general agreement exists on the amount or nature of the most effective training.

A double-periodized year for high jumping, with an indoor and an outdoor macrocycle, is the most common training year for older high jumpers.[3] Bob Myers suggests a training year with the following six phases, which is consistent with current training trends:

- General conditioning: June/July through November
- Specific conditioning (Pre-Competition I): December through January
- Competition I: February through March
- Specific conditioning (Pre-Competition II): April
- Competition II: May through last major meet
- Active rest (Transition/Regeneration)[4]

Athletes break down during heavy load cycles (such as during the general and specific training phases) if all areas of their training have high loads. The peaks should be alternated among strength training, plyometrics, and running. The microcycle (week) should also show the wave pattern of varying loading.

The Athletics Congress's Track and Field Coaching Manual (2nd ed.) suggests the following five-phase, single-periodized program training year:

- Maximal loading base: July through September
- Power development: October through January
- Power transfer: February through April
- Transition/pre-competition: two weeks
- Power retention: competition peak season[5]

For young male high jumpers, the rapid growth of muscular strength between ages 17 and 19 can hamper proper technique development if conditioning work is not mixed with the technical training.[6] From ages 19 to 23 is the "high-performance development phase" for potential elite jumpers, so jumpers should focus on improving their technique and specific fitness, while gaining competitive experience at a high level.

The fastest development for male high jumpers occurs between ages 14 and 15 and between ages 17 and 19, with the "real potential talent" reaching 7′ 1 1/2″ to 7′ 4″ during the latter ages. However, young athletes should not use maximal loads in resistance exercises before ages 18 and 19, because growing athletes are more vulnerable to stress injuries.

Applying the Theory

The high jumper is usually average or above average in height and possesses good spring. He may be a tenacious worker but not necessarily well coordinated. The general test for high jumpers is the jump and reach, the Sargent jump, but it is not an infallible guide. On that test, Dick Fosbury, who high-jumped over 7′ 4″, was outjumped by some weight men on his college team. Also, world-class male high jumpers have been no taller than 5′ 8″ tall. One female American jumper stood 5′ 0″, but she jumped 6′ 0″.

High Jump Tactics

Jumpers must consider their tactics for major and minor competitions. Among the factors that affect the choice of tactics are the following:

- In some tie situations, the smallest total number of jumps decides the winner. Emphasize clearing a height on the first attempt.
- Maximal concentration, speed, and coordination are possible only for 6 to 10 jumps. The jumper should plan the best number of jumps, and use it to determine his starting height.
- A jumper may wait 45 minutes or more between attempts in high-level meets. Such a wait should be practiced on a regular basis.
- Warm-up areas for major meets may be outside the stadium. Practice this situation, with a delay between warm-up and competition.
- Trials and finals are on successive days in major meets. Simulate the meet with two hard days or with morning and evening sessions in a single day.
- Passing heights is useful, but risky. Do not do it in a major meet until practiced in training and at smaller meets.
- Opening heights at major meets may be near the athlete's best. Practice starting at higher heights in some sessions, and take more warm-up jumps before the major meet.
- Prepare for all weather conditions–including rain, wind, and sun.
- Only 90 seconds is allowed for a jump. Use a clock in some practice sessions so the time does not seem restrictive.[7]

Major High Jump Styles

Two major techniques or styles of jumping are commonly in use: the straddle and the flop.

Straddle Style

The straddle, or belly roll, has several variations. It is a very efficient technique, though the Fosbury flop may have mechanical advantages (the center of gravity may not have to rise as far to clear the bar). The *belly roll* may be the best name because it perfectly describes the clearance of the bar. The jumper uses a straight-line approach from the side, taking off from the inside foot and kicking with the outside foot. The athlete clears the bar while face down atop it, rolling around and over it.

Variations of this style, such as the true belly roll, find the jumper in a beautiful layout that perfectly parallels the bar. In the dive straddle, the head clears the bar ahead of the leg, which is more efficient than the nose-to-the-bar style. Although the straddle is less popular, it is still very effective. Christian Schenk, the gold medalist in the 1988 Olympic decathlon, jumped 7′ 5 1/4″ with it.

The approach for the straddle begins from a check mark about eight strides from the takeoff point (Figure 14-1). Most often, the jumper runs toward the bar in a line that forms an angle between 30 and 45 degrees in relation to the crossbar. The speed of the approach varies with the jumper. Some jumpers make a slow approach, relying heavily upon spring for their height, while others make a fast approach, relying on leg strength to enable them to convert their forward momentum to upward momentum. Generally, the last three strides are longer and faster as the athlete lowers the center of gravity and "gathers" for the takeoff. The jumper plants the heel of the takeoff foot solidly, coordinating the "brake" on the forward momentum with a swift upward kick of the lead leg and upward thrust of the arms, designed to divert the momentum upward. On the takeoff, the plant foot is put down out ahead of the jumper's center of gravity. The jump is then coordinated as shown previously.

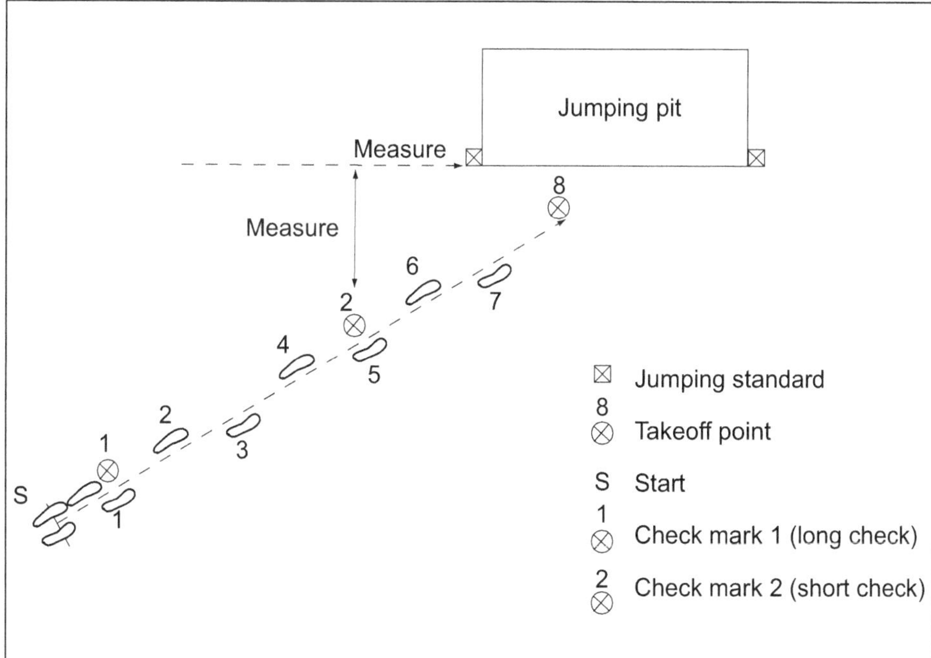

Figure 14-1. Straddle-style approach

The straddle jumper kicks upward, and the lead leg continues over the bar, after which the trail leg clears the bar, so the athlete clears the bar on his stomach. If the height of the jump is great enough, the jumper continues to rotate while falling, landing on his back.

Fosbury Flop

Four advantages of the Fosbury flop, or back layout, make it worth the coach's consideration:

- It is very easy to learn.
- It is a simpler technique, thus having fewer problems.
- It permits greater use of the athlete's natural speed.
- It is more fun to many jumpers than other techniques.

Those advantages do not mean that the form has no risks. Do not overlook one risk: Only a good landing pit should ever be used. The risks of back or neck injury are considerable if any landing area other than a large, deep foam rubber pit is used.

The flop style of jumping is much simpler in practice than it appears. Most athletes take an 8- to 12-step approach, the first step being with the right foot if the jumper plants with the left foot on the takeoff. Some jumpers rock into the first step, though it is mostly a technique of mental focus and preparation, or a personal trait that results from nervousness.

The approach run should be fast but relaxed. Too much speed changes the body lean and hampers the smooth transfer from the run-up to the takeoff.[8] Three approaches are recognized: the curved approach, the J-approach,[9] and the hook approach (Table 14-2).[10]

Approach Styles for the Flop

Curved Approach

- Limited speed
- Difficult to develop consistent stride pattern and length of run-up
- Easier to maintain on a constant curve through takeoff

J-Approach

- Develops more speed
- Provides more consistency
- Blends speed and centrifugal force

Hook Approach

- Provides maximum speed without pause when moving into curve
- Allows acceleration up to takeoff
- Forces emphasis on continual curve running

Table 14-2. Approach styles for the flop

The curve approach is a continuous curve, commonly used by beginning jumpers. The hook approach curves slightly outward before curving toward the bar. It lies between the other two styles, though it is closer to the J-approach. It helps the jumper avoid losing speed when moving from a straight approach into the curve (Figure 14-2).

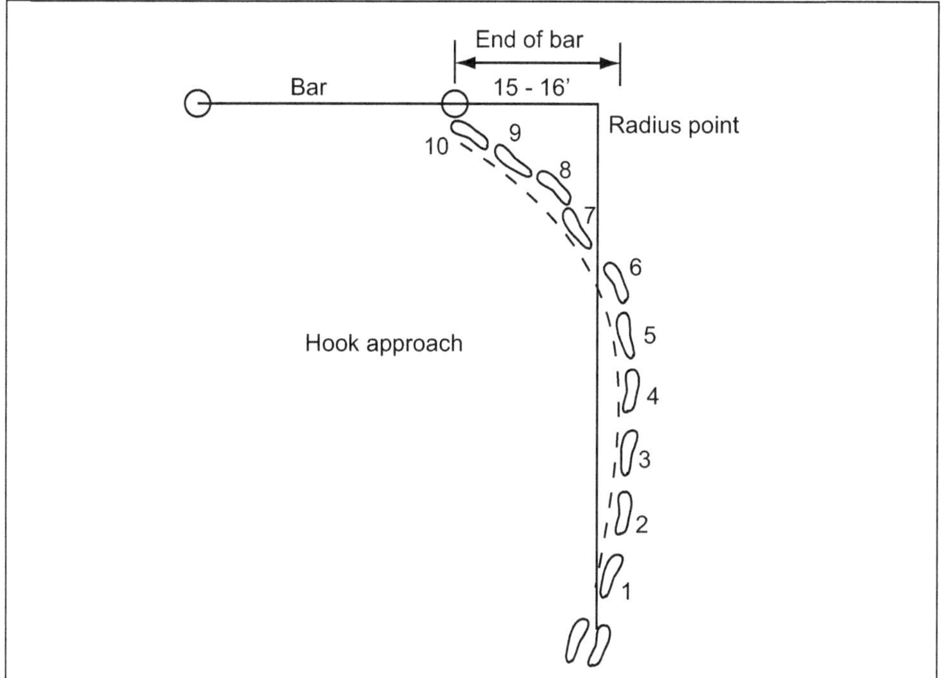

Figure 14-2. Hook approach

The athlete who takes off from the left foot approaches the bar from the right side of the pit (Figure 14-3). The starting point should be measured when the jumper's approach run becomes consistent. Measure the distance to the right of the right standard to a point even with the start of the run, then

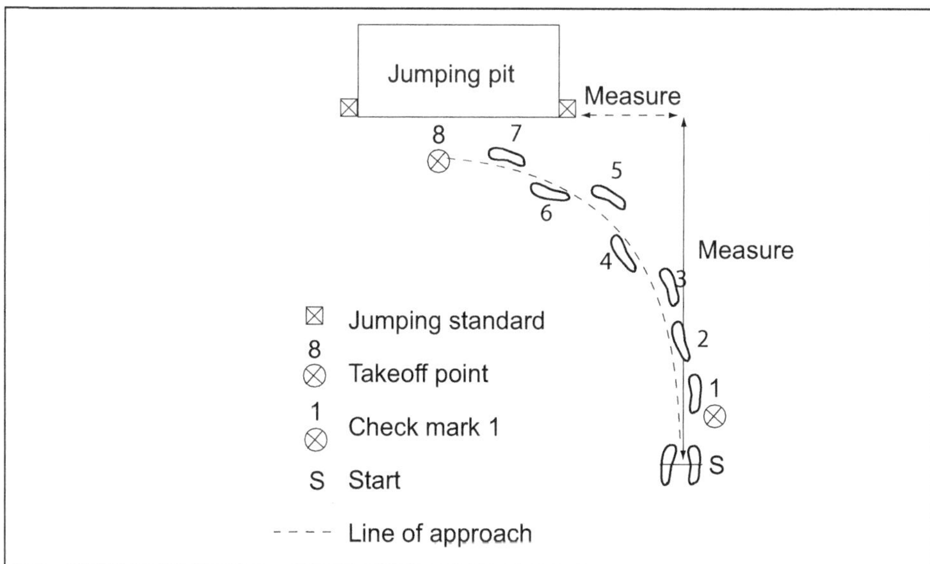

Figure 14-3. Fosbury-style J-approach

measure out from that point to the actual starting position. Though the measurements are in straight lines, the run is a curving approach, similar to an inverted letter J.

The starting point should be measured carefully at a right angle to the nearer of the high jump standards (Figure 14-4). Measure in a straight line extended for either 10m or 32 feet (depending upon the type of tape measure used) from the end of the crossbar. Mark each end of the line and its midpoint (5m or 16 feet). Then make an arc equal to the long line from each end of the baseline. Mark where the arcs cross, and then draw a right-angle line from the midpoint of the baseline.

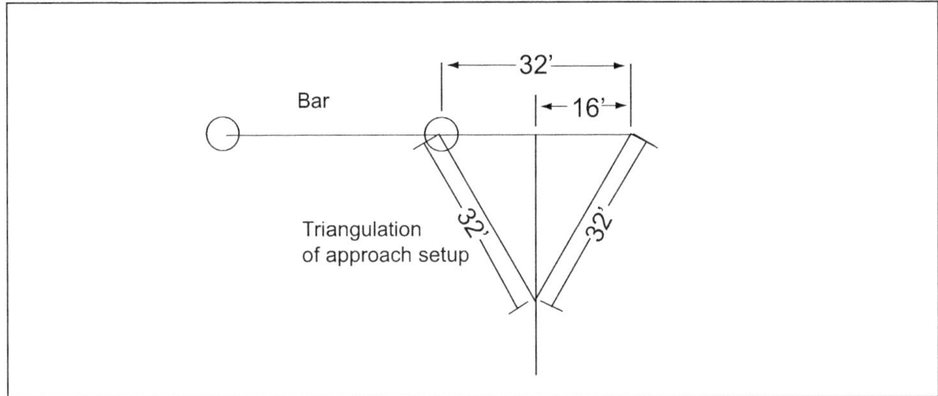

Figure 14-4. Measuring the flop approach

The jumper begins by running straight in at a right angle to the front of the pit rather than toward the takeoff point. Around the fourth or fifth step, the run curves to the left until it points at a very shallow angle relative to the plane of the bar. The jumper gradually accelerates during the run, and then lowers the center of gravity by stretching the stride around the sixth or seventh step. The takeoff stride, which is shorter, finds the body already starting to move upward in the air.

During the takeoff, the kick is coordinated with an upward swing of both arms. The kick is with the upper part of the leg only, a bent-leg kick that gives the sensation of kicking with the knee rather than the entire leg. That kick, combined with the curving run, causes the athlete's back to rotate toward the bar as he rises off the ground. By arching the back, that part of the body clears the bar. The athlete clearing the bar may appear to be lying flat on the back from the head to the knees, with the lower legs still hanging down. The knees and feet are then lifted to clear the bar. An upward swing of both arms can help that movement. The landing in the pit is high on the back or in the upper-neck region, and the jumper may do a backward roll when landing. Otherwise, the landing may be flat on the back.

Training for the High Jump

The first thing for the coach to remember in training high jumpers is that the best style for one athlete is not necessarily best for another jumper. Also, the amount of work that a jumper can tolerate varies greatly from one jumper to the next.

The first thing to do with a group of jumping prospects is to determine their dominant or kicking legs. Have them run over a low hurdle several times, then hand-vault over a sawhorse. This exercise should bring out the kicking leg clearly because each athlete will prefer one leg to the other. Athletes might then be taught the Western roll style of jumping because it is helpful to learn and has great carryover value to the takeoff for the straddle jump. At one time, this progression of learning to jump was considered the proper learning sequence. Though it is not emphasized too much anymore, it is still very helpful.

After the lead foot has been determined, an athlete should work on the check marks. It helps to have two check marks in the approach as a safety factor. The first mark is four steps from the takeoff point, and the second check mark is another four steps out, giving an eight-step approach (Figure 14-1). The last four steps from the check to the takeoff are measured, as is the distance from the check to a line extended from the crossbar and the distance from this juncture to the nearest jumping standard. It is very important to know the jumper's check marks. It is helpful to have a short check mark, in case the jumper has to compete in bad wind conditions. It is easier to vary a short run to hit the takeoff properly than to vary a full run. For floppers, the worst weather condition is rain, making the curved run and takeoff very hazardous.

The jumper warms up, and then works on a routine. The jumper first works on the check marks, then on the takeoff, concentrating on the two-count rise. The last two steps of the approach are longer and faster than the preceding steps, lowering the center of gravity. The jumper drops down slightly, then rises over the last two steps to go into the air with increased momentum. The jumper should try to get both arms and the lead leg rising to aid the momentum and raise the center of gravity.

Form work comes next, with the athlete working from six to eight inches below his best mark at that time of year. If a jumper has a best of 6′ 6″ for the season, then he does form work at 5′ 10″ to 6′ 0″. The jumper might take the last three jumps at increasing heights, but the coach should not permit as many as three misses at a single height. The jumper should be able to finish while feeling that he might have cleared the bar. The jumper also needs to get used to seeing the crossbar at higher heights.

Weight lifting is useful in improving the jumper's spring. Some jumpers do much legwork, emphasizing leg presses. The athlete should be sure to be exercising the muscles within the usual limits of his movement in performing the event. As an example, full squats are risky, and their range of motion is never imitated during high jumping.

Plyometric jumping and bounding exercises have become widespread as a training technique. Although a coach should be cautious when first using them, they are extremely valuable exercises.

Training Program for Floppers

The training program for a flop-style jumper can be a problem to plan, not because of the work involved, but because the jumper who has mastered the form may prefer to do little jumping. Flop jumpers thrive on little or no jumping during the season. A flopper whose form is good during the meets rarely has any reason to jump during the week. If a form problem does appear in a meet, the jumper might work on that aspect of form by jumping on the Monday or Tuesday before a Friday or Saturday meet.

A jumper whose performances begin to get worse may actually be jumping and practicing too much. A flopper is more likely to flourish under the old-fashioned light-training methods than under the modern high-load training methods. The time for perfecting the form with many jumps is during the fall and the winter, when there is plenty of time and no pressure.

Dick Fosbury's training is a good example of the way an athlete might train for this type of jumping after learning the style well. The following schedule is for a typical week during the competitive season, with a meet each Saturday:

- Monday: Sprints and runs up 80 stadium steps, or hopping halfway up stadium steps
- Tuesday: Weight training
- Wednesday: Same as Monday
- Thursday: Weight training
- Friday: Usually light (might repeat Monday's workout)

Fosbury's weight-training program, which he had followed for only two years before the Olympic Games, was as follows (on a Universal Gym):

- Leg presses
    - ✓ 1 v 10 at 390 lbs.
    - ✓ 1 x 8 at 450 lbs.
    - ✓ 1 x 6 at 510 lbs.
    - ✓ 1 x 4 at 540 lbs.
    - ✓ 1 x 2 to 3 at 600 lbs.
- Toe presses
    - ✓ 2 x 25 at 150 lbs.

During the competitive season, he did no shoulder work, did only some of the legwork, and added partial jumping squats with the feet close together and alternating feet on the landing, usually doing two sets of 15 with 135 pounds. Other strength-training exercises are suggested by the coaches cited in the readings listed at the end of this chapter.

High Jump Training Schedules

The common elements of all training schedule sheets are given in Chapter 6. This section will look briefly at the numbered fundamentals that are specific to the high jump schedules. Table 14-3 provides an interpretation of a sample week on the high jump training schedules.

Interpretation of Week One of the Training Schedules		
Monday		Class organization is intended for a physical education unit. Squad organization is listed in the event that fall track is conducted. The objectives and goals of the program are covered. Equipment and responsibility for attendance and separate workouts are discussed.
Tuesday	16.	Easy acrobatics might be done in the gymnastics room, where more equipment is available. Such rudimentary activities as the forward roll and cartwheels can be done at the track.
	4A.	The short check mark is a fundamental drill covered in the section following the schedules.
	14D.	In the general schedule, run 50m, then jog 50m, and repeat the exercise for a distance of 400 to 800m or more.
Wednesday	7.	Squad meeting, time and place to be written on the board in the squad dressing room.
	3.	Weight activities of the athlete's choice or according to the suggestions given in the section on weight training, which is followed by jogging and comfortable running.
	8A or B.	A sauna or swim, depending upon jumper's preference and pool's availability.
Thursday	1A.	In pairs or threes, take a warm-up jog of 400 or 800m. Each runner handles the baton, passing it forward. When the front runner receives the baton, he drops to the rear, and the exercise is continued.
	4A.	Short check work, already mentioned.
	19.	The superscript 6 means the exercise is done six times. Set the bar at an easily cleared height, such as 5 feet. One or more jumpers go through and jump as fast as they can make their clearance and get back to repeat the jump from one to six times. The jumper who misses is through jumping. This exercise is for conditioning and fun.
	14D.	Repeated 50s, already mentioned.
Friday	3.	Weight activities, already mentioned.
	1B.	A run through the park (two to three miles), comfortable pace but with some stress for conditioning.
Saturday	3.	A full workout according to the section on weights or the athlete's already established weight-workout activities.
Sunday		Recreational activities should be included on this day. Sunday can also be a very productive practice day and is very useful in bringing to life the athlete who overdoes Saturday night and would otherwise not revive until Tuesday or Wednesday.

Table 14-3. Interpretation of week one of the training schedules

4A. Short Check Mark

The short check mark is used for learning a method of arriving at a takeoff point that achieves maximum height directly over the crossbar. Usually, four steps are taken from the one check mark to the takeoff. Standing one or two steps from the check, the jumper thinks through the fundamental, if working on one fundamental, and then shuts out the thinking process. The jumper advances the one or two steps to the check, then takes four steps to the takeoff and executes the jump. This distance varies from 18 to 25 feet, depending upon the athlete's needs and stride length. The jumper should take three practice approaches while being observed, and then average the length of the three runs to determine the short check mark. This mark should be measured daily because better physical conditions and weather differences (heat, cold, etc.) cause variations in the approach.

4B. Long Check Mark

The long check mark uses two checks. The jumper begins one or two steps from the first check, then takes four strides to the second check (the short check), then takes another four strides to the takeoff point.

5A. Rhythm Jumping (2-4-6-8)

The athlete pays attention only to developing a rhythm. For learning purposes, the athlete stands at a long check mark and comes in to the jump either counting or having the coach count the even-numbered strides, "2-4-6-8," with "8" being the takeoff. It is for rhythm, for speed, and to get rid of a jerky or uneven approach. The other fundamentals work more smoothly if a good rhythmical approach is achieved.

5B. Settle and Two-Count Rise

This technique is used either consciously or because of the superior coordination of every great high jumper. To acquire this technique, the athlete starts learning with a short check mark. Usually jumpers find that on the second step before the takeoff, they settle and then start to rise on the step before takeoff so that the body weight as well as the momentum is going up at the instant of the takeoff. Some great jumpers have made the settle on the last step before the takeoff, and then started to rise on the same step, taking off on the next step.

5C. Lead Leg and Lead Arm

The lead leg and the lead arm, which are approaching the bar for clearance, should be hurried upward well before the takeoff foot leaves the ground. The lifting of the leg and the arm raises the center of gravity, bringing the total mass of the body nearer the crossbar. The fact that the body mass is going up makes the relative weight of the body mass less. This leg-arm movement must be executed before the takeoff or the physical principle of the "equal and opposite reaction" will tend to destroy the effect of the lift, because the movement will not have the strong base of the takeoff and will be negated by the action of the extremities being in motion at this time.

5D.

A vacant space for use when some unlisted specific is needed in an individual's schedule.

6A. Head

The head is 10 pounds of dead weight that can either help or hinder the jumper. If the chin is raised, the head helps the jumper direct himself upward off the ground. If the chin is dropped, it can hamper the takeoff. If the chin is tipped toward the crossbar, it will lead the body into a premature lean into the bar, a common fault leading to poor jumping.

6B. Layout and Bar Clearance

The center of gravity is what rises, and the body and its extremities rotate around it. The first motion is up; then, by the last actions at the point of takeoff, the body coordination is affected by the arms and legs, turning the body and helping it to "lay out" atop the crossbar. The rotation around the bar is accomplished by lowering the head, which is beyond the bar, and lifting the takeoff leg.

6C. Up and Down—Not Up and Out

Jumpers who use more speed than they can control tend to cover space in the wrong direction. The rule is to use as much speed as can be controlled. The jumper who takes off too close with speed uncontrolled goes into the crossbar. The speed jumper should be farther out than the "stroller." The fast jumper who is going into the bar should experiment with a more acute angle, going down more toward the crossbar as do the floppers using another speed jump.

9A. Takeoff

An exact takeoff spot is a necessity, and check marks must be made that assist the jumper in hitting that spot on every approach run. When the spot is reached, the most important part of the technique is maintaining body position and lift. An outward lean not only makes for a premature turn and striking the crossbar, but it can make the jumper effectively two to four inches shorter by lowering the center of gravity by that distance.

9B. Arm Lift

The left arm almost automatically rises with the right leg. The coordination of the double-arm lift (both arms together) is an acquired one. As the right foot is planted on the last step before the final plant and takeoff, both arms drop back only as far as the plane of the body, then both lift vigorously as the lead (right) leg is driven up toward the crossbar. The arms are near bar height as the takeoff foot leaves the ground. As the body rises, the right arm reaches across the bar, and the most natural thing is for the left elbow to smoothly come to the side and proceed to the rear until the hand is near the hip area. It is also believed helpful for takeoff-leg clearance if the right arm rises, lifting to the outside and triggering a compensating action by the takeoff leg.

9C. Center of Gravity Over Takeoff Foot

The center of gravity should be maintained at as high a position as possible as the takeoff is executed. As the jumper makes the final step, he should pass directly over the takeoff foot. If an out-of-line fault occurs, it should be in the direction of the bar, not away from the bar. Crossing the left foot across the line of approach (and away from the bar) would lower the center of gravity and cause the jumper to lean into the crossbar.

10B. Trial

A warm-up procedure should be acquired for trials and experimented with to determine what is best for competition. The trials themselves are learning situations. A competitive trial exists only to eliminate someone if more entries are available than can be used in the competition. If one jumper is outstanding, he should be an automatic entry but should also compete in the trials for the learning experience. The other jumpers are also learning, but they will also be competing for the other two spots in the dual meet entries.

Let the athletes set the crossbar at a good starting height for each individual, within reason. In Item 10B1, the athlete raises the bar two to three inches after clearing the height, and lowers the bar four inches after missing. One jumper may start at 5′ 6″, while another jumper may start at 6′ 4″. If the weaker jumper misses, he will jump next at 5′ 2″. The better jumper might have the next jump at 6′ 6″ to 6′ 7″—depending upon how good he is and how early in the season it is.

10B2. Two Jumps Two Inches Above Average Best

The jumper who has reached the approximate best and has had two misses at a height may have two more jumps at two to three inches above his best seasonal mark. The jumper should not be allowed three misses, for psychological reasons and because it would put him out of the competition. In practice, the jumper should never take more than two misses at a submaximal height.

11. Alternate From Straddle to Fosbury

This experimental exercise is used for introducing a variety of activity, teaching body control, and perhaps discovering an additional jumping weapon. The jumper works with several different jumping styles, going from the straddle, or belly roll, to the Fosbury flop style of jumping, learning better body control and perhaps discovering whether he can do better with a different form.

16. Easy Acrobatics or Apparatus

If possible, have some apparatus in the practice area. Also, take advantage of the usually superior equipment and instruction of a good gymnastics teacher. It is great exercise for body control, as well as pleasurable and a good change of pace.

17. High Kicking

High kicking is used for work on the takeoff and for timing in the leg lift in relation to the takeoff for straddle jumpers. It consists of short approaches, followed by high kicks with the lead leg toward a high target of some sort. Floppers might practice kicking with the lifting knee.

18. Form Jumping

Form jumping should be done at a minimal height. It is possible to concentrate on the techniques and mechanics without being concerned about the height of the jump. The jumper should acquire the tools, and then do the job in the meet.

19. Speed Jumping

The crossbar is set at an easy height, perhaps a foot under the jumper's best. In rotation, the jumpers take their jumps as fast as they can get into the pit and back out again. A miss puts the jumper out. The winner is the last person out. A solo jumper takes four to eight or so speed jumps.

20. Secondary Event

Every athlete should have a second event, if only for a change of scenery. The jumper should also consider himself a part of the team, and may get the extra point that will win a letter or the team's meet. The greatest high jumper in Oregon history, Les Steers, held the world record for the high jump for well over a decade. He also threw the javelin, hurdled, and pole vaulted.

HIGH JUMP SCHEDULE NAME ______________________ DATE ______________

1. A. Jog 1-2 laps with relay pass, in 2s or 3s
   B. Hendricks Park C. Golf course D. Steps
2. Fartlek A. Varied pace B. Slow, steady pace
3. Weights and jogging
4. Check mark A. Short B. Long
5. A. Rhythm (2-4-6-8)
   B. Settle and 2-count rise
   C. Lead leg and lead arm
   D.
6. A. Head
   B. Layout and bar clearance
   C. Up and down, not up and out
   D.
7. TEAM MEETING
8. Special A. Sauna B. Swim C. Hill
9. A. Takeoff
   B. Arm lift
   C. Center of gravity over takeoff foot
   D.
10. A. Meet B. Trial C. Simulation D. Control test
    (1) Up 2-3 in. on make, down 4 in. on a miss
    (2) 2 jumps at 2 in. above average best
11. Alternate from Straddle to Fosbury
12. With Coach A. B.
14. A. Wind sprints (1) Straight (2) Curve
    B. Hurdle drill: 3 LH, 7-9m apart
    C. Spring and bound
    D. Alternate run and jog, at least 800
    E. Starts (1) 100 (2)
    F. High knee (slow) and fast leg
15. Plyometrics A. Jumps B. Bounding C.
    (1) 1-leg (2) Both legs (3)
16. Easy acrobatics or apparatus
17. High kicking (straddle) A. Basket B. Target
18. Form jumping, 6-12" under best
    A. Short run B. Long run
19. Speed jumping: 4 to 8 fast, or a miss
20. Work on second event
21. A. Videotape B. Film C. Pictures
    (1) Record performance (2) Study
30. Experimental work

Date	Distance	3/4 pace	Date Pace	Goal Pace

M
T
W
T
F
S
S
M
T
W
T
F
S
S
M
T
W
T
F
S
S
M
T
W
T
F
S
S

Table 14-1. Revised high jump training schedule sheet

High Jump NAME DATE September/October

1. A. Jog 1 or 2 laps, relay pass—2s or 3s B. Weights and jog
   C.
2. Fartlek A. Varied pace B. Slow, steady
3. Weights
4. Check mark A. Short B. Long
5. A. Rhythm (2-4-6-8) B. Settle and 2-count rise
   C. Lead leg and lead arm
   D.
6. A. Head B. Layout and bar clearance
   C. Up and down—not up and out
7. Squad meeting
8. Special A. Sauna B. Swim C. Hill
   D.
9. A. Take off B. Arm lift C. CG over take-off foot
   D.
10. A. Trial B. Compete (1) Up 2 in. to 3 in. on a make, down 4 in. on a miss (2) 2 jumps 2 in. above average best
11. Alternate from Straddle to Western roll to Fosbury
12. With coach A. B.
14. A. Wind sprints B. Starts or 1. 110s 2.
    C. High knee and fast leg
    D. Hurdle drill, 3 lows 8 to 10 yds. E. Spring and bound
    F. Alternate run-jog at least 880
15. A. Hendricks B. Laurel C. Steps
16. Easy acrobatics or apparatus
17. High kicking A. Basket B. Target
18. Form jumping A. Short B. Long
    6 in.—12 in. under best
19. Speed jumping—4 to 8 fast, or a miss
20. Secondary event
21. A. Pictures B. Film C.
22. Experimental work

Date	Result	3/4	Date	Goal

M	Class or squad organization
T	16-4A-14F
W	7-1B-8A or 8B
T	6x 1A-4A-19-14F
F	1B-15A
S	3
S	recreation
M	2-4x 1A-14F-4A-5C-18A
T	1B-16-14E
W	1A-14F-5A-5B-14D
T	1B-16-17B
F	1-10A-18A-14F
S	2B
S	recreation
M	1A-14F-4A-5A-18A
T	1B-16-17-14E
W	1-14F-4B-9A-5B-14D
T	1-16-17
F	1-10A1-18A
S	3-14F
S	recreation
M	2-4x2-4x 1-14F-4A-4B-9A-18A
T	1B-14E-14F
W	1-4B-9A-5B-14D
T	1B-16-17
F	6-10x6-10x 1-18A-18B-14F
S	1B-14F
S	recreation

Sheet 14-2. High jump training schedule

High Jump NAME DATE January

1. A. Jog 1 or 2 laps, relay pass—2s or 3s B. Weights and jog
   C.
2. Fartlek A. Varied pace B. Slow, steady
3. Weights
4. Check mark A. Short B. Long
5. A. Rhythm (2-4-6-8) B. Settle and 2-count rise
   C. Lead leg and lead arm
   D.
6. A. Head B. Layout and bar clearance
   C. Up and down—not up and out
7. Squad meeting
8. Special A. Sauna B. Swim C. Hill
   D.
9. A. Take off B. Arm lift C. CG over take-off foot
   D.
10. A. Trial B. Compete (1) Up 2 in. to 3 in. on a make, down 4 in. on a miss (2) 2 jumps 2 in. above average best
11. Alternate from Straddle to Western roll to Fosbury
12. With coach A. B.
14. A. Wind sprints B. Starts or 1. 110s 2.
    C. High knee and fast leg
    D. Hurdle drill, 3 lows 8 to 10 yds. E. Spring and bound
    F. Alternate run-jog at least 880
15. A. Hendricks B. Laurel C. Steps
16. Easy acrobatics or apparatus
17. High kicking A. Basket B. Target
18. Form jumping A. Short B. Long
    6 in.—12 in. under best
19. Speed jumping—4 to 8 fast, or a miss
20. Secondary event
21. A. Pictures B. Film C.
22. Experimental work

Date	Result	3/4	Date	Goal

M	New term or start new year
T	Class or squad organization
W	Register–11–3–or classes
T	7–Register–lockers–11–3
F	1–14A–3–15A
S	3–11
S	Recreation
M	1–4A–5B–9A–14F
T	1A–3
W	1–5A–5C–6C
T	1A–3–15A
F	1–14F–5B–5C–9A–14F
S	1A–3–14A
S	recreation
M	1–3–14D
T	1A–5B–4A (2-4x)–4B (2-4x)–5A
W	1–3–14F–15A
T	1–4B–6B–9A
F	1–3–14E–15B
S	1–10–6A–14E
S	recreation
M	1–3–14F
T	1A–4A–4B–5B–5C–6B
W	1–3–14A
T	1A–5A–5B–5C–14B
F	1–3–14A
S	3–14A
S	recreation–3

Sheet 14-3. High jump training schedule

High Jump NAME DATE February

1. A. Jog 1 or 2 laps, relay pass—2s or 3s B. Weights and jog
   C.
2. Fartlek A. Varied pace B. Slow, steady
3. Weights
4. Check mark A. Short B. Long
5. A. Rhythm (2-4-6-8) B. Settle and 2-count rise
   C. Lead leg and lead arm
   D.
6. A. Head B. Layout and bar clearance
   C. Up and down—not up and out
7. Squad meeting
8. Special A. Sauna B. Swim C. Hill
   D.
9. A. Take off B. Arm lift C. CG over take-off foot
   D.
10. A. Trial B. Compete (1) Up 2 in. to 3 in. on a make, down 4 in. on a miss (2) 2 jumps 2 in. above average best
11. Alternate from Straddle to Western roll to Fosbury
12. With coach A. B.
14. A. Wind sprints B. Starts or 1. 110s 2.
    C. High knee and fast leg
    D. Hurdle drill, 3 lows 8 to 10 yds. E. Spring and bound
    F. Alternate run-jog at least 880
15. A. Hendricks B. Laurel C. Steps
16. Easy acrobatics or apparatus
17. High kicking A. Basket B. Target
18. Form jumping A. Short B. Long
    6 in.—12 in. under best
19. Speed jumping—4 to 8 fast, or a miss
20. Secondary event
21. A. Pictures B. Film C.
22. Experimental work

Date	Result	3/4	Date	Goal

Day	Schedule
M	1-4A-4B-5A-5B-14D-14E
T	3-14A
W	1-4A-4B-15A or 15C
T	14E-3
F	2-3x 1-4A-5B2-9
S	Swim or weights
S	recreation
M	1A-14D-5C-14C
T	3-8A or B
W	3x 3x 1-5A-5B-5C
T	Light
F	1-10
S	Sprint & hurdle trials 10:30 am
S	
M	1A-4B-5C-5B-18-Jog
T	1B
W	6x 1A-18-8C or 15A
T	1B
F	1A-4A-4B-5B-5C-14E-14F
S	Jog & 3
S	recreation
M	2x 2x 3x 3-6x 1A-4A-4B-5A-5B-14E-14F
T	1B-8A or 8B
W	1B-16
T	1B-16
F	1A-10A1-10A2
S	3 or 14E
S	recreation

Sheet 14-4. High jump training schedule

High Jump NAME DATE *March*

1. A. Jog 1 or 2 laps, relay pass—2s or 3s B. Weights and jog
   C.
2. Fartlek A. Varied pace B. Slow, steady
3. Weights
4. Check mark A. Short B. Long
5. A. Rhythm (2-4-6-8) B. Settle and 2-count rise
   C. Lead leg and lead arm
   D.
6. A. Head B. Layout and bar clearance
   C. Up and down—not up and out
7. Squad meeting
8. Special A. Sauna B. Swim C. Hill
   D.
9. A. Take off B. Arm lift C. CG over take-off foot
   D.
10. A. Trial B. Compete (1) Up 2 in. to 3 in. on a make, down 4 in. on a miss (2) 2 jumps 2 in. above average best
11. Alternate from Straddle to Western roll to Fosbury
12. With coach A. B.
14. A. Wind sprints B. Starts or 1. 110s 2.
    C. High knee and fast leg
    D. Hurdle drill, 3 lows 8 to 10 yds. E. Spring and bound
    F. Alternate run-jog at least 880
15. A. Hendricks B. Laurel C. Steps
16. Easy acrobatics or apparatus
17. High kicking A. Basket B. Target
18. Form jumping A. Short B. Long
    6 in.—12 in. under best
19. Speed jumping—4 to 8 fast, or a miss
20. Secondary event
21. A. Pictures B. Film C.
22. Experimental work

Date	Result	3/4	Date	Goal

Day	Workout
M	*1A-8B*
T	*1B-8A or B*
W	*7-1A-4B (2x)-9B-9A-19-14D-14F*
T	*Light*
F	*1A-10A1-18-15A*
S	*Light*
S	*Light*
M	*1-14E-4B (4X)-9B (10X)-9C-14E-14D*
T	*1B-8B*
W	*1-4-9A-18-14F*
T	*Jog*
F	*4-10A1-17*
S	*3-16-14E*
S	*recreation*
M	*1A-4-6B-9B-14E-14F*
T	*Easy grass running*
W	*7-4-18*
T	*Light*
F	*Gear ready and/or travel*
S	*First meet (10B-20)*
S	*Light workout*
M	*A.M. 1A-Jog* | *P.M. Spring trip 1A-4-5B-6C-14F*
T	*1A-3* | *Grass running*
W	*1A-Jog* | *1A-18*
T	*1A-3* | *Light*
F	*Travel home—loosen up*
S	*Division early season relay meet*
S	*Loosen up*

Sheet 14-5. High jump training schedule

High Jump NAME DATE April

1. A. Jog 1 or 2 laps, relay pass—2s or 3s B. Weights and jog
   C.
2. Fartlek A. Varied pace B. Slow, steady
3. Weights
4. Check mark A. Short B. Long
5. A. Rhythm (2-4-6-8) B. Settle and 2-count rise
   C. Lead leg and lead arm
   D.
6. A. Head B. Layout and bar clearance
   C. Up and down—not up and out
7. Squad meeting
8. Special A. Sauna B. Swim C. Hill
   D.
9. A. Take off B. Arm lift C. CG over take-off foot
   D.
10. A. Trial B. Compete (1) Up 2 in. to 3 in. on a make, down 4 in. on a miss (2) 2 jumps 2 in. above average best
11. Alternate from Straddle to Western roll to Fosbury
12. With coach A. B.
14. A. Wind sprints B. Starts or 1. 110s 2.
    C. High knee and fast leg
    D. Hurdle drill, 3 lows 8 to 10 yds. E. Spring and bound
    F. Alternate run-jog at least 880
15. A. Hendricks B. Laurel C. Steps
16. Easy acrobatics or apparatus
17. High kicking A. Basket B. Target
18. Form jumping A. Short B. Long
    6 in.—12 in. under best
19. Speed jumping—4 to 8 fast, or a miss
20. Secondary event
21. A. Pictures B. Film C.
22. Experimental work

Date	Result	3/4	Date	Goal

M	1A-5B-4B-18-19-14D
T	1B-17-14E-14F
W	7-1A-5B-9A-18-14E
T	3
F	Light and gear ready
S	Relay meet
S	Field open 11 to 3
M	1-4B-4A-5B-9A-19-14D
T	1B-17-14E-14F
W	7-1A-4B-10A1 and 2-18 jog
T	3
F	1-4B-18 (4-6x)-gear ready
S	Dual meet
S	Church-field open 11-3
M	1-4A-4B-5B-18-19-14D
T	17-3-14E-14F
W	7-1-5B-9A-6B-18-14D
T	3
F	Gear ready
S	Dual meet
S	Light workout
M	7-1-4A-4B-5B-18-19-14D
T	17B-1B-14E-14F
W	7-1-4-10A1 (4-6x)-10A2 (2x)-14F
T	Light
F	Travel
S	Dual meet
S	Home and loosen up

Sheet 14-6. High jump training schedule

High Jump NAME DATE May

1. A. Jog 1 or 2 laps, relay pass—2s or 3s B. Weights and jog
   C.
2. Fartlek A. Varied pace B. Slow, steady
3. Weights
4. Check mark A. Short B. Long
5. A. Rhythm (2-4-6-8) B. Settle and 2-count rise
   C. Lead leg and lead arm
   D.
6. A. Head B. Layout and bar clearance
   C. Up and down—not up and out
7. Squad meeting
8. Special A. Sauna B. Swim C. Hill
   D.
9. A. Take off B. Arm lift C. CG over take-off foot
   D.
10. A. Trial B. Compete (1) Up 2 in. to 3 in. on a make, down 4 in. on a miss (2) 2 jumps 2 in. above average best
11. Alternate from Straddle to Western roll to Fosbury
12. With coach A. B.
14. A. Wind sprints B. Starts or 1. 110s 2.
    C. High knee and fast leg
    D. Hurdle drill, 3 lows 8 to 10 yds. E. Spring and bound
    F. Alternate run-jog at least 880
15. A. Hendricks B. Laurel C. Steps
16. Easy acrobatics or apparatus
17. High kicking A. Basket B. Target
18. Form jumping A. Short B. Long
    6 in.—12 in. under best
19. Speed jumping—4 to 8 fast, or a miss
20. Secondary event
21. A. Pictures B. Film C.
22. Experimental work

Date	Result	3/4	Date	Goal

Day	
M	7-Jog
T	Light
W	Memorial Day Traditional Dual meet
T	1A-4B-10A1-14E
F	1B-17-14F
S	Jog
S	Field open 11-3--Squad picnic 5 pm
M	1-14E-14D-14F
T	1-4-5C-6B-18-14E
W	Light & Jog
T	Light & Jog
F	1-4
S	Light
S	1-5-18-Jog
M	7-1-5-18-Jog
T	Light
W	7-Light
T	Championship starts
F	Championship-High jump qualifying
S	Championship-High jump finals
S	
M	
T	
W	
T	
F	
S	
S	

Sheet 14-7. High jump training schedule

Endnotes

1. Patrick Reid. (1986). The high jump. *New Studies in Athletics, 1*(1), 47-53.
2. V. Nedobivailo. (1984). Weight training for high jumpers. *Track Technique, 87,* 2785.
3. Dragan Tancic. (1986). Organization of high jump training. *Track Technique, 94,* 3013.
4. Bob Myers. (1988). Periodization for the high jump. In Jess Jarver (Ed.), *The Jumps* (2nd ed.). Los Altos, CA: Tafnews.
5. Berny Wagner, Sue Humphrey & Don Chu. (1989). The high jump (Fosbury Flop). In Vern Gambetta (Ed.), *The Athletics Congress's Track and Field Coaching Manual* (2nd ed., pp. 105-116). Champaign, IL: Leisure Press.
6. W. Lonskiy & K. Gomberadse. (1981). Long range training plan for high jumpers. In Jess Jarver (Ed.), *The Jumps* (2nd ed.). Los Altos, CA: Tafnews, 47-49.
7. Andrei Soran. (1988). High jump tactics. *Track Technique, 102*, 3267.
8. V. Ambarov. (1988). Looking at the high jump. *Track Technique 104*, 3329-3330.
9. William H. Freeman, (1971, January). Coaching the Fosbury Flop. *Athletic Journal, 51,* 16, 71-72.
10. Ed Jacoby. (1986). High jump: A technique evaluation. *Track Technique, 97*, 3089-3093.

Core Readings

Fern, Ed. (1990). *Ed Fern's flight school.* Mountain View, CA: Tafnews.

Freeman, William H. (2001). Periodized training for jumpers. In *Peak When It Counts: Periodization for American track and field* (4th ed., pp. 120-130). Mountain View, CA: Tafnews.

Humphrey, Sue, & Doug Nordquist. High jump. (2000). In *USA Track and Field coaching manual*. Champaign, IL: Human Kinetics, 173-197.

Jacoby, Ed, & Bob Fraley. (1998). *The complete book of jumps*. Champaign, IL: Human Kinetics.

Jarver, Jess, ed. (2000). *The Jumps: Contemporary Theory, Technique and Training* (5th ed.). Mountain View, CA: Tafnews.

Martin, David E., Stones, Dwight, Joy, Greg, & Wszola, Jacek. (1987). *The high jump book* (2nd ed.). Los Altos, CA: Tafnews.

Tansley, John. (1980). *The flop book*. Santa Monica, CA: Petersen.

USA Track & Field Coaching Education Program. (2003). *Level II Curriculum: Jumps*. USA Track & Field. Invaluable; revised regularly.

Recommended Readings

Antekolovic, Ljubomir, Iva Blazevic, Mladen Mejovsek & Milan Coh. (2006). Longitudinal follow-up of kinematic parameters in the high jump. *New Studies in Athletics, 21*(4), 27-37.

Bianco, Enrique, David Lease, Elio Locatelli, Yukio Muraki, Dan Pfaff, Efim Shuravetzky & Miguel Velez. (1996). NSA Round Table 31: Speed in the jumping events. *New Studies in Athletics, 11*(2-3), 9-19.

Brüggemann, Gert-Peter, & Adiamatios Arampatzis. Men's high jump. In Harald Müller & Helmar Hommel, eds., Biomechanical Research Project at the VIth World Championships in Athletics, Athens 1997: Preliminary Report. *New Studies in Athletics, 12*(2-3), 66-69.

Chu, Donald A. (1984). The approach pattern in the Fosbury Flop. *Track and Field Quarterly Review, 84*(4), 15-16.

Dapena, Jesus. (1988). Biomechanical analysis of the Fosbury Flop. Parts 1 and 2. *Track Technique, 104,* 3307-3317, 3333; *105,* 3343-3350.

Dapena, Jesús. (1995). How to design the shape of a high jump run-up. *Track Coach, 131*, 4179-4181.

Dapena, Jesús. (1995). The rotation over the bar in the Fosbury-Flop high jump. *Track Coach, 132*, 4201-4210.

Dyatchkov, V.M. (1984). The preparation training phase of top level high jumpers. *Track and Field Quarterly Review, 84*(4), 26-28.

Freeman, Will, Bob Myers & Dan Pfaff. (1995). Factors influencing skill acquisition in the jumps. *Track Coach, 131*, 4176-4178, 4197.

Godoy, Jose. (1989). Training of Javier Sotomayor up to attainment of his high jump world record. Trans. Richard Westerman. *Track and Field Quarterly Review, 89*(4), 20-22.

Hunneshagen, Christina. (2006). "Coaches' Eye"–Technical analysis and fault finding as an internet application for coaching high jump. *New Studies in Athletics, 21*(4), 39-47.

Kerin, David. (Summer 2002). Achieving strength gains specific to the demands of jumping events. *Track Coach, 160*, 5103-5110.

Killing, Wolfgang. (1997). An investigation of special jumping training in the high jump. *New Studies in Athletics, 12*(4), 53-64.

Killing, Wolfgang. (1996). The run-up of elite high jumpers [abstract]. *Track Coach, 134*, 4289-4290.

Mackenzie, Robert J. (Fall 2003). Determining the force the takeoff leg exerts in the long and high jumps. *Track Coach, 165*, 5265-5268.

Mackenzie, Robert J. (Spring 2007). Film measurement of takeoff forces in the jumps, including slowing effects. *Track Coach, 179*, 5717-5722, 5733.

Mackenzie, Robert J. (Summer 2003). What does the takeoff leg really do? *Track Coach, 164*, 5233-5237.

Moura, Nelio Alfano, & Tania Fernandes de Paula Moura. (2001). Training principles for jumpers: Implications for the special strength development. *New Studies in Athletics, 16*(4), 51-61.

Ritzdorf, Wolfgang. (1986). The practice of strength training in women's high jump. *New Studies in Athletics, 1*(2), 81-89.

Schexnayder, Irving. (1994). Special considerations for the high jump approach. *Track Technique, 126*, 4029-4031.

Schiffer, Jürgen. (2005). Selected and annotated bibliography 71: High jump. *New Studies in Athletics, 20*(3), 75-109; *20*(4), 61-96.

Tellez, Kyle. (1993). Elements of the high jump. *Track Technique, 125*, 3987-3990.

Wagner, Berny, Sue Humphrey & Don Chu. (1989). The high jump (Fosbury Flop). In *The Athletic Congress's Track and Field Coaching Manual.* (2nd ed.). Champaign, IL: Human Kinetics, 105-116.

15

The Pole Vault

Record Setters

Gerry Moro	Canadian Olympic Team, 1964; All-American, 1965 (3rd place)

Pole vaulters vary in size as much as any other athletes in track. Vaulters are athletes with good speed, superior coordination, and determination. The pole vault's technical components require years of hard work to master. Because of the time requirement, the best vaulters often are athletes who grew up with the pole, so to speak. The youngster who started vaulting at age 10 has a great advantage over the vaulter who started only after entering high school or college. The early beginners have already learned to handle the pole easily, to feel it as an extension of themselves or to feel that they are an extension of the pole.

Most pole vaulters need an approach of over 100 feet (30m), good relaxation prior to the plant, a smooth, well-placed planting of the pole so the takeoff will be a swift flow off the ground and into position for the swing and rise that precede the turn, and a smooth flow from the turn into the off-the-pole phase. A good landing is also critical because of the height involved.

The technical complexity of pole vaulting makes it one of the most difficult of sports events. It consists of at least six separate "events" that must be combined into a smooth-flowing motion, from the beginning of the run through the planting of the pole, the takeoff, the hang, the rise-turn, the crossing of the bar, and the dismount, or landing.

Pole Vault Theory

The pole vault is the most complex event in track and field. The athlete must try to coordinate two pendulum actions, those of the pole and of his body, which can work at cross purposes. The leader in vaulting for decades, the United States has been surpassed in the last two decades by vaulters from other nations. Coaches agree that vaulters should begin the event between the ages of 12 and 14. While the Americans have emphasized agility, the Europeans have stressed increased strength and conditioning. These latter factors allow the vaulter to use a faster approach and a higher handhold, reaching higher vaulting heights.

The Russians recommend a high vertical pole carry,[1] while others simply prefer that the end of the pole stay above the vaulter's eye level.[2] Late in the approach run, the pole is lowered gradually toward the level of the vaulting box, which adds to the speed of the approach.

The approach falls into the following three phases:

- Start and early acceleration
- Acceleration to top speed
- Pole plant and takeoff foot placement[3]

The first phase, the start and smooth early acceleration, usually has four to six strides. It must be very consistent, just as in the initial phases of other jumps. The second phase, accelerating from the running start to maximum controllable speed, usually has about 10 strides. The pole is usually carried at an angle of 60 to 70 degrees in this phase. The third phase usually has four to six strides. During this time, the end of the pole is lowered to slide into the box, and the takeoff position is reached.

The higher grips, with much stiffer poles used for higher jumps, put added stresses on the body, especially on the back and the shoulders.[4] This added stress is a major reason for the European emphasis on conditioning and strength. The distance that a vaulter can fly above his handhold has changed little in the last two decades. The tale of progress is simply faster approach speeds and higher grips on the pole, which require improved strength.

Although we recommend teaching the vaulter to resist the pole with the lower hand, it may not be entirely possible in a good vault. In fact, some Olympic coaches stress letting the lower arm bend.[5] This technique is best left to more experienced vaulters who are not concerned with ensuring that the pole does, indeed, bend during their vault. More advanced vaulters bend the pole with the pressure of the body through the upper hand and chest, smoothed by dropping the knee at takeoff to lower the center of gravity.

Though most mechanical concerns are the same for vaulters of all levels, beginners have far less time to complete the vaulting sequence than an athlete who clears 18 to 19 feet. The beginner faces the task of dealing with fast-moving actions, while the elite vaulter must learn to hang back and be patient as he rises through the air. Maurice Houvion, who coaches world-class French vaulters, has given an excellent overview of pole vault training.[6]

In the past, Soviet coaches recommended that developing vaulters go through the following stages at about these ages:

- Introductory phase: ages 10 to 12
- Specialization phase: ages 13 to 15
- Establishment phase I: ages 16 to 17
- Establishment phase II: ages 18 to 19
- Final development phase: ages 20 to 23[7]

They give recommended tasks, training loads, numbers of meets, tests, and performance levels for each stage. Their excellent examples show how a coach begins planning the annual training program for a vaulter.

As the athlete becomes more experienced and skilled over a period of years, the proportion of training gradually shifts from more general to more specific conditioning. The components of jumping training and performance are:

- Endurance: fartlek and cross country
- Speed: intervals, starts, and approach runs
- Strength/power: strength training
- Bounding: plyometrics and varied jumping activities
- Technique: from major to minor skill changes[8]

The pre-season training should take at least three months, including at least 120 training sessions, over 200 vaults on a softer pole from short approaches, and over 100 full-approach vaults with the regular pole.[9] The length of the competitive season depends largely on the length of the pre-season training and the volume of work included. The training load during the season should be controlled carefully, allowing enough recovery for good performances. The training volume should be about 20 to 25 percent less per week than in pre-season training. However, the training load should not be decreased too sharply because the athlete may quickly peak, then decline.

The vaulter may use a phase of six to eight weeks to prepare for a major meet, with a training volume of about 90 percent of maximum for the first week or two. The emphasis is on quality vaulting, with good recovery between vaulting sessions (two days of rest after a session of 15 quality vaults, or three days of rest after a session of 25 quality vaults).[10]

Speaking of the European coaches' stress on the importance of overall fitness (contrasted to American coaches' emphasis on technique), Andrzej Krzesinski (who coached a Polish Olympic champion) says, "Present vaulters ought to be strong and powerful, fast, with jumping ability, agility, and nerve."[11] Table 15-1 summarizes his suggested training loads for a world-class vaulter.

Suggested Training Loads for the Elite Pole Vaulter				
Microcycles of Emphasis by Periods				
Component	*Annual Load*	*General*	*Special*	*Component*
Fartlek	60 miles	1	1	—
PV pop-ups	1600	4-3	3	3-2
PV jumps, short run	1000	3-2	1	—
PV jumps, full run	1000	—	2	3
Acrobatics	1000 reps	3	2	1
Hurdle drills	3500 reps	3-2	2	1
Plyometrics	4000 reps	1	3	1
Sprint starts	5 miles	1	1	1-0
Games	21 hours	4	3-2	2-1
Weightlifting	150-170 tons	3	3-2	2-1
Abdominals	1500 reps	3	3	1-0
Shot and medicine ball	3500 reps	3-2	2	2-1
Knee drills	3600 reps	5-4	3	—
Apparatus drill	600 reps	2	2	1
Speed	8 miles	—	1-2	1
Speed endurance	10 miles	—	1	1/2
Other running	85 miles	6-5	6-5	5

Table 15-1. Suggested training loads for the elite pole vaulter

Analysis of Vaulting Technique

The phases of vaulting technique that need to be examined are holding the pole, the run (including check marks and how they are set up), the plant, the takeoff, the rise and hang, the turn and rise, the crossing of the bar, and the dismount. In the following discussion, a right-handed vaulter is used as an example, so the pole is held with the right hand up, but not too far out, and the left hand down the pole.

Holding the Pole

Some vaulters have the mistaken notion that the height of the crossbar (the height that the vaulter is attempting to make at any one time) influences the position of their hands on the pole, which is not true. A vaulter holds the pole where it is most advantageous to him, where he feels he has the best possible control of the pole and is himself in a position in relation to the pole to make maximum use of that control.

The position of the hands on the pole, like the number of steps in an approach, is a matter for the individual athlete to decide, based on experimentation. It should not be changed impulsively. Any changes should be made only when the athlete has time to master them before competition. The height of the hold may vary in some conditions. With a strong headwind or crosswind, the vaulter may use a shorter run and a lower hold. If the wind is at his back, he might use a longer run and a higher-than-usual hold.

Approach

The approach is planned for the vaulter to reach maximum speed as closely as possible to the moment the pole is planted in the box, giving explosive power to the takeoff. Perhaps the vaulter should reach maximum speed as soon as possible so that at the plant he is "freewheeling." This approach might contribute to the smoothness of the vault and be a noticeable advantage to some vaulters. The theory advocates getting the most controlled momentum possible at Point T because longer maintained speed contributes to *fluidity*.

We teach two types of approaches, the long run and the short run. The long run (100 to 130 feet) is generally favored by vaulters and taught as "normal" technique. However, vaulters should learn the advantages of a short run (50 to 70 feet) and practice it as thoroughly as the long one so they will be able to use it whenever special conditions warrant.

When a strong wind is against the vaulters, it is exhausting to get off the ground with a full run and hold. A short run with a low hold is important for such conditions. For practice sessions, it is possible to take many more vaults with the short run and low hold than with the full run. In big competitive meets, also, when the pole vaulting promises to be a long, drawn-out affair, requiring many attempts, the vaulter who can take a short approach and vault from a low hold, at least in the early attempts, will find that he has a great advantage in conserving his energy for his later, higher attempts.

The hand grip is measured from the bottom of the pole to the top of the top hand. The athlete should be vaulting two feet or more above his hand grip before raising the grip. Many athletes try to use a higher grip than they can effectively handle, mistakenly believing that it will enable them to vault higher. A good vaulter should be able to clear 14 feet with a grip of no more than 12 feet to 12′ 6″. The pole is taped, generally made sticky with "firm grip" or a similar substance, giving a more secure handhold. While carrying the pole, the hands are usually gripping the pole about three feet apart.

For a short-run approach, the vaulter uses a low hold on the pole, probably at about 12 feet. This hold should be comfortable. In any situations where exhaustion, rather than another competitor, may contribute to defeat, the vaulter who can conserve his energy with a short run and a low hold will turn a disadvantage into an advantage.

Establishing Check Marks

When measuring and establishing check marks, it is not necessary to work on the pole vault runway. It is almost impossible for an athlete to establish his check marks alone. It would be ideal if the coach could help each vaulter with this procedure at the beginning of the season. Remember to have the athlete carry the pole when establishing the marks. If the coach cannot assist the vaulter in establishing his marks, then vaulters should work in groups or pairs, with the experienced vaulters particularly helping the inexperienced ones.

A vaulter whose stride is so erratic that he cannot reach the takeoff point in the 4-6-10 stride pattern might drop down to a shorter approach, such as a 4-4-8 stride pattern. Sometimes, however, the candidate's stride is so erratic that he simply cannot establish or meet his check marks. What does the coach do? He tries to help the man improve the evenness of his stride. A good drill is to set three low (30-inch) hurdles about nine yards apart and have the vaulter practice hurdling over the side and over the top, not trying for hurdle style but for evenness of stride. It might be very helpful if all vaulters would try competing in the hurdles. It is hard to tell whether hurdling serves as a particularly good conditioning exercise or whether the benefit comes from improved evenness of stride, but a good correlation seems to exist between excellence in hurdling and excellence in vaulting.

For check marks for the short approach, a single mark suffices. Begin by assuming that the approach will be 50 to 70 feet and should take eight strides. Measure back 10 feet from the planting box (standing under the hand grip with the pole planted in the box) for the takeoff point. From there, measure back 50 feet (or however far the vaulter travels in his eight strides) and locate at that point check mark 1. The vaulter goes through the short approach three times; average the distances for his measured short-run check mark.

As an athlete becomes more fit, the check marks tend to change. His stride may be as much as six inches longer at the end of the season, making his short approach about four feet longer. For that reason, check marks should be measured *every day* before practice or competition and changed as necessary. Other factors that influence the stride length—such as the condition of the track and the wind—also vary and need to be considered.

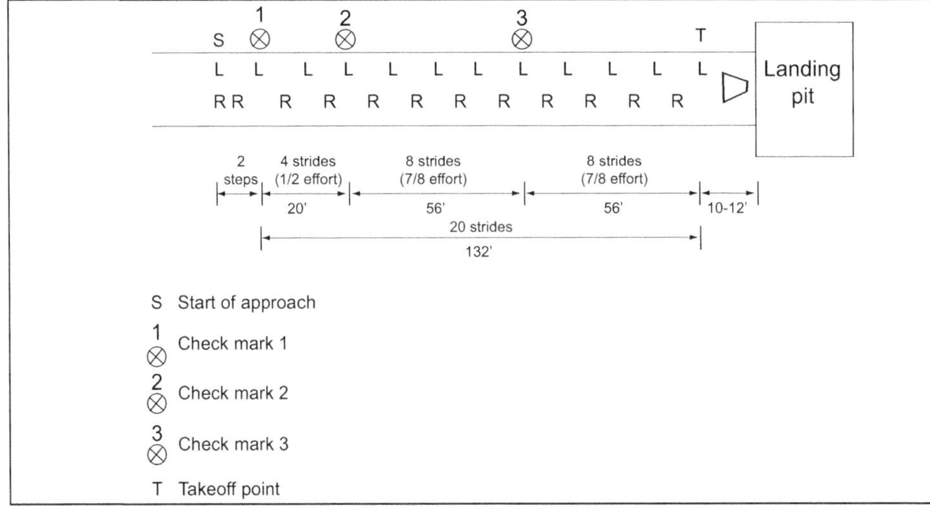

Figure 15-1. Earlier speed approach

The early-speed approach applies the same principles in setting the marks and measuring the stride (Figure 15-1): From the starting point, two steps to check mark 1, then four strides at half speed to check mark 2. From check mark 2 to check mark 3, the vaulter is going at 7/8 speed. From check mark 3 to the takeoff, he goes another eight steps at the same speed, and then plants the pole. The big advantage of the early speed approach for the last 100 feet of the approach run is that the vaulter may have better control of his speed for the pole plant and therefore have better control for the things that follow through the rest of the vault.

Training for the Pole Vault

What do you want the athlete to do, and how do you tell him? The schedule is a continuing line of communication between the teacher and the student, the coach and the athlete. The training schedule lists the fundamentals of pole vaulting and is a day-by-day plan for practicing those items. It also becomes a record of what the athlete did in practice and competition, a diary of his progress and accomplishments.

The patterns that make up the schedules may not all be the best possible for every given individual. However, they provide a plan to work from, a starting point. These schedules have been used successfully by other vaulters. The virtuoso, the truly gifted, may prefer his own adaptations.

The vaulter needs to learn to establish a practice routine. The first step in the routine is work on the short run. Using a run of 50 to 70 feet, the vaulter works at perfecting his technique. He should work on the fundamentals of the pole plant, the takeoff, and the lay back and wait. A general training routine might look like the following:

- Three times a long run (for the steps)
- Three times a short run (also for the steps)
- Work with the short run
    - ✓One to three times working on the plant
    - ✓One to three vaults working on laying back and waiting
    - ✓One to three vaults working on coming off the pole

When working with a short run and low hold, the vaulter should use a pole that reacts like the one he uses for the long run and high hold. A long pole (such as 16 feet) does not react the same if a low hold (such as 11 or 12 feet) is used. Also, the vaulter may at times begin to get tired when he is vaulting. If the vaulter is tired and shows it, he should *stop vaulting* for that day. He runs the risk of emphasizing and setting bad habits of vaulting if he continues.

Pole Vault Training Schedules

Table 15-2 is a translation of the first week of training from the vaulting schedules at the end of this chapter. The numbers on the schedule sheets represent the fundamentals of pole vaulting.

Interpreting the First Week's Training Schedule		
Monday		The class or squad meets for the first time. Equipment is discussed, procedures are explained, goals are recommended for individuals, and such things as hard and easy days with test efforts every 7, 10, or 14 days are explained.
Tuesday	1.	Warm-up.
	14F.	High knee, slow running, almost in place, bringing the knees about hip high. Go for 10m, and then walk for 10m. This exercise is followed by fast leg, barely lifting the feet off the ground, gradually increasing the cadence, and bouncing the ball of each foot off the surface in cadence with a short, very rapid arm action. The vaulter should go about 10m, then rest and repeat the high knee, then the fast leg, for 50 to 100m.
	14D.	The vaulter should run 50m, walk 50m to recover, then repeat until 400 to 800m or more have been covered. This exercise is a conditioning activity.
	16.	Apparatus work, such as ropes, rings, parallel bars, and other apparatus activities.
Wednesday	1A.	Warm up with jogging, relay routine, stretching, and flexibility exercises.
	17.	Run, carrying the pole, which is helpful for conditioning and learning that the vaulting pole is the vaulter's best friend.
	14B.	Set up three low hurdles about 8 to 10 yards apart. This exercise is for evenness of stride.
Thursday	3.	Weight lifting. Most athletes work out weight-training routines of their own. Exercises are suggested in Chapter 2.
Friday	1.	Warm-up.
	14A.	Wind sprints, starting slowly, gradually increasing the speed for about 50m, then gradually decreasing to a jog and recovering for 50m. Cover 400 to 800m.
	17.	Same as Wednesday.
	4A.	Short check-mark drill of 50 to 70 feet. This drill is explained in the section on pole vaulting fundamentals.
	6A.	Another pole vaulting fundamental, explained in the section on fundamentals.
	14D.	Same as Tuesday.
Saturday	3.	Weight training.
	17.	Running with the pole.
Sunday		For relaxation, recreation, and workouts, no day is better day than Sunday.

Table 15-2. Translation of first week of pole vault training

4A. Short Check Mark

A short approach is recommended for early season work because the vaulter can do more vaulting with a shorter run. It is also helpful in competitions that have bad weather conditions, such as rain or a strong headwind or crosswind.

An approach of 50 to 70 feet is used to reach the takeoff point, which is nine feet or more from the vaulting box. The approach is 6 to 10 steps, with a two-step approach to the one check mark (Figure 15-2). With the short approach, a low hold on the pole is used. It should be low enough for positive control in any conditions and high enough for respectable clearance. A handhold of 11′ 6″ will permit a clearance up to 13 to 14 feet. A shorter, calibrated pole should be used for this short-check, low-hold vaulting. When the vaulter can consistently clear 14 to 15 feet, he should acquire a pole with a lower calibration for the short-run practice and for bad weather competition.

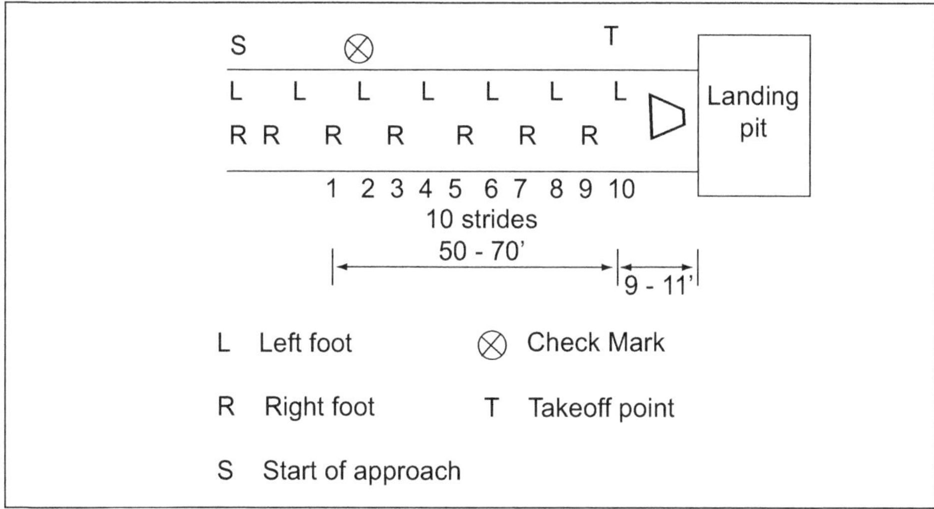

Figure 15-2. Short check mark

The vaulter stands in a forward-leaning position, pole on the ground or at the ready. He concentrates on his total vault, then with a walking-step approach hits the check mark, and gradually accelerates in 10 steps to the T, or the takeoff point. When starting fall or winter training, the vaulter can work on the check mark on the runway or on the track. A right-handed vaulter carries the pole, hits the check with his left foot, and then accelerates through 10 steps to the takeoff. His observer marks the T spot. This run is repeated two more times, and the T marks are averaged to give the length of the short check. This mark is then transferred to the runway. Ten feet (or the proper distance, according to his handhold) from the box, a T mark is placed. The vaulter can now practice his approaches on the runway.

4B. Long Check Mark

The long run and regular high hold are for the time when the parts of the technique, fundamentals, and physical condition are approaching their peak.

Having check marks is as important to the vaulter as navigation points are to the astronaut going to the moon.

The right-handed vaulter stands two steps behind check mark 1 (Figure 15-3). He stands with both feet together or the right foot forward, whichever is more comfortable for him. He should think through the entire technique of his vault before starting his approach. His first step is with his left foot hitting the first check mark.

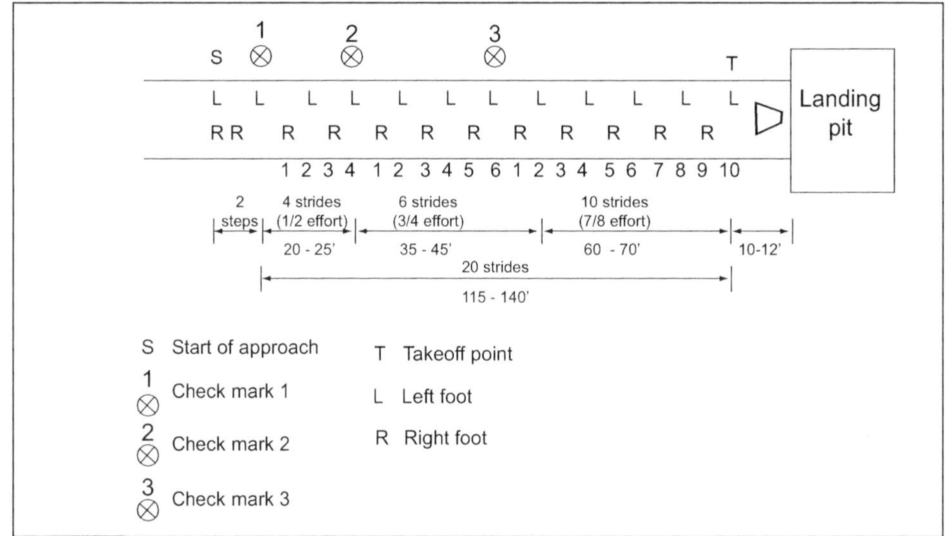

Figure 15-3. Long check mark

Assuming that the stride of the vaulter—going at half-effort at this point—is five feet, he would then take 20 feet to reach check mark 2 with his left foot. This example is not intended to push the vaulter either to try for any particular stride length or to run through an approach when he is establishing his check marks. He should run through this part of the procedure from his starting point before check mark 1 through check mark 2 so he can establish the length of his stride and exactly what this distance should be. The vaulter takes three tries, then uses the average of the three results.

After he has established the distance between check marks 1 and 2, the vaulter works at measuring his stride at 3/4 effort so he can put in check mark 3, which will be six strides after check mark 2. If his stride is six feet, for example, he will cover about 36 feet between check marks 2 and 3. The vaulter now returns to his starting point and run through check marks 1 and 2 to see how close he comes to check mark 3 in six additional strides. Again, the run is done three times, and an average distance is taken.

The next distance is to the takeoff (T), 10 to 12 feet from the box. If the vaulter has become tired or erratic, the procedure is stopped until the next day. To zero in on the takeoff, have the vaulter run the complete approach, marking the track or runway each of the three times. After checking through the first three check marks, the vaulter's intent is to reach a speed that might be called

7/8 effort while taking 10 strides to Point T. If a vaulter's stride at this speed is seven feet, for example, this part of the approach will take 70 feet. He will measure it, taking three trials and averaging their lengths.

The technique of setting the check marks must be practiced and rechecked every vaulting day. Measuring is a must. The champion vaulter is not only an artist; he is a careful technician.

5A. The Pole Plant

The second phase of the vault consists of planting the pole in the vaulting box. It should be accomplished in two or three counts. The vaulter should look at the box rather than the crossbar as he plants the pole. The two planting techniques are the overhand and the straight underhand. Choosing one is simply a matter of personal preference. The plant should not be too hurried. The count or steps should be carefully practiced and a rhythm established.

The pole should be aligned straight into the box and along the vaulter's nose. If it is off to the side, it throws him out of line. The delivery of the pole into the box should be smooth and well timed. The vaulter should try to be rising over the last two steps leading into the plant, so he will seem to float off the ground rather than to be pushing off hard. The vaulter should not pull the pole toward himself during the plant or takeoff, but neither should he hold it out to the side because that would throw him off to the side during his rise.

5B. Takeoff

The pole should be straight overhead during the takeoff, and the head should be hanging in a position about halfway between the hands as they grasp the pole. The lead knee should be quick in leaving the ground. The higher the hold on the pole and the straighter the angle between the pole and the ground, the higher the vaulter will go. The vaulter at this critical stage needs to be on guard against several faults:

- Being off to the side
- Settling down during the last several strides
- Having the arms too bent, which may result in their collapsing as he rises into the air

5C. The Lay Back and Wait (Hang)

The vaulter should not pull the pole toward him, but he should hold the pole away as he rises in order to get into the hang. As the pole bends, he should not sit down because doing so would put more pressure on the pole, a frequent cause of broken poles. Even if the sitting position does not break the pole, it requires greater exertion to get the man off the ground, which means that he could have gone higher and risen more easily had he not dropped into the sitting position.

6A. Pull When Back Is Parallel and Pole "Up"

A vaulter hangs as the pole continues to move upward. Then he tries to get his center of gravity up in the air. Too often, a vaulter watches his feet. When he sees that they are high enough, he believes he is high enough. However, it is not the feet, but the center of gravity, that determines the height of the vault. He should think of the hips or the waist as rising to crossbar height before starting the turn. If he gets the center of gravity up, good things will happen in the pole vault.

6B. The Turn and Rise

If the turn comes too soon, the vaulter may stall the pole. He has to stay behind the pole throughout the bend. The action is like simultaneously performing a curl with the right hand and a press with the left hand. When the hips and the center of gravity are at the height of the crossbar and the bottom of the pole is perpendicular to the ground, then the vaulter should pull and turn. This movement will cause the pole to straighten and the vaulter to rotate around his center of gravity. The lead foot continues up as the turn is completed.

6C. Off the Pole

This step is the final stage of the vault, taking place as the hands are rising and the vaulter's body is clearing the crossbar. The vaulter needs to learn to use his feet and legs to clear the upper body, leaving only the problem of a safe landing, which is no problem if a good landing pad is used.

9. Technical Work

9A. Short-Run, Low-Hold Form Work

Using the short approach, the vaulter works on the aspects of form listed by the letters in Item 6 on the training sheet. Many more productive vaults can be made with a short approach than with the long run.

9B. Long-Run Form Work

This work is done as in Item 9A, practicing on technique, fundamentals, or individual needs, using the full approach with all checks.

10B. Trials

Trials are meant to give progress reports as well as to be learning situations. The starting level of the competition should be within the capability of the weakest or youngest vaulter. The vaulters should rotate turns, with the crossbar going up or down according to the talent of each vaulter.

10B1. Up or Down Six Inches on a Make or a Miss

Move the bar up if the height is cleared and lower the bar if the height is missed. Assume that Vaulter A starts at 12′ 0″ and misses. His next jump is at

11′ 6″. Vaulter B starts at 13′ 0″ (in squad rotation, not according to the height being attempted) and clears it, so his next height will be 13′ 6″. Vaulter A clears 11′ 6″ on his next attempt, so he goes back up to 12′ 0″.

10B2. Two Jumps at Three Inches Above Average Best

When the vaulters acquire some consistency, which usually takes about six weeks, they then occasionally practice above the season's average best mark. Assume that Vaulter B reaches 15′ 3″ and is given two attempts to make the height. He does not get a third attempt, for psychological reasons: three misses would put him out of the competition, and it is preferable that he quit while feeling that he might have made it on that third jump.

10B3. Establish Starting Height for Good or Bad Day

The starting height that the vaulter can use with assurance should be established according to the runway, the weather, and the vaulter's ability. The vaulters should jump in rotation and move the standards to their capability.

11. Higher Grip and Check Mark Adjustment

Some vaulters too easily change their handholds. The height of the vaulter's hold should not change until he has mastered the technique to a near-maximum height. The vaulter should especially not vary his hold out of hope or panic in competition. When the vaulter is ready, then he should start with a three- to six-inch (possibly as much as 12-inch) increase in the handhold. His routine must be reestablished, including the variations in check marks, the changes in timing to a longer hang, and possibly the delayed releases of the pole's stored energy at the turn and the off-the-pole phases of the vault. Those changes may take several vaulting sessions. They should start with no crossbar, working through to a successful simulated competition.

16. Easy Apparatus or Acrobatics

The apparatus room and gymnastic equipment offer great opportunity for variation and pleasant exercise. Vaulting skills can be related to this work, but it is most important that the athlete acquire mastery of his bodily movements. Trampoline activities can be useful for developing body control, but great care should be taken for safety reasons.

20. Secondary Event

The secondary event for the pole vaulter may be for competitive pleasure, conditioning, or team points. Temperament is an ingredient necessary to athletic or any other success. Real champions make it work for them. An athlete should have a secondary event for pleasure as well as self-mastery. The champions do; the losers do not.

POLE VAULT SCHEDULE NAME ____________________ DATE ______________

1. A. Jog 1-2 laps with relay pass, in 2s or 3s
   B. Hendricks Park C. Golf course D. Steps
2. Fartlek A. Varied pace B. Slow, steady pace
3. Weights and jogging
4. Check mark A. Short B. Long
5. A. Pole plant
   B. Takeoff UP
   C. Lay back and wait (hang)
   D.
6. A. Pull when back parallel and pole up
   B. Turn and rise, lead foot up
   C. Off the pole
   D.
7. TEAM MEETING
8. Special A. Sauna B. Swim C. Hill
   D.
9. A. Short run, low hold form work
   B. Long run, form work
   C.
10. A. Meet B. Trial C. Simulation D. Control test
   (1) Up or down 6 in. on a make or miss
   (2) 2 jumps at 4 in. above average best
   (3) Establish starting height, good or bad day
11. Higher grip and check mark adjustment
12. With Coach A. B.
14. A. Wind sprints (1) Straight (2) Curve
   B. Hurdle drill: 3 LH, 7-9m apart
   C. Spring and bound
   D. Alternate run and jog, at least 800
   E. Starts (1) 100 (2)
   F. High knee (slow) and fast leg
15. Plyometrics A. Jumps B. Bounding C.
   (1) 1-leg (2) Both legs (3)
16. Easy acrobatics or apparatus
17. Run with the pole 50m, walk 100, go 400
18. Warmup routine
19.
20. Work on second event
21. A. Videotape B. Film C. Pictures
   (1) Record performance (2) Study
30. Experimental work

Date	Distance	3/4 pace	Date Pace	Goal Pace

M
T
W
T
F
S
S
M
T
W
T
F
S
S
M
T
W
T
F
S
S
M
T
W
T
F
S
S

Sheet 15-1. Revised pole vault training schedule sheet

Pole Vault NAME DATE September/October

1. Warm-up A. Jog 1 or 2 laps relay pass
   B. Weights and jog C.
2. Fartlek A. Varied B. Slow, steady
3. Weights
4. Check mark A. Short B. Long
5. A. Pole plant B. Take off up C. Lay back and wait (hang)
6. A. Pull when back parallel and pole "up"
   B. Turn and rise, lead foot up C. Off the pole
7. Squad meeting
8. Special A. Sauna B. Swim C. Hill D.
9. A. Short run–low hold form work
   B. Long run form work
10. A. Trials B. Compete (1) Up or down 6 in. on a make or miss
    (2) 2 jumps at 3 in. above average best
    (3) Establish starting height good or bad day
11. Higher grip and check mark adjustment
12. With Coach A. B.
14. A. Wind sprints B. Starts or (1) 100 (2)
    C. High knee and fast leg
    D. Hurdle drill—3 lows at 8-10 yds.
    E. Spring and bound
    F. Alternate run-jog at least 880
15. A. Hendricks B. Laurel C. Stadium steps
16. Easy apparatus or acrobatics
17. Run with the pole 55 yds., walk 110, go 440
18. Warm-up routine
19.
20. Secondary event
21. A. Pictures B. Film
22. Experimental work

Day	Schedule
M	Class or squad organization
T	1-14C-16-14F
W	1A-17-14D
T	3
F	1-14A-17-4A-6A-14F
S	1-3-17
S	16
M	1-^{3}4A-^{3}5A-^{3}6A-9A-14A
T	1-3-17
W	7-1-^{2}4B-^{2}4A-9A-14A
T	1-3-14F
F	1-^{2}4B-^{2}4A-^{2}5A-9A-14A
S	3
S	3-16
M	1-^{3}4B-^{2}4A-6B-14D-14A
T	1-3-17
W	1-^{2}4A-^{2}4B-^{2}5A-^{2}5B-9A-14D
T	1-3-15B
F	1-^{2}4A-^{2}4B-9A-17
S	3
S	3-14D
M	1-17-^{2}4A-^{2}4B-^{2}5A-^{2}6B-9A-14D
T	3-14F
W	1-17-^{2}4A-^{2}4B-9A-7
T	1-3-15B
F	1-4A-4B-10A1-14A
S	3
S	3

Date	Result	3/4	Date	Goal

Sheet 15-2. Pole vault training schedule

Pole Vault NAME DATE October/November

1. Warm-up A. Jog 1 or 2 laps relay pass
   B. Weights and jog C.
2. Fartlek A. Varied B. Slow, steady
3. Weights
4. Check mark A. Short B. Long
5. A. Pole plant B. Take off up C. Lay back and wait (hang)
6. A. Pull when back parallel and pole "up"
   B. Turn and rise, lead foot up C. Off the pole
7. Squad meeting
8. Special A. Sauna B. Swim C. Hill D.
9. A. Short run-low hold form work
   B. Long run form work
10. A. Trials B. Compete (1) Up or down 6 in. on a make or miss
    (2) 2 jumps at 3 in. above average best
    (3) Establish starting height good or bad day
11. Higher grip and check mark adjustment
12. With Coach A. B.
14. A. Wind sprints B. Starts or (1) 100 (2)
    C. High knee and fast leg
    D. Hurdle drill—3 lows at 8-10 yds.
    E. Spring and bound
    F. Alternate run-jog at least 880
15. A. Hendricks B. Laurel C. Stadium steps
16. Easy apparatus or acrobatics
17. Run with the pole 55 yds., walk 110, go 440
18. Warm-up routine
19.
20. Secondary event
21. A. Pictures B. Film
22. Experimental work

Date	Result	3/4	Date	Goal

Day	Workout
M	1A-14C-17-16
T	3-14D-15B
W	1A-4B^{3}-14E-16
T	1-4A^{2}-4B^{2}-5B^{2}-14A-8B
F	1-3-17
S	1A-4B^{2}-5A^{2}-6B^{2}-14D
S	15A
M	1A-17-4A^{3}-5A^{2}-6C^{2}-14A
T	1A-3 or 15B
W	1A-4A-5B-5C-9A-14F
T	1A-14D
F	1B-4B-5C-9A-14F
S	3
S	jog
M	1-14D-4A-4B-5C-9B-15A
T	1A-15B
W	1B-5B-5C-9A-15A or B
T	1B-3-8A
F	1A-10A1-10A2-14D
S	1B
S	
M	1A-14C-4B-6A-6C-9B-2B
T	3-8A
W	7-1A-4A-4B-5A-9A-2B
T	3-8A or B
F	1A-5A-10A1-10A2-14D
S	3
S	

Sheet 15-3. Pole vault training schedule

Pole Vault NAME DATE January

1. Warm-up A. Jog 1 or 2 laps relay pass
   B. Weights and jog C.
2. Fartlek A. Varied B. Slow, steady
3. Weights
4. Check mark A. Short B. Long
5. A. Pole plant B. Take off up C. Lay back and wait (hang)
6. A. Pull when back parallel and pole "up"
   B. Turn and rise, lead foot up C. Off the pole
7. Squad meeting
8. Special A. Sauna B. Swim C. Hill D.
9. A. Short run-low hold form work
   B. Long run form work
10. A. Trials B. Compete (1) Up or down 6 in. on a make or miss
    (2) 2 jumps at 3 in. above average best
    (3) Establish starting height good or bad day
11. Higher grip and check mark adjustment
12. With Coach A. B.
14. A. Wind sprints B. Starts or (1) 100 (2)
    C. High knee and fast leg
    D. Hurdle drill—3 lows at 8-10 yds.
    E. Spring and bound
    F. Alternate run-jog at least 880
15. A. Hendricks B. Laurel C. Stadium steps
16. Easy apparatus or acrobatics
17. Run with the pole 55 yds., walk 110, go 440
18. Warm-up routine
19.
20. Secondary event
21. A. Pictures B. Film
22. Experimental work

Date	Result	3/4	Date	Goal

Day	Schedule
M	Register-squad meet-4A(3)-4B(3)-14F
T	3
W	1A-14C-16 or 4A-9A-14A
T	7-3
F	1A-18-4B(3)-20-14A
S	16
S	jog
M	1B-4A(2-3)-4B(2-3)-5A(2-3)-9A-14F
T	3-16
W	1A-4A(2-3)-4B(2-3)-15B(8C) or 15C
T	3
F	1B-14C-4B-18-14F
S	16 or 3
S	jog
M	1A-14C-16-4B(2-3)-4A(2-3)-5B(2-3)-9-14A
T	3-8A or B
W	1A-4B(2-3)-15B (8C)
T	3-15A
F	1-4B-10A1-10A2
S	3 or form work
S	jog
M	1B-14C-6-4B(2-3)-4A(2-3)
T	3-8A or B or sun
W	7-1B-5A-6C-15B (8C)
T	3
F	1B-Gear ready
S	10B Indoors
S	jog

Sheet 15-4. Pole vault training schedule

Pole Vault NAME DATE February

1. Warm-up A. Jog 1 or 2 laps relay pass
   B. Weights and jog C.
2. Fartlek A. Varied B. Slow, steady
3. Weights
4. Check mark A. Short B. Long
5. A. Pole plant B. Take off up C. Lay back and wait (hang)
6. A. Pull when back parallel and pole "up"
   B. Turn and rise, lead foot up C. Off the pole
7. Squad meeting
8. Special A. Sauna B. Swim C. Hill D.
9. A. Short run–low hold form work
   B. Long run form work
10. A. Trials B. Compete (1) Up or down 6 in. on a make or miss
    (2) 2 jumps at 3 in. above average best
    (3) Establish starting height good or bad day
11. Higher grip and check mark adjustment
12. With Coach A. B.
14. A. Wind sprints B. Starts or (1) 100 (2)
    C. High knee and fast leg
    D. Hurdle drill—3 lows at 8-10 yds.
    E. Spring and bound
    F. Alternate run-jog at least 880
15. A. Hendricks B. Laurel C. Stadium steps
16. Easy apparatus or acrobatics
17. Run with the pole 55 yds., walk 110, go 440
18. Warm-up routine
19.
20. Secondary event
21. A. Pictures B. Film
22. Experimental work

Date	Result	3/4	Date	Goal

M	1A-17-9A-4D-Jog
T	3-8A
W	7-1-10A-9A-14A
T	3-8B
F	1-4A-4B-5C-6A-14F
S	3-8A or B
S	jog
M	1A-14C-9B-9A-14A
T	1A-16-8A or B
W	1A-18-4B-6C-9A-14A
T	1A-16
F	1A-10A-10B-14D-14A-Jog
S	3-15A
S	jog
M	1-4B-6A-14D-17
T	16-8A or B
W	1-17-12-4A-5C-6C-17
T	3-16
F	1-4B-6B-9A-14D
S	3-14A
S	jog
M	1-4B-5B-6A-9A-14E
T	3 or 16
W	1-10A-10B-14A
T	1-16-8A or B
F	1-4A-4B-5B-9B-14D
S	15A or B
S	jog

Sheet 15-5. Pole vault training schedule

Pole Vault NAME DATE *March*

1. Warm-up A. Jog 1 or 2 laps relay pass
   B. Weights and jog C.
2. Fartlek A. Varied B. Slow, steady
3. Weights
4. Check mark A. Short B. Long
5. A. Pole plant B. Take off up C. Lay back and wait (hang)
6. A. Pull when back parallel and pole "up"
   B. Turn and rise, lead foot up C. Off the pole
7. Squad meeting
8. Special A. Sauna B. Swim C. Hill D.
9. A. Short run-low hold form work
   B. Long run form work
10. A. Trials B. Compete (1) Up or down 6 in. on a make or miss
    (2) 2 jumps at 3 in. above average best
    (3) Establish starting height good or bad day
11. Higher grip and check mark adjustment
12. With Coach A. B.
14. A. Wind sprints B. Starts or (1) 100 (2)
    C. High knee and fast leg
    D. Hurdle drill—3 lows at 8-10 yds.
    E. Spring and bound
    F. Alternate run-jog at least 880
15. A. Hendricks B. Laurel C. Stadium steps
16. Easy apparatus or acrobatics
17. Run with the pole 55 yds., walk 110, go 440
18. Warm-up routine
19.
20. Secondary event
21. A. Pictures B. Film
22. Experimental work

Date	Result	3/4	Date	Goal

M	*1A-17-18-5A-9B-14D*
T	*1B-16*
W	*1-18-10A1-10A2-9A-5B-Jog*
T	*1-16-14A*
F	*1-18-6B-10-14A*
S	*3-15A or B-8A or B*
S	
M	*1-18-17*
T	*1A-4B-5A-5B-10A2*
W	*1-gear ready or 3-14A*
T	*Travel-1A-14C-4A-4B*
F	*Meet routine*
S	*Travel home*
S	*Loosen up at 1pm-14*
M	*7-1A-14A*
T	*1A-4A-4B-9B-14A*
W	*16*
T	*1-4B-9B-14F*
F	*Gear ready*
S	*Relay meet*
S	*Loosen up at 1 p.m.*
M	*1A-17-4B-5A-9B-14D*
T	*3-14A*
W	*1A-18-9B-10A2*
T	*16*
F	*Gear ready*
S	*Travel to meet-10B*
S	*Loosen up*

Sheet 15-6. Pole vault training schedule

Pole Vault NAME DATE *April*

1. Warm-up A. Jog 1 or 2 laps relay pass
   B. Weights and jog C.
2. Fartlek A. Varied B. Slow, steady
3. Weights
4. Check mark A. Short B. Long
5. A. Pole plant B. Take off up C. Lay back and wait (hang)
6. A. Pull when back parallel and pole "up"
   B. Turn and rise, lead foot up C. Off the pole
7. Squad meeting
8. Special A. Sauna B. Swim C. Hill D.
9. A. Short run-low hold form work
   B. Long run form work
10. A. Trials B. Compete (1) Up or down 6 in. on a make or miss
    (2) 2 jumps at 3 in. above average best
    (3) Establish starting height good or bad day
11. Higher grip and check mark adjustment
12. With Coach A. B.
14. A. Wind sprints B. Starts or (1) 100 (2)
    C. High knee and fast leg
    D. Hurdle drill—3 lows at 8-10 yds.
    E. Spring and bound
    F. Alternate run-jog at least 880
15. A. Hendricks B. Laurel C. Stadium steps
16. Easy apparatus or acrobatics
17. Run with the pole 55 yds., walk 110, go 440
18. Warm-up routine
19.
20. Secondary event
21. A. Pictures B. Film
22. Experimental work

Date	Result	3/4	Date	Goal

M	1A - 4A (2X) - 6B (2-4X) - 5A - 9A - 14A
T	1B - 3
W	7 - 1A - 4 - 6A - 10A2 - 9A - 14D
T	1B - 16
F	Meet preparation
S	Premeet - compete - after meet
S	3 or 15B
M	1B - 4 (3X) - 5A (3X) - 5C - 9A - 14A
T	3 - 8A or B
W	7 - 1A - 4B (3X) - 10A1 - 9A - 14D
T	Jog - 8A or B
F	Light
S	Meet routine
S	16
M	1A or 17 - 4B - 5A - 5C - 9A - 14E
T	1B - 14C - 14D
W	1A - 4B - 10A - 9A - 14F
T	3 - 8B - 14A grass
F	Light
S	Dual meet
S	1A - 11 - 9B
M	17 - 16 - 8A or B
T	1A - 11 - 10A - 9A - 9B
W	3 - 16 - 8A or B
T	1A - 18 - 11 - 9B - 9A
F	Light
S	Compete
S	1A - recheck grip - 11

Sheet 15-7. Pole vault training schedule

Pole Vault NAME DATE *May*

1. Warm-up A. Jog 1 or 2 laps relay pass
   B. Weights and jog C.
2. Fartlek A. Varied B. Slow, steady
3. Weights
4. Check mark A. Short B. Long
5. A. Pole plant B. Take off up C. Lay back and wait (hang)
6. A. Pull when back parallel and pole "up"
   B. Turn and rise, lead foot up C. Off the pole
7. Squad meeting
8. Special A. Sauna B. Swim C. Hill D.
9. A. Short run–low hold form work
   B. Long run form work
10. A. Trials B. Compete (1) Up or down 6 in. on a make or miss
    (2) 2 jumps at 3 in. above average best
    (3) Establish starting height good or bad day
11. Higher grip and check mark adjustment
12. With Coach A. B.
14. A. Wind sprints B. Starts or (1) 100 (2)
    C. High knee and fast leg
    D. Hurdle drill—3 lows at 8-10 yds.
    E. Spring and bound
    F. Alternate run-jog at least 880
15. A. Hendricks B. Laurel C. Stadium steps
16. Easy apparatus or acrobatics
17. Run with the pole 55 yds., walk 110, go 440
18. Warm-up routine
19.
20. Secondary event
21. A. Pictures B. Film
22. Experimental work

Date	Result	3/4	Date	Goal

Day	A.M.	P.M.
M	*Jog*	*1A–4B–5A–5C–9A–14D* (*3* over 4B, *3* over 5A, *3–6* over 5C)
T	*Jog*	*3*
W	*Jog*	*7–1A–18–10B2–14A1*
T	*Jog*	*Light*
F		*Light*
S		*Be good, be tough, be relaxed* *Traditional meet*
S		*Pole plant and swing*

Day	
M	*14F – easy 14D*
T	*1A–18–10A–9A–14C*
W	*7–15B or grass run*
T	*1A–4A–4B–5A–14D* (*2* over 4A, 4B, 5A)
F	*Light*
S	*Dual meet*
S	*Grass run*

Day	
M	*1B–4B–5A–5C–9A or B–14E* (*3* over 4B, *3* over 5A, *3–6* over 5C)
T	*3 and light*
W	*1A–4B–5B–10B2*
T	*Light*
F	*Light*
S	*Championship*
S	*Grass run*

Day	
M	
T	
W	
T	
F	
S	
S	

Sheet 15-8. Pole vault training schedule

Endnotes

1. Vitaly Petrov & Sergei Bubka. (1985). Pole vault clinic (after the lecture). *Track and Field Quarterly Review, 85*(4), 33.
2. Rick Attig. (1987). Understanding pole vault mechanics. *Track and Field Quarterly Review, 87*(4), 25-32.
3. J. Nikolov. (1986). The structure of the pole vault run-up. *Track Technique, 94*, 3012.
4. J. Nikolov. (1987). The contemporary take-off. *Track Technique, 98*, 3124-3125.
5. Andrzej Krzesinski. (1983). Mt. SAC Relays pole vault clinic. *Track Technique, 86*, 2734-2739.
6. Maurice Houvion. (1986). Perfect vaulting technique. *Track Technique, 95*, 3027-3036.
7. V. Jagodin, V. Kurbatov, & J. Volkov. (1981). Systematic development of pole vaulters. In Jess Jarver (Ed.), *The jumps* (2nd ed., pp. 72-74). Los Altos, CA: Tafnews.
8. Derek Boosey. (1980). *The jumps: Conditioning and technical training*. West Heidelberg, Victoria, Australia: Beatrice.
9. V. Jagodin & V. Tshunganov. (1981). Periodization in pole vault training. In Jess Jarver (Ed.), *The jumps* (2nd ed., pp. 81-82). Los Altos, CA: Tafnews.
10. William H. Freeman. (1989). *Peak when it counts: Periodization for the American track coach*. Los Altos, CA: Tafnews.
11. Andrzej Krzesinski. (1983). Pole vault: The total program. *Track Technique, 84*, 2679-2682.

Core Readings

Bemiller, Jim. Pole vault. (2000). In *USA Track and Field coaching manual* (pp. 199-216). Champaign, IL: Human Kinetics.

Ferry, Brian. (1998). *Modern pole vaulting: Analyzing the superior "Russian" style and adapting it to American vaulting*. Mountain View, CA: Tafnews.

Freeman, William H. (2001). Periodized training for jumpers. In *Peak When It Counts: Periodization for American track and field* (4th ed.). Mountain View, CA: Tafnews, 120-130.

Ganslen, Richard. (1980). *Mechanics of the pole vault* (9th ed.). Published by the author.

Jacoby, Ed, & Bob Fraley. (1998). *The complete book of jumps*. Champaign, IL: Human Kinetics.

Jarver, Jess, ed. (2000). *The Jumps: Contemporary Theory, Technique and Training* (5th ed.). Mountain View, CA: Tafnews.

Risk, R. B. (1991). *Risker's vault camp* (2nd ed.). n.p.

USA Track & Field Coaching Education Program. (2003). *Level II Curriculum: Jumps*. USA Track & Field. Invaluable; revised regularly.

Recommended Readings

Adamczewski, Horst, & Bettina Perlt. (1997). Run-up velocities of female and male pole vaulting and some technical aspects of women's pole vault. Trans. Jürgen Schiffer. *New Studies in Athletics, 12*(1), 63-76.

Arampatzis, Adiamatios, Gert-Peter Brüggemann, & Falk Schade. Pole vault. In Harald Müller & Helmar Hommel, eds., Biomechanical Research Project at the VIth World Championships in Athletics, Athens 1997: Preliminary Report. *New Studies in Athletics, 12*(2-3), 69-73.

Armbrust, Wayne. (1993). Energy conservation in the pole vault. *Track Technique, 125*, 3991-3994, 4005.

Bailly, Joël, Roman Botcharnikov, Leszec Klima, Francisco Martinez Lucia, Peter M. McGinnis, Dave Nielson, Dick Railsback & Julian Shuravetsky. (1997). NSA Round Table 33: Pole vault. *New Studies in Athletics, 12*(1), 23-38.

Bianco, Enrique, David Lease, Elio Locatelli, Yukio Muraki, Dan Pfaff, Efim Shuravetzky & Miguel Velez. (1996). NSA Round Table 31: Speed in the jumping events. *New Studies in Athletics, 11*(2-3), 9-19.

Bubka, Sergei. (1989). My training [abstract]. *Track Technique,108*, 3456.

Botcharnikov, Roman. (1996). The continuous chain model in the pole vault. *Track Coach, 135*, 4301-4304.

Bussabarger, David. (Summer 2003). A comparison of the long jump and pole vault takeoff actions. *Track Coach, 164*, 5241-5242.

Bussabarger, David. (Fall 2001). Launching into the vaulting action. *Track Coach, 157*, 5017-5018.

Bussaberger, David. (Spring 2007). Technical analysis of Yelina Isinbayeva. *Track Coach, 179*, 5713-5716.

Bussabarger, David. (Fall 2002). A technique critique of Dmitriy Markov. *Track Coach, 161*, 5134-5136.

Bussabarger, David. (Winter 2002). A technical critique of Stacy Dragila. *Track Coach, 158*, 5033-5034.

Nielsen, Dave. (Summer 2002). Response to "Imperfect form". *Track Coach, 160,* 5111-5113.

Bussabarger, David. (Fall 2002). Reply to Nielsen's critique. *Track Coach, 161*, 5157.

Bussabarger, David. (Summer 2002). A technique critique of Svetlana Feofanova. *Track Coach, 160,* 5101-5102, 5120.

Bussabarger, David. (Summer 2005). Variations in the execution of the vertical extension. *Track Coach, 172*, 5490-5491.

Ebbets, Russ. (Summer 2005). If you build it...Interview with Rick Suhr. *Track Coach, 172*, 5492-5499. Pole vault training & indoor facility.

Grabner, Stefanie. (1997). Kinematic analysis of the women's pole vault. Trans. Jürgen Schiffer. *New Studies in Athletics, 12*(1), 47-61.

Grabner, Stephanie. (2004). Technical and conditioning aspects of the women's pole vault. *New Studies in Athletics, 19*(3), 43-54.

Hay, James. (1998). Biomechanical considerations about jumping training. *New Studies in Athletics, 13*(1), 90-91.

Hay, James G. (1988). The approach run in the pole vault. *Track Technique, 106*, 3376-3377, 3396.

Houvion, M. Maurice. (1982). The preparation of the pole vaulter for advanced levels: 6 meters in 2000. *Track and Field Quarterly Review, 82*(4), 38-41.

Johnson, Jan. (Fall 2001). Beginning pole vaulting progressions and formulas. *Track Coach, 157*, 5008-5010.

Johnson, Jan. (1996). Solutions for a vertical world. *Track Coach, 136*, 4329-4330, 4357. PV

Kernan, John. (1994). A pole vault training area for high schools and colleges. *Track Technique, 126*, 4021-4023, 4036.

Krykorka, Zdenek. (1990). Observing Bubka in training [abstract]. *Track Technique, 113*, 3618.

Krzesinski, Andrzej. (1989). The European concept of the pole vault [abstract]. *Track Technique, 109*, 3488.

Krzesinski, Andrzej. (1983). Pole vault: The total program. *Track Technique, 84*, 2679-2682.

Kerin, David. (Summer 2002). Achieving strength gains specific to the demands of jumping events. *Track Coach, 160*, 5103-5110.

Mackenzie, Robert J. (Spring 2007). Film measurement of takeoff forces in the jumps, including slowing effects. *Track Coach, 179*, 5717-5722, 5733.

McGinnis, Peter M. (1997). Mechanics of the pole vault take-off. *New Studies in Athletics, 12*(1), 43-46.

McGinnis, Peter. (1989). Pete's pointers for perfect pole vaulting. *Track Technique, 109*, 3472-3474.

Miller, Antonina, & Viktor Jagodin. (Spring 2005). Peculiarities in the preparation of female pole vaulters [abstract]. *Track Coach, 171*, 5475-5476.

Müller, Harald. (2000). Interview: Sergej Bubka. *New Studies in Athletics, 15*(3/4), 61-63.

Nikonov, Igor. (2000). Women become pole vaulters. Trans. Kuulo Kutsar. In Jess Jarver, ed., *The Jumps: Contemporary Theory, Technique and Training* (5th ed.). Mountain View, CA: Tafnews, 73-76.

Paar, Colin. (1988). An analysis of Pierre Quinon's vault technique. *Track Technique, 104*, 3326-3327.

Schade, Falk, & Gert-Peter Brüggemann. (2006). The pole vault at the 2005 World Championships in Athletics: A preliminary report. *New Studies in Athletics, 21*(2), 57-66.

Schiffer, Jurgen. (1993). About Bubka's training [abstract]. *Track Technique, 123*, 3934.

Schiffer, Jürgen. (1997). Selected and annotated bibliography 41: Pole vault. *New Studies in Athletics, 12*(1), 95-107.

Schiffer, Jürgen. (2004). Selected and annotated bibliography 67: Pole vault. *New Studies in Athletics, 19*(3), 87-140.

Seese, Eddie. (Winter 2006). Pole vault coaches check list. *Track Coach, 174*, 5573.

Smith, Steve. (1982). Pole vault. *Track and Field Quarterly Review, 82*(4), 44-45.

Thompson, Mike. (Winter 2003). Troubleshooting in the pole vault. *Track Coach, 162*, 5172-5176.

Tidow, Gunter. (1991). Model technique analysis for the pole vault. *Track Technique, 114*, 3642-3648, 3653.

VerSteeg, Russ. (Fall 2005). Improving as a pole vaulter: Play hard, play smart, play together. *Track Coach, 173*, 5520-5523.

Wetter, Jochen. (1997). NSA interview: Wanpei Wang. *New Studies in Athletics, 12*(1), 39-40. Chinese vault coach, female wold medalist

Young, Michael A. (Fall 2002). A technical model for pole vault success. *Track Coach, 161*, 5129-5133.

16

The Long Jump

Bowerman's Best

26' 2 2/4"	Bouncy Moore 1970

Record Setters

Bouncy Moore NCAA champion; two-time U.S. champion; two-time All-American

Mel Renfro	All-American, 1962	25' 11 3/4"
Tom Smith	All-American, 1969	26' 1/4"

"One giant leap for mankind" was taken on the surface of the moon by Neil Armstrong during the summer of 1969. In the Mexico City Summer Olympics in 1968, Bob Beamon made a great leap for posterity when he smashed the world long jump record with a phenomenal leap of 29' 2 1/2" (8.90m). How did it happen? A superb athlete, perfect conditions, and great competition combined to produce it. Although altitude is cited as a major factor, in fact only about two inches of the leap are a possible effect of altitude. It was a supreme athletic achievement, perhaps the all-time greatest performance breakthrough.

Long Jump Training Theory

The bottom line for long jumpers is their speed and power at the takeoff board.[1] In fact, as their velocity increases, the height and length of the jump increase even if the takeoff angle is lower.[2] To give an idea of the effect of the length of the approach run, most jumpers approach their maximum velocity (for controlled long jumping speed) at the following rates:

- 70 to 75 percent after 6 steps (10 to 11m)
- 85 to 90 percent after 10 steps (21 to 22m)
- 96 to 98 percent after 14 steps (30 to 31m)

- 100 percent after 17 steps (38 to 39m)
- Takeoff after 19 steps[3]

The two or three strides before the last stride of the approach tend to be longer than average, while the stride into the takeoff is shorter (though recent biomechanical research suggests that the final step should be slightly longer, rather than shorter). The two-count rise (raising the center of gravity during the last two steps) starts with a slightly longer step, combined with landing flat-footed. This technique lowers the center of gravity and results in a rising center of gravity during the last two steps. This gradual rise helps overcome the inertia of the body's horizontal motion, making the transition to vertical motion easier.

The critical element of the approach is proper sprinting technique, beginning with a gradual acceleration. The stride pattern should be very consistent. Though some coaches suggest a flat-footed takeoff, only limited evidence suggests its use by jumpers. The key to the jump is controlled speed. Speed is useful *only* if the jumper can fully control it.

An analysis of world-class female long jumpers shows that the American edge in pure talent, as seen in sprint performances, does not suffice for the long jump.[4] Instead, better planned, more thorough training in the Eastern European nations has overcome much of the American raw talent advantage. Besides their more intensive training, Eastern European athletes are tested regularly on a battery of control tests designed to assess their specific conditioning and progress in training, with the records kept for year-to-year comparisons of performance and reaction to training.

Training for the Long Jump

Training injury is a very real risk in the long jump, so long jumpers should not take too many jumps in any one session, nor should they jump too often. They are athletes blessed with both agility and speed. Speed alone does not make a really good jumper, though most male world-class long jumpers are capable of 10.5 seconds or faster for 100m.

The even has seen exceptionally speedy runners, such as Jesse Owens and Carl Lewis. As well as fleet of foot, they were also very agile. Long jumpers should be well coordinated, with explosive reactions. This event may also attract the most strongly competitive athletes.

The basic jump involves a run of 120 feet or more, with relaxation during the last 20 to 30 feet, an attempt to go high into the air after the takeoff, then landing with as much outward reaching of the feet as possible. The jumper tries to go into the air from a gradual rise to the board over the last two steps. This technique is sometimes referred to as the "two-count rise." For example, consider a female jumper who hits the takeoff board with her left foot. On the third and fourth strides before hitting the board, she settles down, lowering her center of gravity to hit a low point when she puts down her left foot two strides before she hits the board. Some jumpers accomplish this settling action by slightly lengthening the stride for a step or two. She then rises, so that her center of gravity has already begun its ascent by the time she hits the board. This technique overcomes the inertia of horizontal motion. She hits the low point by landing flat on the left foot, then rises onto the right foot, then rises to the left foot, which hits the board, and then she drives upward into the air.

An excellent training technique is the use of short-run pop-ups. These exercises are done with a run of 50 feet or less, usually taking an eight-step approach. The jumpers work on the two-count rise, doing pop-ups from the area in front of the takeoff board, trying to fly off the runway and get good height in their jumps.

The two biggest problems long jumpers encounter in action are bad check marks and bad takeoffs. Consider the check marks first. How long should a jumper's approach run be? Probably 120 feet or so would be enough. Most world-class jumpers take 120 to 140 feet. Some jumpers who take as much as a 150-foot approach run (with no legal limit) are probably wasting energy rather than gaining benefits. Jumpers using an overly long approach often do not improve after the second jump, probably because they become fatigued. Most people can reach their top sprinting speed in 40 yards, so a longer run is rarely of any benefit.

You would probably find as many ideas on the number and location of check marks as you would long jumpers and coaches. Some jumpers use only

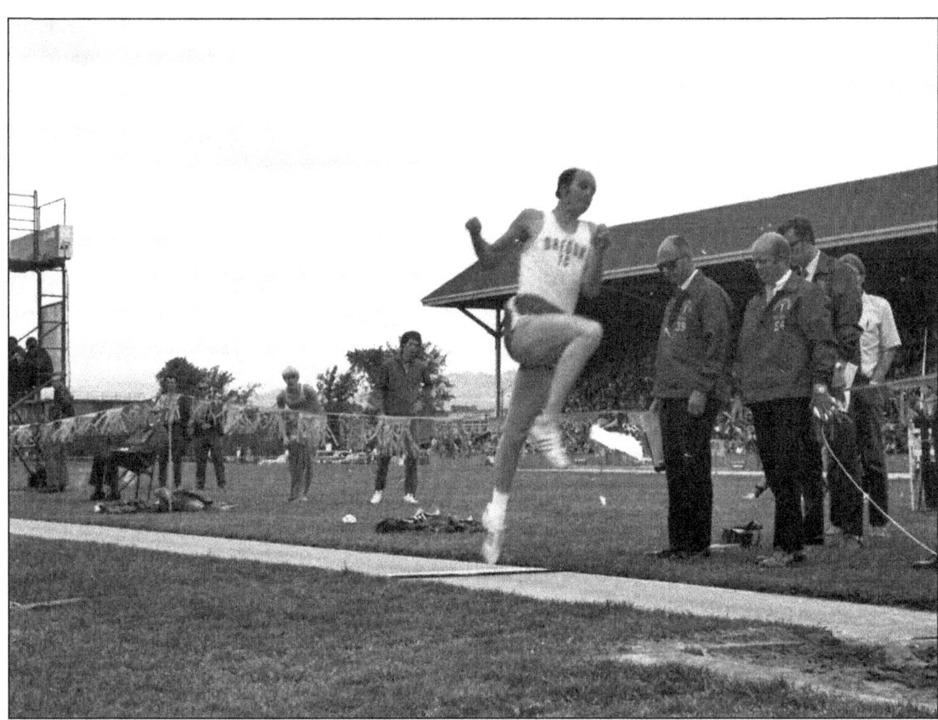

Photo 16-1. Tom Smith, 26′ 0″ long jumper

one check mark, located at the start of the full approach, while others use two or three check marks. Three check marks is likely the most useful number. The first is at the start of the long approach. The jumper leaves this mark running at half effort for four strides. He then hits the second mark, at which point he accelerates to 3/4 or 7/8 speed, running for the next six steps, at which point he hits the final check mark. This mark is 10 steps from the takeoff board. This part of the approach is run at full speed, or as close to it as the jumper can keep under control and convert to upward momentum when the jump occurs.

Many views can be found for what is desirable in the use of check marks. A jumper can use a 2-4-6 set of check marks (similar to Figure 16-2) or any other combination that is found most useful for his own particular jumping style. One highly recommended practice is to have two check marks two steps apart (hitting both marks with the same foot) somewhere in the middle of the approach run. If the first mark is missed, any stride adjustment can be checked quickly. If both marks are missed, the jumper can terminate the run at that point rather than risk wasting a jump. However, the jumper should be aware that major meets allow only 90 seconds for a completed jump.

Some jumpers may have trouble with their check marks in the switch from high school to college jumping. Because some high schools use a 24-inch-wide takeoff board, the switch to hitting the collegiate board, which is only eight inches wide, may be a major adjustment.

A jumper should keep in mind the benefits of the short run (8 to 12 strides) in the competitive situation. Facing a strong head wind, the jumper may find it especially tiring or difficult to jump well after a full approach battling the wind. In this case, the jumper should use the short approach instead. It saves energy on the approach run, energy that can be applied to additional speed to give a jumping edge over those who are sticking with the more exhausting long run. Also, if the jumper has opened with two fouls, leaving only one jump to make the finals, the surer short run is safer to use.

On the takeoff, the jumper should hit the board and pass over the plant foot, not reach out for the board. Actually, the last stride (onto the board) is slightly shorter than the other approach strides, so essentially the jumper "runs off the board" because he is rising through the last two strides. However, some coaches advocate "stamping" the foot on the board.

Also, the jumper should take care not to bring the kicking foot across the body, misdirecting the line of flight to the side. At the takeoff board, the jumper should shift his line of sight from the board to the horizon. The chest should be kept up, and the jumper should concentrate on getting knee lift off the board. The movements in the air are done only to keep the body balanced in flight and to prepare for the landing. While in the air, the primary considerations are getting the feet extended forward (not letting them drop toward the pit) and holding the hands up and out.

Putting a mark in the pit is actually of little real benefit (and is also illegal), for after the jumper has left the ground, the laws of physics determine how far he will go. Nothing done in the air will cause the body to travel any farther, nor can anything be done to shorten the flight of the center of gravity.

The only effect the jumper has on the distance of the jump after takeoff is the extension of the legs and feet. If they are dropped too quickly, the jumper will land before the center of gravity would have landed, thus getting a poorer jump. If they are kept up and extended perfectly, they can land as much as two feet or more ahead of the center of gravity. This, then, is the importance of extending the feet, for it can make a difference of three or more feet between the distance achieved by two jumps that are equal in all other respects. In other words, although the center of gravity may travel 20 feet, the jump could vary from 17 to 23 feet. Thus, the proper use of arms and legs is extremely important.

Long Jump Training Schedules

A training schedule sheet is used for communication and for the convenience of the long jump coach and athlete. Table 16-1 provides an interpretation of a sample week on the long jump training schedules. The numbers and common interpretations are explained in Chapter 6. The following are used particularly for long jump training.

4. Check Mark

The long jump check mark is a critical fundamental. The jumper should first establish a short check mark to use when jumping against the wind, or when two fouls have been made in the preliminaries and a "must" jump is necessary to qualify for the finals. The short check is important in training for other fundamentals, also.

4A. Short Check Mark

The short check mark is a one-mark approach, the distance being 50 to 70 feet, depending upon the length of the athlete's strides. The approach is 10 strides in most cases, though one variation uses a short check of eight strides. Figure 16-1 illustrates the stride pattern for a 10-stride short approach for a jumper who steps on the board with the left foot.

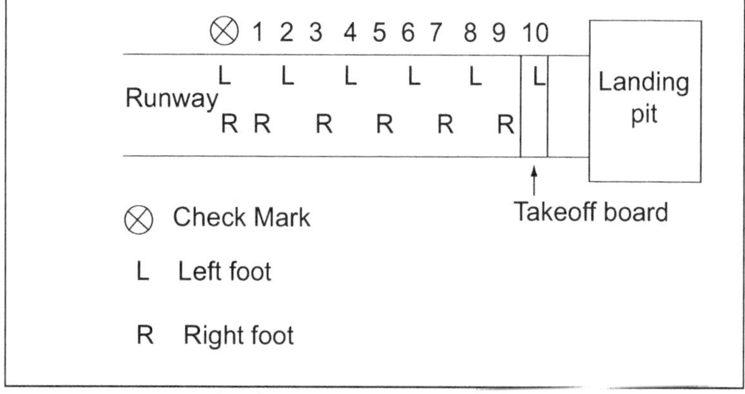

Figure 16-1. Short check approach

Interpreting the First Week's Training Schedule		
Monday		Organization: The physical education class or squad meets to discuss objectives and goals. The teacher or coach explains responsibilities for regular attendance or for separate individual workouts. Use and care of facilities are also explained.
Tuesday	1A.	In groups of two or three, jog one or two laps of the track. A relay fundamental is used, with the joggers carrying a baton and passing it forward as they jog single file. When the baton reaches the jogger at the head of the line, he drops to the rear and begins passing the baton again.
	14D.	Run 50m, then jog slowly or walk for 50m, until 400 to 800m or more have been covered.
	3.	Weight-training activities according to the schedules or the routine of the athlete.
Wednesday	1A.	Warm-up activities already described.
	4A.	Short check mark.
	14F.	High-knee drill, followed by the fast leg described in detail in Chapter 10.
Thursday	3.	Weight-training activities.
	16.	Acrobatics or apparatus work of a gymnastic nature.
Friday	1A.	Warm-up routine.
	1B.	A run to Hendricks Park and two times up the short hill, which is about 50m long.
Saturday	3.	A weight-training session, followed by a jogging session.
	14D.	Alternating runs and jogs or walks of 50m for 400 to 800m.
Sunday		Recreational activities are recommended. Workout procedures are gradually worked into the program as the year progresses. For those who need training and exercise, Sunday is a day to restore physical well-being.

Table 16-1. Interpreting the first week's training schedule

Finding the starting point for a jumper's approach run is like locating a target with mortar fire. Have the jumper start from the takeoff board and run 10 strides up the runway two or three times: mark the location of the 8th stride each time. Then, mark the average of the three marks as a starting check mark and have the jumper begin practicing with it. This approach is long enough for practicing most technique work, except for perfecting the full approach run.

4B. Long Check Mark

This mark has several variations. The most commonly used mark is the 4-8-10 pattern. Using "S" for the start (Figure 16-2), check marks 1, 2, and 3, and "T" for takeoff, a procedure for establishing the marks is the following.

Start the athlete at S and the coach or observer on the runway or track about 20 feet away. Two walking steps lead to check mark 1 with the left foot.

Running at half speed and gradually speeding up, on the fourth step the jumper is at check mark 2. The observer marks the location of this step, and the procedure is repeated for a total of three efforts. The average distance, usually 20 to 25 feet, establishes the first two check marks.

The procedure is repeated for check mark 3. The jumper begins at S and reconfirms check marks 1 and 2 while going through three runs, running at 3/4 effort, gradually increasing the speed. The observer again marks each of the three efforts and takes the average, eight steps being taken from check mark 2 to check mark 3.

The T mark is established in the same manner, with the speed gradually increasing from 7/8 to 9/10 effort. It may be necessary for the jumper to establish the T mark on another day, particularly if his fitness level is low.

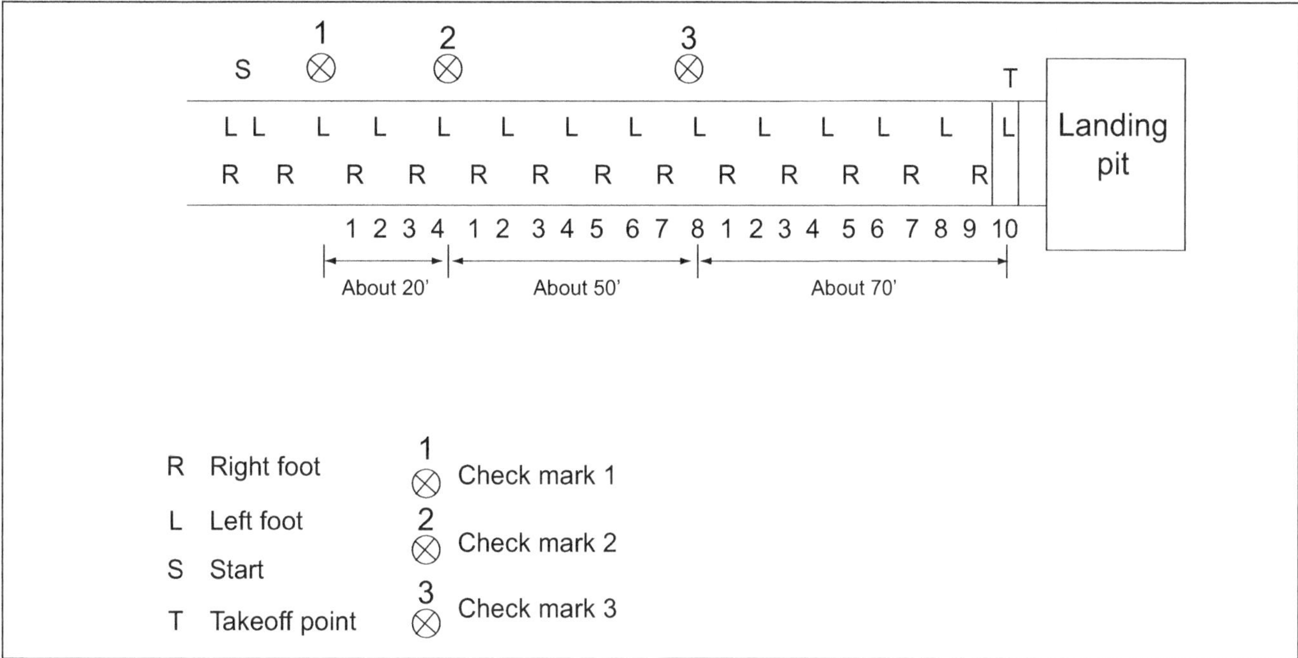

Figure 16-2. Long check approach

4A1. Short Run, Height

This drill emphasizes the slight settle on the second-to-last step, a slight rise on the next-to-last step, and final lift at the takeoff. The perfect jump would find the jumper's center of gravity rising at an angle of close to 45 degrees (in reality, this angle is impossible to achieve), with the maximum height achieved at the midpoint of the jump.

4A2. Short Run, Landing

This landing is a reflex action. The between-the-feet or over-the-feet action is the most common landing. The feet must be dropped soon enough for the forward momentum to carry the jumper over the feet, or a slight spread of the

Photo 16-2. Ross Blackman, 26′ 1″ long jumper

feet should be used to let the jumper go between the feet, forcing the hips forward. This action (the same as in Item 9A) also depends on the jumper's reaching forward and through between the knees.

A second excellent method is landing with one knee slightly stiffened (also used in Item 9B). At the instant of foot contact with the landing surface, the opposite arm and hand reach across the body, while the arm on the same side as the locked knee is moved outward. This action causes a rotation around the feet. This landing is difficult to coordinate and is only for the very agile athlete.

4C. Check Mark, Takeoff

The takeoff in this drill is for the emphasis of having the takeoff foot under the hip, not across the center of gravity. A cross-step by the takeoff foot (planting the foot across the line of the run to the board) would cause a compensating motion across the body by the arm opposite the takeoff leg and also would cause the lead leg to cross over the line of the approach to the pit. Not only would the takeoff be spoiled, but the flight would be a fight for balance, resulting in a poor landing.

5. Height Work

Height work is of such importance that not only is it treated within check mark fundamentals, but it is also a separate fundamental requiring special attention. In a 20-foot jump, the center of gravity should reach its peak height at a point 10 feet from the takeoff. The body should be perpendicular to the ground at the midpoint of the jump.

6. Flight

Two major methods of body control in the air are used in preparation for landing. Neither propels the center of gravity any farther. The importance of the flight is to gain balance so the feet can be thrust as far forward as possible and so the center of gravity can move forward past the feet at impact without the hands or buttocks making sand marks.

6A. Hitch-Kick

As the takeoff foot pushes off the board, the lead knee is brought to hip height, followed by the takeoff leg coming into a running position, then extending, and the lead leg coming up into the extended position for a one-and-a-half-step "walk in the air." Very long jumpers might use a two-and-a-half-step walk. Only those who can benefit from the technique should use it. It is strongly recommended that the one-and-a-half-step style be mastered before the athlete even plays with the two-and-a-half-step style.

6B. Hang

At the takeoff, the lead knee is raised and the arms lift. As the lead knee is lowered, the takeoff leg is brought alongside, but the legs are spread and the knees are slightly bent. The jumper, with arms overhead and the legs hanging down, appears to hang until past the midpoint of the jump, when the legs and arms are brought forward and the jumper awaits the pull of gravity for the landing.

9. Landing

This work was described with the check mark work. It may be practiced with either the long or the short approach (Items 8A and 8B with 4A and 4B, respectively).

10B. Test Effort

The coach or the athlete should record the results of this effort in the lower left area of the training sheet. The 3/4 to 7/8 effort is a usual procedure for practice. No benefit is derived from an athlete being exhausted on Tuesday or Wednesday. The trials are a learning and technique procedure. Assuming a jumper has an average of 22 feet in competition, a reasonable trial or test jump would be 20 feet. A "hot" practice effort might well equal or better the competitive average, but technique combined with controlled progress should produce the big jumps at the big meets.

11A. Feather the Board

The technique strived for with this step is to achieve a running up into the air rather than a pounding of the takeoff board. It is believed that an emphasis up, rather than down, gives maximum lift.

11B. Pound the Board

Pound the board means exactly what it says. It is a technique used by many fine jumpers and advocated by many coaches. The jumper should use what suits him and gets results. Heel bruises and muscle pulls are the great dangers in the pounding technique. In practicing either this or the feathering takeoff technique, the jumper should take off either in front of the board or on the grass, rather than from the board.

11C. Over the Foot

The coach or a teammate should watch the jumper from the rear to determine that the takeoff foot is directly under the hip. Otherwise, a crossover would cause many compensating equilibrium problems that would detract from the jumping distance.

11D. Two-Count Rise, Height

The two-count rise (Figure 16-3) is a very important technique. The jumper settles on the third-to-last step (left foot for a left-footed takeoff, two steps out), is just barely rising on the next-to-last step, and gives the final propulsion and lift on the last step. Theoretically, if the body is already rising, it not only weighs proportionately less but also utilizes the body's momentum to detract from the body's weight. The jumping leg has a tremendous advantage in lifting a mass that is already moving upward.

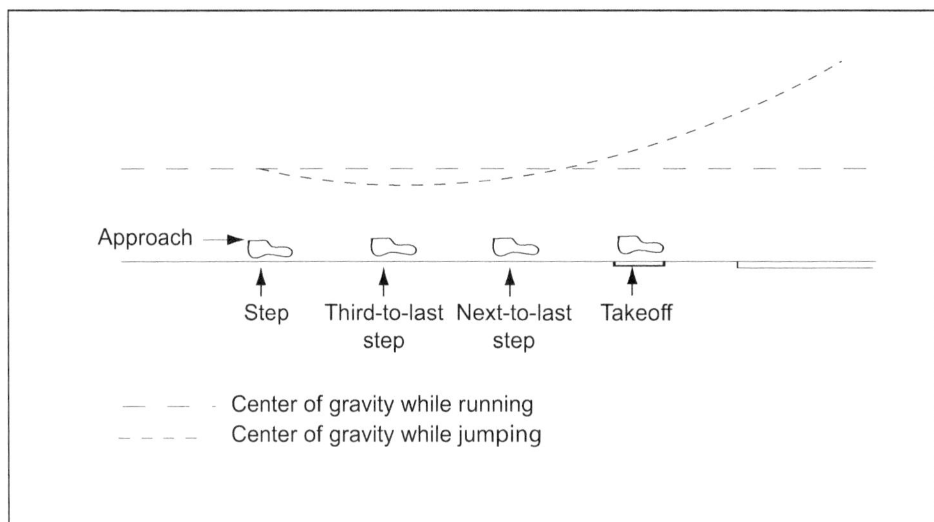

Figure 16-3. Two-count rise

11E. Off Platform

A platform of plywood with one edge on a two-by-four makes an inclined plane with a slight elevation, which enables the jumper to artificially attain additional height, giving more time to practice body control in the air.

20. Secondary Event

A secondary event might be the relay, the 100, or sometimes the triple jump. The dangers of the triple jump are the same as those of the long jump: heel bruises, muscle pulls, back problems, and such. If an athlete limits himself to a total of four to six jumps in both events combined, perhaps it would then be a good double. However, the jumper may turn out to be only fair in both events, yet great if he concentrated on only one event.

LONG JUMP SCHEDULE NAME ______________________ DATE ______________

1. A. Jog 1-2 laps with relay pass, in 2s or 3s
   B. Hendricks Park C. Golf course D. Steps
   (1) Short hill (2) Long hill
2. Fartlek A. Varied pace B. Slow, steady pace
3. Weights and jogging
4. Check marks A. Short run B. Long run
   (1) Height (2) Landing (3) Takeoff
5. Height work
   A. Emphasize body control
   B. Apparatus
   C. Takeoff
   D.
6. Flight A. Hitch-kick 1-1/2 B. Hang C.
7. TEAM MEETING
8. Special A. Sauna B. Swim C. Hill D.
9. Landing A. Over the feet B. Around the feet
   C.
10. A. Meet B. Trial C. Simulation D. Control test
   (1) 3/4ths to 7/8ths effort (2) Full effort
   (3)
11. Short run and jump, relax last 4 steps
   A. Feather the board B. Pound the board
   C. Over the foot D. 2-count rise: height
   E. Off platform F. Landing
12. With Coach A. B.
14. A. Wind sprints (1) Straight (2) Curve
   B. Hurdle drill: 3 LH, 7-9m apart
   C. Spring and bound
   D. Alternate run and jog, at least 800
   E. Starts (1) 100 (2)
   F. High knee (slow) and fast leg
15. Plyometrics A. Jumps B. Bounding C.
   (1) 1-leg (2) Both legs (3)
16. Easy acrobatics or apparatus
17.
18. A. 300-150-100 B. 100-200-100
19.
20. Work on second event
21. A. Videotape B. Film C. Pictures
   (1) Record performance (2) Study
30. Experimental work

Date	Distance	3/4 pace	Date Pace	Goal Pace

M
T
W
T
F
S
S
M
T
W
T
F
S
S
M
T
W
T
F
S
S
M
T
W
T
F
S
S

Sheet 16-1. Revised long jump training schedule sheet

Long Jump NAME DATE *September/October*

1. A. Jog 1 or 2 laps, relay pass 2s or 3s B. Weights and jog
   C.
2. Fartlek A. Varied pace B. Slow, steady
3. Weights
4. Check marks A. Short B. Long 1. Height
   2. Landing C. Take off
5. Height work A. Emphasize body control B. Apparatus
   C Take off D.
6. Flight A. Hitch-kick 1½ B. Hang C.
7. Squad meeting
8. Special A. Sauna B. Swim C. Hill D.
9. Landing A. Over the feet B. Around the feet
   C.
10. Test or trial—compete, record below
    A. 3/4 to 7/8 effort B. Full effort C.
11. Short run and jump—last 4 steps relax A. Feather the board
    B. Pound the board C. Over the foot
    D. 2-count rise—height E. Off platform F. Landing
12. With Coach A. B.
14. A. Wind sprints B. Starts—go 30-50 yds.
    C. High knee and fast leg
    D. Hurdle drill 3 lows 8-10 yds. apart
    E. Spring and bound
    F. Alternate walk-run 55 yds., go 880
    H.
15. A. Hendricks B. Laurelwood 1. Short hill 2. Long hill
    C. Stadium steps D.
16. Acrobatics or apparatus
17.
18. A. 330-165-110 B. 110-220-110 C.
19.
20. Secondary event
21. A. Pictures B. Film C. Videotape

Date	Result	3/4	Date	Goal

M	*Class or squad organization*
T	*1A-14F-3*
W	*1A-4A-14C*
T	*3-16*
F	*1A-15A-15A1 (2x)*
S	*1B-14F*
S	*weights and long walk*
M	*1A-9A (4-8x)-14F*
T	*1B-3-Jog*
W	*7-1A-14C-14D-14E-14A*
T	*1B-3-Jog*
F	*1A-14F-11F-14F*
S	*3 or 15A*
S	*weights and run*
M	*1A-14E-15A1 (3x)-15A2 (3x)-14F*
T	*1A-3-8A*
W	*1A-14E-14A-14E-14D*
T	*1A-3-14F*
F	*1A-14E-15A1 (2x)-15A2 (2x)-Jog*
S	*jog Hendricks Park*
S	*jog Hendricks Park*
M	*1A-14C-9A-8A or B*
T	*3-Jog*
W	*1A-4A (2x)-4B (2x)-14D-14B-Jog*
T	*1B-14F-Jog*
F	*1A-4A-10A (3x)-Jog*
S	*Help on track trials or run SPRINT or hurdle*
S	*run*

Sheet 16-2. Long jump training schedule

Long Jump NAME DATE October/November

1. A. Jog 1 or 2 laps, relay pass 2s or 3s B. Weights and jog
   C.
2. Fartlek A. Varied pace B. Slow, steady
3. Weights
4. Check marks A. Short B. Long 1. Height
   2. Landing C. Take off
5. Height work A. Emphasize body control B. Apparatus
   C Take off D.
6. Flight A. Hitch-kick 1½ B. Hang C.
7. Squad meeting
8. Special A. Sauna B. Swim C. Hill D.
9. Landing A. Over the feet B. Around the feet
   C.
10. Test or trial—compete, record below
    A. 3/4 to 7/8 effort B. Full effort C.
11. Short run and jump—last 4 steps relax A. Feather the board
    B. Pound the board C. Over the foot
    D. 2-count rise—height E. Off platform F. Landing
12. With Coach A. B.
14. A. Wind sprints B. Starts—go 30-50 yds.
    C. High knee and fast leg
    D. Hurdle drill 3 lows 8-10 yds. apart
    E. Spring and bound
    F. Alternate walk-run 55 yds., go 880
    H.
15. A. Hendricks B. Laurelwood 1. Short hill 2. Long hill
    C. Stadium steps D.
16. Acrobatics or apparatus
17.
18. A. 330-165-110 B. 110-220-110 C.
19.
20. Secondary event
21. A. Pictures B. Film C. Videotape

Date	Result	3/4	Date	Goal

M	1-14C-18B-110 in 15-16
T	1-3-14E
W	7-1-4B-4A-5C-14D-11D (4X)-20
T	3-14C
F	1-4A-4B
S	15A or B
S	3
M	1-5-4A-4B-20-11D-Jog
T	3-16-8A
W	1-14E-4B-10A-18B (2X)-Jog
T	3-8A or B
F	1-14E-4A-4B-14D-18B (2X)-Jog
S	15A or 3
S	18A or 3
M	1A-1C-14D-4B (2-4X)-5D (2-4X)
T	3
W	7-1C-14B-11A-11D-18A
T	3
F	1-4B-9-15A
S	10 and sprint or hurdle trial
S	3
M	1-14A-14D-4B-11C (2-4X)-11D (2-4X)-14A
T	3
W	1-14C-4A-4B-11F-11B1 (2X)-11B2 (2X)-Jog
T	3
F	1-14B-4B-11D-18A
S	3
S	15A or B

Sheet 16-3. Long jump training schedule

Long Jump NAME DATE January

1. A. Jog 1 or 2 laps, relay pass 2s or 3s B. Weights and jog
   C.
2. Fartlek A. Varied pace B. Slow, steady
3. Weights
4. Check marks A. Short B. Long 1. Height
   2. Landing C. Take off
5. Height work A. Emphasize body control B. Apparatus
   C Take off D.
6. Flight A. Hitch-kick 1½ B. Hang C.
7. Squad meeting
8. Special A. Sauna B. Swim C. Hill D.
9. Landing A. Over the feet B. Around the feet
   C.
10. Test or trial—compete, record below
    A. 3/4 to 7/8 effort B. Full effort C.
11. Short run and jump—last 4 steps relax A. Feather the board
    B. Pound the board C. Over the foot
    D. 2-count rise—height E. Off platform F. Landing
12. With Coach A. B.
14. A. Wind sprints B. Starts—go 30-50 yds.
    C. High knee and fast leg
    D. Hurdle drill 3 lows 8-10 yds. apart
    E. Spring and bound
    F. Alternate walk-run 55 yds., go 880
    H.
15. A. Hendricks B. Laurelwood 1. Short hill 2. Long hill
    C. Stadium steps D.
16. Acrobatics or apparatus
17.
18. A. 330-165-110 B. 110-220-110 C.
19.
20. Secondary event
21. A. Pictures B. Film C. Videotape

Date	Result	3/4	Date	Goal

M	Recheck all gear-squad or class organize
T	1-9A-15A-locker arrangements
W	1A-11D-14D-14F
T	7-1B-8A
F	1A-14C-11D-14F
S	1A-14A or C
S	jog the halls
M	1A-14C-4A-11A-14A
T	7-3-14F
W	1A-14C-4A-11D-14F
T	3-8A or B or Jog
F	1A-14C-4B-11A-14A
S	3-14D
S	or 8A
M	1-14F-4B-11C-18A
T	14F-8A
W	2-4x 1-14C-4B-10A short run-14A
T	14F-14C
F	1A-4B-11A-11D-18A
S	3-15A-15C
S	
M	1-4B-4A-9A-11A-14F
T	3
W	2x 2x 1A-4B-4A-9D-18B-18C-14F
T	Light
F	Gear ready
S	Compete indoors
S	Light

Sheet 16-4. Long jump training schedule

Long Jump NAME DATE February

1. A. Jog 1 or 2 laps, relay pass 2s or 3s B. Weights and jog
   C.
2. Fartlek A. Varied pace B. Slow, steady
3. Weights
4. Check marks A. Short B. Long 1. Height
   2. Landing C. Take off
5. Height work A. Emphasize body control B. Apparatus
   C Take off D.
6. Flight A. Hitch-kick 1½ B. Hang C.
7. Squad meeting
8. Special A. Sauna B. Swim C. Hill D.
9. Landing A. Over the feet B. Around the feet
   C.
10. Test or trial—compete, record below
    A. 3/4 to 7/8 effort B. Full effort C.
11. Short run and jump—last 4 steps relax A. Feather the board
    B. Pound the board C. Over the foot
    D. 2-count rise—height E. Off platform F. Landing
12. With Coach A. B.
14. A. Wind sprints B. Starts—go 30-50 yds.
    C. High knee and fast leg
    D. Hurdle drill 3 lows 8-10 yds. apart
    E. Spring and bound
    F. Alternate walk-run 55 yds., go 880
    H.
15. A. Hendricks B. Laurelwood 1. Short hill 2. Long hill
    C. Stadium steps D.
16. Acrobatics or apparatus
17.
18. A. 330-165-110 B. 110-220-110 C.
19.
20. Secondary event
21. A. Pictures B. Film C. Videotape

Date	Result	3/4	Date	Goal

Day	Workout
M	2x 2x 6-10x 3-6x 1-4A-4B-5A - 5B-14D-14E
T	3-14A
W	3x 3x 7-1-4A1-4A2-15A or 15C or 8C
T	14E-3
F	2-3x 1-4A-15A or B, 1 and 2-14E
S	8B or 3
S	long walk
M	1A-14D-5C-14C-Jog
T	3-8A or B
W	3x 3x 1-5A-5B-5C
T	Light
F	1-10-8C
S	Sprint and hurdle trials
S	
M	1-14A-14C-11D-14E-14C
T	3-16
W	7-14B-4B-4A-14F
T	3-8A or B
F	2x 1-4A-18A-18B-15A
S	8-15A
S	3
M	1A-14D-5C-14C
T	3-8A or C
W	3x 3x 7-5A-5B-5C-15
T	3-8A
F	1-10-run a 275-15
S	
S	

Sheet 16-5. Long jump training schedule

Long Jump NAME DATE March

1. A. Jog 1 or 2 laps, relay pass 2s or 3s B. Weights and jog
   C.
2. Fartlek A. Varied pace B. Slow, steady
3. Weights
4. Check marks A. Short B. Long 1. Height
   2. Landing C. Take off
5. Height work A. Emphasize body control B. Apparatus
   C Take off D.
6. Flight A. Hitch-kick 1½ B. Hang C.
7. Squad meeting
8. Special A. Sauna B. Swim C. Hill D.
9. Landing A. Over the feet B. Around the feet
   C.
10. Test or trial—compete, record below
    A. 3/4 to 7/8 effort B. Full effort C.
11. Short run and jump—last 4 steps relax A. Feather the board
    B. Pound the board C. Over the foot
    D. 2-count rise—height E. Off platform F. Landing
12. With Coach A. B.
14. A. Wind sprints B. Starts—go 30-50 yds.
    C. High knee and fast leg
    D. Hurdle drill 3 lows 8-10 yds. apart
    E. Spring and bound
    F. Alternate walk-run 55 yds., go 880
    H.
15. A. Hendricks B. Laurelwood 1. Short hill 2. Long hill
    C. Stadium steps D.
16. Acrobatics or apparatus
17.
18. A. 330-165-110 B. 110-220-110 C.
19.
20. Secondary event
21. A. Pictures B. Film C. Videotape

Date	Result	3/4	Date	Goal

Day	
M	1A-14B-14E-11D (3-5x)-11A (3-5x)-14F
T	3-14F (3x)
W	7-1C-14E-14A (2-4x)-9C (2-4x)-9A (2x)-9B (2x)-14D-14F
T	3-14F or set of 300-200-1-
F	1C-4A (3x)-4B (3x)-5A (3-4x)-9A-Jog
S	3-Jog
S	park run

Day	
M	1A-14C-14E-14B (3x)-4A (3x)-4B (3x)-run 110 (4x)
T	14A-3
W	7-1C-4B (3x)-4A2 (3x)-14D
T	3-14A
F	Gear ready and jog
S	Meet routine-compete-after meet routine
S	run

Day	A.M.	P.M.
M	1A-3	1-4A (2x)-4B (2x)-5C (2x)-14F
T	Jog	1-14E-20-4A (2x)
W	Light	Light
T	1-14E	1-14C-4B (2x)-4B1 (2x)-4B2 (2x)-14F
F	Jog	Gear ready-light exercise
S	Meet routine-compete-after meet routine	
S		

Day	
M	
T	
W	
T	
F	
S	
S	

Sheet 16-6. Long jump training schedule

Long Jump NAME DATE April

1. A. Jog 1 or 2 laps, relay pass 2s or 3s B. Weights and jog
   C.
2. Fartlek A. Varied pace B. Slow, steady
3. Weights
4. Check marks A. Short B. Long 1. Height
   2. Landing C. Take off
5. Height work A. Emphasize body control B. Apparatus
   C Take off D.
6. Flight A. Hitch-kick 1½ B. Hang C.
7. Squad meeting
8. Special A. Sauna B. Swim C. Hill D.
9. Landing A. Over the feet B. Around the feet
   C.
10. Test or trial—compete, record below
    A. 3/4 to 7/8 effort B. Full effort C.
11. Short run and jump—last 4 steps relax A. Feather the board
    B. Pound the board C. Over the foot
    D. 2-count rise—height E. Off platform F. Landing
12. With Coach A. B.
14. A. Wind sprints B. Starts—go 30-50 yds.
    C. High knee and fast leg
    D. Hurdle drill 3 lows 8-10 yds. apart
    E. Spring and bound
    F. Alternate walk-run 55 yds., go 880
    H.
15. A. Hendricks B. Laurelwood 1. Short hill 2. Long hill
    C. Stadium steps D.
16. Acrobatics or apparatus
17.
18. A. 330-165-110 B. 110-220-110 C.
19.
20. Secondary event
21. A. Pictures B. Film C. Videotape

Date	Result	3/4	Date	Goal

M	7-1-14C-4A-4B-11D-1C
T	1-14C-3
W	1-4A-4B-14E-14A
T	1-4B-Jog-3
F	Light
S	Meet
S	Jog and 8A or 8B
M	7-1-14C-5B-14A 7 at 4:45 p.m.
T	1-4B-11-14F
W	1-14E-14D.
T	1-4B-11A-11D-14E
F	Light
S	Big meet-relay and long jump
S	Jog
M	7-14C-4B-14A
T	1-4B-11D-11F-Jog
W	1-14E-11-14F
T	1-4B-4A-11D
F	Travel and loosen up
S	Compete
S	1-8A-Jog
M	7-1-14A-4B-14E-14F
T	1-4B-11A-4B1-14F
W	3
T	1-4B-11D
F	Light
S	Dual meet-away
S	Home-8A-Jog

Sheet 16-7. Long jump training schedule

Long Jump NAME DATE May

1. A. Jog 1 or 2 laps, relay pass 2s or 3s B. Weights and jog
   C.
2. Fartlek A. Varied pace B. Slow, steady
3. Weights
4. Check marks A. Short B. Long 1. Height
   2. Landing C. Take off
5. Height work A. Emphasize body control B. Apparatus
   C Take off D.
6. Flight A. Hitch-kick 1½ B. Hang C.
7. Squad meeting
8. Special A. Sauna B. Swim C. Hill D.
9. Landing A. Over the feet B. Around the feet
   C.
10. Test or trial—compete, record below
    A. 3/4 to 7/8 effort B. Full effort C.
11. Short run and jump—last 4 steps relax A. Feather the board
    B. Pound the board C. Over the foot
    D. 2-count rise—height E. Off platform F. Landing
12. With Coach A. B.
14. A. Wind sprints B. Starts—go 30-50 yds.
    C. High knee and fast leg
    D. Hurdle drill 3 lows 8-10 yds. apart
    E. Spring and bound
    F. Alternate walk-run 55 yds., go 880
    H.
15. A. Hendricks B. Laurelwood 1. Short hill 2. Long hill
    C. Stadium steps D.
16. Acrobatics or apparatus
17.
18. A. 330-165-110 B. 110-220-110 C.
19.
20. Secondary event
21. A. Pictures B. Film C. Videotape

Date	Result	3/4	Date	Goal

M	1-4-5A-11D-9A-20-15F
T	3-Jog
W	1-4-11D-9A-14E-14F
T	3-Jog
F	Travel and loosen up
S	Major meet
S	Home-1-14C-8B-8A
M	Jog
T	Jog
W	Twilight meet or trials
T	11C-11D-11F
F	4A-4B-15A
S	Squad picnic
S	walk or jog
M	1-4A-4B1-11C-14E-jog
T	1-4B-14A
W	Jog-3
T	Jog-4
F	1-4A-4B-Jog
S	3x 1-14E-4B-10A
S	Jog and weights
M	4x 1-14E-14A-14B-pop-ups--75 yards-jog
T	2-3x 1-14E-4A-4B-Easy 14D
W	Easy grass running
T	Easy grass running
F	Qualify
S	Championship
S	

Sheet 16-8. Long jump training schedule

Endnotes

1. Gerd Osenberg. (1983). Performance factors in the long jump. *Track Technique, 86*, 2754.
2. Tom Tellez. (1980). Long jump. *Track and Field Quarterly Review, 80*(4), 8-10.
3. Yukio Muraki. (1984). Fundamentals of approach running and takeoff. *Track Technique, 89*, 2845.
4. Adrian Samungi. (1985). The training of world class women long jumpers. Track Technique, 92, 2922-2927.

Core Readings

Freeman, William H. (2001). Periodized training for jumpers. In *Peak When It Counts: Periodization for American track and field* (4th ed.). Mountain View, CA: Tafnews, 120-130.

Jacoby, Ed, & Bob Fraley. (1998). *The complete book of jumps*. Champaign, IL: Human Kinetics.

Jarver, Jess, ed. (2000). *The Jumps: Contemporary Theory, Technique and Training* (5th ed.). Mountain View, CA: Tafnews.

Tellez, Kyle, & Kathy James. Long jump. (2000). In *USA Track and Field coaching manual*. Champaign, IL: Human Kinetics, 141-157.

USA Track & Field Coaching Education Program. (2003). *Level II Curriculum: Jumps. USA Track & Field*. Invaluable; revised regularly.

Recommended Readings

Arampatzis, Adiamantios, & Gert-Peter Brüggemann. (1999). Mechanical energetic processes in long jump and their effect on jumping performance. *New Studies in Athletics, 14*(4), 37-44.

Balius, Xavier, Andreu Roig, Carles Turró, Josep Escoda & Juan Carlos Álvarez. (2000). Enhancing measurement acuity in the horizontal jumps: The DTL Project and the Rieti '99 experience. *New Studies in Athletics, 15*(2), 21-27.

Balius, Xavier, Andreu Randor Eckschmiedt & Attila Mecseki. (2000). Rieti's 2000 DTL report. *New Studies in Athletics, 15*(2), 29-32.

Bianco, Enrique, David Lease, Elio Locatelli, Yukio Muraki, Dan Pfaff, Efim Shuravetzky & Miguel Velez. (1996). NSA Round Table 31: Speed in the jumping events. *New Studies in Athletics, 11*(2-3), 9-19.

Bosco, Carmelo. (1991). Biomechanical observations of the long jump takeoff [abstract]. *Track Technique, 115*, 3682-3683.

Bradshaw, Elizabeth J., & Brad Aisbett. (2006). Visual guidance during competition performance and run-through training in long jumping. *Sports Biomechanics, 5*(1), 1-14.

Burnett, Angus. (Spring 2002). Relevance of jumping exercises to field event athletes [abstract]. *Track Coach, 159*, 5090.

Bussabarger, David. (Summer 2003). A comparison of the long jump and pole vault takeoff actions. *Track Coach, 164*, 5241-5242.

Dapena, Jesús. (Summer 2005). Steep takeoff angles near 45 degrees are not reasonable for the long jump. *Track Coach, 172*, 5481-5485.

Dickwach, Hartmut, Erich Drechsler & Bettina Perlt. (1993). The development of Heike Drechsler's jumping ability [abstract]. *Track Technique, 125*, 4002.

Freeman, Will, Bob Myers & Dan Pfaff. (1995). Factors influencing skill acquisition in the jumps. *Track Coach, 131*, 4176-4178, 4197.

Gaonkar, G. V. (Summer 2003). The development of the extension phase of the takeoff. *Track Coach, 164*, 5238-5240.

Hay, James. (1998). Biomechanical considerations about jumping training. *New Studies in Athletics, 13*(1), 90-91.

Hay, James G. (1988). The approach run in the long jump. *Track Technique, 105*, 3339-3342, 3362.

Hay, James G. (1994). The current status of research on the biomechanics of the long jump. *Track Technique, 128*, 4089-4093.

Hay, James G., John A. Miller & Ron W. Cantera. (1987). Biomechanics of elite long jumping. *Track Technique, 101*, 3229-3232.

Homenkova, L.S., ed. (1994). Training for jumping events. *Track and Field Quarterly Review, 94*(4), 44-52.

Hommel, Helmar. (1995). An interview with Heike and Erich Drechsler [abstract]. *Track Coach, 133*, 4255-4256.

Jaonkar, J. V. (Summer 2004). Development of the takeoff in horizontal jumps [abstract]. *Track Coach, 168*, 5379-5380.

Jeitner, Gerhard. (Fall 2001). A long-term training structure for jumping events [abstract]. *Track Coach, 157,* 5025-26.

Johnson, Carl. (1995). Strength training for jumpers and speed athletes. [abstract]. *Track Coach, 132*, 4225.

Kerin, David. (Summer 2002). Achieving strength gains specific to the demands of jumping events. *Track Coach, 160*, 5103-5110.

Koh, Timothy J., & James G. Hay. (1991). Active landings and performance in the long jump. *Track Technique, 118,* 3756-3758.

Koyama, Hiroyuki, Yuya Muraki & Michiyoshi Ae. (2005). Effects of an inclined board as a training tool on the take-off motion of the long jump. *Sports Biomechanics, 4*(2), 113-129.

Larkins, Clifford. (1989). The takeoff drill for the long jump. *Track Technique, 107,* 3415-3418, 3427.

LeBlanc, Steve. (Fall 2001). The role of active landings in the horizontal jumps. *Track Coach, 157*, 5019-5020.

Linthorne, Nick. (Spring 2005). The color of the plasticine indicator board in the horizontal jumps. *Track Coach, 171*, 5466-5468.

Locatelli, Elio. (1993). Sprinting speed as a basis of the men's long jump [abstract]. *New Studies in Athletics, 8*(3), 93-94.

Lohmann, Wolfgang. (1985). Principles of beginners' training in jumping events. *Track Technique, 91*, 2891-2892, 2899.

Mackenzie, Robert J. (Fall 2003). Determining the force the takeoff leg exerts in the long and high jumps. *Track Coach, 165*, 5265-5268.

Mackenzie, Robert J. (Spring 2007). Film measurement of takeoff forces in the jumps, including slowing effects. *Track Coach, 179*, 5717-5722, 5733.

Mackenzie, Robert J. (Summer 2003). What does the takeoff leg really do? *Track Coach, 164*, 5233-5237.

Mackenzie, Robert J. (Winter 2004). What is the optimum takeoff angle in the long jump? *Track Coach, 166*, 5292-5294.

Mackenzie, Robert J., Lindsay Leonard, Tara DeSilva & John Morgan. (Spring 2004). A simple way for long jumpers to achieve greater height in the takeoff. *Track Coach, 167*, 5329-5335; Schexnayder, Boo. (Fall 2004). A critique. *Track Coach, 169,* 5413; Mackenzie, Robert. (Winter 2005). Mackenzie replies to Schexnayder. *Track Coach, 170,* 5439-5441, 5445.

Mackenzie, Robert. (Winter 2005). Mackenzie replies to Schexnayder. *Track Coach, 170,* 5439-5441, 5445.

Mackenzie, Robert J., et al. (Winter 2006). A reexamination of the optimum takeoff angle in the long jump. *Track Coach, 174*, 5561-5569.

Madella, Alberto. (1996). Speed in the horizontal jumps: Muscular properties or cognitive treatment? *New Studies in Athletics, 11*(2-3), 127-132.

Miladinov, Ognyan. (2006). New aspects in perfecting the long jump technique. *New Studies in Athletics, 21*(4), 4-25.

Moura, Nelio Alfano, & Tania Fernandes de Paula Moura. (2001). Training principles for jumpers: Implications for the special strength development. *New Studies in Athletics, 16*(4), 51-61.

Müller, Harald, & Gert-Peter Brüggemann. LJ. In Harald Müller & Helmar Hommel, eds., Biomechanical Research Project at the VIth World Championships in Athletics, Athens 1997: Preliminary Report. *New Studies in Athletics, 12*(2-3), 56-59.

Muraki, Yuya, Michiyoshi Ae, Toshiharu Yokozawa & Hiroyuki Koyama. (2005). Mechanical properties of the take-off leg as a support mechanism in the long jump. *Sports Biomechanics, 4*(1), 1-16.

Myers, Bob. (1990). Improving the penultimate step in the jumping events. *Track Technique, 112*, 3583-3584.

Myers, Bob. (1991). Restoration for jumpers. *Athletics Science Bulletin, 3*(1), 1-6.

Myers, Bob. (1989). Training for the jumps and multi-events. *Track Technique, 108*, 3449-3452; *109*, 3492-3493 [corrections].

Nielsen, Dave. (1996). Efficiency rating for the long jump. *Track Coach, 136*, 4331-4333.

Polosin, Andrei. (Summer 2001). Runup velocity in the long jump [abstract]. *Track Coach, 156*, 4995.

Popitshev, M. (1994). The development of the jumping capacity of young athletes. [abstract]. *Track Technique, 127*, 4066-4067.

Popov, Vladimir. (1996). An optimal [horizontal jumps] approach run. [abstract]. *Track Coach, 135*, 4322.

Popow, Grigorij I., & Wladimir I. Ljach. (2002). Long and triple jump training on pneumatic run-up surfaces. Trans. Jürgen Schiffer. *New Studies in Athletics, 17*(3/4), 55-60.

Rosenthal, John. (1988). Igor Ter-Ovanesyan on the long jump. *Track Technique, 102*, 3263-3264.

Roundtable: Horizontal jumps. (Winter 2004). *Track Coach, 166*, 5305-5309. Participants: Craig Hilliard, Dan Pfaff, John Boas & Gary Bourne.

Schiffer, Jürgen. (2005). Selected and annotated bibliography 69-70: Long jump. *New Studies in Athletics, 20*(1), 69-114; 20(2), 51-96.

Schulek, Agoston. (Summer 2004). Long jump training with supramaximal speeds [abstract]. *Track Coach, 168*, 5381.

Schutze, Heinz. (1993). Development of jumping power. [abstract]. *Track Technique, 122*, 3904.

Slepica, James. (1991). Training the young athlete for the horizontal jumps. *New Studies in Athletics, 6*(3), 43-48.

Smith, Philip Graham, & Adrian Lees. (Spring 2003). "Balance" in horizontal jumps [abstract]. *Track Coach, 163*, 5221.

Tidow, Gunter. (1990). Models for teaching techniques and assessing movements in athletics: The long jump. *Track Technique, 113*, 3607-3615, 3620.

Woodruff, Catherine. (Winter 2003). Prevention of hamstring injuries in the long jump. *Track Coach, 162*, 5168-5170, 5187.

17

The Triple Jump

Bowerman's Best

50′ 4 1/2″	Marc Hadenfield	1973

A prospective triple jumper needs several natural qualities to be successful. Speed and leg strength are essential. The speed is there, or it is not. The leg strength can be developed. Perhaps the most important factor in successful triple jumping is balance. Finally, rhythm is necessary because the triple jump is, as its title implies, a series of jumps rather than a single effort.

Analysis of the Triple Jump

The triple jump has been called the "hop, step, and jump." The first part of the action is called the "hop," because the jumper lands on the takeoff foot. This action of taking off and landing on the same foot requires considerable leg strength if the jumper is to continue through the other two phases of the jump. From the landing at the end of the hopping phase, the jumper moves into a step, pushing from the takeoff foot, and landing on the opposite foot, preparatory to the last phase of the action: the jump. The jump is simply a normal long jumping action. If the triple jumper takes off on the left foot (placing that foot on the board when beginning the jumping sequence), the step pattern will be takeoff (left foot) to land (left foot) at completion of hop, to land (right foot) at completion of step, to land (both feet) in pit at completion of jumping phase.

The approach run for the triple jump is similar to the run for the long jump, with the primary exceptions that it is not generally as long as the long jump run, and the two-count rise is not used. The triple jumper is primarily seeking controlled speed at the point of the takeoff.

At the takeoff, the jumper does not want to get much height off the board. The action off the board is very similar to the normal sprinting action. The jumper should try to hit the board with the hips a bit more forward than in the normal sprinting position. The jumper wishes to conserve as much horizontal momentum as possible. This momentum at the time of takeoff must last through all three takeoffs. The jumper must hit the board both balanced and relaxed. Balance at this point is very important because any imbalance at the takeoff would result in a loss of power and control later in the jump.

On each landing, the landing foot should be pulled back quickly just before it strikes the ground. This maneuver allows the jumper to preserve momentum through the landing and the later takeoff actions. If the foot is not pulled backward, it acts as a brake when the jumper lands, lessening potential momentum for the next jumping phase.

The coach and the jumper should listen to the footstep rhythm of the jump as it is performed. It should be regular for all three portions of the jump. If the middle portion sounds too quick, the stepping phase is probably not performed properly.

The step is usually the hardest part of the jump to learn and develop properly. The jumper must try to develop strength equally in each leg. He will generally use the same leg for taking off in both the long jump and the triple jump.

Jumpers use the double-arm swing, a coordinated swinging action of both arms in the same direction and at the same time in certain portions of the jump. This move consists of a forward and upward swing of both arms at the time of the takeoff of each phase of the jump. It is used by expert jumpers to give additional impetus to each phase of the jump. It requires much practice, but if mastered, it benefits the jumper considerably. The trend, however, is now toward a single-arm swing on the hop, then double-arm swings, as in Jonathan Edwards' 60' 1/4"/18.29m world record.[1]

Triple Jump Training Theory

Just as in the long jump, in the triple jump the operative word is *speed*. The European approach is to find good sprinters and train them as long and triple jumpers.[2] Most important is the takeoff speed, the acceleration across the takeoff board; next is the rhythm of the jump, distributing a fairly even part of the jump to each of the three phases. Coaches and researchers are not in complete agreement on the ideal relative distribution of the phases.

However, all jumping schools hold similar views on the critical role of the step phase. They suggest a step equal to 28 to 30 percent of the total jump. This step focuses the evaluation of the balance of the jumper's style. The step is the most useful part of the jump for beginners to try to improve after they master the approach run. The hop should be the training focus after the step. The reasons for this sequence are:

- The beginner's step is usually far short of optimal, but it can greatly improve the overall distance.
- When beginners focus on improving the hop, they tend to shorten their step until they are proficient.[3]

Technique Training

The basic factors in maintaining horizontal velocity through the three phases of the jump include the following:

- A proper ratio between the hop, step, and jump phases
- A low (flat) takeoff angle for the hop and the step
- Using the arms (to maintain velocity and aid balance)
- An erect body posture (and head up) throughout
- Pawing action of the contact leg (landing ahead of the center of gravity and pulling through)[4]

The technical complexity of the triple jump, along with the extreme stretching and landing stresses, make it an event with high injury risk. The high injury rate may result from poor preparation in the first several years of jumping.[5] The following training factors help the jumper decrease the likelihood of injury:

- Long-term planning is essential.
- Emphasize technique development during the early training years.
- Emphasize quality before quantity.
- Learn correct lifting techniques early (age 15).
- Use stretching exercises to develop muscle elasticity.
- Always jump with an active landing action.
- Adjust the length of the approach to the level of technique (shorter approach for poorer technique).
- Execute large portions of the technique training with jumps that are near competition level (with high horizontal speed).
- Never do technique training when fatigued.

The triple jump is a very complex event, so it has many technical aspects to master. Table 17-1 summarizes the major faults found, along with their causes and how they can be corrected.

Triple Jump Training

One competitive suggestion for teachers and coaches is: do not use an athlete in both the long jump and the triple jump. Among the several reasons for this suggestion, the primary is that both events are very hard on the athlete's legs.

Triple Jump Technique Faults and Causes		
Fault	*Causes*	*Corrections*
Inconsistent steps	Overstriding Looking at the takeoff board Variation in first 3-4 steps (emotion or fatigue)	Emphasize high knee action with a stride length decrease and a stride rate increase Focus the eyes above the head and past the board Use run-throughs as part of the warm-up on technique days (at least twice a week)
Hop too high	Flexing the knee too much two steps out Knee drive and arm blocking is past 90 degrees Arm blocking is past shoulder level Transition problems of using same takeoff foot for long and triple jumps (need different actions)	Run off the board (forward, not up) Exaggerate the arm and knee blocking at 90 degrees (for the knee) and the shoulder level (for arms)
Over-rotating	Too much forward lean at takeoff (places center of gravity ahead of base of support)	Place takeoff foot in front of hips, with upper body kept upright
Lateral deviation	Dropping the shoulder below the level position Driving the knee and arms across the body's center line, instead of straight ahead	Keep the shoulders as level as possible Move the arms and knee straight forward and backward
Poor timing of arms to leg	Coordination problems. Learn how to use both arms with a jumping motion	Use repeated bounding and short approach drills to imitate the whole motion
Short step	Hop is too high Hop is too long	Emphasize a controlled hop (about 35% of total jump) Try not to go very high. The jarring effect of a high hop makes recovery difficult
Inability to take off on step or jump	Landing from a hop or step that is too high Landing with the center of gravity too far forward Not using the arms and free leg forcefully and through the full range of motion Landing on the ball of the foot	Emphasize a flat trajectory Use the arms and legs together to develop maximum forward momentum Land heel first or mid-foot, followed by a pawing action Land with the foot comfortably in front, not directly below the hips
Poor trail leg position	Heel never comes close to the hip Leg angle is less than 90 degrees or is not parallel to the ground when making contact with the ground	Hold the leg parallel to the ground until contact (allows greater range of motion to generate more knee drive to carry to the next phase)
Decelerating from phase to phase	Too high a hop Too long a hop Lateral deviation No control of speed at takeoff	Emphasize going out, not up Keep the shoulders level through all phases Practice approaches, with the hop only into the pit or other soft surface, to learn how long a hop can be handled
Premature landing	Not keeping the head toward the knees long enough Not extending the legs or keeping them extended	Hold the leg extended, with the head close to the knee position until the heels land

Table 17-1. Triple jump technique faults and causes

The risk of injury with much jumping is great with either event. If the jumper were to compete in both events, the risk of injury would be more than doubled—as are the coach's chances of losing the athlete.

Also, an athlete tends to be better in one or the other of the two events. Only at a low level of accomplishment would he be likely to show equal levels of achievement in the events. Few international-class jumpers in either event have been better than national class (which is significantly different) in the other. Generally, the long jumpers have better speed, while the triple jumpers have better leg strength, which they can utilize despite their lesser natural speed.

The teacher should watch the prospects, looking for rhythm and balance. Hurdlers are often good prospects because they usually have those traits. Rhythm can be developed by jumping first from standing jumps, then going to jumps taken from a short run of three steps or so. While jumping, the athletes should always wear heel cups or pads for their protection.

Training Drills

Several types of drills are used as vital parts of triple jump training. Three types of drills are:

- Rhythm drills
- Power bounding
- Box drills

The rhythm drills use a five- to seven-step approach, followed by 10 consecutive jumps, with any combination of landings (i.e., any combination of hops and steps). The primary object of these drills is to work on the rhythm of the hopping and the stepping. The drills are judged by their sound pattern and the distance covered in the 10-step sequence. As athletes improve, the distance they cover increases, while the time needed for the series decreases. Covering 120 feet in 5.5 seconds indicates that a male athlete would be a good triple jumper.

The power-bounding drills can focus on either height or distance. Several variations of the drill can be used. The athlete does intervals of 50 to 100 meters on soft surfaces, hopping on either one leg or the other, working on either the height or the length of the hops. This exercise is performed six to eight times, as fast as the athlete can go. The jumper might also work on a hop-step drill. In this drill, the jumper also covers 50 to 100 meters, except that he alternates the hopping (H) and stepping (S) (e.g., H-S-H-S-H-S), working on the double-arm action and trying to develop a more powerful lead leg.

The box drills are done with boxes of various heights, with 18 inches the most common height. Boxes 18 inches high by 20 inches across in the jumping direction by 30 inches long can be used. Usually, three to five boxes are used. They are spaced at intervals along the runway or on the grass. At first, the boxes are only a few yards apart. As the jumpers become more adept, the boxes can be moved farther apart.

One drill is to go over the boxes, stepping on the ground with the takeoff leg and stepping on the boxes with the opposite foot. The purpose of the drill is to get the jumper in the habit of raising the stepping leg, which is necessary to get onto the box and also to get a long step in the actual jump. Another drill (with the boxes farther apart) is to work on both hopping and stepping. The athlete hops between the boxes, then steps over a box, hops close to the next box, steps over again, and so forth. If the athlete takes off from the left leg (LL), the pattern would be LL, box, RL, box, LL, box, RL, and so forth, always with a hop over and a step between. Because of the boxes, the jumper learns to get the trail leg up fast. In performing the step, the jumper needs to learn to get both legs up, with one leg forward and the other to the rear.

Rope jumping is also a good leg-strengthening exercise. The athlete jumps on one leg for 30 seconds, then rests for 15 seconds or so, then jumps for an equal period of time on the other leg. During the fall training, jumpers generally work on drills three days a week, with box drills on Mondays and Fridays and rhythm drills on Wednesdays. Fall is a good time for building the athlete's strength and sense of the general movements, leaving the period immediately before the season for more specific technique work.

A warm-up routine is used for the triple jump, as for the other events. After jogging and flexibility exercises, followed by the high-knee (slow), fast-leg drill, the jumper works on power bounding. Next, the athlete performs several series of three triple jumps taken with approaches of varying lengths. The first three jumps are taken from a stand. The next three jumps are taken with a 30-foot approach run. Three jumps are taken from a 60-foot approach, and then three jumps are taken with a 90-foot approach. Actually, this amount is quite enough jumping for a triple jumper, and it may even be more than he should do, except on rare occasions. The other workouts consist of drills and selected sprinters' exercises. The coach should be careful not to overwork triple jumpers, exposing them to needless injury. The most important training principle is one that no triple jumper should forget: "Triple jumpers are made."

Triple Jump Training Schedules

TRIPLE JUMP SCHEDULE NAME ____________________ DATE ____________

1. A. Jogging and flexibility; high knee, fast leg
   B. Hendricks Park C. Golf course D. Steps
2. Fartlek A. Varied pace B. Slow, steady pace
3. Weights and jogging
4. Bounding drills
   A. Height) LR for
   B. Distance) 50-100m
   6-8 repeats as fast as you can control
   C. Hop-step drill, double arm action, powerful
   lead leg (50-100 meters) 6-8 repeats
5. Rhythm drills: 5-7-9 step approach
   A. S - S - S - J
   B. H - H - H - S - J
   C. LL RR LLL R LL - 10 step sequence for time and
   distance - 124'/38m is excellent
6. Box drills
   R R R R R
   A. L | | L | | L | | L | | L | |
   step leg UP to get on box

   B. L |‾| R |‾| L |‾| R |‾| L |‾| R
   L R L R
   C. L | | R | | L | | R | | L
   R R L
   D. R | | L | | R | | PIT 13' between boxes
   Reverse RRLRRL to LLRLLR
   E. R | | R-L | | R-R | | L-R | | R PIT
   10' between boxes
   Reverse RRLRRLRR to LLRLLRLL
   L L
   F. R-R | | R-L | | R-R | | PIT
   16' to 1st box, 10' between boxes
   L L L
   G. R | | R | | R | | PIT
   Begin 8' between boxes, try for 20'
   R L L
   H. R | | R | | L | | PIT
7. TEAM MEETING
8. Special A. Sauna B. Swim C. Film D.
9. Short approach A. Standing
   B. 3-step C. 5-step
   D. 7-step
   E. 9-step F. 11-step
10. Full approach A. Meet B. Trial
    C. Simulation D. Control test
    (1) Check marks (2) Jumping
12. With Coach A. B.
14. A. Wind sprints (1) Straight (2) Curve
    B. Hurdle drill: 3 LH, 7-9m apart
    E. Hill work
    F. Rope jumping: 30 secs., 15 secs. rest
15. Intervals A. 100 B. 150 C.200 D. 250
    E. 300 F. 400 G. 600-400-300-200-100
20. Work on second event
21. A. Videotape B. Film C. Pictures
    (1) Record performance (2) Study
30. Experimental work

Date	Distance	3/4 pace	Date Pace	Goal Pace

M	
T	
W	
T	
F	
S	
S	
M	
T	
W	
T	
F	
S	
S	
M	
T	
W	
T	
F	
S	
S	
M	
T	
W	
T	
F	
S	
S	

Sheet 17-1. Revised triple jump training schedule sheet

Triple Jump NAME DATE September/October

1. Warm-up routine to include A. Jogging-flexibility B. Easy high knee, fast leg
2. Fartlek A. Holmer B. Lydiard
3. Weight routine
4. Bounding drills A. Height, B. Distance } L.R (50-100 yds.) 6-8 repeats fast as you can control
   C. Hop-step drill—double arm action—powerful lead leg (50-100 yds.) 6-8 repeats
5. Rhythm drills: 5-7-9-step approach
   A. S - S - S - J
   B. H - H - H - S - J
   C. LL RR LLL R LL—10 successive—for time and distance—124 ft.—excellent! D.
6. Box drills
   A. L □ L □ L □ L □ L □—step leg up to get on box (R R R R R)
   B. L □ R □ L □ R □ L □ R
   C. L □ R □ L □ R □ L (L R L R)
   D. R □ L □ R □ Pit (R R L) |4m|
   Reverse RRLRRL to LLRLLR
   E. R □ R—L □ R—R □ L—R □ R Pit | 10 ft. |
   Reverse RRLRRLRR to LLRLLRLL
   F. R—R □ R—L □ R—R □ Pit (L L) | 16 ft. | | 10 ft. |
   G. R □ R □ R □ Pit (L L L) 8 ft. work for 20 ft.
   H. R □ R □ L □ Pit (R L L)
7. Squad meeting
8. Special A. Sauna B. Swim C. Film D.
9. Short approach triple jump A. Standing B. 3-step C. 5-step D. 7-step E. 9-step F. 11-step
10. Full approach A. Check marks B. Jumping C. Competition or trial
11. Rope jumping: 30 sec., 15 sec. rest
12. Hurdle X drill
14. Intervals A. 110 B. 165 C. 220 D. 300 E. 330 F. 440 G. 660-440-330-220-110
15. Hill work A. Laurelwood B. Emerald St. C. Stadium steps

Day	Workout
M	1AB-14C (6-8x)
T	1AB-3-2A
W	15A-7
T	1AB-3-2B
F	1AB-14G-14A (4x)
S	1AB-3-2A
S	
M	1AB-14E-14C-14A (3x 3x 3x)
T	1AB-3-2A
W	15A
T	1AB-3-2A
F	1AB-14D-14A-2B (4x 4x)
S	1AB-3-2A
S	
M	1AB-4AB-14G-14A (6x)
T	1AB-3-2B
W	1AB-12-15A
T	1AB-3-2A
F	1AB-4ABC-5ABC-14D-14A (3x 4x 4x)
S	1AB-3-2B
S	
M	1AB-4ABC-5A-5B-5C-14G-14A (5x 4x 3x 3x)
T	1AB-3-2B
W	1AB-12-15A-8C
T	1AB-3-2A
F	1AB-4ABC-5A-5B-5C-14F-14E-14C-14B (4x 3x 3x 2x 3x 4x)
S	1AB-3-2A
S	

Sheet 17-2. Triple jump training schedule

Triple Jump NAME DATE November

1. Warm-up routine to include A. Jogging-flexibility
   B. Easy high knee, fast leg
2. Fartlek A. Holmer B. Lydiard
3. Weight routine
4. Bounding drills A. Height } L.R (50-100 yds.)
   B. Distance }
   6-8 repeats fast as you can control
   C. Hop-step drill—double arm action—powerful lead leg (50-100 yds.) 6-8 repeats
5. Rhythm drills: 5-7-9-step approach
   A. S - S - S - J
   B. H - H - H - S - J
   C. LL RR LLL R LL—10 successive—for time and distance—124 ft.—excellent! D.
6. Box drills
   A. L □ L □ L □ L □ L □—step leg up to get on box (R R R R R)
   B. L □ R □ L □ R □ L □ R
   C. L □ R □ L □ R □ L (L R L R)
   D. R □ L □ R □ Pit (R R L; 4m)
   Reverse RRLRRL to LLRLLR
   E. R □ R—L □ R—R □ L—R □ R Pit (10 ft.)
   Reverse RRLRRLRR to LLRLLRLL
   F. R—R □ R—L □ R—R □ Pit (L L; 16 ft. | 10 ft.)
   G. R □ R □ R □ Pit (L L L; 8 ft. work for 20 ft.)
   H. R □ R □ L □ Pit (R L L)
7. Squad meeting
8. Special A. Sauna B. Swim C. Film D.
9. Short approach triple jump A. Standing B. 3-step
   C. 5-step D. 7-step E. 9-step F. 11-step
10. Full approach A. Check marks B. Jumping
    C. Competition or Trial
11. Rope jumping: 30 sec., 15 sec. rest
12. Hurdle X drill
14. Intervals A. 110 B. 165 C. 220 D. 300
    E. 330 F. 440 G. 660-440-330-220-110
15. Hill work A. Laurelwood B. Emerald St.
    C. Stadium steps

Day	Schedule
M	1AB-4AB-5ABC-14C-14G (3x 14C, 4x 14G)
T	1A-3
W	1A-12-15A
T	1A-3
F	1AB-4ABC-6ABCD-14E-14C-14A (3x 6ABCD, 2x 14E, 2x 14C, 4x 14A)
S	1A-3-2A
S	
M	1AB-4ABC-5ABC-14C (3x 5ABC, 6x 14C)
T	1AB-3-2A
W	15A-8C
T	1AB-3-2A
F	1AB-4ABC-6BCDE-14D-14G (3x 6BCDE, 3x 14D)
S	1A-3-2A
S	
M	1AB-4ABC-5AB-5C-14F-14E-14C-14A (5x 5AB, 3x 5C, 2x 14F, 3x 14E, 4x 14C)
T	1A-3-2B
W	1AB-15A-7
T	1A-3-2B
F	1AB-4ABC-9ABC-14G (3x 9ABC)
S	1A-3-2B
S	
M	1AB-4ABC-5AB-5C-14D-14B-14A (5x 5AB, 3x 5C, 3x 14D, 3x 14B, 3x 14A)
T	1A-3-2B-8C
W	1AB-12-15A
T	1A-3-2B
F	1AB-4ABC-6CDEF-14E-14C-14A (3x 6CDEF, 3x 14E, 3x 14C, 3x 14A)
S	1AB-3-2B
S	

Sheet 17-3. Triple jump training schedule

Triple Jump NAME DATE December

1. Warm-up routine to include A. Jogging-flexibility
   B. Easy high knee, fast leg
2. Fartlek A. Holmer B. Lydiard
3. Weight routine
4. Bounding drills A. Height / B. Distance } L.R (50-100 yds.)
   6-8 repeats fast as you can control
   C. Hop-step drill—double arm action—powerful lead leg (50-100 yds.) 6-8 repeats
5. Rhythm drills: 5-7-9-step approach
   A. S - S - S - J
   B. H - H - H - S - J
   C. LL RR LLL R LL—10 successive—for time and distance—124 ft.—excellent! D.
6. Box drills
   A. L □ L □ L □ L □ L □—step leg up to get on box (R R R R R)
   B. L □ R □ L □ R □ L □ R
   C. L □ R □ L □ R □ L (L R L R)
   D. R □ L □ R □ Pit (R R L) |4m|
   Reverse RRLRRL to LLRLLR
   E. R □ R—L □ R—R □ L—R □ R Pit |10 ft.|
   Reverse RRLRRLRR to LLRLLRLL
   F. R—R □ R—L □ R—R □ Pit (L L) |16 ft.| |10 ft.|
   G. R □ R □ R □ Pit (L L L) 8 ft. work for 20 ft.
   H. R □ R □ L □ Pit (R L L)
7. Squad meeting
8. Special A. Sauna B. Swim C. Film D.
9. Short approach triple jump A. Standing B. 3-step
   C. 5-step D. 7-step E. 9-step F. 11-step
10. Full approach A. Check marks B. Jumping
    C. Competition or Trial
11. Rope jumping: 30 sec., 15 sec. rest
12. Hurdle X drill
14. Intervals A. 110 B. 165 C. 220 D. 300
    E. 330 F. 440 G. 660-440-330-220-110
15. Hill work A. Laurelwood B. Emerald St.
    C. Stadium steps

Day	Schedule
M	1AB-4ABC-5AB (5x)-5C (3x)-14G-14A (4x)
T	1AB-3-2A
W	1AB-12-15B
T	1AB-3-2A
F	1AB-4ABC-6DEFG (4x)-14D (5x)
S	1AB-3-2A
S	
M	1AB-4ABC-5A (6x)-5B (5x)-5C (4x)-14G-14A (4x)
T	1AB-3-2A
W	1AB-12-15B (3-5x)
T	1AB-3-2A
F	1AB-2B
S	1AB-4AC-9BCD (2x)-14E (2x)-14C (2x)-14A (2x)
S	
M	
T	
W	
T	
F	
S	
S	
M	
T	
W	
T	
F	
S	
S	

Sheet 17-4. Triple jump training schedule

Triple Jump NAME DATE January

1. Warm-up routine to include A. Jogging-flexibility
   B. Easy high knee, fast leg
2. Fartlek A. Holmer B. Lydiard
3. Weight routine
4. Bounding drills A. Height / B. Distance } L.R (50-100 yds.)
   6-8 repeats fast as you can control
   C. Hop-step drill—double arm action—powerful lead leg (50-100 yds.) 6-8 repeats
5. Rhythm drills: 5-7-9-step approach
   A. S - S - S - J
   B. H - H - H - S - J
   C. LL RR LLL R LL—10 successive—for time and distance—124 ft.—excellent!
   D.
6. Box drills
   A. L □ L □ L □ L □ L □—step leg up to get on box (R R R R R)
   B. L □ R □ L □ R □ L □ R
   C. L □ R □ L □ R □ L (L R L R)
   D. R □ L □ R □ Pit (R R L) | 4m |
   Reverse RRLRRL to LLRLLR
   E. R □ R—L □ R—R □ L—R □ R Pit | 10 ft. |
   Reverse RRLRRLRR to LLRLLRLL
   F. R—R □ R—L □ R—R □ Pit (L L) | 16 ft. | | 10 ft. |
   G. R □ R □ R □ Pit (L L L) 8 ft. work for 20 ft.
   H. R □ R □ L □ Pit (R L L)
7. Squad meeting
8. Special A. Sauna B. Swim C. Film D.
9. Short approach triple jump A. Standing B. 3-step
   C. 5-step D. 7-step E. 9-step F. 11-step
10. Full approach A. Check marks B. Jumping
    C. Competition or Trial
11. Rope jumping: 30 sec., 15 sec. rest
12. Hurdle X drill
14. Intervals A. 110 B. 165 C. 220 D. 300
    E. 330 F. 440 G. 660-440-330-220-110
15. Hill work A. Laurelwood B. Emerald St.
    C. Stadium steps

Day	Workout
M	1AB – 4AB – 14C (6X)
T	1AB – 3 – 2B
W	1AB – 12 – 15B – 7
T	1AB – 3 – 2A
F	1AB – 4BC – 6EFGH (3X) – 14D (4X) – 14A (4X)
S	1AB – 3 – 2B
S	
M	1AB – 4ABC (4X) – 5A (3X) – 5B (3X) – 5C – 14G – 14A (4X)
T	1AB – 3 – 2B
W	1AB – 10A – 15B
T	1AB – 3 – 2A
F	1AB – 4ABC – 5AB (3X) – 9ABC (3X) – 14E – 14C (2X) – 14A (3X)
S	1AB – 3 – 2B
S	
M	1AB – 4ABC – 10A – 5ABC (4X) – 14G – 14A (3X)
T	1AB – 3 – 2B
W	1AB – 12 – 10A – 15B
T	1AB – 3 – 2A
F	1AB – 4ABC – 10A – 6FGH (4X) – 14F – 14E (2X) – 14C (3X) – 14A (3X)
S	1AB – 3 – 2B
S	
M	1AB – 4AB – 10A – 5AB (3X) – 9CDE (3X) – 14G – 14A (4X)
T	1AB – 3 – 2B
W	1AB – 10A – 15B – 7
T	1AB – 3 – 2A
F	1AB –
S	1AB – 10C
S	

Sheet 17-5. Triple jump training schedule

Triple Jump NAME DATE *February*

1. Warm-up routine to include A. Jogging-flexibility
   B. Easy high knee, fast leg
2. Fartlek A. Holmer B. Lydiard
3. Weight routine
4. Bounding drills A. Height } L.R (50-100 yds.)
   B. Distance }
   6-8 repeats fast as you can control
   C. Hop-step drill—double arm action—powerful lead leg (50-100 yds.) 6-8 repeats
5. Rhythm drills: 5-7-9-step approach
   A. S - S - S - J
   B. H - H - H - S - J
   C. LL RR LLL R LL—10 successive—for time and distance—124 ft.—excellent! D.
6. Box drills
   A. L □ L □ L □ L □ L □—step leg up to get on box (R R R R R)
   B. L □ R □ L □ R □ L □ R
   C. L □ R □ L □ R □ L (L R L R)
   D. R □ L □ R □ Pit (R R L) | 4m |
   Reverse RRLRRL to LLRLLR
   E. R □ R—L □ R—R □ L—R □ R Pit | 10 ft. |
   Reverse RRLRRLRR to LLRLLRLL
   F. R—R □ R—L □ R—R □ Pit (L L) | 16 ft. | | 10 ft. |
   G. R □ R □ R □ Pit (L L L) 8 ft. work for 20 ft.
   H. R □ R □ L □ Pit (R L L)
7. Squad meeting
8. Special A. Sauna B. Swim C. Film D.
9. Short approach triple jump A. Standing B. 3-step
   C. 5-step D. 7-step E. 9-step F. 11-step
10. Full approach A. Check marks B. Jumping
    C. Competition or Trial
11. Rope jumping: 30 sec., 15 sec. rest
12. Hurdle X drill
14. Intervals A. 110 B. 165 C. 220 D. 300
    E. 330 F. 440 G. 660-440-330-220-110
15. Hill work A. Laurelwood B. Emerald St.
    C. Stadium steps

Day	Schedule
M	1AB-4ABC-5ABC-14G-14A (4x)
T	1AB-3-2B
W	1AB-12-15B
T	1AB-3-2A
F	1AB-4ABC-6DEFG-14D-14A (4x, 3x, 3x)
S	1AB-3-2B
S	
M	1AB-4ABC-5ABC-14G-14A (4x)
T	1AB-3-2B
W	1AB-10A-15B-7
T	1AB-3-2A
F	1AB-10A-14C (6-8x)
S	1AB-4AC-9DEF-2B (3x)
S	
M	1AB-4ABC-5ABC-14D (3-5x)
T	1AB-3-2B
W	1AB-10A-15B
T	1AB-3-2A
F	1AB-4AC-6EFGH-14G-14A (4x, 4x)
S	1AB-3-2B
S	
M	1AB-4AC-10A-5ABC-9CDE-14C-14A (3x, 4x, 4x)
T	1AB-3-2B
W	1AB-10A-15B
T	1AB-3-2A
F	1AB-10A-14B-14A (2x, 3x)
S	1AB-4AC-10A-9EF-10B-14G (2x, 2x)
S	

Sheet 17-6. Triple jump training schedule

Triple Jump NAME DATE March

1. Warm-up routine to include A. Jogging-flexibility
   B. Easy high knee, fast leg
2. Fartlek A. Holmer B. Lydiard
3. Weight routine
4. Bounding drills A. Height, B. Distance } L.R (50-100 yds.)
   6-8 repeats fast as you can control
   C. Hop-step drill—double arm action—powerful lead leg (50-100 yds.) 6-8 repeats
5. Rhythm drills: 5-7-9-step approach
   A. S - S - S - J
   B. H - H - H - S - J
   C. LL RR LLL R LL—10 successive—for time and distance—124 ft.—excellent! D.
6. Box drills
   A. L □ L □ L □ L □ L □—step leg up to get on box (R R R R R)
   B. L □ R □ L □ R □ L □ R
   C. L □ R □ L □ R □ L (L R L R)
   D. R □ L □ R □ L Pit (R R) | 4m |
   Reverse RRLRRL to LLRLLR
   E. R □ R—L □ R—R □ L—R □ R Pit | 10 ft. |
   Reverse RRLRRLRR to LLRLLRLL
   F. R—R □ R—L □ R—R □ L Pit | 16 ft. | | 10 ft. |
   G. R □ R □ R □ L Pit 8 ft. work for 20 ft.
   H. R □ R □ L □ L Pit
7. Squad meeting
8. Special A. Sauna B. Swim C. Film D.
9. Short approach triple jump A. Standing B. 3-step
   C. 5-step D. 7-step E. 9-step F. 11-step
10. Full approach A. Check marks B. Jumping
    C. Competition or Trial
11. Rope jumping: 30 sec., 15 sec. rest
12. Hurdle X drill
14. Intervals A. 110 B. 165 C. 220 D. 300
    E. 330 F. 440 G. 660-440-330-220-110
15. Hill work A. Laurelwood B. Emerald St.
    C. Stadium steps

Day	Workout
M	1AB-4AC-10A-5ABC-14G-14A (3x)
T	1AB-3-2B
W	1AB-10A-15B-7
T	1AB-3-2A
F	1AB-4AC-6EFGH (4x)-14D (3x)-14A (3x)
S	1AB-3-2B
S	
M	1AB-4AC-10A-5ABC-14G-14A (3x)
T	1AB-3-2B-8C
W	1AB-10A-15B
T	1AB-3-2A
F	1AB-4AC-9DEF (3x)-14D (3x)-14A (3x)
S	1AB-3-14C (3x)-14A (3x)
S	
M	1AB-4AC-10A-5ABC-14G-14A (4x)
T	1AB-3-2B
W	1AB-4AC-10A-9CDE (2x)-14C (3x)-14B (3x)-14A (3x)-7
T	1AB-3-2A-8C
F	1AB-
S	1AB-10C
S	
M	1AB-4AC-10A-5AB-14G-14A (3x)
T	1AB-10A-3-2B
W	1AB-10A-9CDE (2x)-14D (2x)-14C (2x)-14A (3x)-7
T	1AB-10A-3(light)-2A-8C
F	1AB-
S	1AB-10C
S	

Sheet 17-7. Triple jump training schedule

Triple Jump NAME DATE April

1. Warm-up routine to include A. Jogging-flexibility
   B. Easy high knee, fast leg
2. Fartlek A. Holmer B. Lydiard
3. Weight routine
4. Bounding drills A. Height / B. Distance } L.R (50-100 yds.)
   6-8 repeats fast as you can control
   C. Hop-step drill—double arm action—powerful lead leg (50-100 yds.) 6-8 repeats
5. Rhythm drills: 5-7-9-step approach
   A. S - S - S - J
   B. H - H - H - S - J
   C. LL RR LLL R LL—10 successive—for time and distance—124 ft.—excellent! D.
6. Box drills
   A. L □ L □ L □ L □ L □—step leg up to get on box (R R R R R)
   B. L □ R □ L □ R □ L □ R
   C. L □ R □ L □ R □ L (L R L R)
   D. R □ L □ R □ Pit (R R L) | 4m |
   Reverse RRLRRL to LLRLLR
   E. R □ R—L □ R—R □ L—R □ R Pit | 10 ft. |
   Reverse RRLRRLRR to LLRLLRLL
   F. R—R □ R—L □ R—R □ Pit (L L) | 16 ft. | | 10 ft. |
   G. R □ R □ R □ Pit (L L L) 8 ft. work for 20 ft.
   H. R □ R □ L □ Pit (R L L)
7. Squad meeting
8. Special A. Sauna B. Swim C. Film D.
9. Short approach triple jump A. Standing B. 3-step
   C. 5-step D. 7-step E. 9-step F. 11-step
10. Full approach A. Check marks B. Jumping
    C. Competition or Trial
11. Rope jumping: 30 sec., 15 sec. rest
12. Hurdle X drill
14. Intervals A. 110 B. 165 C. 220 D. 300
    E. 330 F. 440 G. 660-440-330-220-110
15. Hill work A. Laurelwood B. Emerald St.
    C. Stadium steps

Day	Schedule
M	3x 2x 1AB-4AC-10A-6EFG-14G-14B-7
T	1AB-10A-3-2B-8C
W	2x 2x 3x 1AB-10A-9CDE-14D-14C-14B
T	1AB-10A-3 (light)-2A-8C
F	1AB
S	1AB-10C-7
S	
M	1AB-4AC-10A-5ABC-14G-7
T	1AB-10A-3-2B-8C
W	2x 3x 4x 1AB-4AC-10A-5ABC-14D-14C-14A
T	1AB-10A-3 (light)-2A
F	1AB
S	1AB-10C-7
S	6x 1AB-14A
M	3x 1AB-4AC-10A-6DEF-14G-7
T	1AB-10A-3-2B-8C
W	3x 3x 1AB-10A-5ABC-14C-14A
T	1AB-3 (light)-2B
F	1AB
S	1AB-10C-7
S	1AB-4AC-3
M	3x 1AB-4AC-10A-5ABC-14G-14B-7
T	1AB-10A-3-2B
W	2x 3x 3x 1AB-10A-9CDE-14D-14A
T	1AB-10A-3 (light)-2B
F	1AB
S	1AB-10C-7
S	4x 4x 1AB-14C-14A

Sheet 17-8. Triple jump training schedule

Triple Jump NAME DATE May

1. Warm-up routine to include A. Jogging-flexibility
   B. Easy high knee, fast leg
2. Fartlek A. Holmer B. Lydiard
3. Weight routine
4. Bounding drills A. Height, B. Distance } L.R (50-100 yds.)
   6-8 repeats fast as you can control
   C. Hop-step drill—double arm action—powerful lead leg (50-100 yds.) 6-8 repeats
5. Rhythm drills: 5-7-9-step approach
   A. S - S - S - J
   B. H - H - H - S - J
   C. LL RR LLL R LL—10 successive—for time and distance—124 ft.—excellent! D.
6. Box drills
   A. L □ L □ L □ L □ L □—step leg up to get on box (R above each box)
   B. L □ R □ L □ R □ L □ R
   C. L □ R □ L □ R □ L (L R L R above boxes)
   D. R □ L □ R □ Pit (R R L above; |4m|)
   Reverse RRLRRL to LLRLLR
   E. R □ R—L □ R—R □ L—R □ R Pit (|10 ft.|)
   Reverse RRLRRLRR to LLRLLRLL
   F. R—R □ R—L □ R—R □ Pit (L, L above; |16 ft.| |10 ft.|)
   G. R □ R □ R □ Pit (L L L above; 8 ft. work for 20 ft.)
   H. R □ R □ L □ Pit (R L L above)
7. Squad meeting
8. Special A. Sauna B. Swim C. Film D.
9. Short approach triple jump A. Standing B. 3-step
   C. 5-step D. 7-step E. 9-step F. 11-step
10. Full approach A. Check marks B. Jumping
    C. Competition or Trial
11. Rope jumping: 30 sec., 15 sec. rest
12. Hurdle X drill
14. Intervals A. 110 B. 165 C. 220 D. 300
    E. 330 F. 440 G. 660-440-330-220-110
15. Hill work A. Laurelwood B. Emerald St.
    C. Stadium steps

Day	Schedule
M	1AB-4AC-10A-6DEFG (2x)-14G-7
T	1AB-3-2B
W	1AB-10A-9BCD (2x)-14D (3x)-14A (3x)
T	1AB-3(light)-2B
F	1AB-10A
S	1AB-10C-7
S	1AB-10A-9DEF (2x)-2B
M	1AB-10A-14G-14A (3x)-7
T	1AB-3-2B-8C
W	1AB-4AC-10A-5ABC-14D (2x)-14A (4x)
T	1AB-3(light)-2A
F	1AB-
S	1AB-10C-7
S	1AB-10A-14C (5x)
M	1AB-4AC-10A-6DEFG (2x)-14G-7
T	1AB-3-2B-8C
W	1AB-4AC-10A-5AB-14D (3x)-14A (3x)
T	1AB-10A-3(light)-2A
F	1AB
S	1AB-10C-7
S	1AB-10A-9BCD (2x)-14A (4x)
M	1AB-4AC-10A-14G-14A (4x)-7
T	1AB-3-2B
W	1AB-4AC-10A-5ABC-14C (6x)
T	1AB-3(light)-2A
F	1AB
S	1AB-10C-7
S	1AB-10A-4ABC-2A

Sheet 17-9. Triple jump training schedule

Triple Jump NAME DATE June

1. Warm-up routine to include A. Jogging-flexibility
   B. Easy high knee, fast leg
2. Fartlek A. Holmer B. Lydiard
3. Weight routine
4. Bounding drills A. Height } L.R (50-100 yds.)
   B. Distance }
   6-8 repeats fast as you can control
   C. Hop-step drill—double arm action—powerful lead leg (50-100 yds.) 6-8 repeats
5. Rhythm drills: 5-7-9-step approach
   A. S - S - S - J
   B. H - H - H - S - J
   C. LL RR LLL R LL—10 successive—for time and distance—124 ft.—excellent! D.
6. Box drills
   A. L □ L □ L □ L □ L □—step leg up to get on box (R over each box)
   B. L □ R □ L □ R □ L □ R
   C. L □ R □ L □ R □ L (L R L R over boxes)
   D. R □ L □ R □ Pit (R R L over boxes) |4m|
   Reverse RRLRRL to LLRLLR
   E. R □ R–L □ R–R □ L–R □ R Pit |10 ft.|
   Reverse RRLRRLRR to LLRLLRLL
   F. R–R □ R–L □ R–R □ Pit (L, L over boxes) |16 ft.| |10 ft.|
   G. R □ R □ R □ Pit (L L L over boxes) 8 ft. work for 20 ft.
   H. R □ R □ L □ Pit (R L L over boxes)
7. Squad meeting
8. Special A. Sauna B. Swim C. Film D.
9. Short approach triple jump A. Standing B. 3-step
   C. 5-step D. 7-step E. 9-step F. 11-step
10. Full approach A. Check marks B. Jumping
    C. Competition or Trial
11. Rope jumping: 30 sec., 15 sec. rest
12. Hurdle X drill
14. Intervals A. 110 B. 165 C. 220 D. 300
    E. 330 F. 440 G. 660-440-330-220-110
15. Hill work A. Laurelwood B. Emerald St.
    C. Stadium steps

Day	Workout
M	1A-1B-4A-4C-10A-5ABC-14D [3X]-14C [3X]-14A [3X]-[illegible]
T	1A-1B-3-2B
W	1A-1B-4A-4C-10A-9CDE [2X]-14F-14E [2X]-14C [3X]-14A [4X]
T	1A-1B-3-2B
F	1A-1B-4A-4C-10A-5AB-14A [6X]
S	1A-B-4A-4C-10A-6DEF [2X]-14G-14A [4X]
S	1A-1B-10A
M	1A-1B-4A-4C-5ABC [2X]-9BCD [2X]-14D [3X]-14A [3X]
T	1A-1B-3-2B-8C
W	1A-1B-10A-5AB-14C [4X]
T	1A-1B-10A-14A [3X]-8C
F	10C
S	10C
S	
M	
T	
W	
T	
F	
S	
S	
M	
T	
W	
T	
F	
S	
S	

Sheet 17-10. Triple jump training schedule

Endnotes

1. Vitold Kreyer. (2000). The key to Jonathan Edwards' success. In Jess Jarver, ed., *The Jumps: Contemporary Theory, Technique and Training* (5th ed.). Mountain View, CA: Tafnews, 145-149.
2. Dave Norris. (1988). Run-ups in the horizontal jumps. *Track Technique, 104*, 3329.
3. John Crotty. (1988). The hop phase of the triple jump. *Track Technique, 102*, 3261-3262.
4. Andy Heal. (1985). Horizontal velocity in the triple jump. *Track Technique, 92*, 2944-2945.
5. Klaus Kubler. (1987). Triple jump injuries. *Track Technique, 100*, 3202-3202.

Core Readings

Bullard, Ernie, & Knuth, Larry. (1977). *Triple jump encyclopedia*. Pasadena: Athletic Press.

Freeman, William H. (2001). Periodized training for jumpers. In *Peak When It Counts: Periodization for American track and field* (4th ed.). Mountain View, CA: Tafnews, 120-130.

Hayes, Dean. Triple jump. (2000). In *USA Track and Field coaching manual*. Champaign, IL: Human Kinetics, 159-171.

Jacoby, Ed, & Bob Fraley. (1998). *The complete book of jumps*. Champaign, IL: Human Kinetics.

Jarver, Jess, ed. (2000). *The Jumps: Contemporary Theory, Technique and Training* (5th ed.). Mountain View, CA: Tafnews.

USA Track & Field Coaching Education Program. (2003). *Level II Curriculum: Jumps*. USA Track & Field. Invaluable; revised regularly.

Recommended Readings

Bauer, Joachim. (1995). Analysis of audible signals in the triple jump [abstract]. *Track Coach, 131*, 4194.

Bianco, Enrique, David Lease, Elio Locatelli, Yukio Muraki, Dan Pfaff, Efim Shuravetzky & Miguel Velez. (1996). NSA Round Table 31: Speed in the jumping events. *New Studies in Athletics, 11*(2-3), 9-19.

Boas, John. (Winter 1998). Strength training for jumpers [abstract]. *Track Coach, 142*, 4546.

Boni, Mario, Benazzo, Francesco, Castelli, Claudio, & Barnabei, Giuseppe. (1986). Jumper's knee. *New Studies in Athletics, 1*(2), 65-80.

Bourne, Gary. (1995). Specificity in horizontal jumps training. [abstract]. *Track Coach, 131*, 4193.

Brüggemann, Gert-Peter, & Adiamatios Arampatzis. Triple jump. In Harald Müller & Helmar Hommel, eds., Biomechanical Research Project at the VIth World Championships in Athletics, Athens 1997: Preliminary Report. *New Studies in Athletics, 12*(2-3), 59-66.

Burnett, Angus. (Spring 2002). Relevance of jumping exercises to field event athletes [abstract]. *Track Coach, 159*, 5090.

Dickwach, Hartmut. (1992). Multiple jumps in the training of triple jumpers [abstract]. *Track Technique, 120*, 3838.

Donley, Milan. (1992). Speed, technique and statistics in the women's triple jump. *Track Technique, 121*, 3861-3864.

Freeman, Will, Bob Myers & Dan Pfaff. (1995). Factors influencing skill acquisition in the jumps. *Track Coach, 131*, 4176-4178, 4197.

Golubtzov, Anatoly. (1994). Development of triple jump for women. [abstract]. *Track Technique, 129*, 4126-4127.

Hackett, Brad. (1995). Triple jump basics. *Track Technique, 130*, 4138-4141.

Hackett, Brad. (1995). Triple jump basics. *Track Coach, 133*, 4246-4247.

Hay, James. (1998). Biomechanical considerations about jumping training. *New Studies in Athletics, 13*(1), 90-91.

Hay, James G. (1995). The case for a jump-dominated technique in the triple jump. *Track Coach, 132*, 4214-4219. Reprinted in Jarver, *The Jumps* (5th ed.), 139-144; Moura, Nelio Alfano. (1996). Is the jump-dominated technique in the triple jump the best for all? [letter]. *Track Coach, 136*, 4352-4353; Hay, James G. (1996). Reply. *Track Coach, 136*, 4353-4354.

Hay, James G. (1994). Effort distribution in the triple jump. *Track Technique, 127*, 4042-4048.

Homenkova, L.S., ed. (1994). Training for jumping events. *Track and Field Quarterly Review, 94*(4), 44-52.

Hommel, Helmar. (1998). NSA photosequence 39: Triple jump: Yoelvis Quesada. New Studies in Athletics, 13(4), 41-46. Commentary by Jörg Elbe.

Hommel, Helmar. (1998). NSA photosequence 40: Triple jump: Jonathan Edwards. *New Studies in Athletics, 13*(4), 47-54. Commentary by Jörg Elbe.

Jaonkar, J. V. (Summer 2004). Development of the takeoff in horizontal jumps [abstract]. *Track Coach, 168*, 5379-5380.

Jürgens, Annelie. (1998). Biomechanical investigation of the transition between the hop and the step. *New Studies in Athletics, 13*(4), 29-40.

King, Ted. (1995). Beyond 18m in the triple jump. [abstract]. *Track Coach, 132*, 4225.

Larkins, Clifford. (1993). A biomechanical analysis of novice triple jump technique. *Track Technique, 122*, 3882-3886, 3906-3907.

Larkins, Clifford, & Melvin R. Raney. (1994). Can triple jumpers really use an equal phase ratios strategy? *Track Technique, 128*, 4081-4086.

LeBlanc, Steve. (Fall 2001). The role of active landings in the horizontal jumps. *Track Coach, 157*, 5019-5020.

Lees, A., & P. Graham-Smith. (Spring 2000). Phase distance characteristics in the triple jump [abstract]. *Track Coach, 151*, 4835.

Mackenzie, Robert J. (Spring 2007). Film measurement of takeoff forces in the jumps, including slowing effects. *Track Coach, 179*, 5717-5722, 5733.

Mackenzie, Robert J. (Summer 2003). What does the takeoff leg really do? *Track Coach, 164*, 5233-5237.

Madella, Alberto. (1996). Speed in the horizontal jumps: Muscular properties or cognitive treatment? *New Studies in Athletics, 11*(2-3), 127-132.

Maraj, Brian. (1999). Evidence for programmed and visually controlled phases of the triple jump approach run. *New Studies in Athletics, 14*(3), 51-56.

Moura, Nelio Alfano, & Tania Fernandes de Paula Moura. (2001). Training principles for jumpers: Implications for the special strength development. *New Studies in Athletics, 16*(4), 51-61.

Popow, Grigorij I., & Wladimir I. Ljach. (2002). Long and triple jump training on pneumatic run-up surfaces. Trans. Jürgen Schiffer. *New Studies in Athletics, 17*(3/4), 55-60.

Roundtable: Horizontal jumps. (Winter 2004). *Track Coach, 166*, 5305-5309. Participants: Craig Hilliard, Dan Pfaff, John Boas & Gary Bourne.

Slepica, James. (1991). Training the young athlete for the horizontal jumps. *New Studies in Athletics, 6*(3), 43-48.

Smith, Philip Graham, & Adrian Lees. (Spring 2003). "Balance" in horizontal jumps [abstract]. *Track Coach, 163*, 5221.

Todd, Douglas. (Winter 1999). Teaching the triple jump. *Track Coach, 146*, 4657-4660. Reprinted in Jarver, *The Jumps* (5th ed.), 125-129.

THE THROWS

Part 5

Mac Wilkins, gold and silver medalist, Olympic Games; world-record holder at 232′ 6″, 1976

18

The Shot Put

Bowerman's Best

68′ 11 3/4″	Neal Steinhauer	1967

Record Setters

Neal Steinhauer	World and U.S. indoor record (67′10″), 1967; NCAA champion, 1965; three-time All-American (1st, 2nd, 2nd)
Pete Schmock	Two-time Olympian; 2nd, NCAA, 1972 (best 66′ 5″; life 69′ 3″)
Mac Wilkins	3rd, NCAA, 1973 (best 63′ 8″; lifetime 69′ 1 1/4″)
Dave Steen	2nd, NCAA, 1963 (best 61′ 11 1/4″), Canadian and British Commonwealth champion

Some of the best potential throwers never enjoy the fierce, lonely effort that is the reward for the months and years of preparation, culminating in the explosion that leads to an Olympic gold medal. Football's demands of time and organization consume the best of the physical giants who might otherwise be a Neil Steinhauer, an Al Feuerbach, or a Randy Barnes. Also, many of the team-sport giants may not be psychologically equipped to face the possibility of having their abilities measured with the absolute objectivity of the individual sport.

The shot put is traditionally considered the strong athlete's event in track and field. Collegiate putters are typically big and strong. The bigger and stronger they are, the more likely they are to be successful. This factor is not as strictly the case with high school shot-putters. Because the high school shot is only 12 pounds for boys and 8 pounds for girls, a smaller athlete who is fast and explosive can compete with the larger athlete at that level of competition. While the college women's shot weight increases only to 4 kg (8.8 lbs.), the men's weight rises to 16 pounds, a significant increase.

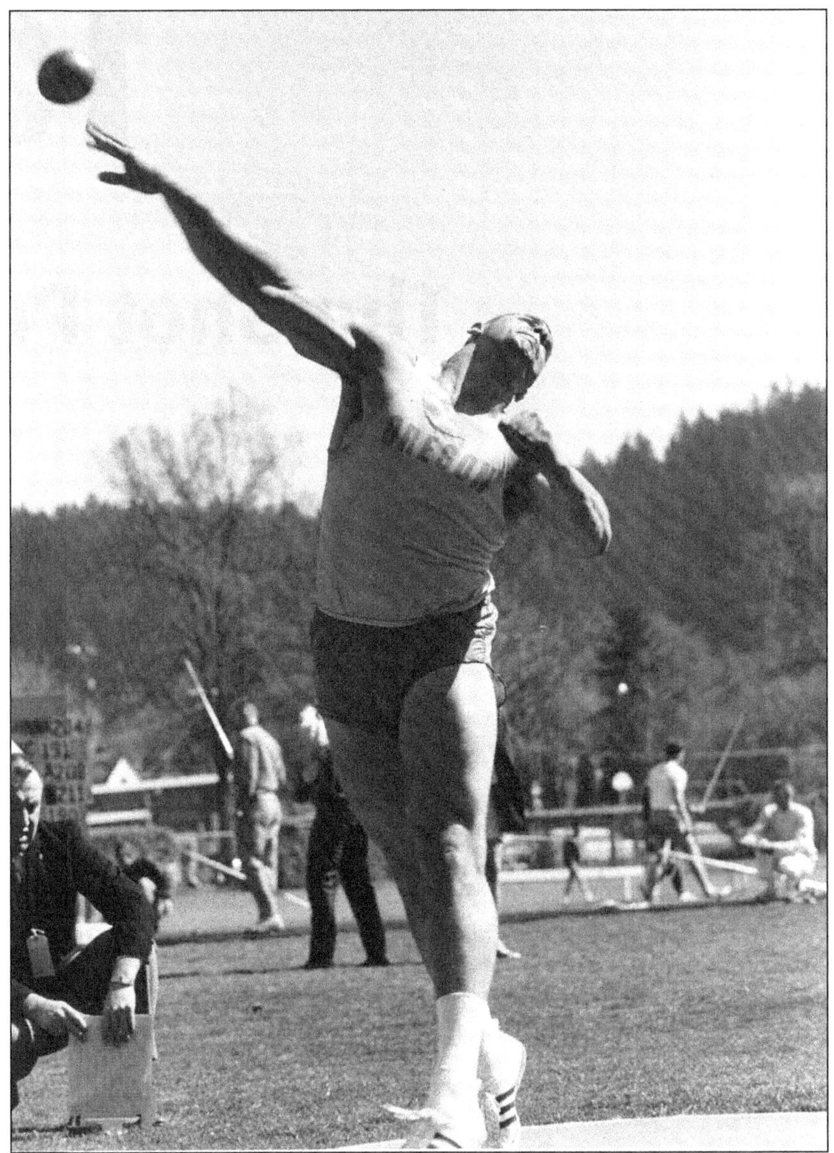

Photo 18-1. Neil Steinhauer, indoor world-record holder at 67′ 10″, 1967

Training Theory

Spectators think of the shot as a very simple event: the biggest, strongest person wins. However, the technique of putting, as well as the training that prepares an athlete for a supreme effort, is really quite complex. Yet, the basic factors that result in the length of a throw are quite simple.[1] They are the shot's release velocity, angle of release, and height of release.

The thrower must develop technique, but the speed-strength factor is extremely important. A thrower must be quick, explosive in movement to accelerate the shot rapidly to an optimal release speed.

The proportionate contributions of the body's muscle groups to a shot put are:

- 50 percent legs
- 30 percent trunk
- 20 percent arms

This point is made to emphasize the importance of proper use of the lower body during the throw. Perhaps the most common fault is "arm throwing," relying on arm strength alone to propel the shot. A throw comes 80 percent from the legs and trunk. According to Harmon Brown:

> *Leg power is the key to success. Throw from the ground up. Lead the throw with the knees and hips. Energy flows from legs, hips to shoulders, arm and implement in a linked series. Rotation of the right foot-knee-hip is* fundamental *to all throws ...The shot is thrown from the* jerk *position—knees bent equally, weight shifting from right to left over the front (left) leg. The left leg exerts most of the explosive power.*[2]

Although absolute strength is important, it is not the primary goal. It is useful only as long as it contributes to speed-strength. Specific strength is more important because although "super strength did not always win, it was explosive strength that produced champions."[3] Explosive strength is developed by using Olympic-style weight lifting (not power lifting) and plyometric jumping exercises.

Better marks in the vertical jump, standing long jump, and 20-meter dash correlate to better performances in the shot put.[4] The most common lifts used by putters include:

- bench press
- snatch
- power clean
- squat[5]

Most putters use one of two styles, the glide (O'Brien) or the spin.[6] The optimal release angle, regardless of style is about 40 to 42 degrees.[7] Each style has its strengths and weaknesses. Although the spin makes higher release velocities possible, it is also less stable, which can result in a poorer release position. Female throwers are still less technically proficient than male throwers,[8] though that may result from the limited depth of competition to date. Varied weight implements (heavier and lighter) can be used to improve technique and release velocity, but no general agreement is found on principles for their use.[9,10] The general trend in training in all events, including the throws, is toward greater quality rather than greater quantity.[11]

A brief word concerning the equipment is necessary because it can affect the distance of the put, though not to the extent possible with different discuses or javelins. The athlete has the choice of iron, steel, or brass instruments. Brass is the smallest shot, but it is not popular with the better putters. Shot-putters want the largest legal implement they can get. This gives them greater leverage to exert while throwing. Some high school throwers have gone so far as to use the larger indoor shot outdoors, when it has been allowed. However, a bird shot-filled instrument is not as good as one of solid metal or of rubber-covered solid metal, because it gives the effect of trying to throw a beanbag.

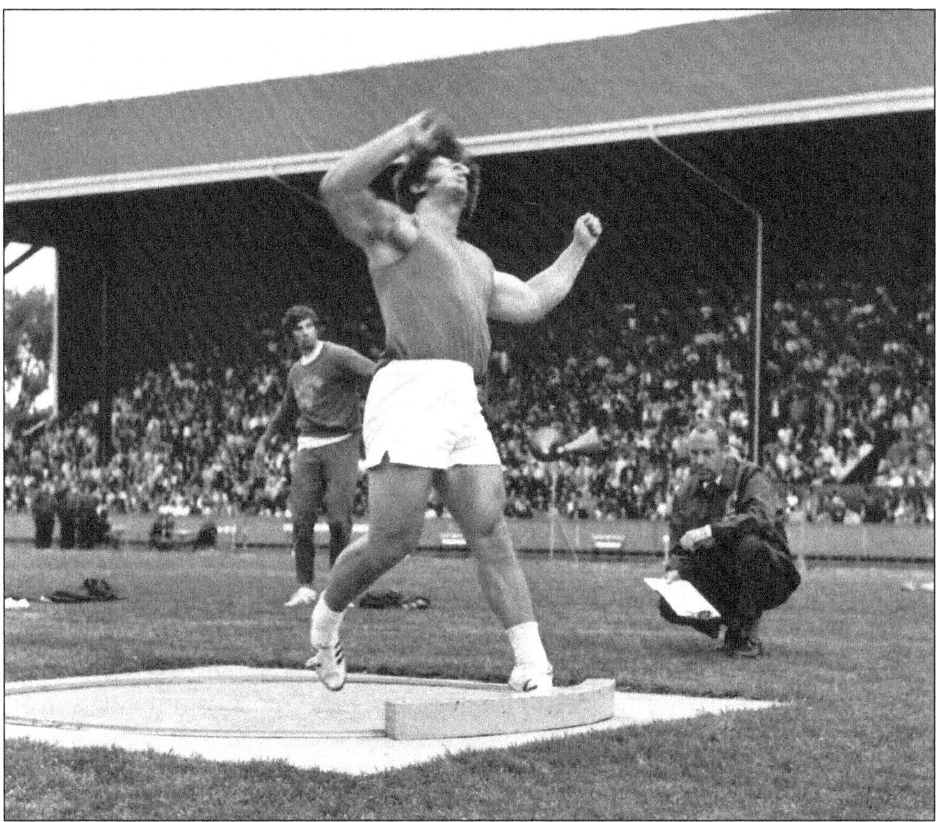

Photo 18-2. Pete Schmock, All-American and two-time Olympian

Technique of the Shot Put

The shot is held at the base of the fingers, where the pads are at the top of the palm. It is held by four fingers (three fingers and the thumb, with the little finger often curled under). Some putters try to hold the shot on the fingers only, but few are strong enough to keep it there, and throwing it that way can hurt the arm all the way to the elbow. The putter should squeeze the shot a bit, helping to keep better control. The elbow should be parallel to the ground and kept behind the shot at all times. The hand might be turned out to keep the elbow in a good position.

Consider a glide thrower who throws with the right hand. He begins crouched at the rear of the circle, facing away from the direction of the throw. The shot is cradled in the hand and held alongside the neck at the chin. The athlete's weight is on the right foot, with the left foot reaching back a bit, in preparation for the movement across the ring.

The athlete begins by raising the left hand or extending it to the rear of the circle. This movement is primarily a matter of attaining balance. The athlete must be in a good state of balance before beginning the movement across the circle.

When the movement begins, the throwing elbow is raised to the side until the arm is parallel to the ground. From this position, the putter carries the shot to the front of the ring to add speed to its movement. In the process of crossing the ring, the athlete lifts, turns, pushes the shot upward, and gives a final flip of the wrist to impart the last bit of momentum to the shot as it leaves the hand.

In the spin (discus-turn) technique, the thrower starts in the rear of the circle with the feet in the position for starting a discus throw. The movements are the same as for the discus, except that the shot is carried next to the neck at the jaw, just as in the glide technique. The release is essentially the same for both styles.

The four stages of the shot-putting action are:

- The move to the center of the circle
- The lift, changing the direction of the shot
- Beginning to turn toward the direction of the put
- Pushing the shot outward until it leaves the hand

These stages are not as separate as the description may suggest. The movement is a continuous, uninterrupted action. According to the laws of physics, the shot weighs less when it is moving, as long as it is pushed along the same line of travel it is already following.

The Shot-Put Routine

The routine is designed to give the shot-putter the feel of what he should be doing when going through the entire putting action. It consists of two groups of exercises, the first group performed in the front area of the circle and the other involving crossing the ring. These exercises should help the putter review the basics of the event, progressing in effort from easy to medium to hard. Although the description is for the glide style, it is performed in the same manner by spin throwers.

The first part of the routine is done with the putter in the front of the circle. Actually, the thrower begins at the start of the final phase of the put, with the body over a flexed right leg and the left leg extended back to the toe board. This part of the exercise is called the *stand*. The shot is held while the athlete goes through the action of the lift and turn, but with one difference: the athlete does not push the shot. The arm goes out to the side, just as though the shot were to be pushed, but the hand stays at the neck area. The shot is allowed to fall from the hand, but it travels only as far as the force of the body, with absolutely no arm action, causes it to go.

The second drill repeats the first one, except that the hand follows (but does not push) the shot as it leaves the hand. The third drill does involve pushing the shot as it leaves, but it is not a hard push. The last standing drill has the athlete lifting, turning, and pushing hard.

The second part of the routine is done by crossing the ring, using the full action of throwing. When crossing the ring in the routine, the thrower should start slow and finish fast. The complete crossing drill is to give the feel of the event rather than to work on the speed of the crossing. The first drill is similar to the second drill from a stand. The athlete crosses the circle, lifts, turns, and lets the shot leave the hand, following it with the hand but not pushing it.

The second, third, and fourth drills with the ring crossing involve pushing the shot at the completion of the action. The second drill has the putter make a medium-effort push. The third drill makes a hard-effort push. On the fourth drill, the athlete tries to explode, unleashing all of his force into the put. At all times, the feet should be spread enough for the athlete to get the hips into the throw.

Photo 18-3. Mac Wilkins, lifetime best of 69′

Some throwers have worked on the final push of the throwing arm by trying to develop a punching action. One exercise used for this action has been for the athlete to work at hitting a punching bag while on his knees, which requires the thrower to push upward at about the angle of the putting action (40 to 42 degrees).

Training for the Shot Put

For the purposes of records, the condensed, coded training sheet shown for the shot put is more practical than one page for every day of training or even every week. Though preparing a written workout may be a bit easier, it can also be sloppier in thought. The workout sheet lists the exercises considered fundamental to training for the shot put. Because all the exercises are listed on the sheet, the coach or teacher is less likely to forget to assign vital portions of the training regime.

The shot-put training schedules are organized so that either an individual or a group, such as the members of a physical education class, can devote a unit of 10 weeks to one or more events. The schedule is a guide, not a dictum.

The routines are introduced and repeated regularly. Technique is introduced early in the schedule, and those points that are most basic to the event are repeated with the greatest frequency. Also included are agility drills, speed work, and possibly a secondary event. The program moves from the simple to the more difficult, with a gradual increase in the planned distance of the throws, so the best technique can be acquired as physical condition and strength improve. The schedules are arranged so that one month's record is available. The three particular values to this system are:

- A complete "book" may be kept on the athlete.
- Comparisons may be made to previous athletes.
- No fundamentals are overlooked (probably the most important value).

The athlete and the coach should try to follow patterns that have been successful, which is one reason for recording and saving the schedule sheets. In training for the technique of the put, it is best to work on only one technical element or phase of the put at a time. Gradually, multiple elements or phases can be put together into the complete put. On the schedule sheet, those elements of the put are listed by letters under Item 6. This listing is primarily to avoid confusion and frustration. The numbered fundamentals are not explained as in the other chapters because they have already been discussed elsewhere in the chapter.

On the fartlek running, the putters should be able to run steadily for at least 20 minutes. Fartlek running is good for the cardiovascular system, and a run of at least 20 minutes is necessary to gain much cardiovascular benefit.

The athletes need to use weight-training activities that develop enough body mass for successful putting. Although training exercises are suggested, the athletes should not rigidly follow someone else's weight-training schedule. Each athlete basically needs to develop his own program of weight-training activities, though younger athletes need considerable (careful) guidance.

The athlete should not be overcoached. By the time athletes are collegians, they should have enough background to know fairly well what activities of this nature are most beneficial for them, if they have been very successful putters. The weight lifters should try to arrange their schedules so they can do their lifting activities together, also they will pick up ideas from each other.

Weight training definitely helps, though it can be overdone. The ultimate object is feet thrown, not pounds lifted. Weight training is done three times a week in the fall, going to two to three sessions per week in the winter, with one (sometimes two) sessions per week in the spring (Tuesday, for a Saturday meet).

The hard-easy schedule is followed to some degree, though not as closely as with running activities. The pattern also varies according to the time of year. For example, in January, the putter might go hard on alternating days, such as Monday, Wednesday, and Friday. In February or early March, preparation for future two-day meets begins. Because the athlete will have to qualify on one day and then throw again the next day in finals, this sequence is simulated in practice. The thrower would go hard on both Monday and Tuesday, with other hard days on Thursday and Saturday. In preparing for a big meet, the thrower might go hard on Monday and Tuesday, then go light until the meet, either on Friday for trials or on Saturday for a one-day meet.

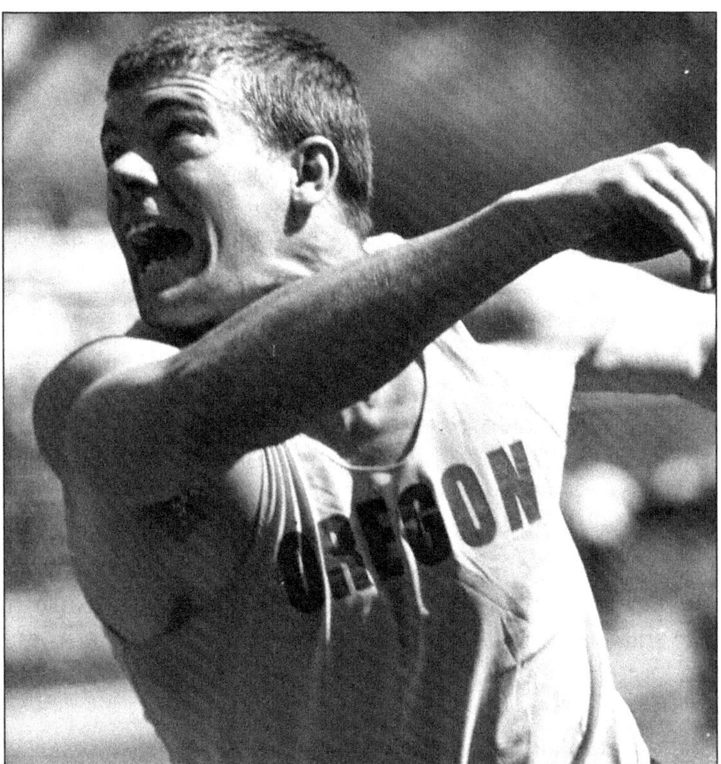

Photo 18-4. Dave Steen, British Commonwealth champion, 1966

Shot-Put Training Schedules

SHOT PUT SCHEDULE NAME ______________________ DATE ______________

1. A. Jog 1-2 laps, easy stretching
   B. Hendricks Park C. Golf course
2. Fartlek A. Varied pace B. Slow, steady pace
3. Weights and resistance activities
4. Routine A. Stand B. Crossing
   (1) Lift (2) Follow (3) Push
5. Effort A. Stand B. Crossing
   (1) Easy (2) Medium (3) Hard
6. Technique A. Stand, shot almost in palm
   B. Crossing, have speed under control
   (1) Comfortable knee bend
   (2) Hip push from cocked position
   (3) Left arm in position, pull for torque
   (4) Eye on ground or target
   (5) Explode on every 3rd or 4th throw
   (6) Lift well before turn
   (7) Squeeze the shot
   (8) Right foot in center of ring
   (9) Target for 3/4ths to 7/8ths effort
   (10) Left foot timing and position
   (11) Reach on put and lean into it
   (12)
7. TEAM MEETING
8. Special A. Sauna B. Swim C. Steps or hill
9. Alternate stand-step-crossing routine
   Same letters as #6
10. A. Meet B. Trial C. Simulation D. Control test
11. Cross ring easy. Feeling of exploding.
    Start slow, finish fast.
12. With Coach A. B.
14. A. Wind sprints
    B. Hurdle drill: 3 LH, 7-9m apart
    C. Spring and bound
    D. Alternate run and jog, at least 800
    E. Starts, go 20-25m
    F. High knee (slow) and fast leg
15. Plyometrics A. Jumps B. Bounding C.
    (1) 1-leg (2) Both legs (3)
16. Tumbling activities
17. Have feeling of low and relaxed.
    No strain at back or in crossing.
18. A. On staying in the ring. B. Lift-turn
19. Ring crossing, feet not too far spread-- go only
    as fast as you can control. Same letters as #6.
20. Work on second event
21. A. Videotape B. Film C. Pictures
    (1) Record performance (2) Study
30. Experimental work

Date	Distance	3/4 pace	Date Pace	Goal Pace

M
T
W
T
F
S
S
M
T
W
T
F
S
S
M
T
W
T
F
S
S
M
T
W
T
F
S
S

Sheet 18-1. Revised shot-put training schedule sheet

Shot-Put NAME DATE September/October

1. A. Jog 1 or 2 laps, easy stretching B. Weights and jog C.
2. Fartlek run A. Varied pace B. Slow, steady
3. Weights and resistance activities.
4. Routine A. Stand B. Crossing (1) Lift (2) Turn (3) Push
5. Effort A. Stand B. Crossing (1) Easy (2) Medium (3) Hard
6. Technique A. Stand-shot almost in palm
   B. Crossing—have speed under control
   (1) Comfortable knee bend (2) Hip push from cock position
   (3) Left arm in position, pull for torque
   (4) Eye on ground or target (5) Every 3d or 4th explode
   (6) Lift well before turn (7) Squeeze the shot
   (8) Right foot in center of ring (9) Target for 3/4 to 7/8 effort
   (a) Stand (b) Crossing (10) Left foot timing and position
   (11) Reach on put and lean into it (12)
7. Squad meeting
8. Special A. Sauna B. Swim C. Steps or hill
9. Alternate stand-step-crossing routine; same letters as item 6
10. Test or compete—record below
11. Cross ring easy. Feeling of exploding. Start slow, finish fast.
12. With coach
14. A. Wind sprints B. Starts, go 25 yds.
    C. High knee and fast leg D. Hurdles
    E. Spring and bound F. Alternate walk-run go 880 or more
15. A. Hendricks Park B. Laurelwood Golf Course
16. Tumbling activities
17. Have feeling of low and relaxed. No strain at back or in crossing.
18. A. On staying in the ring B. Lift-turn
19. Ring crossing, feet not too far spread only as fast as you can control. Same as item 6.
20. Secondary event
21. A. Pictures B. Film C. Video

Date	Result	3/4	Now	Goal

M Organization-equipment-lockers
T Use of equipment-Safety-training times
W 1A-6A(1)-6A(2)-7-14F
T (10 am) 21A-3
F 1A-6A(1)-6A(3)-8C-14F
S 3
S 3-14A-14F or recreation
M 1A-6A(1)-6B(1)-6A(2)-6B(2)-14A
T 7-5A(1)(2)(3)-3-14A
W 1A-6A(3)-6B(3)-17
T 3-8B or 8C
F 1A-6B(6)-11-14C
S 3-14D-14F
S recreation
M 1A-6A(4)-6B(4)-6A(11)-6B(11)-14A
T 3-14F
W 1A-6A(4)-6B(4)-6A(11)-6B(11)-6B(8)-1A
T 3-14F
F 1A-6A(1)-6B(1)-6A(11)-6B(11)-6B(8)
S 3-14F
S recreation
M 1A-6A(11)-6B(11)-6A(1)-6B(1)-17-20
T 3-14A
W 1A-6A(2)-6B(2)-6A(4)-6B(4)-14B
T 3-14F
F 1A-10A-9A(8)
S 3-14F
S recreation

Sheet 18-2. Shot-put training schedule

Shot-Put NAME DATE October/November

1. A. Jog 1 or 2 laps, easy stretching B. Weights and jog
   C.
2. Fartlek run A. Varied pace B. Slow, steady
3. Weights and resistance activities.
4. Routine A. Stand B. Crossing (1) Lift
   (2) Turn (3) Push
5. Effort A. Stand B. Crossing
   (1) Easy (2) Medium (3) Hard
6. Technique A. Stand-shot almost in palm
   B. Crossing—have speed under control
   (1) Comfortable knee bend (2) Hip push from cock position
   (3) Left arm in position, pull for torque
   (4) Eye on ground or target (5) Every 3d or 4th explode
   (6) Lift well before turn (7) Squeeze the shot
   (8) Right foot in center of ring (9) Target for 3/4 to 7/8 effort
   (a) Stand (b) Crossing (10) Left foot timing and position
   (11) Reach on put and lean into it (12)
7. Squad meeting
8. Special A. Sauna B. Swim C. Steps or hill
9. Alternate stand-step-crossing routine; same letters as item 6
10. Test or compete—record below
11. Cross ring easy. Feeling of exploding. Start slow, finish fast.
12. With coach
14. A. Wind sprints B. Starts, go 25 yds.
    C. High knee and fast leg D. Hurdles
    E. Spring and bound F. Alternate walk-run go 880 or more
15. A. Hendricks Park B. Laurelwood Golf Course
16. Tumbling activities
17. Have feeling of low and relaxed. No strain at back or in crossing.
18. A. On staying in the ring B. Lift-turn
19. Ring crossing, feet not too far spread only as fast as you can control. Same as item 6.
20. Secondary event
21. A. Pictures B. Film C. Video

Date	Result	3/4	Now	Goal

Day	Schedule
M	1A-3
T	1A-6A(1)-6B(1)-6B(2)-9AB(1)-20
W	3-14F
T	1A-6A(1)-6B(1)-9AB(8)-14F
F	3
S	
S	
M	1A-3
T	1A-6A(3)-6B(3)-9-14A
W	3-20
T	1A-4 (for distance)-6A(5)-6B(5) -9AB(5)-14F
F	1A-3
S	
S	
M	1A-3-14F or 20
T	1A-5A(4)-9AB(4)-14A
W	1A-3
T	1A-5A(4)-9AB(4)-17-14F
F	1A-3
S	
S	
M	1A-3
T	1A-14F-6A(6)-6B(6)-9AB(6)-17-14A
W	1A-3-14F
T	1A-14A-6A(6)-6B(6)-9AB(6)-11-1A
F	1A-3-14F
S	1A-6A(8)-6B(8)-9AB(8)-11-14A
S	

Sheet 18-3. Shot-put training schedule

Shot-Put NAME DATE November/December

1. A. Jog 1 or 2 laps, easy stretching B. Weights and jog
   C.
2. Fartlek run A. Varied pace B. Slow, steady
3. Weights and resistance activities.
4. Routine A. Stand B. Crossing (1) Lift
   (2) Turn (3) Push
5. Effort A. Stand B. Crossing
   (1) Easy (2) Medium (3) Hard
6. Technique A. Stand-shot almost in palm
   B. Crossing—have speed under control
   (1) Comfortable knee bend (2) Hip push from cock position
   (3) Left arm in position, pull for torque
   (4) Eye on ground or target (5) Every 3d or 4th explode
   (6) Lift well before turn (7) Squeeze the shot
   (8) Right foot in center of ring (9) Target for 3/4 to 7/8 effort
   (a) Stand (b) Crossing (10) Left foot timing and position
   (11) Reach on put and lean into it (12)
7. Squad meeting
8. Special A. Sauna B. Swim C. Steps or hill
9. Alternate stand-step-crossing routine; same letters as item 6
10. Test or compete—record below
11. Cross ring easy. Feeling of exploding. Start slow, finish fast.
12. With coach
14. A. Wind sprints B. Starts, go 25 yds.
    C. High knee and fast leg D. Hurdles
    E. Spring and bound F. Alternate walk-run go 880 or more
15. A. Hendricks Park B. Laurelwood Golf Course
16. Tumbling activities
17. Have feeling of low and relaxed. No strain at back or in crossing.
18. A. On staying in the ring B. Lift-turn
19. Ring crossing, feet not too far spread only as fast as you can control. Same as item 6.
20. Secondary event
21. A. Pictures B. Film C. Video

Date	Result	3/4	Now	Goal

M	1A-14F-6A(6)-6B(6)-9AB(6)-17
T	1A-3-14F
W	1A-14A-6A(6)-6B(6)-9AB(6)-11
T	1A-3-14A
F	1A-3-6A(8)-6B(8)-9AB(8)-11
S	
S	

M	3 (easy and very light)
T	6 (form)
W	1A-14A
T	Light
F	10-Test for distance
S	
S	

M	
T	
W	
T	
F	
S	
S	

M	
T	
W	
T	
F	
S	
S	

Sheet 18-4. Shot-put training schedule

Shot-Put NAME DATE January

1. A. Jog 1 or 2 laps, easy stretching B. Weights and jog C.
2. Fartlek run A. Varied pace B. Slow, steady
3. Weights and resistance activities.
4. Routine A. Stand B. Crossing (1) Lift (2) Turn (3) Push
5. Effort A. Stand B. Crossing (1) Easy (2) Medium (3) Hard
6. Technique A. Stand-shot almost in palm
   B. Crossing—have speed under control
   (1) Comfortable knee bend (2) Hip push from cock position
   (3) Left arm in position, pull for torque
   (4) Eye on ground or target (5) Every 3d or 4th explode
   (6) Lift well before turn (7) Squeeze the shot
   (8) Right foot in center of ring (9) Target for 3/4 to 7/8 effort
   (a) Stand (b) Crossing (10) Left foot timing and position
   (11) Reach on put and lean into it (12)
7. Squad meeting
8. Special A. Sauna B. Swim C. Steps or hill
9. Alternate stand-step-crossing routine; same letters as item 6
10. Test or compete—record below
11. Cross ring easy. Feeling of exploding. Start slow, finish fast.
12. With coach
14. A. Wind sprints B. Starts, go 25 yds.
    C. High knee and fast leg D. Hurdles
    E. Spring and bound F. Alternate walk-run go 880 or more
15. A. Hendricks Park B. Laurelwood Golf Course
16. Tumbling activities
17. Have feeling of low and relaxed. No strain at back or in crossing.
18. A. On staying in the ring B. Lift-turn
19. Ring crossing, feet not too far spread only as fast as you can control. Same as item 6.
20. Secondary event
21. A. Pictures B. Film C. Video

Date	Result	3/4	Now	Goal

Day	Schedule
M	Class or squad organization—3-5A
T	1A-5A(1,2,3)-9AB(1) [3-6x]-14A
W	3
T	7-6B(2) [6-10x] - 9AB(2) [3-6x]-14A
F	3
S	1A-6B(5) [6-10x] -9AB(5) [2-4x]
S	recreation
M	3-14B
T	1A-5A(1,2,3)-5B(1,2,3)-6B(6) [6-10x]-9AB(5) [3-6x]-14F
W	3
T	1A-5B(1,2,3)-6B(6) [6-10x] - 9AB(6) [3-6x]-14A
F	3
S	10(record)—9B(7)-14F
S	recreation
M	3-14B -14F
T	1A-5A(1,2,3)-6AB(8) [6-10x] - 9AB(8) [3-6x] -14F
W	3
T	1A-5B(1,2,3)-6AB(4) [6-10x] -9AB(4) [3-6x]-14F
F	3
S	1A-5B(1,2,3)-6A(6) [6-10x]-9AB(6) [3-6x]-19
S	
M	3
T	1A-8A-6A(1) [6-10x]-6A(4) [6-10x]-9AB(4) [3-6x]-14B
W	3
T	1A-(9AB(9) [4-6x]-17-14F
F	3
S	10 (form work)
S	

Sheet 18-5. Shot-put training schedule

Shot-Put NAME DATE February

1. A. Jog 1 or 2 laps, easy stretching B. Weights and jog
   C.
2. Fartlek run A. Varied pace B. Slow, steady
3. Weights and resistance activities.
4. Routine A. Stand B. Crossing (1) Lift
   (2) Turn (3) Push
5. Effort A. Stand B. Crossing
   (1) Easy (2) Medium (3) Hard
6. Technique A. Stand-shot almost in palm
   B. Crossing—have speed under control
   (1) Comfortable knee bend (2) Hip push from cock position
   (3) Left arm in position, pull for torque
   (4) Eye on ground or target (5) Every 3d or 4th explode
   (6) Lift well before turn (7) Squeeze the shot
   (8) Right foot in center of ring (9) Target for 3/4 to 7/8 effort
   (a) Stand (b) Crossing (10) Left foot timing and position
   (11) Reach on put and lean into it (12)
7. Squad meeting
8. Special A. Sauna B. Swim C. Steps or hill
9. Alternate stand-step-crossing routine; same letters as item 6
10. Test or compete—record below
11. Cross ring easy. Feeling of exploding. Start slow, finish fast.
12. With coach
14. A. Wind sprints B. Starts, go 25 yds.
    C. High knee and fast leg D. Hurdles
    E. Spring and bound F. Alternate walk-run go 880 or more
15. A. Hendricks Park B. Laurelwood Golf Course
16. Tumbling activities
17. Have feeling of low and relaxed. No strain at back or in crossing.
18. A. On staying in the ring B. Lift-turn
19. Ring crossing, feet not too far spread only as fast as you can control. Same as item 6.
20. Secondary event
21. A. Pictures B. Film C. Video

Date	Result	3/4	Now	Goal

Day	Schedule
M	3-14A
T	1A-4-6A(1)-9AB(1)-17-14F
W	3
T	2x 1A-4AB(1, 2, 3)-9-14A
F	Gear ready-weigh shot-7
S	Indoor meet or 10
S	3
M	3-14B or 14F
T	1A-6B(1)-19B(3)-14F-8A-14F
W	1A-3
T	1A-6A(2)-19B(2)-17-19B(8)-11-14A
F	3
S	1A-6A(4)-19B(4)-9-17-14F
S	3
M	1A-3
T	20x 20x 1A-6A(1)-6B(1)-14F
W	1A-3
T	20x 20x 20x 1A-9B(11)-18-6A(3)-11-14F
F	1A-3
S	7-20
S	3
M	20-40x 10-20x 1A-9B(5)-9B(11)-11-14A
T	3-14B
W	20x 20x 20x 20x 1A-9B(11)-18-5B-19B(2)-14F
T	3-14B
F	10
S	3
S	3

Sheet 18-6. Shot-put training schedule

Shot-Put NAME DATE *March*

1. A. Jog 1 or 2 laps, easy stretching B. Weights and jog
   C.
2. Fartlek run A. Varied pace B. Slow, steady
3. Weights and resistance activities.
4. Routine A. Stand B. Crossing (1) Lift
   (2) Turn (3) Push
5. Effort A. Stand B. Crossing
   (1) Easy (2) Medium (3) Hard
6. Technique A. Stand-shot almost in palm
   B. Crossing—have speed under control
   (1) Comfortable knee bend (2) Hip push from cock position
   (3) Left arm in position, pull for torque
   (4) Eye on ground or target (5) Every 3d or 4th explode
   (6) Lift well before turn (7) Squeeze the shot
   (8) Right foot in center of ring (9) Target for 3/4 to 7/8 effort
   (a) Stand (b) Crossing (10) Left foot timing and position
   (11) Reach on put and lean into it (12)
7. Squad meeting
8. Special A. Sauna B. Swim C. Steps or hill
9. Alternate stand-step-crossing routine; same letters as item 6
10. Test or compete—record below
11. Cross ring easy. Feeling of exploding. Start slow, finish fast.
12. With coach
14. A. Wind sprints B. Starts, go 25 yds.
    C. High knee and fast leg D. Hurdles
    E. Spring and bound F. Alternate walk-run go 880 or more
15. A. Hendricks Park B. Laurelwood Golf Course
16. Tumbling activities
17. Have feeling of low and relaxed. No strain at back or in crossing.
18. A. On staying in the ring B. Lift-turn
19. Ring crossing, feet not too far spread only as fast as you can
    control. Same as item 6.
20. Secondary event
21. A. Pictures B. Film C. Video

Date	Result	3/4	Now	Goal

Day	Workout
M	*1A-6A(1)-6B(1)-17-14A-14F-6A(4)-6B(4)*
T	*3-14F-20*
W	*1A-11-17-10 (4x)-10 (4x)-10 (4x)-14A*
T	*3-20-14A*
F	*1A-11-17-10 (4x)-10 (4x)-10 (4x)-10 (4x)-14A*
S	*19-20*
S	*19-20*

Day	Workout
M	*1A-6A(3)-6B(3)-6B(8)-19-14F*
T	*3-20-14F*
W	*7-1A-11-6B(8)-17-14A*
T	*3-20-14F*
F	*1A-8B(8)-11-17-14A*
S	*Exams and jog*
S	

Day	Workout
M	*3-14F-20*
T	*1A-4A-4B-5A-5B-17-14A-14F*
W	*3-20-14F*
T	*1A-11-17-10 (4x)-14A*
F	*Travel*
S	*10-Meet*
S	*Settle in-spring trip*

Day	*A.M.*	*P.M.*
M	*1A-3*	*1A-6B(8)-4A(1,2,3)-4B(1,2,3)-14A*
T	*1-14F*	*1-20-3-14F*
W	*1-3*	*1A-17-6A(8)-6B(8)-14A-14F*
T		*1A-6B(8)-4A-4B-11-14F*
F	*Light*	*Light*
S	*10-Triangular meet*	
S	*Travel home*	

Sheet 18-7. Shot-put training schedule

Shot-Put NAME DATE *April*

1. A. Jog 1 or 2 laps, easy stretching B. Weights and jog
   C.
2. Fartlek run A. Varied pace B. Slow, steady
3. Weights and resistance activities.
4. Routine A. Stand B. Crossing (1) Lift
   (2) Turn (3) Push
5. Effort A. Stand B. Crossing
   (1) Easy (2) Medium (3) Hard
6. Technique A. Stand-shot almost in palm
   B. Crossing—have speed under control
   (1) Comfortable knee bend (2) Hip push from cock position
   (3) Left arm in position, pull for torque
   (4) Eye on ground or target (5) Every 3d or 4th explode
   (6) Lift well before turn (7) Squeeze the shot
   (8) Right foot in center of ring (9) Target for 3/4 to 7/8 effort
   (a) Stand (b) Crossing (10) Left foot timing and position
   (11) Reach on put and lean into it (12)
7. Squad meeting
8. Special A. Sauna B. Swim C. Steps or hill
9. Alternate stand-step-crossing routine; same letters as item 6
10. Test or compete—record below
11. Cross ring easy. Feeling of exploding. Start slow, finish fast.
12. With coach
14. A. Wind sprints B. Starts, go 25 yds.
    C. High knee and fast leg D. Hurdles
    E. Spring and bound F. Alternate walk-run go 880 or more
15. A. Hendricks Park B. Laurelwood Golf Course
16. Tumbling activities
17. Have feeling of low and relaxed. No strain at back or in crossing.
18. A. On staying in the ring B. Lift-turn
19. Ring crossing, feet not too far spread only as fast as you can control. Same as item 6.
20. Secondary event
21. A. Pictures B. Film C. Video

Date	Result	3/4	Now	Goal

M	*1A - 3 - 14A*
T	*1A - 6A(6) 3x - 6B(6) 3x - 9A(4) 4-6x - 9A(2) 4-6x - 14F*
W	*3 - 14B*
T	*1-5A - 6A(7) - 11 - 20*
F	*Easy*
S	*10 - Dual meet*
S	*Your choice*
M	*3 - 14B*
T	*7 - 1A - 6A(6) 3-4x - 6A(4) 3-4x - 9*
W	*3 - 20*
T	*7 - 1A - 6A(1) 3-4x - 6B(1) 3-4x - 11 - 14A*
F	*Easy jog*
S	*10 - Dual meet*
S	*Your choice*
M	*3 - 14B (easy)*
T	*1A - 6A(2) 3x - 6A(6) 3x - 6A(2) 3x - 9 - 14F*
W	*3 - 20*
T	*7 - 1A - 6A(2) 2-3x - 6A(3) 3-4x - 6B(9) - Easy 4x 20*
F	*Travel*
S	*10 - Dual meet*
S	*Home and loosen up*
M	*2 - 14F*
T	*12 - 21B - 5A - 6A - 6B - 9 - 14F*
W	*2 - 20*
T	*12 - 16(8) - 6B(8) - 17 - 19 - 14A*
F	*Gear ready*
S	*10 - Dual meet*
S	*Your Choice*

Sheet 18-8. Shot-put training schedule

Shot-Put NAME DATE May

1. A. Jog 1 or 2 laps, easy stretching B. Weights and jog
   C.
2. Fartlek run A. Varied pace B. Slow, steady
3. Weights and resistance activities.
4. Routine A. Stand B. Crossing (1) Lift
   (2) Turn (3) Push
5. Effort A. Stand B. Crossing
   (1) Easy (2) Medium (3) Hard
6. Technique A. Stand-shot almost in palm
   B. Crossing—have speed under control
   (1) Comfortable knee bend (2) Hip push from cock position
   (3) Left arm in position, pull for torque
   (4) Eye on ground or target (5) Every 3d or 4th explode
   (6) Lift well before turn (7) Squeeze the shot
   (8) Right foot in center of ring (9) Target for 3/4 to 7/8 effort
   (a) Stand (b) Crossing (10) Left foot timing and position
   (11) Reach on put and lean into it (12)
7. Squad meeting
8. Special A. Sauna B. Swim C. Steps or hill
9. Alternate stand-step-crossing routine; same letters as item 6
10. Test or compete—record below
11. Cross ring easy. Feeling of exploding. Start slow, finish fast.
12. With coach
14. A. Wind sprints B. Starts, go 25 yds.
    C. High knee and fast leg D. Hurdles
    E. Spring and bound F. Alternate walk-run go 880 or more
15. A. Hendricks Park B. Laurelwood Golf Course
16. Tumbling activities
17. Have feeling of low and relaxed. No strain at back or in crossing.
18. A. On staying in the ring B. Lift-turn
19. Ring crossing, feet not too far spread only as fast as you can control. Same as item 6.
20. Secondary event
21. A. Pictures B. Film C. Video

Date	Result	3/4	Now	Goal

Day	Schedule
M	1-3-14A-14F
T	7-12-6A(2)-9A(2)-10-17-14B
W	Form work and 20
T	1A-Distance(3x)-11-17-12-Distance(3x)-11-8
F	Travel
S	10-Dual meet
S	Home and loosen up
M	1-3-14F
T	12 with Coach-Technique and target (Aug.-10%)
W	12A-as on Tuesday, 10% less than average.
T	Light-3
F	Light-3
S	10-Twilight meet
S	Your choice
M	Target 10% less than average-3-14A
T	1-4-9AB(5)-18A-11-14A
W	3-14A
T	1-9(11)
F	Light-gear ready
S	10-Northern Division
S	4 puts-3
M	Light-3
T	1-4-9AB(5)-17-14F
W	1-4-11-form work-14A
T	Light
F	Travel
S	10-Pac 8 Meet
S	

Sheet 18-9. Shot-put training schedule

Shot-Put NAME DATE Late May or June

1. A. Jog 1 or 2 laps, easy stretching B. Weights and jog
   C.
2. Fartlek run A. Varied pace B. Slow, steady
3. Weights and resistance activities.
4. Routine A. Stand B. Crossing (1) Lift
   (2) Turn (3) Push
5. Effort A. Stand B. Crossing
   (1) Easy (2) Medium (3) Hard
6. Technique A. Stand-shot almost in palm
   B. Crossing—have speed under control
   (1) Comfortable knee bend (2) Hip push from cock position
   (3) Left arm in position, pull for torque
   (4) Eye on ground or target (5) Every 3d or 4th explode
   (6) Lift well before turn (7) Squeeze the shot
   (8) Right foot in center of ring (9) Target for 3/4 to 7/8 effort
   (a) Stand (b) Crossing (10) Left foot timing and position
   (11) Reach on put and lean into it (12)
7. Squad meeting
8. Special A. Sauna B. Swim C. Steps or hill
9. Alternate stand-step-crossing routine; same letters as item 6
10. Test or compete—record below
11. Cross ring easy. Feeling of exploding. Start slow, finish fast.
12. With coach
14. A. Wind sprints B. Starts, go 25 yds.
    C. High knee and fast leg D. Hurdles
    E. Spring and bound F. Alternate walk-run go 880 or more
15. A. Hendricks Park B. Laurelwood Golf Course
16. Tumbling activities
17. Have feeling of low and relaxed. No strain at back or in crossing.
18. A. On staying in the ring B. Lift-turn
19. Ring crossing, feet not too far spread only as fast as you can control. Same as item 6.
20. Secondary event
21. A. Pictures B. Film C. Video

Date	Result	3/4	Now	Goal

M	1-2-11-17-14F
T	Light
W	3x 10-14A-14F
T	Semi-competition
F	Light
S	3x 1A-3-6B(8)-17-10-14F
S	3x 1A-10-17-14A-14F
M	Jog
T	Jog
W	1-3-6B(1)(2)-17-14A
T	2x 1-3-6B(8)-17-10-14A
F	Jog
S	Jog
S	3x 1-6A(1)-6B(1)(3)-10-9A(8)-17-14A
M	1-3-9A(8)-17-14F
T	Medium-3 puts-14B
W	Light
T	Light
F	Qualify-NCAA meet
S	Finals
S	Home
M	
T	
W	
T	
F	
S	
S	

Sheet 18-10. Shot-put training schedule

Endnotes

1. Bill Black. (1987). The scientific bases of training for the shot put. *Track and Field Quarterly Review, 87*(3), 14-17.
2. Harmon Brown. (1985). Some principles of throwing. *Track Technique, 93*, 2955.
3. George Dunn. (1987). Current trends in shot put training. *Track Technique, 98*, 3118-3123.
4. Black, 15.
5. Bogdan Poprawski. (1988). Aspects of strength, power and speed in shot put training. *New Studies in Athletics, 3*(1), 89-93.
6. John Kenneson. (1987). Rotary shot putting. *Track and Field Quarterly Review, 87*(3), 5-6.
7. Ken Shannon. (1988). Fundamentals for the throws. *Track and Field Quarterly Review, 88*(3), 13-14.
8. Max Jones. (1988). Why can't a woman be more like a man? *Track Technique, 104*, 3331.
9. Ralf Uebel. (1986). The value of different weighted shots in the practice and teaching of shot putters. *Track and Field Quarterly Review, 86*(1), 18-21.
10. L.A. Vasiliyev. (1985). Varied-weight shots in specific power development. In Jess Jarver (Ed.), *The throws: Contemporary theory, technique and training* (3rd ed.). Los Altos, CA: Tafnews, 68-70.
11. Peter Tschiene. (1988). The throwing events: Recent trends in technique and training. *New Studies in Athletics, 3*(1), 7-17.

Core Readings

Amicale des Entraîneurs Français d'Athlétisme, ed. (1987). *The throws: Official Report of the XIVth Congress, European Athletics Coaches Association*. Paris: European Athletics Coaches Association.

Dunn, George D., Jr., & Kevin McGill. (2003). *The Throws Manual* (3rd ed.). Mountain View, CA: Tafnews.

Freeman, William H. (2001). Periodized training for throwers. In *Peak When It Counts: Periodization for American track and field* (4th ed.). Mountain View, CA: Tafnews, 131-139.

Godina, Bill, & Ron Backes. (2000). Shot put. In *USA Track and Field coaching manual*. Champaign, IL: Human Kinetics, 219-233.

Jarver, Jess, ed. (2000). *The Throws: Contemporary Theory, Technique and Training* (5th ed.). Mountain View, CA: Tafnews.

Naclerio, Tony. (1988). *The Teaching Progressions of the Shot Put, Discus and Javelin*. Rockaway, NJ: Author.

Silvester, Jay. (2003). *The complete book of throws*. Champaign, IL: Human Kinetics.

USA Track & Field Coaching Education Program. (n.d.). *Level II: Throws. USA Track & Field*. Invaluable; revised regularly.

Recommended Readings

Aikens, Jim. (Winter 2001). Fremd High school throwing program. *Track Coach, 154*, 4909-4914.

Arbeit, Ekkart, Anders Borgström, Carl Johnson & Yuriy Sedykh. (1996). NSA Round Table 30: The role of speed in the throws. *New Studies in Athletics, 11*(1), 11-16.

Armbrust, Wayne T. (Summer 2004). Understanding non-uniform forces in the throws, with implications for training. *Track Coach, 168*, 5369-5372.

Babbitt, Don. (2006). Endurance training for the throws [abstract]. *New Studies in Athletics, 21*(1), 62-63.

Bakarinov, Juri. (1990). Theoretical aspects of training control for highly qualified throwers. *New Studies in Athletics, 5*(1), 7-15.

Bakarov, Yuriy, Werner Goldmann, Aleksej Ivanov, Anatoli Kvitov, Janne Palokangas, Vladimir Sherstyuk, Peter Tschiene & Mike Winch. (1997). NSA Round Table 35: Shot put. *New Studies in Athletics, 12*(4), 9-24.

Bartonietz, Klaus. (1992). Rotational shot put training [abstract]. *Track Technique, 119*, 3810.

Bartonietz, Klaus. (Summer 2003). Training with varied weight implements [abstract]. *Track Coach, 164*, 5250.

Bartonietz, Klaus. (1992). Werner Günthör's shot technique. [abstract]. *Track Technique, 121*, 3873-3874.

Bartonietz, Klaus, & Anders Borgström. (1995). The throwing events at the World Championships in Athletics 1995, Göteborg—Technique of the world's best athletes Part 1: Shot put and hammer throw. *New Studies in Athletics, 10*(4), 43-63.

Boggis, Don. (Winter 2002). A circuit for young throwers. *Track Coach, 158*, 5047-5048.

Bondarchuk, Anatoliy. (Spring 2002). Individualization of throwing training [abstract]. *Track Coach, 159*, 5090-5091.

Burnett, Angus. (Spring 2002). Relevance of jumping exercises to field event athletes [abstract]. *Track Coach, 159*, 5090.

Dunn, George. (Spring 1999). Crash training to state championship. *Track Coach, 147*, 4681-4683, 4704.

Feuerbach, Al. (1987). Teaching the shot put. *Track and Field Quarterly Review, 87*(3), 4.

Johnson, Carl. (1992). Why hasn't rotational shot putting taken off in the same way that the Fosbury Flop has? *Track Technique, 121*, 3865-3867.

Judge, Larry. (1991). Using the dynamic start in the glide. *Track Technique, 116*, 3700-3703.

Judge, Larry, & Jeffrey Potteiger. (Summer 2000). Using a battery of tests to identify overtraining in throwers [abstract]. *Track Coach, 152*, 4867.

Krevald, Aadu, et al. (Spring 2003). A comparison of shot put techniques [abstract]. *Track Coach, 163*, 5221-5222.

Linthorne, Nick. (Summer 2003). Optimum projection angles in throwing events [abstract]. *Track Coach, 164*, 5252.

Liskowskaya, Natalia. (1990). About my Olympic preparations [abstract]. *Track Technique, 110*, 3522.

Locatelli, Elio. (1997). Difficulties in judging rotational shot put technique. *New Studies in Athletics, 12*(4), 7-8.

Luhtanen, Pekka, Minna Blomqvist & Tomi Vänttinen. (1997). A comparison of two elite shot putters using the rotational shot put technique. *New Studies in Athletics, 12*(4), 25-34.

Marks, Richard. (1985). Specialized strength and technique training for shot and discus. *Track Technique, 91*, 2898-2899.

McGill, Kevin. (1984). Tests of equivalence. *Track and Field Quarterly Review, 84*(1), 50-53.

Miller, Brian P. (1985). Psychological factors in competitive throwing. *Track and Field Quarterly Review, 85*(1), 40-44.

Müller, Harald. (1999). Interview: Astrid Kumbernuss: Part I. *New Studies in Athletics, 14*(2), 59-62. Part II. *14*(3), 59-65.

Oesterreich, Rolf, Klaus Baronietz & Werner Goldmann. (1997). Rotational technique: A model for the long-term preparation of young athletes. *New Studies in Athletics, 12*(4), 35-48.

Paish, Wilf. (Winter 2005). Coaches in a spin—An appraisal of shot putting. *Track Coach, 170*, 5435-5436, 5438.

Post, David. (Winter-Spring 2006). Important flight parameters in the shot put. *Track Coach, 174*, 5571-5572; *175*, 5601-5602.

Probst, Jorg. (Winter 2003). Rethinking the role of strength in the throwing events [abstract]. *Track Coach, 162*, 5186.

Reardon, Jim. (1991). Psychological characteristics of elite junior male and female throwers. *Track Technique, 114*, 3627-3629.

Roundtable: Rotational versus glide technique in the shot put. (Fall 2003). *Track Coach, 165*, 5270-5275. Participants: Steven Lemke, Kirsten Hellier, Rudolf Supko & Scott Murphy.

Scholz, Wolfram. (2006). The throwing events at the IAAF World Junior Championships: A whistle stop on the journey to elite athletics. Trans. Jürgen Schiffer. *New Studies in Athletics, 21*(2), 7-27.

Schiffer, Jürgen. (1997). Selected and annotated bibliography 44: Rotational technique of shot putting. *New Studies in Athletics, 12*(4), 81-98.

Schiffer, Jürgen. (2003). Selected and annotated bibliography 64: Shot put. *New Studies in Athletics, 18*(4), 83-128.

Smith, John. (Summer 2005). A linear approach for rotational shot putting: Working the earth. *Track Coach, 172*, 5500-5503.

Track Coach visits Bill Godina. (1995). *Track Coach, 131*, 4172-4174.

Venegas, Art. (1989). U.C.L.A. shot put-discus conditioning program. *Track and Field Quarterly Review, 89*(3), 6-8.

Young, Michael A. (Winter 2004). Critical factors in the shot put. *Track Coach, 166*, 5299-5304; McGill, Kevin. (Spring 2004). Letter regarding lack of references. *Track Coach, 167*, 5347; Young, Michael A. (Spring 2004). Author's reply, with references. *Track Coach, 167*, 5347-5348.

Young, Michael, & Li Li. (2005). Determination of critical parameters among elite female shot putters. *Sports Biomechanics, 4*(2), 131-148.

19

The Hammer Throw

The first version (1974) of this chapter was written by Arne Nytro of Norway. The later versions (1991 & 2009) were revised by William H. Freeman.

Bowerman's Best

The hammer throw was not a conference event during his coaching years.

People have used the hammer as both tool and weapon for thousands of years. The first known competition was in the Aenoch Taillteann Games in Ireland about 500 B.C. The hammer has been thrown in Scotland since about 300 A.D. From Scotland, the event was introduced into England, where it was a popular sport during the 16th century. The implement of that time was either a blacksmith's hammer or a round stone with a wooden handle.

In the 1860s, the hammer throw was introduced into university sports. The implement evolved into a metal ball at the end of a chain with an attached handgrip. Figure 19-1 shows how the hammer is held with an overlapping grip. The early Olympic champions were Irish or Irish-Americans. Though the hammer throw is an Olympic event of great popularity in Eastern Europe, it has long been the orphan stepchild of track and field in the United States.

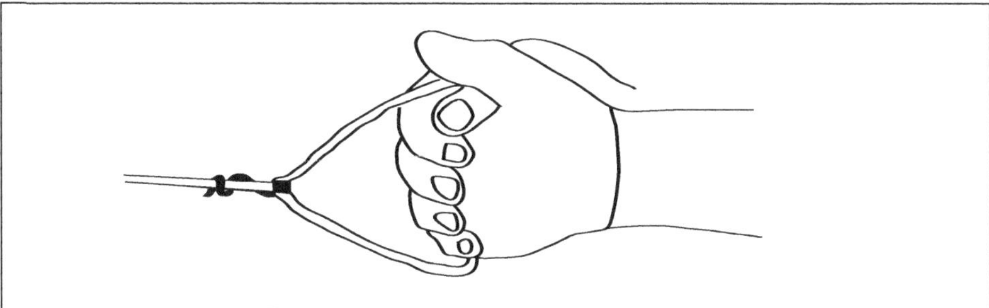

Figure 19-1. Proper hammer grip

Training Theory

For some years now, the leading hammer throwers have come from Eastern Europe. The world record has decisively passed the 80-meter (262′ 5″) range. Throwing distance is affected by the following three factors:

- Release velocity
- Release angle
- Release height[1]

The release velocity appears to be the most important factor. For a 75-meter thrower, a 5 percent speed increase adds 7 meters to the throw, while a 5 percent change in the release angle changes the distance by only 60 cm. The ideal release angle is 44 degrees, though most elite throwers achieve an angle of 38 to 40 degrees. It may be that a thrower cannot rise to the same release speed with a steeper release angle.

Maximum release velocity is achieved by lengthening the path that the hammer follows until it is released. The path is made longer by having a longer radius of rotation, which is done by the counter-position of the pelvis, and extended arms and a relaxed shoulder girdle.

By bending the knees, thereby dropping to more of a sitting position during the turns, the thrower makes the radius of rotation longer. When the thrower extends the arms to their maximum length, while relaxing the shoulder girdle, the arms seem to "stretch" to more than their usual length. The result is a longer radius, a longer pull, and faster velocity of the hammer. Wide winds (preliminary swings) help to set the stage for this movement.

The thrower must minimize the single-support time (when one foot is off the ground during rotation). The hammer is accelerated during the double support, pulled strongly downward as the thrower collapses the knee while the hammer is high in the air. On each turn, the trail leg (the right leg for a right-handed thrower) is picked up and touches down earlier than in the previous turn (Figure 19-2).

Efficient movement with today's technique shows the following elements:

- The trail leg is swung closely around the pivot leg.
- The distance between the feet decreases as the turns progress (from about two feet to about one foot).
- During all turns, a relatively stable triangle is formed between the arms and the shoulder axis.
- The position of the shoulder axis relative to the hip axis is relatively stable.
- The athlete's eyes are focused on the hammerhead.
- The stable rhythmic organization of the first to the last turn is characterized by these points:

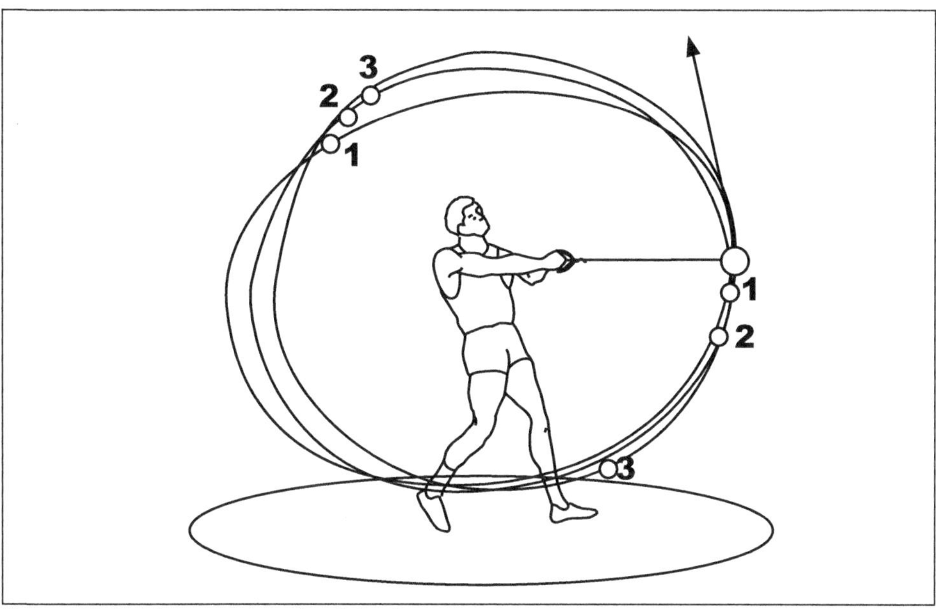

Figure 19-2. Movement path of the hammer

- ✓The position of the hammerhead during the trail foot's touchdown gradually shifts toward the high point.
- ✓As the turns progress, the low point of the hammerhead moves toward the final release path (lower at the low point).[2]

The hammer throw is very technically complex. The East Germans tested prospects at age 13 (Table 19-1). They believe that an athlete must train for 10 to 12 years to become an elite thrower.

East German Standards for 13-Year-Old Hammer Prospects

Height: 5′ 7″
Weight: 121-137 lbs.
Arm span: At least two inches more than height
30m (crouch start): 4.8 seconds
30m (flying start): 4.0 seconds
60m (crouch start): 8.8 seconds
3 two-footed hops: 22′ 4″
3 kg (6.6 lb.) shot: 37′ 9″

Note: Also test the flexibility of the shoulder girdle.

Table 19-1. East German standards for 13-year-old hammer prospects

For the athlete to make long throws as an adult, the technique must be engrained. To do this, lighter hammers are used, so the best junior throwers can reach 80 to 90 meters by age 17 (using a 3-kg hammer, compared to 7.25 kg for the regular hammer). The reason is that the mechanical factors for an 80-meter throw are the same, regardless of the weight of the implement. Thus, the athlete learns the technique of the throw by repeating it with an implement that is light enough to allow him to throw 80 meters, if his technique is correct.

East German researchers noted that "the experiences of the world's best hammer throwers show the great advantages of light implements as far as the perfection of the specific movement capacities and technique are concerned. The aim of the training of young hammer throwers is to achieve long throwing distances without a marked degree of strength development."[3] Table 19-2 shows the youth throwing goals.

East German Performance Goals for Young Throwers

Age	*Meet Hammer*	*Distance*	*Light Hammer*	*Distance*
13	3 kg	55 (180′)	2 kg	60 (197′)
14	4 kg	60 (197′)	3 kg	66 (217′)
15	5 kg	62 (203′)	3 kg	74 (243′)
16	6.25 kg	62 (203′)	3 kg	80 (252′)
17	6.25 kg	68 (223′)	3 kg	86-90 (282′-295′)

Table 19-2. East German performance goals for young throwers

Training uses technique units with drills using wooden sticks, leather balls with straps or wires, medicine balls, and light (2-kg) hammers. Each technical unit must be mastered before the next is attempted, with much use of part-whole learning. Sprint and jump training are used, along with event-specific conditioning and stretching exercises.

For adults, more use is made of strength and speed-strength training. Specific strength training falls into three categories:

- Throwing hammers: different weights, one to four turns
- Strength exercises for shoulder, trunk, and legs (similar to event movements):
  - ✓Standing diagonal throws
  - ✓Jumps with extra loads
  - ✓Trunk exercises with extra loads in swings and turns
- Forms of pulling and leg-strength exercises with barbells, major exercises being the snatch, clean, pull, and squats

Throwers use a double-periodized year, as shown in Figure 19-10. Anatoliy Bondarchuk, the most successful Russian hammer coach, divides the development of hammer throwers into three stages.

Initial Preparation Level: Ages 12 to 14. Three or four sessions per week, 90 to 120 minutes each, including:

- All-around development exercises, sprinting, jumping
- Using light implements (3 to 5 kg)

- Shot-putting (4 to 6 kg) from different positions
- Weight training
- Maximum training load for single session:
  - ✓2 tons of weight lifted
  - ✓15 to 20 hammer throws
  - ✓25 throws with the shot
  - ✓500 meters of sprinting
  - ✓Most training in first (50 to 80 percent) and second (80 to 90 percent) zones of intensity
  - ✓5 percent of training load in higher zones

Special Fundamental Preparation Level: Ages 14 to 18. Five to eight sessions per week, 120 to 150 minutes each, including:

- All-around development exercises, sprinting, jumping
- Use light (5 to 6 kg), normal, and heavy (8 kg) hammers
- Shot-putting (6 to 16 kg) from different positions
- Weight training and special exercises
- Maximum training load for single session:
  - ✓5 to 6 tons of weight lifted
  - ✓25 hammer throws
  - ✓25 throws with the shot
  - ✓1,000 meters of sprinting
  - ✓60 to 70 percent of weights in second zone (80 to 90 percent)
  - ✓25 percent of weights in first (50 to 80 percent) zone of intensity
  - ✓10 to 15 percent of training load in higher zone (90 to 100 percent)

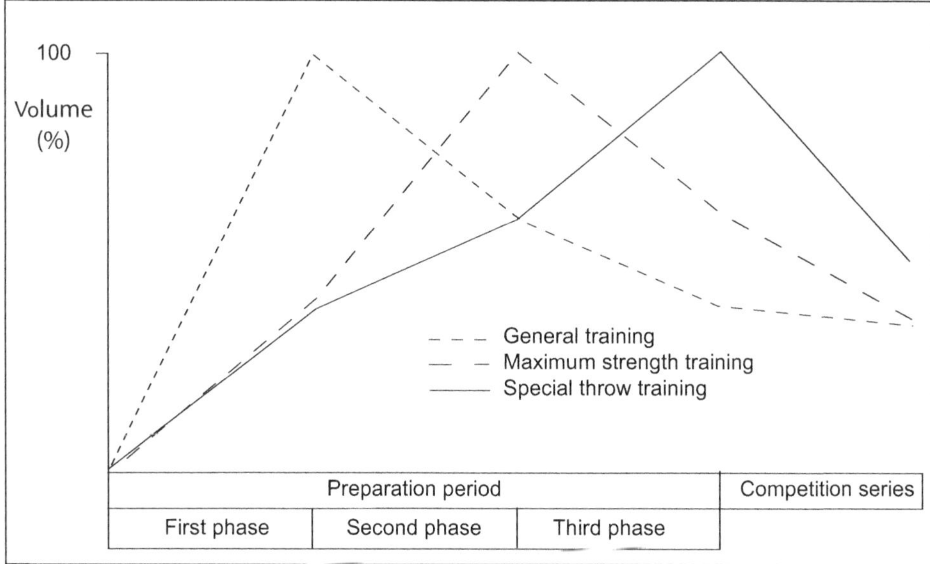

Figure 19-3. Periodized training year for the hammer

Perfecting Acquired Skill Level: Ages 18 and over. Can reach 200 throws a day, but have found that 30 to 40 (sometimes 50 to 60) throws are sufficient. [4]

The Russian throwers mix light and heavy implements with the regulation-weight implement in all of their throwing events. Figure 19-4 shows a single-period macrocycle and the changing training emphasis of the different weights. Figure 19-5 shows a double-period pattern, again one that is appropriate for athletes competing indoors.

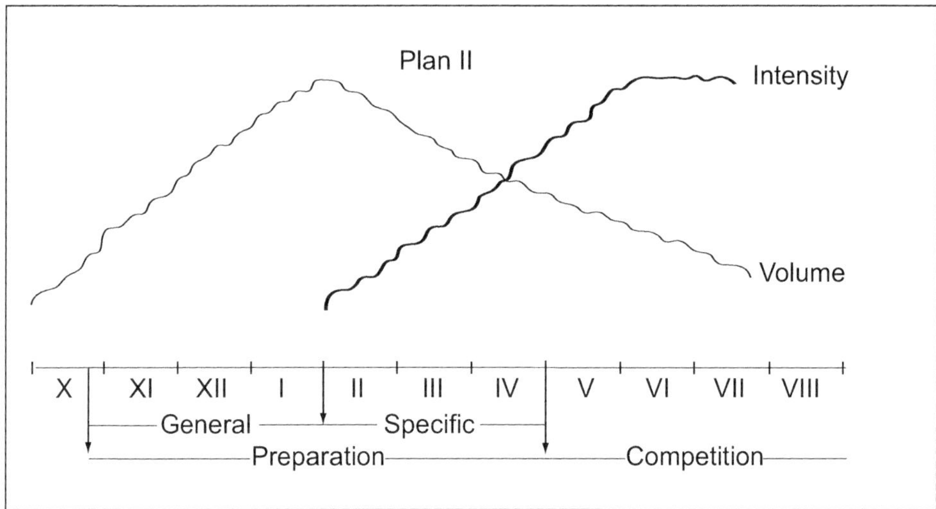

Figure 19-4. Single-periodized year for the hammer

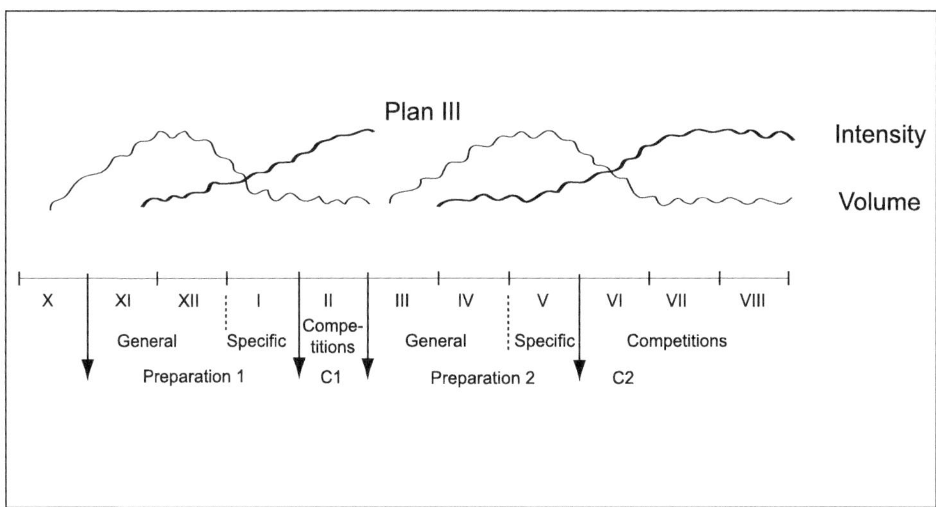

Figure 19-5. Double-periodized year for the hammer

Table 19-3 shows two variations of training by Bondarchuk for elite throwers.[5] Table 19-4 gives another example of elite training loads, with the Soviet use of precise measurement of the training load. The athlete is Yuriy Syedikh, a world-record holder and Olympic champion coached by Bondarchuk.[6] Figure 19-6 shows the relative emphases of types of training across the year, based on Soviet training theory.[7]

Weekly Cycle for Elite Hammer Thrower

Variant I: 5 Days, 10 Sessions

Monday, Tuesday, Friday

❑ Morning Session:
- 10 minutes warming up
- 12 throws with light (6 kg) hammer
- 15 throws with regular (7.25 kg) hammer
- 10 throws with heavier (9 kg) implement

❑ Evening Session:
- 10 minutes warming up
- Weight exercises: 10 tons
  - ✓Snatch: 1.5 tons
  - ✓Twisting: 1 ton
  - ✓Good morning: 1.5 tons
  - ✓Half squat: 4 tons
  - ✓Jumping from half squat: 2 tons

Wednesday and Saturday

❑ Morning Session:
- 10 minutes warming up
- 30 throws with 16 kg weight (50 cm handle), 1-2 turns
- 15 standing long jumps
- 50 throws with 16 kg weight in different kind
- 10 standing triple jumps

❑ Evening Session:
- 10 minutes warming up
- Weight exercise: 5 tons
  - ✓Twisting: 2 tons
  - ✓Jumps from half squat: 1 ton
  - ✓Half squat: 2 tons

Thursday, Sunday

Rest

Variant II: 6 Days, 12 Sessions

Monday, Wednesday, Friday

❑ Morning Session:
- 10 minutes warming up
- 10 throws with light (6.5 kg) hammer
- 10 throws with regular (7.25 kg) hammer
- 10 throws with heavier (8.5 kg) hammer

❑ Evening Session:
- 10 minutes warming up
- Weight exercise: 8 tons
  - ✓Twisting: 2 tons
  - ✓Step test on bench with barbell: 3.5 tons
  - ✓Cleans without splitting: 2.5 tons

Tuesday, Thursday, Saturday

❑ Morning Session:
- 10 minutes warming up
- 100 throws with 16 kg implement in different kind
- 30 standing long jumps

❑ Evening Session:
- 10 minutes warming up
- Weight exercises: 5 tons
  - ✓Twisting: 1.5 tons
  - ✓Good morning: 1.5 tons
  - ✓Jumping from half squat: 2 tons
  - ✓Playing games: 20 minutes (basketball, volleyball)

Sunday

Rest

Table 19-3. Weekly cycle for elite hammer thrower

Increase in Load Volume for Hammer Throwers

Year	*1976* %	*1980* %	*1984* %	*1984* *Absolute values (9 months)*
Training days	100	125	138	222
Total throws	100	118	151	6,332
Barbell training	100	170	198	1,402 (tons)

Table 19-4. Increase in load volume for hammer thrower

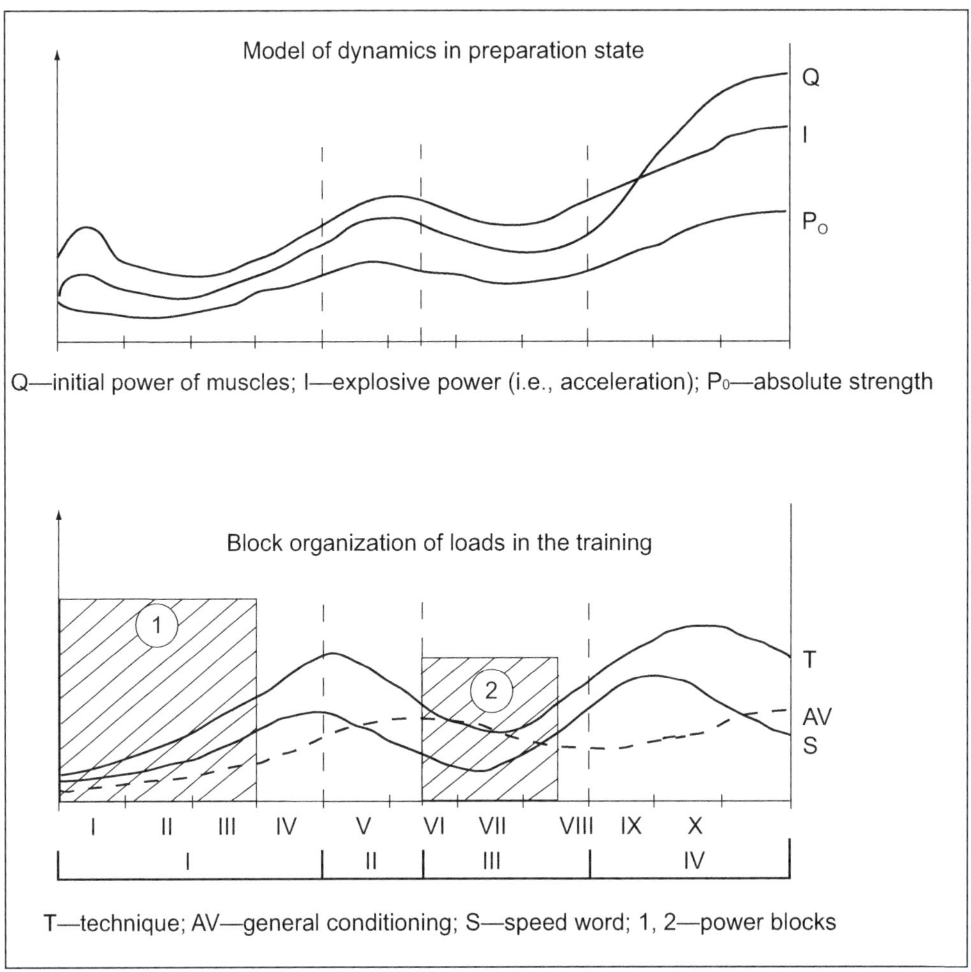

Figure 19-6. Periodized training emphases for the hammer

The Eastern European sport bodies emphasize modeling in developing the training program for each event. Modeling means developing a model of the specific skill patterns, along with tests and standards, that are needed to reach set levels of elite performance. Then the training program is designed to develop those traits, with the standard tests repeated regularly to measure the athlete's progress toward the standard. Table 19-5 shows the former East German model for the hammer throw.[8]

Ladislav Pataki has worked with SyberVision to develop a training videotape that uses visualization techniques and sound imagery as a major part of training for hammer throwers.[9] Together with Ed Burke and Stewart Togher, he developed a highly useful training booklet for learning the hammer throw.[10] It gives one of the clearest programs for learning the hammer, with appropriate skill-training drills.

Photo 19-1. Ken Flax, NCAA champion and Olympian for Bill Dellinger

Technical Components of the Throw

The length of a throw depends upon two things: the speed of the hammer at the moment of the release, and the angle of release. No significant aerodynamic factors come into play, as with the javelin and the discus. The speed of the hammer results from the thrower's muscular power, reaction time, coordination, and physical stature. His ability to use this biophysical background to increase the hammer's speed from the winds through the turns until the release constitutes his technique. The angle of release also depends on the thrower's technique.

From a theoretical point of view, a tall man with a heavy build has the advantage in the hammer, but a small, powerful thrower can also succeed. The hammer thrower must develop optimal muscular power as a base for advanced technique, which takes years of daily training. Even then, he must continue to train to maintain his strengths and to try to overcome weaknesses.

Model Items in Preparation of Hammer Throwers

Throws		
16 kg weight (of 10 kg)	20m (24m)	65′ 7″ (78′ 9″)
18 kg hammer	48-50m	158′-164′
6 kg hammer	88-89m	289′-292′
5 kg hammer	93-95m	305′-312′
7.25 kg shot, backward	21-22m	68′ 11″ - 72′ 2″
Jumps		
Standing long jump	3.40-3.50m	11′2″ - 11′ 6″
Standing triple jump	9.50-9.80m	31′2″ - 32′ 2″
Sargent jump (jump and reach)	95-100 cm	37″-39″
Weights		
Squats	260-280 kg	573-617 lbs.

Table 19-5. Model items in preparation of hammer throwers

Physical Strength Background

The hammer thrower must have overall strength, but these muscle groups should have special consideration in the power training:

- Legs
  - ✓Extensors of the hip (the gluteals and others)
  - ✓Extensors of the knee (the femoris group)
  - ✓Plantar flexors (gastrocnemius and soleus)

- Lower body
  - ✓Twisters of the trunk (obliquis abdominis externis and internis)
  - ✓Muscles controlling the shoulders and arms (trapezius, rhomboids, deltoids, latissimus)
  - ✓Extensors of the trunk (erector spinae, quadratus lumborum)
  - ✓Finger flexors

Mechanical Background

Looking at technique as measured in terms of physical principles, the key word is *speed*, or *velocity*. The thrower tries to build up a high central speed, or angular velocity, during the turns by means of fast footwork (Figure 19-7). At the same time, he tries to maximize the hammer's peripheral, or linear, velocity by combining the central speed with a long radius. That combination requires long arms and a relaxed upper body. The body's axis of rotation is always moving forward in the circle and describing the outline of a cone (circumduction) (Figure 19-8).

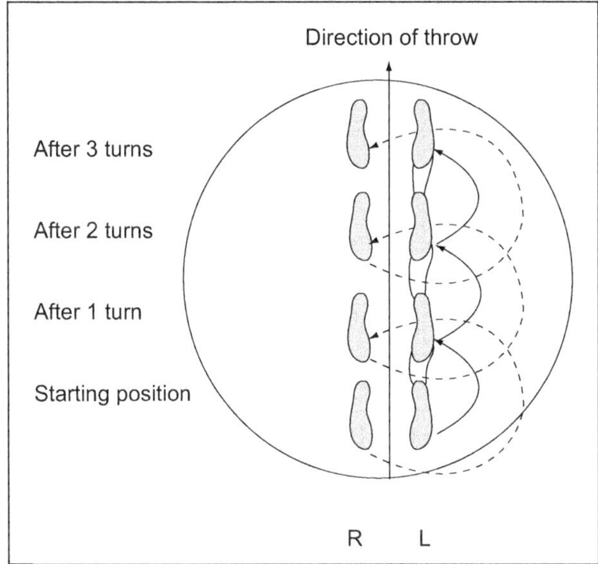

Figure 19-7. Footwork in the hammer throw

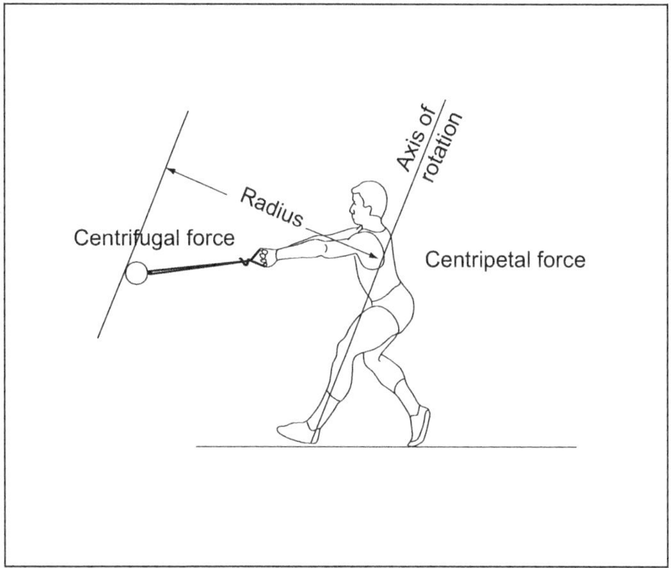

Figure 19-8. Body's axis of rotation during the hammer throw

The fastest central speed and the longest arms give not only the highest speed to the hammer, but also the greatest pull outward (centrifugal force), up to 700 pounds for a throw of 200 feet. To control this force during the turn, the thrower must produce an equal (centripetal) force pulling in the opposite direction. He must keep his knees bent and his lower back straight to control the centrifugal force exerted by the pull of the hammer.

To understand the relationship between the hammer's speed and the angle of delivery, refer to the nomograph that Russian hammer thrower and engineer Anatoliy Samotsvetov constructed (Figure 19-9). Such nomographs can help coaches discover their throwers' potential and correct their faults.

In Samotsvetov's case, he had measured a 200-foot throw. With a stopwatch, he had timed the flight of the hammer, from the release to the landing, as 2.9 seconds. From the nomograph, he can determine that the angle of the release was 33 degrees and the velocity was 82 feet per second. However, using the nomograph, he can also see that if his thrower increased his angle of release to 43 degrees, with the same speed of release, he would have thrown 215 feet.

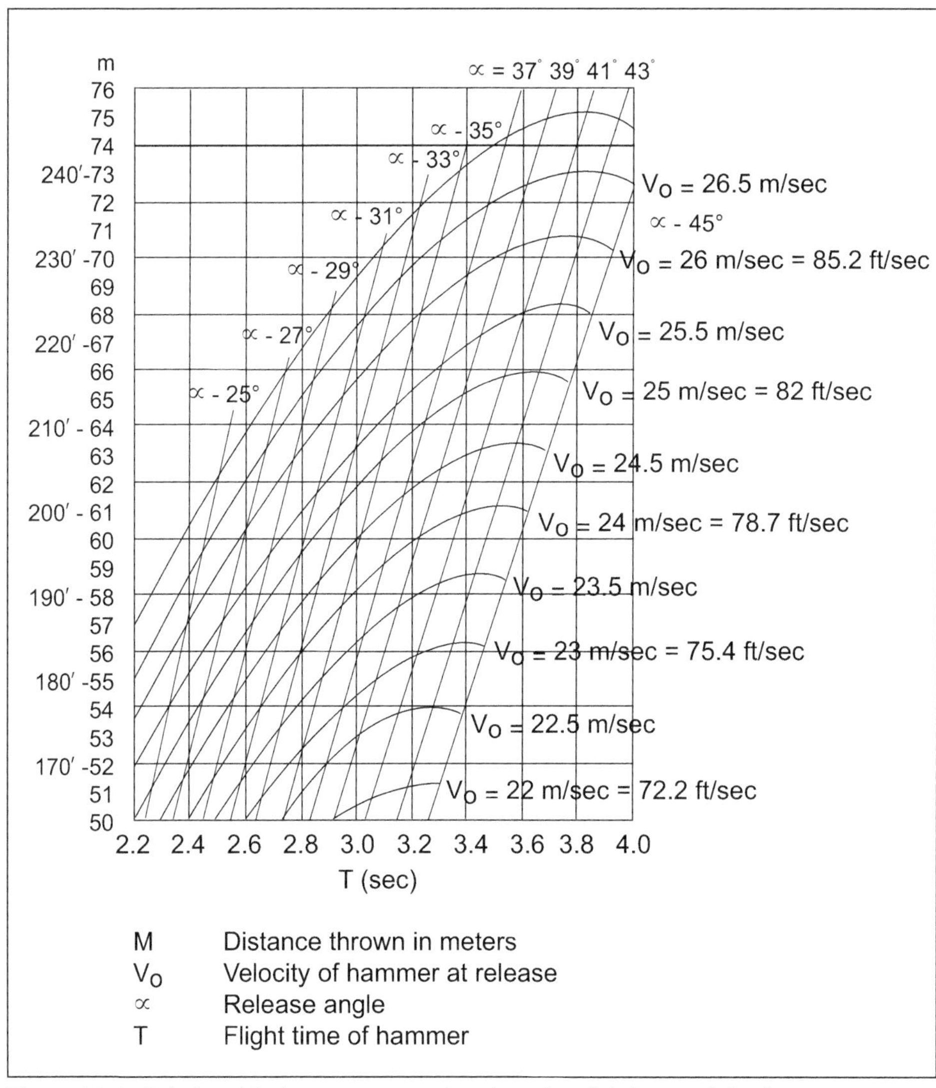

Figure 19-9. Relationship between speed and angle of delivery of the hammer

Common Faults

The following faults are common in each of the areas noted.

In the Starting Position

- Placing the wrong hand on the grip
- Not starting with the hammerhead far enough behind in the preliminary swings
- Bending the elbows and lifting the shoulders
- Bending the trunk forward
- Not bending the knees
- The lowest point of the hammer's swing being too far in front of the athlete
- Not emphasizing the forward and upward part of the swing
- Going too far left with the hands when passing over the head
- Not countering the hips in relation to the shoulders
- Not raising the left heel when turning the trunk right to "meet" the hammer

In the Turns

- Starting the turning of the feet too late and too slow, so the hammer takes the lead
- Not placing the body weight over the bent right leg
- Moving the right leg too slowly and too far from the left in the turn
- Bending the head and upper body forward
- Bending the elbows
- Not turning the left foot 180 degrees, so the thrower ends on the left side of the circle
- Stretching the left knee so the thrower gets too long a turn and ends on the right side of the circle
- The trail of the hammer being too steep

In the Delivery

- The body being too far to the right
- The legs being too extended, so the thrower does not get any power from them and the delivery is too flat
- Using only the upper body in the delivery
- Bending the upper body, the hammerhead touching the ground

After the Delivery

- Stopping the rotation instead of following through
- Stepping out of the front half of the circle

Training for the Hammer Throw

The main goals of training for the hammer throw are to build up general and specific strength and to develop good technique. Roughly one quarter of the training will be allotted to developing technique and the other three quarters to general and special conditioning, using a variety of methods, such as running, games, jumping, flexibility, technical training, and barbell work. The training can be done both indoors and outdoors, depending on local conditions.

Types of Training

Running. Each of the several types of running has its purpose. Jogging is done to warm up, fartlek and long, slow runs develop stamina or cool an athlete off after a hard practice, and sprinting 20 to 40 meters builds up speed.

Games. Games are a combination of running and jumping, but they are more fun. Basketball, volleyball, and soccer are fine for warming up and for recreation.

Flexibility. This training consists of all kinds of arm swings and hip circling to improve these movements and to develop flexibility in the shoulders and the hip region.

Jumping. Jumping is an important training activity because it develops explosive power and speed in the lower extremities. Specifically, broad and high jumps, continuous hops and steps, step-jumping, and rope-skipping develop these skills.

Technical training. This training is important both to the novice, to learn good technique, and to the champion, to try to improve the pattern and speed. Technical training can be done best outdoors, but it is also possible indoors. If the athlete cannot train at the main stadium, it would be worth the effort for him to construct a concrete circle in a quiet place out of the way of activity. Indoors, the athlete can train for technique with sandbags on a rope or with a hammer thrown into a nylon net or a canvas "wall." Technical training for the hammer throw consists of countless swings and turns and releases, practiced in various combinations, with hammers of ordinary weights as well as heavier and lighter implements.

Weight training. Strength is a must for a hammer thrower, and the only way develop strength is to work against resistance. Of the two types of resistance training, isotonic and isometric, the isotonic (dynamic) is recommended. The exercises included in this section (Figures 19-10 and 19-11) are for only that type of training. Strength training can be divided into basic training, with heavy weights, and specific training, with smaller weights. The basic training concentrates on the muscles in the legs, the back, and the arms. The weights used are 70 to 90 percent of the maximum that can be lifted. One to six repetitions are done in three sets. The pauses between the sets are from two to three minutes.

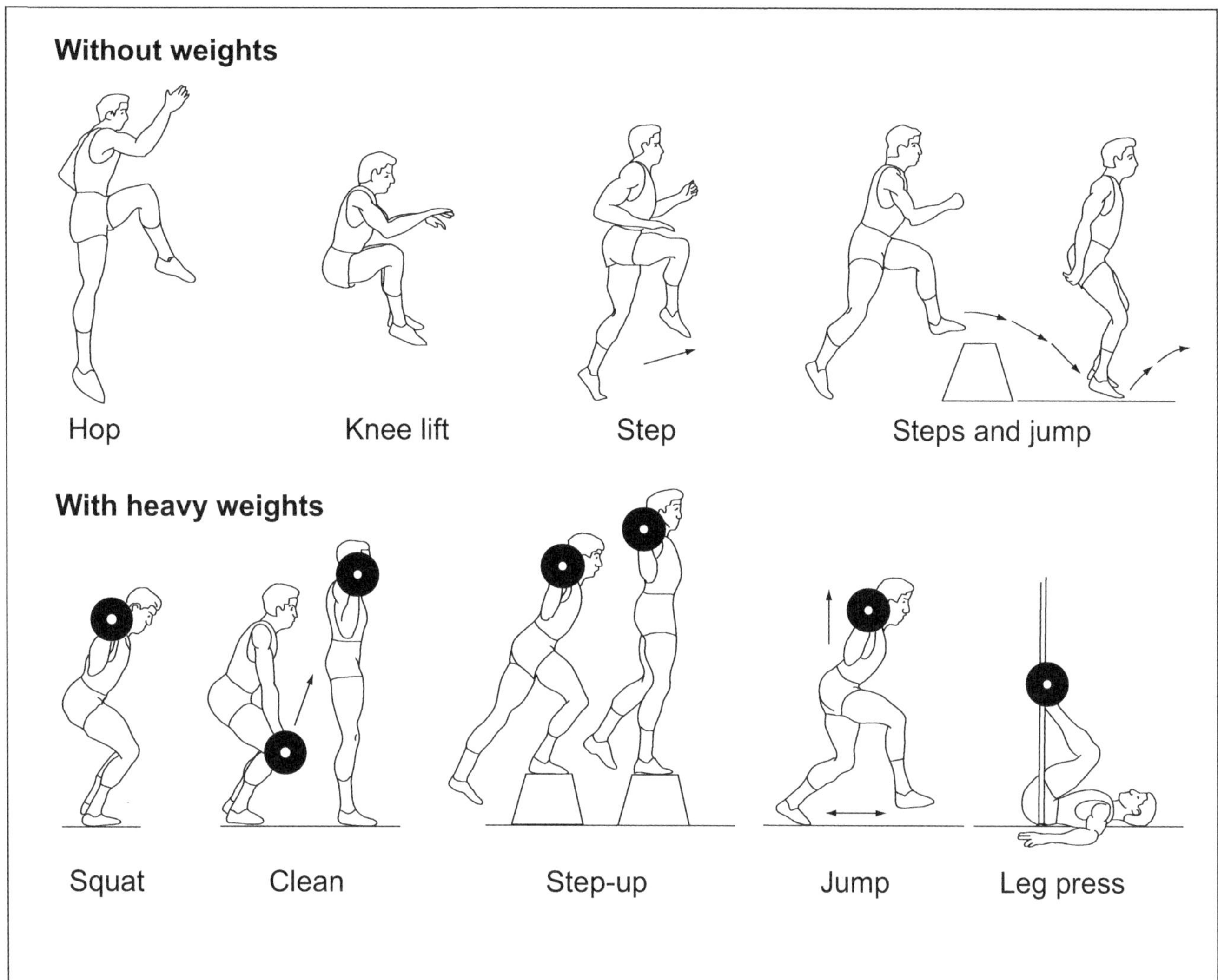

Figure 19-10. Exercises for the lower body

Figure 19-12 shows examples of power exercises. In the specific training, smaller implements and lighter weights are used, such as sandbags, medicine balls, shots, barbell discs, and light and heavy hammers (Figure 19-13). They are all used in exercises that follow the same pattern as the swings, the turns, and the delivery. They are executed as fast as possible and with adequate rest between tries.

Planning the Training Schedule

In all training programs, the athlete must have one plan that encompasses goals over the long term, such as a year, and one or more plans geared toward short-range goals, such as plans for the pre-season months, for competition season, and for days and weeks. All these plans must be flexible enough to accommodate the unpredictable: sickness, injuries, stress from studies, special events, or personal problems.

Figure 19-11. Exercises for the upper body

Figure 19-12. Power exercises

Figure 19-13. Training exercises with small weights

In planning a long-term training program, the athlete should keep certain points in mind:

- In the *off*-season, the aim is to build up and maintain overall physical fitness and strength. At least three days per week should be devoted to this kind of training, and at least one day to technical and more specific training.
- In the competitive season, the athlete still requires two days of all-around training, mixed with auxiliary exercises more specific to the hammer. Technical training should be done two or three days per week.
- The training schedule's ratio of general conditioning to specific training depends largely on the athlete's stage of development. A beginner must spend more time on the basic training than the thrower who has years of practice and several competitions behind him. The experienced thrower must reduce the basic weight training to a level sufficient only to maintain basic strength, and he should spend most of his training time on technique and special weight training.
- The thrower chooses his weights and numbers of repetitions and sets according to his level of development (but within the bounds of accepted training methods).
- Besides weight training and throwing, the athlete should always try to fit in sprints, jumps, and flexibility training. It is best to do this training on the same day as the technical training.
- The number of throws during one "practice day" must never be over 40, and 30 to 40 percent of the throws should be for distance.
- One of the days of technical training should concentrate on special problems of technique, such as:

  ✓Winds and turns without throwing

  ✓Continuous turns (5 to 10) with the hammer or a shot in the hands

  ✓Easy turns with stress on the release
- Warm-up exercises are essential for physical and mental preparedness. The warm-up should always move from slow movements to more vigorous movements; for example, jogging and wind sprints should be followed by calisthenics.

The training load before an important meet is very important, especially during the last two weeks. It determines not only the readiness of the athlete for competition, but also his rate of recovery after competition. The training load for the last 8 to 12 days before competition should be decreased by 50 to 60 percent. During the last week, the number of throws should be reduced to half the number of the previous weeks, and the intensity of the throws should be only 80 to 90 percent of maximum. In short, you should reduce both load and intensity of training before a meet.

Before the meet, the following warm-up is suggested:

- Slow run for 10 to 20 minutes
- Short wind sprints, 20 to 40 meters
- General calisthenics
- Winding the hammer and slow turns
- Two or three easy throws
- One or two harder throws (still not maximum)

Table 19-6 gives a sample year plan. Tables 19-7 and 19-8 give sample training weeks for the preseason and the competition season. As always, these training planes are guidelines, not laws. Sheet 19-1 shows the training schedule sheet for the hammer throw.

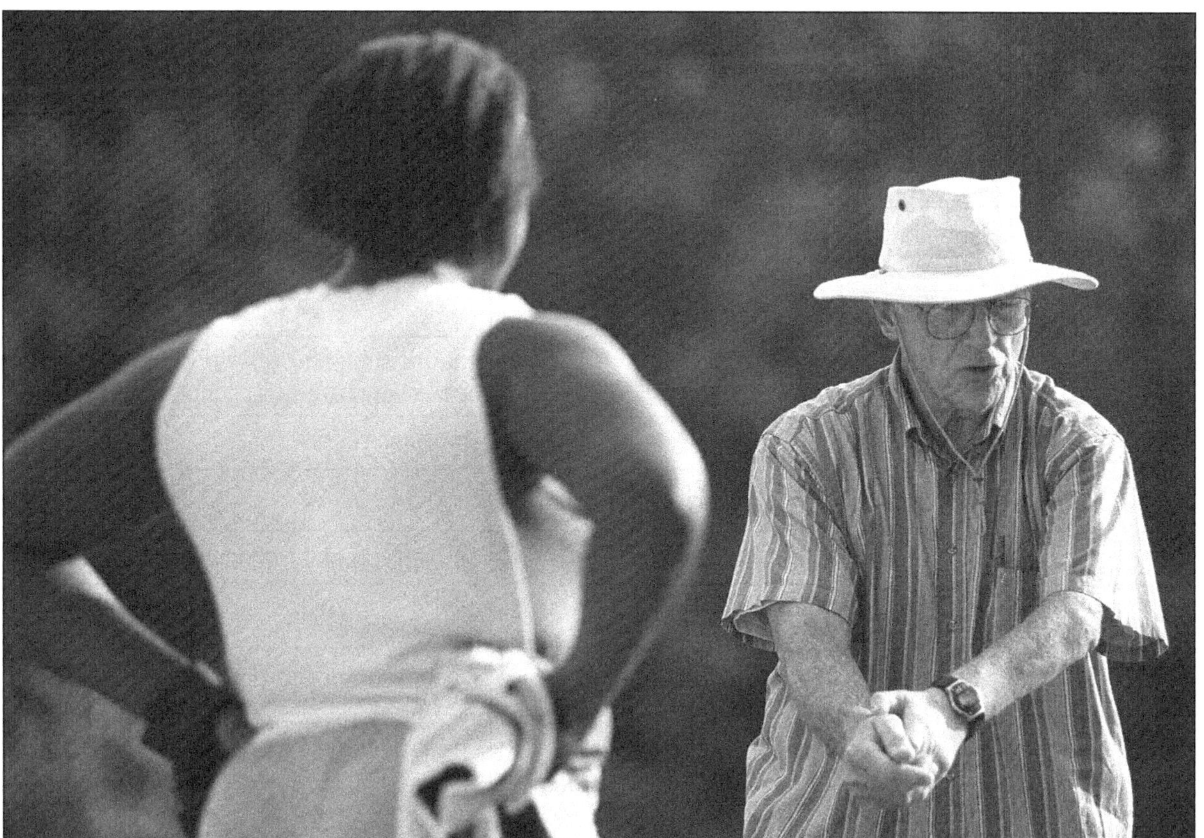

Photo 19-2. Hammer thrower Tamika Powell and her coach Harold Connolly—the most renowned hammer thrower in US track and field history

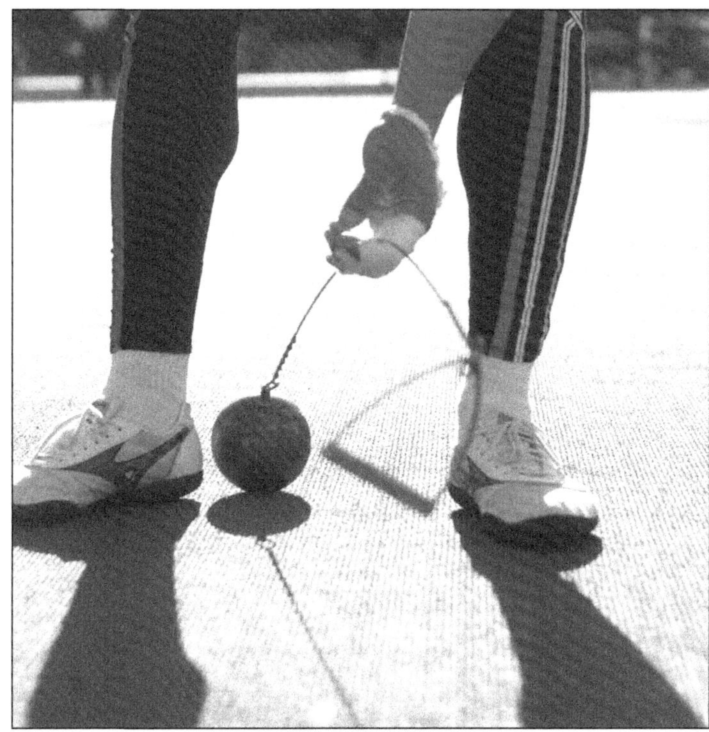

Photo 19-3. In the week before a meet, both the load and intensity of training should be reduced.

Sample One-Year Training Schedule for the Hammer Throw			
	Pre-Season		*Competitive Season*
	September to December (4-5 days a week)	January to March (5-6 days a week)	April to August (4-5 days a week)
Monday	Basic strength training	Fartlek	Basic strength training—long, slow run
Tuesday			Throwing and specific strength training
Wednesday	Basic strength training	Games	Specific strength—light throwing and basic strength, jumps, sprints
Thursday	Technical training	Throwing	Throwing, sprints
Friday	Basic strength training	Specific strength	
Saturday			Competition or throwing; sprints and jumps
Sunday	Throwing, sprints, jumps		
Aim	All-around strength	Specific strength	Preparation for competition—technique
Type of work	Increasing the weights	Same weights; increasing the speed	Reducing the weights

Table 19-6. Sample one-year training schedule for the hammer throw

Sample Week of Pre-Season Training

Monday
- ❑ Warm-up
- ❑ Barbell work
  - ✓Squats: 3 sets of 6
  - ✓Two-handed curls: 2 sets of 10
  - ✓Dead lift: 3 sets of 4
  - ✓Sit-up, with twist: 3 sets of 10
  - ✓Clean: 3 sets of 6
  - ✓Rowing, flat back: 2 sets of 6
  - ✓Leg press (in machine): 2 sets of 6
  - ✓Pull (in machine): 2 sets of 6
- ❑ Exercise for flexibility
- ❑ 1- to 2-mile slow run

Tuesday
No training

Wednesday
- ❑ Warm-up
- ❑ Barbell work
  - ✓Squats: 3 sets of 6
  - ✓Clean: 3 sets of 6
  - ✓Dead lift: 3 sets of 4
  - ✓Good morning, flat back: 3 sets of 4
  - ✓Forward, upward raise: 2 sets of 4
  - ✓Standing, trunk twist and bend: 2 sets of 8
  - ✓Rowing, flat back: 3 sets of 6
- ❑ Exercise for flexibility
- ❑ 1- to 2-mile slow run

Thursday:
- ❑ Warm-up
  - ✓One-handed winds
- ❑ Technical training
  - ✓5 to 10 winds and throws with two hammers or a 25- or 50-pound weight
  - ✓Winds, three turns and throw, with regular hammer; 15 throws with 70% intensity; 10 throws of medium effort.
- ❑ Jumps
  - ✓5-10 x 20-40-meter sprints, standing start
  - ✓5 series of hops, 15 meters on each leg
  - ✓5 series of steps, 25 meters long
- ❑ Auxiliary exercises
  - ✓Arm bending on stallbar or beam, 3 sets of 10
  - ✓Twisting exercises with small weights
- ❑ Exercise for flexibility
- ❑ Slow run

Friday
- ❑ Warm-up
- ❑ Barbell work
  - ✓Squats: 3 sets of 6
  - ✓Bench press: 3 sets of 6
  - ✓Good morning exercise: 2 sets of 6
  - ✓Clean: 3 sets of 6
  - ✓Shoulder shrug: 2 sets of 10
  - ✓Swing bell circling
  - ✓Lying on bench, extended arms twisting
  - ✓Lying down: leg raise and twist
  - ✓Pull (in machine): 2 sets of 6
- ❑ Exercise for flexibility
- ❑ 1- to 2-mile slow run

Saturday
No training

Sunday
Same as Thursday

Table 19-7. Sample week of pre-season training

Sample Week of Competition Training

Monday

- ❑ Warm-up
- ❑ Barbell work
  - ✓One-half squat: 3 sets of 6
  - ✓Clean and jerk: 3 sets of 6
  - ✓Sit-up with twist incline board
  - ✓Step up and down on a box: 20 times
  - ✓Rowing, flat back: 3 sets of 6
  - ✓Leg press (in machine): 2 sets of 6
  - ✓Pull (in machine): 3 sets of 6
- ❑ Exercise for flexibility
- ❑ Jog

Tuesday

- ❑ Warm-up
- ❑ Barbell work
  - ✓Throwing with weights (25- to 50-pound)
  - ✓Throwing a shot backwards, forward, and sideways
  - ✓Pull-up on bar
  - ✓Twisting exercises with the shot in sitting and lying positions
- ❑ 2- to 3-mile slow run

Wednesday

- ❑ Warm-up
- ❑ Throwing
  - ✓Continuous turns
  - ✓20 easy throws
  - ✓10 throws at maximum effort
- ❑ Exercises for flexibility
- ❑ Jog

Thursday

- ❑ Warm-up
- ❑ Throwing
  - ✓Winds and throw without turns
  - ✓20 throws with 3 turns for style
- ❑ Jumps
  - ✓5 series of hops, 15 meters on each leg
  - ✓5 series of steps, 25 meters long
- ❑ Runs
  - ✓Standing start, 5 x 30-meter sprints
  - ✓1-mile slow run

Friday

No training

Saturday

- ❑ Competition

or

- ❑ Warm-up
- ❑ 6 throws, maximum effort, with 3-5 minutes between throws
- ❑ 15 min. jogging
- ❑ 6 more throws at maximum effort as before
- ❑ Wind sprints
- ❑ Exercises for flexibility
- ❑ Jog

Sunday

No training

Table 19-8. Sample week of competition training

HAMMER THROW SCHEDULE NAME ______________________ DATE ______________

1. A. Jog 1-2 laps, easy stretching
   B. Hendricks Park C. Golf course
2. Fartlek A. Varied pace B. Slow, steady pace
3. Weights and resistance activities
4. A. Winds B. Turns C. Release
5. Routine A. Turn and throw B. Cross ring and throw
   (1) One hand (2) Hammer in each hand (3) Regular
   (a) Heavy hammer (b) Light hammer
6. Technique (1) Stand
   (2) Crossing, have speed under control
   (a) Easy (b) Medium (c) Hard
   A. Control of winds
   B. Lift and turn toward front of circle
   C. Collapse knee and drop toward rear of circle
   D. Hips back, arms extended-- long radius of rotation
   E. Explode on every 3rd or 4th throw
   F. Direction across circle
   G. Lift, pull, and explode on release
   H. Target for 3/4ths to 7/8ths effort
   I. Angle of release
   J.
7. TEAM MEETING
8. Special A. Sauna B. Swim C. Steps or hill
9. Special implements, same letters as #6
   A. Light hammer B. Heavy hammer
   C. Shot D. Medicine ball E.
   (1) 4 kg (2) 5 kg (3) 6 kg (4) 16 lb.
   (5) 8 kg (6) 9 kg (7)
10. A. Meet B. Trial C. Simulation D. Control test
11. Cross circle easy. Feeling of exploding.
    Start slow, finish fast.
12. With Coach A. B.
14. A. Wind sprints
    B. Hurdle drill: 3 LH, 7-9m apart
    C. Spring and bound
    D. Alternate run and jog, at least 800
    E. Starts, go 20-25m
    F. High knee (slow) and fast leg
15. Plyometrics A. Jumps B. Bounding C.
    (1) 1-leg (2) Both legs (3)
16. Tumbling activities
17. Jumping drills
    A. High jump B. Long jump
    C. Plyometrics
    D. Hops and steps E. Step jumping F. Rope skipping
18. Work on staying in the circle
19. Games: A. Basketball B. Volleyball C. Soccer
20. Work on second event
21. A. Videotape B. Film C. Pictures
    (1) Record performance (2) Study
30. Experimental work

Date	Distance	3/4 pace	Date Pace	Goal Pace

M
T
W
T
F
S
S
M
T
W
T
F
S
S
M
T
W
T
F
S
S
M
T
W
T
F
S
S

Sheet 19-1. Hammer throw training schedule sheet

Endnotes

1. K. Bartonietz, L. Hinz, D. Lorenz, & G. Lunau. (1988). The hammer: The view of the DVfL of the GDR on talent selection, technique and training of throwers from beginner to top level athlete. *New Studies in Athletics, 3*(1), 39-56.
2. *Ibid.*, 47.
3. *Ibid.*, 51.
4. William H. Freeman. (1989). *Peak when it counts: Periodization for the American coach*. Los Altos, CA: Tafnews.
5. Peter Tschiene. (1988). The throwing events: Recent trends in technique and training. *New Studies in Athletics, 3*(1), 14.
6. Bartonietz, et al., 55.
7. Tschiene, 16.
8. *Ibid.*, 10.
9. Ladislav Pataki. (1986). *Hammer throwing*. Newark, CA: SyberVision.
10. Ladislav Pataki, Ed Burke, & Stewart Togher. (1989). The hammer throw. In Vern Gambetta (Ed.), *The Athletics Congress's track and field coaching manual* (2nd ed.). Champaign, IL: Leisure Press, 177-199.

Core Readings

Amicale des Entraîneurs Français d'Athlétisme, ed. (1987). *The throws: Official Report of the XIVth Congress, European Athletics Coaches Association*. Paris: European Athletics Coaches Association.

Bantum, Ken. Hammer. (2000). Hammer. In *USA Track and Field coaching manual*. Champaign, IL: Human Kinetics, 265-277.

Burke, Ed, Ladislav Pataki & Ken Doherty. (1989). The hammer throw: Fundamental technique and strength plan. *National Strength & Conditioning Association, 11*(4), 8-10, 77-81.

Dunn, George D., Jr., & Kevin McGill. (2003). *The Throws Manual* (3rd ed.). Mountain View, CA: Tafnews.

Freeman, William H. (2001). Periodized training for throwers. In *Peak When It Counts: Periodization for American track and field* (4th ed.). Mountain View, CA: Tafnews, 131-139.

Jarver, Jess, ed. (2000). *The Throws: Contemporary Theory, Technique and Training* (5th ed.). Mountain View, CA: Tafnews.

Johnson, Carl. (1984). *Hammer throwing* (7th ed.). London: British Amateur Athletic Board.

Silvester, Jay. (2003). *The complete book of throws*. Champaign, IL: Human Kinetics.

USA Track & Field Coaching Education Program. (n.d.). *Level II: Throws*. USA Track & Field. Invaluable; revised regularly.

Additional Readings

Agachi, Teodoru, Yuriy Bakarynov, Lawrie Barclay, Guy Guérin, Boris Rubanko, Allan Staerck, Sergey Ivanovich Sykhonosov & Ernö Szabó. (1997). NSA Round Table 34: Hammer throw. *New Studies in Athletics, 12*(2-3), 13-27.

Babbitt, Don. (2006). Endurance training for the throws [abstract]. *New Studies in Athletics, 21*(1), 62-63.

Bakarinov, Yuri. (1990). The hammer throw: Evolution and perspectives. *Soviet Sports Review, 25*(3), 113-116; 25(4), 184-185.

Bakarinov, Juri. (1990). Theoretical aspects of training control for highly qualified throwers. *New Studies in Athletics, 5*(1), 7-15.

Bakarynov, Yuriy, Tapio Korjus, Didier Poppe, Peter Salzer & Wolfram Scholz. (2006). NSA Round Table 42: Age-group competition in the throwing events. *New Studies in Athletics, 21*(2), 85-91.

Bakarynov, Yuriy, Tapio Korjus, Didier Poppe, Peter Salzer & Wolfram Scholz. (2006). NSA Round Table 42: Age-group competition in the throwing events. *New Studies in Athletics, 21*(2), 85-91.

Barclay, Lawrie. (Spring 1997). About Olga Kuzenkova's training [abstract]. *Track Coach, 139*, 4448.

Bartonietz, Klaus, & Anders Borgström. (1995). The throwing events at the World Championships in Athletics 1995, Göteborg–Technique of the world's best athletes Part 1: Shot put and hammer throw. *New Studies in Athletics, 10*(4), 43-63.

Bartonietz, Klaus, Lawrie Barclay & Dean Gathercole. (1997). Characteristics of top performances in the women's hammer throw: Basics and technique of the world's best athletes. *New Studies in Athletics, 12*(2-3), 101-109.

Bertram, Alan. (1993). A visit to the Soviet hammer training camp. *Track Technique, 122*, 3898-3900.

Bomgisser, G. Martin. (2005). An introduction to block training. Review of Bondarchuk's system from a hammer website.

Boggis, Don. (Winter 2002). A circuit for young throwers. *Track Coach, 158*, 5047-5048.

Bondarchuk, Anatoliy. (1988). Constructing a training system, Parts 1 and 2. *Track Technique, 102*, 3254-3259, 3268; *103*, 3286-3288.

Bondarchuk, Anatoliy. (Summer 1998). "Detrimental" exercises in the transfer of training [abstract]. *Track Coach, 144*, 4609-4610.

Bondarchuk, Anatoly. (Fall 1999). Different masses of implements [abstract]. *Track Coach, 149*, 4769-4770.

Bondarchuk, Anatoliy, et al. (Winter 2003). Individuality in throwing training [abstract]. *Track Coach, 162*, 5184.

Bondarchuk, Anatoly. (1987). Secrets to Soviet hammer throw achievement. *Track and Field Quarterly Review, 87*(3), 27-28.

Bondarchuk, Anatoliy. (1996). Speed and strength development of throwers. [abstract]. *Track Technique, 135*, 4320.

Burnett, Angus. (Spring 2002). Relevance of jumping exercises to field event athletes [abstract]. *Track Coach, 159*, 5090.

Cissik, John M. (2000). Conditioning for hammer throwers. *Track and Field Coaches Review, 73*(1), 32-34.

Connolly, Harold. (Summer 2003). Hammer throwing: The right foot liftoff, 180 degrees dilemma. *Track Coach, 164*, 5248-5249.

Connolly, Harold. (1996). Hammer throw technique. *Track Coach, 136*, 4338-4339.

Connolly, Harold. (1988). What makes Syedikh's technique so effective? *Track Technique, 102*, 3260.

Dapena, Jesús. (1990). Some biomechanical aspects of hammer throwing. *Track Technique, 111*, 3535-3539.

Gassner, Greg. (1994). The paradoxical nature of the hammer throw. *Track Technique, 129*, 4113, 4132.

Goldmann, Werner. (1995). Sprinting speed–An asset for throwers. [abstract]. *Track Technique, 130*, 4161-4162.

Hunter, Iain. (2005). The effect of venue and wind on the distance of a hammer throw. *Research Quarterly for Exercise and Sport, 76*(3), 347-351.

Hunter, Iain, & Garry Killgore. (Winter 2003). Release velocity and angle in men's and women's hammer throw. *Track Coach, 162*, 5180-5182.

Jaede, Eberhard. (1991). The main elements of modern hammer throwing technique. *Track Technique, 118*, 3775-3776, 3780-3781.

Joch, Winfried. (1988). Increase in release velocity as the main objective in the throwing events. *New Studies in Athletics, 3*(1), 35-38.

Judge, Larry. (1993). Creating sparks in the 35 lb. weight throw. *Track Technique, 124*, 3960-3965.

Judge, Larry W. (1992). Designing a strength & conditioning program for the thrower. *Track and Field Quarterly Review, 92*(3), 48-60.

Judge, Larry. (Summer 1999). Teaching the women's hammer. *Track Coach, 148*, 4713-4719.

Judge, Larry, & G. Martin Bingisser. (Summer 2006). Rethinking your approach to training for the weight throw. *Track Coach, 176*, 5615-5621.

Judge, Larry, & Jeffrey Potteiger. (Summer 2000). Using a battery of tests to identify overtraining in throwers [abstract]. *Track Coach, 152*, 4867.

Liset, George. (Summer 2004). A conversation with Larry Judge. *Track Coach, 168*, 5362-5366.

Liset, George. (Winter 2004). A kinesiatric model for developing hammer throwers. *Track Coach, 166*, 5310-5313.

Liset, George. (2006). Sensory motor learning: Developing a kinaesthetic sense of the throws. *New Studies in Athletics, 21*(1), 51-56.

McAtee, G., & W. Larry. (2006). Implement selection and training design in the hammer throw [abstract]. New Studies in Athletics, 21(4), 69. From *Modern Athlete and Coach, 44*(2), 9-14.

Otto, Ralph M. (1992). A kinematic analysis of Yuriy Syedikh's world record hammer throw. *Track Technique, 119*, 3797-3801.

Patrick, Steve. (Winter 2003). You want me to do what? (And other stories from a hammer coach). *Track Coach, 162*, 5177-5179.

Piasenta, Jacques. (1997). NSA photosequence 38: Hammer throw: Olga Kuzenkova. *New Studies in Athletics, 12*(2-3), 111-116. Commentary by Guy Guérin, trans. Heather Ross, 111, 117.

Reardon, Jim. (1991). Psychological characteristics of elite junior male and female throwers. *Track Technique, 114*, 3627-3629.

Schiffer, Jürgen. (1997). Selected and annotated bibliography 43: Hammer throw. *New Studies in Athletics, 12*(2-3), 140-157.

Schiffer, Jürgen. (2004). Selected and annotated bibliography 65: Hammer throw. *New Studies in Athletics, 19*(1), 59-96.

Scholz, Wolfram. (2006). The throwing events at the IAAF World Junior Championships: A whistle stop on the journey to elite athletics. Trans. Jürgen Schiffer. *New Studies in Athletics, 21*(2), 7-27.

Syedikh, Yuriy. (1988). TT interview. *Track Technique, 105*, 3357, 3362.

Taylor, Todd. (Winter 2005). Strength training for the hammer throw. *Track Coach, 170*, 5427-5434, 5438. Adapted from Long & Strong Throwers Journal.

Wirth, Allan. (1995). The integration of competitive Olympic weight lifting with discus and hammer throwing. *New Studies in Athletics, 10*(3), 23-28.

20

The Discus Throw

Bowerman's Best

212′ 6″	Mac Wilkins	1973

Record Setters

Mac Wilkins	World and U.S. record (232′ 6″); four-time Olympian (gold and silver medals); NCAA Champion, 1973; six-time U.S. champion; two-time All-American (discus and shot)
Gary Wolf	193′ 2″ 1972
Jerry Stubblefield	4th, NCAA, 1960

At one time, any discus throw of 200 feet was considered exceptional, but today the record is into the 240s. How have athletes progressed this far? Three factors contribute to this development:

- More athletes are throwing in the schools today, and they compete for many more years than before. Not only was Al Oerter a four-time Olympic champion, but he was probably the best technician the world has ever seen. Certainly, he was the best Olympic competitor.
- The throwing facilities are better, and the discuses are now delicate instruments, well balanced and physically prepared to achieve aerodynamic wonders. All-weather surfaces take most of the chance out of footing. Nonskid shoes take care of some of the disadvantages of rain, and the throwing circles are often placed to take advantage of the prevailing winds.
- Technique has evolved from the slow turn, through applied speed and agility, to the careful analysis of body mechanics and use of the principles of physics and aerodynamics.

Discus Training Theory

The three styles of discus throwing are:

- Torque: The thrower rotates on the turn foot, then rotates the lower body when crossing the ring, which causes increased upper-body torque for the release.
- Linear speed: The arms and the legs stay close to the vertical axis for faster rotation; most momentum comes from the sprint across the ring.
- Lineal-rotary: The arms and the legs are out from the vertical axis at the start, then brought in during the turn, which gives a slow-fast progression.[1]

Mac Wilkins, the 1976 Olympic champion (232′ 10″), was the best discus thrower from Bill Bowerman's Oregon program. He stresses the following training points for discus throwers:

- Try to maximize leverage throughout the throw.
- Start with longer, slower movements in the early phases of the throw.
- Learn to block with the left leg and side (for a right-handed thrower).
- Emphasize training and using the lower body.[2]

Photo 20-1. Mac Wilkins, NCAA champion, Olympic champion, world-record holder

A top-level male thrower takes 5,000 to 6,000 high-intensity throws in a year, compared to 2,500 to 3,000 for a 17- or 18-year-old thrower and 3,700 to 4,500 for a young (age 18 to 19) male collegian throwing 160 feet.

A high school thrower should take at least 75 to 100 full throws per week, while college throwers should take at least 100 full throws per week.[3] Only 65 percent of the throws in the pre-season should be with the regulation-weight discus.

An example of the training loads at the elite level is that of Luis Delis (233′ 2″).[4] He can train very intensively only by devoting his full-time energies to training. His training year falls into these four periods (the figures are weekly):

Phase 1: General physical preparation. This phase includes 600 general throws, 40 specific throws, 360 general jumps, sprinting, gymnastics, swimming, and special endurance activities.

Phase 2: Absolute-strength preparation. This phase includes 170 general throws, 375 specific throws, 450 jumps, sprinting, and 6 sessions of absolute-strength training.

Phase 3: Special-strength preparation. This phase includes 270 to 325 specific throws, jumping, sprinting, and 3 sessions of fast-strength training.

Phases 4 and 5: Competition. These phases include 60 to 130 specific throws, jumping, sprinting, and two sessions of competitive-strength training.

Throwers use implements of different weights, but coaches and athletes are still experimenting to find the most effective combinations. Heavier objects work on strength factors, while lighter implements allow more precise technique adjustments and improve arm speed.

Strength training is very important in training for the discus. The most common lifts used by discus throwers include:

- Squat
- Snatch
- Clean
- Dead lift
- Bench press[5]

Wilkins tried to have maximum lifts in the squat five weeks before competition, and in the snatch two weeks before competition. However, he admits that he tended to do too much upper-body lifting during the season.

Wilkins recommended light lifting on the day before a meet, using two sets of five reps of:

- Light squats
- Bench press
- Snatch

This practice is becoming widespread among elite throwers because it prepares the body for maximum effort on the following day (assuming the athlete has tapered for the meet).[6] Another suggestion is two or three sets of three or four reps of barbell exercises at 85 to 95 percent of the thrower's maximum.

Throwers appear to peak at about age 27, when their greatest strength is finally reached.[7] The better junior throwers develop a throwing technique that is slow-fast; that is, they begin the motion slowly through the wind and turn but keep their time in the air (while moving to the front of the ring) very short and accelerate very quickly through the power position and into the release. This technique maximizes their control in the early stages of the throw while increasing the torque that can be applied to the release velocity.

The more advanced throwers vary the release angle of the discus to adapt to changing wind conditions. The discus is highly affected by the wind's speed and direction. A headwind gives the longest throws. The best throwing angles are shown in Table 20-1.

Release Angles for the Discus		
Wind Direction	*Release Angle*	*Angle of Attack*
Headwind	About 27°	-4° (nose angle at 23°)
Tailwind	About 43°	Even
No wind	36°-40°	To -14° (nose angle at 22°-26°)

Table 20-1. Release angles for the discus

With more advanced throwers, the early training, called *general preparation,* is disappearing from the annual program, except during the *regeneration* or *transition* period.[8] The importance of specificity plays a vastly increased role in elite training. At the same time, researchers emphasize the need for individualized training, particularly in the late stages of the year. Each athlete reacts differently to training, with possibly as many as seven different types of throwers, depending upon their personal adaptation to training stresses.

The Discus Routine

The training routine for the discus progresses through the following steps:

- The standing throw
- Stepping into the throw
- Using the turn

The first part of this stand-step-turn cycle is throwing from a standing position in the circle. For the right-handed thrower, the right foot (trail leg) is in the center of the circle, pointing at an angle of 120 degrees or so from the direction of the throw. The left foot is in the front of the circle and a bit to the left of center, so the thrower has room to rotate the hips into the throw. The body is back over the trail leg before throwing. The athlete rotates the body into the throw, keeping a long throwing arm (not bending it) and pulling the discus through the throwing position. The body shifts during the throwing action from the right leg to the left leg, throwing over a relatively straight left leg.

The second part of the routine consists of stepping into the final position and throwing. The turn is not used at this time. When stepping into the final portion, the thrower drops down slightly. Thus, while going into the actual throw, he lifts and "unwinds," like the outer edge of a screw rising as it rotates.

The final part of the routine uses the full turn and throw. From the starting position in the circle, located in the rear of the circle, with the feet planted comfortably facing away from the throwing direction, the athlete turns, moving into the throwing position, and throws. The progression is:

- Turn
- Step (trail-leg plant)
- Step (lead-leg plant, with both feet now in throwing position)
- Throw

The athlete should try to stay close to the center of the ring, allowing room for the follow-through after the throw. When throwing, the athlete should use only as much speed as he can control. Otherwise, the athlete would handicap the throw much more than help it. Also, the athlete should drop down only as low as he can control, then lift and unwind while throwing.

Basic Discus Throw Technique

When studying throwing sequences, athletes and coaches should remember two particular points:

- A sequence covers only a single throw, which may vary in some respects from the athlete's usual throwing form in the most successful throws.
- Each athlete has facets of form that are personal peculiarities, differences that work for him but would not work for many other athletes. A photo sequence is an example of technique, not a law to be rigidly followed.

A right-handed thrower turns on the left foot, keeping the body low and the throwing arm extended and behind the line of the shoulders. While rotating on the foot, the thrower drops the discus down, so it will then rise until it reaches the point of its release. The turn is *very* rapid. The thrower drives off the turning foot, preparing to go into the power position in the center of the ring. At this point, the athlete has bent the lead arm considerably, thereby speeding up the turn—which may or may not be a virtue at this point in the throw because the thrower does not wish to get too much ahead of himself.

The right foot lands and turns into the throwing power position. Then, the left foot comes down in the front of the ring as the thrower lands in a strong position for the last phases of the throw. When both feet have touched down, the weight is over the rear (right) foot in the center of the circle, and the thrower is still down a bit in a semi-crouch. As the athlete brings the discus around to the release position, the body shifts its weight forward toward the front foot, also straightening the legs, so the body is rising. This movement causes the discus to move in a pattern like the edge of a screw, circling in an upward direction. After the release, the thrower reverses the foot position (from left-foot to right-foot support) in the front of the circle, preventing a foul.

Discus Throwing Tips

When throwing the discus, using the entire torso and the legs is important. An "arm" thrower succeeds only against poor competition. While moving into the throw, the thrower rises upward, gradually lifting with the legs and adding to the force applied to the discus. When the throw is being made, the hips are cocked. The right hip is thrown forward like a punch, adding to the power of the throw. If the lead foot is placed directly in front of the body, though, the hips cannot be thrown forward because they have nowhere to go. The thrower should lead into the release of the discus with the nose and chin, which should be pointed straight ahead at the release of the discus.

All the unwinding (of hips, chest, and so forth) must precede the arm. This leading motion gives a sling or whip action to the arm. The farther the discus can be pulled in this manner, the greater the velocity that can be imparted to it. Connected with these actions are the left-arm coordination and the footwork of the throw, which are very important. The direction the discus goes depends on where the left foot points when the hips are cocked. The best throws have a low trajectory, which comes through the thrower's shoulder. The athlete wants a "low screamer" into the wind at an angle of about 22 degrees in relation to the ground. Throws using wooden pegs as targets set in different directions from the throwing circle help develop the ability to throw the discus where it should be going for the greatest benefit to the thrower.

A Typical Training Week for the Discus Thrower

Schedules are given for the entire year for the discus thrower, but the basic training principle is the hard-easy training cycle. An example of one week of training along the suggested hard-easy cycle is provided and can be considered a "typical" week of training.

Monday

- Warm-up routine
  - ✓Four standing throws, working on leading with the chest and the nose
  - ✓Four throws after a turn, working on leading with the chest and the nose
  - ✓Four throws standing, working on a long pull
  - ✓Four throws turning, working on a long pull
  - ✓Four to six throws alternately standing and crossing the ring
  - ✓25-meter wind sprints

Tuesday

- Weight-training work
- Jogging and flexibility exercises

Wednesday

- Same throwing cycles of standing, then turning, as Monday, except working on the following:
  - ✓Keeping the hips ahead of the arm
  - ✓Throwing through the shoulder
  - ✓Left-arm coordination

Thursday

- Weight-training work
- Jogging and flexibility exercises

Friday (Semi-finals)

- Find out how many throws it takes for the athlete to reach the best mark. Throw in sets of three, with five-minute breaks, as in competition:
  - ✓Where do the throws begin to taper off?
  - ✓Where are the longer throws?
- Athletes might throw three and three, sprint for a bit, throw four and four, sprint again, and so forth.

Saturday (Finals)

- Repeat Friday's drill. This regimen prepares the thrower for competing in trials on one day and finals on the following day.

Discus Throw Training Schedules

DISCUS THROW SCHEDULE NAME ____________________ DATE ____________

1. A. Jog 1-2 laps, easy stretching
   B. Hendricks Park C. Golf course
2. Fartlek A. Varied pace B. Slow, steady pace
3. Weights and resistance activities
4. A. Stand, foot in center of ring
   B. Cross the ring C. Stand, step, turn
5. A. Stand (1) Easy (2) Medium (3) Hard
   B. Cross (1) Easy (2) Medium (3) Hard
6. Technique A. Standing throws
   B. Crossing the ring
   (1) Knee bend and lift
   (2) Maximum reach back or torque
   (3) Lead with chest and nose
   (4) Long pull
   (5) Hips cocked to uncocked
   (6) Through the shoulder
   (7) Other arm coordination
   (8) Back knee bend-lift
   (9) Discus flight
   (10)
7. TEAM MEETING
8. Special A. Sauna B. Swim C. Steps or hill
9. Alternate standing and crossing the ring,
   same numbers as #6
10. A. Meet B. Trial C. Simulation D. Control test
    A. 3/4ths to 7/8ths effort B. 9/10ths to full effort
11. Cross ring easy. Feeling of exploding.
    Start slow, finish fast.
12. With Coach A. B.
14. A. Wind sprints
    B. Hurdle drill: 3 LH, 7-9m apart
    C. Spring and bound
    D. Alternate run and jog, at least 800
    E. Starts, go 20-25m
    F. High knee (slow) and fast leg
15. Plyometrics A. Jumps B. Bounding C.
    (1) 1-leg (2) Both legs (3)
16. Tumbling activities for agility
17. Get over rear leg-- lift with legs
18. Position A. Staying in the ring.
    B. Good position at end of turn-- lift and unwind
19. A. Throw into net B. Throw at target
    C. Ring crossing, feet not too far spread, speed
    you can control. Same numbers as #6.
20. Work on second event
21. A. Videotape B. Film C. Pictures
    (1) Record performance (2) Study
22. A. Slow down and be back over rear leg for
    long lift and unwind
    B. Pull the discus-- lift and push with toes
30. Experimental work

Date	Distance	3/4 pace	Date Pace	Goal Pace

M
T
W
T
F
S
S
M
T
W
T
F
S
S
M
T
W
T
F
S
S
M
T
W
T
F
S
S

Sheet 20-1. Revised discus training schedule sheet

Discus Throw NAME DATE September/October

1. A. Jog 1 or 2 laps, easy stretching B. Weights and jog
   C.
2. Fartlek run A. Varied pace B. Slow, steady
3. Weights and resistance activities
4. A. Stand, foot in center of ring
   B. Cross the ring C. Stand, step, turn
5. A. Stand (1) Easy (2) Medium (3) Hard
   B. Cross (1) Easy (2) Medium (3) Hard
6. A. Standing throws B. Crossing the ring
   (1) Knee bend and lift (2) Maximum reach back or torque
   (3) Lead with chest and nose (4) Long pull
   (5) Hips cocked to uncocked (6) Through the shoulder
   (7) Other arm coordination (8) Back knee bend-lift
   (9) Discus flight
7. Squad meeting
8. Special A. Sauna B. Swim C. Steps or hill
9. Alternate standing and crossing the ring, same numbers as in item 6.
10. Trial or competition—record results below
    A. 3/4 to 7/8 effort B. 9/10 to full effort
11. Cross ring easy, feeling of exploding at finish. Start slow, finish fast.
12. With A. Coach B.
14. A. Wind sprints B. Starts, go 25 yds.
    C. High knee and fast leg D. Hurdles E. Spring and bound
    F. Alternate run-walk, go 880 or more
15. A. Park run B. Golf course run
16. Tumbling activities for agility
17. Get over rear leg—lift with legs
18. Position A. Staying in the ring B. Good position at end of turn—lift and unwind
19. A. Throw into net B. Throw at target C. Ring crossing, feet not too far spread, speed you can control. Same as item 6.
20. Secondary event work
21. A. Pictures B. Film C. Video
22. A. Slow down and be back over rear leg for long lift and unwind
    B. Pull the discus—lift and push with toes

Date	3/4	7/8	Goal	Date

Day	Workout
M	Class or squad organization
T	3-14F
W	1A-14B-6A(4)-6B(4)-19B-14F
T	21A-3
F	1-14A-6A(5)-6A(8)-19A-14F
S	3-14F
S	1B
M	1-14A-6A(4) [4x]-9A(4) [4x]-6B(4) [4x]-6A(5) [4x]-14C
T	3-14C
W	7-14A-9A(5)-19B-11
T	3-14A
F	1-14A-6A(1)-19C(5)
S	Choice
S	3
M	1-14A-4C-6A(7) [4x]-6B(7) [4x]-19-14A
T	3-2A
W	1-14F-6A(3)-6B(3)-6A(8)-6B(8)-14A
T	3-8A or 8B
F	1-14A-6A(9)-19B-19C-14F
S	7
S	
M	1-14A-19C(5) [5-10x]-19C(2) [5-10x]-17-14F
T	2B-14A
W	7-1-14A-10A-12-9A(9)-14A
T	3-8
F	1-19C-10A-19B-14A
S	3
S	1-19B

Sheet 20-2. Discus training schedule

Discus Throw NAME DATE October/November

1. A. Jog 1 or 2 laps, easy stretching B. Weights and jog
   C.
2. Fartlek run A. Varied pace B. Slow, steady
3. Weights and resistance activities
4. A. Stand, foot in center of ring
   B. Cross the ring C. Stand, step, turn
5. A. Stand (1) Easy (2) Medium (3) Hard
   B. Cross (1) Easy (2) Medium (3) Hard
6. A. Standing throws B. Crossing the ring
   (1) Knee bend and lift (2) Maximum reach back or torque
   (3) Lead with chest and nose (4) Long pull
   (5) Hips cocked to uncocked (6) Through the shoulder
   (7) Other arm coordination (8) Back knee bend-lift
   (9) Discus flight
7. Squad meeting
8. Special A. Sauna B. Swim C. Steps or hill
9. Alternate standing and crossing the ring, same numbers as in item 6.
10. Trial or competition—record results below
    A. 3/4 to 7/8 effort B. 9/10 to full effort
11. Cross ring easy, feeling of exploding at finish. Start slow, finish fast.
12. With A. Coach B.
14. A. Wind sprints B. Starts, go 25 yds.
    C. High knee and fast leg D. Hurdles E. Spring and bound
    F. Alternate run-walk, go 880 or more
15. A. Park run B. Golf course run
16. Tumbling activities for agility
17. Get over rear leg—lift with legs
18. Position A. Staying in the ring B. Good position at end of turn—lift and unwind
19. A. Throw into net B. Throw at target C. Ring crossing, feet not too far spread, speed you can control. Same as item 6.
20. Secondary event work
21. A. Pictures B. Film C. Video
22. A. Slow down and be back over rear leg for long lift and unwind
    B. Pull the discus—lift and push with toes

Date	3/4	7/8	Goal	Date

Day	Workout
M	1A-4-6A(7)-9A(7)-19B-2B
T	7-1A-20
W	1A-5A-5B-9A(4)-9A(5)-14A
T	1A-3
F	10-20-14F
S	3
S	3
M	1A-14A-6A(4) 4x -6B(4) 4x -9A(4) 4-8x -2A
T	3
W	1A-9A(3)-11-14F
T	3
F	1A-20
S	3
S	3
M	1A-14A 3x -9A(2)-14A
T	10-20
W	7-3
T	1A-14F-4A
F	1A-4-5-11-18A-14F
S	3
S	3
M	1-14A-19C(5) 5-10x -19C(2) 5-10x -22A-14A
T	3
W	1-4A-4B-5AB-9A(5)
T	Light-3
F	1-14A 3x -10A-14A 3x -10A-19C-Jog
S	3
S	3

Sheet 20-3. Discus training schedule

Discus Throw NAME DATE *November/December*

1. A. Jog 1 or 2 laps, easy stretching B. Weights and jog
   C.
2. Fartlek run A. Varied pace B. Slow, steady
3. Weights and resistance activities
4. A. Stand, foot in center of ring
   B. Cross the ring C. Stand, step, turn
5. A. Stand (1) Easy (2) Medium (3) Hard
   B. Cross (1) Easy (2) Medium (3) Hard
6. A. Standing throws B. Crossing the ring
   (1) Knee bend and lift (2) Maximum reach back or torque
   (3) Lead with chest and nose (4) Long pull
   (5) Hips cocked to uncocked (6) Through the shoulder
   (7) Other arm coordination (8) Back knee bend-lift
   (9) Discus flight
7. Squad meeting
8. Special A. Sauna B. Swim C. Steps or hill
9. Alternate standing and crossing the ring, same numbers as in item 6.
10. Trial or competition—record results below
    A. 3/4 to 7/8 effort B. 9/10 to full effort
11. Cross ring easy, feeling of exploding at finish. Start slow, finish fast.
12. With A. Coach B.
14. A. Wind sprints B. Starts, go 25 yds.
    C. High knee and fast leg D. Hurdles E. Spring and bound
    F. Alternate run-walk, go 880 or more
15. A. Park run B. Golf course run
16. Tumbling activities for agility
17. Get over rear leg—lift with legs
18. Position A. Staying in the ring B. Good position at end of turn—lift and unwind
19. A. Throw into net B. Throw at target C. Ring crossing, feet not too far spread, speed you can control. Same as item 6.
20. Secondary event work
21. A. Pictures B. Film C. Video
22. A. Slow down and be back over rear leg for long lift and unwind
    B. Pull the discus—lift and push with toes

Date	3/4	7/8	Goal	Date

M	*1A-6A(4)-6A(5)-6B(3)-9-14F*
T	*3*
W	*1A-21A-17-11*
T	*3*
F	*1-14A*
S	*3*
S	*recreation*
M	*1-14F-6A(2)-6B(2)-11-14A*
T	*3-8A or 8B*
W	*1-14F-6B(4)-11*
T	
F	*10A-10B*
S	*Assist with cross country*
S	*recreation*
M	
T	
W	
T	
F	
S	
S	
M	
T	
W	
T	
F	
S	
S	

Sheet 20-4. Discus training schedule

Discus Throw NAME DATE January

1. A. Jog 1 or 2 laps, easy stretching B. Weights and jog
   C.
2. Fartlek run A. Varied pace B. Slow, steady
3. Weights and resistance activities
4. A. Stand, foot in center of ring
   B. Cross the ring C. Stand, step, turn
5. A. Stand (1) Easy (2) Medium (3) Hard
   B. Cross (1) Easy (2) Medium (3) Hard
6. A. Standing throws B. Crossing the ring
   (1) Knee bend and lift (2) Maximum reach back or torque
   (3) Lead with chest and nose (4) Long pull
   (5) Hips cocked to uncocked (6) Through the shoulder
   (7) Other arm coordination (8) Back knee bend-lift
   (9) Discus flight
7. Squad meeting
8. Special A. Sauna B. Swim C. Steps or hill
9. Alternate standing and crossing the ring, same numbers as in item 6.
10. Trial or competition—record results below
    A. 3/4 to 7/8 effort B. 9/10 to full effort
11. Cross ring easy, feeling of exploding at finish. Start slow, finish fast.
12. With A. Coach B.
14. A. Wind sprints B. Starts, go 25 yds.
    C. High knee and fast leg D. Hurdles E. Spring and bound
    F. Alternate run-walk, go 880 or more
15. A. Park run B. Golf course run
16. Tumbling activities for agility
17. Get over rear leg—lift with legs
18. Position A. Staying in the ring B. Good position at end of turn—lift and unwind
19. A. Throw into net B. Throw at target C. Ring crossing, feet not too far spread, speed you can control. Same as item 6.
20. Secondary event work
21. A. Pictures B. Film C. Video
22. A. Slow down and be back over rear leg for long lift and unwind
    B. Pull the discus—lift and push with toes

Date	3/4	7/8	Goal	Date

M	Week of class organization -3
T	Squad organization-1-3
W	Registration -1-3-16
T	7-1A-4AB-6A(7)-6B(7)-4AB
F	3-5
S	1A-4AB-6A(6)-11-14A
S	
M	1A-3-14A-6A(5)-6B(5)-11-14A
T	1A-3
W	1A-6A(4)-6B(4)-11-4AB-14F
T	1A-3
F	1A-4AB-5-10-4AB-14F
S	3
S	3
M	1A-4AB-9A(8)-17-14A
T	3
W	1A-14A-4AB-6A(1)-6B(1)-11-18A-14F
T	3
F	10(4 to 6 throws)-4AB-14A
S	3
S	3
M	1A-3-14A
T	1A-4AB-9A(1)-14A-14F
W	7-1A-3-14F
T	1A-6A-11-22-14A
F	3-14A
S	1A-4AB-9A(8)-18B-22-14F
S	3-14F

Sheet 20-5. Discus training schedule

Discus Throw NAME DATE February

1. A. Jog 1 or 2 laps, easy stretching B. Weights and jog
   C.
2. Fartlek run A. Varied pace B. Slow, steady
3. Weights and resistance activities
4. A. Stand, foot in center of ring
   B. Cross the ring C. Stand, step, turn
5. A. Stand (1) Easy (2) Medium (3) Hard
   B. Cross (1) Easy (2) Medium (3) Hard
6. A. Standing throws B. Crossing the ring
   (1) Knee bend and lift (2) Maximum reach back or torque
   (3) Lead with chest and nose (4) Long pull
   (5) Hips cocked to uncocked (6) Through the shoulder
   (7) Other arm coordination (8) Back knee bend-lift
   (9) Discus flight
7. Squad meeting
8. Special A. Sauna B. Swim C. Steps or hill
9. Alternate standing and crossing the ring, same numbers as in item 6.
10. Trial or competition—record results below
    A. 3/4 to 7/8 effort B. 9/10 to full effort
11. Cross ring easy, feeling of exploding at finish. Start slow, finish fast.
12. With A. Coach B.
14. A. Wind sprints B. Starts, go 25 yds.
    C. High knee and fast leg D. Hurdles E. Spring and bound
    F. Alternate run-walk, go 880 or more
15. A. Park run B. Golf course run
16. Tumbling activities for agility
17. Get over rear leg—lift with legs
18. Position A. Staying in the ring B. Good position at end of turn—lift and unwind
19. A. Throw into net B. Throw at target C. Ring crossing, feet not too far spread, speed you can control. Same as item 6.
20. Secondary event work
21. A. Pictures B. Film C. Video
22. A. Slow down and be back over rear leg for long lift and unwind
    B. Pull the discus—lift and push with toes

Date	3/4	7/8	Goal	Date

Day	Workout
M	6-10x 1-6A(9)-17-9A(1)-6A(6)-14A
T	3-1A
W	6-10x 6-10x 1-14A-6A(6)-6B(6)-19B-14F
T	3-1A
F	1-21-10-9A(6)
S	3
S	
M	1-14A-3
T	6-10x 6-10x 6-10x 1-14A-19B-6A(5)-6B(5)-9A(5)-14A
W	3
T	4-6x 6-10x 1-14A-19A-6A(3)-10(today or Sat.)-14F
F	3
S	10-20
S	
M	1-3-14A
T	6-10x 6-10x 6-10x 1-14A-6A(3)-9A(8)-9A(6)-14A
W	1-3-8A or 8B
T	4-8x 1-14A-9B-6A(6)-14A
F	Jog-3
S	1-14A-19B-10B-14E
S	
M	1A-3-14B
T	6-10x 6-10x 1A-14A-6A(6)-6B(6)-11-19A
W	3
T	1A-10-20-16
F	3
S	3
S	

Sheet 20-6. Discus training schedule

Discus Throw NAME DATE March

1. A. Jog 1 or 2 laps, easy stretching B. Weights and jog
   C.
2. Fartlek run A. Varied pace B. Slow, steady
3. Weights and resistance activities
4. A. Stand, foot in center of ring
   B. Cross the ring C. Stand, step, turn
5. A. Stand (1) Easy (2) Medium (3) Hard
   B. Cross (1) Easy (2) Medium (3) Hard
6. A. Standing throws B. Crossing the ring
   (1) Knee bend and lift (2) Maximum reach back or torque
   (3) Lead with chest and nose (4) Long pull
   (5) Hips cocked to uncocked (6) Through the shoulder
   (7) Other arm coordination (8) Back knee bend-lift
   (9) Discus flight
7. Squad meeting
8. Special A. Sauna B. Swim C. Steps or hill
9. Alternate standing and crossing the ring, same numbers as in item 6.
10. Trial or competition—record results below
    A. 3/4 to 7/8 effort B. 9/10 to full effort
11. Cross ring easy, feeling of exploding at finish. Start slow, finish fast.
12. With A. Coach B.
14. A. Wind sprints B. Starts, go 25 yds.
    C. High knee and fast leg D. Hurdles E. Spring and bound
    F. Alternate run-walk, go 880 or more
15. A. Park run B. Golf course run
16. Tumbling activities for agility
17. Get over rear leg—lift with legs
18. Position A. Staying in the ring B. Good position at end of turn—lift and unwind
19. A. Throw into net B. Throw at target C. Ring crossing, feet not too far spread, speed you can control. Same as item 6.
20. Secondary event work
21. A. Pictures B. Film C. Video
22. A. Slow down and be back over rear leg for long lift and unwind
    B. Pull the discus—lift and push with toes

Date	3/4	7/8	Goal	Date

Day	Workout
M	3-14F
T	10-20x 1A-6A(9)-11A(1)-11A(5)-14F
W	1B-3-14A
T	1A-22A-20-14A-Gear ready
F	Gear ready
S	10-Meet or trials
S	

Day	AM	PM
M	Jog	1A-3
T	Jog	1A-6A(2)-9A(2)-22
W	Jog	3
T	Jog	4x 1A-10-11-14A
F	Light-gear ready	
S	10-Meet	
S	Home	

Day	Workout
M	1-14A-6A(6)-6B(6)-11-19B-14F
T	1A-3
W	1-10 or 20-19B-18B
T	1-16-14F
F	1-18B-9A(2)-11-14F-9A(3)-18B
S	1A-1B-14F
S	1A-14F

Day	Workout
M	1A-14F-18B-19B-9A(4)-18B-19A
T	1A-3
W	1A-6A(3)-19B
T	1-3
F	Gear ready
S	10-Meet
S	Jog or recreation

Sheet 20-7. Discus training schedule

Discus Throw NAME DATE April

1. A. Jog 1 or 2 laps, easy stretching B. Weights and jog
   C.
2. Fartlek run A. Varied pace B. Slow, steady
3. Weights and resistance activities
4. A. Stand, foot in center of ring
   B. Cross the ring C. Stand, step, turn
5. A. Stand (1) Easy (2) Medium (3) Hard
   B. Cross (1) Easy (2) Medium (3) Hard
6. A. Standing throws B. Crossing the ring
   (1) Knee bend and lift (2) Maximum reach back or torque
   (3) Lead with chest and nose (4) Long pull
   (5) Hips cocked to uncocked (6) Through the shoulder
   (7) Other arm coordination (8) Back knee bend-lift
   (9) Discus flight
7. Squad meeting
8. Special A. Sauna B. Swim C. Steps or hill
9. Alternate standing and crossing the ring, same numbers as in item 6.
10. Trial or competition—record results below
    A. 3/4 to 7/8 effort B. 9/10 to full effort
11. Cross ring easy, feeling of exploding at finish. Start slow, finish fast.
12. With A. Coach B.
14. A. Wind sprints B. Starts, go 25 yds.
    C. High knee and fast leg D. Hurdles E. Spring and bound
    F. Alternate run-walk, go 880 or more
15. A. Park run B. Golf course run
16. Tumbling activities for agility
17. Get over rear leg—lift with legs
18. Position A. Staying in the ring B. Good position at end of turn—lift and unwind
19. A. Throw into net B. Throw at target C. Ring crossing, feet not too far spread, speed you can control. Same as item 6.
20. Secondary event work
21. A. Pictures B. Film C. Video
22. A. Slow down and be back over rear leg for long lift and unwind
    B. Pull the discus—lift and push with toes

Date	3/4	7/8	Goal	Date

M	1A-9A(4)-11-19B-14A-14F
T	1-9A(5)-11-19A-14F-14A
W	7-1A-3-grass
T	1-22A-18B
F	Light and gear ready
S	10-Meet
S	3-10-14F
M	Light
T	1A-6A(8)-6B(8)-22B-19B-14F
W	7-Light
T	1-6A(6)-6B(6)-18B-11-14F
F	Gear ready
S	10-Meet
S	3A-1A
M	1A-18B-9A(5)-11-14A-14B
T	1A (light)
W	1-6A(3)-18B-11-14A-14B
T	Light
F	Gear ready
S	10-Meet
S	1A-18B-9A(3)-11-10-14F
M	Light
T	1-6A(4)-6B(4)-19B-11-3
W	7-Light
T	Gear ready
F	Jog
S	10-Meet
S	3

Sheet 20-8. Discus training schedule

Discus Throw NAME DATE May

1. A. Jog 1 or 2 laps, easy stretching B. Weights and jog
   C.
2. Fartlek run A. Varied pace B. Slow, steady
3. Weights and resistance activities
4. A. Stand, foot in center of ring
   B. Cross the ring C. Stand, step, turn
5. A. Stand (1) Easy (2) Medium (3) Hard
   B. Cross (1) Easy (2) Medium (3) Hard
6. A. Standing throws B. Crossing the ring
   (1) Knee bend and lift (2) Maximum reach back or torque
   (3) Lead with chest and nose (4) Long pull
   (5) Hips cocked to uncocked (6) Through the shoulder
   (7) Other arm coordination (8) Back knee bend-lift
   (9) Discus flight
7. Squad meeting
8. Special A. Sauna B. Swim C. Steps or hill
9. Alternate standing and crossing the ring, same numbers as in item 6.
10. Trial or competition—record results below
    A. 3/4 to 7/8 effort B. 9/10 to full effort
11. Cross ring easy, feeling of exploding at finish. Start slow, finish fast.
12. With A. Coach B.
14. A. Wind sprints B. Starts, go 25 yds.
    C. High knee and fast leg D. Hurdles E. Spring and bound
    F. Alternate run-walk, go 880 or more
15. A. Park run B. Golf course run
16. Tumbling activities for agility
17. Get over rear leg—lift with legs
18. Position A. Staying in the ring B. Good position at end of turn—lift and unwind
19. A. Throw into net B. Throw at target C. Ring crossing, feet not too far spread, speed you can control. Same as item 6.
20. Secondary event work
21. A. Pictures B. Film C. Video
22. A. Slow down and be back over rear leg for long lift and unwind
    B. Pull the discus—lift and push with toes

Date	3/4	7/8	Goal	Date

M	Light
T	Light
W	7-10 (Meet-night)
T	1A-9A(7)-18B-22B-14B-14A
F	Light
S	Light
S	Squad picnic
M	1A-10
T	3x 1-19B-3
W	Light
T	Light
F	1-9A(6)-18B-19B-14A-14F
S	1-9A(8)-18B-17-14F-14A
S	3x 1-19B-3 or form work
M	1-3 (light)-14B
T	3-6x 11-Jog
W	Light
T	Light
F	Qualifying-Pac 8 Meet
S	Finals-Pac 8 Meet
S	
M	
T	
W	
T	
F	
S	
S	

Sheet 20-9. Discus training schedule

Discus Throw NAME DATE June

1. A. Jog 1 or 2 laps, easy stretching B. Weights and jog
   C.
2. Fartlek run A. Varied pace B. Slow, steady
3. Weights and resistance activities
4. A. Stand, foot in center of ring
   B. Cross the ring C. Stand, step, turn
5. A. Stand (1) Easy (2) Medium (3) Hard
   B. Cross (1) Easy (2) Medium (3) Hard
6. A. Standing throws B. Crossing the ring
   (1) Knee bend and lift (2) Maximum reach back or torque
   (3) Lead with chest and nose (4) Long pull
   (5) Hips cocked to uncocked (6) Through the shoulder
   (7) Other arm coordination (8) Back knee bend-lift
   (9) Discus flight
7. Squad meeting
8. Special A. Sauna B. Swim C. Steps or hill
9. Alternate standing and crossing the ring, same numbers as in item 6.
10. Trial or competition—record results below
    A. 3/4 to 7/8 effort B. 9/10 to full effort
11. Cross ring easy, feeling of exploding at finish. Start slow, finish fast.
12. With A. Coach B.
14. A. Wind sprints B. Starts, go 25 yds.
    C. High knee and fast leg D. Hurdles E. Spring and bound
    F. Alternate run-walk, go 880 or more
15. A. Park run B. Golf course run
16. Tumbling activities for agility
17. Get over rear leg—lift with legs

    Position A. Staying in the ring B. Good position at end of turn—lift and unwind

    A. Throw into net B. Throw at target C. Ring crossing, feet not too far spread, speed you can control. Same as item 6.
20. Secondary event work
21. A. Pictures B. Film C. Video
22. A. Slow down and be back over rear leg for long lift and unwind
    B. Pull the discus—lift and push with toes

Date	3/4	7/8	Goal	Date

M	Exams start - 3
T	1A-6A(6)-11A-17-18B-14F
W	Light
T	1A-3X 10 as in Trials
F	1A-3X 10 as in Finals
S	Final exams completed
S	1A - Form work or loosen up
M	17-18B
T	Easy form work
W	Travel and loosen up
T	1st day Prelims - NCAA Meet
F	2nd day Prelims - NCAA
S	Finals - NCAA
S	
M	
T	
W	
T	
F	
S	
S	
M	
T	
W	
T	
F	
S	
S	

Sheet 20-10. Discus training schedule

Endnotes

1. Frank Morris. (1981). The Wilkins style of discus throwing. *Track and Field Quarterly Review, 81(1)*, 22-27.
2. Mac Wilkins. (1987). Technique conditioning drills for the discus throw. *Track and Field Quarterly Review, 87(3)*, 20-23.
3. Vern Gambetta. (1986). TT interview: Mac Wilkins. *Track Technique, 96,* 3053-3055.
4. Hermes Riveri. (1986). Discus training periodization. *Track Technique, 96*, 3058-3059.
5. Ross Dallow. (1987). Mac Wilkins on weight training, mental preparation, diet, technique. *Track and Field Quarterly Review, 87(3),* 24.
6. George Dunn. (1987). Current trends in shot putting. *Track Technique, 98,* 3123.
7. Jan Stepanek & Petr Susanka. (1987). Discus throw: Results of a biomechanic study. *New Studies in Athletics, 2*(1), 25-36.
8. Peter Tschiene. (1988). The throwing events: Recent trends in technique and training. *New Studies in Athletics, 3*(1), 7-17.

Core Readings

Amicale des Entraîneurs Français d'Athlétisme, ed. (1987). *The throws: Official Report of the XIVth Congress, European Athletics Coaches Association.* Paris: European Athletics Coaches Association.

Babbitt, Don. (2000). Discus throw. In USA *Track and Field coaching manual.* Champaign, IL: Human Kinetics, 235-248.

Bartlett, Roger M. (1992). The biomechanics of the discus throw. *Journal of Sports Sciences, 10,* 467-510.

Dunn, George D., Jr., & Kevin McGill. (2003). *The Throws Manual* (3rd ed.). Mountain View, CA: Tafnews.

Freeman, William H. (2001). Periodized training for throwers. In *Peak When It Counts: Periodization for American track and field* (4th ed.). Mountain View, CA: Tafnews, 131-139.

Hay, James G. (1995). Critical characteristics of technique in throwing the discus. *Journal of Sports Sciences, 13,* 125-140.

Jarver, Jess, ed. (2000). *The Throws: Contemporary Theory, Technique and Training* (5th ed.). Mountain View, CA: Tafnews.

Naclerio, Tony. (1988). *The Teaching Progressions of the Shot Put, Discus and Javelin.* Rockaway, NJ: Author.

Silvester, Jay. (2003). *The complete book of throws.* Champaign, IL: Human Kinetics.

USA Track & Field Coaching Education Program. (n.d.). *Level II: Throws.* USA Track & Field. Invaluable; revised regularly.

Recommended Readings

Aikens, Jim. (Winter 2001). Fremd High school throwing program. *Track Coach, 154,* 4909-4914.

Amundsen, Glenn B. (1987). Analysis of four world class discus throwers. *Track Technique, 99,* 3159-3160, 3170.

Arbeit, Ekkart, Anders Borgström, Carl Johnson & Yuriy Sedykh. (1996). NSA Round Table 30: The role of speed in the throws. *New Studies in Athletics, 11*(1), 11-16.

Armbrust, Wayne T. (Summer 2004). Understanding non-uniform forces in the throws, with implications for training. *Track Coach, 168,* 5369-5372.

Babbitt, Don. (2006). Endurance training for the throws [abstract]. *New Studies in Athletics, 21*(1), 62-63.

Badon, Tommy. (1990). Adapting training plans for the prep discus thrower. *Track Technique, 110,* 3503-3505, 3524.

Bakarinov, Juri. (1990). Theoretical aspects of training control for highly qualified throwers. *New Studies in Athletics, 5*(1), 7-15.

Bartonietz, Klaus. (Summer 2003). Training with varied weight implements [abstract]. *Track Coach, 164,* 5250.

Bartonietz, Klaus, Russell J. Best & Anders Borgström. (1996). The throwing events at the World Championships in Athletics 1995, Göteborg–Technique of the world's best athletes Part 2: discus and javelin throw. *New Studies in Athletics, 11*(1), 19-44.

Boggis, Don. (Winter 2002). A circuit for young throwers. *Track Coach, 158,* 5047-5048.

Brown, Harmon. (1984). Training women throwers. *Track Technique, 87*, 2763-2766.

Burnett, Angus. (Spring 2002). Relevance of jumping exercises to field event athletes [abstract]. *Track Coach, 159,* 5090.

Dapena, Jesús. (1993). New insights on discus throwing. *Track Technique, 125,* 3977-3983; Vrabel, Jan. (1994). Are Dapena's insights on discus throwing correct? *Track Technique, 129,* 4114-4115; Dapena, Jesús. (1994). New insights on discus throwing: A response to Jan Vrabel's comments. *Track Technique, 129,* 4116-4119.

Fahey, Thomas D. (Summer 2004). Predictors of performance in elite discus throwers [abstract]. *Track Coach, 168,* 5379.

Gambetta, Vern. (1986). TT interview: Mac Wilkins. *Track Technique, 96,* 3053-3055.

Goldmann, Werner. (1995). Sprinting speed–An asset for throwers. [abstract]. *Track Technique, 130,* 4161-4162.

Harnes, Edward. (1989). Training plan for advanced female discus throwers in Bulgaria. Trans. Freidhelm Endemann. *Track Technique, 106,* 3371-3375, 3393-3395.

Hay, James G., & Bing Yu. (1996). Free-leg action in throwing the discus. *Track Coach, 134,* 4265-4268.

Hay, James G, & Bing Yu. (1996). Weight shift and foot placement in throwing the discus. *Track Coach, 135,* 4297-4300.

Judge, Larry, & Jeffrey Potteiger. (Summer 2000). Using a battery of tests to identify overtraining in throwers [abstract]. *Track Coach, 152,* 4867.

Leutschenko, A., & A, Berestovskava. (1995). Planning of training for elite discus throwers [abstract]. *Track Coach, 133,* 4255.

Linthorne, Nick. (Summer 2003). Optimum projection angles in throwing events [abstract]. *Track Coach, 164,* 5252.

Miller, Brian P. (1985). Psychological factors in competitive throwing. *Track and Field Quarterly Review, 85*(1), 40-44.

Nathan, Simon. (1991). Wolfgang Schmidt at Crystal Palace. *Track Technique, 115,* 3664-3667.

Probst, Jorg. (Winter 2003). Rethinking the role of strength in the throwing events [abstract]. *Track Coach, 162,* 5186.

Pukstys, Tom. (1993). Five weeks with Romas Ubartas, Olympic discus champion. *Track Technique, 124,* 3957-3958.

Rachmanliev, Peter, & Edward Harness. (1990). Long term preparation for advanced female discus throwers. *New Studies in Athletics, 5*(1), 69-92.

Reardon, Jim. (1991). Psychological characteristics of elite junior male and female throwers. *Track Technique, 114,* 3627-3629.

Rudman, Grigori. (Fall 2003). Varied weight implements strategy [abstract]. *Track Coach, 165,* 5284.

Scholz, Wolfram. (2006). The throwing events at the IAAF World Junior Championships: A whistle stop on the journey to elite athletics. Trans. Jürgen Schiffer. *New Studies in Athletics, 21*(2), 7-27.

Schiffer, Jürgen. (2003). Selected and annotated bibliography 63: Discus throw. *New Studies in Athletics, 18*(3), 83-128.

Silvester, Jay. (1986). Points for the discus thrower and coach to ponder. *Track and Field Quarterly Review, 86*(1), 26-27.

Silvester, L. Jay, & Raymond McCoy. (1995). Paths of the discus: A comparison of elite and junior elite discus throwers. *Track Coach, 133,* 4238-4243.

Sinitsin, Aleksandr. (1996). Hints for discus throwers. [abstract]. *Track Coach, 136,* 4351.

Smith, Richard D. (1993). Romas Ubartas and Vytautas Jaras at Rutgers. *Track Technique, 122,* 3893-3894.

The tests of equivalence [throws]. (1984). *Track and Field Quarterly Review, 84*(1), 50-53.

Venegas, Art. (1989). U.C.L.A. shot put-discus conditioning program. *Track and Field Quarterly Review, 89*(3), 6-8.

Wirth, Allan. (1995). The integration of competitive Olympic weight lifting with discus and hammer throwing. *New Studies in Athletics, 10*(3), 23-28.

21

The Javelin Throw

Bowerman's Best

263′ 1″	Les Tipton	1964

Record Setters

Les Tipton	NCAA champion, 1964; U.S. Olympic Team, 1964
Chuck Missfeldt	NCAA champion, 1951
Gary Reddaway	All-American, 1964 (2nd place)
Ron Gomez	All-American (3rd place)
Bill Heikkila	Canadian Olympic Team, 1968; All-American, 1967 (2nd place)
Mac Wilkins	257′ 4″, 1970
Bob Daniel	251′ 3″, 1963

The javelin throw is perhaps the most military of track and field events. To the ancient Greeks, the ability to throw the javelin well was a mark of military prowess, for the javelin was an important weapon of their golden age. Children still play at throwing spears, and then graduate to the intricacies of the javelin. Technique becomes all-important, for the throwing form used with the javelin is not a natural motion. Though the military value of the javelin throw has passed, the beauty of a good throw survives.

Analysis of the Javelin Throw

The thrower begins with a running approach of not more than 120 feet, going into a cross-step on Step 2 of the final five steps. The thrower should accelerate into the cross-step, and then plant the right foot (for a right-handed thrower) to begin the actual throw. The throwing arm is extended back, and the lead arm is across the body. The thrower brings the lead arm around to provide more pull for the throw. The left leg is extended to plant and provide a break on the forward momentum, which will be transferred to the javelin.

When the thrower plants the heel of the left foot, he is already pulling the javelin forward and bringing the left arm around to provide additional pull. The right leg provides additional push, and the torso rotates into the throw. The lead leg is kept rigid, forcing the body to go over it. As the thrower releases the javelin, the pushing right foot is still in contact with the ground, with the thrower continuing forward over the left foot. The thrower lands on the right foot, the fifth step of the final five, stopping his forward movement short of the foul line.

Training Theory

At one time, the javelin was little more than a long, unwieldy stick. Currently, it is an aerodynamically designed precision tool continually undergoing further advances in its design. As a result of the length of the world record (approaching 350 feet), the balancing point of the men's javelin was moved forward in 1985. The result was a javelin that noses down sooner, giving shorter throws but also easing the official's job (fewer flat throws). The javelin is a complicated event because it is highly affected by a mixture of aerodynamic factors. The 1985 change affected the parameters of the "ideal" release and flight pattern.

The East Germans tested potential javelin throwers between the ages of 12 and 14, looking for the performances shown in Table 21-1. As with other tests, these are only guidelines. The East German goal was to have five years of directed training before the athlete could compete in the World Junior Championships (ages 18 to 19).[1] They predicted records of 90m (295 feet) and 80m (262 feet) for men and women, respectively.

East German Youth Selection Standards for Javelin

	Girls		*Boys*	
Exercise	*12-13 Years*	*13-14 Years*	*12-13 Years*	*13-14 Years*
Height	5′ 7″	5′ 7″	5′ 7″	5′ 9"
Baseball throw	180′-197′	197′-213′	213′-230′	230′ -246′
60m dash	8.50	8.40	8.30	8.20
30m flying start	4.25	4.15	4.00	3.90
3 hops, right leg	21′ 4″	22′ 4″-23′ 0″	21′ 4″	23′ 0″
3 hops, left leg	21′ 4″	22′ 4″-23′ 0″	21′ 4″	23′ 0″
Shot put (3 kg for girls, 4 kg for boys)	32′ 10″	36′ 1″	36′ 1″	39′ 4″
800m	2:35.0	2:32.0	2:30.0	2:25.0

Table 21-1. East German youth selection standards for javelin

Research on the current men's javelin suggests that the primary change was in its downward flight.[2] The float largely disappeared. The primary factor in the length of the throw is the speed at the release,[3] though that factor is not as great as before.[4] The new javelin appears to require more technical precision than the old one.

When the javelin is released, two angles are factors:

- *Angle of release:* the path that the throwing hand travels in relation to the ground
- *Angle of attack:* the angle of the javelin in relation to the path that the throwing hand travels

Photo 21-1. Les Tipton, 1964 Olympian

Most throwers release the javelin with a positive angle of attack (the nose higher than the path of the hand). A higher angle of attack may be more a characteristic of lower-level throwers. Indeed, with the new javelin, the ideal throw appears to be "through the point," as is suggested in the training schedules. Coaches are not completely agreed on this, however.[5] Neither is consensus found on the ideal angle of release, though the mid- to upper-30s seems most widely accepted. One study suggests 37 1/2 degrees as the ideal.[6]

A common weakness of poorer throwers on the braking step with the lead leg is to take too short a stride, making it impossible to transfer the momentum fully to the throw. Interestingly, one authority suggests that the new javelin's flight characteristics might make the old fork grip (described later in this chapter) a good technical choice.[7]

An example of training loads is the Finnish program, which includes the following during the training year:

- 7,000 to 13,000 total throws
  - ✓30 to 50 percent with the javelin
  - ✓Others with a variety of weights
- Throwing weights for men
  - ✓Regular javelin (800 grams)
  - ✓800- to 1,000-gram weights
  - ✓400- to 700-gram balls for specific speed
  - ✓1- to 1.5-kg javelins for specific strength
- Throwing weights for women
  - ✓Regular javelin (600 grams)
  - ✓700- to 900-gram weights (10 to 15 percent of throws)
  - ✓400- to 600-gram balls for specific speed
  - ✓1- to 1.5 kg-javelins for specific strength[8]

The bottom line for survival as a javelin thrower is a good base of conditioning, strength, and flexibility. A high throwing volume can lead to spine, shoulder, and elbow injuries. Technique training and the throwing load should increase gradually during the training year, as the conditioning and strength program advances. As an example of the conditioning required for elite performance, the following are the recommended performance levels for a Soviet-era female who throws 70m (230 feet):

- Snatch: 176 to 187 lbs.
- Clean: 220 to 243 lbs.
- Squat: 309 to 353 lbs.
- 60-meter dash: 7.5 to 7.6 seconds
- Short-approach long jump: 18′ 0″[9]

Common Faults of Javelin Throwers

One of the greatest faults, especially with American throwers, is the tendency to throw the javelin to the side rather than bring it across the shoulder. This habit probably results from the common throwing technique used with a baseball, which may be delivered over the elbow, held out to the side of the shoulder, or even thrown sidearm. This throwing form not only results in a poorer throw, but also puts a much greater strain on the arm and elbow than the correct over-the-shoulder delivery.

Another fault is throwing the javelin rather than pulling it. Most of the work in a good javelin throw is done before the hand comes over the shoulder, rather than after the hand has passed the shoulder and is in the process of throwing. Much better results are gained by concentrating on pulling the javelin through the throw.

A great weakness in many throwers is the lack of body pull. The arm is not everything in throwing the javelin. The thrower must coordinate the entire body into the throw. When the athlete learns to throw with the arms the legs and the body, he is beginning to develop from a learner to a thrower.

Premature lift of the left foot (if the thrower is right-handed) also hampers good throwing considerably. This problem may also develop from American ball games, which use a "reverse" of the feet after throwing, much as the shot does. The thrower should stay on the left leg until going over it. The leg should not be pulled out at any stage of the throw because it contributes to the shifting of the athlete's momentum from straight ahead to the launching of the javelin itself.

A final fault is not technical: throwing the javelin hard too often in practice. Notice that all the training described in this section consists of throwing at levels varying from easy throwing to 7/8 effort, but never at full effort. Frequent full-effort throwing usually has one result: injuries, most frequently to the elbow region.

Holding back the effort of the throws does not hamper the success of the thrower. In 1964, Oregon had a thrower with a very bad elbow, Gary Reddaway. In the first meet of the season, in late March, he threw well enough to qualify for the NCAA meet. He was then held out of all other meets until the NCAA Meet in mid-June. He went through his practice routines doing only easy throwing, using a tennis ball. He qualified for the NCAA finals with a single throw of 219' 10". He made a vast improvement on his second throw in the finals to 246' 1 1/2" and finished second as Oregon swept the first three places.

Photo 21-2. Les Tipton, NCAA champion and Olympian

Applied Javelin Training

No ideal size can guide you to look for in the prospective javelin thrower. Top male throwers have been as tall as 6′ 6″, yet the world record has been held by men as small as 5′ 7″ and 165 pounds. The coach is looking for the well-coordinated athlete with a good throwing arm. Tests such as the softball or football throw have been used for locating prospects, but perhaps the most accurate indicator is throwing a ball the same weight as the javelin: 800 grams for men, and 600 grams for women.

Two major ways of holding the javelin are to be considered: the fork grip and the Finnish grip. The fork grip is a simple style, consisting of holding the javelin between the index and middle fingers, with the fingers against the rear of the cord grip of the javelin. This style has been used partly because of its simplicity and partly for other reasons (Oregon's Boyd Brown, who set an American record at 234′ 1 1/2″ in 1940, used the fork grip because he had lost his thumb in an accident). However, the style is rarely seen today.

The Finnish grip consists of laying the cord grip of the javelin through the palm at the middle of the hand, the middle finger encircling the spear at the rear of the cord grip, the thumb around the opposite side of the grip, and the index finger extended back and to the same side of the javelin as the middle finger. Keep in mind that the object is to see how far the athlete can throw the javelin, not how prettily it can be held.

The Finnish approach run, or variations of it, is the most commonly used style in the world today. When reaching the final steps of the approach, the thrower gradually turns the feet slightly to the side of the throwing arm and goes into a fast cross-step or series of cross-steps to get into a powerful throwing position. Although this style is not easy to learn, it allows great use of the thrower's speed. The basic throwing motion, regardless of the grip or approach style, is over the shoulder and close to the ear.

The Javelin Routine

In training, the thrower should progress from standing throws to throws with a short run, then to throws with a full run. This progression is done in a regular routine that is repeated before every workout in which any throwing is done. The standing technique can be done by replacing the javelin with a ball of the same weight.

The first step of the routine is throwing three times from a stand at a target about 30 feet away. The thrower begins with the weight back over the rear leg and the knee bent (the right leg, for a right-handed thrower). The front (left) leg is extended well to the front, pointing in the direction of the throw. The hips are turned at an angle of about 30 degrees away from the line of direction of the throw. The torso is back, with the hips over the rear leg. The right arm (throwing arm) is extended to the rear comfortably, but it is not stretched. The left arm is usually across the chest, leading the torso in rotating into the throw. The hips and legs are used to give additional thrusting power and rotation to the body to impart to the javelin. The javelin is thrown when maximum pull, rotation, and whip of the body have been applied. The thrower works at this last phase of the throw from the standing position for 5 to 10 throws, then progresses to the trotting throws.

The next step in the routine is the 3-4-5 exercise, which consists of going through the last three steps of the approach and throwing the weight or javelin three times at a target about 60 feet away. This step gives the feel of moving the body into the final stages of the throw.

The last step in the routine is taking three throws while going through the approach from the last check mark through the last five steps of the approach. These throws are aimed at a target about 90 feet away. After the routine is completed, the thrower may move on to more warm-up throws with an approach run.

The thrower may work with the trotting throws next. The purpose of the trotting throw is to add momentum to the other mechanics of the throw. With an easy trot of 10 to 20 steps, the javelin or weighted ball is brought back into throwing position, then thrown easily for 50 to 100 feet. This exercise is repeated about five times.

The final stage of the warm-up might be taking several throws, usually about five, with the full-approach run. This stage is especially important for getting the approach pattern and check marks perfected. Three check marks are recommended, though some throwers may use two marks or only one. The first mark is 90 to 110 feet from the rear of the throwing arc, keeping in mind that the rules do not allow a run exceeding 120 feet. From the starting check mark to the second check should be four strides, then another 10 strides to the final check, at the point where the last five strides, including the cross-stepping, begin. The thrower wants to reach the throwing point with as much speed as he can control, though excessive speed hinders successful throwing more than it assists it. You want the athlete to reach the throwing point with good position and control. The last check mark, five strides from the completion of the throw, is about 30 feet or so behind the throwing arc.

After the check marks have been practiced, nine throws with the javelin are taken, but none of them is a hard throw at full effort. Three throws are made at 1/2 effort, followed by three throws at 3/4 effort, and finally three throws at 7/8 effort.

For the progression of throwing in a competitive situation, the check marks should be set up first, then the warm-up cycle taken, followed by one or two throws. The good throws should not be wasted; they should be saved for the competition. The thrower may find it helpful to follow a cycle or pattern such as the following with the competitive throws:

- *First throw:* medium effort only. The primary object of this throw is to get a safe throw, qualifying for the finals at the start of the competition.
- *Second throw:* relatively hard (7/8 to 9/10 effort), a bit of a gamble.
- *Third throw:* attempt to explode with a full effort, a "big" throw.

The same cycle is recommended for the final three throws: medium to hard to explosion.

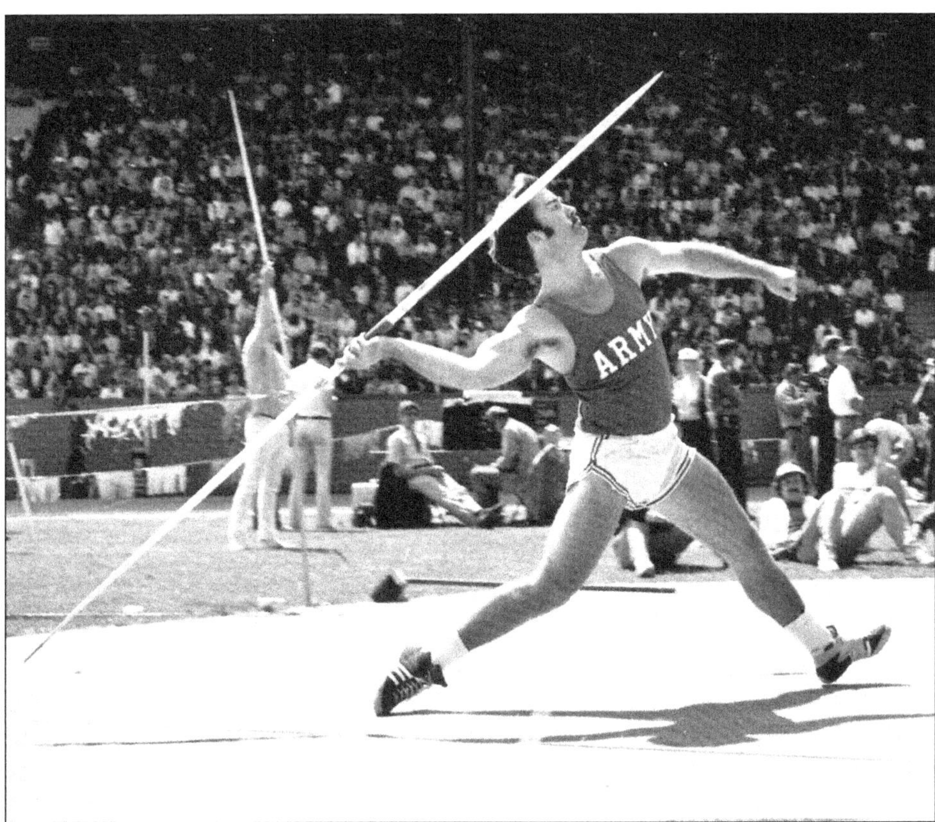

Photo 21-3. A thrower in the 1971 AAU meet

For a general pattern of training, a good practice for the pre-season is to throw on Monday, Wednesday, and Friday. When the season arrives, if the meets are on Saturdays, the throwers throw on Saturday, are off (from throwing) on Sunday and Monday, then throw again on both Tuesday and Wednesday (to help prepare for the experience of two-day competitions later in the season). They do throw on the Thursday and Friday leading into the next Saturday's competition. For a very big meet, no throwing should be done after Monday.

Javelin Technical Points

Several technical points of the approach and throw should be noted at this point. The lead foot comes into the throwing position pointed straight ahead or slightly to the right of the direction of the throw, while the trail foot is pointed slightly to the side. This positioning allows the thrower to rotate the hips into the throw. The lead foot is not moved until the body passes over it.

The lead foot should come down flat. If the landing is made on the heel, the knee is more likely to collapse and absorb much of the momentum of the approach run. Rather, the knee should force the body to pass up and over the leg, passing the body's momentum on to the throw as a summation of forces. The lead arm should not be brought through too fast, or it will get too far ahead of the throw, limiting its effectiveness.

The head should continue looking straight ahead throughout the throwing action, though throwers have a tendency to pull it down to the left while making the throw. The thrower should try either to look ahead or to watch the tip of the javelin. If the head is turned aside, the shoulders may not be squared to the throw, or the legs may not be properly utilized. A very common throwing fault is pulling the front leg from under the body and executing a reverse, rather than going over the leg.

Finally, the faster the javelin is thrown, the lower the trajectory can be. A bit over 30 degrees is considered ideal with the newer javelins. The athlete should always throw through the shaft and to the point of the javelin, trying to send it off at the optimum angle.

Weight training is advantageous for the javelin thrower, as it is for most other athletes. The use of balls of various weights is very beneficial. Some

Photo 21 4. A thrower in the 1971 AAU meet

throwers recommend throwing javelins or balls of various weights above and below the javelin weight. Theory suggests that the lighter implement permits faster arm movement, gradually increasing the speed of the arm strike, which is then applied to the regulation-weight javelin.

Javelin Training Schedules

The first week of the javelin throw training schedules is translated from the numbers to show how the charts are interpreted (Table 21-2). The training week begins on Monday and ends on the following Sunday.

Recommended Training Loads for Soviet Combined Events

	Women	*Men*
Training days	280	280
Training sessions	420	220
Training hours	1,120	1,120
Running at maximum speed (km)	35	40
Repetition runs, 100-600m (km)	85	75
Steady running (km)	1,100	1,200
Hurdling (number of hurdles)	4,000	3,100
Long jumps	900	700
High jumps	1,100	800
Shot puts	2,600	2,300
Javelin throws	3,100	3,000
Weight training (tons)	240	300
Jumping exercises (takeoffs)	11,000	11,000

Table 21-2. Interpreting the first week's training schedule

Photo 21-5. Les Tipton of Oregon, 1971 AAU meet

4A. Short Check Mark

The check marks for the javelin thrower are as important as those used in the jumping events. The elite thrower knows almost to the inch how close he will come to the scratch line. This technique should be practiced on every throwing day.

To establish a short check mark, which is used for technique throwing, for bad weather conditions, or for when the thrower is having a bad competitive day, the thrower begins two steps before the first check mark (Figure 21-1). The first check mark is hit with the left foot (for a right-handed thrower), then the thrower continues for six steps to hit the T with the left foot. The T point is the start of the five-count final approach, which includes the cross-step.

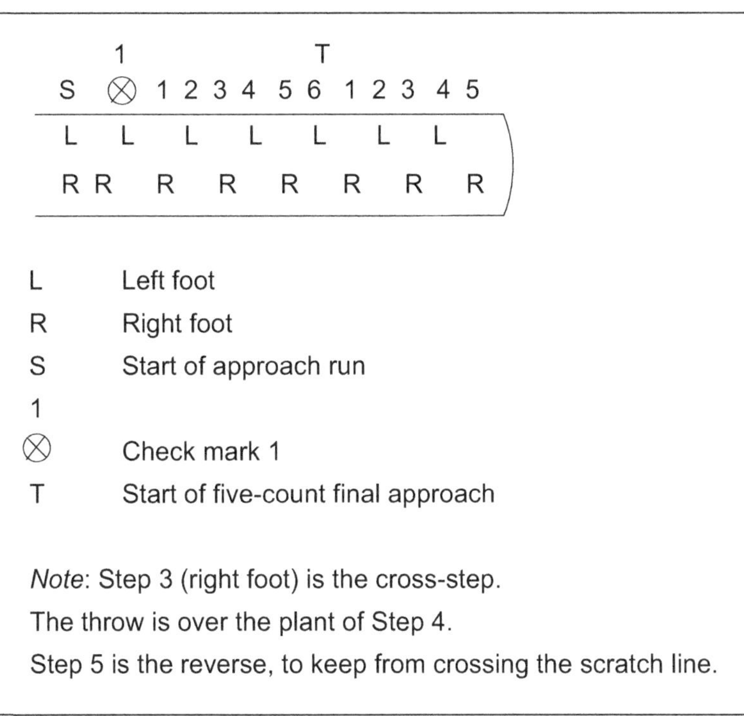

1 T
S ⊗ 1 2 3 4 5 6 1 2 3 4 5
L L L L L L L
R R R R R R R R
L Left foot
R Right foot
S Start of approach run
1
⊗ Check mark 1
T Start of five-count final approach
Note: Step 3 (right foot) is the cross-step.
The throw is over the plant of Step 4.
Step 5 is the reverse, to keep from crossing the scratch line.

Figure 21-1. Short check mark

4B. Long Check Mark

The long check marks are for competitive throwing. The more speed at which the javelin thrower can use control and still get an effective throwing position, the farther the throws should travel. This technique is not easily acquired, so it should be started early in the year and practiced regularly. The rules do not permit an approach longer than 120 feet. Most elite throwers use from 90 feet to the 120-foot maximum.

The athlete stands at the rear of the approach (Figure 21-2), and then takes a four-step trotting start from the start of the run (S), to the first check mark. An observer marks the last step while the thrower repeats the four steps twice. The average for this first part of the approach is about 20 feet. The average of the thrower's three trials is the first check mark.

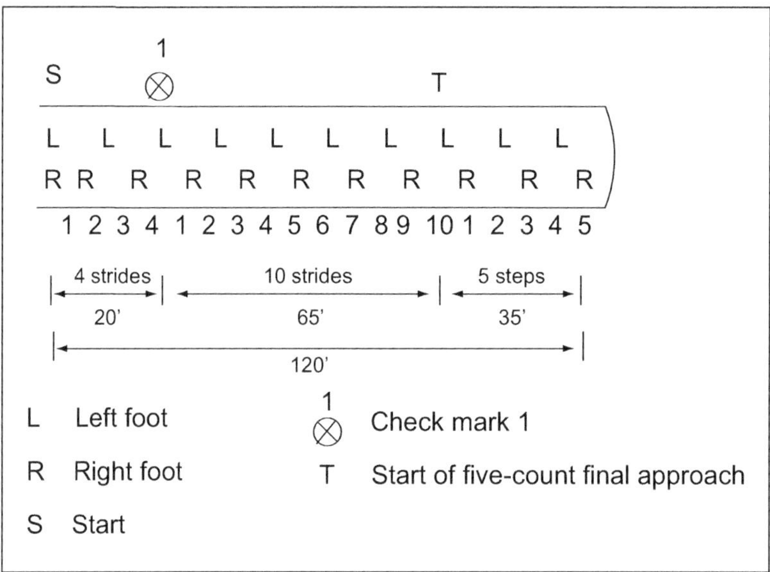

Figure 21-2. Long check mark

The same procedure is followed to establish the distance from the first check mark to T, with three trials made and the distances averaged. However, the athlete runs through the approach from the start (S) through check mark 1 and on through the 10 steps to T, rather than running only the 10 steps. This part of the approach usually averages around 55 to 65 feet.

The final measurement adds the last five steps, including the follow-through. From the starting point, the thrower takes four steps to check mark 1, 10 steps to the start of the final approach (T), and the final five steps, which include the throw and the follow-through. This long run is also done three times for an average. The five-count, or last five steps of the approach, varies from 25 to 35 feet in most cases.

The type of approach as well as the wind and weather conditions can make a great difference in the length of the short approach, and even more dramatic variations in the long approach. Competitive areas vary from soft grass, cinders, and mud to all-weather materials. It is imperative that athletes who aspire to be the best should have among their tools a short as well as a long approach and a full knowledge of their distances on different kinds of approach surfaces.

5A. Stand, Throw 10 to 30 Times

This drill is a routine warm-up drill. From a standing position, the athlete throws the javelin from 10 to 30 feet into a soft surface, gradually increasing the effort of the throws. The drill is also an opportunity to work on technical procedures. *Note:* The lengths of throws suggested throughout this section are for male college throwers and should be modified according to the age, the sex, and the experience level of the individual thrower.

5B. Routine

This drill is a continuation of the warm-up, but it is also a technique drill.

5B1. Three-Step, Throw 45 to 90 Feet

The javelin is already held back in the throwing position. The athlete takes two approach steps (Figure 21-3), and then executes Steps 3, 4, and 5 of the final approach, throwing over the left foot on Step 4.

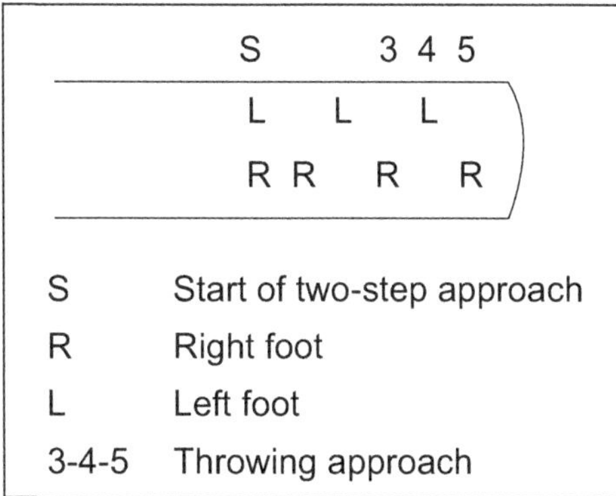

Figure 21-3. Three-step routine

Three easy throws are taken with this approach, with the athlete trying to throw only in the range between 45 and 90 feet. The emphasis is upon perfecting the technique of the approach and the throw, not on distance achieved.

5B2. Five-Step, 90 to 150 Feet

The athlete takes two approach steps to the final check mark, and then executes the five-step final approach and delivery, taking three easy throws (Figure 21-4). The approach should be rhythmical, hitting the check with the left foot (for a right-handed thrower) and going through the five final steps, with Step 3 the cross-step, Step 4 (the left foot) being the plant leg over which the throw is made, and Step 5 the follow-through step.

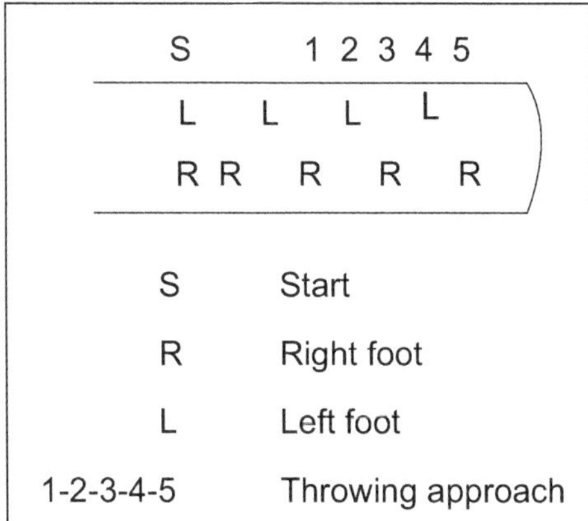

Figure 21-4. Five-step routine

5B3. Run and Throw, 150 to 180 Feet

This drill is the final approach. It is used to gain additional momentum, but the emphasis is on the rhythm of the approach and any technical point that the athlete feels needs attention. Again, these throws are for approach and technique work. No throws are made for distance. The distances listed are general suggestions for male college throwers who can throw from 220 to 260 feet or better.

6A. Short Approach; 6B. Long Approach

As with all other events, concentration on one part of the technique at a time produces the best results. Eventually, the athlete, like a well-timed machine, fits all cogs of the meshing gears together. He then produces gradually increasing efforts as the season progresses. The numbers listed, such as "1" beside "6A", are the numbers of the individual techniques listed under 6A and 6B (and also used in Number 9).

6A1. Position of Feet, Keep Lead Foot Down

This drill's purpose is to provide a throwing foundation while maintaining motion. Starting from the T mark in Figure 21-5, the first step of the five-count approach is a rhythmical, slightly longer, straight-ahead step. At the same time, the javelin starts back toward the throwing position. On the second step, the left foot turns slightly to the right, the javelin is almost back in the throwing position, and the torso is turned partially to the right. On the third step, the right foot is turned slightly to the right (the cross-step), the javelin reaches its final throwing position, and the torso is turned as far to the right as is practical for the individual. The final left-foot position (Step 4) is almost straight ahead, but it is still slightly to the right in its aim. The right-leg momentum is increased by a slight push, the left foot remains planted, and the final step or reverse (Step 5) is made to the final position on the right foot.

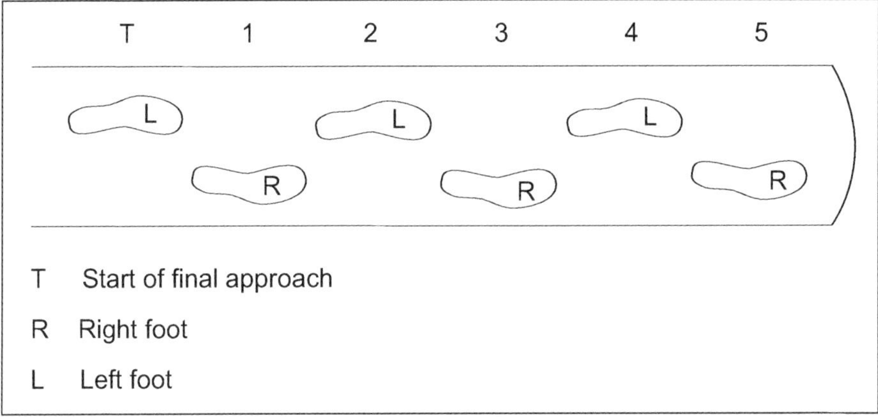

Figure 21-5. Foot position in the final approach

6A2. Rear Foot Under, Over It

On the third step of the final approach, the torso should be turned as far toward a right angle to the throwing direction as the javelin thrower can reach and still be able to pull back into the delivery. This position varies with some individuals. Some excellent throwers keep the torso almost directly ahead, getting a "bow" effect, rather than a "lay back" over the back (right) leg, which is the method most commonly used. The action starts from a slightly bent right knee, and the hip has also been cocked. The torso is turned to the right, and the javelin is back, with the thrower's left arm across the chest or pointed in the direction of the throw. The head and nose are aimed in the direction of the throw. The right knee straightens; the hip thrusts the torso back to a position "across" the direction of the throw (this is a turn of 45 degrees, rather than 90).

6A3. Body to Right, Body Precedes Arm

This position is taken on the third step and continues into the fourth step. The torso is turned to the right to make it easier to pull the javelin back to the throwing position. The left arm should be across the chest or, as some athletes carry it, pointed toward the throwing direction. As the left foot comes down (Step 4), the left arm swings in an arc below shoulder height and comes to the direction of the throw. The torso is turned quickly to the direction of the throw, and the throwing arm flows into the throw.

6A4. Good Pull

The javelin is pulled, as one would pull on a rope. The pull of the body's turn and momentum, which is transferred from the feet to the hips to the torso and finally to the pulling arm, adds momentum to the javelin before the actual throw is made.

6A5. Cock the Hand, Rotate Palm Up

The throwing hand should be rotated up (palm up) as the arm is cocked for the throw. The emphasis on the throwing hand should be to have the palm up at the start of the throw, and the palm down at the finish.

6A6. Over the Shoulder, Close to the Ear

The javelin on delivery should pass over the shoulder and close enough to the head that the head tilts slightly to the left during the delivery. Beware! The sidearm delivery is the most certain way to have elbow injuries.

6A7. Through the Shaft, Keep Tip Low

The shaft should be delivered a bit above 30 degrees. In delivering it, the thrower should watch the point to see that it does not wander to the right or tip up on delivery. As the javelin leaves, all the thrower should be able to see is the "tail-tip," which should appear no larger than a silver dollar. A tipped-up shaft would show the whole javelin and result in a high, bad flight.

6A8. Lead Foot Down Quickly, Pass Over It

The lead foot (Step 4) should come down quickly. The thrower should keep the power and momentum flowing. The left leg is planted quickly, the foot pointed slightly to the right, and the knee almost straight and straightening up into the throw as the body passes over it.

10. Test or Compete, Record Below

The number indicates a trial or an actual throwing all-out. 10B1 is a trial throw of 1/2 to 3/4 effort, 10B2 is a trial throw at 3/4 to 7/8 effort, and 10B3 is a trial throw at 9/10 effort. The best throw is recorded, along with the date, at the bottom of the training sheet.

11A. Start Slow, Finish Fast

The emphasis on the approach run should be to gain momentum with relaxed speed at the end of the throw. The beginner tends to slow down at the end, not only stopping the feet but also stopping the torso. A thrower gains very little from such an approach. It is true, though, that the feet stop in a good approach. The feet stopping at the end of a fast approach make the body a catapult or a whip, which increases the momentum of the javelin before the final throwing motion.

11B. Explosion

The athlete is trying to explode with a burst of energy at the end of the throw. If done well and timed perfectly, the explosion can help the thrower put more into the throw.

11C. Easy-Medium-Hard

This drill is work on a throwing cycle for competition. The first throw is relatively easy, in other words, a "safe" throw, a sure mark. The second throw in the qualifying round would be a bit harder, a medium throw. The last throw is hard, an attempt to explode and get a big improvement in the mark. The same throwing cycle is used in the final round of three throws.

17. Have Feeling of Being Back and Relaxed Over Rear Leg, No Strain

The final throwing position (Steps 3 and 4 in Figure 21-5) is one of a slight lean back over the right or rear leg, which is bent. As the body is turned into the throw, it makes a bow or sling for shooting the "arrow."

18. Work on Staying Behind the Scratch Line

All javelin throwers need some practice in staying behind the scratch line, some because after good throws they wander over the line, causing fouls. A thrower also needs to know how much momentum he can use and still have room for the follow-through.

19A. Throw Ball Into Net

If a net is available, a softball or weighted ball up to 3 pounds can be used to work on technique as well as arm strength and flexibility.

19B. Throw at Target

Target throwing is used to keep the athlete from competing every practice day. It is also used so the athlete can learn to use the wind by varying the direction of approach in the throwing area.

19C. Approach Speed

The thrower should constantly be working for more approach speed. How much speed? Coach Armas Valste of Finland said, "As much speed as you can control." Work regularly to attain greater controlled speed.

20. Secondary Event

A secondary event should be a pleasurable diversion. It may also be a team point winner. Les Tipton, Oregon and Olympic athlete, helped win a dual track meet with a third in the high hurdles.

JAVELIN THROW SCHEDULE NAME ____________________ DATE ______________

1. A. Jog 1-2 laps with relay pass, in 2s or 3s
   B. Hendricks Park C. Golf course D. Steps
   (1) Short hill (2) Long hill
2. Fartlek A. Varied pace B. Slow, steady pace
3. Weights and jogging
4. Check marks A. Short run B. Long run
   (1) Height (2) Landing (3) Takeoff
5. Height work
   A. Emphasize body control
   B. Apparatus
   C. Takeoff
   D.
6. Flight A. Hitch-kick 1-1/2 B. Hang C.
7. TEAM MEETING
8. Special A. Sauna B. Swim C. Hill D.
9. Landing A. Over the feet B. Around the feet
   C.
10. A. Meet B. Trial C. Simulation D. Control test
   (1) 3/4ths to 7/8ths effort (2) Full effort
   (3)
11. Short run and jump, relax last 4 steps
   A. Feather the board B. Pound the board
   C. Over the foot D. 2-count rise: height
   E. Off platform F. Landing
12. With Coach A. B.
14. A. Wind sprints (1) Straight (2) Curve
   B. Hurdle drill: 3 LH, 7-9m apart
   C. Spring and bound
   D. Alternate run and jog, at least 800
   E. Starts (1) 100 (2)
   F. High knee (slow) and fast leg
15. Plyometrics A. Jumps B. Bounding C.
   (1) 1-leg (2) Both legs (3)
16. Easy acrobatics or apparatus
17.
18. A. 300-150-100 B. 100-200-100
19.
20. Work on second event
21. A. Videotape B. Film C. Pictures
   (1) Record performance (2) Study
30. Experimental work

Date	Distance	3/4 pace	Date Pace	Goal Pace

M
T
W
T
F
S
S
M
T
W
T
F
S
S
M
T
W
T
F
S
S
M
T
W
T
F
S
S

Sheet 21-1. Revised javelin training schedule sheet

Javelin Throw NAME DATE September/October

1. A. Jog 1 or 2 laps, easy stretching B.
2. Fartlek A. Varied pace B. Steady pace
3. Weights and jogging
4. Check mark A. Short B. Long
5. A. Stand, throw 10 to 30 times
   B. Routine: throw 3 of each—easy, medium, hard.
   (1) 3 step, 45 ft.-90 ft. (2) 5 step, 90 ft.-150 ft.
   (3) Run and throw, 150 ft.-180 ft.
6. A. Short approach B. Long approach
   (1) Position of feet—keep lead foot down
   (2) Rear foot under—be over it
   (3) Body to right, body proceeds arm (4) Good pull
   (5) Cock the hand—rotate palm up
   (6) Over the shoulder, close to the ear
   (7) Through the shaft—keep tip low
   (8) Lead foot down quickly—pass over it
   (9)
7. Squad meeting
8. Special A. Sauna B. Swim C. Steps or hill
   D.
9. Full run and form throws—numbers as in item 6.
10. Test or compete—record below A. 1/2 to 3/4
    B. 3/4 to 7/8 C. 9/10
11. A. Start slow—finish fast B. Explosion
    C. Easy-medium-hard D.
12. With Coach A. B.
14. A. Wind sprints B. Starts, 25-40 yds.
    C. High knee and fast leg D. Hurdle drill
    E. Spring and bound F. Alternate walk-run, go 880 or more
15. A. Hendricks Park B. Laurel Golf Course C.
16. Tumbling activities
17. Have feeling of back and relaxed, no strain over rear leg
18. Work on staying behind scratch line
19. A. Throw ball into net B. Throw at target
20. Secondary event
21. A. Pictures B. Film C. Video

Date	3/4	7/8	Now	Goal

M	Class or squad organization
T	1A-5A-16-14D
W	3-14D-7
T	1A-4A-19A-14A
F	1A-5A-16-14D
S	3 or 8A
S	recreation
M	3-8A or B
T	1A-5A-6A(7)-4-7 at Student Union
W	3-4 or 8A
T	4-3-16
F	1A-5A-5B-14A
S	3-14D-8A or B
S	recreation-study
M	3-14A-Tuesday 12:30 S.U.
T	1A-5A-5B-14A-12:30 S.U.
W	3-8B
T	1A-4A-3-16
F	1A-Check gear-easy jog
S	1A-4A-4B-10A-14D
S	Usual
M	3-14A
T	1A-6A(2)-6B(2)-5B-4B-14D
W	3-14D
T	14A-3-16
F	1A-6A(2)-6B(2)-19A-14D
S	3
S	Usual

Sheet 21-2. Javelin training schedule

Javelin Throw NAME DATE *October/November*

1. A. Jog 1 or 2 laps, easy stretching B.
2. Fartlek A. Varied pace B. Steady pace
3. Weights and jogging
4. Check mark A. Short B. Long
5. A. Stand, throw 10 to 30 times
   B. Routine: throw 3 of each—easy, medium, hard.
   (1) 3 step, 45 ft.-90 ft. (2) 5 step, 90 ft.-150 ft.
   (3) Run and throw, 150 ft.-180 ft.
6. A. Short approach B. Long approach
   (1) Position of feet—keep lead foot down
   (2) Rear foot under—be over it
   (3) Body to right, body proceeds arm (4) Good pull
   (5) Cock the hand—rotate palm up
   (6) Over the shoulder, close to the ear
   (7) Through the shaft—keep tip low
   (8) Lead foot down quickly—pass over it
   (9)
7. Squad meeting
8. Special A. Sauna B. Swim C. Steps or hill
   D.
9. Full run and form throws—numbers as in item 6.
10. Test or compete—record below A. 1/2 to 3/4
    B. 3/4 to 7/8 C. 9/10
11. A. Start slow—finish fast B. Explosion
    C. Easy-medium-hard D.
12. With Coach A. B.
14. A. Wind sprints B. Starts, 25-40 yds.
    C. High knee and fast leg D. Hurdle drill
    E. Spring and bound F. Alternate walk-run, go 880 or more
15. A. Hendricks Park B. Laurel Golf Course C.
16. Tumbling activities
17. Have feeling of back and relaxed, no strain over rear leg
18. Work on staying behind scratch line
19. A. Throw ball into net B. Throw at target
20. Secondary event
21. A. Pictures B. Film C. Video

Date	3/4	7/8	Now	Goal

M	*1A-3*
T	*Choice*
W	*1A-4A-5A(1)-5A(2)-5A(3)-19B-14D*
T	*3*
F	*1A-4A-4B-10B-14A-10A*
S	*3*
S	*Choice*
M	*1A-3*
T	*Choice*
W	*1A-4A-4B-5A-6A(8)-6A(7)-14D*
T	*3*
F	*1A-4A-4B-5A-6A(3)-17-14D*
S	*3-16*
S	*Usual*
M	*1A-3*
T	*3 or choice*
W	*1A-4A-4B-21-10A-19A-14A or 14D*
T	*Choice*
F	*1A-19A-19B-2A or 2B*
S	*3*
S	*Choice*
M	*1A-3-14A-8*
T	*3*
W	*1A-4A-4B-6A(8)-6B(8)-18-14C-2B*
T	*3-8A*
F	*1A-4A-4B-10(3 short run-3 long run)*
S	*3*
S	*Choice*

Sheet 21-3. Javelin training schedule

Javelin Throw NAME DATE January

1. A. Jog 1 or 2 laps, easy stretching B.
2. Fartlek A. Varied pace B. Steady pace
3. Weights and jogging
4. Check mark A. Short B. Long
5. A. Stand, throw 10 to 30 times
   B. Routine: throw 3 of each—easy, medium, hard.
   (1) 3 step, 45 ft.-90 ft. (2) 5 step, 90 ft.-150 ft.
   (3) Run and throw, 150 ft.-180 ft.
6. A. Short approach B. Long approach
   (1) Position of feet—keep lead foot down
   (2) Rear foot under—be over it
   (3) Body to right, body proceeds arm (4) Good pull
   (5) Cock the hand—rotate palm up
   (6) Over the shoulder, close to the ear
   (7) Through the shaft—keep tip low
   (8) Lead foot down quickly—pass over it
   (9)
7. Squad meeting
8. Special A. Sauna B. Swim C. Steps or hill
   D.
9. Full run and form throws—numbers as in item 6.
10. Test or compete—record below A. 1/2 to 3/4
    B. 3/4 to 7/8 C. 9/10
11. A. Start slow—finish fast B. Explosion
    C. Easy-medium-hard D.
12. With Coach A. B.
14. A. Wind sprints B. Starts, 25-40 yds.
    C. High knee and fast leg D. Hurdle drill
    E. Spring and bound F. Alternate walk-run, go 880 or more
15. A. Hendricks Park B. Laurel Golf Course C.
16. Tumbling activities
17. Have feeling of back and relaxed, no strain over rear leg
18. Work on staying behind scratch line
19. A. Throw ball into net B. Throw at target
20. Secondary event
21. A. Pictures B. Film C. Video

Date	3/4	7/8	Now	Goal

M	Reorganize class or squad
T	3-8B
W	1A-5A-6B-6A-2
T	3-8A or B
F	1A-5A-6B(1)-6A(8)-14A
S	3
S	walk, or recreation
M	3-8A
T	3-16-8B
W	1A-5A-12-6A(5)-6A(3)-19A-14D
T	3-8A
F	1A-5A-6A(5)-6A(7)-14A
S	3
S	2 or good walk
M	3
T	16
W	1A-12(4 pm)-5A-6B(6)-6B(8)-5A
T	3-8A or B
F	1A-14A-6A(1)-6B(1)-6B(7)-14D
S	3
S	3
M	1A-3-14A
T	3-16
W	1A-5A-6A(6)-6A(3)-19A-14D
T	1A-3-14A
F	1A-5A-5B-Easy 11A and B-14C
S	3-2
S	Choice

Sheet 21-4. Javelin training schedule

Javelin Throw NAME DATE *February*

1. A. Jog 1 or 2 laps, easy stretching B.
2. Fartlek A. Varied pace B. Steady pace
3. Weights and jogging
4. Check mark A. Short B. Long
5. A. Stand, throw 10 to 30 times
   B. Routine: throw 3 of each—easy, medium, hard.
   (1) 3 step, 45 ft.-90 ft. (2) 5 step, 90 ft.-150 ft.
   (3) Run and throw, 150 ft.-180 ft.
6. A. Short approach B. Long approach
   (1) Position of feet—keep lead foot down
   (2) Rear foot under—be over it
   (3) Body to right, body proceeds arm (4) Good pull
   (5) Cock the hand—rotate palm up
   (6) Over the shoulder, close to the ear
   (7) Through the shaft—keep tip low
   (8) Lead foot down quickly—pass over it
   (9)
7. Squad meeting
8. Special A. Sauna B. Swim C. Steps or hill
   D.
9. Full run and form throws—numbers as in item 6.
10. Test or compete—record below A. 1/2 to 3/4
    B. 3/4 to 7/8 C. 9/10
11. A. Start slow—finish fast B. Explosion
    C. Easy-medium-hard D.
12. With Coach A. B.
14. A. Wind sprints B. Starts, 25-40 yds.
    C. High knee and fast leg D. Hurdle drill
    E. Spring and bound F. Alternate walk-run, go 880 or more
15. A. Hendricks Park B. Laurel Golf Course C.
16. Tumbling activities
17. Have feeling of back and relaxed, no strain over rear leg
18. Work on staying behind scratch line
19. A. Throw ball into net B. Throw at target
20. Secondary event
21. A. Pictures B. Film C. Video

Date	3/4	7/8	Now	Goal

M	1A-3-14A or 14D
T	1A-6B(5)-6B(2)-6B(6)-14A
W	3
T	1A-5A-5B-4A-4B-14D
F	3-8A or B
S	3
S	study and recreation
M	1A-3-14A
T	1A-4A-4B-6B(2) 3x-6B(6) 3x-5B-14A
W	3
T	1A-4A-4B-5A-5B-6A(2)-19A-14A
F	3
S	1A-5A-6B(2)-11B-14D
S	study or recreation
M	1A-3
T	1A-4A-4B-5A-5B-19B-14D
W	7-1A-3
T	1A-5A-6B(2)-6A(1)-5B-14D
F	3-8A or 8B or 16
S	1A-12-10A-5B-14A or D
S	Usual
M	1A-3-16
T	1A-5A-6B(6)-6B(7)-19B-14A
W	2-8A or B
T	1A-10-12-4B-10-5B
F	3-8A or B
S	3
S	Usual

Sheet 21-5. Javelin training schedule

Javelin Throw NAME DATE *March*

1. A. Jog 1 or 2 laps, easy stretching B.
2. Fartlek A. Varied pace B. Steady pace
3. Weights and jogging
4. Check mark A. Short B. Long
5. A. Stand, throw 10 to 30 times
   B. Routine: throw 3 of each—easy, medium, hard.
   (1) 3 step, 45 ft.-90 ft. (2) 5 step, 90 ft.-150 ft.
   (3) Run and throw, 150 ft.-180 ft.
6. A. Short approach B. Long approach
   (1) Position of feet—keep lead foot down
   (2) Rear foot under—be over it
   (3) Body to right, body proceeds arm (4) Good pull
   (5) Cock the hand—rotate palm up
   (6) Over the shoulder, close to the ear
   (7) Through the shaft—keep tip low
   (8) Lead foot down quickly—pass over it
   (9)
7. Squad meeting
8. Special A. Sauna B. Swim C. Steps or hill
   D.
9. Full run and form throws—numbers as in item 6.
10. Test or compete—record below A. 1/2 to 3/4
    B. 3/4 to 7/8 C. 9/10
11. A. Start slow—finish fast B. Explosion
    C. Easy-medium-hard D.
12. With Coach A. B.
14. A. Wind sprints B. Starts, 25-40 yds.
    C. High knee and fast leg D. Hurdle drill
    E. Spring and bound F. Alternate walk-run, go 880 or more
15. A. Hendricks Park B. Laurel Golf Course C.
16. Tumbling activities
17. Have feeling of back and relaxed, no strain over rear leg
18. Work on staying behind scratch line
19. A. Throw ball into net B. Throw at target
20. Secondary event
21. A. Pictures B. Film C. Video

Date	3/4	7/8	Now	Goal

M	2-14A
T	1A-5A-6A(9)-6A(6)-4B-19B(150-180')-14D
W	1A-3
T	1A-12-10B(190-210')-Target at 200'-14D
F	1A-3-14C
S	Secondary event test
S	Usual
M	3-14A
T	1A-4A-4B-5A-6B(2)-6B(1)-5B-14D
W	3-8A or B
T	1-12-6A(8)-6B(8)-19B-20-8A or B
F	3
S	1-10-14D
S	study
M	3-8A or B
T	1A-4A-4B-5A-5B-6B(2)-6B(1)-17-14A
W	3-8A or B
T	1A-5A-5B-6B(3)-6B(5)-19A
F	3
S	3 or 14A
S	study
M	1A-3-2
T	1A-4A-4B-5A-5B-17-14A
W	1A-4A-4B-3 medium throws-8A
T	3-14D
F	Light and gear ready
S	Travel and compete
S	recreation

Sheet 21-6. Javelin training schedule

Javelin Throw NAME DATE April

1. A. Jog 1 or 2 laps, easy stretching B.
2. Fartlek A. Varied pace B. Steady pace
3. Weights and jogging
4. Check mark A. Short B. Long
5. A. Stand, throw 10 to 30 times
   B. Routine: throw 3 of each—easy, medium, hard.
   (1) 3 step, 45 ft.-90 ft. (2) 5 step, 90 ft.-150 ft.
   (3) Run and throw, 150 ft.-180 ft.
6. A. Short approach B. Long approach
   (1) Position of feet—keep lead foot down
   (2) Rear foot under—be over it
   (3) Body to right, body proceeds arm (4) Good pull
   (5) Cock the hand—rotate palm up
   (6) Over the shoulder, close to the ear
   (7) Through the shaft—keep tip low
   (8) Lead foot down quickly—pass over it
   (9)
7. Squad meeting
8. Special A. Sauna B. Swim C. Steps or hill
   D.
9. Full run and form throws—numbers as in item 6.
10. Test or compete—record below A. 1/2 to 3/4
    B. 3/4 to 7/8 C. 9/10
11. A. Start slow—finish fast B. Explosion
    C. Easy-medium-hard D.
12. With Coach A. B.
14. A. Wind sprints B. Starts, 25-40 yds.
    C. High knee and fast leg D. Hurdle drill
    E. Spring and bound F. Alternate walk-run, go 880 or more
15. A. Hendricks Park B. Laurel Golf Course C.
16. Tumbling activities
17. Have feeling of back and relaxed, no strain over rear leg
18. Work on staying behind scratch line
19. A. Throw ball into net B. Throw at target
20. Secondary event
21. A. Pictures B. Film C. Video

Date	3/4	7/8	Now	Goal

M	3-14A or 14D
T	1A-4A-4B-5A-6A2-6A6-6B2-6B6-19B-14D (3x over 6B2, 3x over 6B6)
W	2-8B
T	1-12-5A-6A2-6B2-6B2-4A-4B-19B (3x over 6A2, 3x over 6B2, 3x over 6B2)
F	Gear ready-jog & stretch-no javelin
S	Compete
S	Form work
M	2-4
T	7-1A-5A-6A6-6B6-6A3-4A-4B-14B (3x over 6A6, 3x over 6B6)
W	1A-4A-4B-3 medium throws-3
T	2-8
F	Jog and stretch
S	Compete
S	Travel home and loosen up
M	1A-3
T	1A-3-14A
W	1A-4-5-6A1-6A3-9B2-9B6-14D (3x over 9B2, 3x over 9B6)
T	1A-3
F	Light-all gear ready
S	Compete
S	Home and loosen up
M	3-14A
T	7-1A-4A-4B-6A8-6A6-9A2-9A6-19A-14D (3x over 6A8, 3x over 6A6, 3x over 9A2, 3x over 9A6)
W	2-8
T	1A-12-5A-4A-4B-9A2-jog (3x over 4B)
F	Gear ready and travel
S	Compete
S	Loosen up-4-5A

Sheet 21-7. Javelin training schedule

Javelin Throw NAME DATE May / June

1. A. Jog 1 or 2 laps, easy stretching B.
2. Fartlek A. Varied pace B. Steady pace
3. Weights and jogging
4. Check mark A. Short B. Long
5. A. Stand, throw 10 to 30 times
   B. Routine: throw 3 of each—easy, medium, hard.
   (1) 3 step, 45 ft.-90 ft. (2) 5 step, 90 ft.-150 ft.
   (3) Run and throw, 150 ft.-180 ft.
6. A. Short approach B. Long approach
   (1) Position of feet—keep lead foot down
   (2) Rear foot under—be over it
   (3) Body to right, body proceeds arm (4) Good pull
   (5) Cock the hand—rotate palm up
   (6) Over the shoulder, close to the ear
   (7) Through the shaft—keep tip low
   (8) Lead foot down quickly—pass over it
   (9)
7. Squad meeting
8. Special A. Sauna B. Swim C. Steps or hill
   D.
9. Full run and form throws—numbers as in item 6.
10. Test or compete—record below A. 1/2 to 3/4
    B. 3/4 to 7/8 C. 9/10
11. A. Start slow—finish fast B. Explosion
    C. Easy-medium-hard D.
12. With Coach A. B.
14. A. Wind sprints B. Starts, 25-40 yds.
    C. High knee and fast leg D. Hurdle drill
    E. Spring and bound F. Alternate walk-run, go 880 or more
15. A. Hendricks Park B. Laurel Golf Course C.
16. Tumbling activities
17. Have feeling of back and relaxed, no strain over rear leg
18. Work on staying behind scratch line
19. A. Throw ball into net B. Throw at target
20. Secondary event
21. A. Pictures B. Film C. Video

Date	3/4	7/8	Now	Goal

M	Light 2 and 14A
T	1A-6A(8)-6A(3)-4A-4B-3x 6A(2)-3x 6A(6)-5B-Jog
W	2-21B
T	Gear ready
F	Preliminaries-Regional or Conference
S	Finals
S	Home and loosen up
M	Easy
T	1A-2x 5B-4A-4B-3x 10B-14A or 14D
W	Help with frosh or JV meet-Jog
T	1A-5B-14A
F	Invitational meet, travel and loosen up
S	Invitational meet, or simulate
S	Usual Sunday routine
M	Runway and form work at Championship area
T	Light
W	Light
T	Qualify for Championship
F	Light
S	Championship finals
S	Usual
M	
T	
W	
T	
F	
S	
S	

Sheet 21-8. Javelin training schedule

Endnotes

1. E. Arbeit, K. Bartonietz, P. Borner, K. Hellmann, & W. Skibbia. (1988). The javelin: The view of the DVfL of the GDR on talent selection, technique and main training contents of the training phases from beginner to top-level athlete. *New Studies in Athletics, 3*(1), 57-74.
2. Wilf Paish. (1986). Some initial observations on the new men's javelin. *New Studies in Athletics, 1*(3), 81-84.
3. Hans-Joachim Menzel. (1986). Biomechanics of javelin throwing. *New Studies in Athletics, 1*(3), 85-98.
4. Anders Borgstrom. (1988). Two years with the new javelin. *New Studies in Athletics, 3*(1), 85-88.
5. Glenn DiGiorgio. (1988). Coaching insights for the new javelin. *Track Technique, 104*, 3318.
6. Randolf Peukert. (1987). Training and biomechanical factors in the development of the javelin throw technique. *Track and Field Quarterly Review, 87*(1), 37-44.
7. DiGiorgio, 3318.
8. Esa Utriainen. (1988). Javelin periodization. *Track Technique, 103,* 3296.
9. O. Ditrusyenko. (1986). New approaches to javelin training. *Track Technique, 95,* 3041.

Core Readings

Amicale des Entraîneurs Français d'Athlétisme, ed. (1987). *The throws: Official Report of the XIVth Congress, European Athletics Coaches Association.* Paris: European Athletics Coaches Association.

Brown, C. Harmon, Bill Webb & Bob Sing. (2000). Javelin. In *USA Track and Field coaching manual.* Champaign, IL: Human Kinetics, 249-264.

Dunn, George D., Jr., & Kevin McGill. (2003). *The Throws Manual* (3rd ed.). Mountain View, CA: Tafnews.

Freeman, William H. (2001). Periodized training for throwers. In *Peak When It Counts: Periodization for American track and field* (4th ed.). Mountain View, CA: Tafnews, 131-139.

Jarver, Jess, ed. (2000). *The Throws: Contemporary Theory, Technique and Training* (5th ed.). Mountain View, CA: Tafnews.

Naclerio, Tony. (1988). *The Teaching Progressions of the Shot Put, Discus and Javelin.* Rockaway, NJ: Author.

Silvester, Jay. (2003). *The complete book of throws.* Champaign, IL: Human Kinetics.

Sing, Robert F. (1984). *The dynamics of the javelin throw.* Cherry Hill, NJ: Reynolds.

Terauds, Juris. (1985). *Biomechanics of the javelin throw.* Del Mar, CA: Academic Publishers.

USA Track & Field Coaching Education Program. (n.d.). *Level II: Throws.* USA Track & Field. Invaluable; revised regularly.

Recommended Readings

Adamczewski, Horst. (1996). *Some biomechanical aspects of the javelin throw.* [abstract]. Track Coach, 135, 4318-4319.

Aikens, Jim. (Winter 2001). Fremd High school throwing program. *Track Coach, 154,* 4909-4914.

Arbeit, Ekkart. (1990). Three years of the new javelin [abstract]. *Track Technique, 110,* 3522.

Arbeit, Ekkart, Anders Borgström, Carl Johnson & Yuriy Sedykh. (1996). NSA Round Table 30: The role of speed in the throws. *New Studies in Athletics, 11*(1), 11-16.

Armbrust, Wayne T. (Summer 2004). Understanding non-uniform forces in the throws, with implications for training. *Track Coach, 168,* 5369-5372.

Auvinen, M., & K. Ihalainen. (1996). Junior World [javelin] Champion Taina Uppa's training, 1993-1994. Trans. Don Welsh. *Track Coach, 134,* 4284-4287.

Babbitt, Don. (2006). Endurance training for the throws [abstract]. *New Studies in Athletics, 21*(1), 62-63.

Bakarinov, Juri. (1990). Theoretical aspects of training control for highly qualified throwers. *New Studies in Athletics, 5*(1), 7-15.

Bartonietz, Klaus. (Summer 2003). Training with varied weight implements [abstract]. *Track Coach, 164,* 5250.

Bartonietz, Klaus, Russell J. Best & Anders Borgström. (1996). The throwing events at the World Championships in Athletics 1995, Göteborg—Technique of the world's best athletes Part 2: discus and javelin throw. *New Studies in Athletics, 11*(1), 19-44.

Boggis, Don. (Winter 2002). A circuit for young throwers. *Track Coach, 158,* 5047-5048.

Borgström, Anders. (2000). The development of the javelin. *New Studies in Athletics, 15*(3/4), 25-28.

Böttcher, Jörg, & Lutz Kühl. (1998). The technique of the best female javelin throwers in 1997. *New Studies in Athletics, 13*(1), 47-61.

Bremicker, Erich. (2000). Why did the senior javelin specification have to be changed? *New Studies in Athletics, 15*(3/4), 29-31.

Brown, Harmon. (1992). Javelin throwing, British style. *Track Technique, 120,* 3824-26;

Brown, C. Harmon, & John Stevenson. (1994). The bio-dynamics of javelin release. *Track Technique, 128,* 4087-4088, 4101.

Burgoyne, Lindsay. (Fall 2002). Stress sites in javelin throwing [abstract]. *Track Coach, 161,* 5156.

Burnett, Angus. (Spring 2002). Relevance of jumping exercises to field event athletes [abstract]. *Track Coach, 159,* 5090.

Goldmann, Werner. (1995). Sprinting speed—An asset for throwers [abstract]. *Track Technique, 130,* 4161-4162.

Gorski, Jeff. (Spring 1999). My dinner with Klaus. *Track Coach, 147,* 4684-4689.

Jianrong, Chen. (1992). Load variations of elite female javelin throwers in a macrocycle. *Track Technique, 119,* 3788-3792.

Judge, Larry W. (1992). Designing a strength & conditioning program for the thrower. *Track and Field Quarterly Review, 92*(3), 48-60.

Judge, Larry, & Jeffrey Potteiger. (Summer 2000). Using a battery of tests to identify overtraining in throwers [abstract]. *Track Coach, 152,* 4867.

Kovacs, Etele. (1987). Complex development of strength, velocity and technique of young javelin throwers. *New Studies in Athletics, 2*(1), 43-45.

Lawler, Peter. (1994). The javelin throw—The past, present and future. *Track and Field Quarterly Review, 94*(3), 47-52.

Lawler, Peter, & Anders Borgström. (2000). Roundtable questions: New javelin for women. *New Studies in Athletics, 15*(3/4), 33-35.

Liebenberg, Terseus. (Summer 2001). Medicine ball training for javelin throwers [abstract]. *Track Coach, 156,* 4996.

Liset, George. (2006). Sensory motor learning: Developing a kinaesthetic sense of the throws. *New Studies in Athletics, 21*(1), 51-56.

Matveyev, Jevgeni. (Summer 2004). A control test for javelin throwers [abstract]. *Track Coach, 168,* 5380.

McGill, Kevin. (1982). Analysis chart for the javelin throw. *Track and Field Quarterly Review, 82*(1), 39-42.

McGill, Kevin. (1994). In search of Seppo. *Track Technique, 126,* 4011-4015.

Morriss, Calvin, & Roger Bartlett. (1996). Biomechanical factors critical for performance in the men's javelin throw. *Sports Medicine, 22*(6), 438-446.

Morriss, Calvin, Roger Bartlett & Neil Fowler. (1997). Biomechanical analysis of the men's javelin throw at the 1995 World Championships in Athletics. *New Studies in Athletics, 12*(2-3), 31-41.

Murakami, Masatoshi, Satoru Tanabe, Masaki Ishikawa, Juha Isolehto, Paavo V. Komi & Akira Ito. (2006). Biomechanical analysis of the javelin at the 2005 World Championships in Athletics. *New Studies in Athletics, 21*(2), 67-80.

Paish, Wilf. (1993). Biomechanics and coaching—A review. *Track Technique, 122,* 3887-3888; Brown, Harmon. (1993). A reply to Wilf Paish. *Track Technique, 123,* 3939-3940.

Probst, Jorg. (Winter 2003). Rethinking the role of strength in the throwing events [abstract]. *Track Coach, 162,* 5186.

Pukstys, Tom. (Spring 2007). Planting, plyos, horsepower, and specificity in planting. *Track Coach, 179,* 5730-5731.

Reardon, Jim. (1991). Psychological characteristics of elite junior male and female throwers. *Track Technique, 114,* 3627-3629.

Rudman, Grigori. (Fall 2003). Varied weight implements strategy [abstract]. *Track Coach, 165,* 5284.

Schiffer, Jürgen. (1998). Selected and annotated bibliography 45: Javelin throw. *New Studies in Athletics, 13*(1), 65-86.

Schiffer, Jürgen. (2004). Selected and annotated bibliography 66: Javelin throw. *New Studies in Athletics, 19*(2), 69-126.

Scholz, Wolfram. (2006). The throwing events at the IAAF World Junior Championships: A whistle stop on the journey to elite athletics. Trans. Jürgen Schiffer. *New Studies in Athletics, 21*(2), 7-27.

White, Scott C. (1986). Introducing the essentials of javelin throwing to beginners. *Track and Field Quarterly Review, 86*(1), 29-34.

Tidow, Günter. (1996). Model technique analysis sheets—Part X: The javelin throw. *New Studies in Athletics, 11*(1), 45-62.

[Utrianen, Esa. (1987). Difference in men's and women's training for javelin. In Amicale des Entraîneurs Français d'Athlétisme, ed. *The Throws: Official Report of the XIVth Congress, European Athletics Coaches Association.* Paris: European Athletics Coaches Association, 55-68.

Young, Michael. (Winter 2001). Developing event-specific strength for the javelin throw. *Track Coach, 154,* 4921-4927.

THE ALL-AROUND ATHLETE

Part 6

Dave Edstrom, 1960 U.S. Olympic Team

22

The Combined Events: Decathlon, Heptathlon, and Pentathlon

Bowerman's Best

7599 Dave Edstrom 1960

Record Setters

Dave Edstrom	U.S. Olympic Team, 1960; not an NCAA event in 1960; high hurdles All-American, 1960 (13.8)

The combined events, the heptathlon and the decathlon, might be called the "acid tests of athletics," for their demands upon the participants are great. The name *decathlon* comes from the Greek *deca,* meaning "ten," because it includes 10 separate events, while *heptathlon* refers to seven events. The competitions last for two days, with the events in the order shown in Table 22-1.

Both competitions are scored by tables devised by the IAAF on a range of 1 to 1,200 points per separate event, with the 1,000-point level roughly equivalent to the "decathlon world record" for that event (no *official* records are awarded, but these are the best marks made in decathlon competition). A score for an inexperienced person of 5,000 total points in the decathlon or 3,000 points in the heptathlon shows potential, provided the weaknesses in any individual event are not too glaring. For men, a score of 7,000 points is beginning to reach national class, while the world-class level begins around 8,000 points. For women, 5,000 points in the heptathlon is national class, and 6,000 points is world class; the women's decathlon is too new to evaluate.

The Combined Events		
Men's Decathlon	**Women's Decathlon**	**Women's Heptathlon**
First Day	*First Day*	*First Day*
100 meters	100 meters	100m hurdles
Long jump	Discus throw	High jump
Shot put	Pole vault	Shot put
High jump	Javelin throw	200 meters
400 meters	400 meters	
Second Day	*Second Day*	*Second Day*
110m hurdles	100m hurdles	Long jump
Discus throw	Long jump	Javelin throw
Pole vault	Shot put	800 meters
Javelin throw	High jump	
1500 meters	1500 meters	

Table 22-1. The combined events

Short versions of the official decathlon and heptathlon scoring tables are shown in Tables 22-7 and 22-8 at the end of the chapter. All implements are official, and all international rules apply, except that

- Only three attempts are allowed in the throwing events and the long jump
- A runner is not disqualified until the third false start
- If the athlete does not start in every event, he is disqualified
- Records cannot be set if the wind exceeds 4m per second in the events with wind-velocity limits

The training for the individual events within the combined events follows the same patterns as for those separate events.[1] However, the sequence of the events in a combined meet affects the performance of the events that follow. For example, going from the shot put to the high jump is not the same as warming up and competing in the high jump as the first or only event of the day.

U.S. athletes no longer dominate in the decathlon. Their recent success in the heptathlon is very unusual. The reason lies in two major changes in international training. Compared to U.S. training systems, the foreign programs carefully plan and record training plans and results, and increase the training loads for both men and women. The result is a gradually developing superiority in the strength and technical events, which reflects more effective training methods.

Table 22-2 shows an example of the increasing training loads. It gives the recommended annual training load for male and female combined-event athletes in the old Soviet Union.

Recommended Training Loads for Soviet Combined Events		
	Women	*Men*
Training days	280	280
Training sessions	420	220
Training hours	1,120	1,120
Running at maximum speed (km)	35	40
Repetition runs, 100-600m (km)	85	75
Steady running (km)	1,100	1,200
Hurdling (number of hurdles)	4,000	3,100
Long jumps	900	700
High jumps	1,100	800
Shot puts	2,600	2,300
Javelin throws	3,100	3,000
Weight training (tons)	240	300
Jumping exercises (takeoffs)	11,000	11,000

Table 22-2. Recommended training loads for Soviet combined events

Theory of Decathlon Training

Basic training goals for the younger male athlete (after a sub-4:40 1500m) might be 700 points for each of the other events, along with 800 points for two to four high-point events. For more advanced athletes, the goals should rise gradually to 800 points per event, with some events ranging toward the 900- to 1,000-point level. This approach has been popular for several decades.

Though the most common training pattern is to practice each event in the order that it occurs in competition, that training pattern needs changes.[2] Recent studies suggest that following such order is not the most efficient way to train.

Polish studies show that greater gains are made by more general training, developing the traits and skills that are shared by several events, thus making more efficient use of training time.[3] For example, aspects of speed training and technique are involved in 7 of the 10 events. The start from blocks occurs three times. Certain basic takeoff patterns are found in all three jumps.

Decathlon training should fall into three stages:

- Ages 14 to 17: Beginning training. Stress building endurance (rather than speed), strength, and mobility.
- Ages 18 to 20: Developing specialized motor skills. Master the technique of the events.
- After age 20: Specialized training. Emphasize dynamic training and making the technical skills automatic. [4]

The first stage uses general physical training to aid the body's growth and development with effective training, rather than overloading it and interfering with the growth process. Endurance (rather than speed) is emphasized because it provides a base for developing speed and strength later. Flexibility and dexterity are developed across a wide range of motor skills. The hurdles and the pole vault are emphasized because they are the most complex events in the decathlon.

During the second stage, the foundations for elite-level motor skills are developed. The training volume is very high, with optimal volumes in running, jumping, strength training, and the mastery of the skills of each individual event. Absolute strength is emphasized, using 75 to 90 percent of maximum in most exercises. Jumping exercises are used, including single-legged and double-legged jumps, along with jumps from a run and over hurdles.

The overall training program uses more intense, complex training methods and higher volumes to improve the athlete's capabilities. The ability to relax is needed because of the length of decathlon competitions. The athlete must conserve his reserves during the intervals between peak efforts.

The third stage uses strength training to develop speed-strength qualities, jumping exercises, and technical training with more advanced skills. Psychological preparation becomes more important. Both coach and athlete must be careful not to over-use jumping exercises or plyometrics; otherwise, the athlete may suffer frequent injuries.

The coach should stress that improvements are gradual. The new decathlete should not expect radical improvements except in new events. A 1980s study of elite athletes showed that they averaged 7,600 points (1962 tables) at age 20.[5] From that point, in four years of competitive growth, they reached a mean score of 8,350 points between ages 24 and 25. Most athletes had explosive improvements in their scores only where attaining their full growth was a factor. For many of the athletes, no improvements were made in some of their high-scoring events.

The composition of the scoring tables is a major factor in planning training. Decathletes perform in a highly subjective environment; the IAAF scoring tables give an edge to the sprinter-jumper. The coach must study the point tables and the athlete's best marks in each event, then plan the training in relation to the tables, trying for the most effective use of training time for potential scoring improvements. Though the scoring tables were revised in 1985, they still favor the sprinter-jumper.

As one study pointed out, more points are lost than are gained in a major competition.[6] For this reason, the most important goal of a young athlete should be to eliminate low-scoring performances in any events. After a stable skill base is developed, the tables can be restudied to probe for potential "easy" events, sometimes easy relative to the scoring table, sometimes relative to the athlete's talents.

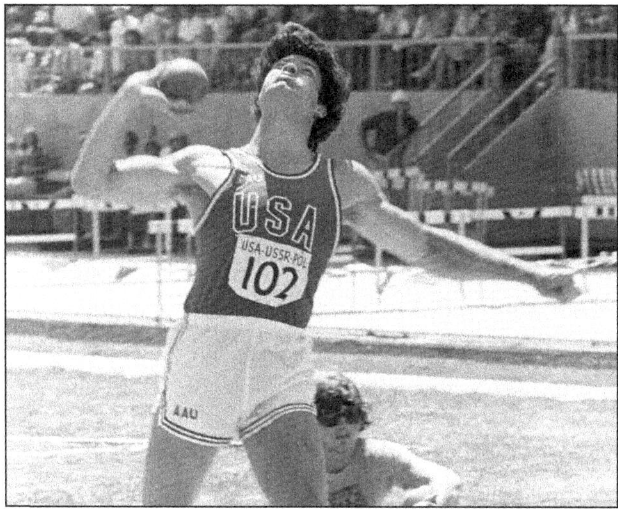

Photo 22-1. Craig Brigham, All-American for Bill Dellinger

Decathlon performances have improved sharply over the last decade. Elite decathlon performers do not develop from untalented youths who became decathletes because they had no single strong event.[7] Those athletes who reach the top are generally among the best even as junior-level athletes.

At the same time, as Table 22-3 shows, performance improvement is not a series of big jumps. It is made up of regular small improvements, a gradual rise in performance over several years (usually four to five years from the national to the elite level).

For the young athlete at the national level (7,500 to 7,700 points), very gradual improvements in performance are the norm for most events, and balance across the events is a clear criterion of success at the highest level. In short, no weak events are found among elite decathletes.

Annual Elite Improvement in the Decathlon

Event	*Early Marks*	*Peak Marks*	*Improvement*	*Annual Gain*
100	11.17	10.96	0.21 seconds	0.05 seconds
Long jump	23′ 4 3/4″	24′ 6 1/4″	1′ 1 3/4″	3 1/2″
Shot put	43′ 10 3/4″	49′ 5 1/4″	4′ 6 1/2″	1′ 1 1/2″
High jump	6′ 6″	6′ 8″	2.0″	1/2″
400	50.02	48.68	1.34 seconds	0.34 seconds
110 hurdles	15.34	14.68	0.66 seconds	0.16 seconds
Discus throw	134′ 3″	152′ 4 1/4″	18′ 1″	4′ 6″
Pole vault	13′ 9″	15′ 4 1/4″	7 1/4″	1 3/4″
Javelin throw	187′ 6″	208′ 2″	20′ 8″	5′ 2″
1500	4:36.12	4:26.88	9.24 seconds	2.31 seconds
Score	7595.51	8352.97	757.46	198.36
Age	*20.36*	*24.51*	*4.15*	

Table 22-3. Annual elite improvement in the decathlon

The performances of elite athletes show that the events that improve the least are the high jump and the flat runs (100, 400, and 1500m). This is not because little training time went into those events. Rather, they are the simplest events in terms of technique. The technical events yield larger point increases as they are mastered. Still, a certain minimal level of skill must be required in every event because those events (except for the 1500) are the earliest "big score" events for juniors.

Much is still to be learned about effective training methods in the decathlon because it involves the interaction of training for events whose major performance traits are not completely compatible.[8] The strength needs for the shot put clash with the body size need for jumping and vaulting, for example. Although the training pattern follows that of the individual events, the coach might prefer a pattern that places the emphasis upon only two or three events during a given phase, allowing more concentrated skill development.

The practice of competing in many individual events during the early season should be limited. The athlete should never compete in an event if he does not have time for a proper warm-up and for concentrating on achieving his goal for that single event in that meet. Rushing from one event to the next results in poor habits of concentration, less effective technique, and an unrealistic sense of what the decathlon is like. In most combined-event competitions, the athlete has from 30 minutes to one hour or more between events (the Olympic Games takes a two-hour "lunch break" for the officials after the second event each day). Competition in individual events should simulate the specific needs of the decathlete, not the needs of a team for an extra few points.

Theory of Heptathlon Training

The points just made about competing in individual events for the decathlon also hold for the heptathlon. Coaches tend to use the talented multi-event athlete as a "big point-man" for the team, but it is detrimental to his chance to become a truly elite combined-event athlete.

The developmental process in the heptathlon falls into the following two stages:

- Learning stage: Emphasize the performance balance across the events and the improvement of conditioning, speed, strength, and endurance.
- Specificity stage: Emphasize increasing the speed, specific strength, speed endurance, and specific endurance.[9]

Bob Myers recommends stressing the following training components in planning the heptathlon training program:

- Speed training: needed for four of the seven events
- Technique training: the common technique factors, as mentioned for the decathlon

- Strength training
  - ✓ General strength: Olympic lifts and power lifts
  - ✓ Specific strength: power or speed-strength, including plyometrics and high-volume technique drills
- Endurance training: base for 800m and for work capacity for extensive training and competition
- Mobility (flexibility): increases the range of motion, improving technique and decreasing the risk of injury
- Recovery: extremely important because of high training volume; includes mental and physical recovery, restoration, active rest, and complete rest (active rest is preferred).[10]

All training should be classified and recorded. An example is the classification of work for combined events, shown in Table 22-4. U.S. heptathletes tend to be deficient in special endurance and strength (both general and specific) compared to their foreign opponents. This deficiency shows in weaker performances in the 800m, the shot put, and the long jump.

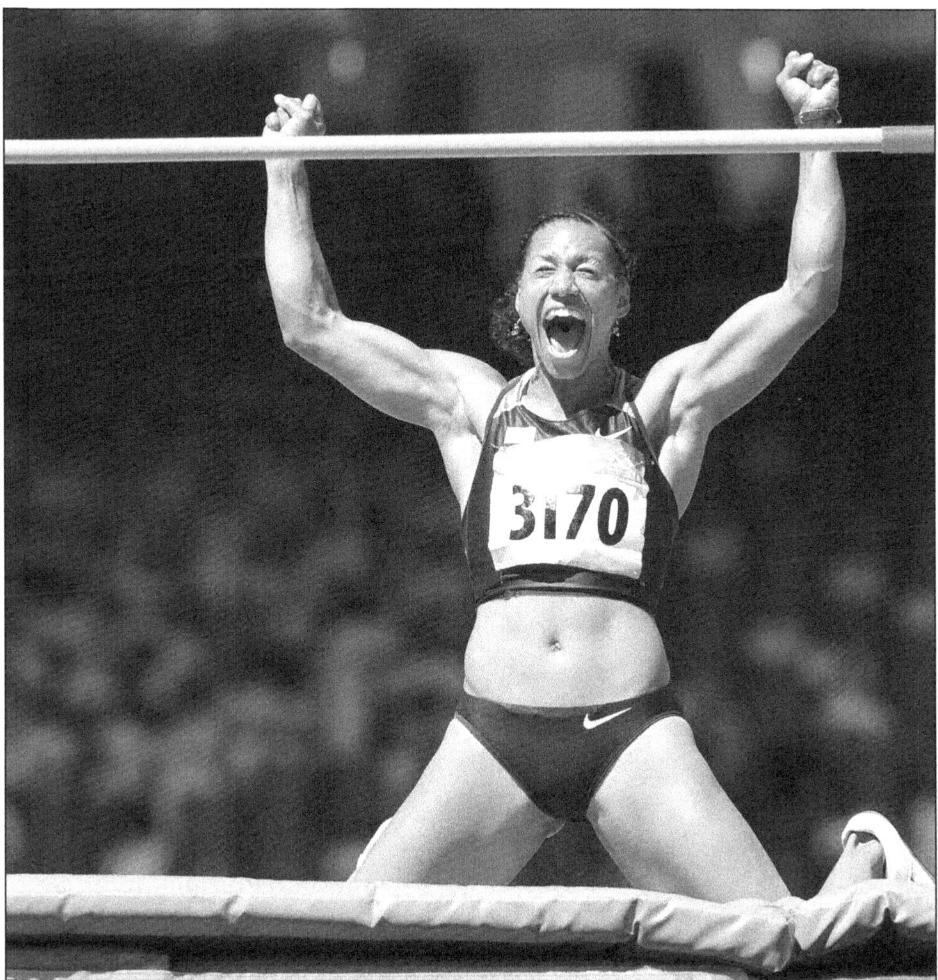

Photo 22-2. Hyleas Fountain of the USA team celebrates after clearing the bar during a heat of the women's heptathlon high jump at the Beijing 2008 Olympics.

Classification of Work for Combined Events		
Type of Training	*Intensity*	*Notes*
Speed • 1-4 sets of 1-4 x 20-60m • 1-5 min. recovery per rep • 5-10 min. recovery per set	95-100%	Run on track from different starting positions
Speed-endurance • 1-3 sets of 2-5 x 60-150m (400-600m total) • 2-5 min. recovery per rep • 8-10 min. recovery per set	90-100%	Run on track
Special endurance • 1-5 x 150-600m (300-1,800m total) • 5 min. to full recovery per rep	90-100%	Run on track
Plyometrics	80-100%	Do on track for multiple contacts, or on track for high intensity
Intensive tempo • 1-4 sets of 2-6 x 100-1,000m; recovery to 110-115 HR	80-90%	Run on grass, if possible
Extensive tempo • 1-3 x 1-3 km, recovery to 120 HR	40-80%	Run on grass
Technique	Varies	
Circuit training	Varies	
Weight lifting	Varies	

Table 22-4. Classification of work for combined events

A broad weekly pattern or microcycle might look like the following:

- Monday and Tuesday: high-volume training
- Wednesday and Thursday: lower-volume training (higher quality; sprinting)
- Friday and Saturday: medium-volume training
- Sunday: total rest or restoration

Within a training session, training should follow the following rough order:

- Technique work
- Sprinting and explosive activities
- Strength training
- Endurance training

Annual Training for the Heptathlon					
	General Preparation (September to November)	*General Preparation (September to November)*	*Early Competition (March to May)*	*Peak (June)*	*Transition (July and August)*
Beginner	Flexibility, intensive tempo, speed, running and lifting, technique work, circuits (weights), Mach drills, extensive tempo, basic drill work	Speed, speed endurance, special endurance, jump circuits, extensive tempo for recovery, total technique work, lifting (lower volume, higher intensity)	Speed, special endurance, very specific drill work, total technique refinement	Sound mechanics, speed, special endurance, competitive-style training	1 month rest, fun, and game-type activities; 1 month active rest (basketball, volleyball); begin lifting, easy circuits, intensive tempo
Intermediate	Flexibility, intensive tempo, speed, speed endurance, fartlek, running and lifting technique, circuits (weights), throws, hurdle, medicine ball, Mach drills, basic drill work, long bounding	Speed endurance, special endurance, lifting (high intensity), intensive technique work, high-volume plyometrics	Special endurance, speed blocks, low-volume lifting maintenance, speed strength or fast lifting plyometrics until crucial meets	Competition technique, speed, special endurance, competition-specific training	2 weeks rest; 2 weeks active rest; 1 month weights (circuits or stage), intensive tempo, sprinting
Elite	Speed, intensive tempo, speed endurance, Olympic lifting technique, circuits, weights, throws and hurdle and jump circuits, corrective drill work (problem solving), long bounding	Speed, special endurance, speed endurance, lower volume of lifting and plyometrics, high volume of special strength drills, restorative work	Special endurance, speed, high volume of event-specific work, maintenance lifting and easy lifting plyometrics up until crucial meets, maintaining high volume of training until end of phase	Speed, special endurance, competition-specific work, lower volume training	2 weeks rest; 2 weeks active rest (basketball, volleyball, swimming); 1 month circuits, technique revamping, intensive tempo, speed endurance

Table 22-5. Annual training for the heptathlon

Myers's recommendations for a general annual plan are shown in Table 22-5.

As noted in a research study of heptathlon performances:

> A willingness to train our women more at the level of the men in intensity, with loadings in proportion to their relative body-sizes, will pay many benefits in the coming years; for in the revolution in women's track and field, the United States has been largely content to follow sluggishly along some distance behind the leaders. The talent has always been there; it is time for American coaches to work at a more thorough development of it.[11]

Applied Training for the Combined Events

Few references give details of decathlon training in actual practice. This section will describe decathlon training at Oregon, which has produced one world-class decathlete. Coaches often fail to realize the potential all-around training that can be gained from decathlon training. Training for the combined events often produces improvements in the specialty events.

Using the Combined Events in Physical Education

Potential for the combined events can be tested with modified competitions, such as the one by Robert Parks[12] for an indoor activity with elementary and junior high school students, or that by Alfred Sylvia[13] for use in high school and college physical education classes. Bowerman used a variation called the "three-quarter decathlon" in university physical education classes for almost 20 years. The most recent version of the scoring table is closely related to the international tables, so it is indicative of genuine decathlon or heptathlon potential. The combined events are strenuous activities (you might even call each a "sport" because they include 7 or 10 events). The short time in which the athletes must produce major efforts creates a need for stamina. The

Modified Decathlons

IAAF Official	*Three-Quarter College*	*Sylvia High School Boys*
100 meters	60 meters	100 meters
Long jump	Long jump	Long jump
Shot put (16 lbs.)	Shot put (16 lbs.)	Shot put (12 lbs.)
High jump	High jump	High jump
400 meters	300 meters	400 meters
110m highs (42")	80m highs (39")	110m lows (30")
Discus (2 kg)	Discus (2 kg)	Discus–H.S.(3 lb. 9 oz.)
Pole vault	Pole vault	Pole vault
JavelinJavelin	Javelin or ball	
1500m run	1200m run	1600m run

Table 22-6. Modified decathlons

psychological considerations are many because the athlete needs long-term powers of concentration to endure the mental strain of up-and-down competition spread over two days.

In any combined event, points are more easily lost than gained, so the key to success is a balance of skill across the range of events. This aspect touches upon the old argument of whether the athlete should concentrate on his specialty event or events to make up for the weak events, or concentrate on the weaker events to not detract so much from the final score. Until the 1960s, the common approach was to focus on one or two "big" events to accumulate a mass of points. This idea is no longer accepted, probably because the opponents are far more talented than in the past.

Also, what happens if the athlete does not come through in the big-point event? He will probably lose. One approach to counteract that risk is to train in all of the events until every event reaches an acceptable bottom-range score. After that, the athlete can work to develop one or more big-point events. If no events are obviously weak, the athlete will not suffer so greatly from an off day.

The Oregon Test: The Three-Quarter Decathlon and Heptathlon

The Oregon Test can be used as a class activity, and it also indicates talent for the combined events. A special scoring table is used because it is a "three-quarter" event: The running events are run at only three quarters of the usual distance.

- 100m is now 75m
- 200m becomes 150m
- 400m becomes 300m
- 800m becomes 600m
- 1500m becomes 1200m
- Men's high hurdles become the 80-meter hurdles
- Women's high hurdles become the 75-meter hurdles

Both hurdle events are set at the high school heights. All other events use standard conditions and implements of the standard size and weight. The student may skip one of the 10 events, taking an automatic 100 points for that event.

The old scoring tables were revised in 1971 and 1988 to be very close to the values of the IAAF tables, giving greater predictive value to potential achievement in a real competition. The tests are spread over three days instead of two, covering a five-day period, with testing on Monday, Wednesday, and Friday.

The decathlon event order might be rearranged on the second day, if wished, such as opening with the hurdles, then the discus, then concluding with the 300m run. Starts are without blocks and running from a three- or four-point start (see Chapter 23 on testing), with the clock begun when the hand is lifted from the track. The long jump is measured from the takeoff point, so all jumps count. The Bowerman tables for both combined events are reproduced in Tables 22-9 and 22-10 at the end of the chapter.

A simpler, quicker scale, but one that cannot be compared to the IAAF tables, is the scale compiled by Sylvia. His tables were amended by the authors to cover 14 events because he suggested that the student be allowed to substitute one of the additional events for one of the 10 regulation events (or his variations of them), usually replacing the javelin, which is not allowed in most states in high school competition, or the pole vault. The range of events allows it to be used for the heptathlon, though the scoring table may have to be modified. Throwing the softball, the football, or the 800-gram weighted ball can be substituted for throwing the javelin, using the same scoring tables. Thus, any of these versions of the combined events might be used in physical education classes (or as an interest-getter for the track team in the fall, in the pre-season, or just after the competitive season has been concluded). The events are as follows.

The Sylvia version can also use the informal aspects of the Bowerman version. No stated length of time is offered for completing this decathlon. The low hurdles are used, set at the low-hurdle spacings (20 yards apart), though the hurdles might be set at the low height with the high-hurdle spacings. One event may be substituted for an additional event, the choices being the 200 and the 800 (scored by Sylvia) and the 3,200 and the triple jump (scored by the authors). His scoring tables are reprinted in Table 22-11 at the end of the chapter.

Each of the versions has its advantages, with the primary advantage of the Sylvia version being its scoring simplicity, while the primary advantage of the Bowerman version is its similarity to the IAAF tables, giving predictive value without requiring the more exhausting full running distances or metric conversions. In all cases, the IAAF competition rules are generally followed, with the modifications mentioned above.

Training Pattern for the Decathlon

We do not give detailed training schedules for the heptathlon because we have not worked extensively with heptathletes. However, Sheet 22-2 gives a suggested form for a heptathlon training schedule sheet. The decathlon training follows the hard-easy principle. Because there are always two consecutive days of competition, the training pattern has two hard days followed by two easy days. The events are practiced in the order in which they are encountered in competition.

On the first hard day, the athlete warms up, and then takes four to six sprint starts. He then does a few short sprints, going 30, then 50m, possibly adding a 70m sprint. He then proceeds to the long jump, where he first works on his check marks, and then he works on pop-ups. He next follows the shot-put routine, first putting from a stand, then crossing the ring and putting, all while working on one aspect of the technique. He then moves to the high-jump area, working first on his check marks, then taking about six jumps working on one of the techniques. He concludes the workout with 4 x 100m and a fartlek run.

On the second hard day, the decathlete warms up, goes through several sprint starts, and then goes to the hurdles. He goes through the X drill, then runs a set of either back-to-back fives or first three, last threes. He then moves to the discus, where he works on one aspect of his technique, first throwing from a stand (with his back foot in the center of the ring rather than hanging over the front of the ring), and then working with the turn. He then works on the pole vault, first setting his check marks, then working on his pole plant, then the takeoff, and finishing with perhaps half a dozen vaults. He then runs through the javelin routine, first throwing the weighted balls from a stand, then going to the 3-4-5 throwing sequence, then the full-count check, then moving several times through the full run. The full-run work is done last during the early season training, but it is done first during the late season training. Finally, the decathlete does what he can handle from a distance workout, usually about a mile of intervals (such as 8 x 200m, or 6 x 300m, or 4 x 400m). He then concludes the second hard day with a fartlek run.

The third and fourth days are easy days, with activities such as jogging and stretching, with perhaps some swimming or weight training. The fifth day is a return to the first day of hard training, beginning the cycle again.

For more specialized training suggestions, or for clarification of the workout sequence, study the chapters on the individual events. The decathlon and the heptathlon are indeed the champion's events, the supreme tests of the true athlete.

Decathlon Training Schedules

The training sheets listing the decathlon workouts are an abbreviation of the regular decathlon training sheets (Sheet 22-1). Sheet 22-2 shows a suggested heptathlon training sheet. The fall training schedules show workouts for only three days per week. During that part of the year, the decathlon is offered as a physical education class. On the days that list no workouts, the track team follows the workouts for each athlete's specialty events.

Almost no new activities appear on the combined-event training sheet that have not already been described in the chapters devoted to the individual events. The events are listed in the order in which they appear in the decathlon competition. For an explanation of the fundamentals of each event, the chapter on that event should be consulted. The few new descriptions that appear here are explained in the sections that follow.

10. Test Effort

These tests are the trials used in the other events. They will be encountered every two to three weeks during training. They are never full efforts, but are attempts at controlled improvement.

DECATHLON NAME ____________________________ __/__ to __/__ 19__

1. A. Jog 1 to 2 laps, easy stretching; high knee (slow), fast leg
   B. Relay
2. Fartlek
   A. Varied pace
   B. Slow, steady pace
   C. Light fartlek
3. A. Jogging and stretching
   B. Weights and jogging
   C. Easy jogging
4. Sprints
   A. High knee, fast leg
   B. Starts: 3 at 1/2, 3 at 7/8; 30m
      (1) Straight (2) Curve
   C. Finish work: 40-60 at 3/4 last 25-40 at 9/10
      (1) 20-40-60m
5. Long jump
   A. Check marks (1) Short (2) Long
   B. Pop-ups, 2-count rise
   C.
6. Shot put
   A. Routine
   B. Standing Put (1) Easy (2) Medium (3) Hard (4) Explode
      a. Lift b. Turn c. Push
   C. Across the ring
7. Team Meeting
8. Special
   A. Sauna b. Swim c. Steps or hill
9. High jump
   A. Check marks (1) Short (2) Long, 2
   B. Takeoff
   C. Clearance
   D. Jumping (1) Low, easy height (2) 4-6 in. below best (3)
   E. HJ rhythm 2-4-6-8 F.
10. Test effort (1) 3/4 distance
    A. 100 B. LJ C. SP
    D. HJ E. 400 F. HH
    G. DT H. PV J. JT
    K. 1500 L.
11. Intervals X. Hurdles Y. Easy
    Z. Fast 20-50 in middle
    A. 50 B. 100 C. 150 D. 200
    E. 300 F. 400 G. 500 H. 600
    (1) Goal pace (2) Date pace (3)
12. With Coach A. B.
14. 110m Hurdles
    A. X Drill (1) 30 in. (2) 36 in. (3) 39 in. (4) 42 in.
15. Discus throw
    A. Routine
    B. Standing throws (center of ring)
       1. Chest and nose lead
       2. Long pull
       3. Hips (cocked to uncocked) ahead of arm
       4. Through the shoulder
       5. Left-arm coordination
       6. Left-arm reach back 7.
          a. Easy b. Medium c. Hard
          d. Explode
    C. Across the ring, numbers as in B
    D. Alternate stand and across
    E.
16. Pole Vault
    A. Check marks (1) Short (2) Long
    B. Approach
    C. Pole plant
    D. Takeoff
    E. Vaulting (1) Low hold (2) High hold
       a. 12 in. below best b.
17. Javelin throw
    A. Standing throws
    B. Trot and throw (1) 345 (2) Full count
       a. Over the shoulder b. Close to ear
       c. Good pull d. Cock the hand
       e. Lead foot down f. Trail foot under
       g. Body turned to side, then precede arm with body
       h. Through shaft; don't tip it up
       i.
    C. Full run X. Check mark
       (1) 1/2 (2) 2/3 (3) 7/8–9/10
    D. Technique target throws
       (1) Standing at 30-60 ft.
       (2) 3-step and throw at 45-90 ft.
       (3) 5-step and throw at 120-150 ft.
       (4) Full run and checks at 150-180 ft.
    E.
18. Sets X. Hurdles (1) 30 in. (3) 36 in.
    A. 100-200-100 1. Goal pace
    B. 150-100-50 2. Date pace
    C. 300-200-100 3.
    D. 600-400-200
19. Weak event work
    A. Throw B. Jump C. Run
    1. Weakest 2. 2nd weakest
20.

Sheet 22-1. Decathlon training schedule sheet

HEPTATHLON NAME ______________________ __/__ to __/__ 19__

1. A. Jog 1 to 2 laps, easy stretching; high knee (slow), fast leg
   B. Relay
2. Fartlek
   A. Varied pace
   B. Slow, steady pace
   C. Light fartlek
3. A. Jogging and stretching
   B. Weights and jogging
   C. Easy jogging
4. Sprints
   A. High knee, fast leg
   B. Starts: 30m, 3 at 1/2, 3 at 7/8
      (1) Straight (2) Curve
   C. Finish Work: 40-60 at 3/4, last 25-40 at 9/10
      (1) 20-40-60m
5. Long jump
   A. Check marks (1) Short (2) Long
   B. Pop-ups, 2-count rise
   C.
6. Shot put
   A. Routine
   B. Standing put (1) Easy (2) Medium (3) Hard (4) Explode
      a. Lift b. Turn c. Push
   C. Across the ring
7. Team Meeting
8. Special
   A. Sauna b. Swim c. Steps or hill
9. High jump
   A. Check marks (1) Short (2) Long–2
   B. Takeoff
   C. Clearance
   D. Jumping (1) Low, easy height (2) 4-6 in. below best (3)
   E. HJ rhythm 2-4-6-8 F.
10. Test effort (1) 3/4 distance
    A. 100H B. HJ C. SP
    D. 100 E. LJ F. JT
    G. 800 H.
11. Intervals X. Hurdles Y. Easy
    Z. Fast 20-50 in middle
    A. 50 B. 100 C. 150 D. 200
    E. 300 F. 400 G. 500 H. 600
    (1) Goal pace (2) Date pace (3)
12. With Coach A. B.
14. 100m hurdles
    A. X Drill (1) 24 in. (2) 27 in. (3) 30 in. (4) 33 in.
       a. Lean b. Trail leg c. Lead leg
       d. Trail arm e. Lead arm f.
    B. Hurdle Starts: (1) 2 at 1/2, 2 at 7/8
       (2) Back-to-back 5s
       (3) First 3, last 3
    C.
15.
16.
17. Javelin throw
    A. Standing throws
    B. Trot and throw (1) 345 (2) Full count
       a. Over the shoulder b. Close to ear
       c. Good pull d. Cock the hand
       e. Lead foot down f. Trail foot under
       g. Body turned to side, then precede arm with body
       h. Through shaft; don't tip it up
       i.
    C. Full run X. Check mark
       (1) 1/2 (2) 2/3 (3) 7/8–9/10
    D. Technique target throws
       (1) Standing at 30-60 ft.
       (2) 3-step and throw at 45-90 ft.
       (3) 5-step and throw at 120-150 ft.
       (4) Full run and checks at 150-180 ft.
    E.
18. Sets X. Hurdles (1) 24 in. (3) 30 in.
    A. 100-200-100 1. Goal pace
    B. 150-100-50 2. Date pace
    C. 300-200-100 3.
    D. 600-400-200
19. Weak event work
    A. Throw B. Jump C. Run
    1. Weakest 2. 2nd weakest
20.
21. A. Videotape B. Film C. Pictures
    (1) Record performance (2) Study
22. Plyometrics A. Jumps B. Bounding
    C.
    (1) 1 leg (2) Both legs (3)
30. Experimental work

Sheet 22-2. Heptathlon training schedule sheet

10A1. 100m, 3/4 Racing Distance

The running events will rarely be contested over the full racing distance. The early trials will be at 60m. The later trials may be longer, moving up to 70 and then 80m.

10E1. 400m, 3/4 Racing Distance

This racing distance will also generally be run at less than the full distance in trials. The most common distance is 300m, though later trials may be at other fractional distances, such as 250 or 350m.

10F1. High Hurdles, 3/4 Racing Distance

For the decathlon classes, the usual trial (and the final exam) is 80m. For other non-class trials, other distances may be used, such as 60, 70, and 75m. For the class, the first trial is over the 30-inch (low) hurdles, the midterm is over the 36-inch (intermediate) hurdles, and the final exam is over the 39-inch (high school) hurdles. The hurdle spacings are not changed: 15 yards to the first barrier, and 10 yards between each hurdle. Few trials will ever be at the full 42-inch international height.

10K1. 1500m, 3/4 Racing Distance

This race will usually be tested either for 1200m or for the full distance. For the decathlon class, the distance is always 1200m.

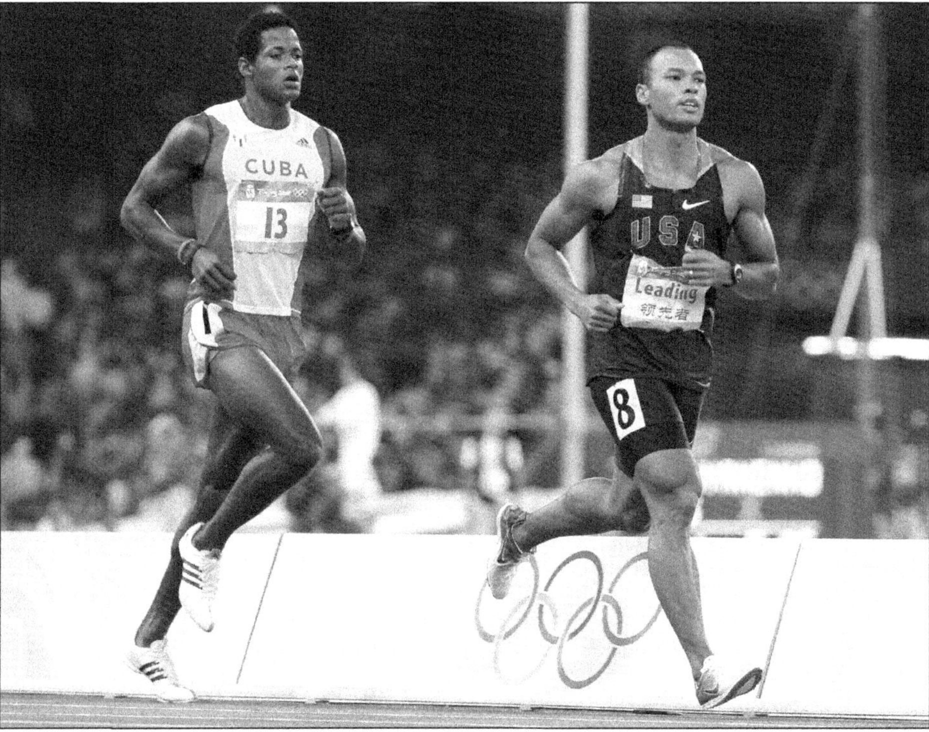

Photo 22-3. Bryan Clay of the USA team leads in the 1500m competition of the men's decathlon at the Beijing 2008 Olympics, in which Clay won the gold medal.

11A1. Intervals, Goal Pace

The distance given is merely an example. The "1" notation for either Number 11 (intervals) or Number 18 (sets) means that the distance is to be run at the athlete's goal pace.

11A2. Intervals, Date Pace

The distance is again an example. The "2" notation means that the given interval or set is to be run at the athlete's current date pace.

11X. Intervals, Over Hurdles

This notation may be used if the decathlete is also training for the 400m hurdles as a dual meet event. A notation of 11EX means run 300m over the hurdles (set at the intermediate hurdle spacings).

11Y. Intervals, Easy

The intervals listed are to be run at a comfortable, relatively easy pace. A listing of "3 x 11CY" means to run an easy 150m three times.

Photo 22-4. Dan O'Brien, gold medalist in the men's decathlon at the 1996 Summer Olympics in Atlanta

11Z. Intervals, Fast 20 to 50 Yards in the Middle of Each Interval

This notation is used for a short interval, such as 100 or 150m, and is an exercise to increase the speed or to learn to accelerate quickly in a race.

18AX. Sets, Over Hurdles

The "A" notation is only an example. The "X" notation, meaning to run over the hurdles, is used if the athlete is training for the intermediate hurdles.

18AX1. Sets, Over 30-Inch Hurdles

The "X1" notation means that the set is run over 30-inch (low) hurdles set at the intermediate hurdle spacings.

18AX2. Sets, Over 36-Inch Hurdles

The "X2" notation means that the set is run over the regular intermediate-height hurdles at the intermediate hurdle spacings.

19. Weak Event Work

On occasion, the athlete will be told to use some of his time in training in one of his weaker events.

19A. Weak Event Work, Throw

The athlete works on one of the weaker throwing events: the shot, the discus, or the javelin.

19B. Weak Event Work, Jump

The athlete works on one of the weaker jumping events: the high jump, the long jump, or the pole vault.

19C. Weak Event Work, Run

The athlete works on one of the weaker running events: the two sprints, the distance run, or the hurdles.

19[A/B/C]1. Weak Event Work, Weakest Event

The choice of the event type is only an example. The "1" notation means to work in the athlete's weakest event in that group of events.

19[A/B/C]2. Weak Event Work, Second-Weakest Event

The "2" notation means to work on the athlete's second-weakest event in that group of events.

Decathlon NAME DATE *September/October*

1. Warm-up A. Jogging and stretching
   B. Relay work
2. Fartlek A. Varied pace B. Slow, steady C. Light
3. A. Jogging and stretching B. Weights and jogging
   C. Easy jogging
4. 100 m A. High knee—fast leg B. Starts C. Finish work
5. Long jump A. Check marks (1) Short (2) Long
   B. Pop-ups, 2-count rise
6. Shot-put A. Routine B. Standing
   C. Across the ring
7. Squad meeting
8. Special A. Sauna B. Swim C. Hill or steps
9. High jump A. Check marks B. Take off
   C. Clearance B. Jumping E. Rhythm
10. Test effort A. 100 meters B. Long jump C. Shot
    D. High jump E. 400 meters F. 110 m G. Discus
    H. Pole vault J. Javelin K. 1,500 m L.
    (1) 3/4 racing distance
11. Intervals X. Easy Y. Hurdles
    Z. Fast in middle 20-50 yds. A. 55 B. 110 C. 165
    D. 220 E. 330 F. 440 G. 550 H. 660 J.
    (1) Goal pace (2) Date pace
12. With coach: A. B.
14. 110 m hurdles A. X drill B. Starts C.
15. Discus throw A. Routine B. Standing
    C. Across the ring D. Alternate stand and across
    E.
16. Pole vault A. Check marks B. Approach
    C. Pole plant D. Take off E. Vaulting F.
17. Javelin A. Standing throws B. Trot and throw
    C. Full run X. Check marks D. Technique throws
    E.
18. Sets Y. Over hurdles A. 110-220-110 (1) Goal pace
    B. 165-110-55 (2) Date pace C. 330-220-110
    (3) D. 660-440-220 E.
19. Weak event work A. Throw B. Jump C. Run
    (1) Weakest (2) 2d weakest
20.
21. A. Pictures B. Film C. Video

M	*Class organization-1A-2B1*
T	
W	*1A-10A1-10C-10B*
T	
F	*1A-10D-10E1*
S	
S	

M	*1A-10F1-10J-2A1 or 11D (35-40)* (8X)
T	
W	*1A-2B2*
T	
F	*1A-10G-10H-2A or 11D (35-40)* (8X)
S	
S	

M	*1A-14A1-9A-9D1-5A1-5B-2C*
T	
W	*1A-14A1-14B3-5B-6A-2B1*
T	
F	*1A-14A1-14B2-9A-9C-6B-2A1*
S	
S	

M	*1A-14A1-15A1-15E1-17B1-2C*
T	
W	*1A-14A1-17A-9A-9D-11C-2C* (3X)
T	
F	*1A-10F1 (30")-9D-15B-2B1*
S	
S	

Sheet 22-3. Decathlon training schedule

Decathlon NAME DATE October/November

1. Warm-up A. Jogging and stretching
   B. Relay work
2. Fartlek A. Varied pace B. Slow, steady C. Light
3. A. Jogging and stretching B. Weights and jogging
   C. Easy jogging
4. 100 m A. High knee—fast leg B. Starts C. Finish work
5. Long jump A. Check marks (1) Short (2) Long
   B. Pop-ups, 2-count rise
6. Shot-put A. Routine B. Standing
   C. Across the ring
7. Squad meeting
8. Special A. Sauna B. Swim C. Hill or steps
9. High jump A. Check marks B. Take off
   C. Clearance B. Jumping E. Rhythm
10. Test effort A. 100 meters B. Long jump C. Shot
    D. High jump E. 400 meters F. 110 m G. Discus
    H. Pole vault J. Javelin K. 1,500 m L.
    (1) 3/4 racing distance
11. Intervals X. Easy Y. Hurdles
    Z. Fast in middle 20-50 yds. A. 55 B. 110 C. 165
    D. 220 E. 330 F. 440 G. 550 H. 660 J.
    (1) Goal pace (2) Date pace
12. With coach: A. B.
14. 110 m hurdles A. X drill B. Starts C.
15. Discus throw A. Routine B. Standing
    C. Across the ring D. Alternate stand and across
    E.
16. Pole vault A. Check marks B. Approach
    C. Pole plant D. Take off E. Vaulting F.
17. Javelin A. Standing throws B. Trot and throw
    C. Full run X. Check marks D. Technique throws
    E.
18. Sets Y. Over hurdles A. 110-220-110 (1) Goal pace
    B. 165-110-55 (2) Date pace C. 330-220-110
    (3) D. 660-440-220 E.
19. Weak event work A. Throw B. Jump C. Run
    (1) Weakest (2) 2d weakest
20.
21. A. Pictures B. Film C. Video

Day	Workout
M	1A – 14A2 – 4B – 15D – 9D – 2C
T	
W	1A – 14A2 – 9D – 6A – 2A1
T	
F	1A – 14A2 – 5A – 5B – 6B – 6C – 2B2
S	
S	
M	1A – 10A1 – 10C – 10D – 2C
T	
W	1A – 10B – 10E1 – 2B2
T	
F	1A – 10F1 (36") – 10G – 10H
S	
S	
M	1A – 14A23 – 5B1 – 10J – 10K – 3C
T	
W	1A – 14A23 – 5B – 16A – 16E – 6A – 2C
T	
F	1A – 14A23 – 16E – 9D or 6B – 6A or 17D
S	
S	
M	
T	
W	
T	
F	
S	
S	

Sheet 22-4. Decathlon training schedule

Decathlon NAME DATE November/December

1. Warm-up A. Jogging and stretching
   B. Relay work
2. Fartlek A. Varied pace B. Slow, steady C. Light
3. A. Jogging and stretching B. Weights and jogging
   C. Easy jogging
4. 100 m A. High knee—fast leg B. Starts C. Finish work
5. Long jump A. Check marks (1) Short (2) Long
   B. Pop-ups, 2-count rise
6. Shot-put A. Routine B. Standing
   C. Across the ring
7. Squad meeting
8. Special A. Sauna B. Swim C. Hill or steps
9. High jump A. Check marks B. Take off
   C. Clearance B. Jumping E. Rhythm
10. Test effort A. 100 meters B. Long jump C. Shot
    D. High jump E. 400 meters F. 110 m G. Discus
    H. Pole vault J. Javelin K. 1,500 m L.
    (1) 3/4 racing distance
11. Intervals X. Easy Y. Hurdles
    Z. Fast in middle 20-50 yds. A. 55 B. 110 C. 165
    D. 220 E. 330 F. 440 G. 550 H. 660 J.
    (1) Goal pace (2) Date pace
12. With coach: A. B.
14. 110 m hurdles A. X drill B. Starts C.
15. Discus throw A. Routine B. Standing
    C. Across the ring D. Alternate stand and across
    E.
16. Pole vault A. Check marks B. Approach
    C. Pole plant D. Take off E. Vaulting F.
17. Javelin A. Standing throws B. Trot and throw
    C. Full run X. Check marks D. Technique throws
    E.
18. Sets Y. Over hurdles A. 110-220-110 (1) Goal pace
    B. 165-110-55 (2) Date pace C. 330-220-110
    (3) D. 660-440-220 E.
19. Weak event work A. Throw B. Jump C. Run
    (1) Weakest (2) 2d weakest
20.
21. A. Pictures B. Film C. Video

Day	Workout
M	1A-14A23-5A-5B-9D-15D-2A1
T	
W	1A-14A23-9D-17D2-17D4-16E-11D (35-40) 4x
T	
F	1A-14A23-6B-6C-5A-15D-2B2
S	
S	
M	1A-14A23-5 or 9 or 16-6 or 15 or 17-2C
T	
W	Choice
T	
F	Choice
S	
S	
M	1A-10A1-10B-10C-10J-3C
T	
W	1A-10C-10D-10E1-3C
T	
F	1A-10F1 (39")-10H-10K1-3C
S	
S	
M	
T	
W	
T	
F	
S	
S	

Sheet 22-5. Decathlon training schedule

Decathlon NAME DATE January

1. Warm-up A. Jogging and stretching
   B. Relay work
2. Fartlek A. Varied pace B. Slow, steady C. Light
3. A. Jogging and stretching B. Weights and jogging
   C. Easy jogging
4. 100 m A. High knee—fast leg B. Starts C. Finish work
5. Long jump A. Check marks (1) Short (2) Long
   B. Pop-ups, 2-count rise
6. Shot-put A. Routine B. Standing
   C. Across the ring
7. Squad meeting
8. Special A. Sauna B. Swim C. Hill or steps
9. High jump A. Check marks B. Take off
   C. Clearance B. Jumping E. Rhythm
10. Test effort A. 100 meters B. Long jump C. Shot
    D. High jump E. 400 meters F. 110 m G. Discus
    H. Pole vault J. Javelin K. 1,500 m L.
    (1) 3/4 racing distance
11. Intervals X. Easy Y. Hurdles
    Z. Fast in middle 20-50 yds. A. 55 B. 110 C. 165
    D. 220 E. 330 F. 440 G. 550 H. 660 J.
    (1) Goal pace (2) Date pace
12. With coach: A. B.
14. 110 m hurdles A. X drill B. Starts C.
15. Discus throw A. Routine B. Standing
    C. Across the ring D. Alternate stand and across
    E.
16. Pole vault A. Check marks B. Approach
    C. Pole plant D. Take off E. Vaulting F.
17. Javelin A. Standing throws B. Trot and throw
    C. Full run X. Check marks D. Technique throws
    E.
18. Sets Y. Over hurdles A. 110-220-110 (1) Goal pace
    B. 165-110-55 (2) Date pace C. 330-220-110
    (3) D. 660-440-220 E.
19. Weak event work A. Throw B. Jump C. Run
    (1) Weakest (2) 2d weakest
20.
21. A. Pictures B. Film C. Video

M	Squad 3-6x 3x organization- 4A-4B - 5B - 11C-2A1
T	3x 4x 1A-14A1-9E-11C-11F (75-80)-2B1
W	7-3B
T	3-6x 3x 1A-4A-4B-5B - 6B1-11C-2A1
F	3x 4x 1A-14A1-9E-11C-11F(75-80)-2B1
S	3B
S	3A

M	6x 1A-14A2-14B2-15D-16A1-11E(50-52)-2B-3B
T	10-15x 10-15x 3x 1A-14A2-14B2-17A - 17B - 18B-18C
W	7-3B
T	6x 1A-14A2-14B2-15D-16A1-11E(50-52)-2B
F	10-15x 10-15x 3x 1A-14A2-14B2-17A - 17B - 18B-18C
S	3B
S	3A

M	3-6x 3x 1A-4A-4B-5B-6B1-11C-2A1
T	4x 1A-10A1 or 10F(60y)-14A1-9E-11F-2B1
W	7-3B
T	3-6x 3x 1A-10A1 or 10F(60y)-4A-4B-5B -11C-2A1
F	4x 1A-14A1-9E-11F(75-80)-2B1
S	3B
S	3A

M	1A-14A2-16A1-16B1-16E1- 6x/11E(50-52)-2A13B
T	10-15x 4x 1A-14A2-15B-16A1-17B1-18C-11B-2B1
W	3B
T	10-15x 10-15x 4x 1A-14A2-16A1-16B1-17A - 17B - 18C - 11B
F	3-6x 3-6x 6x 1A-14A2-15B-15D-16A1-16E1-11E-2A1
S	3B
S	3A

Sheet 22-6. Decathlon training schedule

Decathlon NAME DATE February

1. Warm-up A. Jogging and stretching B. Relay work
2. Fartlek A. Varied pace B. Slow, steady C. Light
3. A. Jogging and stretching B. Weights and jogging C. Easy jogging
4. 100 m A. High knee—fast leg B. Starts C. Finish work
5. Long jump A. Check marks (1) Short (2) Long B. Pop-ups, 2-count rise
6. Shot-put A. Routine B. Standing C. Across the ring
7. Squad meeting
8. Special A. Sauna B. Swim C. Hill or steps
9. High jump A. Check marks B. Take off C. Clearance B. Jumping E. Rhythm
10. Test effort A. 100 meters B. Long jump C. Shot D. High jump E. 400 meters F. 110 m G. Discus H. Pole vault J. Javelin K. 1,500 m L. (1) 3/4 racing distance
11. Intervals X. Easy Y. Hurdles Z. Fast in middle 20-50 yds. A. 55 B. 110 C. 165 D. 220 E. 330 F. 440 G. 550 H. 660 J. (1) Goal pace (2) Date pace
12. With coach: A. B.
14. 110 m hurdles A. X drill B. Starts C.
15. Discus throw A. Routine B. Standing C. Across the ring D. Alternate stand and across E.
16. Pole vault A. Check marks B. Approach C. Pole plant D. Take off E. Vaulting F.
17. Javelin A. Standing throws B. Trot and throw C. Full run X. Check marks D. Technique throws E.
18. Sets Y. Over hurdles A. 110-220-110 (1) Goal pace B. 165-110-55 (2) Date pace C. 330-220-110 (3) D. 660-440-220 E.
19. Weak event work A. Throw B. Jump C. Run (1) Weakest (2) 2d weakest
20.
21. A. Pictures B. Film C. Video

Day	Schedule
M	1A-4A-5B-6A-6B-3x 11C-2A1-3B
T	1A-14A2-15B-16A1-10-15x 17B1-18C-4x 11B-2B1
W	7-3B
T	1A-14A2-16A1-16B1-16E1-1B1
F	1A-6A-6C-9A-9D-18C-3C-4x 11B
S	2A1-3B
S	19-2B2 or 3A
M	1A-14A23-15A-4-6x 15B-16A1-10K1-3C-3B
T	1A-14A2-14B2-16A1-10-15x 16B-10-15x 17A-4x 17B-11F
W	1A-10D-2A2-3B
T	1A-14A23-6x 14B1-6x 15D-15C-16A-16E-4x 11F-2B
F	1A-14A2-14B3-10G-16A-16C-2x 17B-3x 17C-11C-3C
S	1A-10F1-2A1-3B
S	19-2B2 or 3A
M	1A-4A-10A-5A-5B-6A-4x 11C2-2B1-3B
T	1A-14A2-6A-6B-9A-9E-2x 18B2-4x 11B-2B
W	7-1A-10B-2A2-3B
T	1A-4A-4B-5A-5B-6A-11G-2B1-4x 11B
F	1A-14A2-5A-10C-9A-9E-6x 11E2-3C
S	2A1-3B
S	19-2B2 or 3A
M	1A-14A23-15A-4x 15B-16A-10E-2B-3B
T	1A-14A23-14B2-16A1-16B-17A-17B-4x 11F1
W	1A-10H-2A2-3B
T	1A-14A23-6x 14B1-6x 15D-15C-16A-16E-6x 11E2-2B
F	1A-4A-16A-10-15x 17B-10J-2B
S	10F-3B
S	19-2B2 or 3A

Sheet 22-7. Decathlon training schedule

Decathlon NAME DATE March

1. Warm-up A. Jogging and stretching
   B. Relay work
2. Fartlek A. Varied pace B. Slow, steady C. Light
3. A. Jogging and stretching B. Weights and jogging
   C. Easy jogging
4. 100 m A. High knee—fast leg B. Starts C. Finish work
5. Long jump A. Check marks (1) Short (2) Long
   B. Pop-ups, 2-count rise
6. Shot-put A. Routine B. Standing
   C. Across the ring
7. Squad meeting
8. Special A. Sauna B. Swim C. Hill or steps
9. High jump A. Check marks B. Take off
   C. Clearance B. Jumping E. Rhythm
10. Test effort A. 100 meters B. Long jump C. Shot
    D. High jump E. 400 meters F. 110 m G. Discus
    H. Pole vault J. Javelin K. 1,500 m L.
    (1) 3/4 racing distance
11. Intervals X. Easy Y. Hurdles
    Z. Fast in middle 20–50 yds. A. 55 B. 110 C. 165
    D. 220 E. 330 F. 440 G. 550 H. 660 J.
    (1) Goal pace (2) Date pace
12. With coach: A. B.
14. 110 m hurdles A. X drill B. Starts C.
15. Discus throw A. Routine B. Standing
    C. Across the ring D. Alternate stand and across
    E.
16. Pole vault A. Check marks B. Approach
    C. Pole plant D. Take off E. Vaulting F.
17. Javelin A. Standing throws B. Trot and throw
    C. Full run X. Check marks D. Technique throws
    E.
18. Sets Y. Over hurdles A. 110-220-110 (1) Goal pace
    B. 165-110-55 (2) Date pace C. 330-220-110
    (3) D. 660-440-220 E.
19. Weak event work A. Throw B. Jump C. Run
    (1) Weakest (2) 2d weakest
20.
21. A. Pictures B. Film C. Video

M	3x 1A-14A23-4A-5A2-5B1-6A-11G-3C-11CY-3B
T	3x 3x 3x 1A-4C-6B-6C-9A2-9D-11B1-18B2-2B
W	7-1A-14A2-19A1-3B
T	1A-4B-19A2-2A1
F	3x 4x 1A-14A2-15A-16A1-16A2-17CX-3C-11B
S	10:00-10:30-11:00-11:30-12:00-12:30 1A-10A- 10B- 10C- 10D- 10E-3C
S	3C

M	4x 1A-14A23-14B2-15A-18C2-2B-11B-3B
T	10-15x 6x 1A-10A23-14B3-16A-16E-17A-17B-11E2-2B
W	7-1A-19A1-3B
T	1A-14A2-14B1-2A1
F	4x 1A-5A-5B1-6A-9A2-3C-11B
S	10:00-10:30-11:00-11:30-12:15-12:45 1A- 10F- 10G- 10H- 10J- 10K-3C
S	3C

M	14A-19-16-2A1-3B
T	3-6x 3-6x 3x 1A-4B-5A-5B-6A-9A-9D2-11C-3C
W	4-6x 6x 14A23-14B1-15A-15D-16A-16E-17D-11E-3B
T	1A-19-3A
F	3C - Gear ready
S	10 - Early season meet
S	3A

M	14A-19-16-2A1-3B
T	3-6x 4x 1A-4A-5A-5B-6A-9A-9B-11D2-2B
W	3-6x 10-15x 2-3x 14A-15D-16A-16C-17X-17D-18C
T	2x 1A-19-4B or 14B1-11C-3B (light)
F	3C - Gear ready
S	Dual meet
S	3C

Sheet 22-8. Decathlon training schedule

Decathlon NAME DATE April

1. Warm-up A. Jogging and stretching
   B. Relay work
2. Fartlek A. Varied pace B. Slow, steady C. Light
3. A. Jogging and stretching B. Weights and jogging
   C. Easy jogging
4. 100 m A. High knee—fast leg B. Starts C. Finish work
5. Long jump A. Check marks (1) Short (2) Long
   B. Pop-ups, 2-count rise
6. Shot-put A. Routine B. Standing
   C. Across the ring
7. Squad meeting
8. Special A. Sauna B. Swim C. Hill or steps
9. High jump A. Check marks B. Take off
   C. Clearance B. Jumping E. Rhythm
10. Test effort A. 100 meters B. Long jump C. Shot
    D. High jump E. 400 meters F. 110 m G. Discus
    H. Pole vault J. Javelin K. 1,500 m L.
    (1) 3/4 racing distance
11. Intervals X. Easy Y. Hurdles
    Z. Fast in middle 20-50 yds. A. 55 B. 110 C. 165
    D. 220 E. 330 F. 440 G. 550 H. 660 J.
    (1) Goal pace (2) Date pace
12. With coach: A. B.
14. 110 m hurdles A. X drill B. Starts C.
15. Discus throw A. Routine B. Standing
    C. Across the ring D. Alternate stand and across
    E.
16. Pole vault A. Check marks B. Approach
    C. Pole plant D. Take off E. Vaulting F.
17. Javelin A. Standing throws B. Trot and throw
    C. Full run X. Check marks D. Technique throws
    E.
18. Sets Y. Over hurdles A. 110-220-110 (1) Goal pace
    B. 165-110-55 (2) Date pace C. 330-220-110
    (3) D. 660-440-220 E.
19. Weak event work A. Throw B. Jump C. Run
    (1) Weakest (2) 2d weakest
20.
21. A. Pictures B. Film C. Video

M [3-4X] 7-14A234-4B-5A-5B-6B-6C-9A-9D-11C-3C
T [3-6X] [4X] 14A-14B2-15D-16A-16E-17X-17D-18D1-11B
W 1A-14B1-19-3C
T 3C-Gear ready
F 10-Decathlon-first day
S 10-Decathlon-second day
S 3C

M [3-4X] 14A-4A-5A-5B-6B-6C-9A-9D-11E-3B
T 3A-19A-19B-19C-3C
W [6X] 14A-15B2-15D-16A-16E-17X-17D-11E2-3B
T 14A-14B1-19-3C
F 3C-Gear ready
S Dual meet
S 3A

M [2-3X] 14A-4A-5A-5B-6B-6C-9A-9E-18B-3C-3B
T 3A-19A-19B-19C-3C
W [4X] 14A-14B3-15D-16A-16D-17X-17C-11F1-3B
T 14A-14B1 or 4B-19-3C
F 3C-Gear ready
S Dual meet
S 3A

M [2-3X] 1A-4A-4B-6A-6C-9A-9B-11C1-3C-3B
T [6X] 14A-14B1-15A-15C-16A-16C-17X-17D-11E1
W 1A-19B-19A-19C-3B-3C
T 3C-Gear ready
F 10-Decathlon-first day
S 10-Decathlon-second day
S 3A

Sheet 22-9. Decathlon training schedule

Decathlon NAME DATE May / June

1. Warm-up A. Jogging and stretching
   B. Relay work
2. Fartlek A. Varied pace B. Slow, steady C. Light
3. A. Jogging and stretching B. Weights and jogging
   C. Easy jogging
4. 100 m A. High knee—fast leg B. Starts C. Finish work
5. Long jump A. Check marks (1) Short (2) Long
   B. Pop-ups, 2-count rise
6. Shot-put A. Routine B. Standing
   C. Across the ring
7. Squad meeting
8. Special A. Sauna B. Swim C. Hill or steps
9. High jump A. Check marks B. Take off
   C. Clearance B. Jumping E. Rhythm
10. Test effort A. 100 meters B. Long jump C. Shot
    D. High jump E. 400 meters F. 110 m G. Discus
    H. Pole vault J. Javelin K. 1,500 m L.
    (1) 3/4 racing distance
11. Intervals X. Easy Y. Hurdles
    Z. Fast in middle 20–50 yds. A. 55 B. 110 C. 165
    D. 220 E. 330 F. 440 G. 550 H. 660 J.
    (1) Goal pace (2) Date pace
12. With coach: A. B.
14. 110 m hurdles A. X drill B. Starts C.
15. Discus throw A. Routine B. Standing
    C. Across the ring D. Alternate stand and across
    E.
16. Pole vault A. Check marks B. Approach
    C. Pole plant D. Take off E. Vaulting F.
17. Javelin A. Standing throws B. Trot and throw
    C. Full run X. Check marks D. Technique throws
    E.
18. Sets Y. Over hurdles A. 110-220-110 (1) Goal pace
    B. 165-110-55 (2) Date pace C. 330-220-110
    (3) D. 660-440-220 E.
19. Weak event work A. Throw B. Jump C. Run
    (1) Weakest (2) 2d weakest
20.
21. A. Pictures B. Film C. Video

M	1A-4A-4B-5A-5B-6A-9A-9E-18B (2-3x)-3B-3C
T	14A-14B1-15A-16A-16B-17X-17D-11E (4-6x)-2B-
W	1A-4B or 14B1-19A1-19B1-3C
T	3C - Gear ready
F	Qualify - division or conference
S	Finals - division or conference
S	3A
M	1A-19B-19A-19C-3B-2B1
T	14A-19B1-19C1-19A1-3C
W	1A-4A-4B-5A-5B-6A-9A-9D-18C1-3C
T	14A-14B1-15A-16A-16E-17X-17B (3x)-18D1-11B (4x)-3C
F	3A-3B-2B1
S	3A
S	1A-4A-4B-4C-5A-5B-6A-6C (3x)-9A-9B-18C1-3B-3C
M	14A-14B1-15A-15C (3x)-16A-16C-17X-17B (3x)-11E1 (4-6x)-3C
T	3C
W	3C - Gear ready
T	NCAA - Decathlon - first day
F	NCAA - Decathlon - second day
S	3A
S	3A
M	
T	
W	
T	
F	
S	
S	

Sheet 22-10. Decathlon training schedule

Summary of IAAF 2001 Men's Decathlon Scoring Tables

First Day

Points	*100m*	*LJ*	*Imperial*	*SP*	*Imperial*	*HJ*	*Imperial*	*400m*
1100	9.98	8.16	26′ 9 1/4″	20.00	65′ 1/2″	2.31	7′ 7″	44.23
1050	10.18	7.96	26′ 1 1/2″	19.20	63′ 0″	2.26	7′ 5″	44.19
1000	10.39	7.76	25′ 5 1/2″	18.40	60′ 4 1/2″	2.21	7′ 3″	46.17
950	10.60	7.56	24′ 9 3/4″	17.59	57′ 8 1/2″	2.16	7′ 1″	47.17
900	10.82	7.36	24′ 1 3/4″	16.79	55′ 1″	2.11	6′ 11″	48.19
850	11.05	7.15	23′ 5 1/2″	15.98	52′ 5 1/4″	2.05	6′ 8 3/4″	49.24
800	11.27	6.95	22′ 9 3/4″	15.16	49′ 9″	2.00	6′ 6 3/4″	50.32
750	11.51	6.73	22′ 1″	14.35	47′ 1″	1.95	6′ 4 3/4″	51.43
700	11.75	6.51	21′ 4 1/4″	13.53	44′ 4 3/4″	1.89	6′ 2 1/4″	52.58
650	12.00	6.29	20′ 7 3/4″	12.71	41′ 8 1/2″	1.83	6′ 0″	53.76
600	12.26	6.06	19′ 10 3/4″	11.89	39″ 3/4″	1.77	5′ 9 3/4″	54.98
550	12.53	5.83	19′ 1 1/2″	11.07	36′ 4″	1.71	5′ 7 1/4″	56.25
500	12.81	5.59	18′ 4 1/4″	10.24	33′ 7 1/4″	1.65	5′ 5″	57.57
450	13.10	5.35	17′ 6 3/4″	9.40	30′ 10 1/4″	1.59	5′ 2 1/2″	58.95
400	13.41	5.09	16′ 8 1/2″	8.56	28′ 1″	1.52	4′ 11 3/4″	60.40
350	13.74	4.83	15′ 10 1/4″	7.72	25′ 4″	1.45	4′ 9″	61.94
300	14.09	4.56	14′ 11 1/2″	6.87	22′ 6 1/2″	1.38	4′ 6 1/4″	63.57
250	14.46	4.27	14′ 1/4″	6.02	19′ 9″	1.30	4′ 3 1/4″	65.34
200	14.87	3.97	13′ 1/4″	5.15	16′ 10 3/4″	1.22	4′ 0″	67.27
150	15.33	3.64	11′ 11 1/4″	4.28	14′ 1/2″	1.14	3′ 8 3/4″	69.43
100	15.86	3.28	10′ 9″	3.39	11′ 1 1/2″	1.04	3′ 5″	71.96
50	16.54	2.86	9′ 4 1/2″	2.48	8′ 1 1/2″	0.93	3′ 0 1/2″	75.15
1	17.83	2.25	7′ 4 1/2″	1.53	5′ 0 1/4″	0.77	2′ 6 1/4″	81.21

Second Day

Points	*110mH*	*DT*	*Imperial*	*PV*	*Imperial*	*JT*	*Imperial*	*1500m*
1100	13.05	60.89	199′ 9″	5.60	18′ 4 1/2″	83.67	274′ 6″	3:40.78
1050	13.42	58.53	192′ 0″	5.45	17′ 10 1/2″	80.44	263′11″	3:47.21
1000	13.80	56.17	184′ 3″	5.29	17′ 4 1/4″	77.19	253′ 3″	3:53.79
950	14.19	53.79	176′ 5″	5.13	16′ 10″	73.94	242′ 7″	4:00.53
900	14.59	51.40	168′ 8″	4.97	16′ 3 1/2″	70.67	231′10″	4:07.42
850	15.00	49.00	160′ 9″	4.81	15′ 9 1/4″	67.39	221′ 1″	4:14.50
800	15.41	46.59	152′ 10″	4.64	15′ 2 3/4″	64.09	210′ 3″	4:21.77
750	15.85	44.16	144′ 10″	4.47	14′ 8″	60.78	199′ 5″	4:29.25
700	16.29	41.72	136′ 10″	4.30	14′ 1 1/4″	57.45	188′ 6″	4:36.96
650	16.76	39.26	128′ 10″	4.12	13′ 6 1/4″	54.11	177′ 6″	4:44.94
600	17.23	36.79	120′ 8″	3.94	12′ 11″	50.74	166′ 6″	4:53.20
550	17.73	34.30	112′ 6″	3.76	12′ 4″	47.36	155′ 4″	5:01.78
500	18.25	31.78	104′ 3″	3.57	11′ 8 1/2″	43.95	144′ 2″	5:10.73
450	18.80	29.24	95′ 11″	3.38	11′ 1″	40.51	132′ 11″	5:20.10
400	19.38	26.68	87′ 6″	3.18	10′ 5 1/4″	37.05	121′ 6″	5:29.96
350	19.99	24.09	79′ 1/2″	2.97	9′ 9″	33.56	110′ 1″	5:40.41
300	20.65	21.46	70′ 5″	2.76	9′ 0 1/2″	30.03	98′ 6″	5:51.57
250	21.36	18.80	61′ 8 1/4″	2.54	8′ 4″	26.45	86′ 9″	6:03.62
200	22.14	16.08	52′ 9 1/4″	2.31	7′ 7″	22.82	74′ 10″	6:16.84
150	23.03	13.30	43′ 7 3/4″	2.06	6′ 9″	19.12	62′ 8 3/4″	6:31.70
100	24.07	10.44	34′ 3″	1.78	5′ 10″	15.33	50′ 3 1/2″	6:49.08
50	25.41	7.43	24′ 4 1/2″	1.47	4′ 9 3/4″	11.39	37′ 4 1/2″	7:11.24
1	28.09	4.10	13′ 5 1/2″	1.03	3′ 4 1/2″	7.12	23′ 4 1/2″	7:54.11

Note: To approximate the score for hand-times, add 0.24 seconds to the hand-time.

Table 22-7. Summary of IAAF 2001 men's decathlon scoring tables

Summary of IAAF 2001 Women's Decathlon Scoring Tables

First Day

Points	*100m*	*DT*	*Imperial*	*PV*	*Imperial*	*JT*	*Imperial*	*400m*
1100	11.25	62.31	204′ 5″	4.29	14′ 3/4″	62.30	204′ 5″	51.00
1050	11.50	59.85	196′ 4″	4.18	13′ 8 1/2″	59.74	196′ 0″	52.03
1000	11.75	57.39	188′ 3″	4.06	13′ 3 3/4″	57.18	187′ 7″	53.08
950	12.01	54.91	180′ 2″	3.95	12′ 11 1/2″	54.61	179′ 2″	54.16
900	12.27	52.42	172′ 0″	3.83	12′ 6 3/4″	52.04	170′ 9″	55.27
850	12.55	49.92	163′ 9″	3.72	12′ 2 1/2″	49.46	162′ 3″	56.40
800	12.82	47.40	155′ 6″	3.60	11′ 9 3/4″	46.87	153′ 9″	57.56
750	13.11	44.87	147′ 2″	3.48	11′ 5″	44.28	145′ 3″	58.76
700	13.40	42.33	138′10″	3.35	10′ 11 3/4″	41.68	136′ 9″	59.99
650	13.71	39.76	130′ 5″	3.23	10′ 7″	39.08	128′ 2″	61.26
600	14.02	37.19	122′ 0″	3.10	10′ 2″	36.46	119′ 7″	62.58
550	14.35	34.59	113′ 6″	2.97	9′ 9″	33.84	111′ 0″	63.94
500	14.69	31.96	104′ 10″	2.83	9′ 3 1/4″	31.21	102′ 4″	65.37
450	15.05	29.32	96′ 2″	2.70	8′ 10 1/4″	28.57	93′ 8″	66.86
400	15.42	26.65	87′ 5″	2.56	8′ 4 3/4″	25.92	85′ 0″	68.42
350	15.82	23.94	78′ 6 1/2″	2.41	7′10 3/4″	23.26	76′ 3 3/4″	70.08
300	16.23	21.21	69′ 7″	2.26	7′ 5″	20.58	67′ 6 1/4″	71.84
250	16.70	18.43	60′ 5 3/4″	2.10	6′ 10 3/4″	17.88	58′ 8″	73.74
200	17.20	15.59	51′ 1 3/4″	1.93	6′ 4″	15.16	49′ 9″	75.83
150	17.75	12.70	41′ 8″	1.76	5′ 9 1/4″	12.42	40′ 9″	78.16
100	18.40	9.71	31′ 10 1/4″	1.56	5′ 1 1/4″	9.64	31′ 7 1/2″	80.87
50	19.23	6.58	21′ 7 1/4″	1.34	4′ 4 3/4″	6.80	22′ 3 3/4″	84.32
1	20.79	3.11	10′ 2 1/2″	1.03	3′ 4 1/2″	3.87	12′ 8 1/4″	90.85

Second Day

Points	*110mH*	*LJ*	*Imperial*	*SP*	*Imperial*	*HJ*	*Imperial*	*1500m*
1100	13.16	6.79	22′ 3 1/2″	18.54	60′ 10″	1.90	6′ 2 3/4″	4:21.47
1050	13.50	6.64	21′ 9 1/2″	17.81	55′ 5 1/4″	1.86	6′ 1 1/4″	4:28.18
1000	13.85	6.48	21′ 3 1/4″	17.07	56′ 0″	1.82	5′11 1/2″	4:34.99
950	14.20	6.33	20′ 9 1/4″	16.32	53′ 6 1/2″	1.78	5′ 10″	4:41.99
900	14.56	6.17	20′ 3″	15.58	51′ 1 1/2″	1.74	5′ 8 1/2″	4:49.16
850	14.94	6.00	19′ 8 1/4″	14.83	48′ 8″	1.70	5′ 7″	4:56.53
800	15.32	5.84	19′ 2″	14.09	46′ 2 3/4″	1.66	5′ 5 1/4″	5:04.09
750	15.71	5.67	18′ 7 1/4″	13.34	43′ 9 1/4″	1.62	5′ 3 3/4″	5:11.88
700	16.12	5.50	18′ 0 1/2″	12.58	41′ 3 1/4″	1.57	5′ 1 3/4″	5:19.92
650	16.53	5.33	17′ 6″	11.83	38′ 9 3/4″	1.53	5′ 0 1/4″	5:28.24
600	16.96	5.15	16′ 10 3/4″	11.07	36′ 4″	1.49	4′ 10 1/2″	5:36.86
550	17.42	4.97	16′ 3 3/4″	10.31	33′ 10″	1.44	4′ 8 3/4″	5:45.82
500	17.89	4.78	15′ 8 1/4″	9.55	31′ 4″	1.39	4′ 6 3/4″	5:55.17
450	18.38	4.59	15′ 3/4″	8.78	28′ 9 3/4″	1.35	4′ 5″	6:04.97
400	18.90	4.39	14′ 5″	8.01	26′ 3 1/2″	1.30	4′ 3 1/4″	6:15.29
350	19.44	4.18	13′ 8 3/4″	7.23	23′ 8 3/4″	1.24	4′ 3/4″	6:26.24
300	20.03	3.97	13′ 1/4″	6.45	21′ 2″	1.19	3′ 10 3/4″	6:37.95
250	20.66	3.74	12′ 3 1/4″	5.66	18′ 7″	1.14	3′ 8 3/4″	6:50.62
200	21.35	3.50	11′ 5 3/4″	4.87	15′ 11 3/4″	1.08	3′ 6 1/2″	7:04.54
150	22.13	3.24	10′ 7 1/2″	4.06	13′ 4″	1.02	3′ 4″	7:20.21
100	23.03	2.96	9′ 8 1/2″	3.24	10′ 7 1/2″	0.95	3′ 1 1/4″	7:38.60
50	24.18	2.63	8′ 7 1/2″	2.40	7′ 10 1/2″	0.87	2′ 10 1/4″	8:02.16
1	26.40	2.14	7′ 1/4″	1.53	5′ 1/4″	0.77	2′ 6 1/4″	8:48.40

Note: To approximate the score for hand-times, add 0.24 seconds to the hand-time.

Table 22-8. Summary of IAAF 2001 women's decathlon scoring tables

Bowerman Three-Quarters Decathlon Tables

55 Meters

Time	*Pts.*
5.9	990
6.0	960
6.1	920
6.2	870
6.3	820
6.4	770
6.5	720
6.6	680
6.7	640
6.8	600
6.9	560
7.0	510
7.1	480
7.2	440
7.3	400
7.4	370
7.5	340
7.6	310
7.7	280
7.8	250
7.9	220
8.0	190
8.1	170

Long Jump

Ft.	*Pts.*	*A*
26′	1042	7
25′ 6″	1000	7
25′	958	7
24′ 6″	922	6
24′	886	6
23′ 6″	850	6
23′	814	6
22′ 6″	778	6
22′	742	6
21′ 6″	706	6
21′	670	6
20′ 6″	634	6
20′	604	5
19′ 6″	574	5
19′	544	5
18′	514	5
18′	484	5
17′	424	5
16′	364	5
15′	304	5
14′	244	5
13′	196	4
12′	148	4

Shot Put

Ft.	*Pts.*	*A*
60′	976	1.5
55′	886	1.5
50′	796	1.5
45′	706	1.5
40′	616	1.5
35′	526	1.5
34′	508	1.5
33′	490	1.5
32′	472	1.5
31′	454	1.5
30′	436	1.5
29′	418	1.5
28′	400	1.5
27′	382	1.5
26′	364	1.5
25′	346	1.5
24′	328	1.5
23′	310	1.5
22′	292	1.5
21′	274	1.5
20′	256	1.5

High Jump

Ft.	*Pts.*	*A*
7′ 2″	980	25
7′	930	25
6′ 10″	880	25
6′ 8″	832	24
6′ 6″	786	23
6′ 4″	740	23
6′ 2″	696	22
6′	652	22
5′ 10″	610	21
5′ 8″	570	20
5′ 6″	530	20
5′ 4″	490	20
5′ 2″	450	20
5′	412	19
4′ 10″	374	19
4′ 8″	336	19
4′ 6″	300	18
4′ 4″	266	17
4′ 2″	232	17
4′	200	16

300 Meters

Secs.	*Pts.*	*B*
34	1040	7
35	970	7
36	900	7
37	840	6
38	780	6
39	720	6
40	660	6
41	600	6
42	550	5
43	500	5
44	450	5
45	400	5
46	360	4
47	320	4
48	280	4
49	240	4
50	210	3
51	180	3
52	150	3
53	120	3

80m HH

Time	*Pts.*	*B*
10.0	975	18
10.5	890	17
11.0	810	16
11.5	730	16
12.0	655	15
12.5	585	14
13.0	515	14
13.5	450	13
14.0	390	12
14.5	335	11
15.0	285	10
16.0	195	9

Discus

Ft.	*Pts.*	*C*
180′	980	7
170′	910	7
160′	840	7
150′	780	6
140′	720	6
135′	690	6
130′	660	6
125′	630	6
120′	600	6
115′	570	6
110′	540	6
105′	510	6
100′	480	6
95′	450	6
90′	420	6
85′	390	6
80′	360	6
75′	330	6
70′	300	6
65′	270	6
60′	240	6
55′	210	6
50′	180	6
45′	155	5

Pole Vault

Ft.	*Pts.*	*A*
17′	970	8
16′6″	922	8
16′	874	8
15′6″	826	8
15′	778	8
14′6″	736	7
14′	694	7
13′6″	652	7
13′	610	7
12′6″	568	7
12′	526	7
11′6″	484	7
11′	442	7
10′6″	406	6
10′	370	6
9′6″	334	6
9′	298	6
8′6″	262	6
8′	226	6
7′	166	5

Javelin

Ft.	*Pts.*	*C*
250′	1000	5
240′	950	5
230′	900	5
220′	850	5
210′	800	5
200′	750	5
190′	700	5
180′	650	5
170′	600	5
160′	560	4
150′	520	4
140′	480	4
130′	440	4
120′	400	4
110′	360	4
100′	320	4
90′	280	4
80′	240	4
70′	190	5
60′	140	5

1200 Meters

Secs.	*Pts.*	*D*
3:00	1065	10
3:05	1015	10
3:10	970	9
3:15	925	9
3:20	880	9
3:25	835	9
3:30	790	9
3:35	750	8
3:40	710	8
3:45	670	8
3:50	630	8
3:55	595	7
4:00	560	7
4:05	525	7
4:10	490	7
4:15	455	7
4:20	425	6
4:25	395	6
4:30	365	6
4:40	305	6
4:50	255	5
5:00	205	5
5:10	165	4

Key: A: Points per inch B: Points per 1/10th second C: Points per foot D: Points per second
Revised by Freeman (2001)

Table 22-9. Bowerman three-quarters decathlon tables, 2001 revision by Freeman

Bowerman-Freeman Three-Quarters Heptathlon Tables

55mHH

Time	*Pts.*
7.4	1030
7.5	1000
7.6	970
7.7	940
7.8	910
7.9	880
8.0	850
8.1	820
8.2	790
8.3	760
8.4	735
8.5	710
8.6	685
8.7	660
8.8	635
8.9	610
9.0	585
9.1	560
9.2	535
9.3	510
9.4	485
9.5	465
9.6	445
9.7	425
9.8	405
9.9	385
10.0	365
10.1	345
10.2	325
10.3	305
10.4	285
10.5	265
10.6	245
10.7	230
10.8	215
10.9	200
11.0	185

High Jump

Ft.	*Pts.*	*A*
6′ 2″	1080	30
6′	1020	30
5′ 10″	960	30
5′ 8″	900	30
5′ 6″	840	30
5′ 4″	780	30
5′ 2″	720	30
5′	660	30
4′ 10″	600	30
4′ 8″	540	30
4′ 6″	480	30
4′ 4″	430	25
4′ 2″	380	25
4′	330	25
3′ 10″	280	25
3′ 8″	240	20
3′ 6″	200	20
3′ 4″	160	20

Long Jump

Ft.	*Pts.*	*A*
21′ 6″	1042	8
21′	980	8
20′ 6″	932	8
20′	884	8
19′ 6″	836	8
19′	788	8
18′ 6″	740	8
18′	692	8
17′ 6″	650	7
17′	608	7
16′ 6″	566	7
16′	524	7
15′ 6″	482	7
15′	440	7
14′ 6″	404	6
14′	368	6
13′ 6″	332	6
13′	296	6
12′ 6″	260	6
12′	230	5
11′ 6″	200	5
11′	170	5

Shot Put

Ft.	*Pts.*	*B*
55′	990	22
50′	880	22
45′	770	22
40′	670	20
35′	570	20
34′	550	
33′	530	
32′	510	
31′	490	
30′	470	
29′	450	
28′	430	
27′	410	
26′	390	
25′	370	
24′	350	
23′	330	
22′	310	
21′	290	
20′	270	
19′	250	
18′	230	
17′	210	
16′	190	
15′	170	

150 Meters

Secs.	*Pts.*	*C*
18	960	12
19	840	12
20	720	12
21	610	11
22	510	10
23	420	9
24	340	8
25	260	8
26	190	7

600 Meters

Mins.	*Pts.*	*D*
1:35	1020	20
1:40	920	20
1:45	830	18
1:50	740	18
1:55	655	17
2:00	575	16
2:05	500	15
2:10	430	14
2:15	365	13
2:20	305	12
2:25	250	11
2:30	200	10
2:35	155	9

Javelin

Ft.	*Pts.*	*B*
190′	1020	6
180′	960	6
170′	900	6
160′	840	6
150′	780	6
140′	720	6
1130′	660	6
125′	630	6
120′	600	6
115′	570	6
110′	540	6
105′	510	6
100′	490	4
95′	460	6
90′	430	6
85′	400	6
80′	370	6
75′	340	6
70′	310	6
65′	280	6
60′	250	6
55′	230	6
50′	200	6
45′	170	6

Key:
A: Points per inch
B: Points per foot
C: Points per 1/10th second
D: Points per second

Table 22-10. Bowerman-Freeman three-quarters heptathlon tables

Sylvia High School-College Decathlon Tables

100 Meters		Long Jump		Shot Put		High Jump		400 Meters		110m LH		Discus		Pole Vault		Javelin		1600 Meters	
Time	*Pts.*	*Ft.*	*Pts.*	*Ft.*	*Pts.*	*Ft.*	*Pts.*	*Secs.*	*Pts.*	*Time*	*Pts.*	*Ft.*	*Pts.*	*Ft.*	*Pts.*	*Ft.*	*Pts.*	*Time*	*Pts.*
10.8	1200	23′	1200	55′	1200	6′ 4″	1200	49	1200	13.4	1200	165′	1200	14′	1200	200′	1200	4:25	1200
11.0	1100	22′	1150	50′	1150	6′ 2″	1150	50	1100	13.8	1100	150′	1100	13′ 6″	1150	180′	1100	4:35	1150
11.2	1000	21′	1100	45′	1100	6′	1100	51	1000	14.2	1050	135′	1050	13′	1100	160′	1000	4:40	1100
11.4	950	20′	1000	40′	1000	5′ 10″	1000	52	950	14.6	1000	120′	1000	12′6″	1050	140′	900	4:45	1050
11.6	900	19′	900	39′	900	5′ 8″	900	53	900	15.0	950	105′	900	12′	1000	120′	800	4:50	1000
11.8	850	18′	800	38′	800	5′ 6″	800	54	850	15.3	900	95′	800	11′ 6″	950	105′	750	4:55	900
12.0	800	17′	700	37′	700	5′ 4″	700	55	800	15.6	800	90′	700	11′	900	95′	700	5:00	800
12.2	700	16′ 6″	600	36′	600	5′ 2″	600	56	750	15.9	700	85′	600	10′ 6″	800	90′	650	5:05	700
12.4	600	16′	550	35′	500	5′	500	57	700	16.2	600	80′	500	10′	700	85′	600	5:10	650
12.6	500	15′ 6″	500	34′	450	4′ 10″	400	58	650	16.5	500	75′	450	9′ 6″	600	80′	500	5:15	600
12.8	400	15′	450	33′	400	4′ 8″	300	59	600	16.8	400	70′	400	9′	500	75′	400	5:20	550
13.0	300	14′ 6″	400	32′	350	4′ 6″	250	60	550	17.1	350	65′	350	8′ 6″	400	70′	300	5:25	500
13.2	250	14′	350	31′	300	4′ 4″	200	61	500	17.4	300	60′	300	8′	300	65′	200	5:30	450
13.4	200	13′ 6″	300	30′	250	4′ 2″	150	62	450	17.7	250	55′	250	7′ 6″	200	60′	150	5:45	350
13.6	150	13′	200	29′	200	4′	100	63	400	18.0	200	50′	200	7′	100	55′	100	6:00	250
13.8	100	12′ 6″	100	28′	150			64	350	18.3	150	45′	150			50′	50	6:15	150
14.0	50	12′	50	27′	100			65	300	18.6	100	40′	100					6:30	50
				26′	50			66	250										
								67	200										
								68	150										
								70	100										

Alternate Events

200 Meters		800 Meters		3200 Meters		Triple Jump	
Sec.	*Pts.*	*Time*	*Pts.*	*Time*	*Pts.*	*Ft.*	*Pts.*
21.0	1200	1:55	1200	9:30	1200	48′	1200
22.0	1150	1:58	1150	9:50	1150	46′	1150
22.5	1100	2:00	1100	10:00	1100	44′	1100
23.0	1000	2:05	1000	10:10	1050	42′	1000
23.5	900	2:10	950	10:20	1000	40′	900
24.0	850	2:15	900	10:30	900	38′	800
24.5	800	2:20	800	10:40	800	36′	700
25.0	700	2:25	700	10:50	700	35′	600
25.5	600	2:30	600	11:00	650	34′	550
26.0	500	2:35	500	11:10	600	33′	500
26.5	450	2:40	450	11:20	550	32′	450
27.0	400	2:45	400	11:30	500	31′	400
27.5	350	2:50	350	11;40	450	30′	350
28.0	300	2:55	300	12:10	350	29′	300
28.5	250	3:00	250	12:40	250	28′	200
29.0	200	3:05	200	13:10	150	27′	100
29.5	150	3:10	150	13:40	50	26′	50
30.0	100	3:15	100				

Modified by Freeman (1986)

Table 22-11. Sylvia high school-college decathlon tables, modified by Freeman, 1986

Endnotes

1. William H. Freeman. (1989). Periodized training for the combined events. In *Peak when it counts: Periodized training for American track and field.* Los Altos, CA: Tafnews.
2. William H. Freeman. (1986). Decathlon performance success: Progress and age factors. *Track Technique, 96,* 3050-3052.
3. Andrzej Krzesenski. (1984). The specific features of the decathlon. *Track Technique, 89,* 2828-2830.
4. A. Rudski & B. Aptekman. (1986). Stages in the training of decathloners. *Track and Field Quarterly Review, 86*(2), 16-17.
5. Freeman. (1986). 3050.
6. Robin C. Sykes. (1971). Balance: The decathlon keyword. *Track Technique, 45,* 1442-1443.
7. Freeman. (1986). 3051.
8. Freeman. (1989). 82.
9. Bob Myers. (1986). Periodization for the heptathlon: A practical training theory. *Track and Field Quarterly Review, 86*(2), 34-36.
10. Bob Myers. (1989). The heptathlon. In Vern Gambetta (Ed.), *The Athletics Congress's track and field coaching manual* (2nd ed.). Champaign, IL: Leisure Press, 209-218.
11. William H. Freeman. (1986). An analysis of heptathlon performance and training. *Track and Field Quarterly Review, 86*(2), 30-34.
12. Robert C. Parks. (1971). Organizing an indoor decathlon in elementary or junior high school physical education classes. *Track and Field Quarterly Review, 71*(4), 34-35.
13. Alfred J. Sylvia. (1964, April). A decathlon for high school and college. *Athletic Journal, 44, 38, 40.*

Core Readings

Freeman, William H. (1976, April). Decathlon competition organization. *Scholastic Coach, 45,* 34ff.

Freeman, William H. (1986). Factors of decathlon success. *Track and Field Quarterly Review, 86*(2), 4-11.

Freeman, William H. (2001). Periodized training for the combined events. In *Peak When It Counts: Periodization for American track and field* (4th ed.). Mountain View, CA: Tafnews, 140-144.

Hart, Bevan T., & Chris Huffins. (Spring 2006). Development and training techniques of American decathletes. *Track Coach, 175,* 5596-5600.

Marra, Harry. Decathlon. (2000). In *USA Track and Field coaching manual.* Champaign, IL: Human Kinetics, 299-308.

Rovelto, Cliff. Heptathlon. (2000). In *USA Track and Field coaching manual.* Champaign, IL: Human Kinetics, 287-297.

Recommended Readings

Berndt, Axel, & Helmar Hommel. (1995). Report: XIX Congress of the European Athletics Coaches Association: Combined events. *New Studies in Athletics, 10*(2), 87-103; Dick, Frank. Sprint and speed events, 88-89; Higgins, Andy. Endurance and endurance events, 89-90; Hommel, Helmar. New horizons for the men's and women's decathlon, 90-92; Locatelli, Elio. Elastic strength and the jumping events, 92-95; Schäfer, Gertrud. The overall planning of Sabine Braun's heptathlon training and competition since 1989, 96-98; Tidow, Günter. Optimization of strength training, 98-100; Dick, Frank. Training and competition planning, 100-101; Alicea, Angel. The combined events as a basis for the development of athletes, 101.

Ebbets, Russ, ed. (Spring 2005). Combined events roundtable: Dissecting the decathlon. *Track Coach, 171,* 5449-5462. Participants: Matt Candri, Scott Hall, Frank Zarnowski & Kevin Reid.

Etcheverry, Sergio Guarda. (1995). Profile of the decathlete. *New Studies in Athletics, 10*(2),

Freeman, William H. (1986). An analysis of heptathlon performance and training. *Track and Field Quarterly Review, 86*(2), 30-34.

Freeman, William H. (1986). Decathlon performance success: Progress and age factors. *Track Technique, 96,* 3050-3052.

Geese, Rolf. (2000). Decathlon for women. *New Studies in Athletics, 15*(2), 37-40.

Gramantik, Les. (Summer 2000). Aspects of combined events training [abstract]. *Track Coach, 152,* 4866.

Hart, Bevan T., & Chris Huffins. (2003). The development and training of decathletes in the USA. *New Studies in Athletics, 18*(4), 31-36.

Higgins, Andy. (1990). Beyond speed in the decathlon. *Track Technique, 111,* 3544-3546, 3556.

Jenner, Bruce. (1986). Bruce Jenner on the decathlon. *Track and Field Quarterly Review, 86*(2), 26-29.

Jeřábek, Peter. (2003). The preparation of junior athletes for the combined events. *New Studies in Athletics, 18*(4), 37-43.

Jiyingo, Xue, & Huq Xinmin. (1995). Suggestions for the re-compilation of the IAAF scoring tables for the combined events. *New Studies in Athletics, 10*(2), 67-72.

Krátkÿ, Petr, & Jitka Vindušková. (Fall 2005). Performance development trends in the decathlon. *Track Coach, 173,* 5538-5541.

Kunz, Hansruedi. (1994). A conditioning test for the decathlon [abstract]. Track Technique, 128, 4095-4096.

Kuptshinov, R. (1991). A 9000-point decathlon [abstract]. Track Technique, 117, 3740.

Mäkelä, Jarmo, José Luiz Martinez, Brad McStravick, Claude Monot, Lyle Sanderson & Efim Shuravetzky. (1995). NSA Round Table 28: Combined events. *New Studies in Athletics, 10*(2), 29-40.

Maksimenko, G. (1992). The final preparation phase in the decathlon. *Modern Athlete and Coach, 30*(4), 30-33.

McGuire, Rick, & Cliff Rovelto. (Fall 2003). Transitional control in the Combined Events. *Track Coach, 165,* 5276-5281.

McStravick, Brad. (Fall 1997). Long-term planning for combined events [abstract]. *Track Coach, 141,* 4512-4513.

Panteleyev, Viktor. (1998). Preparation of decathletes. *Modern Athlete and Coach, 36*(3), 35-38.

Sanderson, Lyle. (1995). Trends in women's combined events. New Studies in Athletics, 10(2), 13-22. Corrected Figure 3, *New Studies in Athletics, 10*(4), 87.

Schäfer, Gertrud. (1995). The overall planning of Sabine Braun's heptathlon training and competition. *New Studies in Athletics, 10*(2), 57-61.

Schenk, Christian. (1995). The German "Zehnkampf-TEAM"–Approach to an "International Decathlon Team." *New Studies in Athletics, 10*(2), 63-66.

Schiffer, Jürgen. (1995). Selected and annotated bibliography 35: Combined events. *New Studies in Athletics, 10*(2), 75-86.

Shuravetzky, Efim. (1995). An outline of the Australian Decathlon Coaching Programme. *New Studies in Athletics, 10*(2), 43-47.

Tidow, Günter. (2000). Challenge decathlon–Barriers on the way to becoming the "King of Athletes." Part I. *New Studies in Athletics, 15*(2), 43-52. Part II. 15(3/4), 39-44. Part III. 16(1/2), 83-90.

Trkal, Viktor. (2003). The development of combined events scoring tables and implications for the training of decathletes. *New Studies in Athletics, 18*(4), 7-12.

Trkal, Viktor. (Fall 2005). Preparation of combined-event athletes with respect to the men's decathlon point scores. *Track Coach, 173,* 5533-5537.

Ushakov, Aleksandr. (Fall 1997). Construction of decathlon training [abstract]. *Track Coach, 141,* 4514.

Ushakova, Natalia. (Fall 1996). Heptathlon combinations [abstract]. *Track Coach, 137,* 4384.

Váňa, Zdĕnek. (2003). The training of the best decathletes. *New Studies in Athletics, 18*(4), 15-30.

Vinduškovà, Jitka. (2003). Training women for the heptathlon: A brief outline. *New Studies in Athletics, 18*(2), 27-34.

Vinduskovà, Jitka. (Summer 2004). Women's heptathlon training– A brief outline [abstract]. *Track Coach, 168,* 5378-5379.

Westera, Wim. (2006). Decathlon: Towards a balanced and sustainable performance assessment method. *New Studies in Athletics, 21*(1), 39-50.

Yang, C.K. (1987). Decathlon training in preparation for competition. *Track and Field Quarterly Review, 87*(2), 57-58.

Young, Michael. (Summer 2001). Test decathlon for the evaluation of track and field athletes. *Track Coach, 156,* 4985-4987

DIRECTING TRACK AND FIELD PROGRAMS

Part 7

Bill Bowerman during a home meet.

23

Locating and Testing Candidates in School

Few coaches have the good fortune to inherit a team of good athletes. Most coaches begin each year needing new athletes to fill at least several of the events, if not all of them. Do not overlook any prospect in this search. The physical education classes are an excellent source of prospects whether you coach in high school or college.

Coaches benefit from regularly testing the physical education classes in several events. The tests can be mixed with the normal start-of-the-year testing in the classes. The tests described in this chapter are proven indicators of talent in untrained athletes, though other tests can be used as well.

General Comments on Testing and Recruitment

Tests may not be absolute indicators of talent. Some athletes have off days; others are late bloomers. These tests try to discover natural ability without requiring the prospect to have prior training in the events. For that reason, the coach can test prospects on their first day of practice or test everyone in a

Testing Organization

Event	*Test Number*	*Test*	*Site*
High jump	1	Jump and reach	Gym
Long jump (40 yards)	2	Standing long jump	Gym
Sprint and long jump	3	40-yard dash	Field
Hurdles	4	40-yard hurdles	Field
Javelin	5	Ball throw	Field
Triple jump	6	Standing triple jump	Field
Shot put	7	Shot put	Shot area
Distance runs	8	800m run	Track

Table 23-1. Testing organization

physical education class during the first week of school. Athletes do not always realize that they have the talent for a given event, so all prospects should be tested for all events.

If the tests are given in a brief period and several teachers or assistants are available to record the results, the tests can be given quickly to many students. Table 23-1 gives the testing order, Table 23-2 lists the test standards for high school students, and Figure 23-1 shows how to organize a playing field for the tests.

Summary of Test Standards

Event	*Test*	*Male*	*Female*
Sprints	40-yard	5.2 seconds	6.2 seconds
Distances	800m	2:30	3:00
Hurdles	40-yard lows	6.2 seconds	7.5 seconds
High jump	Jump and reach	30″	20″
Long jump	Standing LJ	7′6″	6′ 0″
40-yard		5.2 seconds	6.2 seconds
Triple jump	Standing TJ	24′	19′ high school
		28′	22′ college
	Rhythm and balance		
Pole vault	All-around gymnastic ability		
Shot put	Standing put	20′	18′
Discus	(none; use shot-putters)		
Javelin	800 g ball	Good javelin distance	
	Softball	200′	150′

Table 23-2. Summary of test standards

Students can move from one station to the next as they complete each test, except that the 800 meters is run last in one or two large groups. Athletes or managers can direct some of the events to lessen the number of persons needed to administer the tests. A coach can give all of the tests in one afternoon if the procedure is well organized and carefully explained to the prospects.

Do not consider these tests as the only possible selection factors; a student's strong interest in an event may overcome an early lack of talent for an event. Never underestimate human drive and willpower. Many other tests are also used to indicate event-specific talent. This list is simply one we have found useful for many years.

The coach should try to make the sport popular with the students. He should try to see that it is enjoyed, for this criterion is important for a young person in trying out for a team. No matter how popular a sport may be at first, if the coach does not make it an enjoyable experience, he will lose many prospects and eventually lose any status that the sport might have carried. If a sport becomes popular, much of the recruiting problem is solved.

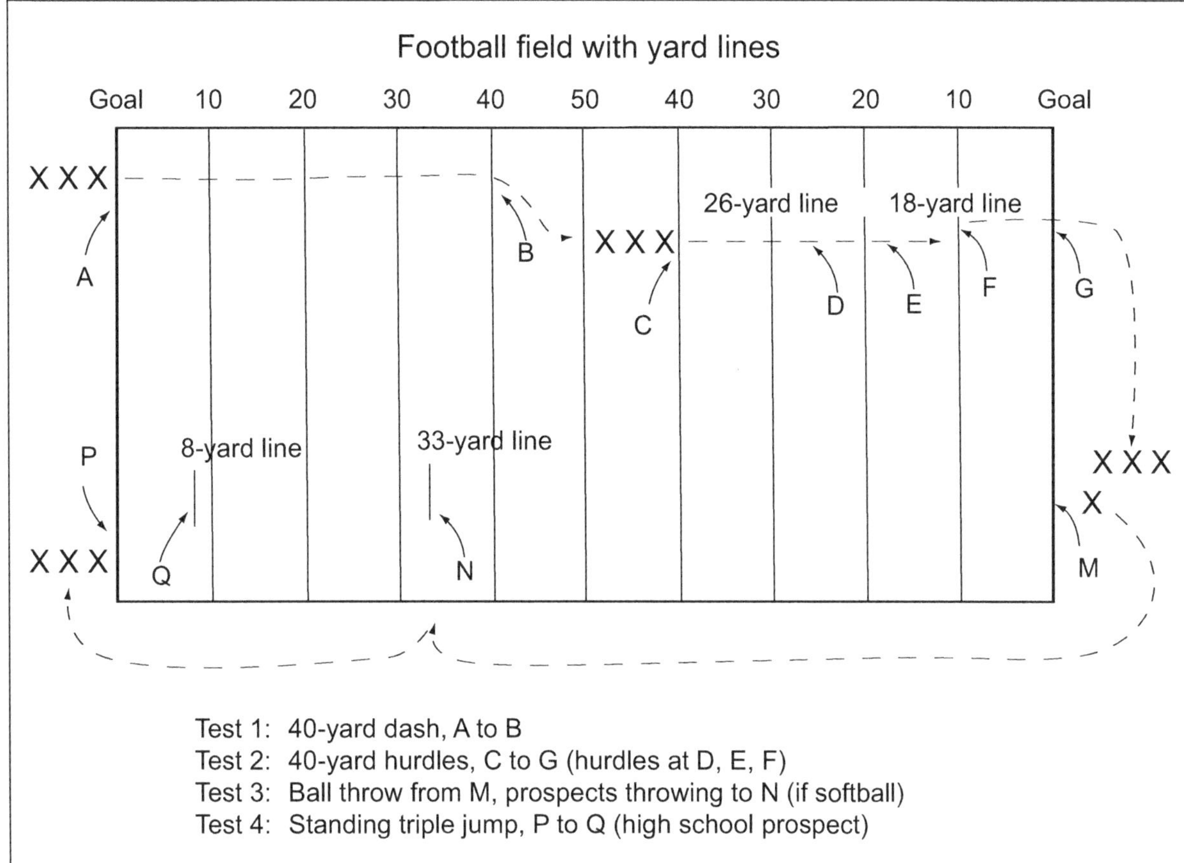

Figure 23-1. Field testing with several teachers available

Convincing a Prospect to Come Out for the Team

Every coach wonders how great an effort to make to get a prospect to come out for the team and to convince the prospect to stay if he shows signs of quitting. Athletic competition has many benefits, but whether those benefits are realized if an athlete stays on a team when he prefers not to be there is uncertain.

Is it worth the continual effort to convince a hesitant athlete to stay on the team? It is likely not. The coach is going to waste much time that is better spent on athletes who appreciate the attention. Also, the team risks losing a valuable member late in the season with no trained replacement. If that loss occurs before the meets begin, however, it might be covered by other athletes. Thus, the effect of a potential dropout on team morale can be minimized. Finally, an athlete may threaten to quit simply to get attention from the coach. Most coaches have enough work to do without pampering prima donnas.

Athlete Tests and Selection Standards

The purpose of these tests is to help select your most likely prospects for each event as quickly as possible. They allow you to locate talent in unsuspected places and to begin more specific training earlier in a program that has a very short season. If you have only two athletes interested in the shot put, you have no trouble deciding who your shot-putters are. However, if all of your athletes complete the battery of tests, you may discover other potential throwers to add to the group.

The distances for the running tests are not the usual racing distances; they simply lend themselves well to testing on a typical, lined football field. Other testing distances may be equally valid. However, the goal is to test the maximum number of prospects in a minimum of time and with a minimum of personnel and equipment.

Sprint Test

The first test is for sprinters. Time each person in a 40-yard dash. Give the test on the football field, starting on the goal line and finishing where the coach is standing on the 40-yard line (Figure 23-2). This site minimizes the risk of injury if prospects fall while running. Have each person go down in a three-point stance (both feet and one hand on the ground) for the start. No one is needed to start the students, if they run one at a time, because the timer starts the watch when the athlete lifts the hand from the ground. Each person is given only one trial because untrained runners rarely improve their sprint times on later attempts.

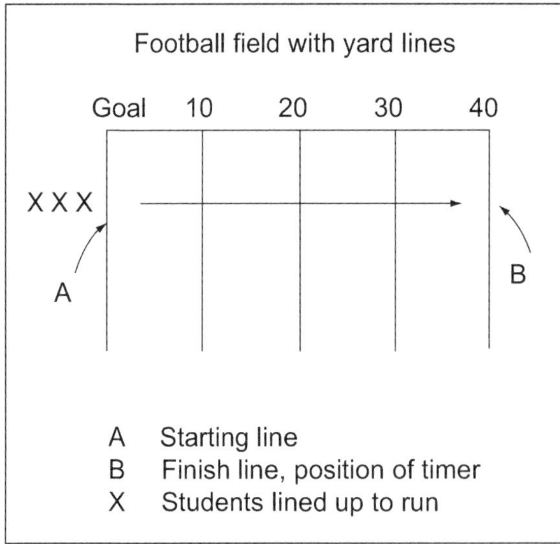

Figure 23-2. Test for sprinters

Hurdling Test

For hurdling prospects a 40-yard distance is also used, but three hurdles are added to the course (Figure 23-3). The first hurdle is 14 yards from the start, and the other two hurdles are at eight-yard intervals past the first one. If you are starting the runners on the goal line, for example, the hurdles will be on the 14-, 22-, and 30-yard lines, with the finish on the 40-yard line. The hurdles are set at low hurdle height (30 inches). For females, reduce the hurdle separations slightly, setting them at 13 1/2, 21, and 28 1/2 yards.

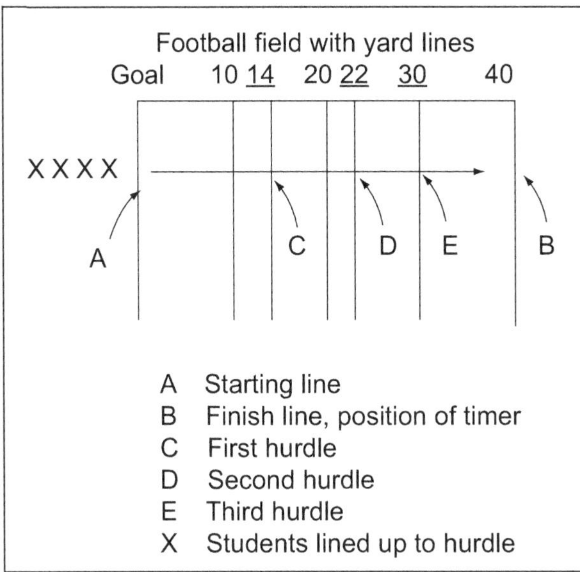

Figure 23-3. Test for hurdlers

Distance Run Test

Find distance runners with an 800-meter run. Divide the class into two groups, one group lined up facing the other and numbered in sequence, with each member of Group 1 having a counterpart in the student with the same number in Group 2. Each runner gets the finishing time of his counterpart and reports it to the recorder, the first runner in Group 1 reporting the time of the first runner in Group 2, and so forth. After one group runs and has its times recorded, the second group runs and has its times reported by the first group. If only runners with the best times are of interest, everyone can run at the same time, with the coach pulling the top runners to the side as they finish.

Other testing distances are equally valid, such as 1,500 meters, one mile, or the Cooper run (12-minute run or 1 1/2-mile run). However, the 800-meter run is sufficient and saves time (and no prospect gets lapped).

High Jump Test

For high jumpers, use the jump and reach (Sargent jump) test. A strip of tape can be placed on the wall, running upward from about 6 feet to 11 feet above the floor. It should be marked at one-inch intervals over that distance, with larger marks and numerals every six inches. Each jumper stands flat-footed next to the wall at the tape and raises an arm so the observer can note how high the jumper can reach with the fingers. He then crouches and jumps, reaching with the hand to touch as high up the strip of tape as possible, while the observer notes the new height (Figure 23-4). Thus, a person with a standing reach of 7′ 3″ and a jumping reach of 9′ 10″ has jumped 31 inches, the difference between the two marks.

This test was more meaningful before the back layout (Fosbury flop) style of jumping appeared in the late 1960s. For "floppers," sprinting speed is as important as the leg spring tested by the Sargent jump. Many elite floppers have tested poorly on the vertical jump, so consider any prospect with moderate spring and good leg speed.

Figure 23-4. Test for high jumpers

Long Jump Tests

Two tests are used in conjunction for long jump prospects. The first is the sprint test, and the second is the standing long jump. This test can be done into the long jump pit, or it can be done indoors on any floor that provides non-slip footing. A strip of masking tape can be placed upon the floor, running outward at a right angle to the takeoff point, beginning four feet from the takeoff point and marked at one-inch intervals to 11 feet (Figure 23-5). Each jumper stands directly behind the takeoff line with the toe of each foot touching the line, and then leaps as far forward as possible. The leap can be into a pit or onto a tumbling mat (mark where the mat's corners should be on the floor because it moves with each landing). Long jumpers require a combination of jumping and sprinting ability.

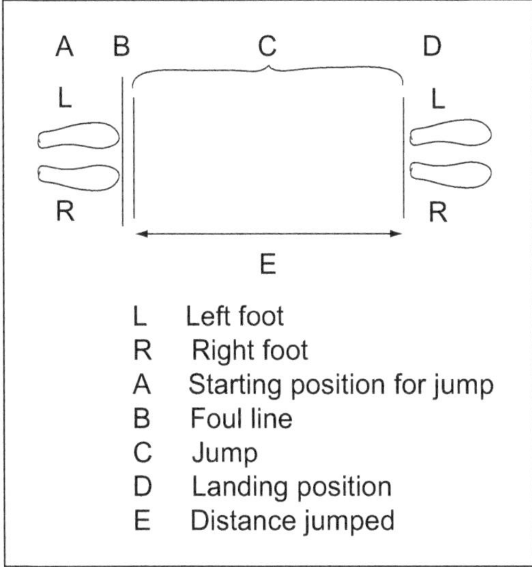

Figure 23-5. Test for long jumpers

Triple Jump Test

The standing triple jump is used to find triple jump prospects. Have a jumper demonstrate the technique first, because it may seem strange to the students. The jumper takes off from one foot, lands on the same foot, goes into a step, landing on the other foot, and then makes a long jump to conclude the sequence (Figure 23-6). Use the same takeoff line as for the standing long jump, but make chalk or masking tape marks at six-inch intervals from 15 to 32 feet away from the takeoff point. If this test is not done with the landing in a jumping pit or on a mat, it should be done on a grassy area, such as the football field. The jumper can "swing" into the jump, starting with one foot behind the takeoff foot to provide some push into the jump. The coach is looking for athletes with good rhythm and balance, so hurdlers are often good prospects.

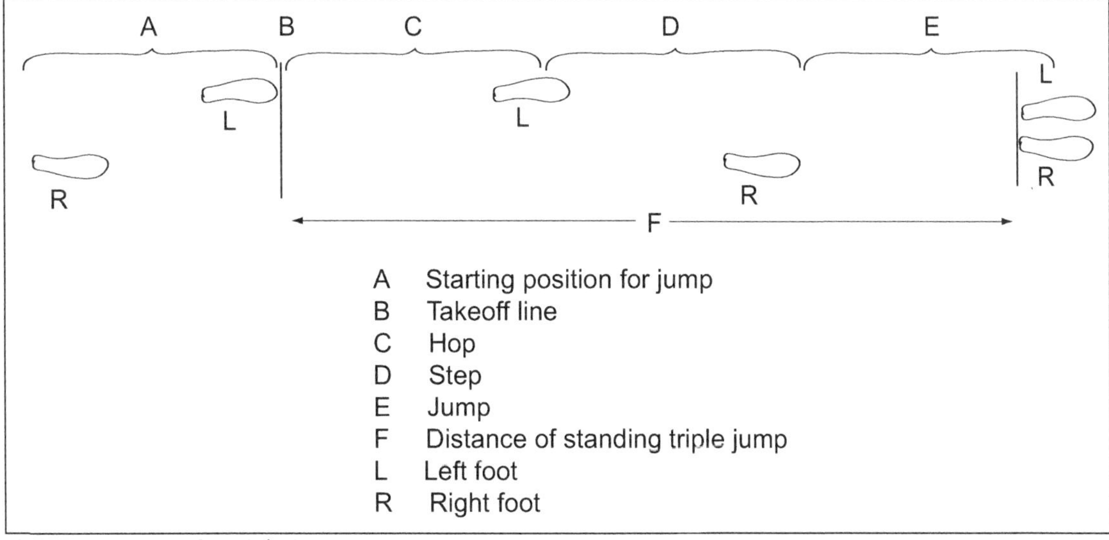

Figure 23-6. Test for triple jumpers

Shot-Put Test

Shot-putters can be found with the standing put. Mark a throwing line on the ground with chalk, then make lines at 10 feet, at 15 feet, and at one-foot intervals from 15 to 30 feet from the throwing line. The prospects take turns throwing from a standing position facing the direction of their throws (no turns are used).

Javelin Throw Tests

Javelin throwers can be found by throwing a softball, a football, or an 800-gram weighted ball (about 1 3/4 pounds). These throws indicate talent (and add years to the life expectancy of the person marking the distances of the throws). The goal line of the football field is used as a throwing line, with the 150-foot mark at midfield and the 200-foot mark at the far 33-yard line (Figure 23-7). The throwers run up to the line however they wish, as long as they do not cross it. The distance an 800-gram weighted ball is thrown gives the closest approximation of how far the javelin can be thrown.

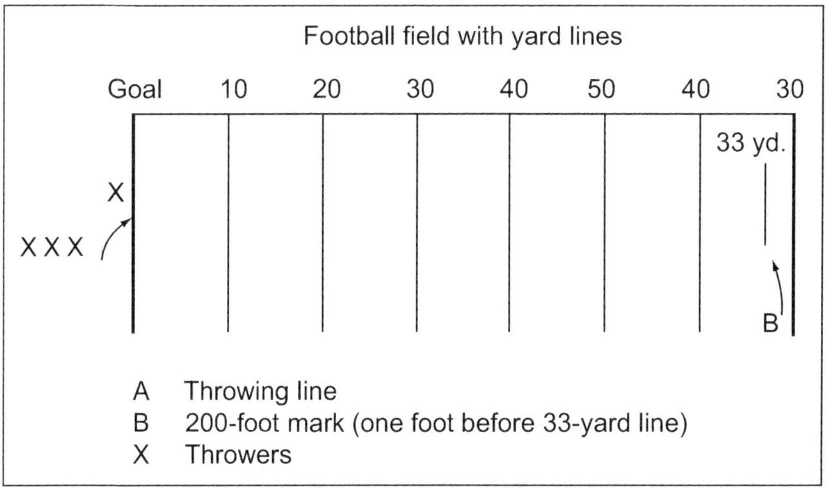

Figure 23-7. Test for javelin throwers

Locating Prospects for Other Events

We have no test that we use to discover discus throwers or pole vaulters. Shot-putters usually throw the discus, eventually showing themselves stronger in one event or the other as they become more competent in their skills. Pole vaulting requires a unique combination of skills that shows most readily in skilled gymnasts. The vaulter is invariably a risk-taker at physical stunts. A pole vaulter may be an athlete who is a fair sprinter, long jumper, and hurdler.

Recommended Readings

Abbot, Angela, Dave Collins & Russell Martindale. (2002). Talent identification: How not to do it! Current "world best" practice? In *12th Commonwealth International Sport Conference (19-23 July 2002, Manchester, United Kingdom) Abstract Book.* London: Association of Commonwealth Universities, 332.

Arbeit, E., Bartonietz, K., Borner, P., Hellmann, K., & Skibbia, W. (1988). The javelin: The view of the DVfL of the GDR on talent selection, technique and main training contents of the training phases from beginner to top-level athlete. *New Studies in Athletics, 3*(1), 57-74.

Bartonietz, K., Hinz, L., Lorenz, D., & Lunau, G. (1988). The hammer: The view of the DVfL of the GDR on talent selection, technique and training of throwers from beginner to top level athlete. *New Studies in Athletics, 3*(1), 39-56.

Collins, Dave, Angela Abbot & Russell Martindale. (2002). Talent identification and development: How would we do it? In *12th Commonwealth International Sport Conference (19-23 July 2002, Manchester, United Kingdom) Abstract Book.* London: Association of Commonwealth Universities, 146.

Dickhuth, H-H. (1993). The limitation of talent identification in running events. [abstract]. *Track Technique, 124,* 3968.

Digel, Helmut. (2002). The context of talent identification and promotion: A comparison of nations. *New Studies in Athletics, 17*(3/4), 13-26.

Foreman, Ken. (1989). The use of talent-predictive factors in the selection of track and field athletes. In *The Athletics Congress's Track and Field Coaching Manual* (2nd ed.). Champaign, IL: Leisure Press, 31-36.

Freeman, William H. (1986). Decathlon performance success: Progress and age factors. *Track Technique, 96,* 3050-3052.

Harksen, Rüdiger. (1998). Report: NACACTFCA Congress in Miami/Florida (USA), October 9 to 12, 1997. *New Studies in Athletics, 13*(1), 87-92; Sanderson, Lyle. Problems of recruiting, motivating and the long-term affiliation of young people to athletics. 91-92.

Headley, N., R. Du Randt & D. J. Venter. (2000). Indicators of potential performance in track and field athletics. In *Book of Abstracts 2000 Pre-Olympic Congress, Brisbane Australia, 7-12 September 2000* (p. 88). Brisbane: Sports Medicine Australia, ICSSPE, ACHPER.

Hemmings, Steph, Alan Nevill & Mary Nevill. (2002). Validation of the 20-M Multi-Stage Shuttle Test as a predictor of peak oxygen uptake in young, elite sports performers. In *12th Commonwealth International Sport Conference (19-23 July 2002, Manchester, United Kingdom) Abstract Book* (p. 373). London: Association of Commonwealth Universities.

Henson, Phil, & Paul Turner. Predictive testing of athletes. (2000). In *USA Track and Field coaching manual* (pp. 19-32). Champaign, IL: Human Kinetics.

Holmes, M. J. (1999). Identifying and developing junior elite athletes. *New Studies in Athletics, 14*(1), 31-40.

Jones, Max. (1988). The test quadrathlon. *Track and Field Quarterly Review, 88*(3), 43-46.

Kutsar, Kuulo. (1991). Hereditary physiological factors in talent identification [abstract]. *Track Technique, 115,* 3681.

Martirisov, E. G. (2001). Body build of sportsmen engaged in Olympic sport events. *Acta Kinesiologiae Universitatis Tartuensis, 6*(supplement), 172-175.

Riordan, Jim. (1987). Talent spotting in Eastern Europe. *Track Technique, 101,* 3214, 3220.

Sanderson, Lyle. (1998). Recruiting and retaining track and field athletes. *New Studies in Athletics, 13*(1), 21-24.

The tests of equivalence [throws]. (1984). *Track and Field Quarterly Review, 84*(1), 50-53.

Thumm, Hans-Peter. (2006). Talent identification in Indonesia: A model for other countries? *New Studies in Athletics, 21*(2), 29-39.

Vernacchia, Ralph A., Richard T. McGuire, James P. Reardon & David P. Templin. (2000). Psychosocial characteristics of Olympic track and field athletes. *New Studies in Athletics, 15*(3/4), 7-21.

Young, Michael. (Summer 2001). Test decathlon for the evaluation of track and field athletes. *Track Coach, 156,* 4985-4987

Ziemainz, Heiko, & Jason Gulbin. (2002). Talent selection, identification and development exemplified in the Australian Talent Search programme. *New Studies in Athletics, 17*(3/4), 27-32.

24

Organizing and Administering the Track and Field Program

A good track and field program must be developed around the concept of community interest in track and field. Local interest in track will do much to assure good track teams, for the more able athletes will be drawn to track more than to other sports. For this reason, the administrative aspect of track athletics must include the community program as well as the school's program itself. On the high school level, a good community program will enhance the school's program immeasurably and provide many future athletes. On the college level, this program will not function so much as a feeder as a community service and as a means of developing community interest in the sport.

Community Track Programs

All-comers summer track programs and jogging programs are good examples of community programs that can be developed either by or through the school. This chapter will describe them as they are practiced in Eugene, Oregon.

A community all-comers summer track program provides many benefits. From the standpoint of the coach, one particular value outweighs the others: it develops a body of spectators for the sport. If young people are competing in the summer meets, many of their parents will come to see the meets.

The many contests involved in a meet are exciting, and they are not difficult to understand. Many persons will discover that they have been missing a good spectator sport. Consequently, when the school has track meets, the body of potential spectators will have grown. Bigger crowds mean more interest, and more interest means more athletes.

A second value lies with the participants themselves. Naturally, they will benefit from the health and fitness standpoint; that is understood. However, many young people are never really exposed to the sport, despite the possibility that they might have considerable natural aptitude for it. Community programs are organized for football, basketball, and baseball—why not track and field? Young people will find it an enjoyable experience, even if they do not develop into future track athletes. Some of them, however, *will* develop into track athletes. Several Olympic athletes were first exposed to track at the all-comers meets in Eugene.

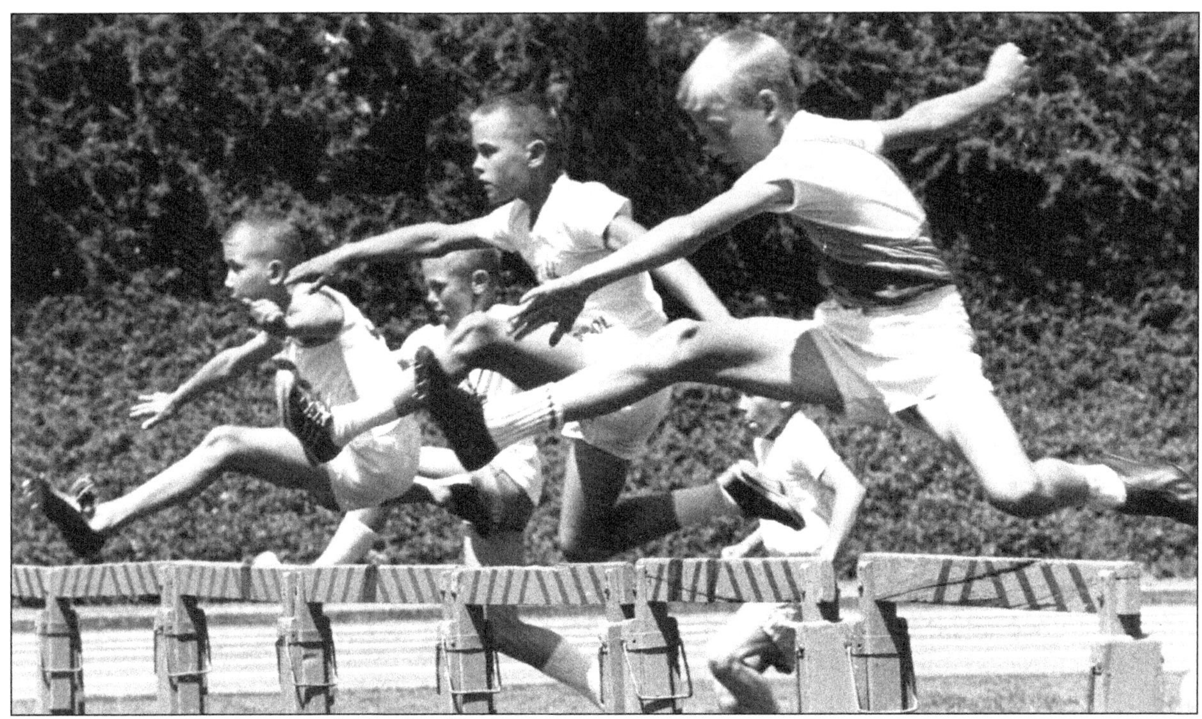

Photo 24-1. Children's meets in the Medford years

The program should reach up as well as down across the age groups. For the young children, the competition is fun, but it does not necessarily require any fine skills that might prove embarrassing to the low-skilled growing child. To the middle school student, it is similar to high school athletics, and it may be interesting from that point of view. To the high school student, it is a chance to compete without the pressure of success or failure involved in team-scored meets, plus it provides a chance to experiment with new events, which is also an aspect of its allure to college athletes. To the graduate of high school or college, it is a chance to continue to compete, even if no longer allied with a team. For older adults, it is a return to the pleasures of competition, or a discovery of those pleasures for the first time. For every competitor, it is an enjoyable social event, for the all-comers meet is decidedly informal. Of course, events are held for both female and male athletes.

The All-Comers Program in Eugene, Oregon

The Summer All-Comers Program was begun in Eugene, Oregon, in 1957 as an attempt to promote summer track and field competition. The original intention was to provide competition for the college athletes. The first meets averaged 30 or 35 competitors, spread over a dozen or more events—not overly impressive for a metropolitan area with over 150,000 people. To expand participation, the high school age groups were added. The number of participants grew. As the bottom age limit continued to drop, the number of entries in the meets snowballed. A typical meet today has hundreds of participants. To make organizing and officiating easier, the meets were split into two meets per weekend. On Friday evening, beginning around 5 p.m., the adult meet (ages 15 and up) is staged, lasting usually until 7:30 or 8 p.m. On Saturday morning, the younger version of the meet is staged from 10 a.m. until about noon, and it is a sight to behold.

All events are subdivided into several age groups, beginning at the bottom with the six-and-under group, and then moving up by two-year groups (7 to 8, 9 to 10, etc.) through the 18-year-olds (17 to 18), followed by an "open" division. In some events, adult masters' categories covering 10-year blocks have been used, where adults aged 40 or older wished to compete (40 to 49, 50 to 59, etc.). Adult categories most common in the jogger's mile. Of course, races are scheduled for the boys and for the girls. To simplify matters and limit the demand for officials, all field events are completed before the running events begin. Through age 12, the short sprint is 60 yards and is contested on the grass infield in heats, with awards to each heat, and no finals. A heat of seven- and eight-year-olds might have 30 or 40 runners.

Photo 24-2. Children's meets in Medford

Competitors are limited in the number of events in which they can enter to prevent monopolizing of the ribbons. All awards, either three or five places, are stamped with the "All-Comers Meet" stamp, the year, and the place of finish. No date, other than the year, and no event designation are used. For children, the entry fee is 25 cents for up to four events. For adults, it is 25 cents for each event. For the six-and-under groups (to enter, they must be able to pronounce their name), the three events are: the 60-yard dash on the grass, the 220-yard run around a turn, and the standing long jump.

To save time on the long jump, a board with the distances is placed alongside the pit, so the length of the jump can be given without using a measuring tape. Since five places are awarded, five pegs are used to mark the leading five jumpers. Anyone not in those five takes the board measurement. After the event is completed, the five leaders have their jumps measured by tape. A similar technique is used in all throwing events, plus the running long jump. Arcs at five-foot intervals are used for the shot, and similar marks assist the discus and javelin.

The hurdle races are shorter races and are also run on the grass, regardless of the age group. For running events, if the number of entries is small for an age group several groups will run together to save time, though the results will still be tabulated separately. Finally, the winners of each event for each age group are typed out and reported to the local newspapers for publication. Seeing his name in the paper increases the athlete's interest in the sport, and seeing their child's name in the paper increases the parents' interest in the sport.

For the adult section, all standard track events that are more common are run, up through the mile. Weeks may alternate between the 3 km and 5 km runs. If interest is sufficient, other races, such as the 3,000m steeplechase, are run.

A jogger's mile, the first running event every Friday evening, beginning around 5:45 or 6:00 p.m., is also included. The men and women run together in this event, since neither sex has a natural advantage over the other. Each runner writes down his predicted time for the mile and turns it in before the race. The person running closest to the estimated time wins. No watches or timing aids are allowed. Speed is no advantage. If one runner runs 5:05 after predicting 5:08, while another predicted 7:00 and ran 6:58, the 6:58 runner would win, being only 2 seconds off. This race is run in two groups. The first race is the "over 7:30," or slow group, those predicting a run no faster than that time. The second race is the "fast group," those running no slower than 7:30 (predicted) and no faster than 5:00. Anyone breaking 5:00 is declared a racer and disqualified. These two races attract entries from 10 years and under to 70 years and older.

The summer meets are held for four or five weekends each summer, beginning on the weekend after the Fourth of July and running through mid-August. The meets are usually preceded by several clinics for young people in the different events, given at schools throughout the community by local teachers and coaches and announced ahead of time in the newspapers and over radio and television.

The summer track program is sponsored by the Oregon Track Club, the successor to the Emerald Empire Athletic Association, a group of local citizens interested in the advancement of track and field in the Eugene-Springfield metropolitan area and the state of Oregon. Incidentally, the experience at putting on large meets regularly had much to do with Eugene winning bids to have the NCAA Track and Field Championships several times, as well as three U.S. Olympic Trials from 1972 to 1980 (and another in 2008), in a metropolitan area that ranked only 139th in the United States in population in 1970.

Community Jogging Programs

The second valuable community program is the jogging program. It performs several vital services, for not only does it acquaint the adults of the community with the track program to some degree, but also it is an excellent public service to the local citizens' state of physical fitness. The jogging boom in the United States began in Eugene, Oregon. Late in 1962, a small group of Oregon distance runners traveled to New Zealand with Bill Bowerman as American representatives for a series of races organized by the sports bodies of the two nations. Bowerman was introduced to a popular activity called "jogging" by the outstanding New Zealand coach Arthur Lydiard.

Deeply impressed by his own miserably unfit showing when jogging with the New Zealanders, some of them in their 70s, Bowerman publicized Lydiard's jogging program on his return to Oregon in January of 1963. He immediately extended an invitation to interested adults to join him in jogging sessions at the Oregon track. A small number of outings brought a mass of hundreds of people swarming over the track at one time. Bowerman stopped at that point and set out to develop a definite, safe jogging program. Working with W. E. Harris, a local cardiologist, he experimented with a group of adults, aged 25 to 66, to discover how much work the typical adult male and female could perform while benefiting, but not undergoing undue stress. The result of the studies was publicized nationwide, bringing correspondence from around the world asking for jogging programs. A small booklet of programs was prepared, and then in 1967, a book of over 120 pages was published, giving the principles and techniques of jogging, plus a number of graduated schedules for getting started and then continuing in jogging.

Jogging is simply a program designed to promote physical fitness by improving the condition of the body's cardiovascular system through a program of regular exercise consisting of slow, easy running. It is not a strenuous exercise program. The key is a quote from Arthur Lydiard: "Train, don't strain." It is the jogger's motto. The ideal is easy, comfortable running. For this reason, anyone running the jogger's mile under five minutes is disqualified. If he is moving that fast, he is no longer jogging; he is running or racing.

The school's track coach is the natural person to promote jogging in the community. This introduction can be done under the auspices of the school itself or through community groups, such as the Department of Parks and Recreation, the YMCA, or any similar interested group. The coach can volunteer to speak to groups on jogging, explaining the principles and demonstrating the techniques, or even better, having his athletes demonstrate the techniques.

Groups could be welcomed if they wish to use the school track for jogging when it is not being used for school activities. Jogging classes or groups might be led at the track by members of the track team. This invitation is excellent community relations, for it benefits the local people in terms of health, and at the same time it makes them a bit more aware of the track team through the influence of the coach and the contact with his athletes. Detailed programs are outlined in the book Jogging, by William J. Bowerman and W. E. Harris, which has been published in many nations around the world.

These two particular programs, the all-comers meets and the jogging program, can be extremely helpful in building a place in the community for the school's track program. They build interest and provide experience while offering activities that will be genuine public services. They should not be expected to be overnight successes; they may take years to develop to the point that major benefits to the community and to the school's programs can be seen. The time invested will be worthwhile.

Non-Varsity School Track Programs

This suggested concern for a strong community program does not mean that the school program should be neglected or played down in any way. However, it should be projected beyond the traditional narrow bounds in which it has been used. The school program of track and field activities should not be limited to the varsity program, for it has much wider applicability to student needs. Two particular phases of the non-varsity program should be considered: the physical education classes and the intramural program.

The school's physical education classes should have as their prime objective the physical fitness of the students, followed closely by providing activities that the students will enjoy and that have carry-over value to their adult life. The track and field activities carry this appeal, as do few of the other competitive sports. The first question asked by the physical education teacher is: what activities can we offer? The second question might concern their value to the students' lives and the school's physical education program.

Three basic units are recommended for the high school curriculum: cross country, track and field, and jogging. Cross country has as perhaps its greatest value the cardiovascular benefits derived from the training. Few sports require as much of the competitor's cardiovascular and respiratory systems. Another positive aspect of cross country is that undersized students hold a small advantage in such competition. The best cross country runners are often the smallest of the school's athletes. The smaller student, at a disadvantage in most sports because of his size, will be happy to find a sport in which he does not begin at a disadvantage.

Track and Field Events

The track and field unit has a great advantage in the variety of activities that it offers. Every student should be able to find some event at which he can be a passable success, and training in all the events gives as well-rounded physical training as can be found in any physical fitness activities. The track and field unit can have several possible variations. The men might have a unit on the decathlon, using the training methods and scoring tables mentioned in Chapter 22. This unit provides some standardization of grading, plus gives natural competition over the whole unit and within each of the 10 sub-parts of the unit. For the women, the pentathlon (100-meter hurdles, long jump, shot-put, high jump, and 200 meters), heptathlon, or the newer women's decathlon might be used.

Jogging

A class in jogging does not give immediate large gains in physical fitness to most young students, but it is more valuable than many activities for its long-term usability. A class involving running aids the student in building a physical fitness base that might be a good start before going into more strenuous physical activities. Students might find it interesting when presented in terms of weight control. Finally, it can be carried out throughout the ordinary person's lifetime with no more equipment than a pair of shoes and no other people required as teammates or competitors. No other lifetime sport can offer this claim. Also, if physical education activities are offered on a five-day-a-week basis, it can be sandwiched into another unit, such as on Tuesdays and Thursdays, as an alternate activity to help prevent boredom with the other activity.

The college physical education program allows a greater variety of course offerings, with more specialized instruction. Activity courses might be offered in track and field, cross country, decathlon, and jogging. In larger schools, some interested students might like a class in road running. Many students might be interested in a jogging class. Classes in track and jogging can easily be used as coeducational activities. Class schedules can easily be adapted from the fall training schedules given in the Chapter 22 on the decathlon, while the jogging schedules in the original 1967 book work well for instructional classes.

Intramural Sports

Intramural sports is another area of potential interest in track and field activities that should not be overlooked by the physical education teacher or athletics coach. Common intramural offerings are a single cross country meet and a single track and field meet. Considerable student interest might result from the offering of a decathlon for the men and perhaps a heptathlon or decathlon for the women.

High schools commonly offer a single cross country intramural race, with the cross country lettermen or team members not allowed to compete. This race often takes place in November, sometimes being called a "Turkey Race" in honor of the Thanksgiving holiday. One variation is to have team competition, either by physical education classes or homeroom units in the high school or by fraternities, dormitory units, or non-affiliated or day-student groups on the college level. Awards might be ribbons, medals, or small trophies. In some cases, the winners (individual and team) might have an award of a turkey given in their name to a needy family.

Track and field competition should be both team and individual competition, organized around units similar to those suggested for cross country. On the college level, sufficient interest in team competition might permit the organization of a small number of dual meets between teams, with all the meets conducted at the same time.

An added fun competition is for "best athlete" in each competition. Freeman has used this with a college track team, using the old "Portuguese Tables." Academics have tried to rate the values of all track and field event performances, though more accurately in the combined event tables. Athletics Canada uses the Mercier Tables online as a way of comparing performances. Using scoring tables such as Mercier's or the "Hungarian Tables," a coach can compare the performance of a shot-putter to a miler, a high jumper to a sprinter. A coach can rank the Top 10 or Top 25 performances for each meet, as well as seasonal bests. Athletes find it an entertaining challenge to be more competitive in their performances.

Decathlon and similar competitions would be individually scored, though variations of team scoring are possible. These events are good to stage to discover the school's best "all-around" athletes. For suggestions on scoring such contests, see Chapter 22 on the decathlon.

Recommended Readings

Baumann, Alex. (2002). Developing sustained high performance services and systems that have quality outcomes. In *12th Commonwealth International Sport Conference (19-23 July 2002, Manchester, United Kingdom) Abstract Book.* London: Association of Commonwealth Universities, 66-71.

Bowerman, William J., and Harris, W. E. (1968). *Jogging.* New York: Grosset and Dunlap.

Bussmann, Gaby. (1999). How to prevent "dropout" in competitive sport. *New Studies in Athletics, 14*(1), 23-29.

Christensen, Scott. (1991). True team track & field. *Track Technique, 117,* 3728-3729.

De Swardt, Arie. (1998). Coaching women–A contribution to the IAAF Year of Women in Athletics. *New Studies in Athletics, 13*(2), 7-9.

Digel, Helmut. (2002). A comparison of competitive sport systems. *New Studies in Athletics, 17*(1), 37-50.

Doherty, Ken. (2007). *Track & Field Omnibook* (5th ed.). Mountain View, CA: Tafnews.

Drewe, Sheryle Bergmann. (2000). An examination of the relationship between coaching and teaching. *Quest, 52,* 79-88.

Ebbets, Russ, ed. (Spring 2003). High school team dynamics round table. *Track Coach, 163,* 5193-5198, 5208. Participants: Greg Isham, Scott Christensen, Oscar Jensen & George Dunn, Jr.

Field, Richard W. (1991). Coach as a role model: What are his salient roles and how do others perceive them? *Track Technique, 117*, 3730-3733.

Fraley, Bob. (Fall 2005). Sports have a huge impact on our culture. *Track Coach, 173,* 5512, 5531-5532. How to improve T&F interest in the U.S., from Pole Vault Standard.

Guthrie, Mark. (2003). Building a successful track & field program. *Coaching track and field successfully.* Champaign, IL: Human Kinetics, 37-44.

Hazen, Jack. (2004). Making a team a team. *Training for cross country.* Mountain View, CA: Tafnews, 80-87.

Hennessy, Geoff. (1996). Problems affecting development of potential trackies. *Track Coach, 135,* 4296, 4324.

Hickey, Christopher. (Summer 2003). Recruiting, training and retaining high school track & field coaches. *Track Coach, 164,* 5225-5232, 5240.

Jegathesan, Manikavasagam. (1999). Athletes' travel management–A necessity, not a luxury. *New Studies in Athletics, 14*(4), 7-13.

Kantola, Rick. (Winter 2005). High school track coach survey results. *Track Coach, 170,* 5417-5421, 5426.

Lammi, Eric. (Summer 2002). Building a successful high school program. *Track Coach, 160,* 5119-5120.

Martindale, Russell J.J., Dave Collins & Jim Daubney. (2005). Talent development: A guide for practice and research within sport. *Quest, 57,* 353-375.

McDonald, Craig, Steve James & Tom Kutschkau. (1989). Elements of a successful prep track program. *Track Technique, 107,* 3403-3408.

McGill, Kevin. (1996). From the Editor. On low performance levels of younger athletes & the new Chula Vista Olympic center. *Track Coach, 134,* 4264, 4279; Reabold, Russ. (1996). Lack of top performance at the younger ages. Track Coach, 136, 4354; McGill, Kevin. (1996). Reply to Reabold. *Track Coach, 136,* 4354, 4357.

Myers, Nicholas D., Deborah L. Feltz, Kimberly S. Maier, Edward W. Wolfe & Mark D. Reckase. (2006). Athletes' evaluations of their head coach's coaching competency. *Research Quarterly for Exercise and Sport, 77*(1), 111-121.

Newland, Bob. (1970). [Eugene, Oregon] *Summer All-Comers Program.* United States Track and Field Federation.

Noakes, Tim. (1991). The dangers of early specialization [abstract]. *Track Technique, 117*, 3741-3742.

Oakley, Ben, & Mick Green. (2001). The production of Olympic champions: International perspectives on elite sport development systems. *European Journal for Sport Management, 8*(1), 83-105.

Rogers, Joseph L. Organizing a successful program. (2000). In *USA Track and Field coaching manual.* Champaign, IL: Human Kinetics, 3-17.

Rushall, Brent, & Norman F. Lavoie. (1983). A call to re-focus serious sport training. *Sports Science Periodical on Research and Technology in Sport, W-1,* 1-5.

Sanderson, Lyle. (1989). Growth and development considerations for the design of training plans for young athletes. *Sports, 10*(2).

Schiffer, Jürgen. (2000). Selected and annotated bibliography 53: Coaching and coaches. *New Studies in Athletics, 15*(2), 75-102.

Shakespear, Wilma. (2002). Developing sustained high performance services and systems that have quality outcomes. In *12th Commonwealth International Sport Conference (19-23 July 2002, Manchester, United Kingdom) Abstract Book.* London: Association of Commonwealth Universities, 73-79.

Spiriev, Bojidar, Attila Spiriev & Gábor Kovács. (1992). *Scoring tables of athletics.* Budapest: Elite.

Zelichnok, Vadim. (2006). From junior star to elite performer [abstract]. *New Studies in Athletics, 21*(1), 66.

25

Organizing and Administering Competitions

Few people realize the difficulties involved in putting on a well-run track and field competition. The meet must be run well to ensure two things:

- The better it is run, the more efficiently the athletes can prepare and the more successfully they can perform.
- The better it is run, the more appeal it will hold for your spectators. The net result of this care will be happier, more successful athletes; happier and more numerous spectators; and a happier, more successful coach. This combination is what every person wants ultimately.

The Meet Director

For most small meets, the track coach is considered the meet director, but he should carefully consider other possibilities. The success of any given meet depends heavily upon the work of the meet director. During a meet, the coach is concerned with helping his athletes, within the bounds of the rules. He cannot successfully fulfill that function and at the same time direct a meet properly. Because of this conflict in duties, both of which are important, he should pick and train a meet director to direct the meets at his school, if at all possible. (Most coaches will react by saying that it is not possible, and 99 out of every 100 of them will be wrong.)

The meet director is the key to the success of the meet. He must be a leader, he must be an administrator, and he must be willing to take charge and run the meet. He will have to be more knowledgeable of the rules than the coach (not as difficult a task as most coaches think), and he must have the resolve to enforce them strictly and fairly, no matter who they affect. He must be skillful in handling people, and he must be as non-partisan as possible. The only aforementioned quality that is not necessary in a good meet director is that the meet director be a "he."

Responsibilities of the Meet Director

The responsibilities of the meet director are many. To clearly understand the duties of the people in charge of running a meet, any person who plans to run a meet should get the appropriate rule books, depending upon his affiliation and the auspices under which the meet is being run.

For some clarifications of the rules and a clearer understanding of what should be done, copies of the IAAF rulebook are highly recommended. The director must keep in mind that variations in rules and specifications occur from one set of rules to another. If an NCAA school puts on a high school meet, it must be run under the high school rulebook. For its own meets, it uses the NCAA rules. If it puts on an open (not limited to colleges) meet, it must also use the USATF rules, while an Olympic Trials and Games must follow the international rules (IAAF). If you are confused, then you know why it is difficult to be a good track coach and meet director at the same time.

The preliminary details of the meet, the major details, must first be determined: when, where, the schedule, and the finances. For a dual meet, you have no real problem. The date and place have been agreed upon, often being set by the conference itself (except for non-conference meets). The time for starting is often set in the same manner. The order of events is either suggested or clearly stated in most rulebooks below the international level, so little problem should be had with that aspect. The time to allow for each event, the methods of seeding, and heat schedules (if required) are also given in the rulebooks, so they should cause little problem.

Expenses

Expenses may be a matter of some concern, especially for the larger meets. For most dual meets, you will find only minor problems, if expenses are even considered. Most small track meets charge little or no admission, so shares of gate proceeds are not a concern. The cost of awards may be defrayed by either having them covered in the annual budget, taking them out of the gate receipts (if there are any), having them donated in some manner, or by charging team or individual entry fees. Track is not a "money sport," so finances usually enter the picture only in very large meets.

Finding a Meet Official

The preparation of the meet officials is the next item of concern. If the officiating is poor, or even the least bit suspect, the meet will not be much of a success. A good number of qualified officials are indispensable to the successful track program. A "spur-of-the-moment" official is often of less value than no official at all, for his lack of knowledge of the rules deters him from doing the athlete justice. As a timer, his work renders times in short races totally worthless. Find some sports-minded or civic-minded people who might be interested in helping with your meets. If possible, interest a civic group, such as the Jaycees or Kiwanis, for they will provide more people and enthusiasm, plus give more of a sense of group cohesion to the task.

Training a Meet Official

When you have found the officials, you are halfway home. Next, they must be trained. Many groups, such as USATF, have set up regular programs for training, testing, and certifying track and field officials. The track coach will be the first instructor, and then when a meet director has been trained, he will either take over the duty of training the officials or share it with the coach. The training should begin with several sessions of reviewing the rules that will be used, in both "the letter of the law" and "the intent of the law." Each official should have his own copy of the rulebook, and he should carry it with him to each meet where he officiates.

After the officials have a good working knowledge of the rules, it would be most beneficial if a field test is provided, so each official could have the opportunity to practice at the track and see the types of situations that he might encounter in an actual competition. This test can be done during time trials or some similar semi-official type of competition. Preferably, the new officials would work under the supervision of an experienced official, so they can be assisted where necessary and evaluated more fairly.

Evaluating the Meet Official

The evaluation of the officials should be based on a combination of performance on a written open-book test on the rules and the official's proficiency test at the track. Each official should also have one or two events or areas in which he specializes. He needs to know the rules in all areas, but he should be certified in specialized areas in which his competence will be high. The USATF has a system of certifying officials on the local, state, and national level, which is a good example of what the coach is trying to develop. Once the meet is provided with officials trained in this manner, 90 percent of the technical snafus encountered in most meets can be eliminated before they begin.

The Track Meet

The meet officials should have a gathering place off the track, so they will not interfere with other events as they come together. They should have some item of identification, preferably an item of clothing such as a cap or shirt or jacket with a suitable emblem and in a suitable color. This system identifies them to the marshals, who have the duty of keeping the competition area clear of non-competitors, coaches, and others who are not supposed to be on the track, and it makes them readily identifiable to the athletes, who may need to find an official in a hurry.

All items used by the officials—such as clipboards, tapes, watches, or rakes—should be kept in a single, off-the-track location, where they can be checked out when they are needed for use and checked in as soon as the event is concluded, thereby avoiding complaints by disgruntled tape-seekers and such.

The officials should know who is in charge of an event and who is their immediate superior, in case any questions come up that they cannot answer or any protests. They must always know either the answer or who will definitely know the answer. Finally, a place should be designated in the stands, or at least off the track, where any officials not actively working on an assigned duty can gather, for they ought to be out of the way and enjoying the meet.

Scoring Contingencies

What if a record is set? How many people never think of that contingency? How many people have lost records because the equipment did not meet the required specifications, or the wind was not gauged, or problems of that nature? At any respectable meet at which the slightest quality of competition occurs, a wind gauge and trained operator should be used. The track and field area must be surveyed and certified by a surveyor, not a groundskeeper with 50-foot tape. The track and all starts, finishes, lane-marking staggers, relay zones, and hurdle markings must be surveyed and certified (in such situations, the all-weather track with permanent is a gift from heaven). Circles and elevation plus throwing

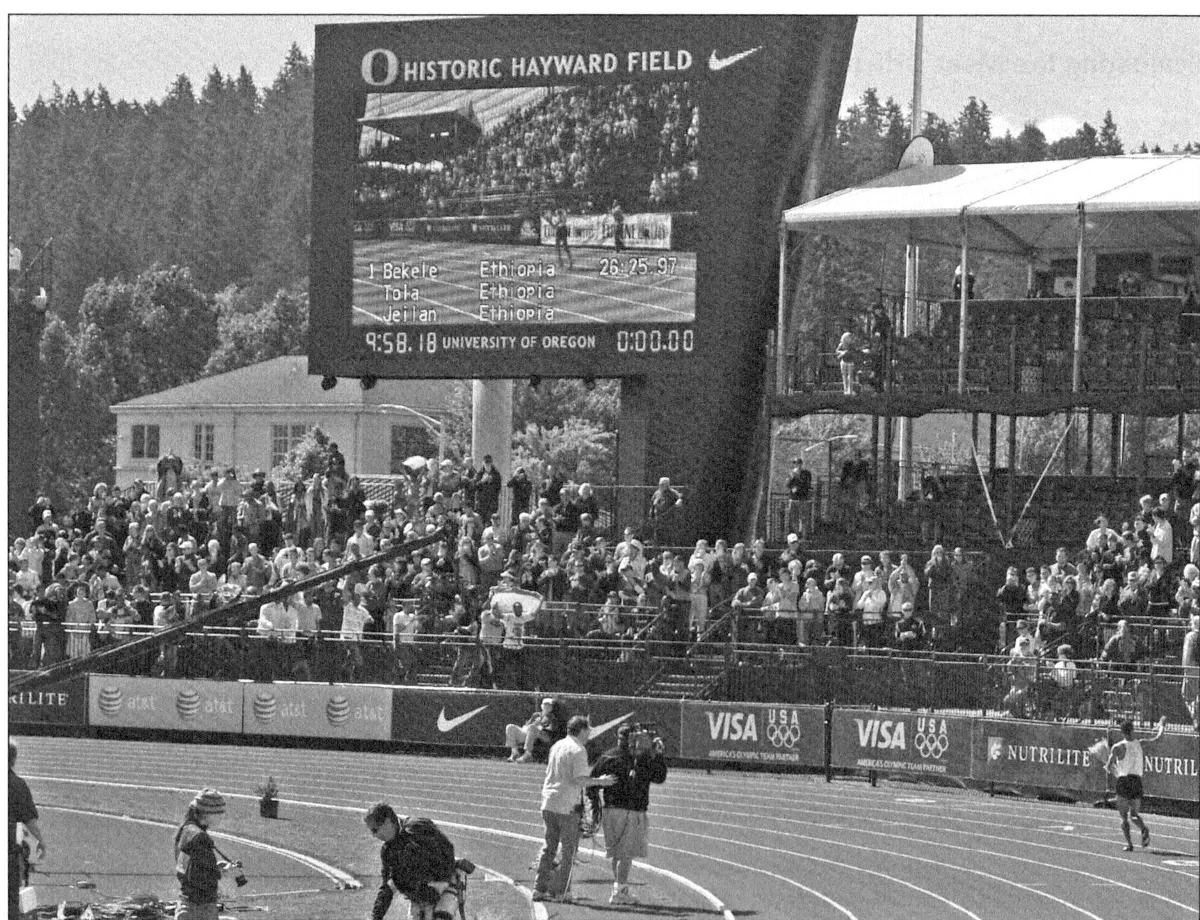

Photo 25-1. Prefontaine Classic, 2008

sectors must be checked. Before the meet, and after a record, implements must be weighed and measured for legality. A last word on weights and measures: a track with a curb has its circumference measured one foot (12 inches) out from the curb; a track with no curb and only a painted line for the inside of the track has its circumference measured only eight inches out from the line. If you are preparing to have an all-weather built, make sure the architect and builder know and understand that fact. The same is true for the surveyor. Many tracks in this nation are one or two yards long per lap because no one thought of that one small rule.

A trained man should handle the weights and measure all field implements. An off-the-track station should be set up, where all implements are weighed and measured, after which they should be marked in a manner known to the event officials (most common is a spot of paint from a spray-can in an agreed-upon color, which should change from meet to meet). If a record is set, the winning implement is checked again for certification.

Finally, the coach should have available a set of records-sheets (applications for records) for any level at which a competitor could conceivably reach. Sets are available for high school records, junior colleges, NAIA, NCAA (all divisions), American (USATF) and world (IAAF). The reason is simple: it is the simplest time to get all the necessary signatures on the paper to certify the record.

Crowd Facilities

The next item to consider in the successful meet is crowd comfort. If the meet is run well, many problems are solved, but suppose no seats are available for the spectators, or they tend to acquire splinters where they are hard to remove? The facility must be comfortable with good seating, placed as close as possible to where the action is. There should also be convenient, clean restrooms available close to the seats, as few spectators come to hike, particularly under stress. If admission is charged, people should be available to collect tickets and direct traffic, especially if any seats are reserved. If possible, concession stands, clean and well run, are good to have, but only if enough spectators are present to warrant them. Keep the people interested and happy, and they will come back. If they will come back, track will grow.

The Meet Announcer

One person is as important to the success of the meet as the meet director, and he is not usually a coach: he is the meet announcer. The meet announcer can put the crowd to sleep (or not disturb their slumbers), or he can get them interested and excited. Every school using an announcer at meets has a customary announcer for all sports events. Is he really the one for the track meet, though? He may not be. The track meet announcer has several characteristics (if he is good):

- He is a good announcer (voice and delivery).
- He likes track very much.

- He is very knowledgeable about track (the rules, the records, the people competing at home and elsewhere).
- He likes to give thorough information, but he is not in love with the sound of his voice.

If any these points are not met, he is not the announcer you want. The first point can be corrected some degree, and the third point can also be corrected, but if he does not pass number two, get a new person.

Many things are desired from an announcer, but the following is what you need the most:

- Accurate information as soon as it is available.
- Thorough information as soon as possible (e.g., what is the height of the bar, what jump is it, how far was that throw, what was his time or place, what and when is the next event).
- Information to help the competitor, such as how long until the next event, the calls for events, running scores, and (if he cannot hear them at the track) accurate lap times for the leader.

Notice that the emphasis is placed upon speed, accuracy, and thoroughness. The announcer should work in that order. The crowd wants results immediately. They want them as accurately as possible (if they are unofficial, announce them as unofficial, for the winner—do not give unofficial place times). As soon as available, they want thorough information. For such instances, the announcer needs an assistant to feed him the information as fast as it happens. An announcer can make a good meet great, and he can make a great meet confusing. Choose and train an announcer with care. You may have to do it yourself.

Publicity and Promotion

Publicity and promotion for the meet are necessary only as the larger meets approach. The coach should make information available for the local news media. Pictures should be available of the better athletes. Written (typed) information should also be available for the media. The coach may have to write everything, including color stories on his team, but if it is necessary, he should do it. Let the local newspaper, radio and television stations know what is going to happen before and after it happens. "During" is their responsibility. If a meet charges admission, press passes or photographers' passes should be available, arranged ahead of time (and with set, strict ground rules against hampering the competition if allowed on the field). Copies of meet schedules and coming events should be sent to all potentially interested bodies well ahead of time, and results should be sent out after the competition is completed (as soon as possible). In a large city, telephone. The more cooperative and helpful you are with the press, the better they will treat you and your team. In the long run, more will get done for sport of track and field.

Many books have chapters on running contests, whether track meets, sports carnivals, or other large sporting events. They will offer further suggestions on running meets and the problems that are encountered. Perhaps the best way to prepare for a large competition is the method used in Eugene, Oregon, to prepare for any kind of competition which has not been put on recently: the dry run.

To prepare for the 1972 United States Olympic Trials Decathlon, four preliminary decathlons were held, three small ones were used to train the meet director and his officials in the peculiarities of the decathlon competition and test their ideas, and then the NCAA decathlon provided a national-class test of the final plans. By the time the actual Olympic Trials began, every person connected with the running of the competition knew exactly what was expected of him, most problems had been anticipated, and the competition ran very smoothly. Only experience works out all the bugs.

The way to success in running meets is to try to foresee anything, no matter how minor, that could possibly go wrong and try to correct it before it happens. This preparation is done mentally in every aspect of the meet as it is being planned. It is then done physically in the dry-run meets or less important competitions where the theories are tested. Finally, it is put into action at the competition itself, hopefully with all the bugs long since corrected. The job of the meet director is to be so thorough that the spectators will think, "Any idiot could run that." If a meet is run well, the officials and meet directors will hardly ever be noticed. How many sports contests can make that claim?

Recommended Readings

Newland, Robert. (June 1967). Oregon summer all-comers track meet program, Track and Field Quarterly Review, 48-60.

Phelps, Dale E. (March 1969). Conducting a track and field meet with inexperienced personnel. Athletic Journal, 49, 28, 30, 110.

Bill Bowerman and the Men of Oregon: The Pursuit of the Collegiate Four-Minute Mile (1954-1973)

William H. Freeman

Presented at the North American Society for Sport History Convention
Banff, Canada
May 28, 2000

Appendix

An Associated Press listing of "notable deaths in 1999" included this statement:

> Bill Bowerman, 88. Track coach who invented modern running shoe and co-founded Nike to put those shoes on everyone from backyard athletes to Olympians.[1]

It is a brief note to close the book on a major force in American track and field athletics, and it ignored his earlier reputation as a great coach.

Concurrently, the opening of the year 2000 led to endless compilations of historical lists of accomplishments and change. *Track & Field News* produced "End-of-Century" features that including a striking (but uncontested) statement: "The choice of the single most memorable track moment of the century was an easy one—Roger Bannister's breaking of the 4:00 barrier in the mile."[2]

During the 20th century, perhaps the most recognized standard in track and field athletics (the premier Olympic sport) was the four-minute mile. Bannister's race on May 6, 1954, resulted in front-page coverage and photographs in the *New York Times,*[3] with sports-section articles on the history of the record and reactions from top milers around the world.[4] In a telling comment that contrasts to sport in 2000, 1500-meter Olympic champion Josey Barthel of Luxembourg said that Bannister deserved the honor:

> Because he works hard and loves running, not for the glory, but for the satisfaction it gives him ... He is an amateur in a real and true sense—in the best English tradition.[5]

To further emphasize the attention on the sub-four mile, it resulted in photo articles in both *Time* and *Newsweek,* with follow-up articles on a good-will visit by Bannister to the United States in the following week.[6]

To further illustrate the intense focus on achieving a sub-four mile in that era, the feature article for the first issue of *Sports Illustrated* was a four-page photo and text report of the Bannister-Landy race at the 1954 British Empire and Commonwealth Games,[7] still one of the most famous races ever run. John Landy of Australia had quickly followed Bannister under the mark, beating his time for a new world record. By the time of the Games in August, they were the only men who had ever broken the barrier, and they were scheduled to race head-to-head. Descriptions of the race included these telling comments:

> Few events in sport offer so ultimate a test of human courage and human will and human ability to dare and endure for the simple sale of struggle…Roger Bannister reigned again as the giant of modern track.[8]

The description was of superhuman sport. Even today, almost half a century after the barrier fell at Oxford, running a mile under four minutes is considered by the public to be a major achievement.

In the United States, one coach became recognized for his production of fast milers: Bill Bowerman of the University of Oregon. On his death on Christmas Eve of 1999, newswriters[9] focused on his legacy as the man who started the jogging boom in the United States with his 1967 book,[10] setting the stage for Cooper's *Aerobics* in the following year; the man who popularized the hard-easy concept of sport training; and the man often called the father of the modern running shoe, for his research that led to the company Nike, co-founded with one of his former milers, Phillip "Buck" Knight.

But during the peak of his coaching career, nearly two decades from 1954 to 1973, Oregon was the home of great milers, and Bill Bowerman was the source of an almost bottomless well of fast racers. From 1956 through 1972, he coached 14 runners who ran sub-four miles or their metric equivalent, with 33 sub-four performances, and another three at exactly 4:00.0. In 1962 at the Compton Relays, his team of four undergraduates ran the 4 x 1 mile relay in 16:08.9, while one returned to win the open mile in 4:00.7.[11] Their new world record cut almost 15 seconds off the old record set by the New Zealand national team, which included two Olympic champions. As an NCAA record, it survived for 37 years.

I must add a small defensive note here on Bowerman's behalf. He always protested being called a coach of milers or distance runners, pointing out that he produced high-level performances in a wide range of events—an Olympic medalist and world record holder at 100 meters, gold medalists and world-record holders at 400 meters and the discus, national collegiate or open champions in the sprints, hurdles, jumps, and throws. He had a career dual-meet record of 114-20, with 24 individual NCAA champions, 38 Pacific 8 Conference champions, 33 Olympians, and 64 collegiate All-Americans (at a time when only the top three finishers were All-Americans).[12] All of these achievements were accomplished while personally writing the training schedule for each athlete and working on the technique of every event with each athlete.

Bill Bowerman was the Oregon coach from 1948 until just before the outdoor season of 1973 when, exhausted by his time as head coach of the United States Olympic Team and devastated by the violence and heavy-handed political machinations he encountered in Munich, he retired in favor of his former runner and protégé Bill Dellinger (who had also been his first NCAA one-mile champion, later a three-time Olympian and 5,000 meter bronze medalist). Newspapers noted that at the time of his retirement, only two coaches had won more NCAA track team titles than Bowerman.[13]

The story of Oregon's four-minute milers is more interesting because when Bowerman arrived in Eugene, he was known as a coach of sprinters, particularly quarter-milers, having produced a number of high school state champions. He inherited only one distance runner: Pete Mundle.[14] Bowerman asked Mundle to research everything he could locate about distance training, then write a paper about it. That paper recommended a combination of interval training and fartlek (which was not widely known in the United States at that time). As Bowerman noted:

> Pete then became the 'guinea pig,' and those experiments laid the groundwork from which the Oregon system of distance training grew. This research led to the discovery of the great value of fartlek to the training program and to the further development of the 'hard-easy' principle of training.[15]

The major influences on the Oregon system, which was fully developed by 1964, were according to Bowerman:

> Gosta Holmer's work with fartlek, observations of John Landy's training before the 1954 British Empire Games, Franz Stampfl's writings on interval training, the theories of Mihaly Igloi, and personal contacts with Arthur Lydiard, plus useful ideas from many fine American coaches.[16]

The final (and critical) point in the development of the system was experimentation: Bowerman never accepted a training principle without experimenting with it and determining its effectiveness and limits.[17]

The simplest way to show the impact of Oregon's sub-four-minute milers is through three key events: the first sub-four race in the United States, the first sub-four race on the University of Oregon campus in Eugene, and the 1962 world record for the four-mile relay. Reaction to those events are the best indicators of how important such a performance was considered in the 1950s and 1960s.

The first sub-4:00 mile in the United States (and the Western Hemisphere) was run in the Memorial Colosseum in Los Angeles on Saturday, May 5, 1956.[18] The occasion was a tour by Australian world-record holder (3:58.0) John Landy. The race was considered so important that it was broadcast live on national radio and television for 15 minutes immediately after the Kentucky Derby, at a time when televised sports events were still uncommon. The race organizers invited a number of prominent collegiate milers, including Ron Delany of Ireland and Villanova (NCAA and Olympic 1500m champion later that year) and Bill Dellinger and Jim Bailey of the University of Oregon. Dellinger had been NCAA mile champion in 1954, then runner-up to his teammate Bailey (an Australian with previous races against Landy) in 1955. Dellinger's 4:10.6 race in 1954 had broken the long-standing Oregon school record of 4:12.4 set by Olympian Ralph Hill in 1930,[19] while in 1955 Dellinger improved to 4:04.6, with Bailey running 4:05.6. Prior to the Los Angeles race, both Bailey and Dellinger had seasonal bests of 4:10.[20]

Oregon newspapers touted the race with daily reports of the competitors expected to challenge Landy, though none seriously considered that he could lose.[21] The 40,000 spectators were shocked when Jim Bailey put on a burst at the close of the race and defeated Landy, missing the world record by less than one second in 3:58.6, with Landy at 3:58.7. The race made headlines across the country, from the *New York Times* to the Oregon dailies, with feature articles in *Time, Newsweek,* and *Sports Illustrated.* National newspapers and magazines published sequence photographs of the dash to the finish line.[22]

Of special interest were the indications of two characteristics of the Oregon training system: undertraining and speed. Bowerman inherited the idea of not overtraining athletes from his college coach, Bill Hayward. It was a characteristic of his approach to training throughout his career. As he put it, "I want my runners to be hungry to race." After Bailey's 3:58.6, reporter Art Litchman noted:

> The experts also found it hard to believe that Bailey had run so little this past week and had jogged only a half mile Thursday and another half mile Friday on the grass back of the hotel in preparation for the race.[23]

In contrast, Landy's race-morning workout consisted of a six-mile run.24 Another report noted that during the summer Bailey loaded lumber as a job and ran only three or four days a week, adding, "He'd like to run more, but his Oregon coach, Bill Bowerman, is a believer in not too much work and keeping the sport a pleasure."25 During this time, coaches and athletes believed that a sub-4:00 record required superhuman training loads and intensities.

At the same time, reporters were awed by reports of Bailey's finishing kick. He ran the last 440 yards in 55.5 seconds, which converts to 55.2 seconds on today's metric tracks. It was an Olympic year, with faster-than-usual performances, yet the fifth-fastest American ran only 4:08.0 (62 seconds per 440), and no man in the world beat Bailey's time that year.[26]

Bailey's race confirmed that Oregon was a school that could produce world-class milers. Indeed, by the next year, the graduating Bailey and Dellinger were replaced by young Jim Grelle, who ran 4:07.1 as a sophomore, finishing second to Olympic Champion Ron Delany at the NCAA meet.[27] By 1959, Grelle had become an NCAA champion and run a 4:01.0 mile (finishing in 56 seconds), and was on the verge of being overshadowed by the next in line, Dyrol Burleson, who ran an NCAA freshman record of 4:06.7 and won the U.S. open championship that year.[28]

Burleson came to the university from less than 20 miles away after setting a national high school mile record of 4:13.2 in 1958. By the time he graduated in 1962, Oregon's position as a school for fast milers was firm. He won the NCAA title all three years of his eligibility (freshman were ineligible for varsity competition at that time), including the fastest mile run in the eastern United States to that time, and finished with an NCAA meet record of 3:59.8 in 1962.[29] By 1962, Oregon runners at been first or second in the NCAA mile for nine straight years, six of them as champion, with 14 top-six places. However, it did not require four years to make Burleson's reputation.

By 1960, four years after Jim Bailey ran the first sub-4:00 mile in the United States, Bowerman and Oregon were widely known for mile runners. Bowerman had published an article on training milers in a major coaching journal, following an earlier effort reprinted in places usually familiar only to college coaches, so high school coaches had their first serious look at how Oregon's milers were trained.[30] The article included sequence photos of back-to-back NCAA champions Grelle and Burleson, and introduced the hard-easy approach to training.

Burleson was already becoming familiar to the American public as a 19-year-old runner, with a short article and photo in *Time,* and a longer lead article in Sports Illustrated, which focused on Bowerman and Hungarian coach Mihaly Igloi and commented of Bowerman that "eight of his runners are capable of 4:10 or faster" (including two post-collegiate runners). Even in 1960, publications commented on his experiments with lightweight running shoes.[31]

However, this media attention was only a prelude to April 23, 1960—noted on the front page of the Sunday *New York Times* as "Burleson, in 3:58.6, Sets Mile Record For an American."[32] Interestingly, while he set a U.S. record, he only tied the university's four-year-old school record. Other coverage included a note and photo in *Sports Illustrated* and a short note in *Newsweek.*[33] In Eugene, however, coverage was intense. The *Eugene Register-Guard* ran a headline above the paper's name on the front page of the Saturday evening paper, following on Sunday with headlines and photos above the newspaper's name at the start of the sports section, and including six photos to mark the event. The reporter commented, "Even the Oregon baseball team was on hand for the mile before it returned to Howe Field and a game with Washington State."[34]

Forty years after the event, it was described in the university's alumni magazine as "one of the most important races in the history of Oregon track and field." "Burley," as he was called, became only the second American under the mark, which "had become a major obsession for runners the world over."[35] Within a month, he was featured on the cover of *Sports Illustrated* with Herb Elliott, the world record holder, under the title "World's Best Miler Meets a U.S. Challenge."[36]

The peak of the Burleson years came with the third major event, headlined in the May 13, 1962, *Eugene Register-Guard* as "Oregon Snaps World Four-Mile Relay Mark."[37] Running at the West Coast Relays in Fresno, the Duck relay team stunned the track world with the magnitude of their record. They cut almost four seconds per runner from a record set not by a collegiate foursome, but by a national team; even more, the New Zealand team had included two Olympic champions, Peter Snell and Murray Halberg, both sub-4:00 runners.

The race reinforced the 1960 articles that focused not on the speed of Oregon's top runner, but on the large number of fast runners. It was a team of undergraduates with two sub-4:00 runners, and two other men under 4:04. *Track & Field News* called the relay effort "one of the most impressive performances in the annals of track," pointing out that they had no assisting competition, lapping their opponents.[38] Indeed, Bowerman had planned to try for the world record in the distance medley relay at the same meet, but conditions became windy and the attempt was cancelled.[39] Within two weeks, Keith Forman became Oregon's next sub-4:00 runner with a 3:58.3 in Modesto, with a last quarter in 56.7 seconds.[40] Famed coach Arthur Lydiard of New Zealand publicly declared Bill Bowerman "the greatest track coach in the world."[41]

Oregon's rise to track prominence was sealed within a month as the team won their first NCAA title in Eugene, resulting in national references to a new "track dynasty,"[42] while the Oregon papers waxed ecstatic, with references to the magnitude and ease of the victory (they would have won even without the 30 points contributed by seniors),[43] even going so far as to produced a celebratory cartoon for the Eugene paper's editorial page.[44]

At that point, Bowerman's and Oregon's reputations were established. Oregon had become a track power, and Bowerman's coaching prowess was nationally recognized. He was making appearances speaking on conditioning and training to the American Medical Association, and he had published articles on his training ideas for the mile and his joint research on proper running mechanics.[45] One result of the four-mile relay record was an invitation to race his milers in New Zealand, where he encountered jogging, which he subsequently researched, then developed into a national fitness craze in 1967.[46] By 1968, *Track & Field News* was referring to "A Coach and a Tradition," focusing on the phenomenal numbers of national-class middle distance runners produced by Bowerman.[47]

Over his career, Bowerman coached about 20 sub-4:00 runners, including postgraduates. Until his death at age 88, runners from across the nation would turn up at his door,[48] if only to (as one New Zealand coach put it) "sit at the feet of the guru." Even in the relative isolation of a retirement home in Fossil, almost 200 miles from the population centers of Oregon, runners and coaches made their way to visit him. As perhaps a final footnote, one that may outlast the laudatory news clippings, his personality was reflected in a motion picture co-written by Kenny Moore, one of his runners and Olympians. *Without Limits* was about Steve Prefontaine, but the picture focused heavily on the relationship between Pre and Bowerman, illustrating Bowerman's obsession with the perfection of performance, but above all, his focus on winning. Pre saw a race as a work of art, a test to show who was toughest, most dominant; Bowerman saw it as a contest with victory as the desired outcome. Thus, he focused on patience and a fast finish, rather than leading and dominating the race, as Pre preferred. Together, they produced one of America's all-time great runners, a man who was still on U.S. all-time top-10 lists 25 years after his premature death. Even so, Pre wanted to hold Oregon's mile record—and ran 3:54.6.[49] He was yet another in the long line.

How did Bowerman achieve this staggering output, especially in a relatively small outpost in the Pacific Northwest? A few years ago, I considered that question in a preface:

> Bowerman's record is in part the result of several personal traits: a deep interest in track; a passion to find the better, more economical way to do anything; constant attempts to provide the "ideal" competitive situation for the athletes; and the belief that anyone could benefit from taking part in sports activities, regardless of the level of the activity.[50]

A local journalist observed:

> Bowerman is an innovator. He develops equipment and improves conditions for [his athletes] with a fervor born of his penchant for technology... His track shoes are the lightest in history and... the Oregon distance runners wear uniforms that weight just 3 3/4 ounces.[51]

However, former Bowerman athlete and Olympic marathoner Kenny Moore probably cut to the core with his simple observation that, "His originality was sometimes so great that it was bewildering."[52]

Perhaps one factor was his lack of ego in the process—not that he did not have great faith in his abilities, but that he did not put his opinion ahead of inconvenient realities, as so many coaches do. As he often said, "God determines how fast you're going to run; I can help only with the mechanics."[53] This statement is not that of a coach consumed with his own wisdom. Several of his statements illustrate his approach to training:

> A teacher is never too smart to learn from his pupils. But while runners differ, basic principles never change. So it's a matter of fitting your current practices to fit the event and the individual. See, what's good for you might not be worth a darn for the next guy[54]...I think determination and intelligence are much more important than talent[55]...You have to apply the principle of how much can this man tolerate to enable him to progress. What are his strengths? How do you develop these strengths and avoid the weaknesses? These things are important for the champion, and they're important for someone coming up...The magic is not in 100 miles; the magic is in the man.[56]

Another writer noted that:

> When discussing the hard-easy training system he developed, which remains a staple for every competitive runner around the world,[57] Bowerman says, "It isn't just saying go hard and go easy. It's knowing how to apply it to the individual."[58]

Kenny Moore provided a sense of the overall process, which was fleshed out in detail by Chris Walsh:[59]

> Experimentation seems to be responsible. "Every kid is different," he said. "Unless you understand that, you can't coach."...Bowerman wrote an individual program for each runner, scheduling two or three weeks of workouts in advance. He tested each man's responses to widely differing types of training, and it was not uncommon for two Oregon milers of equal ability to go an entire season without running the same workout on the same day. In addition he conducted yearly goal-setting sessions to make sure runner and coach had the same ends in mind. He expected runners to understand the principles at work in their training so that they could carry on to physical maturity.[60]

A 1972 interview gave a sense of Bowerman's feelings for his athletes, pointing out:

> He expresses deep affection for his track athletes. "They're such good people," he says. "They help each other all the time. The distance runners are always trying to get another runner to better his time. They're unselfish, and they don't need the emotionalism that other athletes do." [61]

That his affection for and appreciation of his athletes was returned is evident in this note by another journalist, "Admiration, like criticism, runs deep. Steve Prefontaine...says, 'I'll never forget the first time I met him. I felt like I was talking to God. I still do.'"[62]

Bill Bowerman was one of those rare coaches whose importance seemed to increase for decades after he retired. By the time he had been gone from the university for a decade (though still working with the occasional post-collegiate runner), running magazines approached him with near reverence. As an editor wrote:

> [We have] published many articles about the world's greatest coaches and their training philosophies. We've published articles about writers whose books have inspired millions to take up the sport. We've chronicled the exploits of a long succession of sub-4-minute milers. And, of course, we've torn apart thousands of pairs of running shoes to learn how they work and how they could be made better.
>
> In this issue, we cover all the above areas in just one story—[our] profile of Bill Bowerman, the living legend of Eugene, Oregon. Bowerman has influenced our sport more, and in different ways, than anyone else.[63]

The writer of the article was only slightly less effusive:

> There is a solar quality to the career of Bill Bowerman—its influence, in this running life, as protean and fundamental as daylight. Whether you are hoping to run the Olympic Trials or your first 3-mile workout, you stand in direct debt to this man.[64]

The ongoing influence of the chase for the sub-4:00 mile was shown in the 1991 video production *Legends of Hayward Field,* with repeated references to and scenes of milers, along with the remark that the University of Oregon had produced 25 sub-4:00 runners, not including others who ran the metric equivalent of that mark.[65] But looking back to earlier days, by the end of 1962, 10 graduates of American universities were members of the sub-4:00 club. Oregon had produced four of them, while each of the others represented a single school. When Keith Forman hit the line in 3:58.3 in Modesto, he was the seventh collegian to beat the mark, and half of those who preceded him were fellow Ducks.[66]

Today, the sub-4:00 mile is common. British coach Harry Wilson remarked on the perceived difficulty of the mark, saying, "It turns out it wasn't so much like Everest as it was like the Matterhorn; somebody had to climb it first, but I hear now they've even got a cow up it."[67] Yet, it still has that cachet of immortality.

Still, there is a final note on Bowerman and the Oregon sub-4:00 mile tradition that he developed. Perhaps a final startling statistic will demonstrate how strongly identified Oregon's Hayward Field became with the sub-4:00 mile. In 2000, a list of all sub-four runners from the United States (233 of them at that time) showed that 51 of them (22 percent) ran their fastest mile in Eugene. Not 51 marks, but 51 *personal records.*[68] The number of individual sub-4:00 performances probably numbers over 100. No one seems quite sure.

Endnotes

1. Associated Press, "A Roll Call of Notable Deaths in 1999," *The* (Raleigh, N.C.) *News and Observer* (January 1, 2000).
2. *Track & Field News* (March 2000): 4.
3. Drew Middleton, "4-Minute Mile Is Achieved by Bannister in England," *New York Times* (May 7, 1954).
4. Joseph M. Sheehan, "Bannister's Record Feat Is Another Milestone in Eternal Quest for Improvement by Athletes," *New York Times* (May 7, 1954); "Track Stars Pay Tribute to Miler," *New York Times* (May 7, 1954).
5. "Track Stars Pay Tribute," *ibid.*
6. "The Miracle Mile," *Newsweek* (May 17, 1954): 57; "Glory on Foot," *Time* (May 17, 1954): 56-57; "Hurry, Hurry," *Newsweek* (May 24, 1954): 53; "Bungle by a Ninny," *Time* (May 24, 1954): 81; "Hands Across the Sea," *Newsweek* (May 24, 1954): 86; John Lardner, "I've Got a Secret," *Newsweek* (May 24, 1954): 88.
7. Paul O'Neil, "Duel of the Four-Minute Men," *Sports Illustrated* (August 16, 1954): 20-24.
8. *Ibid.*, 21.
9. Carl Cluff and Ken Goe, "Fabled Track Coach Bill Bowerman Dies," *The* (Portland) *Oregonian* (December 26, 1999); John Conrad, "Track Pioneer Dead at Age 88," *Eugene* (Ore.) *Register-Guard* (December 26, 1999); Richard Green, "Nike Co-founder Bill Bowerman Dies," Associated Press (December 26, 1999); Ron Bellamy, "The Legendary Teacher and Coach Made Eugene a Fixture in the World of Track and Field," *Eugene* (Ore.) *Register-Guard* (December 26, 1999).
10. Bill Bowerman and Waldo E. Harris, *Jogging* (New York: Grosset and Dunlap, 1967).
11. "Wow! 3:57.7," *Eugene* (Ore.) *Register-Guard* (May 13, 1962).
12. Carl Cluff & Ken Goe, The (Portland) Oregonian (December 26, 1999): sec. A, 1, 14; The (Portland) Oregonian (March 24, 1973): sec. 3, 1; "Nike Mourns Passing, Celebrates Life of Co-founder William J. Bowerman," http://www.nikebiz.com/media/n_bowerman.shtml.
13. Portland *Oregon Journal* (March 24, 1973): sec. 3, 1.
14. William J. Bowerman and William H. Freeman, *Coaching Track and Field* (Boston: Houghton Mifflin, 1974), 7.
15. *Ibid.*
16. *Ibid.*, 7-9.
17. William H. Freeman, *A Biographical Study of William Jay Bowerman* (Eugene, University of Oregon, 1972), 3-4; Hal Higdon, "The Spirit That's Moved Us," *The Runner* (April 1982): 31.
18. Associated Press, "Oregon's Bailey Beats Landy in L.A.," *Eugene* (Ore.) *Register-Guard* (May 5, 1956).
19. *Track & Field News* (January 1955): 6.
20. "Bailey, Dellinger Prep for Mile," *Eugene* (Ore.) *Register-Guard* (May 1, 1956).
21. "Bailey, Dellinger Prep for Mile;" Associated Press, "Delany Accepts Special Mile Bid," *Eugene* (Ore.) *Register-Guard* (May 2, 1956); "Oregon Mile Stars Depart for LA Race," *Eugene* (Ore.) *Register-Guard* (May 3, 1956); "KERG to Carry Special Mile Race," *Eugene* (Ore.) *Register-Guard* (May 4, 1956).

22. Associated Press, "Oregon's Bailey Beats Landy in L.A.;" Eugene (Ore.) Register-Guard (May 6, 1956); Bob Myers, "Expected: Needles Winner in Derby ++ Unexpected: Jim Bailey Beats Landy," *The* (Portland) *Oregonian* (May 6, 1956); "Landy Upset in 3:58.6 Mile," *New York Times* (May 6, 1956); Gladwin Hill, "Bailey Defeats Landy," *New York Times* (May 6, 1956); Associated Press. "Bailey Enjoys Running; Oregon Miler Loads Lumber During Summer Months," *New York Times* (May 6, 1956); Art Litchman, "Bailey's Yell Fails as Spur," *The* (Portland) *Oregonian* (May 6, 1956); Associated Press, "Bailey Clocks 3:58.6," *Eugene* (Ore.) *Register-Guard* (May 6, 1956); Art Litchman, "'I Knew It Was Bailey! It Wouldn't Have Been Anybody Else'—Landy," *Eugene* (Ore.) *Register-Guard* (May 6, 1956); Bob Robinson, "Bailey Zipped Home Ahead, to U.O.'s Joy!," *Eugene* (Ore.) *Register-Guard* (May 6, 1956); INS, "Bailey Predicts Others Will Conquer 'Barrier,'" *The* (Portland) *Oregonian* (May 6, 1956); Paul O'Neil, "A Day to Remember: The Mile," *Sports Illustrated* (May 14, 1956): 13-14; "A Mile to Remember," *Sports Illustrated* (May 14, 1956): 18-19; "The Anonymous Miler," *Newsweek* (May 14, 1956): 84, 86; "Man with a Mission," *Time* (May 14, 1956): 59; Bert Nelson, "Bailey Over Landy in 3:58.6," *Track and Field News* (May 1956): 4.
23. Litchman, "Bailey's Yell Fails as Spur."
24. "The Anonymous Miler," *Newsweek.*
25. "Bailey Enjoys Running," *New York Times.*
26. *Track & Field News* (January 1957): 9.
27. *Track & Field News* (January 1958): 6; *New York Times* (June 16, 1957).
28. *Track & Field News* (January 1960): 9.
29. *New York Times* (June 19, 1960); *New York Times* (June 18, 1961); *New York Times* (June 17, 1962).
30. Bill Bowerman, "Mile Mechanics and Training Techniques," *Athletic Journal* (January, 1960): 8-9, 11, 63-64; "Training for the 1500 Meter (or Mile) Run," *Clinic Notes* (1956): 81-85; "The Oregon School of Running," *Clinic Notes* (1961): 59-64.
31. "Oregon Flash," *Time* (February 1, 1960): 40; Tex Maule, "Masters of Endurance," *Sports Illustrated* (February 22, 1960): 10-13; Kris Stokes, "Man Behind the Track Stars," *Old Oregon* (March 1960): 6-8.
32. Associated Press, "Burleson, in 3:58.6, Sets Mile Record for an American," *New York Times* (April 24, 1960).
33. "Sparking the Flash," *Sports Illustrated* (May 2, 1960): 7; "Faster, Faster, Faster," *Newsweek* (May 2, 1960): 56.
34. "UO's Dyrol Burleson Runs the Mile in 3:58.6, the Fastest Ever By an American," *Eugene* (Ore.) *Register-Guard* (April 23, 1960); "Mark Falls by Tenth of Second," *Eugene* (Ore.) *Register-Guard* (April 23, 1960); Barney Bartholomew, "Burleson Goes Under Four with 3:58.6 Win," *Eugene* (Ore.) *Register-Guard* (April 24, 1960).
35. Harley Patrick, "Burley's Great Race," *Oregon Quarterly* 79, no. 3 (Spring 2000): 41-42.
36. Tex Maule, "The New Herb Elliott," *Sports Illustrated* (May 30, 1960): 10-13.
37. "Oregon Snaps World Four-Mile Relay Mark," *Eugene* (Ore.) *Register-Guard,* (May 13, 1962); "Wow! 3:57.7," *Eugene* (Ore.) *Register-Guard* (May 13, 1962); Associated Press. "Oregon Sets Mark for 4-Mile Relay," *New York Times* (May 13, 1962).

38. Bert Nelson, "16:08.9 Record for Oregon," *Track and Field News* (May 1962): 1-2.
39. Dick Strite, "Highclimber," *Eugene* (Ore.) *Register-Guard* (May 14, 1962).
40. "For the record," *Sports Illustrated* (June 4, 1962): 69.
41. Tex Maule, "Batch of Surprises in Los Angeles," *Sports Illustrated* (May 28, 1962): 47-50.
42. Tex Maule, "Birth of a New Dynasty," *Sports Illustrated* (June 25, 1962): 74; Joseph M. Sheehan, "Oregon Team First in N.C.A.A. Track," *New York Times* (June 17, 1962).
43. Matt Mitchell, "13,000 See Ducks Take NCAA Meet," *Eugene* (Ore.) *Register-Guard* (June 17, 1962); Dick Strite, "Oregon Wins NCAA Track Crown," *Eugene* (Ore.) *Register-Guard* (June 17, 1962); Dick Leutzinger, "Tarr, Hero of UO Victory, Praises Mates' Toughness," *Eugene* (Ore.) *Register-Guard* (June 17, 1962).
44. Paul Ron, Editorial cartoon: "Running Companions," *Eugene* (Ore.) *Register-Guard* (June 18, 1962).
45. Bill Bowerman, "A Philosophy of Conditioning in Track and Field," in *Proceedings of the Fourth National Conference on the Medical Aspects of Sports* (1963): 20-22; "Track and Field at the University of Oregon," in *Proceedings of the Fourth National Conference on the Medical Aspects of Sports* (1963): 60-66; Donald B. Slocum and Bowerman, "The Biomechanics of Running," in *Proceedings of the Second National Conference on the Medical Aspects of Sports* (Chicago, 1961): 53-58; Slocum and Bowerman, "The Biomechanics of Running," *Clinical Orthopedics* 23 (1962): 39-45; "The Oregon School of Running," in Track in *Theory and Technique,* ed. Thomas P. Rosandich (Richmond, Calif.: Worldwide, 1963): 195-200; Slocum and Bowerman, "The Biomechanics of Running" (pp. 67-73), in *Track in Theory and Technique;* Bowerman and Gwilym S. Brown, "The Secrets of Speed," *Sports Illustrated* (August 2, 1971): 22-29.
46. Bill Bowerman and W. E. Harris, "Jogging: An Adult Exercise Program," in *Proceedings of the Eighth National Conference on the Medical Aspects of Sports* (1967): 57-60; Bowerman and Harris, *Jogging* (New York: Grosset and Dunlap, 1967); William H. Freeman, "Bill Bowerman: Catalyst of the American Jogging Movement," *Canadian Journal of History of Sport and Physical Education* 5 (May 1974): 47-55.
47. Joe Henderson, "A Coach and a Tradition," *Track and Field News* (I June 1968): 20-21.
48. Comment by Barbara Bowerman, December 8, 1999.
49. Kenny Moore, *Best Efforts* (New York: Doubleday, 1982), 114.
50. William H. Freeman, "Dedication to Bill Bowerman: Looking Back and Looking Forward," In *Proceedings of the International Track and Field Coaches Association IX Congress,* ed. George G. Dales (Kalamazoo, MI: N.C.A.A. Division I Track Coaches' Association, 1984): 4.
51. Dan Sellard, "Bowerman," *Eugene* (Ore.) *Register-Guard Emerald Empire* (April 2, 1972).
52. Moore, 53.
53. Hal Higdon, "The Spirit That's Moved Us," *The Runner* (April 1982): 31.
54. Quoted in *The Quotable Runner,* ed. Mark Will-Weber (New York: Breakaway, 1995): 60.
55. Higdon, 33.
56. Higdon, 32.

57. Pete Pfitzinger, "Re-Examining the Hard-Easy Principle," *Running Times* (May 2000): 16.
58. John Brandt, "Bowerman," *Runner's World* (November, 1991): 110.
59. Chris Walsh, *The Bowerman System* (Los Altos, Calif.: Tafnews, 1983).
60. Moore, 61.
61. Dan Sellard, "Bowerman," *Eugene* (Ore.) *Register-Guard Emerald Empire* (April 2, 1972).
62. Douglas S. Looney, "Pretty Soon I'll Find Out If This Honor Is Ashes," *The National Observer* (July 22, 1972).
63. George A. Hirsch, "A Living Legend," *Runner's World* (November, 1991): 8.
64. Brandt, 108.
65. *Legends of Hayward Field* (Eugene, Ore.: Media Craft, 1991, videotape).
66. James O. Dunaway, *The Four Minute Mile* (Los Altos, Calif.: Tafnews, 1967).
67. *Quotable Runner,* 193.
68. All-time list of United States citizens who have run a sub-4:00 mile. http://www.runnersworld.com/stats/mileusa.html

Credits (Photos, Tables, Figures)

Photo Credits

University of Oregon Archives: Page 1, 2-4, II-1, 7-1, 7-4, 7-7, 7-8, 8-1, 9-1, 9-2, 9-7, 10-1, 11-1, 12-3, V-1, 18-1, 18-4, 20-1, 21-1, Back Cover-1; University of Oregon Athletic Media Services: 6-2, 8-4, 9-3, 10-2, 13-1, IV-1, 19-1, VI-1, 22-1; Phil Wolcott, Jr., *Eugene Register Guard:* 12-1; Collection of Barbara Bowerman: Photos 2-2, 6-1, 7-2, 7-3, 7-6, 8-2, III-1, 24-1, 24-2; Courtesy of Nike: 2-3, 8-3; Jeff Johnson: Photos 11-5, 18-3; Geoff Hollister: 2-3, *The News and Observer,* Raleigh, NC: 2-1; William H. Freeman: 2-1, I-1, 7-5, 9-4, 9-5, 9-6, 9-8, 9-9, 9-10, 11-2, 12-2, IV-1, 16-1, 16-2, 18-2, 21-2, 21-3, 21-4, 21-5, Back Cover-2; © Imago Sports/ZUMA Press: 11-6, 22-3, 22-4; © Zsolt Szigetvary/North Foto/ZUMA Press: 11-4; © Astrid Riecken/*Washington Times*/ ZUMA Press: 19-2; © Liao Yujie/Xinha/ZUMA Press: 22-2; © Michael Steele/Allsport: 19-3

Tables Credits

4-1. William H. Freeman. (1989). *Peak when it counts: Periodization for American track & field.* Mountain View, CA: Tafnews, 10.

5-1. N.G. Ozolin in Tudor O. Bompa. (1983). *Theory and methodology of training.* Dubuque, IA: Kendall/Hunt, 210.

5-2. Freeman, *Peak when it counts,* 24.

5-3. Frank W. Dick, (1978). *Training theory.* London: British Amateur Athletic Board, 60-61.

5-4. Tudor O. Bompa. (1987). Peaking for the extended athletics calendar. *New Studies in Athletics,* 2(4), 41.

9-1. Personal Communication from John Underwood, 1985.

9-2. Jürgen Schiffer. (1988). Performance factors in the marathon. *Track Technique,* 105, 3360.

10-3. Hans Torim. (1988). Maximal speed in the sprints. *Track Technique,* 104, 3331.

10-4. Gary K. Winckler. (1989). In *The Athletic Congress's track and field coaching manual* (2ed ed.). Champaign, IL: Leisure Press, 69.

12-2, 12-3, 13-3, 13-4. Brent McFarlane. (1981). Hurdles touchdown times. In Jess Jarver (Ed.). *The hurdles: Contemporary theory, technique and training* (2nd ed). Los Altos: Tafnews, 34-35.

14-1. Patrick Reid. (1986). The high jump. *New Studies in Athletics,* 1(1), 47-53.

14-2. Ed Jacoby. (1986). High jump: A technique evaluation. *Track Technique,* 97, 3089.

15-1. Andrzej Krzesinski. (1983). Pole vault: The total program. *Track Technique,* 84, 2681-2682.

17-1. Adapted from Steve Miller & Scott Bennett. (1989). The triple jump. In *Athletic Congress's manual* (2nd ed.), 140-141.

19-1. K. Bartonietz, L. Hinz, D. Lorenz, & G. Lunau. (1988). The hammer: The view of the DVfL of the GDR on talent selection, technique and training of throwers from beginner to top level athlete. *New Studies in Athletics,* 3(1), 50.

19-2. Bartonietz, et al. *New Studies in Athletics,* 50.

19-6, 19-7, 19-8. Arne Nytro. (1974). The hammer throw. In William J. Bowerman & William H. Freeman. *Coaching track and field.* Boston: Houghton Mifflin, 322, 324-326.

20-1. Kim Bukhantsov. (1988). Wind variations in discus training. *Track Technique,* 104, 3229.

21-1. E. Arbeit, K. Bartonietz, P. Borner, K. Hellmann, K., & W. Skibbia. (1988). The javelin: The view of the DVfL of the GDR on talent selection, technique and main training contents of the training phases from beginner to top-level athlete. *New Studies in Athletics,* 3(1), 57-74.

22-2. Fred Kudu. (1984). Training load in the heptathlon. *Track Technique,* 89, 2883.

22-3. William H. Freeman. (1986). Decathlon performance success. *Track Technique,* 96, 3050-3052.

22-4, 22-5. Bob Myers. (1989). The heptathlon. In *Athletic Congress's manual* (2nd ed.), 214-215.

22-11. Adapted and expanded by William H. Freeman from Alfred J. Sylvia. (1964, April). A decathlon for high school and college. *Athletic Journal,* 44, 38, 40.

Figures Credits

4-1. "Planning the Training Schedule" by B. Klavora. (1980), Coaching Association of Canada: Bridging the Gap Unit, package 7, item 3,1-14.

4-2. Freeman. *Peak when it counts,* 10.

4-3. Freeman. *Peak when it counts,* 11.

5-1. Freeman. *Peak when it counts,* 6.

5-2. Tudor O. Bompa. *Theory and methodology,* 198.

5-3. Tudor O. Bompa. *Theory and methodology,* 198.

5-4. Freeman. *Peak when it counts,* 31.

14-1. William H. Freeman. (1991). In William J. Bowerman & William H. Freeman. *High-performance training for track and field,* 129.

14-2. Adapted from Ed Jacoby. (1987). High jump: A technique evaluation. *Track Technique,* 97, 3090.

14-3. William H. Freeman. In William J. Bowerman & William H. Freeman. *High-performance training for track and field,* 131.

15-1, 15-2, 15-3. William H. Freeman. (1974). In William J. Bowerman & William H. Freeman. *Coaching track and field.* Boston: Houghton Mifflin, 227, 242, 243.

16-1, 16-2, 16-3. William H. Freeman. In William J. Bowerman & William H. Freeman. *Coaching track and field,* 200, 201, 203.

19-1. William H. Freeman. In William J. Bowerman & William H. Freeman. *Coaching track and field,* 314.

19-2. K. Bartonietz, L. Hinz, D. Lorenz, & G. Lunau. (1988). The hammer: The view of the DVfL of the GDR on talent selection, technique and training of throwers from beginner to top level athlete. *New Studies in Athletics,* 3(1), 44.

19-3. Bartonietz, et al. *New Studies in Athletics,* 3(1), 53.

19-4, 19-5. Kevin McGill. (1984). Hammer clinic. *Track and Field Quarterly Review,* 84(1), 49.

19-7, 19-8. Arne Nytro.

19-9. Anatoliy Samotsvetov (1969). Die Wirksamkeit der Abwerfphase beim Hammerwurf. *Leichtathletik,* 20.

19-12. Peter Tschiene. (1988). The throwing events: Recent trends in technique and training. *New Studies in Athletics,* 3(1), 12.

21-1, 21-2, 21-3, 21-4, 21-5. William H. Freeman. In William J. Bowerman & William H. Freeman. *Coaching track and field,* 301, 302, 302, 303, 304.

23-1, 23-2, 23-3, 23-4, 23-5, 23-6, 23-7. William H. Freeman. In William J. Bowerman & William H. Freeman. *Coaching track and field,* 369, 364, 365, 365, 366, 367, 368.

About the Authors

About the Authors

Bill Bowerman was the legendary coach at the University of Oregon, producer of many national champions and Olympians during his 25-season tenure. Winner of numerous track and football state championships as a high school coach, he won four NCAA team titles and produced team members for six consecutive Olympic Games as a collegiate coach. He also served as head coach for the U. S. Olympic Team in 1972. Though known as a coach of sub-4:00 milers, with 20 athletes achieving that mark, he produced world-record holders in the 100, 400, and discus, as well as the 440-yard relay and the 4 x 1 mile relay. He was known as one of the most innovative coaches in the sport, developing widely used training principles (the hard-easy principle) and better running shoes (he was co-founder of Nike). He was also the author of *Jogging,* which launched the running boom in the United States.

Bill Freeman coached track athletes for 30 years, working with athletes from the middle school level through the Olympic Trials levels. He was the director of the combined events competitions at the 1972, 1976, and 1980 U. S. Olympic Trials. A professor of exercise science at Campbell University in North Carolina, his other books include *Peak When It Counts: Periodization for American Track and Field* (4th ed.), which is required reading for USA Track and Field coaching certification, *Physical Education and Sport in a Changing Society* (6th ed.), *The Competitive Runner's Training Book* with Bill Dellinger, and the previous editions of this book, starting with *Coaching Track and Field* in 1974.